CANADIAN

Women

A READER

CANADIAN
Women

· ·

A READER

Wendy Mitchinson
Paula Bourne
Alison Prentice
Gail Cuthbert Brandt
Beth Light
Naomi Black

HARCOURT
BRACE
CANADA

Harcourt Brace & Company, Canada

Toronto   Montreal   Fort Worth   New York   Orlando
Philadelphia   San Diego   London   Sydney   Tokyo

Canadian Cataloguing in Publication Data

Main entry under title:

Canadian women: a reader

ISBN 0-7747-3292-X

1. Women — Canada — History.   2. Women — Canada — Social conditions.   I. Mitchinson, Wendy.

HQ1453.C35   1996   305.4'0971   C95-931316-8

Publisher: Heather McWhinney
Senior Acquisitions Editor: Christopher Carson
Projects Manager: Liz Radojkovic
Editorial Assistant: Martina van de Velde
Director of Publishing Services: Jean Davies
Editorial Manager: Marcel Chiera
Supervising Editor: Semareh Al-Hillal
Production Editor: Laurel Parsons
Production Manager: Sue-Ann Becker
Production Co-ordinator: Sheila Barry
Copy Editor: Margaret Allen
Cover Design: Opus House
Typesetting and Assembly: True to Type Inc.
Printing and Binding: Best Book Manufacturers, Inc.

Cover Art: Kittie Bruneau, *Les bonnes femmes* (1971). Photographed by Patrick Altman. Reproduced by permission of the artist.

This book was printed in Canada.

1   2   3   4   5   00   99   98   97   96

for our families

Acknowledgements

It remains to thank those who have helped us in the production of this book: Carol Cooper, Alyson King, Vered Pittel, Caralee Price, Jim Walker, and the Centre for Women's Studies in Education at the Ontario Institute for Studies in Education.

Note from the Publisher

Thank you for selecting *Canadian Women: A Reader*, by Wendy Mitchinson, Paula Bourne, Alison Prentice, Gail Cuthbert Brandt, Beth Light, and Naomi Black. The authors and publisher have devoted considerable time to the careful development of this book. We appreciate your recognition of this effort and accomplishment.

We want to hear what you think about *Canadian Women: A Reader*. Please take a few minutes to fill in the stamped reader reply card at the back of the book. Your comments and suggestions will be valuable to us as we prepare new editions and other books.

Contents

Introduction

The history of women interested our foremothers — and some of our forefathers — long before the second wave of the women's movement began in Canada. But it was in the early 1970s that the study of Canadian women's history really took off, with the first courses, conference papers, and journal articles in the history of women. Very soon, it seemed important to make the new work more widely accessible, and thus, over the years, a number of essay collections have appeared. The present collection is intended to continue in this tradition and to illustrate new directions and topics in the field. Designed to complement the second edition of our text, *Canadian Women: A History*, the essays collected here introduce students of Canadian women's history to some of today's most exciting new work, as well as to several older studies that deserve to be better known.

Gender makes women's lives profoundly different from the lives of men. As a result, much that we learn from the history of men is problematic for the history of women. The very language often fails to describe women's experience. A particularly complex set of problems surrounds the word "work." To begin with, the generally accepted census definition of "occupation" omits much work that women do in the home — housework, child care, and care of the elderly or the sick. Even less recognized is the unpaid "reproductive" work that women do in the family, both in bearing children and in providing emotional stability and support. These omissions stem directly from the failure to treat unpaid work with the same respect as work for pay. In addition, much of women's paid work goes unrecorded, from taking in sewing or boarders to doing housework or child care for others. Similarly, the words "culture" and "politics" have meanings for women that can differ significantly from those generally accepted. By using "culture" and "politics" anthropologically, we move beyond "high culture" and "party politics" to concepts that encompass ways of thinking and acting, ways of being in the world and seeing the world. Many of the articles in this volume explore the multifaceted dimensions of work, culture, and politics.

We have organized this book into four parts, corresponding to the four sections of the text and to a periodization of Canadian history that we feel best represents the experience of women. Part One explores the history of women in Canada from the period when only the First Nations inhabited the continent to the mid-nineteenth century. By the end of this period, many waves of migration, largely from western Europe, had drastically altered the landscape. By this time, too, industrialization and urbanization were beginning to make serious inroads into older patterns of women's work and cultural life. Part Two deals with the decades from the 1850s to World War I: industrialization, urbanization, and the first women's movement affected many British North American and Canadian women during this period. In Part Three, our attention turns to the decades after World War I and the ways in which different groups of Canadian women faced the many issues of the interwar years, such as changing patterns of marriage and child rearing and work and leisure. Finally, Part Four looks at women's experiences of life in Canada following World War II. The participation of women in the labour force for more years of their lives constituted the major material shift of these years. In addition, the second wave of the women's movement preoccupied many, as did increasing concern for the safety and well-being of women in all spheres of their lives.

Inevitably, temporal markers are artificial. They are the more so when it comes to the life of an individual woman, or the lives of whole groups whose participation has been on the edges of the mainstream. What did the advent of factories, the achievement of prohibition and suffrage, or the movement of married women into the paid labour force mean to women living on Canada's more isolated resource frontiers or on Indian reserves? Did such changes affect the lives of black women, of lesbians, or of poor or immigrant women in the same ways as they affected mainstream women? We have made a special attempt to include essays concerning those women who are most remote from the centres of political or economic power.

We believe that the material structures of people's lives are the most important among the many factors influencing them, and for that reason each part of the book begins with an essay focussing on aspects of women's work experience. Yet we would not limit such influences to the economic, for we are convinced that women's bodies are an important part of the material bases of their lives. Furthermore, as feminists focussing on the experience of women, we also recognize the power of ideas and feelings, of social and political movements, and of cultural and racial as well as gender identities in fixing or altering how people react to the conditions they encounter.

Because Canada is a country of immense diversity, there nearly always seems to be the need for multiple perspectives if we are to get the picture right. Yet, despite such diversity, or perhaps because of it, an increasingly frequent theme of Canadian women's history has been the quest for a unified women's voice. Has such a voice existed? Is there a distinctively Canadian women's experience that can be identified?

While each of the articles that follow explores different aspects of women's diversity, underlying them is a sense that commonality at some level exists, muted though it may be.

To encompass in 21 essays all that Canadian women have done and experienced is, of course, an impossibility. The articles collected here are meant to be suggestive only of the many new topics, sources, and approaches to women's history now being explored in Canada. A few are reissues of earlier important work in Canadian women's history; some rework old seams in new ways; still others take us away from the mainstream entirely, into new worlds that have long deserved examination but are only now finding their historians.

Part One

The Founding Mothers: Beginnings to the Mid-Nineteenth Century

The history of Canadian women in the years prior to the mid-nineteenth century necessarily embraces an almost unimaginably long period of time and a tremendous diversity of experience. The history of aboriginal women alone cannot be easily encompassed: the indigenous people who first inhabited these lands belonged to twelve separate language families and a wide variety of material cultures and geopolitical groups. This period also includes the histories of the early Newfoundland fishery and of New France and Acadia, of the seventeenth- and eighteenth-century settlements of the northern British Atlantic colonies, as well as of the Loyalist and post-Loyalist migrations to eastern and central British North America. As European settlements spread, the fisheries and the fur trade were gradually supplemented, and in some cases supplanted, by forest industries and farming. During the century prior to the 1850s, the north and west saw the birth of new societies based on the fur trade, which eventually developed to include other staple-oriented industries such as gold mining and agriculture.

The European grab for resources, as well as the spread of European religion — not to mention European diseases — wreaked havoc throughout North America. But, for all their suffering, nearly all of the indigenous nations survived. Trade and intermarriage had positive effects for some individuals and groups; others found that they could retreat or adapt, and eventually rebuild. Aboriginal women played key roles in these histories of survival and change, as the first two essays in this collection demonstrate.

European women accompanied or soon followed the fishermen, traders, missionaries, and military men who ventured to the northern regions of the Americas. Among the first French women were the stalwart nuns who played a key role in the establishment of New France and who are the subject of the third essay in our collection. Other women subsequently came as refugees from war, famine, or oppression, as one wave of immigration followed another — from France, the British Isles, the

5

Thirteen Colonies, and later the United States. Very early, women of African origin were to be found among the migrants. The first black women came as slaves of wealthy French colonists, but there were free blacks among the Loyalists fleeing the American Revolution and the refugees of the War of 1812. Later, the Underground Railway brought many more African-Americans who were fleeing slavery.

These migrating women should not be thought of as simply passive partners of men's imperialist ventures or victims of the disasters of their day. Many came voluntarily in search of freedom and opportunity; many shared the European imperialist dream. If they were often soon disillusioned, they also quickly set about the work of building and rebuilding, most frequently sustained by the powerful inspiration of religion. The teaching sisters of New France took charge of female education and dedicated themselves to teaching both the aboriginal and, with more success, the European girls in their care. Pioneer women reacted to the difficulties of their own lives by seeking female support; by the mid-nineteenth century, British North American women had organized women's groups that were taking major initiatives in the realms of religion and social welfare. The fourth and fifth essays in our collection deal with those women who found in spiritual expression and charitable work a central meaning for their lives.

Women Traders in the Maritime Fur Trade

LORAINE LITTLEFIELD

The active economic role of Northwest coast women in the appropriation and distribution of trade goods during the maritime fur trade has been neglected in the literature[1] despite the many historical accounts that document the presence of women in trade transactions, their shrewdness and skill in bargaining, and their role as chief negotiators. The role of women in trade was not a new behaviour arising out of the fur trade and its introduction of new trade goods but a continuation of women's traditional role that had included their active participation in the exchange of trade goods.

SOURCE: Loraine Littlefield, "Women Traders in the Maritime Fur Trade," in Bruce Alden Cox, ed., *Native People, Native Lands: Canadian Indians, Inuit and Métis* (Ottawa: Carleton University Press, 1988), 173–85.

Maritime Fur Trade

From 1785 to 1825, a profitable maritime fur trade flourished on the Northwest coast. The fur resources of this trade were the sea otters that inhabited the ecological niche between the Columbia River to the south and Cook's Inlet to the north. The incentive for this trade was the easy harvest of the sea otter herds and the high demand for their pelts on the Chinese market. The first trading vessel dispatched solely for the purpose of the fur trade was the British *Sea Otter* commanded by James Hanna in 1785.[2] In his brief visit to the coast he obtained 560 pelts which fetched a profit of $20,000 in Canton. The promise of such profits encouraged other traders, and during this period it is estimated that over 450 vessels visited the Northwest coast.[3]

Initially, the main items demanded were iron and copper, with little popularity for trinkets and other trade items. Many vessels stripped themselves clean of everything metal on board in order to appease these demands. However, the coast became saturated with metals within a decade and muskets, blankets, and cloth became the more popular trade items. During the later years, more exotic tastes in trade were expressed in the demand for tobacco, molasses, biscuits, and rum.

Many maritime accounts reveal the desirability and eagerness on the part of the native population to trade. The earliest accounts of exploration[4] noted this eagerness from the start. Later maritime traders,[5] while pleased with this response, were at times astonished at the native shrewdness and mercenary attitude in trade. Indicative of this trading ability is the increased price of sea otter pelts as the maritime trade progressed.[6]

In the beginning of the trade, traders were able to acquire large quantities of sea otter pelts in a fairly short time; however, with the increasing competition and the gradual depletion of the sea otter herds this number decreased considerably. By 1825, the sea otter herds had been so decimated that the maritime fur trade came to a close, and other fur bearing animals and the establishment of permanent fur trading posts now held the most promise for fur trade returns.

Women Traders

While early explorers[7] had noted the presence of women during trade transactions, the first trader to specifically identify women's active participation in trade was an Englishman who recorded his visit and trading experience at Nootka Sound. James Strange,[8] a senior merchant for the East India Company, wrote in his journal in 1786 that in many of his trade transactions with the Nootka Indians, women were not only present, but were principally in control of the trade. He noted also that women traders would increase the price of furs up to three times the price he could have acquired them for if dealing only with their men. This trading activity by Nootka women was confirmed two years later, in 1788, by John Meares,[9] who visited another Nootka community to the south of Nootka Sound at Clayoquot Sound. He too noticed the presence of women during trade transactions, and remarked on their bargaining ability. Like Strange, he complained that women would consistently interfere in his trade transactions and retard the sale until they had procured an additional gift from the transaction.

Other journals described the women on the northern coast of this region as equally shrewd and active in trade transactions. Dixon,[10] one of the first traders to discover the rich fur resources of the Queen Charlotte Islands in 1786, acknowledged that in trade with the Haida the women were equally active and encouraged to come aboard his vessel. Later other traders[11] noted that the Haida men dared not trade their furs without the concurrence of their wives for if they disapproved of a deal it would ultimately fail. Ingraham[12] and Roquefeuil[13] were surprised by instances where men who parted with their furs without the consent of their women were abused in the most cruel manner.

Still other accounts recorded that such an active role in trade was also present among the Tlingit and Tsimshian women. Douglas,[14] accompanying Meares in the *Iphigenia* sailing between Queen Charlotte Islands and Cook Inlet, commented that women with large lip plugs (labrets) commanded the canoes trading alongside his vessel. Later Marchand[15] wrote that Tlingit women at Sitka Sound and Yukatat Bay were consistently present during trade transactions, and the men seldom concluded a deal without consulting them. Similarly, Vancouver,[16] when surveying this northern coastline in 1792, observed that Tlingit and Tsimshian women took the principal role in all commercial transactions involving the purchase of salmon and furs.

South of Nootka Sound, women participated in and controlled trade transactions. Quimper,[17] during his exploration of the Strait of Juan de Fuca, wrote that women were present at Cape Flattery and Waddah Island, and participated equally in the trade of goods. Bishop,[18] a few years later, recorded that women eagerly traded goods while he anchored at the mouth of the Columbia River. When Sturgis arrived in 1804, he observed that he dealt solely with women in all his trade transactions with the Chinook and Clatsop. Similarly, Lewis and Clark, in their daily entries, wrote repeatedly of the active role of women in trade in this region. Lewis[19] described incidents where women either arrived at the post individually or accompanied by their male relatives in order to trade a variety of goods.

While these maritime accounts document the active participation of women in trade throughout the length of the coast, the fur traders differed in their opinions concerning the nature of this participation.

Meares' statement concerning women "interfering" or "retarding" a sale seems to imply that Nootka women were only peripheral participants in trade transactions. However, this statement may reveal more of the fur traders' bias in recording women's roles in trade than it does any sexual variation in roles throughout the coast. For example, the presence of native men in the bargaining process may have been purely a male bias on the part of the European fur traders who were accustomed to directing their trade transactions to men. The lack of terms such as "interfere" and "retard" to describe women's role in trade transactions in later accounts supports this assumption.

Other trade accounts noted that trade transactions needed women's approval in order to succeed. To account for this behaviour, some fur traders felt that women's participation stemmed from a man's respect for her decision-making and not from any other form of formal rights in trade transactions. For example, Alexander Walker,[20] accompanying Strange at Nootka Sound, recorded that Chief Maquinna was principally directed by his young wife Hestoquotto. In Walker's estimation, this control stemmed from her husband's desire to please her and not from any formal authority. Marchand[21] formed a similar opinion in his observation of women's control over trade among the Tlingit. He felt that women's opinions before concluding a bargain were sought only out of polite respect.

However, this view that women's participation in trade was only a product of men's respect for women's decision-making does not explain those cases where men were actually abused for not consulting women before accepting a trade negotiation. Douglas[22] gives a fairly vivid account of a Tlingit woman at Cross Sound, who, when interrupted in her trade transactions, began to strike a man upon his head with a paddle for close to half an hour, and then ended the abuse by slashing his thigh with a knife. Douglas noted that during this violent exchange no one interfered as this seemed to be this woman's right. Such acts of violence and abuse during trade transactions were also witnessed by other traders.[23]

Such observations led some traders to conclude that in many locations of the coast, women were the superior sex and this accounted for their principal role in trade transactions. For example, during his trade with the Haida of the Queen Charlotte Islands, Haswell[24] referred to the wife of Cunneah as the chief of the tribe because of her dominating role in trade transactions. Vancouver[25] and Douglas[26] formed a similar opinion about some of the Tlingit women they met. While later ethnographies written on the Northwest coast have acknowledged that some women did acquire considerable political power within their society, traditionally this power was vested in men.

Nevertheless, these statements of sex superiority may reflect the fur traders' ignorance of the existence of classes within Northwest coast societies. While recent ethnologists have documented the presence of a ranking system that included nobles, commoners, and slaves as an integral feature of Northwest coast societies, not many early maritime traders were perceptive to the existence of classes. For example, both Vancouver[27] and Malaspina[28] believed that Northwest coast societies were fairly egalitarian, and that the concepts of property and class had not yet arisen. This lack of awareness of class may have misled some traders when observing women's behaviour in trade, for women of high class would have had a superior status over any of the men in their tribe. This superiority would have been apparent during trade transactions.

However, while there were many accounts describing trade transactions with chiefs' wives, or women of great authority, there are many more accounts that record the active trading role of women who did not have such power. While class may have influenced the type of goods women traded, it does not seem to have restricted a woman's ability (with the exclusion of slaves) to trade. One account in the historical material which acknowledges that women of all classes traded was written by Ingraham[29] after he arrived at Cloak Bay, off the tip of the Queen Charlotte Islands. He was disappointed to find that this particular village had traded all of its furs to previous maritime traders. He complained that the canoes that came alongside his vessel contained women of the lowest class, for they had only fish, and not furs, to sell.

Lewis,[30] who with Clark spent the winter on the Columbia River, speculated that the economic role of women stemmed from the usefulness of their labour in subsistence production. In the interior of the continent, where women's status was lower, he noted that hunting, the main subsistence activity, excluded women, while on the Columbia River the Chinook and Clatsop women were active drying fish, and gathering wappato roots and berries. This production made a major contribution to the traditional economy and, he believed, gave women a voice in their distribution. Later, fur traders to this region agreed with Lewis's conclusions. Cox[31] believed that women's role in collecting the wappato root allowed them an air of independence that he had not seen evident among the interior tribes.

This speculation that women's role in the distribution of trade goods stemmed from their participation in production has some support, for many trade goods were produced wholly or partially by women. Even at the start of the fur trade, Portlock[32] acknowledged that many of the trade goods brought out to his vessel were made by women. However, cross-cultural studies[33] into women's economic roles have revealed that women's participation in the production of trade goods does not necessarily ensure that women obtain the rights to distribute them. To understand how women on the Northwest coast acquired these rights, we must examine both the economic role of women within the traditional fishing economy and how this role gave them access to trade goods.

Women's Traditional Economic Roles

The traditional economy of the Northwest coast was based largely on marine resources such as salmon, halibut, cod, candle fish, and herring. These fish, which were caught off the coast or in the rivers and streams, appeared seasonally, and often in great quantities. While some were eaten fresh, the majority were dried and smoked to furnish food all year round. At certain seasons, seals, sea lions, sea otters, whales, and other larger marine animals were hunted. Also, according to the season, shellfish and vegetable foods, such as shoots, roots, and berries, were gathered and sometimes dried. Land animals were hunted but were of minor importance in the diet.

Men were the fishermen and hunters. In groups, or individually, they furnished the majority of food. Men were also skilled in woodworking, and made a variety of items such as dishes, bowls, spoons, boxes, and other small items. As well as wood, men carved bone and shell to make arrowheads, fishing hooks, and awls. Among men there was some specialization in production, and, either through skill or heredity, some individuals carved poles and manufactured large canoes and ritual masks.

Women's role in the traditional economy is confirmed in many of the maritime fur trade accounts.[34] They document that women's primary subsistence activities involved the preparation and curing of fish, as well as digging clams, gathering mussels, sea urchins, and other edible shellfish. Also according to the season, women picked berries and shoots which they often dried in the sun and shaped into cakes. Besides helping in food production, women also wove a variety of items such as baskets, hats, trays, fish-nets, aprons, and blankets. These items were made out of plant materials that women gathered, dried, and coiled. Women also made robes out of furs which were first cured and then sewn together. And finally, but not least, women were responsible for the care and nurture of their children.

Maritime accounts record that there was some margin of flexibility in the sexual division of labour that allowed women to fish and hunt, and men to assist in gathering shellfish and plant foods. This flexibility was noted by Von Langsdorff,[35] a visitor to the Russian post at Sitka. He observed that among the Tlingit, women were quite accustomed to firearms and were included in the many hunting expeditions. Also, Vancouver,[36] while surveying the Strait of Juan de Fuca, observed the participation of Klallam men in the gathering of roots and plant materials.

However, there are no historical accounts that document such flexibility in the production of crafts. It seems that, traditionally, women did not carve wood, bone, or shell, and men did not weave baskets or blankets.[37] Whether or not this flexibility in food production was a product of the fur trade, it is hard to judge, but it seems to have been evident

in traditional times. Even then the intensive labour needed for the seasonal, and often unpredictable, food resources of the Northwest coast
may have necessitated a flexibility in the gender-related division of
labour.

While the division of subsistence labour was determined by sex, all
such labour was directed by the needs of the household, which was the
fundamental social and economic unit of the Northwest coast. Each
household was autonomous and consisted of a chief or elder, his related
family, and slaves. The chief's role was to direct the general subsistence
activities of the household. He supervised the men's work, while his senior
wives supervised the women and their slaves. During the summer months,
individual nuclear families within the household dispersed to the many
fishing camps. In the fall, they rejoined their original household group
or made alliances to form new ones.

Apart from the active subsistence practices of drying fish and other
foods, women were responsible for food management and rationing
within the household. Each woman had the product of her family's spring
and summer labour stored in boxes or bundles suspended from the ceil-
ing. While this food was shared by the household, individual women
were responsible for ensuring that these foods were kept dry and free
from insects or mould. Their care in monitoring and rationing this food
was crucial: during the later winter months when food supplies were
scarce, the survival of the household depended upon its stores.

The role of managing the larder may explain the participation of
women in trade. Women were responsible not only for scarcity of food
stores, but also for any surplus that might have been available for trade
outside of the household. However, this role alone would not guarantee
women rights to appropriate and distribute trade goods outside of the
household. On the contrary, many societies have property relations that
allow husbands and elders to systematically appropriate the surplus production of the household. To understand the women's rights to trade
goods, the relations of production that enmeshed all Northwest coast
household resources must be examined.

Property Ownership

The concept of property ownership was well developed on the coast and
was all encompassing. Maritime traders were to discover this fact in their
many transactions with these people.[38] There were two recognizable types
of property: communal and private. Communal property included food
producing areas such as beaches, fishing streams, halibut and codfish
banks, hunting territories, berry grounds, as well as smoke houses, and
dwelling areas. It also included intangible property such as songs, dances,
rituals, and supernatural powers. This property was not owned by one

individual, but was managed and administered by a chief or elder of the household. The chief had power to administer and distribute this property based on lineage rights that placed him as the highest ranking member within the household. Other members of his household, while they did not have rights to distribute communal property, did have user rights based on their hereditary affiliations.

Private property, on the other hand, was owned and distributed by individuals. This property included items such as clothing, tools, ornaments, and other personal effects. Individual men owned their fishing gear and woodworking tools, while women owned household utensils such as knives, baskets, mats, and bowls. The majority of items were made by their owners; however, there was an exchange of tasks within the household whereby men carved bowls and other wooden utensils for women to use, and women made nets, clothing, and mats for men to use. The type and amount of property owned by any one individual depended not only upon gender but also upon that individual's industry and class. Men and women of high class and wealth owned furs, coppers, dentalium shells, slaves, and other prestige items.

Early maritime accounts record the trade of goods that are recognizably women's private property. Women actively participated in the trading of baskets, hats, and their other gender-related crafts. The demand for such trade goods would have ensured women's participation in trade transactions; however, the interest in these goods was often more one of curiosity than one of marketability. While on some voyages there was a conscientious effort to collect material culture for anthropological and ethnographical research, the majority of these trade goods were acquired by individual crew members who were interested in them for their own personal use. While later accounts during the land fur trade indicate an increase in demand for such crafts, in the maritime period, women's participation in trade would have been negligible if the only goods traded were their personal effects and gender-related crafts.

However, there are many reports in the fur trade accounts that document women trading furs, dried fish, and other goods that are recognizably communal property. In some Northwest coast societies, women could have acquired access to communal property by their hereditary status. For example, in the north, where matrilineal descent groups were predominant, women who by their age were the highest members of their lineage might have had an ability to control their own lineage property. However, in other regions of the coast where different descent systems existed, women did not necessarily have the same access. To understand how women throughout the coast acquired rights to trade communal goods during the fur trade, let us consider that women had a specific role in traditional trade that was maintained and continued during the fur trade. The following section reveals this role in trade and examines some of the pivotal factors that might have contributed to this role.

Women's Role in Trade

While each household was self-sufficient and autonomous in the production of its own goods, each household traded for goods that were not locally produced. Trade networks linking neighbouring coastal villages and tribal groups gave individual households access to a great variety of trade goods, as well as diversity of cultural interaction. Traditionally, trade took place during the spring and early summer months before intensive food gathering activities began. At this time, each household established its own trading partnerships with other households in neighbouring villages. These trade partnerships and alliances were maintained through either marriage affiliations or trade monopolies of specific food resources. Food was the primary trade good; crafts and other goods were of secondary importance.

Traditional trade included social and political obligations that were expressed in rituals, feasting, and the giving of gifts. This was an integral part of trade and continued throughout the maritime fur trade period.[39] The participants in this aspect of trade were the elders or the chiefs of the households involved. The goods that they traded or exchanged were viewed as gifts to confirm and maintain the status of the household group and their lineage. They included not only tangible communal property, such as furs and other prestige items, but also intangible property such as the rights to rituals, songs, and medicines. Inadvertently the giving of such gifts also enhanced the prestige of the chief who gave them, for prestige on the Northwest coast did not come from the acquisition of wealth but its generous distribution. The more a chief gave, the more status he gained for himself and his household group.

Women did participate in and contribute to this social and political aspect of trade. Besides their involvement in the welcoming rituals and food preparation for feasting, women also participated in the giving of gifts. The senior women of the household, depending on their status, gave furs and other prestige gifts to the visiting guests. Many of these women were related through kinship or marriage, and consequently these exchanges further enforced the trading alliances. These gifts also confirmed the status of the household group, and in the giving, enhanced the prestige of the women involved.

Once the gift-giving ceremonies were complete, individual families traded with other families on a more informal level. At this level, all individuals (with the exception of slaves) had an opportunity to participate in trade. At this point in the trade transactions, the motives were purely economic and each family tried to maximize its trade returns. The women had a decisive role in this goal. They checked the goods to be traded and kept track of the prices for each item. Sometimes the prices were set by custom, or by the skilful bargaining of the chief; however, at other times women could, through their own shrewdness and experience, manipulate the prices to ensure a better trade exchange.

. . . In a society where status was determined not only by heredity, but also by wealth, this bargaining skill had great potential for increasing a woman's status as well as her household's wealth. Women's participation in this regard would have been further enforced because they need not compromise a chief's reputation for generosity in the prestigious distribution of wealth. A chief's status rested on the distribution of wealth, and not on its accumulation. Thus chieftainship had been given a cultural role definition that excluded some men from maximizing (buying cheap and selling dear) during trade transactions. Women evidently did not labour under such strictures, thus allowing them to control goods distributed outside of the household.

The maritime fur trade differed in many respects from traditional trade in that it did not have the same social and political ramifications as inter-tribal trade. In fact, many maritime traders[40] were quite aggravated by the time-consuming welcoming rituals and feasting that first accompanied trade. Their prime concern was to acquire furs as quickly as possible, and move on. Also, the prestige associated with gift-giving had no place in these exchanges. While many maritime traders were forced into gift-giving exchanges, they recorded their dislike for such practices, and declined as much as possible. Such dislike was further increased when many maritime fur traders[41] discovered that gift-giving exchanges actually increased the price of trade goods. In such trade situations, where maximizing was the sole criterion for exchange, women's participation in trade would have been ensured.

Another element that might have ensured women's participation in trade during the maritime period was the increased competition between tribal groups that the infusion of new wealth encouraged. The maritime fur trade, due to its nature of interaction, brought new disparities of wealth between the tribal groups. With this new uneven distribution of wealth came the increasing need for chiefs and their households to validate their status. To do so, there was an increasing need for each household to accumulate more wealth than the other. Some traders noted this competition among different households in trade transactions. For example, Dixon[42] observed in his trade with the Haida that the furs in each canoe were distinct household property and the trade returns kept secret from each other. In the competitive trade transactions that had only maximizing motives, a woman's role in bargaining and monitoring prices would have been maintained and continued, particularly if she could increase the returns. Many fur trade accounts seem to confirm that women did have this skill from the beginning of the maritime trade.

However, women's economic control over household goods in trade transactions may have continued during the maritime fur trade with the increasing demand upon food stores. While the main motive of the maritime fur traders was to acquire furs, another important trade item was food: when vessels reached the Northwest coast, they were in desperate need of replenishing their provisions. In order to do so, maritime traders became dependent upon the natives of the region to resupply them. In this regard the natives were quite accommodating, and many accounts[43] record instances of women rowing out to the boats to trade food with the crews. Women brought a variety of items such as fresh and dried fish, ducks, shellfish, berries, and shoots.

Many of these foods were produced by women on the spur of the moment while the vessels were anchored in their harbour. During the summer, when food was in abundance and food gathering activities were at their peak, such trading activity probably had no consequence upon the household stores. However, later in the maritime trade period when vessels remained for the winter on the coast, the trade of food provisions had the potential to jeopardize the winter stores of the household group. This increasing demand upon household stores would have increased women's economic power in managing and rationing this food outside of the household for trade transactions.

However, women's active participation in trade during the maritime fur trade may have also increased due to changes in property relations. Drucker,[44] for example, theorizes that the fur trade encouraged the breakdown of communal relations, and fostered private ownership of resources. While it has been argued[45] that women's economic role and participation in the distribution of social production decreases with the formation of private property, there are many cross-cultural instances where private property gave women an increasing role in trade. For example, Afonja[46] and Etienne,[47] in tracing the role of women in trade, noted that within the Yoruba and Baule subsistence economy there was a private but gender-related ownership of property that encompassed all property relations. This gender-related property ownership allowed women rights to trade their own goods.[48]

Gender-related property ownership already existed to some extent on the Northwest coast. If women's control over household goods increased, is it possible that property relations may have been increasingly transformed into private gender-related ownership? Such ownership would have assured women a role in trade with their own gender-related trade goods. There is some evidence in the later ethnographies which indicates that this gender-related property ownership was well entrenched between a woman and her husband at the end of the fur trade. However, such evidence does not reveal whether gender-related ownership increased during this period from that in traditional times.

Conclusion

This paper has examined the role of Northwest coast women in the fur trade, and proposed that this role was not a new behaviour arising from the fur trade, but a continuation of a traditional role that included women in trade transactions. Also, it proposed that some of the key factors that enabled women access to trade goods in traditional trade were the specific relations of production of the Northwest coast, women's role in the management and production of household goods, and a cultural role definition that excluded some men from maximizing in trade transactions.

This paper has also examined how these factors may have increased women's participation in trade during the maritime fur trade. The fur trade, by increasing the frequency and importance of maximizing exchanges, may have increased women's participation in a role that traditionally excluded some men. Also, the increasing demand upon household stores by the maritime crews may have increased women's stewardship of such goods into their use for trade.

Finally, the transformation of communal property to private property may have increased the emphasis upon gender-related ownership of goods giving women increased participation in trade transactions.

NOTES

1. Recent fur trade research by Jennifer S.H. Brown, *Strangers in Blood: Fur Trade Company Families in Indian Country* (Vancouver: University of British Columbia Press, 1980); and Sylvia Van Kirk, *Many Tender Ties: Women in Fur Trade Society* (Winnipeg: Watson & Dwyer, 1980), has revealed the role of women in marriage alliances and their productive role as a labour force. However, this research only portrays women as supporting men's roles and neglects the economic role of women in the appropriation and distribution of trade goods.

2. W. Beresford, *A Voyage Round the World: But More Particularly to the Northwest Coast of America; Performed in 1785–88*, edited by Capt. Dixon and Capt. Portlock (London, 1789), 315.

3. F.W. Howay, "A List of Trading Vessels in the Maritime Fur Trade, 1785–94," *Transactions of the Royal Society of Canada*, 3rd ser. 24, section 2 (1930): 111–34.

4. J. Crespi, *Missionary Explorer on the Pacific Coast, 1769–74*, edited by H.E. Bolton (Berkeley: University of California Press, 1927), 329; F. Mourelle, "Voyage of the 'Sonora' in the Second Bucareli Expedition. . . . The Journal Kept in 1775 on the 'Sonora' by Don Francisco Antonio Mourelle," in *Miscellanies* by Daines Barrington (London, 1781), 503; J. Cook, *A Voyage to the Pacific Ocean Performed under the Direction of Captains Cook, Clerke and Gore, in His Majesty's Ships the Resolution and the Discovery in the Years 1776, 1777, 1778, 1779, and 1780*, vol. 3 (London, 1784), 43.

5. C. Fleurie, *A Voyage Round the World Performed during the Years 1790–92 by Etienne Marchand*, vol. 1 (London, 1801), 92; J. LaPerouse, *A Voyage Round the World in the Years 1785, 6, 7, 8*, edited by M. Milet-Mareau, vol. 1 (London, 1798), 369; J. Meares, *Voyages Made in the Years 1788–89 from China to the Northwest Coast of America* (New York: Da Capo Press, 1967), 141.

6. G. Vancouver, *A Voyage of Discovery to the North Pacific Ocean and Around the World*, vol. I (London, 1798), 348; E. Bell, *A New Vancouver Journal on the Discovery of Puget Sound by a Member of the Chatham's Crew*, edited by E. Meany (Seattle, 1915), 40; J. Espinoza, *A Spanish Voyage to Vancouver and the Northwest Coast in the Year 1792 by the Schooners 'Sutil' and 'Mexicane' to Explore the Strait of Fuca*, translated by C. Jane (London: Argonaut Press, 1930), 90.

7. Crespi, *Missionary Explorer*, 329; Fray Tomas de la Pena, *Diary of Fray Tomas de la Pena Kept during the Voyage of the Santiago — Dated 28 August 1774*, edited by G.B. Griffin, the Sutro Collection, Historical Society of Southern California (Los Angeles: Franklin Press, 1891), 122; B. La Sierra, *Diaries of Benito de La Sierra and Padre Miguel de la Campa Made on Board the Frigate Santiago, 1775* (Mexico: D.F., 1919), 19.

8. J. Strange, *Journal and Narrative of the Commercial Expedition from Bombay to the Northwest Coast of America* (Madras, 1928), 25.

9. Meares, *Voyages Made in the Years 1788–89*, 141.

10. Beresford, *Voyage Round the World*, 208, 225.

11. R. Haswell, "Log of the First Voyage of the Columbia," in *Voyages of the Columbia*, edited by F.W. Howay (Boston, Mass.: Historical Society, 1940), 96; Haswell, "Log of the Second Voyage of the Columbia," in *Voyages of the Columbia*, 325; J. Hoskins, "Narrative of the Second Voyage of the Columbia," in *Voyages of the Columbia*, 372; J. Ingraham, *Journal of the Brigantine Hope on a Voyage to the Northwest Coast of North America, 1790–92*, edited by M.D. Kaplanoff (Mas-

sachusetts: Imprint Society, 1971), 132; J. Caamano, "Extracto Del Diario, 1792," *British Columbia Historical Quarterly* 2 (1938): 205; C. Bishop, *The Journal and Letters of Capt. Charles Bishop on the Northwest Coast of America, in the Pacific and in New South Wales, 1794–1799*, edited by M. Rowe (Cambridge: Hakluyt Society, 1967), 63.

12. Ingraham, *Journal of the Brigantine Hope*, 132.
13. C. Roquefeuil, *A Voyage Round the World between the Years 1816–19* (London, 1823), 104.
14. Meares, *Voyages Made in the Years 1788–89*, 323.
15. Fleurie, *Voyage Round the World Performed during the Years 1790–92*, 242.
16. Vancouver, *Voyage of Discovery*, vol. II, 343, 409.
17. M. Quimper, "Diaro, 1790," in *Spanish Explorations in the Strait of Juan de Fuca*, edited by H. Wagner (Santa Ana, CA, 1933), 123.
18. Bishop, *Journal and Letters of Capt. Charles Bishop*, 125.
19. M. Lewis, *The Lewis and Clark Expedition*, vol. II (Philadelphia and New York: Lippincott Co., 1961), 483, 484, 500, 501, 521.
20. A. Walker, *An Account of a Voyage to the Northwest Coast of America in 1785 and 1786*, edited by R. Fisher and J.M. Bumsted (Seattle: University of Washington Press, 1982), 62.
21. Fleurie, *Voyage Round the World Performed during the Years 1790–92*, 242.
22. Meares, *Voyages Made in the Years 1788–89*, 324.
23. Hoskins, "Narrative of the Second Voyage of the Columbia," 208: Vancouver, *Voyage of Discovery*, vol. II, 324; Beresford, *Voyage Round the World*, 290; Roquefeuil, *Voyage Round the World between the Years 1816–19*, 104; Ingraham, *Journal of the Brigantine Hope*, 132.
24. Haswell, "Log of the Second Voyage of the Columbia," 325, 326.
25. Vancouver, *Voyage of Discovery*, vol. II, 409.
26. Meares, *Voyages Made in the Years 1788–89*, 323.
27. Vancouver, *Voyage of Discovery*, vol. II, 253.
28. A. Malaspina, *Politico-Scientific Voyage Round the World by the Corvettes Descubierta and Atrevida from 1789–94*, translated by C. Robinson (Vancouver: University of British Columbia Press, 1934), 16.
29. Ingraham, *Journal of the Brigantine Hope*, 101.
30. Lewis, *Lewis and Clark Expedition*, vol. II, 532.
31. R. Cox, *The Columbia River* (Norman: University of Oklahoma Press, 1957), 226.
32. Beresford, *Voyage Round the World*, 294.
33. P. Sanday, "Toward a Theory of the Status of Women," *American Anthropologist* 75 (1973): 1682–1700; E. Friedl, *Women and Men: An Anthropologist's View* (New York: Holt, Rinehart and Winston, 1975).
34. J. Jewitt, *The Adventures and Sufferings of John Jewitt Captive among the Nootka, 1903–05* (Washington: Galleon Press, 1975); Fleurie, *Voyage Round the World Performed during the Years 1790–92*, 242; Vancouver, *Voyage of Discovery*, vol. I, 347; G. Franchere, *Narrative of a Voyage to the Northwest Coast of America in the Years 1811, 12, 13, 14*, translated and edited by J. Huntington (Redfield, New York, 1854), 245.
35. G. Von Langsdorff, *Voyages and Travels in Various Parts of the World*, vol. II (New York: Da Capo Press, 1968), 132.
36. Vancouver, *Voyage of Discovery*, vol. II, 262.
37. Collins, "Growth of Class Distinctions and Political Authority among the Skagit Indians during the Contact Period," *American Anthropologist* 52 [1950], maintains that among present-day Salish a man was labelled transvestite if he attempted any of the women's crafts. She noted that the only times there occurred cross-sexual division of labour was in the making of twine and the preparation of reef nets.
38. Espinoza, *Spanish Voyage*, 17; LaPerouse, *Voyage Round the World in the Years 1785, 6, 7, 8*, vol. I, 375.
39. Jewitt, *Adventures and Sufferings of John Jewitt*, 69.
40. LaPerouse, *Voyage Round the World in the Years 1785, 6, 7, 8*, vol. I, 370; Jewitt, *Adventures and Sufferings of John Jewitt*, 59; Beresford, *Voyage Round the World*, 187.
41. Hoskins, "Narrative of the Second Voyage of the Columbia," 265; Ingraham, *Journal of the Brigantine Hope*, 126.
42. Beresford, *Voyage Round the World*, 204.
43. Boit, "Log of the Second Voyage of the Columbia," 382; Quimper, "Diaro, 1790," 110; E. Coues, ed., *The Manuscript Journals of Alexander Henry and David Thompson*, vol. II (Minnesota: Ross and Hines, 1965), 854, 859; S. Patterson, *Narrative of the Adventures and Sufferings of Samuel Patterson* (Washington: Galleon Press, 1967), 73; Meares, *Voyages Made in the Years 1788–89*, 141.
44. P. Drucker, *Indians of the Northwest Coast* (Natural History Press, 1955).
45. M. Rosaldo, "Woman, Culture, and Society: A Theoretical Overview," in *Woman, Culture, and Society*, edited by M. Rosaldo and L. Lamphere (Palo Alto, CA.: Stanford University Press, 1974); K. Sacks, "Engels Revisited: Women, the Organization of Production and Private Property," in *Woman, Culture, and Society*; Sanday, "Toward a Theory of the Status of Women."
46. S. Afonja, "Changing Modes of Production and the Sexual Division of Labour among the Yoruba," *Signs: Journal of Women in Culture and Society*, vol. 7, no. 2 (1981): 299.

47. M. Etienne, "Women and Men, Cloth and Colonization: The Transformation of Production Distribution Relations among the Baule," *Cahiers d'étude africaines*, vol. 65, no. 1 (1977): 41.
48. These authors maintain as well that the historical continuity of women's role in trade was a product of the gender-related ownership of household resources.

Women in Iroquois Society

ELISABETH TOOKER

For over a century, students of comparative social organization have pointed to the Iroquois as an illustration of the extent to which a society can be controlled by women. As a result, Iroquois women have gained an enviable reputation.[1] It is one that has led Judith K. Brown (1970: 156), for example, to remark that Iroquois matrons enjoyed perhaps more authority "than women have enjoyed anywhere at any time" and George Peter Murdock (1934: 302) to write, "of all the peoples of the earth, the Iroquois approach most closely to that hypothetical form of society known as the 'matriarchate.'"

However, not all students of the matter have concurred with this appraisal.[2] The most noted student of Iroquois society, Lewis H. Morgan (1851: 324), observed that "The Indian regarded woman as the inferior, the dependent, and the servant of man, and from nature and habit, she actually considered herself to be so," adding that "This absence of equality in position, in addition to the force of custom, furnishes a satisfactory explanation of many of the peculiarities characteristic of Indian society." And the best Harriet Maxwell Converse (1908: 138) could write of woman's status in Iroquois society was that "She may seem to have been a creature only and not a companion of the red man, yet by comparison with the restrictions, to characterize it by no stronger term, obtaining among *civilized* people, the Iroquois woman had a superior position and superior rights."

These differences of opinion suggest that the place of women in Iroquois society is not well understood. But I believe some of the obscurity surrounding this subject can be dispelled through a consideration of the principles of Iroquois sociopolitical organization — for Iroquois society may well rest on principles quite unlike those to be found in modern industrial societies or, for that matter, agrarian ones. At least, it is the intent of the following to suggest what these principles might be and how inattention has led to contradictory interpretations of the place of women in Iroquois society, as well as to suggest why Iroquois women — probably erroneously — have come to be regarded by so many as wielding exceptional power.

SOURCE: Elisabeth Tooker, "Women in Iroquois Society," in Michael K. Foster, ed., *Extending the Rafters: Interdisciplinary Approaches to Iroquoian Studies* (Albany: State University of New York Press, 1984), 109–123. Reprinted by permission of the State University of New York Press.

The Iroquois Clan and Political Systems

A review of the theoretical literature indicates it is their matrilineal clan system that has given the Iroquois the reputation of being a matriarchy or gynecocracy. But matrilineal clan systems are found in a number of North American Indian societies, and the fame of the Iroquois system does not derive from any basic difference between it and those of other North American Indians. Rather, its renown is largely the result of two accidents of history. First, the political system of the Iroquois was well described by Lewis H. Morgan in 1851 in what was the first ethnography in the modern sense of an Indian people and is still the best single description of Iroquois society. Morgan's study appeared a decade before studies of the evolution of human societies became popular and provided data for the proposition that became widely accepted: that matriarchal systems preceded the patriarchal ones familiar from Scripture. Comparison of American Indian societies to those more familiar to Europeans from their own, ancient, and Biblical history was not then new nor was the idea that human society had progressed. Rather interest in such studies increased in the latter half of the nineteenth century, as is indicated, for example, by the numerous editions of Sir John Lubbock's *The Origin of Civilization and the Primitive Condition of Man*, first published in 1870. To this body of literature Morgan himself contributed *Ancient Society* (1877), a work that attracted the notice of Karl Marx and achieved additional fame when Frederick Engels, carrying out Marx's intention, published a discussion and summary of it as *The Origin of the Family, Private Property and the State* (1942). As a result, the Iroquois matrilineal system became widely known, and so a convenient example of a matriarchical society for those who wished to interpret it thus.

Second, in the mid-1800s when anthropology was developing as a discipline, the Indians west of the Mississippi — and thus the Indians living there who had matrilineal clan systems — were little known to Whites, and some of these Indians, such as those of the Southwest who also have such an organization, were not so prominent in history. In contrast, the Iroquois were famous. In the early decades of the seventeenth century, the Iroquois, through a combination of favorable geographic position and political skill, became the most warlike and powerful Indians in the region. They remained so for a century and a half, holding the balance of power in the Northeast. (That England finally defeated France in their contest for control of this region and so control of the continent was due in some measure to the military and diplomatic aid the Iroquois gave the English.) To Americans in the nineteenth century, interested as they were in their own recent history, Morgan's account of the right of women to select and depose chiefs in the warlike Iroquois society was of more than passing interest.

But although the data collected since Morgan's time indicate that the clan system of the Iroquois does not differ in any fundamental respect from a number of such systems among other North American Indians (Tooker 1971), Iroquois clans do differ in several important respects from the usual textbook definition, indicating the principles on which they rest are not those usually presumed. In the anthropological literature, a "clan"[3] is most often defined as a group consisting of two or more lineages which are assumed to be descended from a common ancestor although the genealogical connection cannot be traced. Iroquois clans are exogamous (or, more properly, were exogamous, for the rule of clan exogamy is not now observed by all Iroquois), and this suggests that the Iroquois might believe that all members of a particular clan are descended from a common ancestor. However, such a presumption is not confirmed in Iroquois tradition. To the contrary, Iroquois tradition states that some personage (variously identified in different accounts) went about giving to groups who were camped together their clan names, naming each such group after an animal or bird he saw nearby (see, for example, Shimony 1961: 55–56; Stern 1933: 142–43; Hewitt 1928: 593–608; Henning 1898: 477–78). There is no tradition indicating that all members of each group were descended from a common ancestor, either human or animal. And, in fact, the relationship of the members of the clan to the "totemic animal" after which it is named more closely resembles the relationship between college students and their college mascot than any of the more exotic relationships mentioned in the anthropological literature. Among the Iroquois, then, clans were groups in which membership was ascribed at birth; they were not primarily a means of retaining knowledge of kinship relations that might otherwise be forgotten as is so often supposed.

Neither is the clan a local residential unit.[4] As in most other North American Indian societies that have clans, members of the same Iroquois clan lived in different villages. In fact, it is this dispersal of clan members that accounts for one of the principal functions of clan affiliation among the Iroquois as well as other North American Indians: the obligation of clan members to provide food and lodging to visitors from other villages who belong to their clan.

Nor did the clan own much property, either sacred or secular.[5] There were no ceremonies belonging to clans, at least none are mentioned in the literature, and those few references to ownership of property by clans are usually an Iroquois shorthand reference to ownership by a family or to ownership of things that may be inherited matrilineally.

However, among the Iroquois as among a number of other Indians, clans owned personal names, and it is this feature of Iroquois clanship that gave Iroquois women such prominence as they had in political affairs. By Iroquois custom, each clan holds a set of personal names. When a child is born, he or she is given a name "not in use." This "baby name" is usually later changed for an "adult name" that is not then "in use," that is, one belonging to someone now deceased or to someone whose name has been changed. Certain of these names are associated with particular obligations (in effect, roles) in the society. The evidence suggests that in the eighteenth and earlier centuries when trade and war were more important in the Iroquois economy, some names were associated with trading privileges and others with war (see, for example, Tooker 1964: 25–26, 44–45). Now, however, only those names designating particular chieftainships in the League and those names (the "Faithkeeper" names) associated with special religious obligations (obligations similar to deacons and deaconesses in some Protestant churches) have such specific associations.

The famed League of the Iroquois was established when the leading chiefs of the Mohawks, Oneidas, Onondagas, Cayugas, and Senecas met in council and decided to end the animosity between them. Just when this meeting was held and so the League founded is not known (it was probably sometime between A.D. 1400 and 1600). In succeeding years, this council of chiefs continued to meet to decide matters of concern to the Confederacy, and the clan-naming practices provided the basis for the perpetuation of the original council of fifty chiefs.[6] When such a chief (variously called in English, League, federal, or sachem chief) died, the senior woman of the clan (termed in English, the clan mother) to which he belonged, in consultation with the other women of the clan, selected the man from her clan who was to be given the name of the deceased chief and so his position. The man who was given this name was then "raised up" and the deceased chief "resuscitated" at a convocation known as the Condolence Council, or Condolence Ceremony — in the past, the first order of business at the councils of the League chiefs. If subsequently he proved unsatisfactory in this office, his name could be taken away. By this action he was "dehorned," that is, had his symbolic horns of office taken from him and so was deposed by the clan mother.

The seeming prominence of women in Iroquois political affairs rests almost entirely on this practice. By Iroquois custom, women did not speak in council, at least not normally. Councils were meetings of men, and council decisions the work of men, not women — however interested women might be in them. Men were the orators, the masters of the art of finding consensus in the welter of differing opinions among them — for the decisions reached by councils had to be unanimous in order to be binding. It was the men, too, who negotiated the treaties with other tribes and with European nations, meeting with representatives of those powers who came to the Iroquois capitals on such missions and sending delegations themselves to the seats of government of other nations. Women could, of course, and did attempt to influence the opinion of men. (One suspects women have always and everywhere tried to defend their own interests in ways that they could, as men have also attempted to defend their own interests.) This is attested by occasional references in the literature to women advising chiefs and to particular men being asked to speak for women (see, for example, Lafitau 1974–1977, 1: 295, 298–99; Stone 1841: 56–60, 154–56), references that have on occasion been taken to mean that women wielded considerable political power. Such an interpretation is usually not applied to comparable kinds of indirect influence women exerted in, say, nineteenth-century England or America. In Iroquois society, as in others, council affairs were the business firstly of men.

It should be further noted that in the councils of the League, men did not exercise this political power for the sole benefit of their clans. Although chosen by clan mothers, League chiefs were not properly representative of the various clans of the Confederacy. To suppose they were is to suppose the Iroquois form of governance was of the representational type familiar in Western society. It was not. By Iroquois custom all decisions had to be unanimous, and in decisions affecting the League, not only did all the League chiefs have to agree but also the people generally. The League chiefs had no police or other coercive power at their disposal to enforce the decisions they made. Their principal power was that of persuasion. If others disagreed with the chiefs' judgment, they could act contrary to the chiefs' decision and so abrogate it. In effect, then, the council of the Confederacy acted as a kind of committee appointed to discuss particular kinds of issues and charged with proposing to the people generally the most reasonable course of action they could find. If all the people generally did not agree with the chiefs' suggestion, they could overturn it by ignoring it.

Attention to this form of governance helps explain why the clans were not necessarily equally represented on the council of the League and why some clans had no representation. (For example, of the eight names belonging to the Seneca, three are held by one clan, two by another, one each by two other clans; three clans have no League chiefs.) It was not essential that they be; it was only essential that differing points of view be taken into consideration in reaching a decision. Neither was it necessary that all members of a clan agree as to the choice of the successor of a chief having a name that belonged to his clan. Although the clan mother was supposed to consult with the other women of her clan in choosing such a successor, the available evidence indicates that she often did not and that her choice was usually a close relative such as a brother or son. In practice, the seeming prerogatives of clans in the selection of chiefs were obligations of certain lineages to staff the League council, to secure its continued existence rather — it is tempting to suggest — as women by giving birth to children insure the perpetuation of the society as a whole. Neither the role of certain women in certain clans nor the clan system generally was primarily a method by which women exercised political power as has so often been supposed.

If, on examination, the political power exercised by Iroquois women proves to have been limited, the economic power wielded by Iroquois women might seem to have been considerable. A number have suggested that it was, among them Brown who asserts that "The high status of Iroquois women was the result of their control of the economic organization of their tribe" (Brown 1970: 164).

Such statements as Brown's — that Iroquois women had dominant control of the Iroquois economy — usually rest on two contentions: (1) that Iroquois women by their labor contributed the major portion of subsistence and (2) that they owned much property, including that used in production. For example, in Iroquois society, the women were responsible for the planting, tending, harvesting, and storing of crops, that is, of corn, beans, and squash — called by the Iroquois either "the Three Sisters," for they were found together like sisters in the fields, or "Our Life Supporters," an indication of the important role of these foods in the economy. It is also reported that women owned the fields and that this property was inherited in the female line. Women also seem to have owned the houses and their stores. These longhouses were multifamily dwellings made of a framework of poles covered with bark sheets, approximately twenty feet wide and as long as required for the number of families who lived in the house. As residence was generally matrilocal,[7] the household was composed of a number of related women and their husbands. Marriages were apt to be brittle. Although monogamy was the rule, divorces were frequent, and consequently, women were the more permanent residents of the longhouse.

However, control by the women of the fields and houses was not the result of their labor in constructing them. Men both cleared the fields and built the houses. These were not inconsiderable tasks; as Trigger (1969: 27) has noted, perhaps "The most arduous agricultural work . . . that of clearing land . . . was men's work." Using stone axes, the men girdled the largest trees, cut down the smaller ones, and cleared the underbrush — a process that had to be repeated often because after a few years the fields became exhausted and new ones had to be cleared. Similarly, as the village was moved every eight, twelve, or twenty-five years (when both the fields that could be cleared and the firewood that could be collected nearby became exhausted, and perhaps also when the houses had deteriorated), men had to construct new houses relatively frequently.

Further, the contribution of men in supplying food was not negligible. The economy of the Iroquois was a mixed one, based on hunting, fishing, and collecting in addition to agriculture. The collecting of wild fruits and plants seems to have been women's activity, but hunting and much of the fishing — more important in the Iroquois economy than has often been recognized — were the responsibility of men. Although it is impossible at this date to make more than an educated guess as to the amount of food men contributed, it should be noted that a diet of corn, beans, and squash — which, aside from sunflowers and tobacco, were the only plants cultivated by the Iroquois — is a monotonous though balanced one. Hence, the contribution of men to it would seem likely to have been of more than casual interest to the Iroquois themselves.

But if the contribution of Iroquois men to economic production was perhaps as significant or almost as significant as that of the women — and therefore Iroquois women cannot be said to have had economic control of the society by virtue of their greater contribution to economic production — it might seem that it was their ownership of agricultural land, houses, and other property that gave Iroquois women this supposed control. Such an interpretation, however, ignores certain characteristics of Iroquois property: much of it lacked durability and hence great economic worth. Agricultural fields quickly lost fertility, and new ones had to be cleared. Their value lasted only a few years, and there was no shortage of fertile land. Houses lasted only a little longer. In a few years, the bark covering dried out, making their destruction by fire an ever-constant danger. The poles may well have rotted in the ground causing some disintegration of the structure, and perhaps the general deterioration of the houses as well as the reported exhaustion of agricultural land and of the firewood supply were factors in the decision to move the village and so rebuild the houses every dozen or two dozen years.

Similarly the implements used in production did not involve great investment in time and labor, nor did they last long. For example, the principal agricultural implement was the digging stick, a straight stick pointed at one end used to plant corn and in weeding. It was easily made, and although a particularly useful tool, it is hard to imagine it was a particularly priceless one. Thus, the likelihood that women owned such agricultural implements rather than men (Brown 1970: 159) was probably of little economic consequence.

What seems to have been important in Iroquois society in establishing rights to what we term "property" was not that idea so central in Western society — namely, ownership of a transferable legal title — but rather use. Property was "owned" by those who used it. Thus, a man "owned" those implements he used; a woman, those she used. In fact, concern with "use" pervades Iroquois society and culture. For example, in the Iroquois view of things, animals, plants, water, and the like were put on this earth for "our use," that is, for the use of human beings. This is evident in the Thanksgiving Speech that begins and concludes most Iroquois ceremonies. Of the earth itself, this speech states:

> And now this is what Our Creator did: he decided, "I shall establish the earth, on which the people will move about. The new people, too, will be taking their places on the earth. And there will be a relationship when they want to refer to the earth: they will always say 'our mother, who supports our feet.'" And it is true: we are using it every day and every night; we are moving about on the earth. And we are also obtaining from the earth the things that bring us happiness. And therefore let there be gratitude, for we believe that she had

indeed done all that she was obligated to do, the responsibility that he assigned her, our mother, who supports our feet. And give it your thought, that we may do it properly: we now give thanks for that which supports our feet. And our minds will continue to do so. (Chafe 1961: 19)[8]

This view of the world probably explains statements to the effect that women "owned the agricultural land." Women, not men, used it, that is, women planted, tended the crops, and harvested them. Men "produced" the fields in the sense that they cleared them, but since they did not use them, they were not regarded as having rights to these fields. Similarly, since houses were used more by women than men in the sense that women spent more time in them than men, they were often regarded as being owned by women. The same principle applied to other kinds of property. Thus, if a piece of property was clearly not being used by someone, another could use it and could claim rights to it so long as he continued to use it. If he ceased to do so, another could use it. As Fey and McNickle (1970: 21) state, "the right was a right to use, not to transfer in the market place."

Property rights, then, were probably of little importance in Iroquois society and, in fact, there was relatively little in the economic organization to "control." What little there was was fairly equally apportioned among individuals in the society.

Iroquois Kinship Terminologies

Some confirmation of the lack of importance of property in Iroquois society comes from an unexpected source: their kinship terminologies. It is often supposed that Iroquois kinship terminologies reflect their clan and moiety system. (Among the Iroquois, clans are grouped into moieties.) For example, in the Seneca system of kinship terminology (the other Iroquois kinship terminologies are similar, see Morgan 1871: 293–376), mother and mother's sister are called by the same term. As both belong to the same clan, it would seem that for this reason, the term "mother" is extended to "mother's sister." Similarly, father and father's brother are called by the same term and both also belong to the same clan. Further, parallel cousins are called by the same terms applied to siblings and cross-cousins by different terms — a practice which, as Tylor (1889) suggested, might reflect a moiety system. (By Iroquois custom, an individual calls members of his moiety "brothers" and "sisters," and members of the opposite moiety, "cousins.")

However, this hypothesis obtains only if the first collateral line is considered. The peculiarities of the Seneca system are such that it does not hold for the second and more distant collateral lines. As Lounsbury (1964: 1079n.) has noted, the now "classic theory" that characterizes the Seneca kinship system as classifying kin according to membership in unilineal descent groups predicts correctly only terms for the closest relatives; beyond that, it predicts, at best, only half the terms correctly.

Morgan, who more than any other writer is responsible for anthropological interest in systems of kinship terminologies, was well aware that matrilineal descent could not account for the Seneca system and others like it (see, for example, Morgan 1871: 475). And it is evident that in the rush to find a better explanation than Morgan's for these systems which began when Morgan's great *Systems of Consanguinity and Affinity of the Human Family* was published, this observation as well as others made by Morgan were overlooked.

What Morgan noted about the Seneca system was that it ignored the distinction most basic in ours: the distinction between collateral and lineal lines. It is a difference, Morgan suggested, that reflects the importance or lack of importance of property in the society. In those societies where property is negligible, Morgan (1871: 14) suggested, "The wider the circle of kindred the greater assurance of safety." The Seneca system and others of the type Morgan termed "classificatory" do this by ignoring in whole or in part the distinction between collateral and lineal kin, seeming to treat collateral relatives as if they were lineal ones. However, Morgan suggested, in those societies in which property is important . . . with "its possession sprang immediately the desire to transmit it to children. . . . [which] was realized by the lineal succession to estates" (Morgan 1871: 492). The "descriptive systems," as Morgan termed them, reflect this concern by distinguishing lineal from collateral relatives.

It is inattention to this difference between Iroquois society and ours, I would suggest, that has led to the presumption that Iroquois society is organized on the same basic principles as ours. But Morgan (1871: 492) may have been correct when he noted:

> It is impossible to over-estimate the influence of property upon the civilization of mankind. It was the germ, and is still the evidence, of his progress from barbarism, and the ground of his claim of civilization. The master passion of the civilized mind is for its acquisition and enjoyment. In fact governments, institutions, and laws resolve themselves into so many agencies designed for the creation and protection of property.

It is as if many anthropologists since Morgan's time, by dropping the word "barbarism" from their vocabulary, have been led to the assumption that the political and social institutions of all societies "resolve themselves into so many agencies designed for the creation and protection of property."

Relationships between Men and Women

Social relationships, then, between various classes of people in Iroquois society, including men and women, were not grounded in control of po-

litical power or economic resources. Rather, the contingencies of life as
the Iroquois had to live it led to dependence on other kinds of relationships, most notably, on reciprocal obligations, for the Iroquois per-
force did not rely on ownership of property but on other individuals.
There were reciprocal obligations between the old and the young, including those between older and younger generations and between older
and younger siblings. Other reciprocal obligations, including that of
burying the dead, were the responsibility of the moieties, and when the
moieties were exogamous, as they are said once to have been, they provided spouses for each other. Still other reciprocal obligations obtained between the chiefs and the people generally. Others involved
the supernatural. These beings have obligations to the people and
the people to them — as the quote given above from the Thanksgiving
Speech illustrates. And, as will be suggested, relationships between men and women also rested on maintenance of reciprocal obligations.

In Northern Iroquoian societies, including those of the Iroquois
proper and the Iroquoian-speaking Hurons, men and women occupied
different domains: the forest and the clearing. Their principal villages
were sparsely populated, having perhaps a few hundred to a thousand
inhabitants, and few in number. For example, in the seventeenth century,
the Iroquois had only thirteen principal villages and some scattered
smaller settlements consisting only of a few houses in the considerable
territory they controlled in what is now upstate New York (a region some
two hundred miles long that stretched from the Mohawk valley in the
east to the Genesee in the west). Nonetheless, these villages, small as
they were, constituted islands of human habitation in a forest sea and
it may be for this reason that the clearing — the village and surrounding
fields — had a special importance to the Iroquois. It was from the village
that the Iroquois ventured out to fish, to hunt passenger pigeons in the
spring and deer and other animals in the fall, to collect maple sap in
the early spring and later greens, berries, and nuts of various kinds,
and to trade and war, returning with the produce so obtained. Since
it was the men who most often left on such expeditions, the village became
more particularly the world of the women as well as that of the people
generally. Further, as the women did all the agricultural work of planting,
tending, and harvesting of crops, the whole clearing (village and fields)
also was regarded as the domain of women. The land beyond the clearing,
the forest, was the domain of men, the land into which they traveled
to hunt, war, and trade and the land they cleared to make the fields
and village.[9]

Rather similarly, each house was the domain of the women, a consequence of the general practice of matrilocal residence. Each longhouse
was occupied by a number of nuclear families related in the matrilineal
line. Women, then, remained part of the household they were born into

although the rebuilding of the village every eight, dozen, or two dozen years meant that a woman lived in several different houses in the course of her lifetime. Men, however, were apt to live in a number of different households in the course of their lifetime (divorce was frequent) as they traveled in and out of the village over the course of a year. In fact, it may well have been that the hunting, war, and trading parties the men so avidly joined (on occasion older men had to restrain some of this enthusiasm to insure that an adequate number of warriors remained to defend the village in case of attack) served as a kind of men's club, an escape from the domination of women. Village and League councils also may have served the same purpose.

Property seems to have figured little in marriage arrangements, for there was little of value to own. Marriage involved not rights to property, but reciprocal obligations between a man and a woman. These obligations were of no small moment, and they proved to be a major obstacle to conversion to Christianity with its idea of the indissolubility of marriage. As one Huron put it, "If we take a wife, at the first whim that seizes her, she will at once leave us; and then we are reduced to a wretched life, seeing that it is the women in our country who sow, plant and cultivate the land, and prepare food for their husbands" (Thwaites 1896–1901, 14:235).

It was the obligation of a man to provide the household in which he was living with the products of his activities away from the village. For this reason, according to Lafitau (1974–1977, 1:340), a mother was in no hurry to have her son marry, for when he did the mother's household was deprived of his economic contribution. In compensation for this loss, a wife was obligated to help her husband's maternal household with their work in the fields and the collecting of firewood (ibid.:348), one of the most important tasks of women. The reported practice of Iroquois mothers' arranging marriages (ibid.:341; Fenton 1951: 43) would seem to have been an attempt to insure that the wife fulfill these obligations. The practice is not reported for the Hurons, and it may be that few Huron marriages were arranged, as Huron men did not make as much of an economic contribution to the households in which they were living as did Iroquois men; Hurons seem to have been less dependent on hunting than the Iroquois were.

These reciprocal obligations between the sexes extended beyond the marriage relationship. Most important, the obligation of women to provide food for men extended to the clan when men were visiting in other villages. On arrival in a village, a man was asked what his clan was so he could be directed to a house where he might expect to be given food and shelter. As has been noted, one of the important functions of the clan was fulfillment of this obligation.

It was also the obligation of the women of the clan to see that important leadership positions were filled, especially those of the League council. But as customarily such positions went to the men of the clan, fathers could not expect their sons to inherit their position, perhaps adding to a man's sense of being a drifter between households run by women.

An Iroquois man's concern, then, seems to have been a constant search for a household that would provide him with food and shelter — a household of mother, wife, or clan member who might be induced to provide these necessities, perhaps in return for such goods and services as he could provide. Women's concerns would seem to have centered on keeping the household running. One task involved obtaining stores, the women of the household often working together to provide the basic provisions (the household held these in common). It was the women who planted, cultivated, and harvested the crops — corn, beans, and squash — that constituted the basic diet. Such food as was furnished by the men supplemented that provided by women. Nonetheless, the women needed the help of men, particularly in clearing the land for cultivation and in building the houses. Since such activities demanded the work of a group rather than a single individual, it was to a woman's advantage to increase the number of men — related by blood or marriage — on whom the household could call for such help, thus extending her kin relations.

But within the village, these kin relationships were extended bilaterally. The matrilineal clan system was not so much a means of distributing property or of organizing life in the village as it was a means of relating to people in other villages beyond the surrounding forest. Men typically dealt with matters beyond the clearing, including political affairs. Hence, the chiefs who did so were men, but their names indicated they had been designated by women as worthy to speak for them and the people generally. On the other hand, visitors to the village needed only to know the name associated with a particular role to be directed to the proper individual and the name of his own clan to be provided with food and shelter.

In summary, the problems that Iroquois women and men had to confront were not those of contemporary western society. They only appear to be when the underlying principles of Iroquois sociopolitical organization are ignored, and the separate elements that make it up pulled from their context and reinterpreted in familiar — to us — ways, with the result that matters of little consequence to the Iroquois are presumed to be of great moment and matters of crucial significance to them overlooked. Perhaps, then, Morgan's (1851: ix–x) admonition given over a century and a quarter ago is apt: "The time has come in which it is befitting to cast away all ancient antipathies, all inherited opinions; and having taken a nearer view of their social life, conditions and wants, to study anew our concerning them."

NOTES

1. An earlier version of this paper was given at the Conference on Women in the Era of the American Revolution held in July 1975 at George Washington University.
2. In addition to the discussion to be found in the general ethnographic literature on the Iroquois, the role of women in Iroquois society has been the subject of a number of papers. These include those by Carr (1884), Beauchamp (1900), Goldenweiser (1915), Hewitt (1933), Randle (1951), Richards (1957; 1974) and Brown (1970).
3. The term "clan" is used here in preference to "sib," "gens," "tribe," "nation," or any other term that has been applied to these social units because in the anthropological literature on North American Indians this is the term most commonly used.
4. A statement made by Johannes Megapolensis in 1644 (Jameson 1909: 178-79) has often been interpreted as meaning the Mohawks had clan villages. But this is the only such reference in the literature, and a contemporaneous remark by Father Isaac Jogues (Thwaites 1896-1901(29): 53, 293) seems to indicate that the Mohawks had multiclan villages at the time.
5. Morgan's (1877: 70-85) summary of the rights, privileges, and obligations of clans is somewhat overdrawn, as a close reading of this passage will indicate. The workings of the Iroquois system are somewhat better described in his *League of the Iroquois* (1851). Nevertheless, Morgan was a more careful observer and more accurate writer than he is often given credit for. For example, if he seems to slight some aspect of Iroquois culture, it is usually because the matter is of little consequence to the Iroquois themselves, and if he seems to dwell too long on other matters, it is because these are of importance to the Iroquois. Further, his theoretical concerns reflect this knowledge. Thus, it is of some interest that one of the first papers he wrote after he became interested in more general and comparative problems rather than in just the Iroquois was on "The Indian Method of Bestowing and Changing Names" (Morgan 1859), a subject that has attracted little attention since then.
6. The number of League chiefs is variously given as forty-eight, forty-nine, and fifty. The number of chiefly names is fifty. However, by custom, no one is given the name of Hiawatha, who with Deganawida founded the League. (Longfellow later gave this name further fame by appropriating it for his poem about Algonquians.) Also, some Iroquois regard two of the Onondaga chiefly names as belonging to one person, while others contend they belong to two different men. Hence, different individuals calculate the total number of League chiefs differently.
7. Richards (1967) has questioned this, but the available evidence seems to indicate that the customary (although not invariant) rule was that of matrilocal residence. For a somewhat similar conclusion, see Trigger (1978: 58).
8. The Thanksgiving Speech is not recited by rote and consequently no two repetitions of it are identical. Nevertheless, the same basic ideas are evidenced in all performances. For other examples of this speech see Foster (1974) and the references listed in Chafe (1961: 301-2).
9. To the best of my knowledge this contrast between forest and clearing was first made by Wallace (1952: 24-28). The idea was further elaborated by Hertzberg (1966: 23-30). Part of the intent of the present discussion is to indicate its usefulness in clarifying certain matters not considered by either Wallace or Hertzberg.

REFERENCES

Beauchamp, William M. 1900. "Iroquois Women." *Journal of American Folk-Lore* 13(49):81-91.
Brown, Judith K. 1970. "Economic Organization and the Position of Women among the Iroquois." *Ethnohistory* 17:151-67.
Carr, Lucien. 1884. "On the Social and Political Position of Women among the Huron." *Reports of the Peabody Museum* 3:207-32.
Chafe, Wallace L. 1961. "Seneca Thanksgiving Rituals." *Bureau of American Ethnology Bulletin* 183. Washington.
Converse, Harriet (Maxwell). 1908. "Myths and Legends of the New York State Iroquois." Arthur C. Parker, ed. *New York State Museum Bulletin* 125:5-195. Albany.
Engels, Friedrich. 1942. *The Origin of the Family, Private Property and the State in the Light of the Researches of Lewis H. Morgan.* New York: International Publishers.
Fenton, William N. 1951. "Locality as a Basic Factor in the Development of Iroquois Social Structure." *Bureau of American Ethnology Bulletin* 149(3):39-54. Washington.
Fey, Harold E., and D'Arcy McNickle. 1970. *Indians and Other Americans: Two Ways of Life Meet.* Rev. ed. New York: Harper and Row.
Foster, Michael K. 1974. "From the Earth to Beyond the Sky: An Ethnographic Approach to Four

Longhouse Speech Events." *Canada. National Museum of Man, Ethnology Division, Mercury Series Paper* 20. Ottawa.

Goldenweiser, Alexander A. 1915. "Functions of Women in Iroquois Society." *American Anthropologist* 17(2):376–77.

Henning, Charles L. 1898. "The Origin of the Confederacy of the Five Nations." *Proceedings of the American Association for the Advancement of Science* 47:477–80. Salem, Mass.

Hertzberg, Hazel W. 1966. *The Great Tree and the Longhouse: The Culture of the Iroquois.* New York: Macmillan.

Hewitt, J.N.B. 1903–1928. "Iroquoian Cosmology." Pp. 127–339 in Vol. 21 and pp. 449–819 in Vol. 43 of the *Annual Reports of the Bureau of American Ethnology for the Years 1899–1900* and *1925–1926.* Washington.

———. 1933. "Status of Women in Iroquois Polity before 1784." Pp. 475–88 in *Annual Report of the Board of Regents of the Smithsonian Institution for 1932.* Washington.

JR = Thwaites, Reuben G., ed. 1896–1901. *The Jesuit Relations and Allied Documents: Travel and Explorations of the Jesuit Missionaries in New France, 1610–1791; the Original French, Latin, and Italian Texts, with English Translations and Notes.* 73 vols. Cleveland: Burrows Brothers. (Reprinted: Pageant, New York, 1959.)

Jameson, J. Franklin, ed. 1909. *Narratives of New Netherland, 1609–1664.* New York: Charles Scribner's Sons. (Reprinted: Barnes and Noble, New York, 1959.)

Lafitau, Joseph-François. 1974–1977. *Customs of the American Indians Compared with the Customs of Primitive Times.* William N. Fenton and Elizabeth L. Moore, eds. and trans. 2 vols. Toronto: The Champlain Society.

Lounsbury, Floyd G. 1964. "The Structural Analysis of Kinship Semantics." Pp. 1073–93 in *Proceedings of the 9th International Congress of Linguists.* Horace G. Lunt, ed. Cambridge, Mass., 1962. The Hague: Mouton.

Lubbock, John. 1870. *The Origin of Civilization and the Primitive Condition of Man; Mental and Social Condition of Savages.* London: Longmans, Green.

Morgan, Lewis H. 1851. *League of the Ho-dé-no-sau-nee or Iroquois.* Rochester, N.Y.: Sage; New York: Newman. (Reprinted as *League of the Iroquois,* Corinth Books, New York, 1962.)

———. 1859. "The Indian Method of Bestowing and Changing Names." *Proceedings of the American Association for the Advancement of Science* 13:340–42.

———. 1871. "Systems of Consanguinity and Affinity of the Human Family." *Smithsonian Contributions to Knowledge* 17. Washington.

———. 1877. *Ancient Society or Researches in the Lines of Human Progress from Savagery through Barbarism to Civilization.* New York: Henry Holt. (Reprinted: World Publishing Company, Cleveland and New York, 1963; Gordon Press, New York, 1976.)

Murdock, George P. 1934. *Our Primitive Contemporaries.* New York: Macmillan.

Randle, Martha C. 1951. "Iroquois Women, Then and Now." Pp. 167–80 in *Symposium on Local Diversity in Iroquois Culture.* William N. Fenton, ed. *Bureau of American Ethnology Bulletin* 149. Washington.

Richards, Cara E. 1957. "Matriarchy or Mistake: The Role of Iroquois Women through Time." Pp. 36–45 in *Cultural Stability and Cultural Change.* Verne F. Ray, ed. *Proceedings of the 1957 Annual Meeting of the American Ethnological Society.*

———. 1967. "Huron and Iroquois Residence Patterns, 1600–1650." Pp. 51–56 in *Iroquois Culture, History and Prehistory: Proceedings of the 1965 Conference on Iroquois Research.* Elisabeth Tooker, ed. Albany: New York State Museum and Science Service.

———. 1974. "Onondaga Women: among the Liberated." Pp. 401–19 in *Many Sisters: Women in Cross-Cultural Perspective.* Carolyn J. Matthiasson, ed. New York: Free Press.

Shimony, Annemarie A. 1961. "Conservatism among the Iroquois at the Six Nations Reserve." *Yale University Publications in Anthropology* 65. New Haven, Conn.

Stern, Bernhard J. 1933. "The Letters of Asher Wright to Lewis H. Morgan." *American Anthropologist* 35:138–45.

Stone, William L. 1841. *The Life and Times of Red Jacket, or Sa-go-ye-wat-ha; Being the Sequel to the History of the Six Nations.* New York and London: Wiley and Putnam.

Thwaites, Reuben G. *See* JR

Tooker, Elisabeth. 1964. "An Ethnography of the Huron Indians, 1615–1649." *Bureau of American Ethnology Bulletin* 190. Washington. (Reprinted: The Huronia Historical Development Council, Midland, Ontario, 1967.)

———. 1971. "Clans and Moieties in North America." *Current Anthropology* 12(3):357–76.

Trigger, Bruce G. 1969. *The Huron: Farmers of the North.* New York: Holt, Rinehart and Winston.

———. 1978. "Iroquoian Matriliny." *Pennsylvania Archaeologist* 48(1–2):55–65.

Tylor, Edward B. 1889. "On a Method of Investigating the Development of Institutions: Applied to Laws of Marriage and Descent." *Journal of the Royal Anthropological Institute* 18:245–69.

Wallace, Anthony F.C. 1952. "The Modal Personality Structure of the Tuscarora Indians as Revealed by the Rorschach Test." *Bureau of American Ethnology Bulletin* 150. Washington.

The Education of Girls by the Ursulines of Quebec during the French Regime*

NADIA FAHMY-EID

The education of girls by the Ursulines of Quebec was based primarily on the philosophy that prevailed in French metropolitan society in the seventeenth and eighteenth centuries. In France and New France, the education of girls was based on a specific definition of their role in society and consequently differed markedly from that of boys. Also, both societies were divided according to social rank and income, which were determining factors in the kind of education a girl would receive. In the colony the education of girls by the Ursulines was unique because society was further divided along ethnic lines — French and Indian.

This discussion will be limited to elementary school education since secondary schooling was not available to girls in either France or New France. In the colony, only the College of the Jesuits in Quebec offered higher education.

Philosophy of the Education of Girls

Although in New France no central organization was responsible for subject matter, pedagogy, or grade levels, the curriculum of the elementary school — petite école as it was then known — was fairly uniform. This uniformity was possible because the program was drawn from homogeneous philosophical and pedagogical sources and was limited in content. Besides the catechism, the girls were taught to read, write, and, in the language of the time, jeter — count with the use of jetons or tokens (usually old copper pennies). At this level, the education offered to girls and boys was almost the same. However, it should be noted that the curriculum for girls invariably included the teaching of "woman's" work (which will be discussed later).

Religion was the cornerstone of the education offered by the petite école, the "school of the popular classes." Since salvation was of para-

SOURCE: Nadia Fahmy-Eid, "L'éducation des filles chez les Ursulines de Québec sous le Régime français," in Nadia Fahmy-Eid and Micheline Dumont, eds., Maîtresses de maison, maîtresses d'école: Femmes, famille et éducation dans l'histoire du Québec (Montreal: Boreal Express, 1983), 49–76. Translated by Sarah Segev and Norma Scotcher.

*Translators' Note: Unless otherwise indicated, direct quotations are our translations.

mount importance, boys and girls received the same religious instruction. In New France girls were sent to school mostly around the time of their First Communion. As in most Catholic societies of the Western world at the time, secular education was secondary to religious instruction, the method favoured to Christianize the masses. In fact, the many treatises on education written in the sixteenth and seventeenth centuries often lamented the ignorance of the masses, referring less to their illiteracy than to their ignorance of basic religious truths and the corresponding moral precepts. Church-approved pedagogical guides and educational manuals circulated freely between France and the colony. The colony's strong ties with the motherland largely explain their similar educational philosophies.

In Quebec the Ursulines and the Sisters of the Congregation of Notre-Dame had much the same objectives for girls' education as their French counterparts. The writings of Marie de l'Incarnation revealed that the Christianization of Indian girls and the religious education of French girls were of utmost importance. In his letters of authorization written in 1676 to the Sisters of the Congregation of Notre-Dame, the Bishop of Quebec, Monsignor de Laval, reiterated: ". . . one of the best means to ensure our congregation's devotion, and the best manner to preserve and augment our parishioners' piety is by providing children with instruction and a good education; knowing that the Lord has blessed our Sister Bourgeoys and her companions . . . we have authorized and authorize the establishment of the religious order of the said Bourgeoys and the novices who have joined her or who will join her in the future, permitting them to live together as a community."

While religious instruction was stressed more for young girls, it was also available to boys. However, only girls were taught domestic arts. Here, too, the teachers in New France merely followed the general educational philosophy of the time; the education of girls, particularly those of the popular classes in seventeenth- and eighteenth-century France, focussed primarily on domestic skills, especially needlework. The following pedagogical treatises written by Catholic educators in Louis XIV's France are unanimous about the importance of the domestic work of women: De Fénelon, *Traité de l'éducation des Filles*, 1687; Abbé Claude Fleury, *Traité du choix et de la méthode des études*, 1689; Charles Rollin (rector of the Université de Paris in 1694), *Traité des études*, 1726. Accordingly, the curriculum, which minimized academics and emphasized the teaching of household arts, was eminently suited to the nature and social role of women. It should be noted that daughters of the nobility were taught more refined skills. For example, Madame de Maintenon, the founder of St. Cyr, taught her students embroidery, lacework, and so on. However, these students were in the minority, as were the convent boarders of l'Assomption, Sacré-Coeur, or the Ursulines of both France and the colony. For most of the students of the *petites écoles*, instruction in domestic arts, including needlework, provided early training for their future in a society where roles and tasks were defined according to class and gender. In addition to the teaching of catechism, reading, and writing, the Augustines' curriculum in France emphasized: "For the good of our young girls . . . as well as for the families they will one day raise . . . they must learn to sew and do the different kinds of woman's work." The constitution of the Ursulines of Rouen stated the importance of teaching girls to "sew and carry out other honest tasks appropriate to their sex." The Ursulines of Quebec also stressed this kind of education. In her writings Marie de l'Incarnation explained that besides catechism, reading, writing, and basic arithmetic, the nuns felt it important to teach the girls "all the tasks peculiar to their sex, all that a girl should know."[1] In fact, Monsignor Laval confirmed that the Sisters of the Congregation of Notre-Dame "raised little girls in the fear of God and taught them good Christian morals. They also taught them to read, write and carry out other tasks of which they were capable."

Thus, the educational philosophies in both the colony and France were inspired by the same sources. In Quebec the philosophy was shaped by the church's guidelines of strict orthodoxy and by some central ideas which held that, fundamentally, young girls should become good Christians first and then be groomed for the future roles assigned to them by society — mothers and housewives. As will be discussed later, these roles varied little, regardless of the social class of the pupils.

PROGRAMS

The educational policies and objectives of the program offered by the *petites écoles* in New France were directly related to the socioeconomic factors which determined whether a pupil attended school as a boarder (*pensionnaire*) or as a day student (*externe*), and to the French/Indian ethnic factor which was peculiar to this frontier society. Tuition for boarders varied with the "class" of the institution and the clientele. The cost associated with this kind of education was prohibitive for the popular classes because girls of rural and urban working-class families made a twofold contribution to the household: domestic and financial. As such, not only did the families have to pay for their daughters' education, they also had to be prepared to do without this dual contribution. Consequently, girls of modest means could only be day students, paying little or no tuition for this kind of education. Clearly, the division between boarders and day-pupils was directly linked to social class, and the education offered to each group differed as a result.

With respect to this division, a perfect analogy between schools in New France and the motherland is impossible because of the unique circumstances surrounding the colony's existence. Within the colonial perspective of the time, demand from France dictated production in the colony, thus preventing New France from fully exploiting its resources and filling its coffers. What riches the colony had were more uniformly distributed than in France, and social classes were less sharply defined. Generally, life in this frontier society was difficult and great fortunes were few. This economic reality precluded high tuition fees for girls' boarding schools. In fact, the cost of education remained low throughout the French regime and decreased further in the years following the Conquest. In addition to the colony's unique socioeconomic situation, its geography — the distance between home and school, the harshness of the climate, and the short growing season — at times made boarding school the only viable form of education for girls in rural areas. Yet, during the French regime there were but nine convents in the countryside: five were founded in the seventeenth century, four in the eighteenth century. These convents, run by the Sisters of the Congregation of Notre-Dame, usually lodged two or three nuns, but it is unclear whether they were all teachers. Neither these modest institutions nor their alternatives, such as the missions set up in several rural parishes, could bridge the gap between urban and rural education. This disparity may be viewed as a new distinction, or as an extension of the boarder versus day-pupil division and further explains the qualitative and quantitative differences in the content and level of programs offered to girls in New France.

Furthermore, the ethnic variable (previously discussed) is linked to the unique circumstances surrounding the colony's existence and is reflected in the different educational programs offered to French and Indian girls.

Lastly, the make-up of the teaching community also influenced the educational programs for girls in New France. Depending on the provisions of their respective constitutions (cloistered order for the Ursulines, or secular order for the Sisters of Notre-Dame, who enjoyed relatively unrestricted movement) and the human and socioeconomic geography of their apostolate, the religious communities of New France each tended to offer somewhat different programs of education. This tendency became more pronounced with time, lasting until the beginning of the nineteenth century.

Education of Indian Girls

From the start, Indian girls — Huron, Algonquin, Montagnais and some Iroquois — were taught separately from French girls. Around 1668 the Crown ordered the integration of the two groups; the results of the experiment were unconvincing, and this attempt at assimilating the Indians was short-lived. The annals of the convent confirm that "by the end of the year (1668), only one little Savage remained at the seminary in Quebec, and our sisters went back to teaching in separate groups."

The curriculum and methods used to teach native girls were different for day-pupils and boarders, also called seminarians. Furthermore, the boarding students who attended school for only five to six months of the year (usually during the hunting season) were considered "temporary" pupils and were offered an educational program that differed from their "permanent" counterparts. However, most of the students were day-pupils and received only religious instruction; a small minority learned to read and write. The chronicles of the Ursulines, as well as letters written by Marie de l'Incarnation, attest to the heterogeneous nature of the day-pupils. From different Indian nations and social ranks, this varied and ever-changing group of men and women of all ages had different motivations for coming to the convent. The nuns knew very well that most often these "heathens" came to them for material aid rather than salvation. In 1641, Mother Marie de l'Incarnation spoke of "eight hundred visits from Savages whom we succored as best we could."[2] That same year she wrote: "There are times when the Savages almost die of hunger. They sometimes go three or four leagues [fifteen to twenty kilometres] to find miserable wood berries or wretched roots that we could scarcely suffer in our mouths. We are so afflicted at seeing them in such starvation that we scarcely dare look at them. Judge for yourself whether it is possible not to strip oneself of everything on these occasions."[3] The need for sustenance was even more pronounced in the winter when the ranks of the needy included old people who could not join in the hunt. "If they were not cared for at that time they would die of hunger in the cabins,"[4] the Venerable Mother stated. The education offered to these "makeshift" students was minimal. The annals of the Ursulines recount that "they [the nuns] did not object to the frequent visits of these good Savages, who suffered from such hunger. The sisters' charity was twofold: they had them pray to God, gave them food and sent them on their way with an encouraging word." Further on, the chronicler continues: "During this period, around 1662, 70 to 80 Huron girls came to class every day, just like our day-pupils. After having them say their prayers, sing hymns and recite the catechism, we explained and taught Christian doctrine. We then gave them *sagamité* [a popular native dish made of black prunes, bread, maize, Indian meal, and suet or lard]." The nuns understood that they could not separate material aid from spiritual guidance, the first often a precondition for the second. This concept was explained by the founder of the Ursulines, who in one of her letters described a "feast" for a large group of natives: "This is how we win souls to Jesus Christ, we entice them with the promise of sustenance." She continued on the subject: "After instruction and prayers we feast them according to their fashion."[5] At the end of the letter she concluded: "It is a singular consolation to us to deprive ourselves of all that is most necessary in order to win souls to Jesus Christ."[6]

Both day-pupils and "temporary" seminarians received religious instruction in their native tongues, which the Ursulines had to learn. Studying under Father Le Jeune, Mother Marie de l'Incarnation and Mother

Sainte-Croix learned Algonquin, and Mother Saint-Joseph learned Huron. In 1640 Mother Marie wrote: "We study the Algonquin tongue, which is very difficult." The following year she added: ". . . there are many thorns in learning a speech so contrary to ours . . . the desire to speak does much."[7] Evidently, this "desire to speak" was a strong motivating force for Marie de l'Incarnation: her proficiency in Algonquin, and subsequently in Iroquois, was such that she composed works in both languages. She elaborated: "As these matters are very difficult, I am resolved that before my death I shall leave as much writing as I can. Between the beginning of last Lent and Ascension Day, I wrote a big book in Algonkin [sic] about sacred history and holy things, and also an Iroquois dictionary and an Iroquois catechism that is a treasure. Last year I wrote a big dictionary in the French alphabet; I have another in the Savage alphabet."[8]

To prepare the temporary boarders, who remained at the school a few months (sometimes just a few days) for baptism or communion, the nuns enlisted the help of the permanent boarders. In a way, "the oldest and most educated" became the religious instructors of the newcomers, responsible for "welcoming these temporary boarders. They had to explain the doctrine of Jesus Christ using the question and answer method used in the instruction of catechism, interpret holy pictures and tell them stories to hold their attention." On this subject, Father LeJeune wrote: "There is one girl, not more than eight years old, who teaches the younger ones, helps them examine their conscience and teaches them to never hide a sin."

The educators also endeavoured to teach these temporary boarders household arts. "I have begun to show them needlework," wrote Madame de la Peltrie in 1640. That same year, the Jesuit *Relations* adds: "They are wonderfully clever in performing all their little tasks and the small household duties that we teach them."[9] This kind of instruction, in addition to the teaching of catechism, was clearly an attempt to introduce the girls to a certain way of life — to Western mores.

Following the Crown's directive to assimilate the natives, the colonial educators for a while went beyond proselytizing and added a cultural dimension to their program. The first Mother Superior of the Ursulines, who along with the other nuns was sceptical of this ambitious but unrealistic program, commented with a touch of humour: "A Frenchman would more easily become savage than a Savage a Frenchman."[10] She continued on the subject of the native boarders: ". . . of a hundred that have passed through our hands we have scarcely civilized one."[11]

Certainly, assimilation was somewhat more successful with permanent than with temporary boarders. However, the scarcity of quantitative data makes it difficult to determine who these permanent boarders were. Sporadic information exists as to their number and the circumstances of admission, but there is little on the duration of their stay. For example, the annals of the convent tell us that "in the month of August, Father Raguenau brought us eight seminarians. In this same month of August 1650, came to us Elizabeth Astache of the Algonquin nation. After having been at the seminary for some time, she died." The founder of the Ursulines merely commented that there were "just as many temporary as permanent boarders." In 1654 she noted: "We have some Huron girls that the Reverend Fathers have judged suitable to be reared by us as French girls. . . ."[12] The following year, she wrote of the Iroquois: "Their ambassadors . . . admired our Savage seminarists [sic] when they heard them singing the praises of God in three different tongues. They were delighted to see them so well reared in the French way." Later, still on the subject of the Iroquois ambassadors, Mother Marie added: "They got singular pleasure from seeing and hearing our seminarists [sic], among others a little Huron of ten or eleven years whom we are rearing as a French girl. She can read, write, and sing in three tongues — namely Latin, French, and Huron."[13] Without specifying the number, Marie de l'Incarnation again wrote: "We have assimilated several savage girls, Huron and Algonkin [sic], who later married Frenchmen and were happy together." However, she explained that "nonetheless, we only assimilated a few poor orphan girls in our care, and those whose parents wished their daughters to be reared in this manner."

Various reasons accounted for a boarder's "permanent" status: young Indian girls entrusted or "given to" the Ursulines by the Jesuit Fathers, young orphaned girls taken in by the nuns, young girls or young ladies seeking or offered sanctuary from undesirable fiancés, husbands, or suitors, and so forth. The permanent boarders also varied in age; Marie de l'Incarnation confirmed that "in the case of Savage girls, we take them at all ages."[14] According to the records, the nuns took in "babies who not only required care during the day but kept the nuns awake at night." The chronicler continues: "In 1643 Mother Marie de Saint-Joseph took in a frail little creature a few months old, brought to the parlor by a poor, disconsolate mother." The Relation by Father Vimont (a Jesuit) also speaks of the nuns taking care of "three little orphans who needed a wet-nurse." The data, however, indicate that babies in the seminary were the exception and that the Indian boarders ranged from five to twelve years old. One could well imagine the difficulty these children had in adapting to such a completely different milieu and way of life. Still, records of that time are replete with examples of the native boarders' piety and devotion. While very few became the object of a hagiographic biography like Thérèse, the Huron girl, the letters of Marie de l'Incarnation as well as the Jesuit Relations are filled with testimonials and anecdotal accounts of the pious and exemplary behaviour of the native boarders. They write of Marie Amiskouevan, whose "docility, modesty, and obedience could make one believe she was a well-bred French girl," and of Marie-Magdeleine Abatenau, who "at age seven, does everything she is told with such good behaviour and good grace one would take her for a girl of rank."[15] Marie-Ursule Gamitiens was five or six years old and "is no sooner awake than she prepares herself to pray to God. She says her rosary during Mass and sings hymns in her Savage tongue."[16] Marie de l'Incarnation wrote that Agnes Chabdikouechich, "who has made very great progress . . . in the knowledge of the mysteries and, as well, in good manners, spoke and wrote with ease not only her native tongue but also French. . . . She was so devout, we thought to bring her into our Order, but she died in the woods, book in hand, praying to God."[17]

It is primarily the zeal with which the Indian seminarians prayed and their promptness to confess and do penance that elicited glowing testimonials in their regard. They were praised for being docile and obedient. Marie de l'Incarnation wrote the following to her son, who seemed incredulous at the exemplary behaviour of so many Indians: "If our Savages are as perfect as I tell you? . . . There are Savages as there are Frenchmen. Among them there are the more and less devout, but generally speaking, they are more devout than the French."[18]

Despite this piety and devoutness which the educators mentioned so often, few native girls seemed to have had the religious calling. The chronicler of the Ursulines comments: "There are about eight young girls who, according to our Mother Superiors could have become nuns and who would have devoted their lives to God but for the accidents which Providence failed to prevent. The two Savage girls who became nuns at the Congregation around 1685 both died young, and the same fate befell those who became sisters of the Hôtel-Dieu at Quebec." It is unclear whether these "accidents" happened by chance or because the young Native girls had difficulty adapting to a singular and specific way of life for which their original culture had in no way prepared them. Though few in number, historical records do speak of the unhappiness that some Indian boarders felt at having been forcibly transplanted into such a foreign environment. In a letter to a "lady of rank," Marie de l'Incarnation wrote of the difficulties the sisters experienced in getting their first boarder to adapt to her new life. This ten-year-old Indian girl was yet another of Madame de la Peltrie's godchildren: "The first Savage seminarist [sic] that was given to us, Marie Negabamat by name, was so used to running in the woods that we lost all hope of keeping her in the seminary. The Reverend Father Le Jeune, who had persuaded her father to give her to us, sent two older Christian girls with her. These remained with her for some time in order to settle her, but to no avail, for she fled into the woods four days later, after tearing to pieces a dress we had given her."[19] The founder also wrote that "there are still others that go off by some whim or caprice; like squirrels, they climb our palisade, which is high as a wall, and go to run in the woods."[20]

Although other seminarians who resented being separated from their families expressed their will to leave in less spectacular ways, they were no less determined. Such was the case with seven-year-old Nicole Asse-panse, about whom Marie de l'Incarnation wrote: "This girl has a mind so open that she is as capable of instruction as a girl of twenty. She was only five months in the seminary and was able to recount the prin-cipal points of our Faith and knew the catechism and Christian practices perfectly. . . . The girl nevertheless could not leave her mother whose only child she was, but she said, 'Though I wish to go, it is not because I lack for anything. I eat as much as I wish, the virgins give me fine clothes and love me very much, but I cannot leave you.' "[21]

Yet, for those Indian girls whose protests led to depression or ill-health, the first Mother Superior realized that there was no point in keeping them "by force or by entreaties,"[22] explaining, "Others are here only as birds of passage and remain with us only until they are sad, a thing the Savage nature cannot suffer; the moment they become sad, their parents take them away lest they die."[23]

The end of the seventeenth century was characterized by steadily declining Indian enrollment. While no single cause seems to have been at the root of this decline, the following reasons may provide some ex-planation: the moving of Indian nations away from Quebec, the taking over of Indian missions by the Sisters of the Congregation of Notre-Dame (a non-cloistered, hence more mobile congregation), and the real-ization that the long-term goal of assimilating Indian girls was a failure. In her writings, the chronicler of the Ursulines, after mentioning the presence at the convent of the "last Indian girls to form a separate class after 1700," states that "around 1725, the Indian boarders had all but disappeared." In fact, it was around this time that the Ursulines, when taking their vows, ceased to mention the instruction of Indian girls.

The Education of French Girls

DAY-PUPILS

"It was first as day-pupils that French young ladies attended the school of the Ursulines when the sisters lived in the Lower Town," reports the Order's annalist. To explain the raison d'être of a day-school, she specifies: "In the Institute of Ursuline Nuns, a day-school that does not charge tuition is deemed as essential as a boarding school, for it affords poor and rich alike the opportunity to benefit from education."

Not only was the day-school system ideally suited to the children of poor families, it also provided a solution to the overcrowding in the "Louvre," the name the nuns had jokingly given their small house on the quay.

The absence of day-school records makes it difficult to establish the annual enrollment of day-pupils. While there are some quantitative data on boarders, the information available on day-pupils is based primarily on general accounts which refer to the school population as a whole, that is, to both day-pupils and boarders. In 1652 Marie de l'Incarnation described how "the day after our arrival in Quebec, French and Savage girls alike were brought to us in great numbers so that we could educate them in good morals and piety."[24] On the subject of French girls, the founder of the Ursulines commented in 1664, "There is not one that does not pass through our hands."[25] Four years later she wrote, "I do not know the number of externs [day-pupils] for in winter the snow obliges them to remain at home. We have those of Upper Town and Lower Town. The French bring their daughters from a distance of sixty leagues [300 kilometres]."[26]

The chronicler of the Ursulines wrote that in 1687 there were about 50 day-school pupils. Additionally, records indicate that at the beginning of the eighteenth century there were more day-pupils than boarders, who numbered 55 to 60.

Marie de l'Incarnation painted the moral and psychological profile of day-girls as follows: "These girls are docile, they have good sense, and they are firm in the good when they know it."[27] She explained, however, that she could not look after their moral welfare quite as well as if "they were cloistered." Evidently, because they were more numerous and transient than boarders, day-pupils were not as closely supervised.

As was previously discussed, day-girls were taught reading, writing, and counting, but the emphasis was on religious instruction. One may assume that day-pupils were entitled to the same kind of education as short-term boarders. According to the founder, the school-mistresses had to apply themselves strenuously to teach those boarders in one year "reading, writing, calculating, the prayers, Christian habits, and all a girl should know."[28] Although this education would be considered minimal by today's standards, it reflected to a large extent the attitudes of the time — an era that expected little of girls, especially those of modest means.

BOARDERS

Three years after their arrival in New France, the Ursulines finally had their own convent. Built for them in the Upper Town in 1642, this building housed a residence for the nuns and a separate boarding school for French and Indian girls. Both the founder of the Ursulines and the chroniclers used different terms to designate schools for French and Indian students: "boarding school" for French girls and "seminary" for Indian girls.

At the time, the Ursuline convent was the only educational institution for girls in the colony; however, extraordinary circumstances forced the boarding school to close on several occasions. A fire which destroyed the convent closed the school from December 1650 to June 1652 and forced the Ursulines to seek shelter at the Hôtel-Dieu for three weeks. They then moved into Madame de la Peltrie's house next door to the ravaged convent. A second fire closed the school again in October 1686; the convent was restored with the help of the colonists and reopened its doors in November 1687. The siege of Quebec by the English in the fall of 1687 again forced the boarding school to close, this time for more than a year. During this time, the Ursulines provided asylum to refugees, thus creating a situation which the chronicler of the Ursulines describes as follows: "Not only was our house filled with lay people, but our classroom for day-pupils became cluttered with furniture and goods; it served to store the belongings of those who had brought them."

Save these few short interruptions, the boarding school had an unbroken existence, even after the Conquest in 1760. According to the annals of the convent, "eighteen to twenty French girls" comprised the first group to attend the boarding school. Their names, moreover, were inscribed in the registers of the time. While there is more statistical information on boarders than on day-pupils, the data are sporadic at best. Thus, one must resort to estimates in order to paint a general picture of student enrollment during that time. Over the years, various factors influenced enrollment. In 1668 the desperate financial situation of the Ursulines forced Mother Marie to send some boarders home: "We are limited to sixteen French girls and three Savages."[29] The following year she wrote about enrollment to a nun at Tours: "The colony has grown, and now we usually have 20 to 30 boarders." As the population increased, so did the number of students. The Ursuline chronicler records that "around 1700 there were on average 60 boarders," and that "in 1793 there were still 40 boarders despite the small-pox epidemic that ravaged Quebec." Was the chronicler correct in concluding that "the number of boarders was constantly on the rise?" In fact, in 1750 the nuns had to open another class to accommodate the increasing number of students. However, a comparison of the chronicles' figures between 1641 and 1719 indicates a total of 1,206 boarders, or an annual average of twelve, thus confirming that the increase was not constant but varied considerably.

From its inception the boarding school kept a School Register for French and Indian Girls which paints a picture of the geographical and social origins of the boarders. According to this register (rather difficult to decipher), kept until 1717, the majority came from Quebec. However, a significant minority came not only from surrounding parishes Île d'Orléans, Château Richer, Neuville, and so on) but also from greater distances, such as Trois-Rivières. Marie de l'Incarnation sometimes mentioned that they also had boarders from Montreal, notwithstanding the Sisters of the Congregation of Notre-Dame's active presence in that town.

Just as their geographic origins were diverse, so too were the boarders' social origins: the registers for the two decades following the opening of the boarding school reveal that of the 81 families whose daughters studied under the Ursulines, 9 belonged to the nobility, 41 to the bourgeoisie and 31 to the lower class (commonly referred to as *petites gens*). The annals stressed that only the social elite attended the boarding school: "This is confirmed by the names that grace our registers — magistrates, interpreters well-versed in Savage tongues, doctors, merchants and businessmen of all kinds. . . . Note too, the names of illustrious and valiant officers." According to the chronicler, these girls of such gentle birth had to behave in a manner befitting their class and as such "not allow themselves to be swayed by the appeal of life's transitory honours or crushed by its tribulations, but always behave as paragons of Christian virtue."

This glowing description of the young girls attending the boarding school contrasts with Mother Marie's rather negative perception of their undisciplined behaviour. She expressed these feelings in some of her letters; for example, she wrote the following to her son in 1652: ". . . the French girls would be real brutes without the education they receive from us and need even more than the Savages. . . ."[30] Some fifteen years later, the founder seemed not to have changed her mind about these students and reiterated: "Thirty girls give us more work in the boarding school than sixty would in France."[31]

It seems that young girls in France were more conservative than their counterparts in the colony. Based on Marie de l'Incarnation's accounts, the sociogeographic setting of New France was conducive to more liberal ways of thinking and behaving. Certain situations and sociogeographic characteristics peculiar to this frontier society constituted in the eyes of the nuns a definite source of "moral disorder." As the founder wrote in one of her letters, circumstances at times made it necessary for some parents to leave their daughters at home in the care of men (family, friends, neighbours, or hired help). In a letter to her son she described this kind of situation: "Great care is taken in this country with the instruction of the French girls, and I can assure you that if there were no Ursulines they would be in continual danger for their salvation. The reason is that there are a great many men, and a father and mother who would not miss Mass on a feast-day or a Sunday are quite willing to leave their children at home with several men to watch over them. If there are girls, whatever age they may be, they are in evident danger, and experience shows they must be put in a place of safety. In a word, all I can say is the girls in this country are for the most part more learned in several dangerous matters than those of France."[32]

Nonetheless, the nuns must have been generally satisfied with the education they provided, and the changes that they were able to bring about in the behaviour of their students, for in the same letter in which Mother Marie expressed her concerns, she also affirmed: "Our Reverend Fathers and Monsignor our Prelate [Bishop Laval] are delighted with the education we give the young girls. They let our girls receive communion as soon as they are eight years old, finding them as well instructed as they could be."[33] The Jesuit Fathers echoed such testimonials on various occasions, as did Father Raguenau in the *Relation* of 1651: "Experience teaches us that the girls who have been with the Ursulines feel the benefit of their stay there throughout their lives, and that in their households the fear of God reigns more than elsewhere, and they bring up their children much better therein."[34] Seventeen years later, in the *Relation* of 1668, Father Le Mercier also stated: "The Ursuline Mothers have had so great success in the instruction of the girls who have been confided to them . . . that in visiting the households of Canada, and each house in particular, it is very easy to distinguish, by the Christian education of the children, the mothers who have come out of Ursuline houses from those who have not had that advantage."[35]

To complete the social profile of the clientele of boarders, one must go beyond the moral assessment and value judgements of life in the colony and examine the financial dimension: the cost of attending boarding school. Some students remained for a year or more; others for a few months, just long enough to prepare for First Communion. The Mother Superior wrote: ". . . several board with us for only a short while. . . . Some of them are left with us by their parents till they are of an age to be provided, either for the world or for religion."[36] The annual boarding fee, which varied with the length of stay, was approximately 120 *livres* and appears to have remained constant throughout the French regime. This must have been a major expense for many colonial families since at the end of the 1660s, 120 *livres* represented the yearly wages of a "skilled worker." However, the Ursulines designed a sliding scale of boarding fees in light of the economic hardships in the colony, which were more pronounced during the seventeenth century, a period characterized by frequent wars and financial instability. Mother Marie de l'Incarnation frequently wrote of the harsh reality of the country's poverty — a reality that she and her companions had to come to terms with. One of the hardships was the scarcity of money in circulation in the colony. The Company of One Hundred Associates, with its barter policy, preferred the colonists to pay in kind — in this case, pelts — rather than with money. Consequently, the nuns often found themselves having to accept payment in kind for part of or even the entire boarding costs. The chronicles of the community contain several examples of this form of payment, such as the fee paid in 1646 for a Mademoiselle C. (whose name the chronicler discreetly withholds, referring to her as "belonging to one of the country's prominent families").

Received January 13	3½ cords of firewood
Received March 6	4 cords of firewood
Received March 13	1 12-pound pot of butter
Received November 13	1 fattened pig, 1 barrel of peas, one barrel of salted eels

Despite this kind of arrangement, which should have compensated for the scarcity of money in circulation, many families still could not afford their daughters' tuition. In a letter dated September 1660, Mother Marie wrote of this problem, noting that it cost more to educate French girls than Indian girls: "The expenses at the Seminary are many, not because we have many Savage boarders but because we receive many French girls whose parents do not have the means to pay their daughters' board. And we must say that the French girls cost us by far much more to feed and care for than do the Indian girls. God is the Father of us all, and we must hope that he will help us to help them."

This help came in the form of bursaries (*fondations*) provided by generous benefactors, notably Madame de la Peltrie, who was the foremost contributor in the community. Her donations, earmarked for total or partial payment of some tuition fees, alone represented 3,405 *livres*, or 41 percent of all the bursaries granted between 1641 and 1662. In 1660 Madame de la Peltrie, commonly referred to as "our Mother and benefactress" by the chronicler of the Ursulines, established six 100-*livre* bursaries for the education of poor girls, to be granted upon her death. The Jesuits were just as important a source of funds, since between 1652 and 1660 they contributed 3,330 *livres*, or 40.2 percent of all tuition fees paid until that date. In 1660 Monsignor de Laval became the third highest contributor with 535 *livres* or 18.5 percent of all the *fondations* established until 1662. By contrast, the state's contribution (disbursed by the governors, d'Ailleboust of Coulonges and Voyer of Argenson) was but a meagre 20 *livres*.

However, the generosity of the benefactors depended more on the recipients' social standing than on their true financial needs; consequently, moneys were not distributed equitably. Thus, of the 81 families who received grants for their daughters between 1642 and 1662, nine were of the noble class and received larger bursaries than families of the bourgeoisie. Accordingly, the families of eight of these nine school-age girls were able to pay for the education of their daughters. The bursaries received by 41 bourgeois families allowed them to pay for the education of only 51 of their 105 school-age daughters. During this same period, the *petites gens* — labourers and small land owners — received bursaries for only 33 of their 73 girls. While allowing more girls to attend boarding school, this system of grants did not resolve the social inequities in education. Although boarding school was not the exclusive domain of the nobility and bourgeoisie, girls from the popular classes were a minority. To a large extent, this reality explains the enriched — perhaps more refined — program that was available only to boarding students.

The scattered accounts in the Ursuline chronicles reveal that while the nuns taught a more advanced program of French to boarding students, they were also concerned with teaching grammar to day-pupils. The chronicler of the Order at Trois-Rivières recounts the extent to which grammar books were scarce before and after the Conquest: "Grammar books were so rare that the day-school only had one; it was placed on a desk in the middle of the room, opened to a page held in place by a wood frame. Each student took turns to learn the lesson of the day, and only the schoolmistress was allowed to turn the pages of the treasured book." Still, it is difficult to assess just how extensive the girls' knowledge of grammar was, since the chronicles (for both Quebec and Trois-Rivières) are vague on this subject.

Little information is available on the teaching of what was known as "art and decorative art" during this period. Clearly, the nuns excelled in this area, whether in needlework, embroidery on silk or bark (most often used to decorate altars), or the gilding of statues, tabernacles, or reliquaries. The annals speak of Jeanne Le Ber, a girl of gentle birth, who, following the example of the nuns, showed such an affinity for the arts of embroidery and gilding that she "soon equalled her teachers." Hers was probably not an isolated case, and most of the young girls who stayed long enough at the boarding school likely learned these arts.

While little is known about the grammar and art programs taught to boarding students, there is some evidence that the program as a whole was more complete and "refined" than the one available to day students (who were not only more transient than boarders but also non-paying). It bears repeating that most of these boarders came from prominent families; consequently, not only did they have to become good Christians but they also had to live up to the requirements and social standards of their elite class. Thus, the chronicler at Trois-Rivières justifies the greater emphasis on teaching the girls to behave and think in a certain way than on the depth and breadth of the program. In fact, she relates on the subject: "We did not seek to impart to these girls tremendous knowledge — this was not appropriate for women — but sought to instill in them that refined way of thinking, that wondrous ability to make good conversation, the gift of good letter-writing, all these things which, after virtue, make up a good education and a refined woman." The Quebec annalist adds that the nuns felt the need "to accustom the girls to speak correctly and with ease, to present themselves gracefully, and to learn, as the rule states, the morals of the most honest and virtuous Christians who live honourably in the world."

Behind this educational program one finds a portrait of the ideal future woman as envisioned and expected by society in a given era and social milieu. In order to create this female ideal who was both graceful and articulate, the teaching of theatre was considered the method of choice: reciting in public, verbal sparring matches, recitals, poems, and pastorals (short plays of religious and moral nature). The boarders performed on special occasions such as religious feasts, end-of-year award ceremonies, or receptions for distinguished guests. The chronicler of Quebec explains the context and objectives of these kinds of oratorical exercises: "It is a practice in our classrooms that with the advent of certain holidays, and especially at Christmas time, we have the children learn a pastoral or other religious play by heart, not only to develop their memories and fill their minds with good things but also to develop graceful carriage and gestures. Each child has a role in these exercises. We try, as much as possible, to accommodate the personalities and tastes of the young girls."

It would be interesting to examine some of these theatrical exercises more closely. Although replete with naïvete, they merit attention less for their intrinsic literary qualities than for their educational purposes and the cultural framework in which they were written.

The education of girls in New France was based on a specific definition of women. Upon closer examination, it is clear that several socialization models influenced women. Both the ethnic (French/Indian) and social class (boarders/day-pupils) variables contributed to the definition of these models and influenced their application. However, whether instruction was provided to French or Indian girls, day-pupils or boarders, whether it was academic or socioreligious, the education of girls under the Ursulines of Quebec had one common characteristic: it was based on a general concept of women, their nature as well as their place and role in society. This concept existed at a particular time in history (the Old Regime) and in the geopolitical context of a frontier society that faced unique material challenges: the economic constraints of the colony's resources and production, and a harsh climate. Compared to the schooling available to girls in France and boys in the colony, the Ursuline community offered girls a unique kind of education.

NOTES

For full references consult the original article, "L'éducation des filles chez les Ursulines de Québec sous le Régime français," by Nadia Fahmy-Eid.

1. Francis Parkman, *The Old Regime in Canada* (Boston: Little, Brown & Company, 1874), p. 365.
2. Joyce Marshall, translator, *Word from New France — The Selected Letters of Marie de l'Incarnation* (Toronto: Oxford University Press, 1967), p. 94.
3. Marshall, p. 90.
4. Marshall, p. 74.
5. Marshall, p. 74.
6. Marshall, p. 75.
7. Marshall, p. 89.
8. Marshall, p. 334.
9. Reuben Gold Thwaites, *The Jesuit Relations and Allied Documents — Travels and Explorations of the Jesuit Missionaries in New France, 1610–1791* (Cleveland: 1896-1901), Vol. 23, p. 51.
10. An Ursuline of Quebec, *The Life of the Venerable Mother Mary* (France: C. Paillart, 1813), p. 85.
11. Marshall, p. 341.
12. Marshall, p. 216.
13. Marshall, p. 222.
14. Marshall, p. 336.
15. Marshall, p. 72.
16. Marshall, pp. 72–73.
17. Marshall, p. 73.
18. Marshall, pp. 131–32.

19. Marshall, pp. 71–72.
20. Marshall, p. 336.
21. Marshall, p. 73.
22. Marshall, p. 336.
23. Marshall, p. 336.
24. An Ursuline of Quebec, p. 82.
25. An Ursuline of Quebec, p. 82.
26. An Ursuline of Quebec, p. 83.
27. Marshall, p. 335.
28. Marshall, p. 335.
29. Marshall, p. 335.
30. Marshall, p. 204.
31. Marshall, p. 335.
32. Marshall, p. 335.
33. Marshall, p. 336.
34. Thwaitcs, Vol. 36, p. 173.
35. Thwaites, Vol. 51, p. 211.
36. Marshall, pp. 335–36.

"A Woman's Awakening": Evangelical Belief and Female Spirituality in Mid-Nineteenth-Century Canada

MARGUERITE VAN DIE

> My dear Mother, Mrs. Margaret Hammond, being near the close of her life, and looking back upon it, considers that she is called upon to leave her testimony for the glory of God, to the power of his grace, who called her in her youth and brought her from darkness to light and from the thraldom of sin into the glorious liberty of the children of God, and sustained her in her pilgrimage even down to old age. She has pressed upon me to take up the pen which I do, not from choice but from necessity, as she is incapacitated through age and infirmity.
>
> Her daughter
> Sarah Jane[1]

Why, one might ask, should a mother and her daughter in Lanark County, Canada West, in 1861 consider an obscure life of such importance as to warrant a written memoir? And further, as is already apparent in the brief preface, why should the narrative be cast in imagery evoking the stages of an arduous journey to an ideal destination? Even more to the point, why should either of these questions be of concern to us today?

In answer to all three of these questions, we are reminded that for some time now feminist historians have been reconstructing the scholarly canon in such a way as to make "the study of women's roles and visions,

SOURCE: Marguerite Van Die, "'A Woman's Awakening': Evangelical Belief and Female Spirituality in Mid Nineteenth-Century Canada," paper presented to the Canadian Historical Association, Kingston, 1991.

power and oppressions central to historical analysis."[2] Such reconstruction stresses the need to listen to women's own words and self-definitions. To Margaret Boyd Hammond and her daughter, the importance of the life about to be chronicled lay precisely in the fact that its subject as a young girl had experienced a religious conversion, joined a Methodist society, and entered into "the glorious liberty" of the thousands of men, women, and young people caught up in the evangelical revivalism of the eighteenth and nineteenth centuries.

As evangelicals they were part of a larger configuration of denominations which in Canada included the Methodists, the Baptists, the United and Free Church Presbyterians (joined after 1861 into the Canada Presbyterian Church), as well as significant numbers within the Church of England and the Church of Scotland. Experiential and scriptural in their approach to the Christian religion, organized and vocal in the dissemination of their beliefs, and activist in implementing their vision of a morally transformed nation, evangelicals have increasingly come to attract the attention of religious historians. The dynamic nature of their creed and temper has come to be recognized as a critical factor in the modernization and eventual secularization of American society.[3]

It is in this discourse on the role of evangelicalism as part of the larger process of modernization, that the concerns of religious historians have come to intersect with the research of feminist scholars. In their efforts to chart the changes in women's economic, social, and political positions, the latter have been particularly attracted to two expressions of evangelicalism in America: women's enthusiastic participation in the revivals of the Second Great Awakening (1800–1840), and in the many benevolent and moral reform associations which were part of the evangelical outreach to society.[4]

In both cases the opportunities provided to women have been viewed with some ambivalence, as offering, in the words of Ruth Compton Brouwer, "a paradoxical pattern of opportunities and constraints."[5] Understood as marking an important transition from an agrarian based to a commercial and industrial economy, revivals have been seen to provide for women a brief opportunity to engage in unconventional and anti-ritualistic behaviour. It has also been pointed out, however, that in the long term, women's position deteriorated as they were re-integrated and re-socialized to meet the demands of the new commercial and industrial state. It has therefore been argued that, increasingly in this new male bourgeois hegemony, women were confined to the private sphere, to a world "bounded by kitchen and nursery, overlaid with piety and purity, and crowned with subservience."[6] This narrowly prescribed female role, which Canadian as well as American feminist historians have come to designate as the Cult of True Womanhood, meant that middle class women could be allowed access to the public world only through participation in voluntary religious societies.[7] Created especially to protect the home and to provide a wider social role for feminine nurturing qualities, these societies became for nineteenth-century women, in the words of Anne Firor Scott, "what business and public life were to aspiring young men."[8]

Suggestive as such analysis is in demonstrating women's move from revivals to voluntary reform societies, moral crusades and eventually women's rights campaigns, it has recently come under challenge by other feminist scholars. In part influenced by postmodern philosophy and deconstruction, scholars like Joan Wallach Scott have urged a broadening of gender as an analytical category, the abandonment of a search for single origins, and have pressed for a conceptualization of processes "so interconnected that they cannot be disentangled."[9] In addition, scholars have suggested that such categories as the separation of spheres, which labelled women as private beings, bear little relation to the actual lives of nineteenth century women.[10] This is of special relevance to Ontario, where, as Marjorie Griffin Cohen has demonstrated, industrialization with its accompanying separation of home and workplace influenced the lives of women at a significantly slower pace than in Great Britain and the United States.[11]

Such self-criticism is especially important in the recovery of women's religious experience, for it calls into question the pervasiveness of the Cult of True Womanhood and its accuracy as a symbol to assess the experience of religiously-minded women in the nineteenth century. Moreover, by viewing gender not simply as a metaphor for role formation, i.e., woman's role, but rather as an organizing principle which sees the domestic world as the central point of investigation, feminist theoreticians are recognizing that the history of women's religious experience cannot be seen as separate from that of men.[12] Studies such as those by Mary P. Ryan and Leonore Davidoff and Catherine Hall, regional in their focus and painstakingly minute in their collection and analysis of data, have broken new ground by investigating the intersection between religion, class, and gender in the domestic world of evangelical piety.[13] Comparable research remains to be done for Canada, and will require detailed quantitative work in order to examine gender participation in the various evangelical denominations. However, quantitative patterns of evangelical piety can only be arrived at if they are based on an analysis of a more subjective and qualitative nature which explores how evangelicalism shaped individual self-understanding and behaviour. My focus will be on this more modest concern, namely to explore the way evangelical religion informed the experience and consciousness of a number of women in Canada during the period 1830 to 1875, and was itself, in turn, profoundly influenced by female spirituality.

The choice of this period is deliberate, for it follows upon the intensive revivalism of the early decades of the century and ends just before the national organization in Canada of two major denominations, the Methodists and the Presbyterians, and such important women's organizations as the W.C.T.U., the W.M.S., and the Y.W.C.A. Perhaps because of its position "betwixt and between," this period has remained under-studied by both feminist and church historians in Canada. These were, however, the decades which have usually been associated with the Cult of True Womanhood, and they should provide fruitful insight into the background of women's participation in benevolent and moral reform societies. Although women's participation in these societies has received considerable attention in Canadian feminist historiography, the motives of such participation have largely been attributed to socio-economic factors.[14] The language of evangelical piety has received little attention, and scholars have treated only tangentially their subjects' own professed strong belief in and commitment to a worldview which transcended time and space and which figures so prominently in the obituaries, correspondence, diaries, and memoirs of nineteenth-century religiously-minded women.[15] Hence a primary purpose will be to reconstruct some of the parameters of evangelical belief and female spirituality in the period under examination.

Rather than interpret the term "spirituality" through such concepts as "mentalité" or "personal attitudes of life," as some recent studies have undertaken, I propose a more precise definition which takes seriously evangelical women's own self-understanding.[16] For them, the doctrines of sin, salvation and sanctification through a life of service distinguished evangelicals from "unawakened" or "merely moral" Christians, and these were the doctrines which provided the framework to their spiritual autobiographies, memoirs, eulogies, and obituaries.[17]

Largely invisible in the denominational press, women were able to leave traces of their religious faith only in private correspondence, diaries, and memoirs, and in the odd instance, in published accounts. While those writings which I have been able to recover make manifestly clear that their authors were not "leisured," they were all literate, white, financially comfortable, British or Canadian born, and resident on farms and in rural villages and urban centres in central Canada and the Maritimes. A few had found employment as school teachers, but the lives of the majority were defined by the demands of marriage and motherhood and circumscribed by the boundaries of farm, family, and church. Indeed only a few appear to have been able to live out their faith beyond their family confines by actively participating in voluntary religious associations.

Heterogeneous and incomplete as these sources are, they are complemented by a more uniform, but highly stylized source, the ministerially written obituary. Intended to encapsulate the evangelical rites of passage and be a witness to the eternal salvation of the deceased, such obituaries also implicitly address the feminist concern that a woman's complete life cycle, and not merely isolated events, be considered. At the same time, they draw attention to the theology and religious values promoted by the male hierarchy of the various denominations. Ministers and educators ultimately defined the nature of lay piety, and therefore it will be necessary as well to examine denominational publications and private ministerial diaries, sermons, and correspondence. Since the Cult of True Womanhood was primarily a prescriptive rather than a descriptive concept to define women's religious role, these publications are an important source in ascertaining the extent to which evangelicalism attempted to define gender.

Historians have pointed out that the period 1830–1875 was a time of stabilization and consolidation for Canadian evangelicalism, as various denominations consciously began to make use of the term "evangelical" in their self-definition.[18] Part of a transatlantic movement, they were able in this endeavour to draw on a wide array of publications which addressed specifically the expected lifestyle and values of individual members. Educators and ministers did not overlook the duty of the sexes. In moral theology courses, for example, in several of the colleges of the Maritimes and central Canada, students were exposed to the textbook *Elements of Moral Science* (1835), by an American Baptist educator, Francis Wayland. There, in a lengthy chapter, "Duties Which Arise from the Constitution of the Sexes," readers were reminded of the duties of husbands, wives, and children towards one another. While Wayland adopted a largely protective position towards the female sex, he made it unequivocally clear that in a case of difference of opinion between husband and wife, "the duty of yielding devolves upon the wife." Should any woman ponder the possibility of resistance, she was reminded that, "the act of submission is in every respect as dignified and lovely as the act of authority, nay, more, it involves an element of virtue that does not belong to the other."[19]

Wayland's view that woman's virtue could best be expressed through self-effacement was not left buried in college textbooks. It found a didactic echo in short stories, letters and articles in the denominational journals, and in ministerial addresses to the fairer sex. "Prefer the company of your husband to that of your dearest friends. Have no private separate interest in view," an assembly of women was instructed by the Reverend John Tawse, a Presbyterian minister sent to Eversley (King), Ontario, from Scotland by the evangelical Glasgow Colonial Society in 1837.[20] Even in the rare instance that a female voice can be heard addressing other women in the periodical press, her call is that of submission. Thus in one of a series of letters on spiritual concerns in the Methodist *Christian Guardian* in 1852, the renowned female holiness evangelist Phoebe Palmer responded to the veiled resentment of a young mother whose infant child prevented her from church attendance. Palmer's answer was to remind her reader of the sterling example of Susannah Wesley, mother of seventeen, who always managed to set aside time for personal devotion, and who unfailingly maintained her husband Samuel's "lordly prerogative . . . quite to the bounds that Scriptural propriety might warrant, and perhaps a little beyond what the gallantry and republicanism of the present day would justify."[21]

Evidence such as this, much of it drawn from the same American periodicals used by feminist historians like Barbara Welter to construct the Cult of True Womanhood, attests to acceptance of the conventional definition of woman's role by the hierarchy of Canada's evangelical denominations. Their definition of gender, however, did not stop with women, for the periodical press of the 1830s to 1850s displayed an equal zeal in spelling out the duties of men with respect to their families.[22] It should be noted, as well, that the evangelical concept of gender which was emerging during these years represented part of a much larger concern, namely the propagation and transmission of the faith to the next generation. Thus in addition to articles on "woman's true sphere" and "the formation of character in young men," there was an even greater effort to instruct parents on the importance of family worship and the need for childhood religious training.[23] In the words of Francis Wayland, "the eternal destiny of the child is placed in a most important sense in the hands of its parents."[24]

While the periodical press implicitly assumed that the responsibility of family religion fell first and foremost upon the father as head of the household, it also drew attention to woman's special nature as "a Heaven-commissioned angel of mercy to man in his miserable fallen state."[25] Since woman's principal duty was to redeem, every activity and decision contained grave moral implications. The Congregationalist mother, for example, was warned during the 1842 Christmas season that even such a simple choice as to spend time preparing her children's dress rather than attending to the needs of the Bible, Tract and Missionary Societies might leave a lasting negative impression upon a youthful mind.[26]

At the same time, as attempts were being made to socialize women into the awesome demands of evangelical religion, such instruction was not to be seen as a substitute for conversion. Throughout this period considerable ink was spent in outlining the experiential nature of "real religion" and reminding parents of the importance of encouraging their children to seek conversion by instructing them "of their relation to God and the Redeemer, of their sins, and their wants, and of the method they must take to procure pardon for the one, and the relief of the other."[27] This concern, quoted from the Congregationalist *Harbinger*, found concrete echo in the obituaries in the Methodist *Christian Guardian*. An examination of 216 obituaries of women during the period 1870–1873 showed 77% making specific mention of conversion.

It is of interest that in these accounts of the spiritual life of the deceased, the eulogists did not make a sharp distinction in the lifestyle before and after conversion, but rather pointed out the exemplary piety which had characterized the life of their subject from early childhood. Of Isabella Rorke of Toronto, for example, it was noted that already "at a very early period she gave evidence of religious impressions."[28] In the case of Melissa Ann Ketcheson of Sidney, Ontario, attention was drawn to her Christian parents who already when she was very young "gently and prayerfully endeavoured to lead her in the paths of righteousness."[29]

Not only is there an emphasis on the Christian homelife of the young women in these accounts, but it also becomes clear from private correspondence and diaries as well as obituaries that parents were playing an important role in the conversion of their daughters. Writing home concerning a revival of religion in 1844 at the female Burlington Academy where she was a teacher, Jane Van Norman concluded her account with an expression of gratitude to God for having privileged her with believing parents.[30] Ann Appleby, a Methodist who settled in the Belleville area in the 1830s and who left a detailed account of her conversion as a young girl in Leeds, England, paid tribute not only to the exemplary piety of her mother, but also to the assistance offered by her father and her sister.[31] Fragmentary evidence from obituaries suggests that such an experience was shared by other young women.[32]

The age of conversion, too, bears mentioning. Of the sampled obituaries stating an age of conversion, three-quarters mentioned that their subject had been converted before her thirtieth birthday, with over half being between ages 18 and 29. Moreover, in an age when young women assumed family responsibilities in their mid-twenties, the majority recorded conversion before marriage. These findings parallel the conversion pattern in male obituaries and private papers, and show that for both young men and women raised in an evangelical environment, conversion continued to be an integral part of piety.[33] For both, conversion frequently was experienced during late adolescence, during a time when new responsibilities and changed pattern of life were about to replace the old and familiar.

While there is much that is similar in the conversion accounts of both men and women, their different roles in life and the cultural expectations placed upon them do appear to suggest certain differences. Young men could look forward to leaving the home and taking control of their own destiny as they tried to carve out a living in a new and competitive environment. Young women, on the other hand, remained in the home, and faced a future shaped by marriage, child-bearing and family responsibilities.[34]

For evangelicals the home was not simply a place to hang one's hat. As Colleen McDannell has illustrated in a detailed study of the Christian home in Victorian America, and as Canadian evangelical writers took pains to emphasize, home was a sacred space, claimed by a family member's most intimate feelings.[35] Nurtured in a Christian home, young evangelical women did, however, have to break out of this protected environment and take up new responsibilities and enter into their own family arrangements. As may be expected, conversion accounts often reveal a direct connection between the disruption of family life through the death of a close relative and the beginning pangs of religious conversion. Eliza Chipman, a young Baptist from Cornwallis, Nova Scotia, for example, found that the unexpected death of a brother was for her the beginning of a period of deep anxiety and concern about her own lack of preparedness. In a similar manner Mrs. John Edgecombe of Fredericton, N.B., who as a girl had been "naturally possessed of a disposition exceedingly light and trifling," experienced a radical change upon receiving a letter from a dying brother.[36]

The awakening to one's sinful condition was part of a regular pattern in conversion accounts reaching back into the Puritan period, as Jerald Brauer has demonstrated in an analysis of the various stages of conversion.[37] In obituaries this period is often captured in shorthand by such phrases as "she was led to see and feel the necessity of a change," or "convinced of sin," or more fully, "a failure to bear her cross as taught by the Saviour which was the cause of many hard conflicts with the enemy."[38]

A critical component of the conversion experience, this time of awakening has received little attention from historians. Scholars like Carroll Smith-Rosenberg and George Rawlyk who have examined the role of women in the Second Great Awakening have used the insights of Victor Turner and other anthropologists to draw attention to the "anti-structural liminality" of women's unconventional and uninhibited behaviour during the revivals.[39] For the young women of this study, however, converted during a later period, or raised in evangelical homes, references to such behaviour during conversion are very rare. If the term "liminality" can be used at all, it applies not to their experience immediately following conversion, but rather to the period of anxiety and alienation which preceded it. Often this was accompanied by a lack of interest in the amusements of their peer group, and a critical posture towards customs and habits which formerly had been accepted without question. While less fascinating than the enthusiastic and liberating outbursts of the revival, this liminal period was in fact crucial in a young woman's personal appropriation of the faith. Studies of the morphology of conversion by Brauer and others have argued that this period of awakening was greatly foreshortened in the post-Puritan period, but only recently, thanks to Susan Juster's fine analysis of the gendering of evangelical cultures in eighteenth-century Massachusetts, has there been a conscious distinction of the different ways in which men and women experienced conversion.[40] For some young women this time of awakening appears to have stretched over months and even years. It deserves, therefore, to be re-integrated into our understanding of the evangelical conversion.

To conceptualize what evangelicals experienced and understood by conversion it is helpful to take some critical distance from the terminology and imagery which they employed in their accounts. A later observer, William James, the psychologist, writing in 1902, attempted to define conversion as "the process, gradual or sudden, by which a self hitherto divided, and consciously wrong inferior and unhappy, becomes unified and consciously right superior and happy, in consequence of its hold upon religious realities."[41] Equally insightful is the approach taken by John Welch in an analysis of the spirituality of the sixteenth-century Spanish mystic Teresa of Avila. Combining Victor Turner's structural analysis with Carl Jung's depth psychology, Welch portrays conversion and union with God as part of the human individuation process whereby a person moves from structure to anti-structure and back again to structure through a series of transitional or liminal experiences expressed in powerful imagery.[42] Both of these definitions take the view that conversion is not a sudden event of brief duration, but rather a central event in an inner journey of awareness, where thought and activity become focused away from the self and directed towards God and one's neighbours.

Harriet Dobbs Cartwright of Kingston recalled that during her period of awakening as a young Anglican in Dublin, a new sense of time as part of eternity began to make her acutely aware of "the fleeting value of this life." Religious faith began to transform itself from customary practice and belief to becoming a matter of intense personal experience. In the months which followed Harriet's awakening to her sinful state, she became, as she recalled, increasingly "sensible of my own lost and ruined state by nature — I *felt* that I was a sinner as well as believed it on the authority of God's Word." Accompanying this sense of alienation from self and from God there was frequently also a lack of harmony in family relationships. Harriet, who prior to this time had been a dutiful daughter, began to experience an intense dislike for social outings and parties, objected to what she now called "adorning" herself for such vain activities, and resisted at times to the point of disobeying her mother.[43]

For women like Harriet this period of awakening was a time of shift in life pattern and views, a change which has often been associated with adolescence. Not surprisingly, evangelical colleges were frequently the location for such an alteration of perspectives. Here academic as well as personal influences combined to create a period of unrest and re-evaluation, an experience all the more powerful because it was shared with one's peers. Jane Van Norman described to her parents in 1844 a "glorious revival" at the Burlington Academy which was resulting in the conversion of almost all of the young women in attendance.[44] The future president of the Canadian W.C.T.U., Letitia Youmans, who that same year attended the Cobourg Ladies Seminary, noted that such a revival was not an isolated incident, but a regular recurrence. "In many instances, a thoughtless, giddy girl, with no special leaning to any religious denomination, was brought under the influence of divine truth, soundly converted to God, and then sought a home in one of the churches most congenial to her views, and was ever after a consistent Christian."[45]

The evidence that the nature and length of awakening in the conversions of the nineteenth century were influenced by gender is fragmentary but suggestive. Analysing the relationship between the sex ratio of converts and preaching style during the First Great Awakening, Cedric

Cowing has noted that men responded much more quickly and decisively than women to preaching which stressed the imminence of retribution and the terrors of hell. While men were moved to conversion by such shock tactics, sudden conversions among women were rare.[46] More research is needed to determine whether this pattern changed during the Second Great Awakening as the image of a God of judgement in evangelical Calvinism became replaced by the more accessible portrayal of God as a loving Father.[47] However, the personal accounts of women's religious experience and obituary details do point to the conclusion that sudden conversions for women continued to be rare.

There may be good reason for this. Conversion for evangelicals was seen in the first place not as a matter of human effort but as the work of God, and therefore required a new birth, an annihilation of the self and a re-centering of the will. Philip Greven has pointed out in his probing analysis of evangelical child-rearing, "It was only after their wills had been broken that individuals could know they had experienced their new birth."[48] For young women raised in a culture which expected female behaviour to be self-sacrificing and submissive, and who had never been encouraged to develop an independent will, the new birth was decidedly more problematic than it was for their male peers. For men there was a clearer distinction between the world's definition of masculinity and the ideals of evangelical manhood. Young women, raised in a middle class family, on the other hand, found role expectations before and after conversion to be the same.

This does appear to have prolonged the anguish of the new birth for some women. Conversion, aimed at the breaking of the will, confronted a woman in the most vulnerable place in her psychological makeup. As a result, for some young women, given societal role-definition, their own inner insecurity proved to be an obstacle to experiencing the assurance of divine forgiveness. This, for example, appears to have been the case of Mary Weldon of Dorchester, New Brunswick, and Virtue Vey, of Saint John's, Newfoundland.[49] In the memorial of the latter, written by her husband, a Methodist minister, it was noted that even though she had been awakened to sin and able to put her faith in the atonement of Christ, "her subsequent experience was greatly influenced by a natural timidity of disposition, which led her to dwell on her own unworthiness, and those numerous deficiencies which her tender conscience perceived."

Influenced even in conversion by societal conditioning, evangelical women remained subject to the same expectations and limitations as other members of their sex. Nevertheless, their experience of awakening and conversion did result in a number of subtle but important differences. As evangelical Christians they had been encouraged since childhood to engage in self-examination and to expose their innermost thoughts and feelings before God. Conversion or the new birth was a means whereby the negative self-image which often resulted from such introspection was exchanged for a new experience of God and a deeper integration of self into the transcendent world of space and time. Convinced of their sinfulness, they had finally relied for forgiveness on the atonement of Christ, and they knew at least temporarily a peace that came through self-surrender. God was now no longer seen as a source of condemnation, but as a loving parent. As one Presbyterian writer explained, using the word *Abba* or father for God, a favourite evangelical New Testament image:

> Children naturally cry "Father" to their earthly parent. It is one of the first things they learn. They do not thus call upon God; but when he comes to Christ, and feels the Father's smile, the Father's arms, the Father's love, he cries "Abba."[50]

For Harriet Dobbs Cartwright this experience of God as *Abba* was the supreme turning point in her spiritual life. Even in recalling it in her autobiography written for the benefit of her husband, as they crossed the Atlantic as newlyweds, her usually didactic, self-analytical writing style is temporarily transformed into a lyrical song of praise. In so doing, she unwittingly underscored the re-centering which had taken place. "Oh what strong consolation! What anchor of the soul! What a refuge from distress and anxiety — from weariness & turmoil & evils, from within and without," was the way in which she recalled the psychological benefits of conversion. "From this hour it has been the dearest wish of my heart to promote my Redeemer's glory," she concluded.[51]

Both her assurance of a new understanding of self and of God, and her promise of a new consecration are repeated in the conversion accounts of other evangelical women. The Methodist father of Mary Ann Humphries, for example, was surprised and delighted to hear his daughter speak publicly in church of her conversion, for "her natural diffidence was so extreme that he could never have expected to hear her voice in a public congregation."[52] At the Cobourg Ladies Seminary (as at institutions for men such as Victoria College in the same town) the emphasis was placed on conversion as a time of consecration to the service of God. Letitia Youmans recalled that during a Friday evening service she had responded to the principal's request that "those who would enlist in His service make it known by rising." As she recalled, "I then rose and from that moment I felt that I was committed to the service of God."[53] As an emphasis upon the soundness of conversion, and upon the inner assurance of eternal salvation, obituaries frequently detailed the signs of consecration shown in the life of the deceased. In the obituary of Mrs. Philenia Smart, wife of a Free Church Presbyterian minister in Brockville, it was pointed out that "we have the best of all evidence, a long and consistent life, and profession of attachment and conformity to Christ."[54]

Expressed in the imagery of evangelical piety and gender definition, this process of self-awareness and affirmation which resulted from conversion is not easy for us to grasp today. As a result, feminist historians who have made a correlation between revivalism and the Cult of True Womanhood appear to have overlooked that conversion, rather than marking a brief hiatus in the socialization of women from the values and relationships of an agrarian society into the hegemony of the new commercial and industrial state, may actually *have retarded* such a development.[55] To suggest how evangelicalism was able to maintain some of the values and folkways of an agrarian society against the excessive individualism and rationalization associated with industrialization, we must enter into the area of popular religion. This then leads us also to examine briefly the lives of young evangelical women after conversion, as they assumed the responsibilities of their faith and marital state and formed a new network of family and denominational ties.

The first of these relationships formed as a direct result of conversion was with the community of believers, and in most evangelical denominations conversion was followed by the decision to apply for full church membership. Some six months after her conversion, Eliza Chipman, for example, was able to record solemnly in her journal, "I have entered into covenant with God's people, have cast my lot with them, the excellent ones of the earth, and have been received into the bosom of the Baptist Church."[56] Those wishing to become full members and take part in the Lord's Supper in the Presbyterian Free Church were subjected to a lengthy process of interrogation by the governing consistory.[57] While Methodists did not stipulate conversion as a prerequisite for membership, the phrase "she united immediately with our Church," frequently follows upon the reference to conversion.[58] For all the denominations, however, clearly defined conditions of membership continued to convey a conscious awareness of sectarian differences as well as a distinction between "real" and merely nominal Christians.

On a more personal level, conversion also opened the way to intimate relationships with members outside one's family as women shared the anxiety of religious awakening or the joy of assurance of forgiveness. Ministers played a crucial role in the conversion of many young women, and later in the stylized form of memoir or obituary were given special mention, and frequently referred to in terms of "spiritual father" to convey this sense of new relationships. For older women, a title such as "a mother in Israel" conjured up biblical images of nurturer and provider and conveyed a signal of special female stature in obituaries. References to "sisters" with whom women shared their spiritual concerns also indicate that the bonds of family had been transferred to a wider yet still intimate community.[59]

Relationships such as these were of special value in providing continuity and stability in lives disrupted by death, marriage, immigration, and early widowhood. Ann Appleby experienced all of these, but her memoirs still show a clear strand of continuity. In New York City, to which she had immigrated with her first husband she was able in 1837 to join a combined women's prayer meeting of the Mulberry Street and Allen Street Methodist Episcopal Churches, led by Sarah Lankford, sister to the famed holiness preacher Phoebe Palmer. It was there that Ann appears to have experienced that second crisis in Methodist spirituality, known as entire sanctification, the second blessing, or Christian perfection.[60] Later, when she moved to Belleville, and remarried, she joined yet another group devoted to encouraging spiritual growth, and led by a prominent church woman, Jane Clement Jones. Even in advanced age, in the 1860s, Ann continued to draw on her spirituality as a source of contact with younger members of her sex, as she sent off letters of spiritual counsel to a "Dear Young Friend," or evinced a lively interest in reports of a "gracious movement" among young girls at a recent prayer meeting, and their subsequent attendance at the Methodist class conducted by Mrs. Jones.[61]

Such contacts not only provided continuity between life in the old world and the new, childhood and the responsibilities of adulthood, but also were a means to transcend the bonds of womanhood which relegated women to domesticity and the private sphere. Much has been written about the manner in which nineteenth-century women were able to reach beyond the confines of the home by becoming involved in moral improvement and benevolent societies. As evangelical wives and mothers, women could also call, however, on spiritual power to bridge the space between the home and the workplace of their men. For Jane Van Norman, teaching at the Burlington Academy, the world of Methodist class meetings, evangelical literature, and private devotional life provided a bond in the letters which she regularly wrote to her fiancé, a recently widowed farmer.[62]

In Belleville, Jane Clement Jones, for thirty-eight years a class leader for "young ladies," in 1869 took over in addition the leadership of the senior boys' Bible class. Immensely popular, it drew upon a large number of young men enrolled in Belleville's Albert and Ontario Business College. In the 14 years she taught this class, some 707 young men came under her influence. Here, as with the young women, her purpose was the conversion of her students, a goal neatly summarized in the words of a song pasted on a page of her roll book: "My class for Jesus! nothing less can save, can sanctify, can bless . . ."[63]

A position such as that of Jane Clement Jones was no doubt exceptional and was dependent on a male constituency which was willing and interested in sharing her sense of ultimate values. For women, it was, however, easier on the whole to integrate sacred with secular concerns than was the case for men working outside the home. While some women like Harriet Dobbs Cartwright and Eliza Chipman were able to find support in a shared faith with their clergymen husbands, the journals and memoirs of others reveal a greater spiritual intimacy with a heavenly Father than with the earthly father of their children.[64] Catherine Bell Van Norman, a young housewife in Burlington confined to her home through convalescence in 1850, worried a great deal about the moodiness and inattentiveness of an overworked husband. Her assessment of the male predicament, "I think that if they [men] would talk more about religion they would enjoy themselves more," revealed a viewpoint which was more a matter of gender than she may have realized.[65]

The men with whom many evangelical women were able to forge strong ties were ministers. Regretting the sudden death of a female parishioner, William McLaren, a Free Church minister in Belleville in the 1860s, mused: "she was one of those hearers who gave strength to a minister."[66] In women's obituaries, especially in the Methodist *Christian Guardian*, ministers described in detail their spiritual contacts with the deceased, extolled their exemplary piety, and not infrequently made special reference to the hospitality they had extended to travelling preachers.[67] While such praise had an obvious didactic intent, it also reflected the appreciation of an itinerant ministry, who continued to be dependent on the generosity and hospitality of the religious community.

Confined by the demands of farm and family life, women were able to draw on evangelical religion to create bonds of intimacy and to form community in ways which were becoming more difficult for the majority of men. Their ability to continue to place temporal events within eternal time provided meaning and purpose to the limitations of their daily existence, even though these varied according to their particular circumstances. For Anna Bellamy, a busy Presbyterian farm wife in the early 1850s in North Augusta in eastern Ontario, the days were long and demanding. Respite appeared to come only on Sundays when she could record in her journal that she had spent time "reading the Word," or could look back on the administration of the sacrament as a time of "consolation" and "improvement."[68] For Catherine Bell Van Norman, a rare outing to Sunday "meeting," followed by the opportunity to meet new people at the Methodist class meeting, offered a treasured possibility of escape from the narrow confines of home life.[69]

Gender and religion reinforced one another in this appropriation and application of the faith, but this faith also assured women of a unique status. The reason, as Gwen Neville Kennedy, a cultural anthropologist, has noted, is that women are placed by culture in an ambiguous situation; as childbearers they are part of the natural world, but as wives and mothers they are also essential to the ongoing task of civilization.[70] In this position between the natural and the cultural, nineteenth-century evangelical women were able to influence particularly the lives of their sons. Even after the latter had left the nurturing environment of an evangelical home and had struck out on an independent career they continued to experience the controlling influence of a mother's piety.[71]

"No matter how desperate your case may be, he [Christ] is all powerful and once encircled in his loving arms you are safe in eternity," admonished the mother of young John Francis Norris, a Methodist who later became editor of the *Montreal Star* and the *Victoria Day Colonist* and was beginning to show a lack of fervour towards his family as well as his religion.[72] "Dear Thomas, possessing the feelings and bowels of a Mother it is impossible but I should always feel deeply anxious for the salvation of each soul I have brought into the world," wrote Mary Shenston to her son, whose life in St. Catharines, Ontario, away from home, was leading him to question the principles of the Baptist faith in which he had been raised.[73] Even Egerton Ryerson, editor of the Methodist *Christian Guardian*, could not escape the admonition of his mother: ". . . my son be continually on your guard, you have need to believe firmly, to pray fervently, to work abundantly; live Holy daily; watch your heart; guide your senses; redeem your time; love Christ and long for Glory."[74]

The fact that letters such as these were saved and treasured is indicative of the influence which evangelical mothers were able to exert over the lives of their sons. As mothers, they played a critical role in the religious socialization of a new generation of evangelicals, for by training the child's conscience, they were laying the groundwork for future conversion. Evangelicals took great pleasure in recounting examples of spiritually directed maternal influence. They were the stuff of pious tracts and the drama of deathbed parting admonitions.

More than a concern for the propagation of the faith was at stake here. Mothers also reminded their sons of a world which they had left, but which through childhood training they had internalized and continued to value. "The warm comfortable world of the family contrasts starkly with the rational technical world of town and city life," Neville Kennedy has noted, and has perceptively observed that woman's role has been especially idealized in periods of excessive socio-economic change.[75] The nineteenth-century was such a time, and rare are the memoirs of evangelical ministers, educators, and successful businessmen which fail to attribute their rise from obscurity to the formative influence of a mother's piety.[76]

A mother's piety which was able to set the vicissitudes of life in the marketplace within the context of eternity, and reconcile sacred with secular time, appeared to provide a measure of security in a world in constant flux. Nowhere was the fragility of life more apparent than in the pervasive spectre of death in an age when female life expectancy in Canada in 1851 was only 41.4 years, and the infant mortality rate measured 184.1 per 1000 population.[77] It is in their confrontation with the personal tragedy of the loss of loved ones that the spirituality of evangelical women is expressed most clearly. Recalling how she had been unable to part with her two-year-old son, Catherine Bell Van Norman wrote, "but I was enabled by the assisting grace of God to keep silent and submit to his holy and righteous will." Resignation also contained comfort, for as she mused, reflecting on the possibility of her own death, "I know that I have a little sainted babe in heaven, who will be among the first to welcome me there."[78] Such a thought sustained many, for it provided a bridge between temporal and eternal time. As one son reflected on the death of his mother at age 80, some 35 years after the loss of four of her children, "for long she had felt that a large part of her own life's interest had been transferred already to that other sphere 'beyond time and space.'"[79] Thus the death of children made one's own death, especially for women more advanced in years, a less frightening prospect.

For old as well as young, death in the nineteenth century was a public event, shared by family and friends. To evangelicals one's final moments summed up one's whole life, for death was not merely an ending of life, but its culmination. A person whose life had been shaped by her response to the transcendent, would, it was expected, find her last thoughts directed to God.[80] Thus final words to family members provided an awesome opportunity for evangelization. Many women were to be remembered by the final words of hope or admonition which they had been able to address to family members. Obituaries tell of sisters who through death were able to help convert their siblings, of mothers who left a lasting spiritual impact on husbands and children, and even of cases where parents were converted through the words of a dying daughter.[81] Family members were not the only ones present at such scenes, for the bonds of sisterhood were also often visible, as a dying woman requested friends to sing a favourite song or read a meaningful passage of Scripture.[82]

It is at this point that we turn for a final glance at the testimony of Margaret Hammond with which this study began. "I am now unable for active life," she dictated to her daughter Sarah. "My work in that respect appears to be done, but I can sit and recount the mercies of my heavenly Father — the dangers he has brought me through, His precious gifts to me. . . . The gift of His Holy spirit that enlightened my mind . . . and has continued with me through life even down to old age and now gives me a prospect of an inheritance incorruptible, undefiled and that fadeth not away."[83] For evangelical women like Margaret Hammond, religious faith had been a means of reconciling the gap between the world that "ought to be" and the contradictions and ambiguities of the world that was. This reconciliation would be complete only in death, but already in life one might begin to forge ties with fellow travellers to this new world. The language to express this vision and experience was that of evangelical Protestantism. As evangelicals they knew what women have begun more recently to emphasize: that it is in the telling of one's experience through words and images that one begins to own it and allow it to shape one's life. If as feminists we wish to understand their experience, we must therefore take pains to hear the words of evangelical piety.

However, the language and images they used were also distinctly relevant to the place and time in which they lived. Here too we need to listen to women's words. In our reconstruction of that world as historians of religion we must go beyond the institution, the ministry, the printed texts, and an uncritical acceptance of the categories of modernity. When instead we make the domestic world and the spirituality of evangelical women the central point of our investigation, we do not encounter a world of dynamic socio-economic change and institutional growth, but a world narrowly circumscribed by the parameters of kinship, community, of birth and death. What we encounter is a distinctive evangelical culture, within but also separate from the rest of society. With its own values, ranks and community networks, this culture depended for its continuity and integrity in large part on the spirituality of its female participants.

"Woman rules the world now," proclaimed a Congregational writer in 1856. "Her empire is the affections. Endowed by her Creator with finer sensibilities, more constant in her attachment, and possessing more fortitude and perseverance than man, the power is already hers."[84] These words I would argue are not just one more example of the Cult of True Womanhood. Rather, they represented the empowerment of a "women's awakening," but also a call to women to reclaim a world in danger of disappearance.

NOTES

1. Typescript Family History and Testimony of Mrs. Henry Hammond (née Margaret Boyd) (1790–1861). In possession of the author. I thank J. William Lamb for this source, and for the Diary of Ann Appleby (note 31).
2. Carroll Smith-Rosenberg, *Disorderly Conduct: Visions of Gender in Victorian America* (New York: Oxford University Press, 1985), 11.
3. For evangelicalism in Great Britain see David Bebbington, *Evangelicalism in Modern Britain: A History from the 1730s to the 1980s* (London: Allen & Unwin, 1989); in the United States see Leonard I. Sweet, ed., *The Evangelical Tradition in America* (Macon, Ga.: Mercer University Press, 1976); in Canada see Michael Gauvreau, *The Evangelical Century: College and Creed in English Canada from the Great Revival to the Great Depression* (Montreal and Kingston: McGill-Queen's University Press, 1991).
4. See for example: Smith-Rosenberg, *Disorderly Conduct*, 109–164; Nancy A. Hewitt, *Women's Activism and Social Change, Rochester, New York, 1822–1872* (Ithaca: Cornell University Press, 1984); Carolyn DeSwarte Gifford, "Sisterhoods of Service and Reform: Organized Methodist Women in the Late Nineteenth Century. An Essay on the State of the Research," *Methodist History* 23:2 (October 1985): 15–30.
5. Ruth Compton Brouwer, *New Women for God: Canadian Presbyterian Women and India Missions, 1876–1914* (Toronto: University of Toronto Press, 1990), 9.
6. Smith-Rosenberg, *Disorderly Conduct*, 13.
7. For an early expression of this concept see Barbara Welter, "The Cult of True Womanhood," *American Quarterly* 18 (Summer 1966): 151–174, and "She Hath Done What She Could: Protestant Women's Missionary Careers in Nineteenth-Century America," in *Women in American Religion*, ed. Janet Wilson James (Philadelphia: University of Pennsylvania Press, 1980): 111–125.
8. Anne Firor Scott, "On Seeing and Not Seeing: A Case of Historical Invisibility," *The Journal of American History* 71:1 (June 1984): 7–21.
9. Joan Wallach Scott, *Gender and the Politics of History* (New York: Columbia University Press, 1988), 42.
10. Ibid., 15–27. See also Elizabeth Fox-Genovese, "Culture and Consciousness in the Intellectual History of European Women," *Signs* 12:3 (1987): 529–547; Jane Flax, "Post-Modernism and Gender Relations in Feminist Theory," *Signs* 12:4 (1987): 621–643; Joy Parr, "Nature and Hierarchy: Reflections on Writing the History of Women and Children," *Atlantis* 11 (1985): 39–44.
11. Marjorie Griffin Cohen, *Women's Work, Markets and Economic Development in Nineteenth-Century Ontario* (Toronto: University of Toronto Press, 1988), 3–28, 118–158 especially.
12. See note 10, and Judith Newton, "Family Fortunes: 'New History' and 'New Historicism,'" *Radical History Review* 43 (1989): 5–22.

13. Mary P. Ryan, *Cradle of the Middle Class: The Family in Oneida County, New York, 1790–1865* (Cambridge: Cambridge University Press, 1981); Leonore Davidoff and Catherine Hall, *Family Fortunes: Men and Women of the English Middle Class, 1780–1850* (London: Hutchinson, 1987).

14. See, for example, Linda Kealey, ed., *A Not Unreasonable Claim: Women and Reform in Canada, 1880s–1920s* (Toronto: The Women's Press, 1979). Most recently, Ruth Compton Brouwer, while recognizing the religious motives of missionary women, still focuses on those reasons "that went beyond faith and altruism," *New Women for God,* 8.

15. A fine exception to this observation is Katherine M.J. McKenna, "The Union between Faith and Good Works: The Life of Harriet Dobbs Cartwright, 1808–1887," paper presented to the Canadian Women's Studies Association, Victoria, B.C., June 1991. See also Virginia Lieson Brereton, *From Sin to Salvation: Stories of Women's Conversions, 1800 to the Present* (Bloomington: Indiana University Press, 1991), which analyses the formulaic nature of conversion accounts.

16. See Carolyn Walker Bynum, *Jesus as Mother: Studies in the Spirituality of the High Middle Ages* (Berkeley: University of California Press, 1982), 3–8, for a discussion of current use of the term. For a less focused use see Amanda Porter, *Feminine Spirituality in America: From Sarah Edwards to Martha Graham* (Philadelphia: Temple University Press, 1980); Gayle Graham Yates, "Spirituality and the American Feminist Experience," *Signs* 9:1 (1983): 59–72.

17. See, for example, Daniel B. Shea Jr., *Spiritual Autobiography in Early America* (Princeton: Princeton University Press, 1968); David Leverenz, *The Language of Puritan Feeling: An Exploration in Literature, Psychology, and Social History* (New Brunswick, N.J.: Rutgers University Press, 1980); Charles E. Hambrick-Stowe, *The Practice of Piety: Puritan Devotional Disciplines in Seventeenth-Century New England* (Chapel Hill: University of North Carolina Press, 1982).

18. See Goldwin French, "The Evangelical Creed in Canada," in *The Shield of Achilles: Aspects of Canada in the Victorian Age,* ed. W.L. Morton (Toronto: McClelland and Stewart, 1968), 15–35. William Westfall notes that the term "evangelical" came to be consistently used by the Methodists in the 1830s. William Westfall, *Two Worlds: The Protestant Culture of Nineteenth-Century Ontario* (Montreal and Kingston: McGill-Queen's University Press, 1989), p. 233, n. 83.

19. Francis Wayland, *The Elements of Moral Science* (Cambridge, Mass.: Belknap Press, 1963), 285.

20. "Duties of Wives to Their Husbands," John Tawse Papers. Presbyterian Church Archives.

21. "Faith and Its Effects," *Christian Guardian,* 10 November 1852, p. 17.

22. See for example: "Influence of Marriage," *Christian Guardian,* 26 January 1870 (Methodist); "A Boy's Character," *Good News* (1863): 607–608 (Canada Presbyterian); "Make Home Pleasant for Boys," *Christian Messenger,* 25 December 1856, 1 (Baptist).

23. See for example: "Hints for a Christian Family," *Good News* (1863): 622; "Rules for Home Education," *Canadian Baptist,* 7 June 1860, 4; "On Worldly Amusements," *British North American Wesleyan Magazine* (1840): 633–641 (hereafter referred to as *BNA Wesleyan*); "Importance of Early Piety," *Ecclesiastical and Missionary Record* (September 1854): 174 (Presbyterian Church of Canada) (hereafter referred to as *Record*); "Family Worship," *Harbinger,* 15 March, 1843, 39–40 (Congregational).

24. Wayland, *Moral Science,* 292.

25. Correspondent of *Independent,* "Woman's Sphere," *Record* (March 1856): 86.

26. "To Mothers," *Harbinger,* 15 December, 1842, 179.

27. "Real Religion," *Good News* (1863): 68.

28. *Christian Guardian,* 30 March 1870, 51.

29. *Christian Guardian,* 29 June 1870, 101.

30. Jane Van Norman to her parents, 21 October 1844. Correspondence Jane Van Norman and A. Dunham Emory, 1844(?)–1857. United Church of Canada Archives (UCA hereafter).

31. Diary of Ann Appleby (1796–c. 1862), on loan to the author from Margaret Deacon, Toronto.

32. See, for example, "Sketch of the Life and Death of Margaret Irving, Who Died in Her Seventh Year," *Record,* 10 September 1854, 148; and "Memoir of Mrs. John Hale," *BNA Wesleyan* (November 1842): 401–405.

33. Of the 146 male obituaries in the *Guardian* during 1870–1873, 104 (71%) noted an age of conversion. Of these, 70 (67%) stated the age to be between 12 and 29.

34. For an excellent analysis of gender differences in nineteenth-century revivalism see Kathryn Kish Sklar, *Catharine Beecher: A Study in American Domesticity* (New Haven: Yale University Press, 1973), 31–38.

35. Colleen McDannell, *The Christian Home in Victorian America, 1840–1900* (Bloomington: Indiana University Press, 1986).

36. *Memoir of Mrs. Eliza Ann Chipman,* eds. Allen B. and Caroline E.B. Robertson (Hantsport, N.S.: Lancelot Press, 1989), 5. "Memoir of Mrs. John Edgecombe," *BNA Wesleyan* (1841): 535–536.

37. Jerald C. Brauer, "Conversion: From Puritanism to Revivalism," *Journal of Religion* 58 (1978): 227–243.

38. See for example obituary of Maria A. Forward, *Christian Guardian,* 16 March 1870.

39. Smith-Rosenberg, *Disorderly Conduct,* 129–164; G.A. Rawlyk, *Ravished by the Spirit: Religious Revivals, Baptists, and Henry Alline* (Montreal and Kingston: McGill-Queen's University Press, 1984), 116–119.

40. Brauer, "Conversion," 238–243; Leonard I. Sweet, "Views of Man Inherent in New Measures Revivalism," *Church History* 45 (June 1976): 206–221. Susan Juster, "'In a Different Voice': Male and Female Narratives of Religious Conversion in Post-Revolutionary America," *American Quarterly*

41 (March 1989): 34–62; *Disorderly Women: Sexual Politics and Evangelicalism in Revolutionary New England* (Ithaca, NY: Cornell University Press, 1994).

41. William James, *The Varieties of Religious Experience* (Harmondsworth: Penguin Books, 1982), 189.

42. John Welch, *Spiritual Pilgrims: Carl Jung and Teresa of Avila* (New York: Paulist Press, 1982), 7–28.

43. Journal of Harriet Dobbs Cartwright, Cartwright Papers, Public Archives of Ontario (hereafter PAO).

44. Jane Van Norman to her parents, 21 October 1844. Correspondence Jane Van Norman with A. Dunham Emory, 1844(?)–1857, UCA.

45. Letitia Youmans, *Campaign Echoes* (Toronto: William Briggs, 1893), 61.

46. Cedric B. Cowing, "Sex and Preaching in the Great Awakening," *American Quarterly* 20 (Fall 1968): 624–644.

47. See, for example, Ann Douglas, *The Feminization of American Culture* (New York: Avon, 1978), 143–196.

48. Philip Greven, *The Protestant Temperament: Patterns of Child-Rearing, Religious Experience and the Self in Early America* (New York: New American Library, 1977), 93.

49. "Memoir of Mrs. Virtue Vey," *BNA Wesleyan* (February 1846): 321–328.

50. "'Abba Father,'" *Good News* (1863): 358.

51. Journal of Harriet Dobbs Cartwright, Cartwright Papers, PAO.

52. "Memoir of Mrs. Mary Ann Humphries," *BNA Wesleyan* (Supplement 1843): 3.

53. Youmans, *Campaign Echoes*, 53.

54. "The Late Mrs. Smart," *Record* (January 1856): 38.

55. Deborah M. Valenze, *Prophetic Sons and Daughters: Female Preaching and Popular Religion in Industrial England* (Princeton: Princeton University Press, 1985) makes this argument. Valenze's analysis of the role of popular religion as a means to preserve the values of an agrarian society in industrial England is a suggestive model for Canada in the mid-nineteenth century, where denominational consolidation and the creation of the commercial state occurred significantly later than in England. More research needs to be done on the role of immigration in extending and preserving early nineteenth-century British agrarian ways and popular religious practices within Canada during the period of this paper.

56. *Memoir of Mrs. Eliza Ann Chipman*, 14.

57. Those seeking membership in the Free Presbyterian Church in Brockville in the 1840s, for example, were subjected to thirteen probing questions. Two of these were, "Have you repented of your sins so far as you know them? Is it your desire to shun all sin, in every form & above all do you desire to walk worthily as a Christian all your life long?" William Smart Papers, Box 1:10, UCA.

58. See for example, obituary of Mrs. Esther Brown, *Christian Guardian*, 5 January 1870, 3.

59. See, for example, the Diary of Ann Appleby, pp. 4–5.

60. For the prevalence of the doctrine of entire sanctification within Methodism see, for example, John Leland Peterson, *Christian Perfection and American Methodism* (Nashville: Abingdon, 1956).

61. Diary of Ann Appleby, "Draft of letter to 'Dear Sister Young.'"

62. Jane Van Norman to A. Dunham Emory, 1 January 1848, Correspondence Van Norman/Emory, UCA.

63. J. William Lamb, *Bridging the Years: A History of Bridge Street United/Methodist Church, Belleville, 1815–1990* (Winfield, B.C.: Wood Lake Books, 1990), 115.

64. Ann Appleby, for example, makes only brief mention of her first husband, and none of her second, and states that after her conversion she had hoped to stay single in order to be of greater use to God. She was, however, overruled by her family, "who thought that I should marry, which state I entered into in the fear of the Lord." Ann Appleby Diary, p. 3.

65. *Catherine Bell Van Norman: Her Diary, 1850*, ed. Ethel V. Gudgeon (Burlington: Burlington Historical Society, 1981), 23.

66. Photocopy of Diary, 24 February 1866, William McLaren Papers, Presbyterian Church Archives.

67. See, for example, obituary of Mrs. Nancy Day, *Christian Guardian*, 19 January 1870. For a parallel expression in British Wesleyanism in pre-1850 England see Valenze, *Prophetic Sons and Daughters*, 42.

68. Photocopy Mrs. Anne B. Bellamy Diary, 1854–1855, PAO.

69. *Catherine Bell Van Norman: Her Diary*, March 1850.

70. Gwen Kennedy Neville, *Kinship and Pilgrimage: Rituals of Reunion in American Protestant Culture* (New York: Oxford University Press, 1987), 66–67.

71. For a more complete analysis of the role played by theology in cementing such a relationship between evangelical mothers and sons see Marguerite Van Die, *An Evangelical Mind: Nathanael Burwash and the Methodist Tradition in Canada, 1839–1918* (Montreal and Kingston: McGill-Queen's University Press, 1989), 20–37.

72. [1868 or early 1869] J.F. Norris Family Papers, Box 1:8, British Columbia Archives.

73. Mary Shenston to Thomas Shenston, 23 November 1853, T.S. Shenston Papers, Toronto Reference Library.

74. C.B. Sissons, *Egerton Ryerson: His Life and Times*, vol. 1 (Toronto: Clarke, Irwin, 1937), 224.

75. Kennedy Neville, *Kinship and Pilgrimage*, 67–68.

76. For examples see Van Die, *An Evangelical Mind*, 24–25.

77. Roderic P. Beaujot and Kevin McQuillan, "The Social Effects of Demographic Change: Canada, 1851–1981," *Journal of Canadian Studies* 21:1 (Spring 1986): 59.
78. *Catherine Bell Van Norman: Her Diary*, 23.
79. Typed Draft of Biography, Chapter XIII "Margaret Proctor," Nathanael Burwash Papers Box 28:634, UCA.
80. I thank Clifford G. Hospital for this observation. Sermon "The Wesleyan Heritage," delivered at St. George's Cathedral, 3 March 1991.
81. For an example of a daughter converted at a mother's deathbed, see obituary Miss Hannah Walker, *Christian Guardian*, 12 January 1870; of parents hopefully converted by a dying daughter, obituary Margaret Ann Morris, Ibid. An especially detailed account of female influence at deathbed can be found in "Memoir of Miss Brown," *BNA Wesleyan* (July 1846): 41–52.
82. See for example "The Late Mrs. Smart," *Record* (January 1856): 39.
83. Typescript Family History and Testimony of Mrs. Henry Hammond.
84. "Woman's Sphere," *Record* (March 1856): 38.

"Femmes Fortes" and the Montreal Poor in the Early Nineteenth Century

JAN NOEL

A recent travelling exhibition of Lower Canadian portraits from the first half of the nineteenth century elicited comments from gallerygoers about how stern the women looked. As early as the 1840s though, advice columnists in Canadian newspapers had encouraged their middle class readers to lighten up. Women were told to dress nicely, stop nagging, and smile:

> Woman does not truly appreciate her mission in domestic life . . . weighted down by cares — as a wife she is different from what she was as mistress. She is employed in drudgery for her children and her household. She neglects her dress — she forgets her manners. Her husband sees the change . . . He flies to the tavern, the billiard table![1]
>
> How simple is the secret of feminine beauty. Let a country girl have a face rough enough to grate nutmegs on. Yet how the wraiths of sunshine dance around her once she illuminates it with a *smile*! — Let the fair sex take heed.[2]

Men, on the other hand, were saddled with the whole burden of seriousness. An artist even repainted the early nineteenth century family portrait of wealthy fur trader William McGillivray a few decades later to meet more exacting standards of manliness. The original sweet paterfamilias presenting his wife with fruit was replaced by a more aggressive father, standing guard over his family with a rifle. More indicative of an earlier sensibility is William Berczy's 1809 portrait of the Woolseys, a Quebec mercantile family. Male and female figures vie with each other in gorgeous display of bows and trimmings, rich fabrics and golden buttons. The two boys are pretty in bright green with big ruffled

SOURCE: Jan Noel, "'Femmes Fortes' and the Montreal Poor," in L. Muir and M. Whiteley, eds., *Changing Roles of Women in the Christian Church* (Toronto: University of Toronto Press, 1995). Reprinted by permission of University of Toronto Press Incorporated. © University of Toronto Press 1995.

collars. The classically robed daughter with a doll is no more frivolous than her uncle lounging in the window with a flute. Though paterfamilias does tower over the family, he is quite dapper, and perhaps vies with his seated old mother for authority. She is a purposeful figure, so closely associated with work that she poses with her sewing basket and scissors. Her son in his gold vest with his hand resting in his pocket has perhaps delegated protection of the family to the one truly *macho* figure in the portrait, the sinewy brown Labrador straining at his leash.

One grows more appreciative of Lower Canada's unsmiling matrons, with their work spread out before them, when one understands how busy they were. Not just at home, either. Women in the first decades of the nineteenth century were leading the response to a pressing urban problem, the surge of British immigrants into Lower Canadian ports after the Napoleonic Wars ended in 1815. Montreal, for example, which had only about nine thousand people then, saw its summer population swell by several thousand more. For four decades the flow would continue, flooding the town with many who were homeless, orphaned, or ill. In those days when people of the comfortable classes still lived downtown, begging streetpeople came right up to their doors and knocked.

After they heard enough of the knocking,[3] a number of energetic women decided to create a better system. Some worked to enlarge existing institutions while others established new social welfare services. A number of the hospitals, hostels and childcare agencies they established between 1800 and 1832 were so useful that they continue to exist, in altered form, even today. It will be shown in this essay that women provided most of the organised social welfare in Montreal and its environs in the first two decades of the nineteenth century. They were still initiating major projects as late as 1832 when cholera created an emergency in the town. Women drawn from both major language groups founded and operated organised help for people unable to provide their own food, clothing, fuel, childcare, housing or health care. French Canadians even have a term for these administrators in skirts: *femmes fortes*. *Femmes fortes* became more rare after 1840 as public enterprise by bourgeoise women would begin to seem crude, and to face the handicap of increasing legal constraints. After the early nineteenth century decades under review here, projects were increasingly initiated by male clergy, laymen or government officials. Women would continue to supply much of the labour but were less apt to supply the direction.

Appreciation of this leadership of early efforts contributes to an understanding of the stages of the history of women — a history that has not always been progressive. Indeed, there seems to have been more independent action at the beginning of the nineteenth century than in subsequent decades. This was to some extent a post-Conquest carryover from the days of New France in which gender roles had been rather loosely defined.[4] Then, women not only bore children and kept house but often provided much of the family's livelihood; they also played an important part in shaping public endeavour, particularly in the welfare field.

As their unsmiling early nineteenth century portraits suggest, these women did not believe their primary role was to please. Nor did they sally forth onto the streets primarily to show off their hats. Indeed, the oft-repeated notion that women joined organisations due to idleness or boredom rings particularly false for this period. Society still had many aspects of the *ancien régime*, which saw both women and men producing and exchanging commodities. Farms could not function without women's dairying, poultrykeeping and gardening. Households required the textiles manufactured by Lower Canada's thirteen thousand weavers, mostly female,[5] as well as the soap and candles they made. Since few ready-made clothes were imported, women's dressmaking was equally essential. Shops and workshops were often a family enterprise in a way later waged work was not. Montreal historians have confirmed that the female proportion of the labour force (27%) was larger in 1825 than it was at the end of the nineteenth century.[6]

Not only were female workers more numerous, they also had a surprisingly wide range of occupations. Women still had the skills, for example, to make the clothing and household items which fetched £700 at an 1831 charity bazaar in Montreal. To these events women also brought retailing experience, not a hobby but a livelihood for the thirteen female "traders," twelve grocers or drygoods dealers, seven tavernkeepers and one auctioneer listed among about 1500 occupations in the 1819 Montreal directory.[7] Throughout the century, women would work as grocers and tavernkeepers, boardinghouse keepers, dressmakers and teachers; but the traders and a few skilled female artisans such as the tinplate manufacturer and tallow chandler hint at an earlier and wider pre-industrial range. So do the female blacksmiths, coachmakers, gardeners, innkeepers, mercers and farmers identified in Jacques Viger's 1825 census. Nuns who ran the hospital, assisted by the elderly women living there, made clothes and ornaments the North West Company traded to the Indians; they also printed and bound books and worked in the fields of their seigneurie. The frequent use of women's own last names rather than that of their husbands during this period also suggests a certain independence,[8] an independence that must have owed something to the wives' extensive and varied economic production.

Certainly in comparison to the later nineteenth century, this society placed more weight on social class and less on gender. Few men enjoyed a marked educational advantage over women. In government and the professions, career training was still somewhat rudimentary. Manners, names and family ties opened doors. Social contacts were essential, and gentlewomen played a large part in cultivating them.[9] Until 1849,[10] female property owners had the right to vote, and French civil law in the early nineteenth century entitled wives and widows to a more secure portion of family property than existed under British law.[11] Domestic service in 1820 also tended to be more a function of class than of gender;[12] it was with the subsequent identification of woman and home that the manservant would fall out of fashion. Childrearing, too, was still an avocation rather than a destiny. Children were often raised by others: the Upper Canadian Governor's wife, Elizabeth Simcoe, left four young daughters in England while she came to Canada for five years, and Canadian families of various classes sent young children away from home to schools or apprenticeships. Although British and American conduct literature was already preaching "separate spheres" to the elite by the late eighteenth century, the idea was still somewhat novel among the Canadian middle classes until the 1840s; then prosperity, the rapid growth of towns, occupational diversification, public schools and better communications (which carried a rash of family newspapers and advice literature) would all work together to deal a decisive blow to the old family economy.[13] In the early nineteenth century, women tended to be somewhat at home in the public domain. They did not step into the street as timid amateurs when they undertook public relief work. Also, because of the less discriminatory property and civil laws, they probably enjoyed more discretionary spending power and more authority than would their daughters and granddaughters later in the century. In many ways early nineteenth century women were less constrained than later Victorian Canadians who had gender distinctions drummed into them and fortified by an array of gender-based regulations and institutions. These more fluid circumstances help explain women's energetic public welfare activity.

Most of women's social welfare work in this period was religiously motivated or church-related. Yet often such work crossed denominational lines. The well-worn Protestant/Catholic dichotomy does not explain this early nineteenth century period as well as another which distinguishes between more wealthy Established church "insiders" and less wealthy, more reform-minded Evangelical church "outsiders." "Establishment" work emanated from the three churches established in Canada in the seventeenth and eighteenth centuries, the Churches of Rome, England and Scotland, all receiving state support for some or all of the period under review. By 1800 all three of these denominations were firmly rooted in Canadian soil and had experience with its multicultural, multidenominational reality. Fittingly, they shared church buildings: the Anglicans worshipped for some time at the Catholic Récollet Church, later sharing a building with the Scots. They had also learned to live not only with the religious beliefs of others but also with their moral failings. The St. Gabriel Street Presbyterian Church, for example, tolerated the indiscretions of a minister who drank too much, and quietly baptized fur magnates' children conceived in various beds.[14] Similarly the Catholics took in foundlings without asking about their origins, one Mother Superior noting that "prudence and delicacy forbids us to put any question on that score."[15] "Established" efforts tended to draw on the resources of Montreal's elite: private bequests, fundraising efforts such as bazaars, church or neighbourhood collections, and government subsidies. In contrast to American evangelical denominations, these churches derived from countries with fairly rigid class systems, pre-Revolutionary France and anti-Revolutionary Britain (with an added conservative injection of American Loyalists). Lower Canada's elite generally belonged to these churches, as did the majority of its poor.

The Established tradition produced most of the recorded female benevolence in this early period. This is seen both in the work of the Catholic nuns and the primarily Protestant Female Benevolent Society. Springing from the traditional order, these groups embodied classic Canadian virtues of conciliation and compromise. They had learned to cooperate with various denominational and ethnic groups. Their ability to work with powerful men was also important to their success. If these virtues had a corresponding vice, it was perhaps a proclivity to bend too much to the prevailing winds, be they the windy advice of ambitious clergymen, or the tendency to place increasing burdens of self-sacrifice on overworked members when a change of system might have better served both donors and recipients of aid.

I. Establishment Social Welfare: The Nuns

Catholic nuns continued to carry the major burden of social welfare in Montreal for at least a half-century after the British Conquest of 1760. From the seventeenth century, Congregational nuns had provided free schooling to working class children; they added two new Montreal locations to their Notre Dame motherhouse in the early 1830s.[16] Other groups of nuns had cared for the orphaned, indigent, aged and ill. Beginning as a dedicated group of missionaries funded by government, private donors, and their own lands and labours, the nuns had long provided services that had compared favourably with hospital care and female education in France.[17] After the Conquest, despite financial difficulties, their role was enhanced. Having cared for British as well as French cases during and after the Seven Years' War (a blend of charity and *politique*), the nuns were permitted to remain and to recruit in Canada at a time when the Jesuit and Récollet orders were forbidden to do so and vocations to the parish priesthood were not keeping pace with population growth. By 1825 nuns outnumbered clergymen in Montreal by four to one. Moreover, from the beginning of the nineteenth century, the government was regularly funding their work in Lower Canada's three urban centres. The sum of £17,103 was awarded to Montreal nunneries between 1800 and 1823 to help pay for the care of growing numbers of sick and homeless in the expanding town.

One of the recipients was the Hôtel Dieu, located on the bustling business street of St. Paul. This thirty bed hospital consisted of two wards until its late-1820s expansion. The Hôtel Dieu benefited from the volunteer ward visiting by Dr. William Selby, while the nuns carried on the day-to-day work as administrators, apothecaries, ward supervisors, and (combining pre-industrial doctoring with practical caretaking) sisters who might best be described as "nurse-practitioners."

The Hôpital Général, run by Madame Youville's Grey Nuns since 1737, was a larger establishment with about eighty sickbeds. Unlike the Hôtel Dieu (which turned away children, maternity cases, communicable diseases and several other categories), the Hôpital had an open door. It nursed a number of indigent invalids along with wealthier pensioners. By sheltering a number of Irish orphans and other victims of a typhus outbreak in 1822-23, the Hôpital received Legislative commendation for preserving the town's "uncommon degree of health at that time." In 1823 it treated 485 Protestant and 367 Catholic patients, of whom apparently only 41 died.[18]

This large and useful establishment owed its prosperous condition to capable superiors such as Thérèse-Geneviève Coutlée, its director from 1792 to 1821. The daughter of a day labourer, Coutlée had entered the convent in 1762, and was early singled out for her intelligence and judgement. When appointed superior, Coutlée had wept at the responsibility. However, she soon displayed the business acumen not unusual in eighteenth century women. The Hôpital was in financial difficulty due to the French government's failure to pay certain annuities. Coutlée did her best to restore sound footing: she rented out part of the land, and developed workshops where the nuns made candles and vestments, embroidered cloth, and bound books, exercising a range of craft skills typical of the *ancien régime*. For part of Thérèse-Geneviève Coutlée's regime the sisters also still toiled in the fields to feed their community; but the premature death of several nuns apparently persuaded the superior their overtaxed energies were better used indoors. Doctors, legislative councillors and all parties involved in the 1824 Enquiry spoke with respect of the dedication of the religious women and their "great and unremitting exertion" to feed, clothe and care for all those in their charge.

The Hôpital Général's Foundling Street Location bespoke its other major function, to receive abandoned infants. The nuns sent these out to wetnurses, paying the nurses, providing them with baby clothes and visiting to check up on their small charges. At age two the babies were brought back to the Grey Nuns and sent out for adoption or contractual placement with "respectable families."

This infant care, which might have been one of the nuns' more cheerful tasks, was in fact the grimmest. As Montreal developed into a major port, military centre and reception point for immigrants and displaced habitants, increasing numbers of children were abandoned. The nuns received seventeen infants in 1760, thirty-nine in 1800, and eighty-six in 1823.[19] Many arrived at the Grey Nuns' door nearly dead, some brought in carts from considerable distances. Between 1800 and 1823, more than three-quarters of the foundlings received by the nuns — 841 of 1207 — died after being sent out to nurse, most of them in the first month of life. This contrasted with a 25% infant mortality rate in Montreal generally. Questioned about this by the Legislative Council Committee in 1824, the Grey Nuns' Superior, Marguerite Lemaire St. Germain (who succeeded Coutlée in 1822), attributed it to "the bad state in which we receive them, which proceeds from that shame which induces the mothers to resort to the utmost means of concealing the offspring of their crime from the eyes of the world."[20]

Concerned by the deathrate and also by the expense of caring for the growing numbers of foundlings, the government Committee expressed the opinion that the system itself was defective. Their research indicated that high mortality rates characterised foundling hospitals everywhere. They felt that the moral effect of these institutions was pernicious: giving unwed mothers a place to send their infants was "calculated to weaken that mainspring of a healthy population, matrimony, and to blunt or destroy . . . parental affection by encouraging mothers to abandon their offspring." Besides being an "incitement to vice and licentiousness," foundling hospitals swallowed up public money. As a result the 1824 Committee recommended phasing out the system as soon as possible. The gulf between their scientific aspirations and Mother St. Germain's charitable realism appears in the proceedings:

> Query: What is the System in respect to them?
> Answer: Not understanding completely the object of the query I am not able to answer it in a satisfactory manner: all that I have the honor to say to you, is, that we attend to all the details, and we bestow all the care that forsaken, unsupported and unprotected children can inspire.

Despite the Council's laudable concern for systemic change, Mother St. Germain may have understood the situation better: given Montreal's large military and transient population, closing the foundling hospital would probably have increased infanticide rather than lowering illegitimacy.[21] Indeed the Committee had no alternative forms of prevention or care to suggest, and the foundling work would continue for decades to come. Yet laywomen soon began to take steps to help women in childbirth, relieving at least some of the desperation that led to abandonment of infants.

At the same time that the numbers of foundlings increased, the Grey Nuns also accepted the burden of housing insane patients. The situation was Dickensian. The afflicted lived in six-by-eight foot cells with grated windows. The nuns eschewed corporal punishment and, according to their physician, fed the patients "if anything too well." Although the sisters cleaned and cleaned, a noxious smell arose from the cells. The building's riverside location added winter damp to the pungent atmosphere. There was no exercise yard and no room for one. The situation, the Hôpital's physician asserted, was "more likely to . . . increase insanity than to cure it."[22] Remarkably, forty-nine of the eighty-four mental cases the nuns received between 1800 and 1823 had been discharged as "cured or relieved." Here too was a system recognized as obsolete; but in this case the Legislative Council was able to propose an alternative, a government asylum based on the famous mental asylum in Glasgow with facilities for classification, treatment and exercise. Such an institution would eventually be built at Beauport in 1845. In the meantime, however, the nuns cared for up to eight patients, while that many again overflowed into the town jail. In 1818 the Grey Nuns made an unwonted refusal of a £2000 government grant allocated for building more cells for the insane, "as it would increase what is in itself bad and inadequate to the object" of helping the mental cases.

The nuns had successfully made the transition to a new regime by diplomacy with their British rulers and by the continuing tradition of dedicated care, broadened now to include non-Catholics. Above all, they survived and grew because they filled a vital need, to which the large grant from a parsimonious government stands testimony. There were no other hospitals available until 1816 and no sizeable Protestant institution until 1822, despite the preponderance of Protestant patients. Both the Hôpital Général and the Hôtel Dieu continued to provide services for decades, the latter functioning to this day as a teaching hospital in connection with the Université de Montréal. One cannot contemplate with satisfaction the primitive treatment the nuns' charges received and the seemingly calm acceptance of appalling conditions. Without the nuns, however, such cases would have marched more surely and swiftly to the alternate destinations of jailhouse and grave.

II. Establishment Social Welfare: Laywomen

So important was the nuns' contribution to early nineteenth century welfare that Protestant benevolence to some extent simply picked up the pieces that fell outside the nuns' wide net. The founders of the Female Benevolent Society were struck by the plight of immigrants arriving in 1815. The Benevolent Society's approach to poverty displayed much of the same religious tolerance and female initiative seen in the work of the nuns. Apparently the first permanent English-language voluntary relief association in Montreal, it filled a major gap in the town's welfare services.[23] Like the convents, it looked to the powers of the land for support, and worked within the established order. The women who were most active in initiating the Benevolent Society, Eleanor Gibb, H.W. Barrett and the widow Janet Finlay Aird, worshipped at the St. Gabriel Street Church connected with the Church of Scotland.[24] Mrs. Gibb, from a tailoring family, might be suspected of an interest in fashion; but in fact she spent many of her waking hours among those in rags.

This trio and a handful of their friends placed a notice in Montreal newspapers and bookstores shortly before Christmas in 1815 that "a number of Ladies, deeply impressed with the destitute situation of the poor, wish to form a society to relieve indigent women and small children, the sick, the aged and the infirm poor of the city."[25] To achieve their aim they fashioned a structure that involved a directress and a board of twelve managers. To support their work they persuaded the Reverend Robert Easton, pastor of the St. Peter Street Scottish Secession congregation, to preach a charity sermon, which he did on a Sunday night in September, 1816.

The sermon was no revolutionary manifesto. Easton accepted the class system; he counselled his hearers to be prudent in their giving, retaining whatever was necessary for the support of their "rank and credit in the world." Yet he acknowledged the common humanity of the poor: "Whoever wears the human form challenges our respect, and, being found in a state of wretchedness, is entitled to relief."[26] Most notable is what the sermon did *not* do. Scarcely any mention was made of benevolent activity as a womanly or motherly endeavour. Easton dwelt instead on compassion as "one of our natural endowments . . . a sentiment of nature . . . a maxim of true religion." He appears to have been aware of the upsurge of such benevolence in Britain and the United States, and towards the end of his sermon he did mention this work as highly becoming to members of the female sex and a good example to their daughters. In contrast to later nineteenth century ministerial counsels, however, there was a refreshing emphasis on the common humanity of givers and recipients of aid. Charitable workers were generic good samaritans, rather than gendered nurturers.

In the Society's first year the members used their £190 treasury to give food, firewood, clothes, and medicine to about sixty adults and forty-five children, mostly drawn from the several thousand immigrants who began annually to inundate a town then numbering about nine thousand. Some of this group were unfit to go on to the usual immigrant destination of Upper Canada, so Benevolent Society members rented a small house in the Récollet suburb which they named the House of Recovery. They hired several housekeepers, while the twelve managers took turns supplying and visiting the house. By 1817–18 the Society was helping some 370 people a year including twenty "permanent charges" and the annual treasury had grown to £1200. Supplementing their efforts from 1818 was another voluntary society for the Relief of Emigrants, which included Catholic, Presbyterian and Anglican ministers, formed to arrange westward passage for destitute but ablebodied immigrants. By 1820 the Benevolent Society was sending five hundred people a year by this agency, agreeing in return to open a soup kitchen for hungry immigrants in one of its houses.[27]

Alongside this immigrant work, the Society cared for a number of women in childbirth as well as some forty invalids unable to gain admission to the Hôtel Dieu. Securing discarded bedding from the military barracks, they moved their sick patients into a larger house on Craig

Street which had three wards and could hold twenty-four patients. When this experiment proved viable, doctors and businessmen such as John Richardson and William McGillivray began plans to give the city a permanent General Hospital. The Benevolent Society's historian later recorded that "the large Craig Street house to which the patients from the House of Recovery were moved was the first General Hospital, the direct result of the efforts of the Ladies' Benevolent Society on behalf of the sick poor."[28] Doige's *Montreal Directory* of 1819 corroborates the claim:

> the bright example of superior benevolence evinced by the female sex in this institution has at length aroused the energies of the gentlemen, who have lately caused a public dispensary to be established, which . . . the increase of the population and the difficulties of the times . . . has made necessary.

With the hospital passing into the hands of a male committee and the clergy beginning to address itself to immigrant aid, the women expanded another arm of their work. Increasingly the Benevolent Society turned to helping children, "the prospect of training a rising generation to industry and sobriety being so much more promising than that of reforming those whose habits have become fixed."[29] Several committee members worked to establish a National School while others formed a committee of the Society for Promoting Education and Industry.[30] In 1822 they opened the Protestant Orphan Asylum, directed by Janet Aird with H.W. Barrett as secretary. Many of its twelve managers had previously served as managers of the benevolent society.

The charity flourished, growing in numbers and prestige. The seventy-three members of 1816 increased to eighty-one by 1819. It appears to have been an upwardly mobile group. The founders were of the middle class; besides Eleanor Gibb, who belonged to a family of merchant-tailors who outfitted Montreal's elites, Janet Aird and H.W. Barrett were also from mercantile families. By 1817, though, Mrs. Ogden, wife of the Chief Justice, was the Society's second directress. In 1819 there was an influx of "several ladies of the first respectability . . . who had not before honoured the meetings."[31] The move towards exclusive work with children fit genteel conceptions of feminine duty better than did work with adult street people. A new sensibility is suggested, too, by the gradual replacement of the earthy "Female" in the Society's name with the more refined term "Ladies," made official in the society's reconstituted charter in 1832.

Ladies or not, the membership remained capable of taking to the streets in a crisis. A cholera epidemic reached the town with the arrival of the ship *Carricks* from Dublin on 8 June 1832. Within a week 261 people died in Montreal; 632 died the following week and 166 the next; that year the city saw 2500 cholera-related fatalities. Many Montrealers fled to the country in terror, and refugees huddled in the barns and granaries on the outskirts of town. The members of the Ladies' Be-

nevolent Society went out in pairs to canvass the town streets for donations to help the victims. They collected £500, to which was added
£100 collected by a male citizens' committee. Again the Society established a soup kitchen to feed the hungry, along with a house to receive
destitute widows and children, and an employment office for domestics.
With medical services volunteered by Dr. John Stephenson, the women
also ran a house for the homeless and for invalids released from the
General Hospital but still convalescing.

By 1833 the Society had effectively demonstrated its usefulness. At
its public general meeting a resolution was unanimously passed that the
members had "as far as funds had permitted . . . fulfilled their pledge
to the public to relieve all those who were in real want and distress
from the ravages of the cholera" and further resolved that the Society
should be permanent. The Montreal Sanitary Committee transferred its
£50 balance to the Ladies' Benevolent Society, and Stephenson offered
his services and supplies for an indefinite period. Two prospective
teachers for the orphanage were sent for training in the Lancastrian and
Infant School methods. The financial future looked promising: along
with £228 raised at a Government House Bazaar, the group also received
£100 from the government, the first of a long series of such grants for
the orphanage.[32]

The Ladies' Benevolent Society was an effective organisation — so
much so that it is still functioning in Montreal as a childcare organisation
after amalgamating with several other groups. Its longevity can be attributed to several factors. First, its members were dedicated: the same
names recurred on the membership and managerial rolls year after year,
with some families serving for generations. Secondly, its ecumenical
membership made it acceptable in Montreal's multicultural setting.
Thirdly, the society showed a tendency to order and system as opposed
to trends and enthusiasms. Early in its history, clear lines of responsibility
and an endowment fund were both in place. This soundness, along with
the status of its members, helped ensure success in securing government
support as well as free care from physicians, charity sermons from clergy,
and other important donations of goods and services. That in turn made
possible the hiring of a small paid staff. A pioneering Protestant orphanage, it led the way for a number of such institutions founded in
other colonial towns after 1850[33] in addressing problems endemic to volunteer organisations.

The most notable aspect of Montreal Benevolent Society welfare
is the centrality of the work of women. They did not operate peripherally
but initiated the response to a pressing public need, and sustained it.
The Society's 1920 historian wrote that "the authority of older histories
and statistics [established] the fact that this Society was the pioneer philanthropy of British Montreal, and that its work led directly to the founding of the Montreal General Hospital and the Protestant Orphan Asylum
and to an organised assistance for that vast throng of immigrants con-

tinually progressing towards Upper Canada."[34] As late as 1820 other groups were still so ephemeral that the Ladies' Benevolent Society was the only Protestant charity mentioned in the *Montreal Directory* of that year. A workhouse had a brief career from 1819 until it folded four years later.[35] Apart from that, there appears to have been little besides a bread line at the Récollet Church to supplement the organised relief work of the nuns and laywomen. Until the opening of the commodious Montreal General Hospital in 1822, the institutions for the ill in Montreal were also founded and administered by women.

The 1820s and 1830s would see an increase in benevolent activities. Catholic laywomen, for example, began the Dames de Charité in 1827 to provide housing, education and employment to needy women and children. The hope was expressed in Doige's 1819 *Directory* that men would soon follow women's lead in the benevolent field. By 1839 this too had come to pass; a directory writer then boasted of Montreal's vigorous charitable activity relative to its size and wealth, with a plethora of societies devoted to relief, reform, and immigrant aid.[36] By that time men's groups were directing many of the projects. Although they were no longer alone in the field, women did continue to direct several major efforts, as seen in the Benevolent Society's vigorous response to the cholera epidemic. There were also several emanations from the Dames de Charité — a Catholic orphanage erected in 1832 and the hostels of Emilie Tavernier-Gamelin, which grew into the extensive work of today's Sisters of Providence.[37]

In the 1830s these lay groups continued the ecumenical tradition established by the nuns. Some women joined both Catholic and Protestant groups. Marie C-J. LeMoyne, owner of the seigneurie of Longueuil and widow of Captain David Grant, served as the first president of the Catholic Orphanage and second president of the Protestant one.[38] In 1831 Catholic and Protestant women co-sponsored a notable bazaar that netted £710, which appears to have been divided with the best of will on all sides:

One-third to the Ladies of the R.C. Church	237
Montreal General Hospital	175
Orphan Asylum	108
National School	40
Br. and Canadian School	40
Infant School	30
8 Protestant Clergy for the poor, 10 each	80

The Catholic women saluted their colleagues by promptly returning £50 of their own grant to the Protestant Montreal General Hospital.[39]

III. Evangelical Innovations

In contrast with these societies which were rooted in the established churches, the evangelicals were more disruptive. In the period under review they were only beginning the social crusading that became their trademark. In Montreal they were drawn from various denominations outside the three established churches, such as Methodists, Congregationalists and the group of American Presbyterians who had broken away from the Church of Scotland group in Montreal; later recruits came from the Free Kirk. A number of the evangelicals, including some "American" Presbyterians, hailed from the British Isles; but more significant were the roots many others had in the "Burnt Over Districts" of New York and New England, centres of the Second Great Awakening (a revival largely financed and attended by women).

The evangelicals' root conviction was that all human beings must subscribe to a pure biblical faith and a single standard of morality. Moreover, this daunting goal had an imminent deadline. Montreal evangelicals shared the widespread millennial expectations of Awakened America and post-Wesleyan Britain. Tending to discern the Second Coming of Christ in passing stormclouds, they hastened to save the world before it was too late. They saw the Antichrist in churches accommodating double or multiple standards, or corrupted by accretions of non-biblical ritual or dogma. To their credit the evangelicals — often craftspeople or shopkeepers who were not uninterested in upward mobility — were brave about attacking harmful customs, no matter how long established or well entrenched. They were ready to bear rebuff or ridicule for what they thought right; this remained true even of many of them who ascended to Montreal's higher social circles (surprising the Governor, for example, by lecturing him on teetotalism at his own banquet).[40]

What is more, dedicated evangelicals believed that the most lowly scrap of humanity deserved sustained attention (though not all the lowly welcomed the zealot's penetrating gaze). They accepted the need to feed and clothe beggars to put them in suitable state to hear the Word of God. They also went deeper, recognizing the more lasting effect of touching hearts and changing minds. Their belief in the redeemability of the inner person caused them to protest a whole range of brutal practices that ignored the existence of conscience by assuming desirable conduct must be forced rather than taught or inspired. Evangelicals fought slavery, and the use of the lash on sailors and soldiers and on the young. They believed that the consciences of children and others must be awakened and trained to do what was right so that external constraints could be removed. To the extent that society made immoral demands on its weaker members, society itself must be changed.[41]

In the early nineteenth century, the evangelical sense of urgency and its mission to teach opened a door for female endeavour. Indeed, it is among the evangelicals that one catches flickers of rebellion against the established order that seem altogether lacking in established churchwomen with their cordial relationship with the powers of the land. At a time when Sunday schools were often the only access to literacy available to working class children, Lucy Hedge established one in Montreal;

founded in 1817, it was claimed to be the first such institution in the city. Hedge, one of the founding members of Montreal's American Presbyterian congregation, had been educated in Litchfield, Connecticut; her pastor there had been the renowned American evangelist and reformer Lyman Beecher. Apparently the school she founded ossified and fell into other hands. This elicited a seeming *coup d'état* meeting held at Hedge's house in 1826 in which she, her sister and fifteen other women and men signed a manifesto declaring the school's constitution totally inadequate and insisting on a new one directed to the religious and moral improvement of the young of all classes without distinction. The staff, they demanded, was to consist of "persons of both sexes, all of whom shall be actively employed in the school."[42] This work soon led to outreach to children in other parts of the city. Hedge worked with a committee to form the British and Canadian School for educating children of the labouring classes which opened in 1821 in the Craig Street house where the Benevolent Society had earlier operated the General Hospital.[43] In the 1830s the church [American Presbyterian] itself had five hundred children enrolled in several Sunday schools as well as a large Free School.[44] It was by that date considered sufficiently useful to warrant government support.[45]

Most of the evangelical women's public activity, however, was in more controversial realms than teaching the poor the three R's. Women in Laprairie encountered priestly opposition to their distribution of French language Bibles, which was underway by 1826. Evangelical women in Montreal followed suit, and were in possession of sufficient funds to hire a city missionary in 1830.[46] These women were more interested in spreading the gospel than in doing social welfare work. This caused a reaction in the Catholic community, with the priests forbidding their parishioners to accept the Bibles or attend the Sunday schools.

Equally unpopular, but of much greater significance for social welfare, was temperance work. Well into the 1840s in Canada some zealous temperance advocates suffered dismissal from jobs and regiments, and censure by church congregations for "speaking out too frankly on certain points." Nevertheless, temperance work in that hard-drinking society was, as scholars have begun to recognize, a humanitarian endeavour. Historians of women have long treated temperance with respect, as a politicizing agent in the suffrage campaigns. Partly because of the excesses of the post-1850 prohibition movement, even those who appreciate this benefit have tended to analyse the attack on alcohol as melodrama, as middle class status-seeking, or as social control: in all events a distraction from the deeper problems that drove people to drink. The movement did contain all these elements; but recent research tends to confirm early temperance workers' claims that heavy drinking was a severe social problem in its own right, causing or exacerbating violence, family abuse or neglect, accidents and many alcohol-related health problems.[47]

Evangelical women in the Canadas supported this important reform from its inception. Indeed their participation predates the years of 1826 to 1828 that historians have identified as its start.[48] G.W. Perkins, a Presbyterian missionary who later served as pastor of Montreal's American Presbyterian church, wrote in 1822 of an earlier society. The family of Mrs. John Forbes ran the local store in the little logging settlement of Russelltown, about forty kilometres south of Montreal. Energetic and resourceful, Mrs. Forbes was concerned about conditions in her neighbourhood, which had no minister and was by several accounts "fearfully intemperate."[49] American-born, she may have been influenced by the Second Great Awakening and the temperance work accompanying religious revivals in the States after 1815. She undertook to have a church built by raising subscriptions on both sides of the border and organising a local dressmaking operation to bring in additional funds. Perhaps in reaction to the succession of dissolute doctors, teachers and even preachers who passed through the village, Forbes also

> commenced . . . the formation of a temperance society. . . . The proposal at first met with universal neglect and even derision. Still she persisted; through private conversation, and the distribution of tracts and papers, she endeavoured to disarm prejudice. Her efforts were so far successful that she ventured at length to request a meeting of a few of the neighbours at her own house for the purpose of forming a temperance society. . . . She conversed with them individually, and a society was formed.[50]

Evangelical women in the Montreal Temperance Society would continue this tradition in 1840 by sending the first of a series of temperance circuit riders out to preach the cause across the Canadas in 1840, a crusade that would soon be expanded by the wealthy businessmen of that Society. Thus, beginning in 1822, temperance leadership by evangelical women appeared in Canada a half-century earlier than is generally recognised. As outsiders, the evangelicals were willing to attack a social custom entrenched at all levels of society — in a way that nuns and other "established" churchwomen with their gentlemen supporters and government funds were not likely to venture.

Female activists were overshadowed during the 1840s. Montreal's merchant princes would then begin to incorporate zealous reformers in their ranks, born-again, evangelical businessmen, ardent Presbyterians such as John Redpath with his sugar empire, the Lyman pharmaceutical magnates and the Mackay brothers who made a fortune in drygoods. These men turned the women's wooden hospices and rented houses into the great pillared and iron-railed institutions of Victorian Canada. While philanthropic laymen replaced the hard-living fur traders at Montreal's social summit, the powerful Bishop Bourget created and controlled a new network of Catholic welfare institutions, and the paeans praising woman's place in the home grew deafening. Thereafter men would tend to supply the direction to major welfare efforts while women continued to supply much of the labour.

At the beginning of the century, things had been different. The field was dominated by women. In the first decade the nuns worked virtually alone in social welfare. In the second and third decades, a number of laywomen, mostly in connection with the established Churches, took charge of social cases falling outside the nuns' network. The older benevolence associated with the established Churches acted to relieve the growing numbers of urban poor. It did so without enquiring too closely into either the lifestyle of those who begged or the shortcomings of society. Yet these churchwomen alleviated human suffering in a time when little other relief was available; they left a legacy of interdenominational co-operation rather than bitterness. Clearly the work was solid, for the nuns and the Ladies' Benevolent Society built institutions which continued to evolve, and endure to this day.

The evangelicals, beginning as outsiders because of American origins or lower status, dispensed a critique along with their charity. Their dogmatism and proselytisation fostered decades of ill will. Yet in refusing to accept the maxim "the poor we have always with us" and preferring to "go teach all nations," they determined to go beyond relieving distress to root it out. In so doing they initiated in Canada one of the nineteenth century's most important reforms, the temperance movement which addressed a serious problem for society in general and women in particular, and eventually mobilized the latter to reclaim their basic civil rights.

Together, established and evangelical forms of Christianity produced notable female activism in the Montreal vicinity in the early nineteenth century. The period instructs us in feminine service that was not subservient. A former Londoner then living in Montreal compared this activity favourably to that of British women, saying that "Montreal, though not equal to London in the number of its females, far surpasses that metropolis in the activity, capability and independence of the female mind and spirit."[51] With their hospitals, asylums and dispensaries, Mother Coutlée, Eleanor Gibb, Madame Grant and their associates shaped the first response to the problems of immigrants arriving in the port city in desperate need of help, and of the growing numbers of indigenous poor. Evangelical women began to address underlying ills of addiction, brutality and ignorance. Many of these endeavours won the co-operation of clergymen, physicians and politicians. The initiative, however, arose from the "capability and independence of the female mind and spirit." A smile might have added to their beauty. It could scarcely have added to their worth.

NOTES

1. *Stanstead Journal*, Nov. 16, 1848.
2. *Stanstead Journal*, July 19, 1847.
3. Hungry beggars going door to door occasioned the founding, for example, of the Montreal Dames de Charité in 1827, who recorded "on prit en considération l'extrême misère que souffre par le manque de nourriture, un très grand nombre de pauvres de cette paroisse de Montréal, et on

résolut alors de soulager et d'apporter un remède plus efficace à leurs infortunes, que celui qui résulte des aumônes qu'ils reçoivent journellement, dans les quêtes qu'ils fond [sic] de porte en porte. . . ." Cited in M-C. Daveluy, *L'Orphelinat catholique de Montréal (1832-1932)*, Montréal, 1933, 290.

4. Jan Noel, "New France: Les femmes favorisées," *Atlantis* 6, 2 (Spring 1981), 81-82. For a fascinating discussion of changing attitudes in subsequent decades see Allan Greer, "La république des hommes: les Patriotes de 1837 face aux femmes," *Revue d'histoire de l'Amérique française* (hereafter *RHAF*) 44, 4 (printemps 1991).

5. Isidore Lebrun, *Tableau statistique et politique des Deux Canadas* (Paris, Londres: Treutel et Würtz, 1833), 389-90.

6. J-P. Bernard *et al*, "La Structure Professionnelle de Montréal en 1825," *RHAF* 30, 3 (déc 1976), 397-99.

7. Thomas Doige, *An Alphabetical List of the Merchants, Traders and Housekeepers Residing in Montreal* (Montreal: Lane, 1819), 48-183.

8. See for example the St. Paul's Church, Montreal, baptismal records, where until the 1840s the child's parents are usually recorded as "John Brown and his wife Mary Jones." This usage was also found in the French Canadian community.

9. For a detailed study of this phenomenon see Katherine McKenna, "The Life of Anne Murray Powell, 1755-1849: A Case Study of the Position of Women in Early Upper Canada" (Ph.D. dissertation, Queen's University, 1987), 28.

10. Women were also briefly deprived of the right to vote by the Lower Canadian Assembly in 1834, but this law did not survive the Rebellion period.

11. Clio Collective, *Histoire des femmes au Québec* (Montréal: Quinze, 1982), 82-85, 150-52. The choices available to women under Lower Canadian marriage laws, and some of their implications — and the rudimentary state of our knowledge about the implications are discussed in B. Bradbury *et al*, "Property and Marriage: The Law and the Practice in Early Nineteenth-Century Montreal," *Histoire sociale/Social History* 26, 51 (mai-May 1993), 9-39.

12. Claudette Lacelle, *Urban Domestic Servants in 19th Century Canada* (Ottawa: Parks Canada, 1987), 31-32.

13. Jan Noel, "Dry Millennium: Temperance and a New Social Order in Mid-19th Century Canada and Red River" (Ph.D. dissertation, University of Toronto, 1987), 116-33.

14. Robert Campbell, *History of the Scotch Presbyterian Church, St. Gabriel Street, Montreal* (Montreal: Drysdale, 1887), 52, 262-63. Jennifer Brown, "Children of the Early Fur Trades," in *Childhood and Family in Canadian History*, ed. Joy Parr (Toronto: McClelland and Stewart, 1982), 52-53.

15. Legislative Council of Lower Canada, *Journal*, 1824, Appendix 1, "Report from the Special Committee . . . upon the Establishments in this Province, for the reception and cure of the Insane, for the reception and support of Foundlings, and for the . . . sick and infirm Poor . . ." (hereafter JLCLC 1824 appx. 1).

16. Doige, 17, *Annuaire de Ville-Marie*, Première Année, 1863: Origines, Utilité et Progrès des Institutions Catholiques de Montréal (Montréal: Senécal, 1864), 144-45.

17. F. Rousseau, "Hôpital et société en Nouvelle-France: l'Hôtel Dieu de Quebec à la fin du XVIIe siècle," *RHAF* 31 (juin 1977), 47. Noel, "Femmes favorisées," 87-88. While Canadian female literacy was not particularly high, the gap between the sexes was smaller than that existing in contemporary France, England and New England. Allan Greer, "The Pattern of Literacy in Quebec, 1745-1899," *Histoire sociale/Social History* 11, 22 (nov-Nov. 1978), 332.

18. JLCLC 1824 appx. 1; *Annuaire*, 1864, 70.

19. JLCLC 1824 appx. 1.

20. This was asserted for a later time, in the 1860s. *Annuaire*, 1864, 63. By that time babies were also sent by train, often in carpetbags, from as far away as Quebec City and Upper Canada. J-C. Robert, "The City of Wealth and Death, 1821-71," in *Essays in the History of Canadian Medicine*, eds. W. Mitchinson and J. Dickin McGinnis (Toronto: McClelland and Stewart, 1988), 31, and Peter Gossage, "Les enfants abandonnés à Montréal au 19e siècle: la crèche d'Youville des Soeurs Grises, 1820-1871," *RHAF* 40, 4 (printemps 1987), 537-59.

21. Despite changing judicial responses, the leading causes of infanticide remained the same in Quebec for three centuries: desperation of young unwed mothers with no resources to raise a child and fearful of disgrace, family disapproval or dismissal from employment. Marie-Aimée Cliche, "L'Infanticide dans la région de Québec (1660-1964)," *RHAF* 44, 1 (été 1990), 31-59.

22. JLCLC 1824 appx. 1.

23. "Until the founding of this society, the only sources of relief for the poor were the Hôtel Dieu, the convents and the bread line." PAC, MG 28, I388, Vol. I, 1933 typewritten history, Montreal Ladies' Benevolent Society.

24. Campbell, 114, 143.

25. Mrs. C.A. Pearce, *A History of the Montreal Ladies' Benevolent Society* (Montreal: Lovell, 1920), 9.

26. Robert Easton, *A Sermon Delivered before the Members of the Female Benevolent Society in Montreal, Sept. 18, 1816* (Montreal: N. Mower, 1816), 4.

27. Alfred Sandham, *Ville-Marie* (Montreal: G. Bishop, 1870), 289; Pearce, 14-15.

28. Pearce, 18; Sandham, 290.

29. Pearce, 14.
30. *Montreal Almanack of Lower Canada Register for 1831* (Montreal: Rbt. Armour, 1831), 144–46.
31. Pearce, 15.
32. *Historical Sketch of the Montreal Protestant Orphan Asylum* (Montreal: J. Lovell, 1860), 10.
33. Patricia Rooke and R.L. Schnell, "The Rise and Decline of British North American Protestant Orphans' Homes as Woman's Domain, 1850–1930," *Atlantis* 7, 2 (Spring 1982), 22, situate the beginning of most Protestant orphanages after 1850. For the elaborate set of rules developed over time see Montreal Ladies' Benevolent Society, *Rules . . . Confirmed at the Extraordinary General Meeting . . . April 1874* (Montreal, 1874).
34. Pearce, 7.
35. Fecteau, 193–94.
36. N. Bosworth, ed., *Hochelaga Depicta* (Montreal: Wm. Grieg, 1839), 1880–93, 205, 210–11.
37. D. Robillard, *Emilie-Tavernier-Gamelin* (Montréal: Éditions du Méridien, 1988); Daveluy, *L'Orphelinat catholique*, 295ff; H. Lapointe-Roy, *La Charité bien ordonnée* (Montréal: Boréal, 1987), 82–83; *Annuaire*, 1864, 77–78; *Dictionary of Canadian Bibliography* (hereafter, DCB) IV 178, VII 301.
38. She was also sister-in-law to the president of the Ladies' Benevolent Society, Mrs. John Richards.
39. Figures have been rounded. Source: Lady Aylmer, *Recollections*, typescript, 73; also Daveluy, 305.
40. Rev. J. Wood, *Memoir of Henry Wilkes* (Montréal: Grafton, 1887), 134.
41. For a Foucault-inspired interpretation of this internalisation as a stage in state formation, see Jean-Marie Fecteau, *Un nouvel ordre des choses: la pauvreté, le crime, l'Etat au Québec de la fin du XIXe siècle à 1840* (Outremont: VLB, 1989).
42. American Presbyterian Church (Montreal), Sunday School Records, United Church Archives, Lennoxville, Quebec.
43. *Montreal Almanack* 1831, 145; Sandham, 104.
44. *Hochelaga Depicta*, 114; American Presbyterian Church Records, A 523, 2 and 3, United Church Archives, Lennoxville, Quebec.
45. In Montreal's hinterland, evangelicals also organised to address poverty and illiteracy. A Baptist revival in Potton Township, Brome County, for example, led to the formation of a Female Benevolent Society in 1826. About fifty members made and sold cloth to help poorer neighbours in various ways, which included the purchasing of books for a Sabbath school. Rev. Ernest Taylor, *History of Brome County* (Montreal: Lovell, 1908 and 1937), vol. 1, 230–33; vol. 2, 112.
46. American Home Missionary Society Correspondence 1826–30, United Church Archives, Toronto, esp. Rev. I. Purkis to Absolom Peters, May 1826, and S. Marsh to A. Peters, Oct. 1830; see also *Montreal Almanack*, 1831, which records a Montreal Ladies' Bible Association and a (female) Montreal Domestic Missionary Society.
47. See for example Ian Tyrell, *Sobering Up* (Westport, Conn.: Greenwood, 1979), and Ruth Bordin, *Woman and Temperance* (Philadelphia: Temple U., 1981) on the American movement; my own *Dry Millennium* (Toronto: University of Toronto Press, 1995) on Canadian temperance shares this basically favourable assessment, particularly of the early temperance movement.
48. The movement has been dated from the appearance of a group in Gloucester, New Brunswick, in 1826, and in Montreal, Brockville, Leeds County, the Niagara peninsula, and Beaver River, Nova Scotia, in 1827–28. Ruth Spence, *Prohibition in Canada* (Toronto: Dominion Alliance, 1919), 38–39; R.D. Wadsworth, *Temperance Manual* (Montreal, 1847), 4–5; F.L. Barron, "The Genesis of Temperance in Ontario, 1828–50" (Ph.D. dissertation, University of Guelph, 1976), 36–37.
49. G.W. Perkins to Absolom Peters, American Home Missionary Society Correspondence, United Church Archives, Toronto; Robert Sellars, *History of the County Huntingdon and the Seigniories of Chateauguay and Beauharnois from the First Settlement to the Year 1838* (Huntingdon: Gleaner, 1888), 29, 462–71.
50. Perkins to Peters, AHMS correspondence, July 1822. The date on the inside of the letter is simply July '22 which leaves some ambiguity about whether 22 refers to the day or the year; but on the outside of the letter is written "will Mr. Judd take this to New York 1822." While Perkins does not name the woman in question, her identity is supplied by E. McDougall in "The Presbyterian Church in Western Lower Canada" (Ph.D. dissertation, McGill University, 1969), 271. See also Sellars, 472.
51. Pearce, 23.

Part Two

The New Pioneers:
The Mid-Nineteenth Century
to the End of the Great War

The tremendous changes that occurred in the period from the middle of the nineteenth century to the end of the Great War laid the groundwork for Canadian society as we know it. In 1867 the colonies of Canada East and Canada West, New Brunswick, and Nova Scotia joined in Confederation; in the decades that followed, the goal of a Dominion from sea to sea was completed. Nationalism and imperialism were two ways Canadians chose to define the newly formed nation. For most English Canadians, no conflict between the two existed; nationalism could best be expressed by maintaining and reinforcing strong links with the British Empire.

The background to these political events and ideologies was the continuing economic development of the nation. In the settled regions, household production gave way to the beginnings of a factory system that co-existed with sweatshops, the "putting-out" of industrial work into workers' homes, and artisan workshops. The vast forest, mineral, and hydro-electric resources of central British Columbia, Ontario, and Quebec helped fuel this development, as did foreign capital from Great Britain and increasingly from the United States. By the end of World War I a full-blown industrial society had emerged, albeit with strong remnants of the earlier economic systems still in place in various regions and locales.

Industrial development was predicated on cheap labour, and this period saw the increased entry of immigrants, especially from non-English-speaking countries. They and other working-class Canadians endured harsh and unsafe working conditions and low pay with little public acknowledgement of their plight or appreciation of their efforts. Yet they continued to come, thereby underlining the even harsher realities of the societies they were leaving behind.

Across regional, class, race, religious, and ethnic divisions, women participated fully in the economic transformation of Canada. Indeed, without them, it is unlikely that the transformation would have occurred.

As well as bearing children who were the work force of the future, women provided a cheap and efficient work force in themselves. Most of their work was unpaid, absorbed into the family economy, but even when irregular or unpaid, it was vital.

The uneven economic expansion of these years was mirrored in population growth. Many of the immigrants who came in the early years of the twentieth century were attracted by the offer of free homestead land in the region west of Ontario. At the same time as new regions were being settled, many Canadians and immigrants moved into urban areas. In 1851 more than four-fifths of the British North American population lived in rural regions; by 1921 the number of rural and urban Canadians was about equal. Women led this shift in the population, as they moved to the cities for employment opportunities created by the new industrial economy. Consequently women outnumbered men in most cities, just as men tended to form the majority in rural and frontier areas.

Canada's expansion, industrialization, and rapid urbanization resulted in densely populated areas that accentuated the problems of poor sanitation and contagious disease. The concentration of factories in certain sections of the larger industrial centres created pollution and filth in the areas surrounding them. Intemperance, crime, delinquency, and prostitution were seen as social problems and appeared to be worsening. Nor was life in the rural areas idyllic. Many farmers' sons and daughters were lured to cities by the prospect of paid employment, a trend that resulted in rural depopulation in some regions, and a sense of an agrarian lifestyle under siege.

In response to such problems, a vigorous, generally white and middle-class reform movement was in place by the middle of the century. Women were actively involved in mixed-sex reform groups, and even more so in organizations of their own. Existing women's groups expanded their activities and began to join in more formalized associations, often on a national scale. In such groups, women worked together for the improvement of society and also, increasingly, for their own rights. Prohibition and women's suffrage were among their most important goals, and both were largely achieved by the end of World War I.

Women were by no means of one mind, however. Many in English Canada shared the nationalism and imperialism of the era. They were hostile or indifferent to the needs of the immigrants from non-English-speaking countries as well as to all those of different racial origin, however long their residence in Canada. Differences in class, region, and religion also continued to be divisive. On a more ideological level, women often disagreed about the proper female role in society, and even prohibition and the vote were contested terrain.

The articles in this section show, to begin with, the variety of work experience of Canadian women in the nineteenth and early twentieth centuries. A second theme is violence against women. Finally, we include some of the new elements for improvement in women's situation.

Native Women of the Northern Pacific Coast: An Historical Perspective, 1830-1900

CAROL COOPER

The fur trade and missions are generally viewed as having a negative impact upon the roles and status of native women. Eleanor Leacock and others have argued that, in egalitarian societies such as the Montagnais of eastern Canada, women's status deteriorated rapidly with the inception of the fur trade and was further eroded under the influence of the Jesuit missionaries. According to this interpretation, the fur trade upset traditional balances by placing a new emphasis upon production for exchange. Since men were the principal producers of furs, their work became more highly valued in native economies. As the use of European foodstuffs and clothing increased, women's traditional activities were further devalued and they became more economically dependent upon males. With the relations of production thus disturbed, it was only a matter of time before the ideological sphere was similarly affected. Missionaries inculcated notions of female subservience among their male parishioners, and the autonomy of native women was severely reduced in the mission settlements. While these interpretations have merit for the egalitarian societies of the northeast, it is necessary to avoid facilely extending such findings to all native groups throughout Canada. Among the ranked societies of the northern Pacific coast, for example, the status of women did not decline appreciably as a result of fur trade and missions. Instead there was considerable continuity in the roles and status of coastal women. As Laura Klein has noted of their Tlingit neighbours, the Nishga and Tsimshian women studied here moved from a position of strength in the traditional era to a position of strength in the mission era.[1]

It is necessary to note that this position of strength did not automatically imply equality with men. Males most frequently filled the highest political and ceremonial roles among the Nishga and Tsimshian. Still, the ranked nature of Nishga and Tsimshian societies meant that there was always a certain potential for women to amass political and economic power. When viewed from a cross-cultural perspective, the opportunities for these native women probably far exceeded those of nineteenth-century Euro-Canadian women. A woman of ability and high rank could become a chief and her authority would be respected by her male peers. As late as the 1890s women held several of the hereditary

SOURCE: Carol Cooper, "Native Women of the Northern Pacific Coast: An Historical Perspective, 1830-1900," *Journal of Canadian Studies* 27, 4 (Winter 1992-93), 44-75. Reprinted with permission.

chieftainships among the Tsimshian. Despite missionaries' attempts to curb their autonomy and to confine Nishga and Tsimshian females to the domestic sphere, high-ranking women continued to assume active roles as councillors, making decisions on the public affairs of the mission settlements.

Women also exercised considerable control over the production and distribution of food supplies and other economic resources in the fur trade and mission eras. They received recognition for the skilled management of resources, because the surplus they produced became the basis of trade and generated wealth for distribution in the potlatch. Contributions to the potlatch were of particular importance in the status-conscious native societies of the northern Pacific coast. The presence of the Euro-Canadian fur-trading interests offered further opportunities for women to create wealth by exchanging food items and other goods of their own manufacture. Some females engaged directly in the trade of furs, assuming roles as intermediaries between their tribes and the fur traders. As a capitalist economy developed on the northern Pacific coast, women took an active role as inside workers in the salmon-canning establishments. Their continuing contribution to the economic welfare of their households and lineages was thus an important factor in the maintenance of Nishga and Tsimshian women's status in the period under study.

The Nishga and Coast Tsimshian occupy the northernmost coastal regions of British Columbia. When the land-based fur trade commenced in 1831, the Coast Tsimshian resided in nine separate villages along the Skeena River. Later they joined in one settlement at Fort Simpson when the Hudson's Bay Company relocated its establishment there in 1834. Their neighbours, the Nishga, who spoke a separate dialect of Tsimshian, inhabited numerous villages along the Nass River valley. Within each Nishga and Tsimshian village resided the members of several exogamous clans, such as the Killerwhale, Eagle, Raven, and Wolf.[2] Clans were segmented into still smaller groups known as matrilineages. These matrilineages, who traced their descent to a common clan ancestress, played a more immediate role than the clan in the day-to-day lives of the Nishga and Tsimshian.

The members of a matrilineage corporately owned territories such as fishing sites and hunting grounds, and these resources were shared according to rank. Membership in a matrilineage was lifelong. Although a woman joined her husband's residential group at marriage, she never abandoned her membership in or loyalty to her own matrilineage. In addition, at birth her children automatically assumed their mother's clan and lineage affiliation. The matrilineal organization of Tsimshian and Nishga society entailed some complex rules of inheritance. Because offspring were considered to be members of their mother's lineage, males succeeded their maternal uncles rather than their fathers as chieftains or heads of lineages. Similarly, property passed from a man to his sister's son or daughter when a suitable male heir was unavailable.

Despite the fact that inheritance of property and position was traced through the female line, there is no clear correlation between matriliny and elevated status for women. In the past there has been a tendency to assume that matriliny implied extensive economic powers and control of political institutions by women. Much of this confusion results from a misunderstanding of the Iroquois, a matrilineal society wherein women owned the majority of lands and clan mothers selected the chiefs of the League of the Iroquois. However, recent studies have shown that the power of Iroquois women did not result from the matrilineal organization of their society. Instead, their position derived from their control of the production and distribution of food supplies. Alice Schlegel's analysis of several matrilineal societies also reveals that matriliny *per se* cannot be used to predict women's status. However, she does note that "it is probable that the importance of the woman as the linking factor in the descent group gives to womanhood a dignity that may be lacking in societies that do not have this belief." Such findings are consistent with the case of the Nishga and Tsimshian, where women were not considered the equals of men but a certain respect accrued to them for their role as the "crest carrier." Crests were important symbols which included both genealogical and spiritual elements. They were represented on most of the material items of the lineage and imbued the user of these goods with an important sense of identity and belonging. The privilege of displaying these crests was again inherited from the mother.[3]

The sexual division of labour in Nishga and Tsimshian societies also raises some complex questions about women's status. There was a traditional separation of tasks between men and women: men hunted, fished, and engaged in war; women were responsible for childcare, processing fish, collecting berries and tubers such as potatoes, and ensuring that sufficient supplies of food were available for the winter months. Taboos associated with menstruation generally prohibited women from hunting large game or handling fish nets and weirs, since the native peoples believed that a woman could render the equipment ineffective through her touch. Upon initial consideration the roles of women appear quite restrictive. Still, it is important to recognize that there was considerable interdependence between males and females in northern coastal societies, and some flexibility in the sexual division of labour was possible. Among the Tlingit, a northern coastal group which neighboured and interacted freely with the Tsimshian, there were examples of women who fished and hunted.[4] Their Nishga counterparts obtained small mammals such as groundhog and traded these skins to women of other tribes.

Women also played many important supportive roles in hunting and fishing. During the eulachon fisheries each spring, women accompanied their husbands and steered the canoes while their spouses harvested the fish. Nishga, Tsimshian, and neighbouring Haida women were excellent canoeists, for they received instruction in paddling and guiding a canoe from the time they were six years of age. Tsimshian wives often followed their husbands on deer hunts and served as packers, bearing animal carcasses to the camp. According to the Nishga and Tsimshian belief system, success in hunting was also dependent upon the conduct of both man and wife. While her husband hunted, a woman was expected to prepare special foods and refrain from bathing or cutting her hair in order to ensure his good fortune.[5]

At other times, women's participation in procuring and processing food supplies was more direct. The shellfish, berries, seaweed, nuts, bark, and other items collected by women accounted for an estimated 16 to 25 percent of the Tsimshian diet. In addition, women were solely responsible for the preservation of fish, which composed more than 50 percent of the Nishga and Tsimshian food supply.[6] Yet these women did not simply collect and process the food; they also managed the supply throughout the year and controlled its distribution. As noted earlier, women were responsible for deciding what proportion of the food supply should be allocated for immediate use and what might be devoted to trade or distributed in feasts. They not only meted out the food for the potlatch ceremonies sponsored by their husbands, but they also contributed to potlatches held by their own lineages. Women traded fish and various foods to other native groups for potlatch goods. Later they exchanged seaweed, shellfish, and potatoes with the Euro-Canadian fur traders in order to obtain manufactured items such as blankets for distribution by their lineages at feasts. Women's involvement in food production and distribution thus had significance not merely at the domestic level but also at the public level, because their contributions were acknowledged before other lineages and visiting tribes during the potlatch ceremonies.

The importance of women in the production and distribution of food supplies was ritually expressed through the rules governing the processing of eulachon, a species of fish that was second only to salmon in the diet of the Nishga and Tsimshian. Once the eulachon were caught each spring, women assumed control of processing. Men could not engage in the preparatory activities lest they offend the spirit forces which "sent" the eulachon. It was vital to propitiate the forces which controlled the eulachon, for the arrival of this fish marked the end to a winter's hunger and signalled the production of valuable oil which could be exchanged for food and potlatch goods in intertribal trade networks. As late as the 1870s, a special woman, who was "sedate and solemn," was chosen to prepare a fire for cooking the first eulachon. After she completed the cooking according to strict rituals, the woman ordered that the fish be honoured and divided it up among each family. Women's distributive role was thus symbolized in these acts.[7]

While women's roles in food production and distribution were extensive, their involvement in war was more limited. Women were expected to observe certain rituals to aid their husbands' success in war, but few participated directly in battle. A middle-aged woman of high position commonly travelled with the warriors and assumed the function of steerswoman or "canoe chief," a role which both reflected and augmented her prestige within the tribe. Female shamans might also attend the fighting because these women were believed to have the ability to predict or influence the outcome of battles. Some women such as the chieftainess Nishlkumik (Victoria Young) of the Gilutsau tribe of the Coast Tsimshian engaged in actual combat against opposing tribes. Despite taboos upon the use of weaponry, Nishlkumik employed guns and knives in a struggle with another Tsimshian group in the 1850s.[8] On the whole, however, males controlled the instruments of war. This fact had some negative implications for the status of women. Women were often unable to defend themselves against raiding tribes, particularly in the fur trade era when guns were used more extensively. Women were thus most frequently enslaved by other tribes.

The exclusion of women from military activities also meant that they could not use this avenue to increase their prestige as their brothers and husbands did. A successful warrior garnered respect from his lineage and his village as a whole; the spoils of war also contributed to his wealth. Still, there were no organized warrior societies analogous to those of the Blackfoot and other interior tribes. Among the societies like the Blackfoot, political and economic influence was achieved by passing through various levels of the warrior associations after the completion of successful military endeavours. On the northern Pacific coast, amassing wealth through successful exploitation of resources and trade was an equally if not more important means to prestige and public power than warfare. Significantly, these were activities in which Nishga and Tsimshian women could readily engage.

Scholars often point to the division of labour in the production of crafts and ceremonial objects as a further indication that women occupied a subordinate position in northern coastal societies. They argue that women's crafts were of lesser importance because they were of a secular or utilitarian nature, while men's were more highly valued because they produced the sacred art of the tribe and designed the crest figures.[9] It is true that only men served as *gitsonkt*, or carvers of the sacred devices which were employed in the ceremonies of the Nishga and Tsimshian. Yet women's role in art may have been more significant than previously imagined, particularly in the production of the "button blanket," the production of which flourished during the fur trade era. They served to identify the individual through their crest emblems and were believed to impart a certain "power" to the wearer. Men designed the crests to be placed upon these robes, but women had an important role in the

choice of colours, the placement of the designs, and the actual construction of the garments. Such considerations were not insignificant. The
"power" of the garment depended upon the skill and spiritual inspiration
of both the designer and the sewer.[10]

The ceremonial activities of northern Pacific societies were also differentiated by gender, but each played significant roles. The ceremonial
lives of the Nishga, Tsimshian, and their neighbours centred largely upon
the potlatch. Potlatches in fact assumed more than one form. Housewarming potlatches celebrated the completion of a new dwelling. The
mortuary potlatch commemorated the passing of a chief or lineage head.
During these ceremonies, goods were distributed to guests and titles were
validated in the presence of witnesses. The Anglican missionary, William
Duncan, who witnessed a housewarming potlatch in 1858, related that
the female relatives of the host invited the women of the camp separately
and they feasted as a group apart from the men. Such treatment did
not imply inferiority, however, for as Duncan observed, "the women always took precedence" in the order of invitation and their participation
in the feasting procedure was considered as important as the men's.[11]

The Hudson's Bay Company records also reveal that women hosted
both mortuary and housewarming potlatches. In 1841, Soudal (Shoudal),
the daughter of the Tsimshian head chief Legaic and wife of Company
head officer Dr. John Kennedy, hosted a large potlatch "in commem-
oration of her deceased brother." The powerful Nishga chieftainess Neshaki hosted feasts and erected an impressive totem pole in honour of
her dead brother Neeskinwaetk (Nishkinwetk), during the 1860s. In addition, women engaged in the rivalry potlatches which became more common with the increased wealth associated with the fur trade. The purpose
of these feasts was to eclipse one's rivals by a lavish distribution of goods
which demonstrated the wealth and prestige of the host. Madame Arthur,
another Tsimshian woman of high rank, conducted such a feast in opposition to Soudal's potlatch in 1841. Two influential Kaigani Haida
women who were visiting Fort Simpson on a trading mission in 1838
engaged in rivalry potlatches and both "threw away property" in order
to assert their respective importance.[12]

Even when women did not serve directly as hosts of the potlatch,
they still received recognition for the goods which they contributed to
the ceremonies. Women made valuable donations of blankets, cotton,
rice, and other materials which were distributed to guests during the
feasts. Coast Tsimshian women obtained these supplies in an exchange
system which operated rather independently of native males. First, the
Tsimshian women gathered up crabs and seaweed for trade with the
Hudson's Bay Company. Sheaves of tobacco were obtained in the exchange. The Tsimshian women then traded the tobacco to Nishga women
in return for groundhog or marmot skins. The groundhog skins might
be distributed directly to guests at the potlatch or they could be traded
once again to the Company for woollen blankets, a high-value item which

was also dispensed during feasts. If a woman, particularly one of high rank, perceived that her contributions were not adequately recognized, she was free to voice her displeasure. In one instance, Nishlkumik felt greatly insulted by her father, the Eagle chief Rapligidahl. She supplied him with valuable goods for his potlatch but believed he did not sufficiently acknowledge her donations. To restore her own pride and that of the lineage she represented, she hosted a grand potlatch which dwarfed the feast held by her father. Rapligidahl was humiliated and peace was subsequently restored between father and daughter.[13]

Some elements of Nishga and Tsimshian ceremonial life such as full membership in their most prominent "secret societies," known as the "cannibals" and "destroyers," were apparently closed to women. Neighbouring Haida women could not participate in the most important dancing societies of their tribes, while Nishga and Tsimshian women are generally believed to have been official members of only the first two levels of their people's secret societies. The secret societies consisted of four graded associations in which spirit powers were conveyed to initiates. Possession of these powers brought considerable prestige to the holder. The reputation and influence of the heads of the two highest societies extended far beyond the confines of the village and were known all along the coast. While the ethnographic record indicates that women could not engage in these prestige-building activities as "cannibal" or "destroyer" members, at least one instance in the 1880s contradicts this opinion. A visiting missionary noted that a Tsimshian woman performed a "smash dance" in his presence and went about a village destroying the property of others, a privilege which belonged only to "destroyer" members.[14] This occurrence raises some important questions as to whether women were excluded from the highest societies on the basis of gender *per se*. It is important to recall that the "cannibals" and the "destroyers" drew their members mainly from the highest-ranking chiefs of their communities. The lack of visibility of women in these two societies could be mainly attributable to the fact that far fewer women were chiefs in the first place rather than to exclusive policies based on gender.

Even if women did not participate as full members, they were still considered important enough to be privy to information about the inner workings of the highest secret societies. In contrast to cultures where women were thought unfit to share in religious celebrations with men, Tsimshian women regularly observed the ceremonies and attended the "cannibal" initiate during his induction into the society by offering their arms to be bitten. The bite of a "cannibal" initiate was a badge of honour and women with these marks were respected throughout their communities. Women also occupied prominent positions in the "dancers" and the "dog-eaters," the first two levels of the secret societies. The admission of girls into these organizations was considered of great importance, and families devoted as much time and resources to girls' initiations as they did to boys' entry into the "dancers" and "dog-eaters." Fathers or maternal uncles often went to considerable expense to ensure that the initiation ceremonies of their daughters or nieces were properly conducted. In 1858, the head chief Legaic sponsored the initiation of his ten-year-old daughter, who later became Sarah Legaie (sic), into the "dog-eater" society. The girl was secreted away for many days during her initiation and then returned in an elaborate and costly display in order to demonstrate her newly gained spirit "power."[15]

The ceremonial complex discussed above provided the most prestigious and visible means of obtaining sacred power, but there were other avenues for accessing the spirit world, and these were open to all males and females save for the *wa'ayin*, or the lowest-ranking persons, and slaves. During illness, a revelatory dream, vision, or other spiritual experience might occur, indicating that a person had the power to heal and to discern the future. Upon recovery, a period of training under a shaman commenced, and eventually the student would be able to practise shamanic activities on his or her own. In Tsimshian society, shamans were usually distinct from native doctors. Although both treated illness and other problems such as infertility, they differed in technique. The latter specialists, who were often women as well, used bloodletting, herbs, and other medications as their means of treatment. Shamans, by contrast, employed supernatural techniques in order to heal, for they had the ability to communicate with the spirit world and to discern and remove evil presences from the bodies of their patients. While healing was probably their major activity, shamans also predicted the outcome of wars or hunting expeditions and were often asked to use their prophetic abilities to disclose sources of food during times of famine. Missionaries such as Robert Doolan, who evangelized the Nishga in the 1860s, noted that shamans were often female and that both men and women had confidence in their abilities. Shamanic activity brought considerable prestige and wealth to its practitioners, since patients had to pay for successful treatment. In 1865 a curing session could bring as much as three boxes of valuable eulachon oil and seven blankets. The respect and influence enjoyed by female shamans was of a lasting nature. As will be shown, they occupied prominent civic and spiritual roles in the mission villages, long after their conversion to Christianity and abandonment of shamanic practices.[16]

Throughout the era of the land-based fur trade, native women continued many of their traditional economic and spiritual functions, while expanding their activities in areas such as trading. Long before the arrival of whites, intertribal trading networks flourished in northern Pacific regions. Goods such as foodstuffs, abalone for decorative and ceremonial purposes, hides, and ceremonial coppers were traded over hundreds of miles. It is difficult to determine precisely what role women played in these exchanges. Pregnancy and the care of nursing infants restricted the amount of time women could devote to the arduous trading trips to the interior, for these journeys could occupy several months of the year. Because lineage and village chieftains were most frequently male, it is probable that men normally conducted both long-distance trade and negotiations for high-prestige items such as copper shields. Yet women were not unaccustomed to trading. Women of neighbouring tribes regularly exchanged goods. Nishga and Tsimshian women traded valuable commodities such as eulachon oil along with other items of their own production, such as dried salmon, to the Haida women who visited from the Queen Charlotte Islands. When European and American traders began to appear on the coast in the 1780s in order to obtain sea otter hides and other items, some Haida and Tsimshian women exchanged fish and furs with them. Other women exerted a more indirect yet considerable influence by overseeing and approving the negotiations between their male relatives and the Europeans.[17]

Native men continued to conduct most of the transactions in the land-based fur trade which began in the 1830s. In some respects the fur trade could be viewed as detrimental to the economic roles of women. The fur trade reinforced the importance of hunting, a male activity. Females were for the most part excluded from directly obtaining furs. Still, it should be recalled that the collective nature of Nishga and Tsimshian society meant that neither the furs themselves nor the goods received in trade were considered solely the property of male heads of households. Instead, the items received would be used to raise the status of the lineage in the potlatch ceremonies, and be redistributed to male and female members of the house according to rank. As well, on some occasions men may have simply served as trading delegates for women. The Kaigani Haida chieftainess Ilowen, for instance, permitted her male relatives to trade beaver skins for her at Fort Simpson. The decision to allow men to act as their representatives did not indicate a lack of confidence on the women's part, but instead probably reflected the Euro-Canadians' habit of dealing with males in all business transactions. Regardless of their prejudices, the Company officials often found themselves trading directly with very powerful chieftainesses. During the 1830s the former wife of the head chief, Legaic, regularly traded a large number of beaver skins and other furs to the fort on behalf of her lineage, and Scutsay, or Scotseye, a Kaigani chieftainess, was one of the most important traders at Fort Simpson before her death in 1839.[18]

By the 1860s, the number of women traders at Fort Simpson, especially those of Nishga and Tsimshian descent, appears to have increased. In addition to trading provisions such as potatoes and salmon, these women bartered large quantities of marten and other skins for goods such as regatta cotton and rice. Some bypassed the Hudson's Bay Company altogether, exchanging furs with American seafaring traders who offered rum. The increase in the number of female traders stemmed in part from the fact that more women became lineage heads or chieftains after the mid-century. As Margaret Blackman notes of the Haida, deaths associated with the smallpox epidemics in 1836 and 1862 left many positions open. According to Hudson's Bay Company records, mortality from smallpox was greatest among the males of the Nishga and Tsimshian tribes as well. Women were thus left to fill chiefly roles and to assume the important names and trading rights associated with these positions.[19] Yet some women such as Nishlkumik and Neshaki were playing significant roles as traders long before the deaths of their brothers, who were likely the nominal heads of their lineages. Their rise as traders stemmed from the fact that these women wielded great personal influence within their own societies. The Hudson's Bay Company officials also understood the importance of women such as Neshaki and Nishlkumik in furthering trade relations with their respective tribes. William McNeill, who became the chief factor of Fort Simpson in 1851, was clearly aware of Neshaki's influence, for he married her after the death of his first wife.

Neshaki's career as a trader is of considerable interest. Her activities were not simply confined to trading the furs trapped by her own family or lineage. Instead, she adopted a traditionally male role as an intermediary or "middle-man" between the Company and the Nishga groups who dwelt in the Nass River valley. The Company supplied her with goods and credit in order to attract trade from the Nishga. She brought their furs to Fort Simpson and on occasion travelled as far as Victoria, 500 miles south. On one trading trip she collected 160 martens, 6 lynx, 26 fishers, and 30 beavers from the Nishga, a yield which exceeded the combined total of the Kaigani and Cumshewa Haida's trade at Fort Simpson for the same period. In 1863, the chief factor Hamilton Moffat, who succeeded McNeill, noted that Neshaki's exchanges alone were "sufficient to make the monthly trade look very well."[20]

Neshaki was able to operate successfully in both native and fur trade society. Her influence among the Nass people may have increased with her marriage to McNeill, since she could obtain favourable trading terms for them. Yet she distinguished herself by her own actions and demonstrated her autonomy in her dealings with both her former native husband, Sakauwan, and McNeill. Sometime in the 1860s Sakauwan, a Nishga Eagle chief, tried to shame Neshaki for leaving him and marrying McNeill. He denounced her as a "woman of the bleached Victoria," and challenged her to respond to his taunts by erecting a totem pole. Neshaki was equal to the challenge. She sent a lavishly decorated canoe to her former husband and erected a totem pole in honour of her dead brother Neeskinwaetk. These actions served to humiliate Sakauwan and lifted Neshaki further in the estimation of her people. McNeill also had to accept her independent nature, for Neshaki continued to act as a trader at Fort Simpson for some years after his retirement to Victoria. Neshaki not only impressed native and white men with her confidence and self-reliance, she also served as a role model for many of the high-ranking young women of the Nass valley. The Anglican missionary Robert Doolan

observed that young women gathered around her for instruction in behaviour and Christianity. Many girls followed her to points such as the
Tsimshian Christian village of Metlakatla.[21] Just as male chiefs often
served as the transmitters of new information, beliefs, and technology
to their tribe, so too did Neshaki.

Marriage to Hudson's Bay Company employees helped to promote
the trading activities of native women and their families. To a large extent
these unions were influenced by indigenous customs, for marriage had
always been a means of cementing alliances between native trading
partners. The matrilineage probably continued to arrange marriages of
their nieces and daughters to the Euro-Canadian traders as they had
done in the pre-contact era. The Hudson's Bay Company normally discouraged marriage to native women, but some flexibility was possible
at the northern coastal forts, since Company officials conceded that native
wives were important in fostering trade relationships with groups such
as the Tlingit.[22] The Company's local representatives at Fort Simpson
also quickly appreciated how vital Nishga and Tsimshian wives could
be to their own happiness and to the prosperity of the Fort. The first
marriage between a Tsimshian woman and a Hudson's Bay Company
trader occurred in 1832 when Soudal, the daughter of Legaic, married
the chief officer of the Fort, Dr. John Kennedy. It was through Soudal's
influence that the Company obtained a new site for Fort Simpson. At
her husband's request, she convinced her father to allow the Company
to use his tribe's land on Rose Island, some miles south of the Nass.
Soudal's diplomatic skills also proved invaluable when a war erupted
between the Tsimshian and Haida in 1832. The Hudson's Bay Company
officials were powerless to intervene directly lest they incur enmity on
both sides. Kennedy once again entreated Soudal to approach her father
and his tribe, the Gispaxloats. Legaic agreed to end the fighting, for
Soudal convinced him that sufficient blood was spent and the Haida
were no longer a threat.[23]

The maintenance of their own family connections and friendships
was vital to the native wives of Company employees, especially in cases
where the marriage dissolved. When separations occurred, women and
their children were able to be successfully reintegrated into the lineage.
Because Nishga and Tsimshian children continued to derive their clan
affiliation and status from their mothers, the fact that the child was
of mixed descent appeared to have no negative bearing upon his or her
status within the tribe. Tsimshian oral traditions claim that fairness of
skin and hair were looked upon with favour and that a child of mixed
descent "in the village gets every thought."[24] Such contentions are borne
out by the fact that mixed-blood offspring of high-ranking women often
played prominent roles in the community throughout the fur trade and
mission periods. Some of the leading Tsimshian chiefs in the period
1875 to 1900 were of mixed descent. Two such men, Alfred Dudoward
(Skagwait) and David Swanson, were among the highest-ranking chiefs

at Port Simpson (formerly Fort Simpson) in 1900 and were frequently called upon by their tribes to represent them in land negotiations and other meetings with the governmental authorities.

Grandparents and lineage relatives readily adopted children of mixed descent in cases where the mother died and the father was unable or unwilling to care for the child. In addition, Nishga and Tsimshian peoples never censured native women who chose to leave or had been cast off by their white husbands. Divorce was relatively simple in native society. Since women had considerable autonomy in Nishga and Tsimshian societies, they were often the first to separate when the marriage proved unsatisfactory. Nishga partners sometimes performed a brief ceremony known as *Llin*, which formally dissolved the bonds and obligations between a man and his wife, but most divorces were signified by the removal of either partner to their own quarters.[25] Divorce from a white was conducted in a similar manner.

Maltreatment such as beatings appears to have been a major factor in most cases of divorce involving native women and white husbands. In 1842, a French-Canadian servant of the Company named Maurice gave his wife "a drubbing because of her misconduct." She quickly returned to her own people, taking her child with her. Families did not allow such abuse to go unchecked. One chief severely beat a Company servant named Turcotte when the man struck his daughter. Families provided native women with an important network of support, and the threat of retaliation probably deterred many servants and officers of the Fort from mistreating their wives. On the whole, the Company employees tended to value their native wives as important helpmates and sources of emotional and physical support, so much so that William McNeill remarked "The women of this place have some '*way*' [sic] to turn the men's brains, more so than in any other part of the world."[26]

From an economic perspective, native women retained considerable independence even after their marriages to Company employees. They were not solely dependent upon their husbands' wages, for they continued to share in the resources and potlatch activities of their lineages. In addition, some native wives of Company employees and other Nishga and Tsimshian women were regularly employed by the Company in jobs which were vital to the maintenance of the Fort. During the spring they sorted seed potatoes for planting. In the summer they bound tobacco and collected and dried seaweed for sale by the Company to other native groups. In July and early August they dried squirrel skins and beat bear skins to prepare them for shipment to the Company's outside markets. They constructed lime ovens to produce materials used in shingling the roofs of the Fort buildings. Until late September they were also engaged in planting and weeding the gardens. Although the precise number of women employed at the Fort is not known, as many as 60 were sometimes engaged in any one task. In many instances Company officials at Fort

Simpson preferred to employ native women rather than their male counterparts because they claimed that the women were more reliable and efficient workers. It is likely that women performed better because the nature of the tasks required teamwork. In the traditional economy, Nishga and Tsimshian women had generally worked in cooperative units when drying fish, picking berries, and processing other foods. Although males shared their bounty with their lineages, men's activities, such as hunting, tended to be more solitary in nature. Thus, they had less opportunity to prepare themselves for working as a team with other males at the Fort. In contrast, women worked well together, so much so that by the 1850s they replaced males entirely in many tasks about the Fort. Their work was time-consuming and difficult, but it provided them with a source of income separate from that of their husbands. They were able to purchase goods such as cotton and tobacco for their own use or to trade to others. At the same time, women gained experience in working under the direction of Euro-Canadians, thus preparing them for the decades ahead when jobs in the canneries and other types of paid labour became available.[27]

The expanded opportunities for women in trade and employment at the Fort were offset by many disruptive elements, which increased in number with the influx of white settlers into southern centres such as Victoria in the 1850s. Although the Nishga and Tsimshian were more isolated from the full effects of settlement than southern groups such as the Kwakiutl, they did travel to the new centres. As well, some unsettling influences such as alcohol found their way directly into Tsimshian territories. Alcohol use, escalation of the number of slave raids by other native groups, and prostitution were all symptomatic of the disorganization in native societies resulting from contact with whites. The Hudson's Bay Company had ceased trading alcohol to native peoples in any large quantity by the 1840s, but within a decade American ships and settlements in Washington territory, as well as traders at Victoria, commenced a profitable trade in rum and whisky. While alcohol use was not so pervasive as to interrupt the subsistence activities of the Nishga and Tsimshian, liquor was heavily employed in ceremonial activities, particularly during the winter season. Elite men and women were regularly intoxicated during the several weeks when feasts were held. The use of alcohol led to a rise in the number of deaths by shooting. In most cases these shooting incidents were not part of normal warfare but more often resulted from drunken quarrels between lineages dwelling in the same village. Though women normally did not take part in the fighting, they were often killed or maimed by stray bullets. William Duncan also reported that the incidence of spousal violence increased by the 1850s as a result of intoxication. Even women of chiefly rank such as Waahtl, the wife of Legaic, were victims of beatings by their husbands during drunken rages. To some degree the family networks which formerly discouraged the mistreatment of women by their husbands and protected them from spousal violence became less effective as alcohol consumption increased.[28]

The security of women was also threatened by the rising number of slave raids between 1830 and 1870. By the late 1830s, officials of the Hudson's Bay Company reported that slave raids were the principal cause of "predatory warfare" along the northwest coast. Southern tribes such as the Newettee, a Kwakiutl people of Vancouver Island, were far more frequently the prey of the Haida and Tsimshian, but women of the latter groups were also susceptible to capture during intertribal warfare. Men were clearly ascendant in military matters. During the fur trade, the increased use of guns, which were traded only to native males, meant that women were subjected to greater violence and more frequent threats of enslavement. Yet even in pre-contact times, women had been the principal victims of slave raids. Marauding tribes often attacked groups of females and children while the men were away hunting and could not defend them. Men were also less favoured as slaves since their captors assumed they would be too difficult to manage. An 1845 census of a Stikine Tlingit tribe, a northern neighbour of the Tsimshian, indicates that 56 out of 93 slaves — roughly 60 percent — were female. Treatment of these individuals varied greatly from tribe to tribe and from family to family, but in general slaves performed the most menial tasks in the village. They could not marry nor could they participate in the ceremonial and spiritual activities which gave meaning to the lives of their masters. Slaves remained with their captors unless they were traded to another group or were ransomed by their own families. Any children belonging to these women, either at the time of their abduction or born of liaisons with their captors, were considered permanent slaves.[29]

Changes in the native economies resulting from the fur trade led to an increase in slave raids after 1830. With the wealth generated by the trade, high-ranking men and women could afford to purchase more slaves. Slaves were important sources of labour and a major commodity in trade with other tribes. In addition, the prestige and wealth of a lineage was indicated by the number of slaves it held. Yet by the 1850s, such considerations were becoming secondary to the profits which could be reaped by selling slave women, their daughters, and other women of low rank into white-operated prostitution. In 1855, Hudson's Bay Company officials at Fort Simpson remarked that the northern Kaigani Haida and Tsimshian were taking south as many as 60 women at a time for purposes of prostitution. Native males were most frequently responsible for selling these women into prostitution, but some high-ranking Tsimshian women also took females to the settlements. According to one observer the sale of a woman into prostitution could bring at least $200. Sometimes female children as young as nine years of age were taken to American territory or to Victoria to serve its large transient population of gold miners.[30] Slaves could not expect their families to protect them, as all their lineage connections were severed upon enslavement. Resistance to forced sale for prostitution would have been futile since their captors held the power of life and death over them. Thus, for the most powerless women of Nishga and Tsimshian society, the changes associated with the fur trade and the coming of settlement served to degrade them further.

While it is clear that a certain proportion of slave women and wa'ayin were forced into prostitution, some caution is necessary in regard to allegations that families engaged in the widespread sale of their wives, daughters, and sisters to white procurers and pimps. As late as 1890, British Columbia newspapers and missionary reports repeatedly charged that fathers and other male relatives were regularly selling their daughters to whites in order to obtain goods for potlatches. The Department of Indian Affairs investigated such charges beginning in 1891, and found that they were largely unfounded. The Indian agent who served the Nass and Skeena regions firmly denied that any women were sold by their Tsimshian and Nishga relatives.[31] Admittedly, the presence of missions and Indian agents meant there were more controls placed upon native societies by 1890, but certain factors operated to ensure that the sale of female family members was limited in the earlier periods as well. As discussed earlier, disruptive elements such as alcohol and population decline obviously undermined native family structures and affected the degree to which lineages could protect their kinswomen. Yet we should not overestimate the extent of this decline. In most cases lineages offered considerable support to their members as late as the twentieth century. Ties of affection remained important but concerns about the status of the lineage also persisted. Lineage members would not permit their kinswomen to be treated as chattel for sale by husbands and fathers, since such treatment would reflect poorly upon the status of the entire lineage. Within the lineage itself there were further controls which would have discouraged uncles or other matrilineal relatives from forcibly selling a woman into prostitution. Although the coercion of slaves and other individuals outside the ranking system was tolerated, the cooperative and collective nature of the lineage meant that authority could not be wielded in an arbitrary way against its full members. Even the power of heads of households and chiefs was limited in this fashion.

Far more common than forced sales of female family members for prostitution were the voluntary liaisons between native women and white men in return for goods to be used in trade or potlatching. Economic changes associated with the decline of the fur trade and the growth of commercial interests in the south were largely responsible for the increase in sexual activity for payment. Commercial developments to the south meant that a wide range of new goods were available, but these items were often difficult for the Nishga and Tsimshian to obtain because of the cash-deficient nature of their economies. By engaging in sex for payment or goods, women were able to gain access to these goods. There was also an indisputable link between growing alcohol consumption and the increase in paid sexual encounters between northern coastal women and white men. Hudson's Bay Company officials at Fort Simpson maintained that large numbers of women who engaged in sex for payment at Victoria, and on the ships which regularly plied the coast, did so in order to obtain whisky and rum. As a result, women were among the major purveyors of alcohol to both the Tsimshian and the employees of the Company at Fort Simpson.[32]

At present our understanding of the impact of prostitution upon the status of native women is limited. Historical studies of prostitution in Canada are few, particularly in regard to native women. The lacunae of data are largely responsible. It is difficult to estimate the numbers of native women who engaged in prostitution, or to know the circumstances of their entry into this activity. Nor is it a simple matter to follow their lives once they became prostitutes, particularly in the case of slave women who were sold as prostitutes. Prostitution has been described as an unequal exchange between sexual partners, wherein women have low social status and few defences against abuse or exploitation. For native women who practised prostitution, physical and emotional abuse by white males were no doubt common. At the same time, prostitution served to lower the status of all native women in the estimation of whites, regardless of whether or not the native women actually engaged in this activity. Prejudice and the lack of contact between "polite" white society and native peoples often led the whites to stereotype native women. As a result native women as a group tended to be viewed as degraded and inclined to prostitution.[33] Yet within their own societies, there was little censure of women who engaged in sexual activity for payment.

There is little evidence of institutionalized prostitution in aboriginal society. Still, there were always certain women of high rank who were considered "lucky" or able to impart luck and power to those with whom they had intercourse. The oral traditions of the Tsimshian relate that chiefs sometimes offered valuable presents for the privilege of engaging in sex with these women, even though they might be the wife of another chief. Such practices continued in the fur trade era. In 1853, the Tsimshian chief Cushwhat paid the wife of a Company employee to sleep with him. As Julia Cruikshank has noted, sexual relations were also often a way of cementing alliances among peoples of different tribes. Thus, there was no particular stigma attached to payment for sex *per se*. Such views on sexuality did not imply that Tsimshian and other native societies were without rigid moral standards, for they were especially concerned with such matters as guarding the chastity of young unmarried women. Adult women, however, were freer to determine their own sexual and reproductive lives. In any case, it is unlikely that many of the women who engaged in voluntary sexual activities for payment considered themselves as prostitutes by vocation, nor did their families regard them in this light. This fact alone permitted Nishga and Tsimshian women to retain their self-respect and their status within their lineage. Francis Poole, who visited their Haida neighbours in the 1860s, remarked that families and friends showed no manner of disrespect towards Haida women who engaged in prostitution on a temporary basis. The women themselves often looked upon such activities as a "mode of serving their kindred," by obtaining goods for their lineage to distribute at potlatches.[34]

A problem remains as to how the forced sale of slave women and women of low rank, as opposed to the voluntary activities noted above, affected the general standing of Nishga and Tsimshian women within their communities. Did the "traffic in women" or the tendency to regard certain women as commodities for sale mean that the status of all women fell in the estimation of native males? No definite answer can be advanced, but it does appear that native men compartmentalized their feelings toward slave and low-ranking women versus other female members of their societies. Slaves and *wa'ayin* were regarded as being outside the social system. As such, slaves in particular were always regarded as commodities which could be disposed of at the will of the owner. It is thus unlikely that attitudes towards these slave women influenced the position of Nishga and Tsimshian women as a whole.

One of the most disastrous consequences of the increase in sexual activities between native women and whites was the rise in the incidence of venereal disease. By the 1860s, many women were ill or dying from diseases contracted at Victoria and on the ships. Hudson's Bay Company records and missionary reports for the 1860s indicate that rates of infection with syphilis and other diseases rose dramatically, particularly among native women and the native wives of Company employees. Greater infant mortality and sterility related to such diseases were reported among all groups, but especially among the Haida. Precisely how these developments affected the status of native women remains problematic. Still, from the example of the Nishga alone, it does appear that individual women were held responsible for bringing this "scourge" to their peoples. Nishga men feared for the safety of the female relatives who had infected their tribesmen with venereal disease contracted at Victoria. They were concerned that these men might retaliate by killing the women who had brought them the disease.[35]

The missionaries, who began to arrive on the northern coast in the 1850s, hoped that a by-product of their newly established Christian villages would be the termination of prostitution of Nishga and Tsimshian women, both on the whisky ships and at the southern settlements. In this goal the missionaries were partially successful because they were able to use the backing of the colonial authorities and the threat of gunboats to remove the whisky traders from the northern coast. By the 1860s they had also effectively employed the threat of British gunboats to suppress the intertribal raids which had so long supplied women for prostitution. Enslavement was further reduced as the missionaries influenced chiefs to free their captives. A sense of relief from the fear of abduction was now possible for native women. Yet the mission era introduced some disruptive elements itself, for the missionaries demanded far-reaching cultural changes of their converts. Missionaries expected native peoples to abandon their traditional belief systems and tried to impose Victorian standards of domesticity and submissiveness upon native women.[36] Still, Nishga and Tsimshian women did not passively accept the teachings of the missionaries. For the most part, these women retained their self-confidence in their dealings with the missionaries and often obtained Christian instruction on their own initiative.

In order to understand why Nishga and Tsimshian women were able to retain their autonomy and resist the pressures to conform to the missionaries' notions of female submissiveness, it is important to understand the circumstances of their conversion. As Clarence Bolt and others reveal, the Tsimshian and their neighbours were never so thoroughly demoralized through contact with whites that they had little choice other than to accept Christianity. Despite the disruptive influences of alcohol and population decline due to smallpox and other diseases, native values and spiritual beliefs were not automatically eroded. Although an in-depth analysis of the native response to Christianity cannot be attempted here, it is clear that many Nishga and Tsimshian accepted Christian instruction while maintaining their confidence in the existing spiritual complex. For them, conversion was more of an additive process, as these women and men interpreted the teachings of the missionaries in indigenous ways and blended Christianity with traditional beliefs. Interestingly, Nishga and Tsimshian women of chiefly rank were often the first to seek instruction in Christianity, rather than lower-class women, who can be regarded as the most demoralized members of these cultures with the least stake in the maintenance of the traditional belief system and social structure. Shortly after William Duncan's arrival at Fort Simpson in 1857, high-ranking women began to attend classes conducted by him.[37] While receiving instruction they continued to participate in traditional ceremonies despite the missionary's censure of these activities.

A number of women of chiefly status accompanied Duncan to the Christian village of Metlakatla at its establishment in 1862. A rare opportunity to study their motivations for conversion exists because the Anglican Bishop, the Right Reverend George Hills, visited Metlakatla in 1863 and recorded the testimonials of several female and male converts. Tah-tiks, a twenty-four-year-old woman, revealed that sickness and the dissolution of her family were major factors in her conversion. Yet this feeling of alienation was not universal. Loosl, a high-ranking woman and wife of the chief Quathray, exhibited considerable interest in the physical manifestation of Christ, remarking that she was struck that "He came down among us." Oo-ah, the wife of the chief Thrak-sha-Kawn, stated that she was drawn to Christianity because "the spirit helps us." Such statements were consistent with traditional beliefs, for the Nishga and Tsimshian believed that spirit powers took compassion upon humans and gave them both spiritual and material assistance.[38] Neshaki revealed that her interest in Christianity had developed over several years. Although she continued to engage in many traditional ceremonies, she simultaneously instructed others in Christianity, particularly the young women of her tribe at Angida on the Nass. Neshaki's endeavours sometimes brought her into conflict with the missionaries because they felt she was assuming too much responsibility for instruction. The missionaries were no doubt unaccustomed to a woman competing with their authority in this manner.

Repeatedly, powerful women such as Neshaki influenced their own people and members of surrounding tribes to seek out Christianity. In 1874, Elizabeth Dudoward Lawson, a Tsimshian chieftainess of the Gitando tribe at Fort Simpson, attended meetings of the Methodist Church at Victoria. She was impressed with what she had learned and later influenced her son, Chief Skagwait, and many other Tsimshian to convert. It was through her efforts that the Tsimshian invited the Methodists to establish a mission at Fort Simpson. In 1877, the Methodists employed the services of Victoria Young (Nishlkumik) in order to establish a mission among the Nishga. Though Tsimshian, Nishlkumik commanded considerable respect from these neighbouring tribes. According to the Methodists she helped lay the foundations for their later success with the Nishga. Victoria Calder (or Negawon), a Nishga chieftainess of a powerful wolf lineage, was responsible for the conversion of several members of her tribe to Methodism during the late 1870s. Both the local Methodist missionaries as well as visiting dignitaries from eastern Canada treated her with particular respect and acknowledged her as the leader of the Christian village of Greenville, despite the presence of a number of male chiefs in the settlement. While women were barred from roles as priests and ministers, they still took an active role in the life of the mission. Tsimshian of both sexes recognized the inconsistencies in a religion which declared that all were equal before God, yet denied women a role in the priesthood. They were accustomed to women taking important public roles in their traditional ceremonials. Thus, they queried their Bishop why a woman might "preach in a loud voice on the street" but not in the church.[39] It is likely his response that St. Paul willed it so was less than satisfactory to them.

Missionary records provide scant information about the experiences of native women of middle and lower rank. Some women may have followed the example of the members of their lineage in converting. Others saw Christianity as a means to increase their own prestige. In one instance, a Nishga woman who was the wife of a carver became very haughty upon conversion and did not wish to associate with others who still wore traditional dress. Slave women viewed the missions as a means to freedom, since they provided refuge for women who escaped from traditional villages where slavery was still practised. One such woman travelled 150 miles on her own in order to reach Metlakatla. At the missions, these women could now marry and set up their own households. Some former slave women were employed as interpreters by the missionaries. They were ideally equipped for this employment since they were often traded to several different groups during their captivity and learned many languages. While ex-slaves might be given positions of some importance by the missionaries, it is important to note that their status did not rise accordingly in the estimation of the native peoples. They were never fully accepted by the native residents of the mission villages. If unmarried, they resided with other former slave families. If they did marry and bear children, their sons and daughters carried the stigma of being descended from slaves.[40] The example of the slave women thus illustrates the need to measure native women's status not by Euro-Canadian standards but according to the values of the native peoples themselves.

On the whole, Nishga and Tsimshian women exercised considerable autonomy in their decision to convert. It is true that some women followed the examples of their uncles who were lineage heads, and many husbands and wives converted together. Yet, equal numbers converted in spite of opposition from their families and husbands. Relatives sometimes destroyed books and writing instruments belonging to female converts. Tsimshian women such as Nayahk, a shaman's wife at Fort Simpson, were ridiculed by their husbands for seeking Christian instruction but continued to pursue an independent course of action and eventually influenced their spouses to convert. Still others chose the traditional ways over Christianity despite the conversion of their husbands or male relatives. Yet conflict between the sexes over the question of conversion was never as intense among the Nishga and Tsimshian as it was in some other native groups such as the Montagnais. During the seventeenth century, Montagnais women tried to resist the proselytization efforts of the Roman Catholics because they feared that settlement in mission villages would only undermine their own economic roles and subject them to much closer control by their husbands.[41]

On the northern Pacific coast women may have felt more secure about their positions, for the only group of women who offered serious opposition to the missions were the female shamans. Reverend Alfred Green, a Methodist missionary active on the Nass during the 1880s, experienced considerable resistance from these women. The Anglican missionary Robert Tomlinson, who evangelized the Nishga a decade earlier, found that female shamans and the wives and female relatives of male shamans influenced their tribesmen to avoid conversion. These Nishga women probably feared they would suffer a loss of prestige and authority associated with their roles as shamans were Christianity to take hold. Yet when female shamans did convert, they often played very prominent roles in the mission villages, sometimes more so than their male counterparts. During the pre-mission era, shamans commanded respect from the community as a whole, not merely from their own particular lineage or house. There are some indications that the spiritual capabilities of the shamans may have allowed them to rival or sometimes exceed chiefs in power. In any case, people continued to look to them for guidance after conversion. Katherine Derrick, a former shaman who converted to Methodism in 1888, became a prominent member of the Greenville community and influenced many of her tribe from the Nishga village of Kitwinsilth to relocate there. Nox Stabah, another Nishga shaman, became the leader of a women's church group known as the White Cross at the Anglican mission of Aiyansh. There was a certain continuity in the spiritual aspects of her role, for women actively sought Nox Stabah's advice on sacred matters and she conducted prayer groups for their benefit.[42] Another facet of her work with the White Cross was nursing the sick of the community. It is ironic that because nursing was considered women's work and not within the proper sphere of activities for males, female shamans such as Nox Stabah had more opportunities than male shamans to continue their roles and influence as healers.

In some instances, women who evinced a positive interest in Christianity at the outset of missionization later found the discipline of the mission villages to be oppressive. In such cases they asserted their autonomy by abandoning the mission settlements and returning to their traditional ways. After a brief stay at Metlakatla, one woman decided to return to Fort Simpson, where she could participate in potlatch ceremonies and be free of the missionaries' interference. She must have perceived some value in the teachings of the missionaries, however, because she left her young son with them to receive schooling and Christian instruction. Girls often escaped from the boarding institutions at Metlakatla because they were accustomed to much autonomy in their own societies and could not tolerate the harsh treatment and corporal punishment meted out by the missionaries.[43] One young woman named Sophia informed the missionaries that she was going to the Nass fisheries and would not return to Metlakatla, for she found the "restraints of the mission too great," and she could do as she wished in the company of her mother and brother. Other young women who were residents at the Crosby School for Girls in Port Simpson physically challenged the matron of that institution, and spat upon her when she attempted to enlist them in domestic chores against their liking.[44] Such instances testify to the continuing autonomy and self-confidence of Nishga and Tsimshian girls and women.

Women clearly resented the intrusions of the missionaries upon their personal lives. They were particularly resistant to the missionaries' efforts to prevent them from divorcing their spouses. Despite the institution of formal Christian marriage ceremonies and the missionaries' prohibitions upon divorce, husbands and wives continued to separate. In 1872, Tomlinson commented that one of the major problems facing his mission was the "brittle nature" of Nishga marriages. His co-worker, James

McCullagh, made similar complaints as late as the 1890s. Missionaries encountered the same difficulty at Metlakatla, which had the reputation of being the most rigidly controlled of the Christian villages. Duncan and the Metlakatla Council, which consisted of 10 of the most prominent males in the settlement, passed jail sentences and fines upon individuals who committed adultery. The threat of incarceration must have existed in cases of divorce, too, for one woman told Duncan she would gladly accept imprisonment rather than stay with her current mate.[45] Others who found themselves in unsatisfactory marriages simply left the confines of the mission village and returned to their own relatives.

The missionaries believed that they would have more success inculcating notions of modesty and domesticity in native women if they offered the proper training to girls at an early age. Accordingly, young girls were instructed in the domestic arts such as cooking, sewing, and knitting. By the 1890s, such instruction was regularly received at boarding institutions at Metlakatla and Port Simpson. Boys learned trades such as smithing and cooperage. Critics of native education often charge that males were given at least a modicum of training for wage labour, while females received few skills to prepare them to participate in the industrial economy. Thus, female graduates were relegated to low-paying jobs as domestics or confined to roles within the home.[46] Yet in the northern Pacific coast, several factors intervened to mitigate the effects of the missionaries' educational system.

In the first place, the application of these educational principles was by no means uniform. At mission centres outside Metlakatla and Port Simpson, the majority of children attended day schools rather than boarding institutions prior to 1900. Here, curriculum was the same for boys and girls. Both sexes received basic skills of literacy and numeracy and their enrolment rates were roughly equal.[47] But even when female children attended boarding schools on the northern coast, the type of education they received did not necessarily restrict their economic opportunities. As Joanne Fiske has shown in her study of the Lejac Boarding School in the northern B.C. interior, Carrier women actually became more employable than their male counterparts as a result of the domestic education they received. Carrier women, who neighboured the Tsimshian on their interior border, found employment as nursing assistants, waitresses and cannery workers as a result of their training. In contrast, the opportunities for Carrier males to employ their skills as farmers or tradesmen were few. A similar argument could be made for Tsimshian women. Education in domestic skills, basic numeracy and literacy prepared them well for the type of work available to women on the northern coast before 1900. Their male counterparts found only limited demand for the carpentry and smithing skills they had acquired, but the domestic skills possessed by women were particularly desired by the salmon canneries, which offered the main opportunity for paid employment on the northern coast. Canners admitted that they frequently offered employment to native fishermen simply to ensure that their wives would come to work at inside jobs in the canneries.[48]

Each spring and summer, women were able to find employment at canneries on the Skeena River in Tsimshian territory and at several points on the Nass River. Canneries hired a large complement of female labourers to perform such functions as cleaning fish, and packing and soldering cans. An estimated one-third of all cannery employees in British Columbia were female. In the mission-operated cannery at Metlakatla, the ratio was as high as one-half. Although women were given the most repetitive and lowest paying jobs at the canneries, the opportunity to work outside the home meant that they were not reduced to a position of irrelevance in the new capitalist economy, as were women in many other native societies. The economic position of Nishga and Tsimshian women at the end of the nineteenth century thus contrasts greatly with groups such as the Dakota of the northern plains of the United States in the same time period. Patricia C. Albers' study of Dakota women reveals that opportunities for these women contracted as the fur trade ended and a capitalist economy developed. Dakota women were not considered for jobs as agricultural workers or for other wage labour. As a result they were increasingly confined to the domestic sphere. This did not occur to a similar degree on the northern Pacific coast. In addition to cannery work, Tsimshian and Haida women found employment at dogfish oil production facilities on the Queen Charlotte Islands. Haida women were actually shareholders in one such operation conducted by the Methodists at Skidegate. Hundreds of Tsimshian, Nishga, and Haida women and their husbands also found seasonal employment as hop-pickers in Washington State beginning in the 1870s. Others packed freight to the Omineca mines. A few Tsimshian and Tlingit women were hired as interpreters by ethnologists such as Franz Boas who began to appear on the coast in the late 1880s. Boas preferred to hire native women, regarding them as far more intelligent and knowledgeable than their male counterparts.[49]

Flexible arrangements for childcare allowed Nishga and Tsimshian women and their northern neighbours to pursue employment outside the home. Because women's labour was in such demand by the canneries, cannery operators permitted women to bring their infants to work with them. Infants were strapped onto the mothers' backs while the women proceeded with their tasks. Obviously, the conditions of the canneries, which were damp and poorly ventilated, were not always conducive to the health of the infants, but the efficiency of women cannery workers indicates that the infants' presence did not interfere with their mothers' work. By the early twentieth century, cannery operators instituted a rudimentary form of daycare in order to retain their female workers. Elderly Tsimshian women were enlisted to look after the infants in a separate room while their mothers laboured. Women could also draw upon the services of female relatives for childcare and assistance in household duties. The nuclear family did not become the norm during the mission era despite the missionaries' efforts to encourage this development. Extended families continued to include widowed mothers of the heads of the households, and unmarried aunts and sisters, all of whom cooperatively undertook domestic tasks.[50] By relying on this network of female relatives, a woman was free to travel to the cannery sites or hop fields in order to earn an income. Although it is not entirely clear how women disposed of the monies they earned, the major portion probably went to the support of their families. The reduction of the potlatch activities due to the missionaries' influence, and the anti-potlatch law of 1884 meant that fewer resources were allocated to traditional feasting and ceremonial activities. Still, women used their earnings to increase their own prestige and that of their lineage by contributing jewellery, blankets, and sums of money to the missions. These donations were made in public ceremonies and thus served to validate the status of the contributors, in a more limited but nonetheless similar way to the potlatch.

In addition to performing wage labour, women continued many of their traditional economic activities. The welfare of the household and lineage still relied heavily upon women's labour, particularly in the production of food. Although some Euro-Canadian foods such as flour, tea, rice, and sugar were regularly purchased by 1900, salmon and eulachon were still the main components of native diets. Families continued to move seasonally to the fisheries, and women processed a large proportion of the Tsimshian and Nishga food supply. Women gathered berries, mollusca, and seaweed, grew potatoes, and dried salmon and eulachon. Surpluses of items such as soapberries and seafood were exchanged with women of interior tribes for other food or money in some instances. The missionaries also served as their customers for goods such as fish, woven mats, and potatoes. According to the missionaries, Nishga women were extremely shrewd negotiators and were always conscious of the prices charged by their competitors.[51] Thus, the significant roles of Nishga and Tsimshian women in production and distribution continued largely unaltered.

Elements of change and continuity were also evident in the public roles of Nishga and Tsimshian women during the late 1800s. As mentioned earlier, the highest public positions, such as village chieftainships, were most often assumed by men. Still, the public and domestic spheres were not as sharply separated in northern coastal tribes as they were in Euro-Canadian society. Women exercised considerable influence upon such decisions as the allocation of resources and even intertribal relations, on occasion. One American woman who visited the Tlingit in 1885 noted that the rights and political powers of Tlingit females would "astonish the suffrage leaders of Wyoming and Washington territory." Such observations could be readily extended to the Tsimshian, since the Tlingit and Tsimshian shared a similar culture and social structure and freely intermarried. Like their Tlingit counterparts, Tsimshian women served as conservators of the laws and customs of their people, and acted as councillors and chiefs.[52]

When mission villages were established, formal definitions of "public" roles and concepts of "citizenship" were instituted. In both the Anglican and Methodist mission villages, citizenship applied only to the adult males of the settlement. In principle, only they could serve as councillors and constables. At Metlakatla, the taxpayers were men. Male taxpayers were also theoretically the only ones permitted a voice in law-making and public works in the villages. Yet, in spite of these regulations, women did assume roles as councillors at the mission villages. At the Methodist settlement at Port Simpson, Victoria Young served as a chief and councillor, and Victoria Calder assumed similar roles at Greenville. Significantly, neither of these women held their positions through any magnanimity on the part of the missionaries. Instead, these women held power because the native peoples themselves continued to acknowledge them as leaders and sought their advice. As a chief, Calder represented the Nishga in protests against the survey of their land in 1888 and demanded payment be made for all lands surrendered. In 1896 Victoria Young and others joined in a three-way struggle between the Tsimshian, Department of Indian Affairs, and Hudson's Bay Company over disputed territories at Port Simpson.

In addition to Young and Calder, a number of other women also served as hereditary chiefs during the 1890s, including Sarah Legaie and Anna Sebassa of Metlakatla, and Julia Legaie of Port Simpson. Julia Legaie's tribe, the Gispaxloats, supported her installment as chief in opposition to a male heir who also had claims to the chieftainship at the death of their uncle in 1890. Women also had a quasi-public role through their participation in the church guilds, such as the Anglican White Cross and the Methodist Epworth League. These organizations performed evangelical duties, but they also collected funds necessary for the maintenance of the mission village through producing goods for sale to outside markets. In some cases, as at Aiyansh, the women of the White Cross conducted public works such as road-building.[53] These associations not only provided an important sense of solidarity among the women, they also meant that women maintained a certain visibility within the community as a whole and were not merely confined to the household sphere.

While women were sometimes able to circumvent regulations and participate in mission councils, the Indian Act presented them with a more rigid system of government. Of course, at a most fundamental level, the Indian Act circumscribed the participation of many women in the affairs of their communities by excluding those who married non-Indians from band membership and legal status. These discriminatory features of the Act were not removed until 1985. But it was the Indian Advancement Act (of 1885) which ultimately curtailed Nishga and Tsimshian women's roles as councillors by redefining the nature and composition of band councils and setting up a municipal form of government. The Indian Advancement Act required acceptance by the band before it became effective. This acceptance was slow to evolve, but by 1900 the Tsimshian villages of Metlakatla and Port Simpson accepted the Indian Advancement Act, as did the Nishga centres of Kincolith and Aiyansh. According to the Indian Advancement Act, chiefs and councils were to be elected for a fixed term by male suffrage. Women could neither elect nor serve as councillors.[54] They no longer had veto power over the decisions made by males. The full impact of this legislation was not immediately apparent. Matters such as resource allocation were still settled at the level of the household or lineage. In addition, hereditary chiefs, who were sometimes women, did not suddenly lose their power but continued to be consulted on political and economic matters. Yet the new rules meant that women were restricted in regard to official roles in negotiations with the federal and provincial governments concerning land claims and use in the twentieth century.

The period between 1830 and 1900 witnessed considerable alterations in the lives of native women of the northern Pacific coast, but change was never linear. Positive developments such as the expansion of access to sources of wealth and prestige during the fur trade era were offset by disruptive elements such as alcohol and prostitution. Yet Nishga and Tsimshian women demonstrated a remarkable degree of strength and adaptability. In the past, scholars have argued that women of native societies were more conservative than their male counterparts.[55] Certainly there was continuity in Tsimshian and Nishga women's roles as mothers and wives; they maintained the home and passed on important traditions to their children. But they also embraced change when they perceived it as beneficial. They readily accepted items of Euro-Canadian material culture which made their every-day tasks less arduous. They expanded their roles as traders, entered the labour force as cannery workers, interpreters and freight packers, and were active participants in the functions of the mission villages.

The ability of native women to adapt to the changing circumstances of the fur trade and missions is clear. Determination of their status under these new conditions is a more complex matter. Formal political power is but one measure of status. Economic control of production and distribution, informal influence over the decision-making process, and degrees of personal autonomy are also key determinants.[56] As we have seen, in each of these areas Nishga and Tsimshian women maintained much of their former position by 1900. Several factors helped to ensure that their status was not eroded despite the coming of the fur trade and missions. The redistributive nature of the Tsimshian economy meant that women had access to the wealth generated by the fur trade, for they continued to share the resources of their lineages according to rank. At the same time, their traditional participation in intertribal exchange prepared them to assume roles as traders and intermediaries in the land-based fur trade and directly acquire wealth.

Because Nishga and Tsimshian women continued to play a vital part in production for both exchange and use, they were not marginalized as were many native women during the fur trade era. Nor did the importance of Nishga and Tsimshian women's traditional economic functions diminish even as industrial development commenced. On the one hand, the isolation of the Nishga and Tsimshian allowed the women to carry on many of their traditional productive roles such as gathering and processing fish. The rate of white settlement and industrial development was gradual and small enough that it did not significantly erode Nishga and Tsimshian maritime resources and traditional gathering sites before 1900. On the other hand, the nature of development in the region also permitted women to take an active part in the new economy, for a female labour force was vital to the operations of the canneries.

Nishga and Tsimshian women retained their status to a large degree because of their continuing economic importance in their communities; kinship arrangements, however, may also have been influential in determining their position. As has been shown, matriliny itself is not a guarantor of status for women, but the particular kinship structure of Nishga and Tsimshian society was such that women were able to play active parts in their own lineages as well as in the household headed by their husbands. These arrangements meant that there was a multiplicity of roles for women, each of which carried important rights and duties. For example, in her role as a maternal aunt, a woman often played a major part in negotiating the marriage arrangements of her sister's sons. These activities had important consequences for the lineage, since marriages served to ally families and extend their resource base. In the case of a chief, a properly negotiated marriage might ensure that his community had important economic connections in other villages. In her role as a paternal aunt, the same woman might be involved in such diverse activities as the naming ceremonies of her brother's children and the memorial feasts. The latter ceremonies persisted, albeit in an attenuated fashion, throughout the mission era, and continued to mark the succession of hereditary leaders of the community. Participation in such functions once again ensured that women's influence was not confined to the domestic sphere alone, but was exerted at the public level as well.[57]

Along with these externally applied measures of women's status, the native peoples' assessments of women's importance must be considered. The Nishga and Tsimshian of the nineteenth century clearly understood the interdependence of the sexes and recognized how vital women were to the welfare of their households, lineages, and villages. This interdependence finds no better expression than in the native peoples' own words. In 1894 at the celebration of a marriage, a Nishga chief conveyed the mutual responsibilities of man and woman:

... when a man gets married his wife must watch his canoe to see if it stays wet when the sun shines on it. If she does not, the canoe will split. But even then it is not lost altogether. The husband sews the split together and ties a rope around it, the canoe can be used again. Thus the wife should help her husband because her negligence would be of disadvantage to both. If she makes a mistake however, her husband should not just stand and scold or mistreat her, but try to help because when both work on it together, things will run more smoothly again.[58]

NOTES

The author wishes to acknowledge the support of the Social Sciences and Humanities Research Council of Canada Doctoral Fellowships Program.

1. Eleanor Leacock, "Montagnais Women and the Jesuit Program for Colonization," in *Women and Colonization: Anthropological Perspectives*, ed. Mona Etienne and Eleanor Leacock (New York: Praeger Publishers, 1980), 25–42; Carol Devens, "Separate Confrontations: Gender as a Factor in Indian Adaptation to European Colonization in New France," *American Quarterly* 38 (1986), 461–80; Laura Klein, "'She's One of Us You Know': The Public Life of Tlingit Women: Traditional, Historical and Contemporary Perspectives," *Western Canadian Journal of Anthropology* 6 (1976), 173.

2. Clan membership cut across village and tribal lines. For instance, members of the Nishga Wolf clan who resided on the Nass considered themselves to be related to Tsimshian individuals of the same clan. Even though they might not necessarily be connected by blood, they could not intermarry. Persons of the same clan were also expected to provide hospitality to visiting clan members and on occasion they might be asked for support in times of war.

3. Paula Webster, "Matriarchy: A Vision of Power," in *Toward an Anthropology of Women*, ed. Rayna Reiter (New York: Monthly Review Press, 1975), 145; Margaret Blackman, "The Changing Status of Haida Women: An Ethnohistory and Life History Approach," in *The World Is as Sharp as a Knife: Essays in Honour of Wilson Duff*, ed. Donald N. Abbott (Victoria: Provincial Museum of British Columbia, 1981), 74; Judith K. Brown, "Economic Organization and Position of Women among the Iroquois," *Ethnohistory* 17 (1970), 151–67; Alice Schlegel, *Male Dominance and Female Autonomy: Domestic Authority in Matrilineal Societies* (n.p.: HRAF Press, 1974), 141; Doreen Jensen and Polly Sargent, *Robes of Power: Totem Poles on Cloth*, University of British Columbia Museum of Anthropology, Museum Note 17 (Vancouver: University of British Columbia, 1986), 6; Alfred P. Niblack, *The Coast Indians of Southern Alaska and Northern British Columbia*, U.S. National Museum *Annual Report*, 1888 (Washington: U.S. National Museum, 1890; reprint ed., Johnson Reprint Co., 1970), 259.

4. Laura Klein, "Tlingit Women and Town Politics," Unpublished Ph.D. dissertation, New York University, 1975, 166.

5. Francis Poole, *Queen Charlotte Islands: A Narrative of Discovery and Adventure in the North Pacific*, ed. John W. Lyndon (1872; West Vancouver: J.J. Douglas Ltd., 1972), 259; Viola Garfield, "Tsimshian Clan and Society," *University of Washington Publications in Anthropology* 7 (1939), 267; Livingstone Jones, *A Study of the Thlingets of Alaska* (1914; New York: Johnson Reprint Company, 1970), 166; Robert Doolan, *Journal*, 1 June 1865, Church Missionary Society, *Records* "Papers and Correspondence" (1822–1900), Microfilm Series CMS/A105.

6. R.W. Nolan, "The Utilization of Fish Resources by the Coast Tsimshian: Predicting Optimal Patterns of Exploitation," Unpublished M.A. thesis, Trent University, 1977, 158.

7. William Henry Pierce, *From Potlatch to Pulpit: Being the Autobiography of Rev. Wm. Henry Pierce, Native Missionary to the Indian Tribes of the Northwest Coast of British Columbia*, ed. J.P. Hicks (Vancouver: The Vancouver Bindery, 1933), 111; William Duncan, *Journal*, 17 April 1860, CMS/A105.

8. Garfield, *Tsimshian Clan and Society*, 262; Thomas Crosby, *Up and Down the North Pacific Coast by Canoe and Mission Ship* (Toronto: The Young Peoples' Forward Movement, Missionary Society of Methodist Church of Canada, 1914), 384.

9. Marjorie Mitchell and Anna Franklin, "When You Don't Know the Language Listen to the Silence: An Historical Overview of Native Indian Women in B.C.," in *Not Just Pin Money: Selected Essays on the History of Women's Work in British Columbia*, ed. Barbara Latham and Roberta Pazdro (Victoria: Camosun College, 1984), 21.

10. Mary Jane Schneider, "Women's Work: An Examination of Women's Roles in Plains Indian Arts and Crafts," in *The Hidden Half: Studies of Plains Indian Women*, ed. Patricia Albers and Beatrice Medicine (Latham, Md.: University Press of America, 1983), 102; Nancy Lou Patterson, "Review Essay: 'The Spirit Sings,'" *Native Studies Review* 3 (1987), 143; Jensen and Sargent, *Robes of Power*, 81.

11. Duncan, Annual Letter to the Church Missionary Society, n.d., February 1858 CMS/A105.

12. Hudson's Bay Company Archives (hereafter, HBCA), Fort Simpson (Nass) *Journal*, 29 November 1841, B201/a.5, fo. 27; Marius Barbeau, *Totem Poles*, Vol. Two, National Museum of Canada, Bulletin No. 119, Anthropological series 30 (Ottawa: National Museum of Canada, 1951), 11; HBCA Fort Simpson (Nass) *Journal*, 17 July 1838, B201/a.4, fo. 34.

13. HBCA Fort Simpson (Nass) *Journal*, 7 September 1840, B201/a.5, fo. 23; Garfield, *Tsimshian Clan and Society*, 199; "The Controversy of Nishlkumik and Rapligidahl," in *Tsimshian Narratives: Trade and Warfare*, Volume 2, Collected by Marius Barbeau, ed. George F. Macdonald and John J. Cove. Canadian Mercury Series, Directorate Paper No. 3 (Ottawa: National Museum of Canada, 1987), 57-58.

14. Salvation Army Archives, Port Simpson News Clipping File, 13A3, Lt. Col. Friedrich, "Among the Coast Indians," *All the World* 24 (November, 1903), 606.

15. Duncan, *Journal*, 20 November 1858, CMS/A105.

16. Robert Doolan, *Journal*, 15 October 1865, CMS/A105; Jones, *The Thlingets of Alaska*, 226; Charles Harrison, *Ancient Warriors of the North Pacific: The Haida, Their Laws, Customs and Legends with Some Historical Account of the Queen Charlotte Islands* (London: H.F. & G. Witherby, 1925), 94; Doolan, *Journal*, 21 May 1865, 1 November 1865, CMS/A105.

17. "The War of the Gispaxloats and the Haida," *Tsimshian Narratives* Vol. 2, 389; Loraine Littlefield, "Women Traders in the Maritime Fur Trade," in *Native Peoples, Native Lands: Canadian Indians, Inuit and Metis*, ed. Bruce Alden Cox (Ottawa: Carleton University Press, 1987), 173-85.

18. HBCA Fort Simpson (Nass) *Journal*, 28 July 1837, B201/a.3, fo. 118, 15 April 1839, B201/a.4, fo. 89, 12 May 1839, B201/a.4, fo. 97.

19. HBCA Fort Simpson (Nass) *Journal*, 5 August 1857, B201/a.8, fo. 106; Margaret Blackman, *During My Time: Florence Edenshaw Davidson, A Haida Woman* (Seattle: University of Washington Press, 1982), 35-38; James Gibson, "Smallpox on the Northwest Coast, 1835-1838," *B.C. Studies* 56 (1982-83), 61-81; HBCA Fort Simpson (Nass) *Journal*, 19 October 1836, B201/a.3, fo. 75.

20. HBCA Fort Simpson (Nass) *Journal*, 31 May 1858, B201/a.8, fo. 141, 28 June 1858, B201/a.8, fo. 141, 10 June 1863, B201/a.9, fo. 13.

21. Barbeau, *Totem Poles*, Vol. 2, 11; Doolan, *Journal*, 25 October 1865, 18 November 1865, CMS/A105.

22. Sylvia Van Kirk, *Many Tender Ties: Women in Fur-Trade Society, 1670-1870* (London: Watson & Dwyer, 1980), 31.

23. "War between the Haida and the Gispaxloats," in Franz Boas, *Tsimshian Mythology*, Bureau of American Ethnology, Thirty-first Annual Report, 1909-1910 (Washington: Government Printing Office, 1916), 389.

24. Pierce, *From Potlatch to Pulpit*, 8; "Copper Nail's Legend," *Tsimshian Narratives: Tricksters, Shamans and Heroes*, Vol. 1, 205.

25. James B. McCullagh, *Red Indians I Have Known* (London: Church Missionary Society, n.d., c. 1917), 13; Garfield, *Tsimshian Clan and Society*, 235.

26. HBCA Fort Simpson (Nass) *Journal*, 28 March 1842, B201/a.6, fo. 40, 24 November 1856, B201/a.8, fo. 73; HBCA Fort Simpson (Nass) *Journal*, 11 February 1856, B201/a.8, fo. 34.

27. HBCA Fort Simpson (Nass) *Journal*, 6 March 1856, B201/a.8, fo. 38, 25 June 1856, B201/a.8, fo. 53, 2 July 1856, B201/a.8, fo. 54, 19 October 1857, B201/a.8, fo. 115; James A. McDonald, "Trying to Make a Life: The Historical Political Economy of the Kitsumkalum," Unpublished Ph.D. dissertation, University of British Columbia, 1985, 84.

28. HBCA Fort Simpson (Nass) *Journal*, 1 January 1863 B201/a.8, fo. 3; Doolan, *Journal*, 8 May 1865, CMS/A105; Duncan, *Journal*, 6 June 1859, CMS/A105.

29. HBCA Fort Simpson (Nass) *Journal*, 22 June 1838, B201/a.4, fo. 26; Niblack, *The Coast Indians of Southern Alaska and Northern British Columbia*, 253; HBCA Fort Stikine, *Miscellaneous Items*, "Census of the Stikine Population, 1845," B201/z.1, fo. 1; Garfield, *Tsimshian Clan and Society*, 272.

30. HBCA Fort Simpson (Nass) *Journal*, 21 May 1855, B201/a.8, fo. 5; HBCA Fort Simpson (Nass) *Journal*, 9 February 1859, B201/a.8, fo. 161; Rt. Reverend George Hills, Bishop of Columbia, "Columbia Mission Occasional Paper, June, 1860," *Report of the Columbia Mission, 1860* (London: Rivington's, 1860), 28.

31. National Archives of Canada, RG10 Indian Affairs, Black Series, Volume 3846, file 57045-1, Microfilm Reel C-10193, A.W. Vowell to Deputy Superintendent of Indian Affairs, 25 February 1891, Agent Morrow to A.W. Vowell, 25 May 1906.

32. Henry S. Wellcome, *The Story of Metlakahtla* (London: Saxon & Co., 1887), 26; HBCA Fort Simpson (Nass) *Journal*, 5 August 1857, B201/a.8, fo. 106.

33. Canadian Advisory Council on the Status of Women, *Prostitution in Canada* (Ottawa: Canadian Advisory Council on the Status of Women, 1984), 3-17; Susan Johnston, "To Be Happy You Must Be Good: British Columbia Women's Response to Nineteenth Century Social Conventions," Unpublished B.A. essay, University of British Columbia, 1989, 54.

34. "The Purchase of Nahahulk," *Tsimshian Narratives*, Vol. 2, 48; HBCA Fort Simpson (Nass) *Journal*, 18 January 1853, B201/a.7, fo. 50; Julia Cruikshank, "The Role of Northern Canadian Indian Women in Social Change," Unpublished M.A. thesis, University of British Columbia, 1969, 77; Poole, *Queen Charlotte Islands*, 313; Newton H. Chittenden, *Report of an Exploration of the Queen Charlotte Islands for the Government of British Columbia* (Victoria: Government of British Columbia, 1884), 18.

35. Crosby, *Up and Down the North Pacific Coast*, 271; Doolan, *Journal*, 3 June 1866, CMS/A105.
36. Mary E. Young, "Women, Civilization and the Indian Question," in *Clio Was a Woman: Studies in the History of American Women*, ed. Mabel E. Deutrich and Virginia C. Purdy (Washington: Howard University Press, 1980), 98–110.
37. Clarence Bolt, "The Conversion of the Port Simpson Tsimshian: Indian Control or Missionary Manipulation?" in *Sa Ts'E: Historical Perspectives on Northern British Columbia*, ed. Thomas Thorner (Prince George: College of New Caledonia Press, 1989), 159–76; Duncan, *Journal*, 18 February 1859, 26 February 1859 CMS/A105.
38. Rt. Reverend George Hills, Bishop of Columbia, "Extract of the Journal of the Bishop of Columbia," *Report of the Columbia Mission, 1863* (London: Rivington's, 1863), 63; Philip Drucker, *Cultures of the North Pacific Coast* (San Francisco: Chandler Publishing Co., 1965), 86.
39. United Church Archives. Methodist Church of Canada (MCC), *Fifty-Sixth Annual Report of the Missionary Society of the Methodist Church of Canada, 1879–1880*, xvi; General Secretary of the Methodist Missionary Society, "Notes of a Tour among the Missions of British Columbia," *Missionary Outlook* 5 (November, 1885), 168–69; Bishop William Ridley, *Snapshots from the North Pacific*, ed. Alice J. Janvrin (London: The Church Missionary Society, 1903), 82.
40. Doolan, *Journal*, 29 January 1866, CMS/A105; Wellcome, *The Story of Metlakahtla*, 85; Garfield, *Tsimshian Clan and Society*, 271.
41. Rt. Reverend Hills, "Extract of the Journal of the Bishop of Columbia," 63; Leacock, "Montagnais Women and the Jesuit Program for Colonization," 25–42; Devens, "Separate Confrontations," 461–80.
42. Robert Tomlinson, Annual Letter to the Church Missionary Society, n.d. 1868, CMS/A105; A.E. Green, 14 March 1888, quoted in *Missionary Outlook* 8 (July, 1888), 109; McCullagh, *Red Indians I Have Known*, 46.
43. Reverend and Mrs. A.E. Gribbell, who served briefly at Metlakatla in 1867, claimed that Duncan stripped a girl naked and then beat her. It is impossible to know whether a sexual offence was involved or if Duncan was attempting to teach the girl submission, since Reverend Robert Doolan, who also witnessed the incident, disputed the Gribbells' charges and claimed the girl was clothed. In any case, this extreme form of discipline of young girls was unknown in traditional native societies of the northern Pacific coast. Duncan, *Journal*, 5 March 1867, CMS/A105; Tomlinson, Letter to Dean Cridge, 24 January 1867, CMS/A105.
44. Kate Hendry, *Letterbook*, 1 June 1883, Provincial Archives of British Columbia (PABC); "Reminiscences of Miss Agnes Knight at Bella Bella, Port Simpson and Cape Mudge, 10 July 1885 — 23 October 1887," PABC Typescript, 20.
45. Tomlinson, Annual Letter to C.M.S., 5 June 1872, CMS/A105; James B. McCullagh, "The Indian Potlatch: Substance of a Paper Read before the Church Missionary Society Annual Conference at Metlakahtla," *Caledonia Interchange* n.s. (1899), 13; Duncan, *Journal*, 25 February 1867, CMS/A105.
46. Laura Waterman Wittstock, "Twilight of a Long Maidenhood," in *Comparative Perspectives of Third World Women: The Impact of Race, Sex, Class*, ed. Beverly Lindsay (New York: Praeger Publishers, 1980), 207–28.
47. Enrolment figures for boys and girls in 1898 at six mission day-schools among the Tsimshian (T) and Nishga (N) were as follows:

	Boys	Girls
Aiyansh (N)	11	14
Kincolith (N)	13	13
Lakalzap (N)	34	22
Metlakatla (T)	26	27
Pt. Essington (T)	20	20
Port Simpson (T)	53	32

Department of Indian Affairs, *Annual Report for the Year Ended 1897* (Ottawa: S. Dawson, 1898), 322–23.
48. Joanne Fiske, "Life at Lejac," in *Sa Ts'E*, 257–61; National Archives of Canada, RG10 Indian Affairs, Black Series, Vol. 3908, file 107297-2, Microfilm Reel C-10160, "Minutes of a Royal Commission at Victoria Involving Fishing Privileges of Indians in British Columbia, 1915."
49. Mitchell and Franklin, "When You Don't Know the Language Listen to the Silence," 26; Jean Usher, *William Duncan of Metlakatla: A Victorian Missionary in British Columbia*, National Museums of Canada Publications in History, No. 5 (Ottawa: National Museum of Canada, 1974), 74; Patricia C. Albers, "Autonomy and Dependency in the Lives of Dakota Women: A Study in Historical Change," *Review of Radical Political Economics* 17 (1985), 109–34; Kathleen E. Dalzell, *The Queen Charlotte Islands, 1744–1966* (Terrace, B.C.: C.M. Adams, 1966), 67; Rolf Knight, *Indians at Work: An Informal History of Native Indian Labour in British Columbia, 1858–1930* (Vancouver: New Star Books, 1978), 82; Franz Boas, in *Ethnography of Franz Boas*, editor and compiler Richard Rohner (Chicago: University of Chicago Press, 1969), 23.
50. National Archives of Canada, RG10, Indian Affairs, Black Series, Vol. 4045, file 351,304. Microfilm Reel C-10178, G.J. Desbarats to D.C. Scott, 11 July 1916; Garfield, *Tsimshian Clan and Society*, 280.
51. Doolan, *Journal*, 17 May 1865, CMS/A105; Pierce, *From Potlatch to Pulpit*, 115.
52. Eliza Ruhamah Scidmore, *Alaska: Its Southern Coast and the Sitkan Archipelago* (Boston: D. Lothrup

and Company, 1885), 182; Niblack, *The Coast Indians of Southern Alaska and Northern British Columbia*, 253; Duncan, Annual Letter to C.M.S., n.d. February 1858, CMS/A105.

53. Crosby, *Up and Down the North Pacific Coast*, 385; Department of Indian Affairs, *Annual Report for the Year Ended 1897*, 480; "Once When the Gitando Tried to Take the Power of Legex" (H.D. Pierce, informant) Columbia University. *The Beynon Manuscripts*. File 122; Blackman, "Changing Status of Haida Women," 74; James B. McCullagh, "A Transformed People: The Appliance of Civilizations as the Result of Evangelization," Church Missionary Intelligencer n.s. (July, 1896), 511; Pierce, *From Potlatch to Pulpit*, 67.

54. Wayne Daugherty and Dennis Madill, *Indian Government and Indian Act Legislation, 1868–1951* (Ottawa: Department of Indian and Northern Affairs, 1980), pt. 2, 19.

55. Louise Spindler, *Menominee Women and Culture Change*, American Anthropological Association Memoir 91, Pt. 2, Vol. 64 (1962), 99.

56. See Carol C. Mukhopahdyay and Patricia J. Higgins, "Anthropological Studies of Women's Status Revisited, 1977–1987," *Annual Review of Anthropology* 17 (1988), 461–95.

57. Blackman, "Changing Status of Haida Women," 70; Garfield, *Tsimshian Clan and Society*, 222, 233; Mariane Boeschler, *The Curtain Within: Haida Social and Mythical Discourse* (Vancouver: University of British Columbia Press, 1988), 105.

58. Boas, "Letter from Kincolith, British Columbia, 11 October 1894," in *Ethnography of Franz Boas*, 165.

"The Children, the Cows, My Dear Man, and My Sister": The Transplanted Lives of Mennonite Farm Women, 1874–1900

ROYDEN K. LOEWEN

On 1 May 1881 thirty-seven-year-old Maria Kornelson Ens of Cub Creek Township, Jefferson County, Nebraska, wrote to her relatives in the Mennonite East Reserve in Manitoba.[1] Her letter was one of scores that served to express and maintain ties between the two Mennonite communities, rooted in kinship, a common history, and an association with a single church congregation, the conservative Mennonite Kleine Gemeinde.[2] In 1874 the 170 families of this small Mennonite group had migrated to North America from the German-speaking colonies of southern Russia. Although they split paths, with sixty families settling in Nebraska and 110 families in Manitoba, close ties were rigorously maintained.[3] Developing church differences in the two communities after 1880 did little to undermine these relationships. The composite portrait of Mennonites as an ascetic, communal-oriented, pacifist, German-speaking religious body seeking freedom from the threat of military service in imperial Russia is well established in historical writing. Sometimes this portrait overshadows the fact that each community was made up of real men and women who organized their lives in single-family households and wider kinship groups.[4]

SOURCE: Royden K. Loewen, " 'The Children, the Cows, My Dear Man and My Sister:' The Transplanted Lives of Mennonite Farm Women, 1874–1900," *Canadian Historical Review* 73, 3 (1992), 344–373. Reprinted by permission of University of Toronto Press Incorporated. © University of Toronto Press.

Maria Ens's 1881 letter, written to bolster that social network, lets us glimpse the details of her world as a Mennonite farm woman. Like other letters, this one began with a statement of religious devotion, reflecting on life's transiency and on the mercies of God. But it moved quickly to a four-part description of her social world: the first dealt with her "two youngest" children, Anna and Jacobchen, who had both been quite ill during Easter; the second described her farmyard activities, which included milking the cows that "gave plenty of milk," setting chicken and goose eggs, and planting potatoes; the third reported the activities of her "Lieber Mann," her "dear husband," who was "occupied with the field work" and was "planting the last of the wheat today"; and, finally, she sent word to her sister-in-law to write "a little on a small piece of paper," for receiving letters "is the only joy we can have with one another here on earth." These were the components of Maria Ens's world, a world in which most activities were intrinsically tied up in the Mennonite household, which in turn was anchored to a pervasive kinship network that transcended the distance between Nebraska and Manitoba.

The Mennonite women of Cub Creek and the East Reserve between 1874 and 1900, the Kleine Gemeinde Mennonites' first generation in North America, lived complex lives. Such lives were only one variation of a myriad of different worlds that farm women in North America encountered and fashioned. They fit the typology of neither the peasant or yeoman household nor the fully commercialized and mechanized farm. Even Ester Boserup's paradigm of productive women in a culture of shifting cultivation and nonproductive women in a male-dominated plough culture fails to capture or explain the world of Mennonite women.[5] Instead, we need to pay close attention to the particular historical and economic circumstances of this group, as they grafted their North American experiences onto a well-established religious culture and farm economy. In North America, traditional pursuits, self-sufficiency, modest lifestyles, partible inheritance practices, and kinship ties met up with rising living standards, land availability, and farm commercialization and mechanization. The result was a life oriented to both economic production and biological reproduction, extended to both the hearth and the farmyard, and ordered by both patriarchalism and elements of female power.

Studies that explain the world of farm women with reference to the exigencies of the rural household economic unit are especially useful in understanding the lives of Mennonite women. Undergirding this historiography are scholars who have argued that a household mode of production, relying on the productive input of women, remained relevant long after the development of a capitalist, market economy. Harriet Friedmann, for example, found that on the North American grasslands it was the self-reliant "household commodity producers" who adapted most quickly to frontier conditions, while large, mono-crop commercial enterprises were more vulnerable to periods of limited cash income and labour shortages.[6] Other scholars, such as Kathleen Conzen, have described the particular success of ethnic farm households in reproducing themselves within a pluralistic, industrialized society as they turned all their resources to securing the "generational succession" of land.[7]

The importance of the household in shaping the lives of farm women has been the focus of many recent studies in North America, as in Europe. Works by Veronica Strong-Boag, Sara Brooks Sunberg, and Mary Kinnear on Canadian prairie farm women, and Joan Jensen, Cornelia Butler Flora, and Jan Flora on women in the United States, have each outlined the important roles that farm women held as household producers.[8] Similar conclusions have been drawn of farm women in England, Greece, Germany, and France.[9] Martine Segalen's study of small, mixed-production French farms has argued that women's indispensable roles as farm producers provided them with important degrees of power, despite their gender-defined work roles and their legal inferiority.[10] The status of these women was based on the household's central focus for both men and women: here the daily life of both members of the couple "merged with that of the household"; here the primary "function of the house [was] . . . its function on the farm"; here the "economy of the farm [was] a function of the family cycle"; and here "direct ownership [wove] a series of emotional ties between household and dwelling."[11] In contrast to the women of more commercialized and economically specialized farms, described recently by rural historians Paul Voisey, Marjorie Griffin Cohen, and Jon Gjerde, the women in Segalen's study were neither domesticated nor proletarianized.[12] The family farm that was geared to self-sufficiency, mixed production, and generational succession provided women with status.

The primacy of the household economic unit carried the Mennonite women into the modern world of a marketplace economy without significantly altering their lives as producers. The women who settled in the bloc settlements of Manitoba and Nebraska in the mid-1870s had already adjusted to a more commercialized farm economy in southern Russia. Economic and social reforms and the development of a global wheat trade after 1860 had transformed the lives of the Mennonite farmers in Russia.[13] After 1860, for example, new land sources, improved transportation links, high international wheat prices, and a large cheap labour pool had intensified agriculture. The rise of commercial wheat production separated the territories of men and women in an unprecedented way; rising living standards, the wares of travelling merchants, and the employment of female Russian workers had encouraged women to spend more time in the domestic world of children and well-furnished houses.[14] Still, the founding of daughter colonies on lands once occupied by Russian serfs and state peasants allowed the Mennonite farm household, with its values of strict social boundaries, agrarian economic pursuits, partible inheritance, and kinship ties to flourish; and in this context women maintained important social and economic roles.

This world, composed of both change and continuity, was transplanted to North America. Here, too, there were developments that threatened to undermine the productive roles of women: early field mechanization allowed men to control the grain division of the farms; the distance to marketplaces made the selling of products a responsibility of the men alone; larger families confined women more often to their houses; and a growing economy allowed women to contemplate lives in clean, roomy, frame houses, complete with windows and white plastered walls, and fitted with store-bought kitchen wares, furniture, and sewing machines.[15]

Other characteristics of the new land, however, encouraged Mennonites to establish old ways of life. An abundance of unsettled land allowed the Mennonite partible inheritance system to operate, bequeathing land to young women and encouraging their husbands to settle on that land in acts of matrilocality. In the context of pioneering conditions and a mixed farm economy, women continued to be producers, especially in the farmyard, and hence maintained an important economic status. The founding of new village settlements along kinship lines ensured the transplantation of traditional female social networks, while the establishment of ascetic, sectarian villages encouraged women to pursue household self-sufficiency in food, clothes, and medicine and thus to maintain ethnic social boundaries.

A strong and meaningful identification with the farm household and an active participation in female social networks were thus maintained. The household and the social networks ensured a larger measure of continuity than change between 1874 and 1900. Not until the turn of the century, with rising land shortages, fuller farm commercialization, rising urbanization, and cultural integration with the outside world, were these old ways of life significantly threatened. So long as new land sources could be found, ascetic lifestyles maintained, and a mixed farm economy pursued, Mennonite farm women would find their role models in neither the suffragist nor the "ideal woman." Their lives in the farm household provided them with a significant degree of meaning, status, and power.

Like women of other ethnic groups, Mennonite women faced changes on their arrival in North America. Some of those changes encouraged a domestic world; especially important was a high birth rate that directed women in Cub Creek and the East Reserve to a life of bearing and rearing small children. Diaries and birth records reflect this reality. Letters indicate that the caring of children was a consuming endeavour: "Little Jacob woke me last night at 1 A.M. with a very severe cough which one could hardly bear to listen to," wrote Maria Ens in a typical letter in 1884, "and I hardly knew what to do as I had to stay with him all night."[16] It was an emotional bond that surpassed all others: "We have had a tragic [experience]," wrote Aganetha Brandt Klassen of Manitoba in 1892, "on the 27th of February our daughter, Frau Heinrich Friesen, was taken from our side after a . . . three year illness, toward the end of which she was in great pain; but it was especially difficult for her to leave her eight children motherless."[17] It was her role as a mother that often confined the woman to a private world; when the house of Abram and Anna Reimer of Cub Creek burned to the ground in 1882, neighbours reported that it had been an especially critical situation as "she was at home alone with the children while he was in town."[18]

While children were centrally important in shaping the lives of Mennonite women in Russia, there is evidence that they became even more so in North America. Birth rates were high throughout the first generation and at the turn of the century stood at 4.9 per cent in Cub Creek and 4.8 per cent in the East Reserve. In addition, mortality rates declined from 2.7 per cent in southern Russia in the 1850s to 1.7 per cent in the East Reserve and 1.2 per cent in Cub Creek around the turn of the century.[19] As a result, the number of Mennonites in Cub Creek increased from 378 to 673 between 1880 and 1900, while the population of the three Kleine Gemeinde village districts in the East Reserve increased from 450 to 857. Along with the total population, family sizes also grew. Between 1880 and 1900 the size of the average family increased from 5.6 to 6.1 in the East Reserve and from 6.3 to 6.6 in Cub Creek.[20] Mennonite families varied greatly in size at different points in their developmental cycle. Thus, while families of the elderly or newly wed might number only two persons, middle-aged couples might have more than nine children.

The rising number of children in the new world accompanied the decreasing marriage age for women. Marriage ages had been dropping for some time. In Russia during the 1850s, for example, the average Mennonite Kleine Gemeinde male married at 24.4, the average female at 22.0. By the time of the 1874 migration, that age had fallen to 23.1 and 21.2 for men and women, respectively. While marriage ages for men did not change significantly during the first generation in North America, they did change for women. During the 1890s the average male in the East Reserve married at 23.0 years and in Cub Creek at 22.5, only a slight change from the 1860s. The marriage age of women, however, dropped significantly, to 19.3 in the East Reserve and to 19.1 in Cub Creek.[21] These demographic changes, coupled with the fact that the vast majority of women in the communities under study practised little fertility control and thus gave birth to their first child between ten and twelve months of marriage, contributed to a higher proportion of children in the communities.[22]

Women's preoccupation with children also seems to be underscored by a growing demand for female servants during these years. Diaries are filled with references to men travelling distances of up to thirty miles to hire maids. On 28 April 1879, for instance, farmer Abram Penner of the East Reserve, whose thirty-two-year-old wife was bedridden and pregnant with her sixth child, drove the fifteen miles from Blumenort to Heuboden to pick up a maid, only to discover that she and her family had left the East Reserve. He was then compelled to go to neighbouring Gruenfeld, where he "got P. Toews' Katrina for two weeks."[23] Letters also refer to maid shortages. On 11 June 1877 Isaak Loewen of the village of Rosenort wrote to enquire about a maid near Blumenort: "We have heard that there is a girl available in Schoenthal," wrote Loewen to his brother, "send us notice if she is available, for we must have a girl!"[24] High birth rates also resulted in a demand for wet nurses, who sometimes could ask for and receive more than fifty cents a day for their services.[25]

It is evident from the salaries of female servants and their job descriptions that much of their work was domestic. Indeed, they often received only 40 per cent of the male servants' salary. In April 1891, for example, forty-five-year-old Gerhard Giesbrecht of Steinbach, in the East Reserve, was able to reduce his debt with neighbour Cornelius Loewen by $19.35 after working for him for nineteen and a half days; in the same year the thirty-seven-year-old widow Elisabeth Toews earned only seventy-five cents after washing for the Loewen household for two days.[26] A similar disparity existed for teenaged labourers. In 1892 the children of the Rev. Peter Reimer of the East Reserve village of Blumenort would "help out" at the neighbouring Plett household whenever time allowed; Reimer's teenaged sons Peter and Cornelius helped the Pletts with their threshing and seeding at fifty cents a day, while their older sister, seventeen-year-old Maria, helped with the washing for thirty-five cents a day.[27] Washing the clothes of more children, and the walls and floors of new frame houses, pointed women to a new preoccupation with antiseptic cleanliness.

A growing degree of domesticity for women was also encouraged by a steadily increasing level of field mechanization and its associated division of labour, with men working the fields and women spending their time near and in the house. While Mennonite women had been doing less field work in southern Russia, where Ukrainian women were often hired to reap the wheat with scythes and Ukrainian men were employed to haul the grain to the threshing floor on the farmyard, field mechanization in North America consolidated the men's hold on the grain division of the farm. Settlement reports in the first years in North America indicated that women had initially worked on the fields: John Lowe, secretary in the Canadian Department of Agriculture, noted on his visit to the East Reserve in 1877 that "every man, woman and child is a producer. Women were ploughing in the fields, thatching roofs and girls were plastering houses."[28] The introduction of the mechanical reaper, the threshing machine, and the "up-right" steam engine by 1880 turned grain production once more into a male activity. As Boserup noted, the mechanization of a given aspect of the farm inevitably encourages male control of it.[29]

Women who did work in the fields tended to be young, unmarried women who were helping out in a male world in which the male most often was a father or close relative. In August 1883 school-teacher Abram R. Friesen of the East Reserve hired Maria Friesen, his sister, to help tie sheaves that he had earlier cut with the mechanical reaper; he noted that in one day "I and Maria tied 3.5 acres."[30] In February 1884 when Jacob Ens in Cub Creek set out to husk 500 bushels of corn, it was he and his single sister, Maria, who did the work.[31] In most instances women worked the fields only during times when the men and the boys were operating the machines; the binders, threshing machines, steam engines, and ploughs were the tools of the men. The work of the girls was more labour-intensive. It was they who pulled the mustard plants, dug the potatoes, stooked the grain sheaves, reaped the loose grain the binder had missed, and cut the twine on the sheaves on the threshing machine.

The work patterns on the forty-acre farm of Johann Dueck of the East Reserve village of Gruenfeld are indicative of the sexual division of labour that was shaped by the introduction of machinery. In 1888 the eldest child of the Dueck household was seventeen-year-old Anna. She was followed in age by brother Gerhard, fifteen, sister Katherina, fourteen, twins Jacob and Helena, twelve, and two younger siblings. Because Anna was the eldest, she often operated the plough and helped with the threshing. There were signs in Dueck's diary, however, that Anna's role would not be permanent; the entry for 30 June read: "Frank [the hired hand] ploughed the new land, the girls pulled mustard"; the entry for 8 July stated: "the girls mounded the potatoes, the boys harrowed"; the 13 August notation indicated: "I began cutting with the binder . . . Anna tied [sheaves]." This division of labour became established as the boys grew older. In April 1891 as Gerhard hauled products to the city, Anna worked for "H. Loewens"; in May, as Gerhard seeded and harrowed, Anna "worked at Goossens"; in July as Gerhard disc-harrowed the summerfallow, Anna worked for "the Toewses." Now that Gerhard was old enough to perform field duties, Anna moved on to the domestic service or farmyard duties of the Duecks' neighbours.[32]

That women's work tended to keep them close to the house is apparent also from farmers' "workers lists," kept during harvest to identify the crew's fireman, "separator man," "bagger man," engineer, water boy, and other posts. They demonstrate that while young women sometimes worked as "sheave cutters," they were quickly relegated to domestic duties if men became available. In September 1884 East Reserve farmer Gerhard Kornelson hired only one woman, "die Jacob Barkmansche," as part of the fifteen-person threshing crew — but it was not to pitch sheaves or shovel grain; her job was to "make food." A year later Kornelson's workers once again included only men, except for worker thirteen, Maria Friesen, whose job designation was "inside."[33]

What were the effects of larger families, field mechanization, and roomier houses on the status of women? While it is clear that these changes encouraged women to remain in or closer to the house, women also maintained close ties to the household economy and hence maintained their status as household producers. Historians sometimes argue that increased family size reflects household economic strategies. Some frontier historians, for example, have argued that lower marriage ages and larger families resulted from an abundance of farmland and perceived economic opportunity.[34] Other historians have suggested that high birth rates reflect community labour shortages and a value placed on child labour. Hans Medick explained that the growing number of children in proto-industrial English families was related to earlier ages of marriage for women at a time when "child labour, [increasing] in both its intensity and duration . . . was in fact a vital necessity for the rural cottage workers' families."[35] A parallel with Mennonite families practising intensive agriculture in labour-dear North America is not unwarranted. At least one scholar examining Old Order Amish society has concluded that high birth rates result from the status associated with child bearing, important because it helped "provide the hands that maintain the system."[36]

The importance of children in maintaining the household is evident. Children were expected to begin helping with the milking, herding, and stooking after the age of six, and began working full-time when boys left school at the age of twelve and girls at the age of eleven. A major moment in the family life cycle occurred when children finally allowed the family to become self-reliant in its labour needs. In 1877 Sarah Janzen Friesen of Cub Creek wrote to her relatives with the proud news that "we are now helping ourselves entirely with the help of our own children."[37] In 1894 Gerhard Kornelson of the East Reserve noted that the harvest was noteworthy because "the children are helping in a greater way; especially as they can haul [the sheaves home] without me."[38] When children reached the age of majority at twenty-one, another important moment in the life cycle arrived; parents saw their children marry and begin their households. Thus, the deeply held cultural value of "generational succession" was realized.

Just as it is possible to argue that children did not sever the woman's tie from the economy of the farm, but rather consolidated it, it can likewise be argued that farm mechanization altered, but did not reduce, women's economic role and status on these farms. By 1880 field mechanization ended the need for women grain reapers and for their work on the threshing floor, but there remained the considerable and significant economy of the farmyard. The fact that the average size of the Kleine Gemeinde Mennonite farm was less than sixty cultivated acres at the turn of the century (63.4 acres in Nebraska in 1900 and 54.1 acres in Manitoba in 1898) and that households continued to rely on mixed products ensured that women's production of farm products would remain highly valued.

Some of these farm products were required to guarantee household self-sufficiency in food. Self-sufficiency reflected a cultural value, but it was also required in the relatively primitive economy of both Nebraska and Manitoba in the 1870s and 1880s, especially because both settlements lay some distance from large metropolitan centres. In this context, women's work in securing food was absolutely crucial to the family's survival. Food supplies were purchased only occasionally, and usually with an eye to tiding the household over to the next garden season. While agricultural census records can only hint at the level of food self-sufficiency, diaries can more fully ascertain that level. The dietary record of one East Reserve farmer reflects the important role that the wife exercised in the household economy. Gerhard Kornelson of Lichtenau calculated in 1888 that he and his wife had consumed 933 pounds of flour, 48 pounds of meat, 40 pounds of lard, 50 pounds of butter, 20 bushels of potatoes, 25 pounds of roots, and 120 pounds of wheat.[39] These figures indicate not only their self-sufficiency in food, but the significance of the wife's labour in sustaining her household. The value of the products from the fields in this diet, such as the wheat for the flour and the oats for meat production, was $19, while the food produced in the farmyard, the domain of the woman, amounted to $43. The dietary supplements of coffee, sugar, fruit, fish, and brandy, purchased on trips to the city, remained minor budgetary items during the first generation in North America and did not change this equation significantly.

The mixed farms of both the East Reserve and Cub Creek also relied on female-produced table foods to provide part of the early household's income. Diaries of East Reserve farmers note that it was not unusual for farmers to market such products as chickens, butter, eggs, sauerkraut, onions, and potatoes in Winnipeg during the early 1880s.[40] Indeed, these diaries indicate that such shipments of farmyard-produced table foods to Winnipeg accounted for more than half of the East Reserve household's annual income of approximately $300 during the first decade in Manitoba. Illustrative of this practice as well are letters from Cub Creek. Maria Ens's letter of May 1881, for example, noted that "on Monday we drove to [Fairbury] as we had some wheat, and some eggs and butter."[41] Census records from Cub Creek for 1880 and 1885 underscore the importance of women in the farm economy as well; they indicate, for instance, that the average Mennonite household in the township produced 252 pounds of butter, 110 dozen eggs, and 30 bushels of potatoes annually.[42]

Women's economic roles in the farm household continued in the 1880s and 1890s despite a decline in the reliance on these table foods for farm income. Indeed, as egg and vegetable sales decreased, butter, cream, and whole milk sales increased. Dairy farming in both Cub Creek and the East Reserve became more important after both communities began de-emphasizing the Mennonite tradition of wheat growing. Low wheat prices at the end of the 1870s, coupled with poor soils in Manitoba and excessive moisture in Nebraska, encouraged farmers to turn from their beloved wheat to feed grains such as corn in Nebraska and oats in Manitoba.[43] Both of these feed grains encouraged a new focus on cattle production. So, too, did the construction of five cheese factories in the East Reserve between 1889 and 1893, and the coming of a railway through the heart of Cub Creek in 1886, developing a direct link to the creamery in nearby Fairbury. The number of milch cows increased during the 1880s and 1890s. Between 1883 and 1905 the average number of cows per East Reserve household increased from 3.1 to 8.2, while in Cub Creek that number increased from 2.8 in 1880 to 5.6 in 1885.[44]

Although the farmyard gained in importance in the commercial makeup of the Mennonite farm, there is little evidence that men took a more active role in diary operation. Instead of marketing butter in the cities as they had before, men now sold fluid milk to the local cheese factory, and as before, it was the men who maintained the breeding stock, fences, wells, and buildings, dispersed the manure, and hauled the hay in from the fields. Women merely turned their energies from butter churning to the milking of more cows and preparing either the cream or the whole milk for shipment. Marjorie Griffin Cohen has observed that women were no longer "central" to dairying once "activity moved from household craft production to more capital intensive factory production."[45] This observation, however, does not account for relatively small, unmechanized dairies that relied on household labour and were primarily geared to household social reproduction.

That women maintained an active role in the dairies is evident from diaries and logbooks. It was the women who maintained the birthing records of cows and the wives who were the head milkers.[46] When, during times of childbirth or illness, wives were unable to do the milking, milk maids were hired to do the chores. During the summer of 1890, for example, when Anna Wiebe Reimer of Steinbach bore a child, the fourteen- and fifteen-year-old daughters of neighbour Johann Reimer were hired to milk "314 times at 5 cents a time" for a total of $15.70.[47] Young girls were socialized quickly to understand the territories of their sex: one family history notes that "small and slightly built, but wiry [Justina Brandt of Manitoba] was milking cows at the . . . age of six."[48] Women thus continued to work the farmyard and to produce marketable products.

Reinforcing the status derived from productive work was the centuries-old Mennonite practice of bilateral partible inheritance that often provided women with land of their own.[49] Typically, brides in traditions practising primogeniture could expect to inherit little more than a dowry consisting of moveable property, usually a cow and a few household furnishings. One study of women in a turn-of-the-century Kansas community observed that "giving girls property . . . [was] like turning one's deed over to another family."[50] By contrast, the 1857 Mennonite "Teilungsverordnung," the inheritance by-laws of the Molotschna Mennonite Colony of southern Russia, stipulated clearly that sons and daughters were to share equally in the inheritance of their parents. The twenty-five articles of this church-sanctioned ordinance discriminated between men and women in only some respects: on the death of the husband, for example, article 4 indicated that the widow must elect a "Mann zum Kurator" who was to provide counsel and be informed of all major business transactions; article 6 specified that upon the death of a spouse, a widow must be guaranteed the inheritance of a cow, while a widower was guaranteed a horse. The main articles, however, were egalitarian. Article 11 stipulated that "in the order of inheritance [all] the descendant children shall be the first."[51]

Especially important for women, daughters as well as wives, were the articles outlining procedures in the event of the death of only one of the spouses. Article 12 indicated that six weeks after the death of one spouse, and before any announcement of remarriage, the "surviving spouse . . . shall be awarded half of the net estate and the other half shall be designated to the other descendants." Any farmer whose wife died was required to issue half the farm in equal shares to each of his children. Article 8 which indicated that "the inheritance of dependent children . . . may remain in the farm without interest until the age of majority" assured the continued economic survival of the farm. It also ensured that, on turning twenty-one, daughters were often entitled to a significant inheritance. Because of the high mortality rate among women of childbearing age, it was not unusual for Mennonite children to have an inheritance awaiting them when they reached the age of majority and for marriageable women to own land.

This inheritance procedure also sanctioned the practice of dividing farmland equally to both sons and daughters on a farmer's retirement. It was also encouraged by the frontier conditions of free land in Manitoba and cheap railway lands in Nebraska. While Mennonite farmers, as farmers of other ethnic groups, strove to establish sons on land of their own through low interest loans or by outright gifts of land, daughters were often helped in similar fashion. Female landownership, however, is not always borne out by official land titles. In Manitoba, for example, Mennonites superimposed their open-field system onto the square-grid homestead survey, leaving little record of who actually owned which piece of land. Female landownership is evident in Cub Creek, Nebraska, where Mennonites did not use the open-field system and where women often left their inherited land registered in their own names even after marriage. Indeed, fifteen of the eighty Mennonite landowners in Cub Creek in 1900 were women, and only one of these women was widowed.[52]

These records also indicate the process by which women acquired land. The accounts of two Cub Creek families demonstrate that the process could differ. The first case involved the simple reception of land through inheritance after the death of both elderly parents; in 1892 three married daughters and two married sons, aged thirty-eight to forty-nine, each received 209 acres from the estate of their parents, Jacob and Maria

Ens, on the eastern edge of Cub Creek. In the second instance, two daughters of a landowner from the western sections of the township received land on two different occasions. In 1891, just after the death of his first wife, fifty-nine-year-old Jacob Klassen divested himself of 200 acres, almost half his total acreage; the land was equally divided among his youngest five children, aged thirteen to twenty-nine, including a fourteen-year-old daughter, Sara. His eldest daughter, Katherina, who had received land shortly after her marriage in 1879, received nothing. In 1896, when Klassen retired, he turned over the remaining 300 acres to his children, giving a piece to each child including his two daughters.[53]

The significance of women owning land is multifaceted. Boserup has suggested that the ending of female ownership of land in colonial Africa severely undermined women's status.[54] Several studies of the bilateral partible inheritance system in present-day rural societies have argued that women who bring inherited land into a marriage have a greater role in farm management than those who do not.[55] While this is difficult to substantiate in a historical study, it is known that women who inherited land were often able to attract their husbands to settle in the woman's village where the woman had more familial ties than did the man. Both the Ens and Klassen daughters of Cub Creek, for example, secured matrilocal households. The husbands of the Ens women, Peter Brandt, Peter Hildebrandt, and Johann Thiessen, settled in the Ens village of Rosenthal, despite the fact that none of these men had any close relations of his own in that part of the township.[56] Similarly, inherited land attracted the husbands of the Klassen sisters to settle on the western side of the township in the Klassen village of Neuanlage. Neither Abram Rempel nor Isaak Friesen, who married the Klassen daughters and who resided in Cub Creek in 1900, owned land of their own.[57] A letter from 1896 explains why at least one of these men owned no land; "Abram Rempel," notes the letter, "has sold [his farm] and at the present is living on his wife's land near her parents."[58] Similar patterns of matrilocality existed in each of the villages in Manitoba: in Blumenort and its five satellite villages, for example, twenty-nine of the seventy-one marriages consummated between 1874 and 1900 resulted in matrilocal residence.[59]

The practice of matrilocal residence was especially frequent in those marriages in which the groom hailed from a poorer family and the bride from a well-to-do family. In these cases the groom often worked for his father-in-law until the birth of the first child, when the young couple would be provided with land of their own. With the wife's additional dowry of a cow and the husband's of a horse or a cow, the couple would begin farming. While census records do not indicate the nature of a woman's kinship ties with other villagers, genealogical records do and they hint at high degrees of matrilocality in rural Mennonite society. Mennonite inheritance practices clearly presented women with tools to exercise important degrees of influence at crucial points in the household's life cycle.

Transplanted inheritance practices also ensured that Mennonite women could become the recipients of important sums of money at any time in their life. In 1892, for example, Elisabeth Reimer Plett of the East Reserve, who had been an infant when her mother died in 1870, turned twenty-one and received 324 rubles from the estate's administrator in Russia.[60] In 1883 forty-one-year-old Elisabeth Rempel Dueck, also of the East Reserve, received 484 rubles after her remaining parent died in Russia.[61] The most important source of inheritance for women came on the death of their husbands, when they were assured control of half the estate. In each community there were a number of wealthy widows. In fact, tax rolls indicate that the average size of an East Reserve widow's farm in 1898 was 52.5 cultivated acres, just slightly less than the overall average farm size of 54.1 acres. Other widows who liquidated their assets were in the position of loaning their money to poorer community members. While financial records from the East Reserve show that widows often borrowed money from the church-run loaning agency, they also reveal that the two largest contributors to this financial program during the 1880s were two well-to-do widows, Widow Plett and Widow Johann Loewen.[62]

The fact that widows owned their own capital and land allowed them to maintain a measure of autonomy in their old age. It was they who owned the small retirement houses located in the back yards of their youngest child's farm. In 1889, for example, it was the duty of Gerhard Kornelson to move "my mother's house" from Blumenort seven miles south to Lichtenau.[63] And it was the widows who paid for their lodging as they became infirm. The logbook of eighty-five-year-old Aganetha Brandt Klassen of Rosenhof noted in August 1901, for instance, that she paid her son Jacob Klassen ten dollars for her board since moving to his house on 24 May.[64] Mennonite inheritance practices that granted women a measure of economic status early on in life also enabled widows to maintain important degrees of independence later in life.

Women also exerted a certain degree of independence outside their households. Mennonite women during these years, as women in other communities, were accorded little formal status in society's public sphere; only men sat on the ruling "Lehrdienst" of the church and on the "Schulzenbott," or general village council, and only men's names were used to designate women in the public arena. Even the public forums such as the annual school examination exercises, the "Pruefungen," attracted few women. In the March 1890 Steinbach, Manitoba, examination, for instance, only seven of the thirty-three guests were women.[65] In fact, not until the coming of the more evangelistic and individualistic churches around the turn of the century did the women of the East Reserve and

Cub Creek participate in formal associations. Mennonite religious values, demanding the cultivation of strict social boundaries, ensured that Mennonite women would not participate in women's organizations of the wider society.[66] The literary society of Fairbury, near Cub Creek, regularly debated such themes as "the greater moral influence" of women, but, of course, it was unmentioned in the letters of Mennonite women.[67] Indeed, it was not till 1903 when the Mennonite women of Cub Creek organized a sewing circle, and not till 1908 when the evangelistic Bruderthaler Mennonite church in the East Reserve began electing women as Sunday school teachers, that avenues of formal associations were opened to Mennonite women.[68]

The only women to have a public profile in Mennonite society were the midwives and female lay doctors practising herbal medicine. Within the community social boundaries that separated the Mennonites from the wider society, these women were accorded public deference.[69] Midwives, who bore the double duty of attending the births of children as well as preparing the dead for burial, were noted to have been "appointed by the church" to be the "pioneers" in a "skill" that was to be in "great demand."[70]

Even greater public deference was paid to female lay doctors who practised herbal medicine, and who treated both men and women. Women lay doctors of the Mennonite communities did not escape the opposition of the male-dominated medical establishment of the host society; they were, however, strongly supported by the male leaders of the Mennonite communities. When travelling women "doctors" visited Mennonite communities, men made special note of their presence. In February 1884 a certain Frau Baerg arrived in the East Reserve and men dutifully spread the word that patients could see her in the village of Steinbach. Later in 1884 it was a Frau Neufeld who came to practise medicine, and once again men put out the notice that she could be seen for consultation at her rented room in Steinbach.[71] When Frau Neufeld attended church in the village of Blumenort, the village mayor, Abram M. Friesen, noted the event in his diary.[72] When another woman doctor, Frau Thiessen, visited Steinbach in 1888, a local farmer described how she set up shop "here at A. Reimers' where she lectured and 'doctored' for three days" and attracted a clientele of men and women from surrounding villages. The observer himself saw the "doctor" and recorded her "recipe" in the family diary.[73]

So supportive was the Mennonite community of Frau Thiessen that, in 1895, when the male-dominated Manitoba College of Physicians served her a $50 fine for practising medicine without a licence, she received immediate sympathy. Her predicament was reported at length in the weekly *Mennonitische Rundschau* by a male writer. He described how "the beloved Frau Thiessen, who is know as a 'doctor' throughout Southern Manitoba, has recently been fined . . . by several English doctors." The writer added that "it is very strange that a woman who has tirelessly worked to dispense her own wisdom should be persecuted," and concluded by calling for Mennonites to help pay her fine.[74]

The avenue of social interaction that took most women outside the bounds of their households was an informal one; it was the network of female relationships that close kinship ties and proximity to other women within the Mennonite village encouraged. Rural histories often note the loneliness of farm women and their dependence for wider social interaction on their husbands.[75] Historians of urban immigrants, in contrast, have noted how informal female networks, often based on kinship, ensured the smooth transplantation of communities to North America.[76] With respect to recreating informal female networks, the Mennonite group settlers were more akin to urban immigrants than to the more individualistic Anglo-Canadian and Anglo-American farm settlers. The group migration not only tied women together in a common life experience, it also brought women of particular kinship groups together in a single village.

The migration allowed kin, once separated in land-tight southern Russia, to settle close to each other. Not only did Mennonites establish their farms in "street" or "line" villages, they also tended to settle in kinship groups. Each of the six large twenty-household Kleine Gemeinde villages established in Nebraska and in Manitoba were dominated by two or three extended families; and in the twelve small ten-household villages, a single extended family dominated. Within such settings Mennonite women, unaccompanied by their men, visited their next of kin or female cousins several times a week. Sometimes elderly women visited their married daughters: "On 9 March 1889," wrote grandfather Abram Reimer of Blumenort, Manitoba, in his diary, "I walked to Abram Friesens"; my wife went to Abram Penners' [the household of her forty-seven-year-old daughter, Elisabeth]." On 14 March, Mrs. Reimer visited Elisabeth again; two days later, on 16 March, Elisabeth received a visit from her mother-in-law and a friend.[77]

Sometimes it was only the bearing of a child or sickness that disrupted such visits; a noteworthy event occurred in the life of Elisabeth Kornelson of the East Reserve in January 1885 when she left her house for "the first time" after giving birth to a daughter and visited "her sister, Widow Friesen" on one day and "her mother-in-law" on the next.[78] Mennonite villages were hubs of social interaction, involving women of all ages and marital status visiting and receiving visitors. In a set of entries in March 1891, Johann Dueck of Gruenfeld noted that on one Sunday his sixteen- and eighteen-year-old daughters visited the homes of different friends within the village; on the following Monday his wife visited her sister-in-law and the elderly neighbour Frau H. Reimer; and the next day, Tuesday, Frau Johann Friesen of a village thirty miles distant dropped in for a visit.[79] Informal social networks such as these were to assure that women possessed independent social avenues outside the household.

When the 1874 migration separated relatives and friends, letter writing ensured a continued network. Maria Ens's 1881 letter, for instance, expressed appreciation for letters from her sister-in-law. Not only were such letters written, they inevitably referred to other women, in effect casting an even wider network. In February 1877 Katherina Janzen Klassen of Nebraska wrote to her sister in Manitoba because "on Monday we were at siblings H. Ratzlaffs' and they told us that the 'Klaas Brandtsche' had written that you, dear sister, were not well and that you could stand some comforting."[80] Many other letters written by women and addressed to women and telling of their lives on the farm, their childbirths, the agonies of seeing children die, attest to the existence of close female networks within the Mennonite communities. Letters and visits between women, especially those within a particular kin group, took them beyond their domestic base. In lieu of formal women's associations, these ties provided women with relationships that were autonomous of their husbands.

A final characteristic of the transplanted world of Mennonite farm women is the most difficult to assess — the conjugal relationship. Men and women rarely wrote about their relationships, and other indicators of the nature of these relationships, such as nonverbal communication or private conversations, are not available to historians. Men and women sometimes did record feelings of love for each other. Among examples are a series of letters exchanged by a young Manitoba couple who were separated during the harvest of 1890, just six months after their wedding: twenty-three-year-old Isaak Loewen addressed each of his letters to "my very heart-loved Elisabeth" and ended them with assertions such as "I am well, although without you I am quite lonely." Elisabeth's letters were in the same vein, beginning each paragraph with the phrase "and now my dear man" and confessing her anxieties of being separated from her husband.[81] Deeply expressed emotions could also come after the death of a spouse. During the months after his wife, Anna, died in 1894, sixty-two-year-old Jacob Regehr of the East Reserve frequently recorded his grief of separation: "it was a very sorrowful day," he wrote on 21 August 1894, "as I just cannot forget the spirit of my wife; oh, it is so difficult for my heart when I remember the past in this way!"[82]

Usually, however, marital relationships are described not in terms of emotional bonds of love and affection but in a common identification with a household. It was an identification demanded by the community. When in 1884 farmer Johann Broeski threatened to beat his wife and then abandoned her, the church brotherhood excommunicated him.[83] A similar fate met well-driller Isaak Plett when, shortly after his marriage in 1886, he abandoned his wife and small child, sold his well-drilling machine, and took the train to Chicago.[84] The church also acted in 1883 when Katherina Goossen reportedly put her husband in great misery by "resolutely continu[ing] the mutiny on him."[85]

More important than church sanctions, however, in consolidating the conjugal unit was the exigency of the household. No doubt, the frequent references by letter writers to the "health of my dear wife" or "sickness of my dear man" were expressions of sympathy, but they were also admissions of interdependence.[86] Even when husbands recorded the agony of seeing their wives die they usually couched the account with references to a family without a mother. When farmer Jacob Klassen of Cub Creek lost his wife in 1890 he noted in a letter that only "the Lord is helping me carry [this] cross. Sarah [age thirteen] is sick . . . Without mother we are not at the best. Things are really wanting, but what can one do?"[87] Similarly, when wives lost their husbands, it was a loss for the household: when "father, Peter Toews, passed away," noted one family historian, "Mrs. Toews found herself left alone with a large family and in poor financial circumstances . . . Mrs. Toews with her grown-up daughters and her sons . . . looked after the farm [but] she also earned money by sewing." The author notes, however, that it was only when Toews remarried at the age of forty-nine that "her financial circumstances improved considerably."[88]

That women identified closely with the household farm, and considered their lives complementary to those of their husbands, is evident in the manner in which they wrote to their friends and relatives. Almost inevitably women signed off those letters with reference both to themselves and to their husbands: when Margaretha Friesen wrote to her relatives in Manitoba in the 1890s it was a letter from "Jacob and Margaretha Friesen"; when Elisabeth Loewen wrote to her sister and brother-in-law in Nebraska in the late 1870s it was signed "Elisabeth and Isaak Loewen."[89]

Important as well was the fact that women letter writers, like Maria Ens in 1881, referred to the economy of the whole farm. There were some differences in the way in which men and women wrote their letters. Men, more often than women, described church affairs; women, more often than men, wrote about children. When husband and wife described the state of the household economic unit, their perspectives differed as well. Men more often spoke about size, number of acres put to wheat, size of the dairy herd, and configuration of buildings. Women wrote more about the yield and the health of crops. Men reported more often on cereal grains and cattle herds, while women described the gardens and the nature of fall slaughters.

Both women and men, however, wrote about the farm economy. In June 1877 Anna Ratzlaff of Cub Creek closed a letter begun by her husband in which he wrote about church schisms; she wrote about the children and then closed with a description of the fall harvest: "Now I will report to you," wrote Anna, "that we are thinking of soon cutting the rye which has grown tall. The wheat and barley also look good. If conditions remain we can expect a very good harvest — the grasshoppers have not yet done much damage. The potatoes are doing well, as are the laying hens and the garden vegetables."[90] In November of the same year Elisabeth Loewen of Manitoba also finished a letter begun by her husband. After describing her family's health and inviting her in-laws to a visit, she noted that "we have slaughtered two good pigs and also slaughtered some 35 chickens also of good quality; wheat we received 500 bushels from 24 acres, however there was much smut in it; barley we received 115 bushels from four acres; potatoes, however, yielded very poorly, only about 10 bushels and of those many were green."[91]

Despite an increase in farm commercialization during these years, women's letters from the 1890s contained similar expressions of identification with the household economy. In June 1893 Margaretha Sawatsky Friesen of Cub Creek responded to a letter from an aunt in Manitoba. Friesen began with the usual enquiries about health, asking about her friends, die Jansche and die Thiesche, and reporting that "my dear man is very busy with the planting of corn." She then proceeded to report about the farm, noting that "we have 40 acres in corn, 15 acres oats, 30 in wheat" and reporting that "this spring we sold two horses . . . two oxen . . . three dozen hens . . . seven pigs." She noted the income from each of these sources and then listed the present inventory of livestock and poultry.[92] In July of that year she wrote again. This time her letter began with a detailed report of the painful experience of her Cub Creek aunt, Maria Wiens, who gave birth to a daughter, Sarah, but then, just six hours after "all the work was over and the pain receding," complications arose and "this little Sarah died." Despite this tragedy Friesen did not omit reporting on the farm. On the second page of the letter she abruptly noted, "now I must also report . . . about the harvest; the cutting is about completed . . . and presently all is consumed with threshing." She reported on the poor yields from the dry conditions and about the work of her husband with the threshing crew.[93] Ratzlaff, Loewen, and Friesen were mothers and keepers of the house; they were also farm producers, vitally interested in family sustenance and in the economic state of the household. It was on the basis of this common pursuit that the woman's relationship with her husband was shaped.

The world of Mennonite farm women between 1874 and 1900 was intrinsically tied to the household and to a pervading kinship network. The women under study were accorded little public recognition in Mennonite society and participated in no formal women's organizations during these years. Within the farm household and the extended family, however, women did possess important degrees of status. During the first generation of Mennonite settlement in Manitoba and Nebraska the household still ordered the activities of both men and women in a joint and complementary life. Women were actively involved in the economic advancement of the family farm. So long as the domestic group, the single-family household, remained more important as the turning-point of Mennonite society than either the church or the village association, women's roles would change little.

The new setting in Manitoba and Nebraska introduced some changes to women's lives. Indeed, there were some signs of increased domesticity during these years; women bore more children as marriage ages dropped, mechanization consolidated men's role as grain producers, and distance from the marketplace ensured that marketing would be the domain of men alone. These changes, however, did not separate women from the productive side of the farm household. The continued household economy, bound up as it was in the life cycle of the family, ensured that the role of women as mothers would not be divorced from the world of men. Moreover, the mixed nature of the farm economies in both Cub Creek and the East Reserve ensured that women would continue to play important roles as household producers. Women prepared commodities for the marketplace and provided the sustenance in the pursuit of household self-sufficiency. They milked the cows and manufactured the butter; they tended the chicken flocks, setting the hens on eggs and slaughtering the chickens; they managed the vegetable gardens and orchards.

Even more important than their work roles was the culture of Mennonite inheritance in which women were viewed as potential owners of land. The bilateral partible inheritance system ensured that women received more than a token cow at marriage; within the Mennonite's inheritance system all children were to be accorded an equal measure of land and livestock. Matrilocal residence was evidence of the kind of status women in line for the patrimony of land could possess. This ownership, coupled with their work roles, provided women with a strong tie to the household. It was a tie that was evident in their letters to their next of kin, which inevitably provided a detailed report of the state of the farm economy.

Within the close-knit Mennonite villages of Cub Creek and the East Reserve, women could also find avenues that led them outside the household. Some women, like the female lay doctors, caught the attention of the public world, but most women interacted outside their households only in the private world of other women. Close-knit village life was the setting for female networks that were sustained on a daily or weekly basis. Replicated kinship networks within those villages were especially important in the maintenance of relationships between women.

By the end of the century, land shortages, mortgages with outside lending agencies, a burgeoning farm economy, and increasing urbanization began to threaten these traditional lives in Cub Creek and the East Reserve. However, there were signs that a strong ideological commitment to the agrarian household by a majority of the children of the Kleine Gemeinde Mennonite immigrants would ensure the continuation of these lifestyles into the twentieth century. When urbanization encroached on the family farms, colonization projects led to the migration of 25 per cent of the East Reserve and 50 per cent of Cub Creek families to Alberta and Kansas. This outmigration relieved the population pressures in the old settlements and allowed the vast majority of Kleine Gemeinde descendants to continue an agrarian existence.[94] Thus, in the majority of Kleine Gemeinde Mennonite communities, the rural household was reproduced; the farm family continued to supply most of the household's labour, consume most of its products, and shape the manner in which resources were transferred from one generation to another.[95]

Within their farm households, the first generation of women in the East Reserve and Cub Creek were to experience few challenges to an established way of life. Women's work roles in the farmyard, their identification with the economic activities of their husbands, their relationships with women in their kin groups, and their children, who were a crucial part of the household strategy, were the components of a world in which these rural farm women were to maintain important degrees of status and power. Their children, their cows, their men, and their sisters were the central features of the transplanted worlds of immigrant Mennonite women.

NOTES

I wish to thank Professors Kathy Jones, Mary Kinnear, Gerald Friesen, John Thompson, James Curry, and Morris Mott, who commented on earlier versions of this article. I am also grateful for the comments of the CHR reviewers.

1. Dave K. Schellenberg, Steinbach, MB, Gerhard E. Kornelson Papers (GEK), Maria Kornelson Ens to Gerhard Kornelson, 1 May 1881. The East Reserve was an eight-township land bloc set aside by the Canadian government in 1873 for the exclusive settlement of Mennonites from Russia. It was located thirty-five miles southeast of Winnipeg. In 1883 the reserve became the Hanover Municipality and in the 1890s it was opened up for settlement by other ethnic groups. Cub Creek Township, located sixty miles southwest of Lincoln, Nebraska, was a land bloc owned by the Burlington and Missouri River Railroad Company until 1874, when Mennonites and other German-Americans purchased the land.

2. The three Kleine Gemeinde townships were centred around the villages of Steinbach, Blumenort, and Gruenfeld (Kleefeld). For confessional histories of the Mennonites in North America between 1874 and 1900 see Frank Epp, *Mennonites in Canada: The History of a Separate People, 1786–1920*, vol. 1 (Toronto 1974); and Theron Schlabach, *Peace, Faith, Nation: Mennonites and Amish in Nineteenth-Century America* (Scottdale, PA 1988). For specific works dealing with the Kleine Gemeinde Mennonites see Delbert Plett, *The Golden Years: The Mennonite Kleine Gemeinde in Russia, 1812–1849* (Steinbach 1985), *Storm and Triumph: The Mennonite Kleine Gemeinde, 1850–1874* (Steinbach 1986); and Henry Fast, "The Kleine Gemeinde in the United States, 1874–1943," in D. Plett, ed., *Profiles of the Kleine Gemeinde, 1874* (Steinbach 1989), 87–140.

3. The Kleine Gemeinde Mennonite migrants, numbering only about 900 people, were a minority among the 10,000 Mennonites from Russia who settled in Kansas and neighbouring states during the 1870s and the 8000 Mennonites who came to Manitoba. The Kleine Gemeinde were, however, a representative group of the conservative Mennonites who migrated to North America after new military service laws were announced in Russia. Some 32,000 Mennonites remained in Russia.

4. Despite the Mennonites' "group migration" and the importance of the religious congregation in their society, the primary social unit of the Mennonites was the household, the chief unit of production and residence of the domestic group, with close emotional ties to other households within the wider kinship group. The Mennonite domestic group at this point in history was primarily a nuclear or simple family that could be supplemented at various points in its developmental cycle by extra unmarried orphan children, unrelated servants, widowed relatives, or married sons or daughters and their spouses requesting a temporary place of residence. The domestic unit could thus vary in size: from two members when the married couple first established their own household or when they reached old age, to four to seven members when the first children were born and a servant was employed, to ten to fifteen members when the couple reached middle age and their

unmarried and married children and a widowed relative all lived with them. The unit was smaller than stem or extended families in which several generations of married spouses and their children lived together at all times, and which practised impartible inheritance. For theoretical studies of the household, family, and kinship group see Martine Segalen, *Historical Anthropology of the Family* (New York 1986), 13ff; Alan Barnard and Anthony Good, *Research Practices in the Study of Kinship* (London 1984), 79ff; Richard R. Wilk and Robert McC. Netting, "Households: Changing Forms and Functions," in R. Netting et al., eds., *Households: Comparative and Historical Studies of the Domestic Group* (Berkeley 1984), 1–28; and Jack Goody, "The Evolution of the Family," in P. Laslett, ed., *Households and Family in Past Time* (Cambridge 1972), 103–24.

5. Ester Boserup, *Woman's Role in Economic Development* (New York 1970).

6. Harriet Friedmann, "Household Production and the National Economy: Concepts for the Analysis of Agrarian Formations," *Journal of Peasant Studies* 8 (1980): 158–84; "Simple Commodity Production and Wage Labor in the American Plains," *Journal of Peasant Studies* 6 (1978): 71–100; "World Market, State and Family Farm: The Social Bases of Household Production in the Era of Wage Labour," *Comparative Studies in Society and History* 4 (1978): 545–86.

7. Kathleen Conzen, "Peasant Pioneers: Generational Succession among German Farmers in Frontier Minnesota," in S. Hahn and J. Prude, eds., *The Countryside in the Age of Capitalist Transformation* (Chapel Hill, NC 1985), 259–92; for a description of the household mode of production from another period see James Henretta, "Families and Farms: 'Mentalité' in Pre-Industrial America," *William and Mary Quarterly*, 35 (1978), 3–32.

8. Veronica Strong-Boag, "'Pulling in Double Harness or Hauling a Double Load': Women, Work and Feminism," *Journal of Canadian Studies* 21 (1986): 32–52; Mary Kinnear, "'Do You Want Your Daughter to Marry a Farmer?' Women's Work on the Farm, 1922," *Canadian Papers in Rural History* 6 (1988): 137–53; Sara Brooks Sunberg, "Farm Women on the Canadian Prairie Frontier: The Helpmate Image," in V. Strong-Boag and A. Clair Fellman, eds., *Rethinking Canada: The Promise of Women's History* (Toronto 1986): 95–106; Cornelia Butler Flora and Jan L. Flora, "Structure of Agriculture and Women's Culture in the Great Plains," *Great Plains Quarterly* 8 (1988): 195–206; Joan M. Jensen, "'You May Depend She Does Not Eat Much Idle Bread': Mid-Atlantic Farm Women and Their Historians," *Agricultural History* 61 (1987): 29–46. These studies could be contrasted to earlier studies such as Rosemary Ball, "'A Perfect Farmer's Wife': Women in 19th Century Rural Ontario," *Canada: An Historical Magazine* 3 (1975): 3–21, which concludes that "domesticity and dependence were the essential qualities of women in rural, nineteenth-century Ontario."

9. Mary Bouquet, "Production and Reproduction of Family Farms in Southwest England," *Sociologia Ruralis* 30 (1990): 227–44; Ernestine Friedl, "The Position of Women: Appearance and Reality," *Anthropological Quarterly* 40 (1967): 97–108; Robert Lee, "Family and 'Modernization': The Peasant Family and Social Change in Nineteenth-Century Bavaria," in R. Evans and W. Lee, eds., *The German Family* (London 1981), 84–119.

10. Martine Segalen, *Love and Power in the Peasant Family: Rural France in the Nineteenth Century*, trans. S. Matthews (Chicago 1983).

11. Ibid., 53, 63, 72, and 75.

12. Jon Gjerde, *From Peasants to Farmers: The Migration from Balestrand, Norway to the Upper Middle West* (Cambridge 1985), 222ff; Paul Voisey, *Vulcan: The Making of a Prairie Community* (Toronto 1988), 27, 95–96; Marjorie Griffin Cohen, "The Decline of Women in Canadian Dairying," *Histoire Sociale/Social History* 17 (1984): 307–34.

13. James Urry, *None but Saints: The Transformation of Mennonite Life in Russia, 1789–1889* (Winnipeg 1989); David Rempel, "The Mennonite Colonies in New Russia: A Study of Their Settlement and Economic Development from 1789–1914" (Ph.D. dissertation, Stanford University 1933).

14. Boserup, *Woman's Role*, 66, suggests this pattern occurred when men of "plough cultures" hired women farm labourers from other cultures.

15. Manitoba Department of Mines and Natural Resources, Winnipeg, Homestead Patent Applications, 7-6E, 6-6E, 5-6E, 6-1E, 5-1E, allows for a survey of thirty-six houses built between 1874 and 1879 in Manitoba settlements and indicates that early houses had an average living area of 676 square feet. Similar evidence for the construction of roomy houses in the Cub Creek settlement can be found in a letter to the *Chicago Daily Tribune* in January 1875 in which Cornelius Jansen notes that the Cub Creek Kleine Gemeinde have gone "to work to erect buildings, and by this time [they are all sheltered] in their own comfortable houses." Clarence Hiebert, ed., *Brothers in Deed to Brothers in Need: A Scrapbook about Mennonite Immigrants from Russia, 1870–1885* (Newton, KS 1974), 205.

16. GEK, Maria Ens to Gerhard Kornelson, 4 Feb. 1884.

17. Mennonite Heritage Centre (MHC), Winnipeg, David Klassen Papers, Aganetha Brandt Klassen to anon., 23 March 1892.

18. John K. Loewen Papers (JKL), C.J. Loewen family, Giroux, MB, Jacob Klassen to Johann Janzen, 29 Dec. 1881.

19. Evangelical Mennonite Conference Archives, Steinbach (EMCA), box 36, East Reserve Kleine Gemeinde Seelenliste, 1894–1903; *Mennonitische Rundschau*, 7 Jan. 1903 and 1 Jan. 1904; Helmut Huebert, *Hierschau: An Example of Russian Mennonite Life* (Winnipeg 1986), 72.

20. Rural Municipality of Hanover, Steinbach (RMH), Hanover Tax Assessment Roll, 7-6E, 6-6E,

5-6E, 1898; Nebraska State Historical Society, Lincoln (NSHS), Population Census, Cub Creek, Jefferson County, 1900.

21. These statistics derived from Peter Toews, "Genealogy Register of Kleine Gemeinde Migrants, 1879," in Plett, ed., *Profiles of the Kleine Gemeinde, 1874*, 5-59; NSHS, Population Census, Cub Creek Precinct, Jefferson County, Nebraska, 1900; Provincial Archives of Manitoba, Winnipeg (PAM), Population Census, La Verendrye, Manitoba, 1891.

22. See family genealogies of extended Kleine Gemeinde Mennonite families at EMCA and Steinbach Bible College, Steinbach.

23. EMCA, Abram R. Reimer, "Tagebuch, 1870-1873, 1879-1888," 28 May and 4 June 1879, 26 Sept. 1888.

24. JKL, Isaak Loewen to Peter Loewen, 11 June 1877.

25. Cornelius Loewen paid $1.25 a week in 1876. Loewen, "Tagebuch," 1 Aug. 1876. Klaas Reimer paid $4.60 a week in 1884. P.J. Reimer, Steinbach, Klaas R. Reimer, "Memoirs, 1857-1890," trans. P.U. Dueck.

26. EMCA, John C. Reimer Papers, Cornelius B. Loewen, "Rechnungsbuch," April and Oct. 1891. Another example of this disparity dates from August 1883 when Maria Friesen, a forty-year-old spinster from the East Reserve, hired her neighbour, Gerhard Kornelson, to haul five loads of hay for her cow and paid him $1.00 a day for his labour. In return she washed for the Kornelson household for 40 cents a day. See GEK, Kornelson, "Tagebuch, 1882-1900," Aug. 1883.

27. Gerhard Reimer, Goshen, IN, Peter R. Reimer, "Tagebuch, 1892"; Kornelson, "Tagebuch." For other allusions to women receiving 40 cents a day while men received $1.00 a day see Mennonite Heritage Village Archives, Steinbach (MHVA), Cornelius Loewen, "Tagebuch, 1863-1892," 5 Oct. 1883; MHVA, Heinrich W. Reimer, "Rechnungsbuch, 1890-1930," 28 July 1890.

28. Quoted in E.K. Francis, *In Search of Utopia* (Winnipeg 1955), 77.

29. Boserup, *Woman's Role*, 53. See also Segalen, *Love and Marriage*, 181; Bouquet, "Production and Reproduction," 239.

30. EMCA, boxes 4 and 29, Abram R. Friesen, "Tagebuch, 1870-1873, 1876-1884."

31. GEK, Jacob Ens to Gerhard Kornelson, 4 Feb. 1884.

32. EMCA, unfiled, Johann Dueck, "Diary, 1887-1892," trans. John Wohlgemuth.

33. Kornelson, "Tagebuch," 13 Oct. 1884 and 12 Oct. 1885. A further example of these gender roles appears in an 1886 letter; when twenty-eight-year-old Margaretha Reimer of Cub Creek contemplated a relocation to Manitoba she was assured there would be work for her but she "need not work in the fields." P.J. Reimer Steinbach, MB, Klaas R. Reimer Papers, Klaas Reimer to Margaretha Reimer, nd [1886].

34. Gjerde, *From Peasants to Farmers*, 203.

35. Hans Medick, "The Proto-Industrial Family Economy: The Structural Function of Household and Family during the Transition from Peasant Society to Industrial Capitalism," *Social History* 3 (1976): 302.

36. Julia Erickson and Gary Klein, "Women's Roles and Family Production among Old Order Amish," *Rural Sociology* 47 (1981): 293.

37. JKL, Sarah Janzen Friesen to Johann Janzen, 23 June 1877.

38. Kornelson, "Tagebuch."

39. PAM, N47, E.K. Francis, "In Search of Utopia" (unpublished draft).

40. Kornelson, "Tagebuch"; Loewen, "Tagebuch"; A.R. Friesen, "Tagebuch," 24 Sept. 1883; A. Reimer, "Tagebuch," 1 Sept. 1880; A.M. Friesen, "Tagebuch," 26 Aug. and 1 Dec. 1884.

41. JKL, Ens to Janzen, 1 May 1881.

42. NSHS, Agricultural Census, Cub Creek, 1880 and 1885.

43. The percentage of acres dedicated to wheat in Cub Creek shrank from 50 per cent in 1880 to 19 per cent in 1890, while corn increased from 9 per cent of cropland to 51 per cent. In Manitoba, individual farmers who had concentrated up to 59 per cent of their cropland to wheat in the late 1870s turned to oats during the 1880s, a crop closely associated with cattle production. NSHS, Agricultural Census; A. Reimer, "Tagebuch," June 1879; Martyn Bowden, "Changes in Land Use in Jefferson County, Nebraska, 1857-1957" (M.A. thesis, Nebraska University 1959), 81; John Warkentin, "Mennonite Settlements in Southern Manitoba: A Study in Historical Geography" (Ph.D. dissertation, York University 1960), 181 and 182; Royden Loewen, "Ethnic Farmers and the Outside World," *Journal of the Canadian Historical Association* 1 (1990): 195-214.

44. RMH Tax Rolls, Hanover, NSHS, Agricultural Census, Cub Creek, 1880 and 1885.

45. Griffin Cohen, "Decline of Women in Canadian Dairying," 334.

46. As late as 1919 Maria Reimer Unger of Blumenort, Manitoba, regularly recorded the birth of calves in her diary, noting the event as the cow's "milk renewal," the time that the cow became "frisch milch." See Peter U. Dueck, Steinbach, Maria Reimer Unger, "Tagebuch, 1919." Also see EMCA, box 152, interviews with Sara Reimer Kroeker, 9 Dec. 1983; Anna Baerg Penner, 22 Dec. 1983; Margaret Siemens Reimer, 23 Dec. 1983.

47. MHVA, H.W. Reimer, "Rechnungsbuch, 1890-1930."

48. Lenore Eidse, ed., *Furrows in the Valley: Rural Municipality of Morris, Manitoba: 1880-1980* (Morris 1980), 454.

49. For a survey of the bilateral impartible inheritance system in different parts of Europe see Walter Goldschmidt and Evelyn Jacobson Kunkel, "The Structure of the Peasant Family," *American Anthropologist* 73 (1971): 1058-70. For a note on the thirteenth-century Flemish origin of this practice

see E.K. Francis, "Mennonite Institutions in Early Manitoba: A Study of Their Origins," *Agricultural History* 22 (1948): 144-55.

50. Flora and Flora, "Women's Culture," 201.

51. MHC, "Teilungs Verordnung von der Molotschna, 1857"; EMCA, *Teilungs Verordnung von der Molotschna aus Russland eingewanderten Mennoniten Gemeinden in Manitoba* (Winnipeg 1902).

52. Jefferson County Courthouse (JCCH), Fairbury, NE, Land Plat of Cub Creek, 3-3E, 1900.

53. JCCH, Numerical Index, Lands, Jefferson County, 1870-c.1930.

54. Boserup, *Woman's Role*, 53ff.

55. Sonya Salamon and Ann Mckey Keim, "Land Ownership and Women's Power in a Midwestern Farming Community," *Journal of Marriage and the Family* 41 (1979): 109-119; Ernestine Friedl, "The Position of Women: Appearance and Reality," *Anthropological Quarterly* 40 (1967): 97-108.

56. Fast, "Kleine Gemeinde," 107, 110, and 102.

57. *Mennonitische Rundschau*, 20 July 1904; JCCH, Land Plat, 1900; JCCH, Numerical Index, 1870-c.1920, Cub Creek Precinct; NSHS, Population Census, Cub Creek Precinct, 1880 and 1900; Elizabeth Classen Rempel, *Genealogy of the Descendants of Jacob Klassen, 1792* (North Newton, KS 1971).

58. JKL, Cornelius and Maria Friesen to Johann Janzen, 16 March 1896. Ironically, Jacob, the eldest of the Klassen sons, received his wherewithal to begin farming in 1881, shortly after marrying Maria Thiessen, the daughter of one of the wealthiest men in Cub Creek. In a letter in 1881, Jacob Klassen Sr. noted that his son was "living with [his wife's] parents" and that the young couple was planning to establish their own farm shortly as they were anticipating receiving "part of the acreage [from her parents] this summer." JKL, Johann Klassen to Johann Janzen, 29 Dec. 1881.

59. These statistics are derived from the biographical sketches in Royden Loewen, *Blumenort: A Mennonite Community in Transition* (Blumenort, MB 1983), 265-324. Blumenort's five satellite settlements are Blumenhof, Neuanlage, Greenland, De Krim, and Schwagershof. Patrilocality accounted for thirty-three household formations and nine formations involved a husband and wife hailing from the same village. For examples of matrilocality in other villages see John R. Dueck et al., *Descendants of Jacob and Maria L. Dueck, 1839-1986* (Steinbach 1986), 71; Gertrude Klassen, ed., *The Family Book of David and Aganetha Klassen, 1813-1900* (Rosenort, MB 1974), 342.

60. Peter Reimer, "Tagebuch," 16 Dec. 1892.

61. Dietrich Dueck, Spanish Lookout, Belize, CA, Abram L. Dueck Papers (ALD), Abram L. Dueck to Isaac Friesen, nd [1883].

62. EMCA, box 126, "Kleine Gemeinde Rechnungsbuch, 1847-1883." Widow Plett deposited $600 and Widow Johann Loewen deposited $336.65. This combined sum amounted to 38 per cent of the $2500 capital pool in the church fund.

63. Kornelson, "Tagebuch," 6 June 1889.

64. MHC, David Klassen Papers, 38, Aganetha Brandt Klassen, "Tagebuch," Aug. 1901.

65. Kornelson, "Tagebuch," March 1890. In 1889, five of twenty-two guests were women. Ibid., 3 March 1890.

66. For a discussion of farm women in the public domain in Canada see Strong-Boag, "Pulling in Double Harness"; Jeffery Taylor, "Dominant and Popular Ideologies in the Making of Farm Women in Early Twentieth Century Manitoba," presented to the Canadian Historical Association, University of Prince Edward Island, May 1992.

67. Fred Stafford, "Jefferson County and Fairbury, Nebraska" (M.A. thesis, University of Nebraska 1948), 109.

68. *Mennonitische Rundschau*, 23 Sept. 1903; "Bruderthaler Protokollbuch, 1908."

69. For one analysis of the role midwives played in maintaining the boundaries of ethnic communities see Charlotte Borst, "Wisconsin's Midwives Are Working Women: Immigrant Midwives and the Limits of Traditional Occupation, 1870-1920," *Journal of American Ethnic History* 9 (1989): 24-59.

70. Eidse, *Furrows*, 328 and 458. See also EMCA, box 152, interview with Sara Reimer Kroeker, Steinbach, Manitoba, 29 Dec. 1983; Loewen, *Blumenort*, 219; EMCA, box 137, Anna Toews, "Midwife Records, 1893-1932"; Peter J.B. Reimer and David Reimer, eds., *The Sesquicentennial Jubilee: Evangelical Mennonite Conference, 1812-1962* (Steinbach 1962), 35.

71. ALD, Abram Dueck to Peter Rempel, 15 Feb. and 15 Dec. 1884; Henry Friesen, Greenland, MB, Abram M. Friesen, "Tagebuch, 1884-1908," 4 April 1892.

72. A.M. Friesen, "Tagebuch," 15 May 1892.

73. Kornelson, "Tagebuch."

74. *Mennonitische Rundschau*, 3 July 1890. For a parallel account of legally barring female lay doctors by university trained male doctors see Barbara Ehrenreich and Deidre English, *Witches, Midwives and Nurses: A History of Women Healers* (New York 1971), 17ff.

75. Kathleen Storrie, ed., *Isolation and Bonding: The Ecology of Gender* (Toronto 1987); Voisey, *Vulcan*, 31ff; Kinnear, "Do You Want Your Daughter to Marry a Farmer?" 150.

76. Virginia Yans McLaughlin, "Patterns of Work and Family Organization: Buffalo's Italians," *Journal of Interdisciplinary History* 2 (1971): 299-314; J.E. Smith, "Our Own Kind: Family and Community Networks in Providence," *Radical History Review* 17 (1978): 99-120; Corinne Azen Krause, "Urbanization without Breakdown: Italian, Jewish and Slavic Immigrant Women in Pittsburgh," *Journal of Urban History* (1978): 291-306.

77. A. Reimer, "Tagebuch."

78. Kornelson, "Tagebuch," 23 and 24 Jan. 1885.

79. Dueck, "Tagebuch."

80. JKL, Katherina Klassen to Isaak W. Loewens, 1 Feb. 1877.

81. Bernard P. Loewen, Cuauhtemoc, Mexico, Isaak J. Loewen to Elisabeth Penner Loewen, 5 and 19 Oct. 1890; Elisabeth Loewen to Isaak Loewen, nd.

82. EMCA, box 93, Jacob Regehr, "Tagebuch, 1894–1898."

83. A.M. Friesen, "Tagebuch," 17 July 1884.

84. ALD, Abram Dueck to Bernard Dueck, 22 Jan. 1896.

85. ALD, Abram Dueck to Jacob Kroeker, 6 July 1883.

86 MHC, David Klassen Papers, Aganetha Brandt Klassen to anon., Tiegenhoff, Prussia, 1888.

87. JKL, Jacob Klassen to "Liebe Geschwister," 18 Sept. 1890. A similar sentiment is recorded in 1885 at the death of the wife of merchant Klaas Reimer of the East Reserve; Reimer recalled that "it was very hard for me, this parting: but what can one do? . . . So I was left behind with 14 children in this world full of grief and sorrow." Reimer, "Denkschrift," 11.

88. John C. Reimer, ed., Familienregister der Nachkommen von Klaas und Helena Reimer (Steinbach 1958), 170.

89. Both sets of letters are addressed to Johann Janzen, Giroux.

90. JKL, Anna Ratzlaff to Johann Janzen.

91. JKL, Elisabeth Loewen to Peter and Anna Loewen.

92. JKL, Margaretha Friesen to Johann Janzen, 12 June 1893.

93. Ibid., 24 July 1893.

94. Klassen, David Klassen, 15; Meade County Historical Society, Pioneer Stories of Meade County (Meade, KS 1985), 144.

95. For a full three-generational study of the Kleine Gemeinde Mennonites see Royden Loewen, Family, Church, and Market: A Mennonite Community in the Old and New Worlds, 1850–1930 (Toronto: University of Toronto Press, 1993).

Sweated Labour: Female Needleworkers in Industrializing Canada

ROBERT McINTOSH

There are "scores, hundreds, of women in this city whose only means of subsistence is by their needle. They are paid starvation wages, viz., 6 cents each for making shirts, 17 cents for making and pressing pants, 75 cents for coat and vest, etc. In the words of a skeleton living on Maitland St. with a sick girl: 'I have to work with my needle until midnight to earn the money to buy bread for tomorrow. And this is my hard experience every day of the week, and every week of the year.'"[1]

The clothing industry emerged gradually in Canada during the 19th century, as the site of production shifted from the household (for use) to larger-scale manufacture for the market. By the end of the century, the industry was one of the largest employers in manufacturing in industrial centres such as Montréal, Toronto, and Hamilton, and remained so until well into this century.[2] Unlike most contemporary manufacturing industries, the clothing trades were a major source of wage labour for women, who typically accounted for 70 to 80 per cent of all needleworkers.[3] While the clothing industry extended across the country, it

SOURCE: Robert McIntosh, "Sweated Labour: Female Needleworkers in Industrializing Canada," Labour/Le Travail 32 (Fall 1993), 105–138. Reprinted with the permission of the editor of Labour/ Le Travail. © Committee on Canadian Labour History.

was based in central Canada. By 1901 at least 7500 women in Ontario and nearly 9000 in Québec worked in their homes at garment manufacture. Many more, including more than 5500 in Ontario and nearly 1800 in Québec, worked in small contract shops.[4]

Rife with sweating by the close of the 19th century, the garment trades exhibited some of the most deplorable working conditions faced by any worker.[5] An analysis centred on the operation of the capitalist system helps to account for the grossly depressed labour standards, interminable hours of work, and wretched pay within the garment trades. It cannot explain why sweated needleworkers were overwhelmingly female.

Jacques Ferland argued recently that "labour history has all too often neglected [the] wedding of capitalist oppression and patriarchal domination."[6] The terms and conditions of this wedding warrant close scrutiny. Capitalist society emerged within an existing patriarchal context, "a set of social structures and practices in which men dominate, oppress, and exploit women."[7] Capitalism and patriarchy, analytically distinct, interacted in complex, manifold, and frequently contradictory ways. Capitalist social relations adapted, used, and exploited — but never subsumed — patriarchal attitudes and practices.[8]

Historical narrative details this interaction. Women's subordinate role within the traditional household, whereby they assisted and supplemented the work of men, made them, in the context of industrial capitalist growth, of ready use to employers in search of cheaper, easily victimized, workers.[9] The initial disadvantage women faced was compounded by discrimination on the part of trade unions, which sought for decades to restrict or exclude women's wage labour as part of the struggle for the male breadwinner wage.[10]

If the interrelation between class and gender provided the context in which female sweated labour emerged, it also shaped responses to sweating. At one level, seamstresses who sweated at home were inoffensive to patriarchal norms. These women did not desert home duties and children by taking on wage labour outside the home, nor did they steal "men's" jobs. They did not toil at "rough work in hot sweaty environments in close physical proximity to unrelated men."[11]

Eventually, however, the pervasiveness of sweating came to be unsettling to patriarchal standards. Female sweating jeopardized male incomes in the clothing trades, and for this reason drew the hostility of men as wage-earners. The profound degradation associated with sweated labour threatened women's ability to perform their designated duties as homemakers and mothers. Evidence linking sweating with the emergence of slums became clearer and stronger. Chronic occupational diseases undermined women's capacity to function as mothers. The sweated trades exploited the labour of many children. Extremely poor pay, in tandem with the demoralization and degradation associated with sweating, led to the seamstress's close ties with the prostitute.[12]

Patriarchal unease intersected with concerns to mute the most destructive aspects of the capitalist system. Sweating revealed starkly how terribly damaging unchecked market forces could be. On this question a coincidence of interests emerged toward the end of the 19th century. The liberal state, concerned to "legitimize" the system, took steps to mute its most destructive aspects. On this point trade unions, on behalf of the interests of their working-class constituents, lent their support. Likewise, private and organized philanthropy, moved by humanitarian impulses, struggled to secure the legislation which some hoped would maintain what they viewed as the essential elements of their society.[13]

Consensus formed most readily concerning women. Patriarchal arguments regarding women's role and place resonated with capitalist concerns to perpetuate by timely reforms a class-based, market-driven society. If society was to be saved, reform had to begin with women.[14]

The Rise of Sweating

The integrity of the traditional clothing trades had been maintained by means of formal apprenticeships. Apprentices, while subject particularly at the outset of their period of indenture to menial tasks, generally were initiated into all aspects of clothing manufacture, including the measuring and cutting of cloth, sewing, and the pressing of the completed garment.[15]

By the 1820s and 1830s, expanding markets owing to urban growth, immigration, and improved transportation (with the construction of canals, railways, and roads) brought traditional clothing manufacture under pressure.[16] Traditional garment manufacture had been largely custom-work. Clothing was made to measure, manufactured on the premises, under the supervision of the master tradesman and retailed directly to the public. Increasingly, particularly in men's clothing, there was a shift from custom to readymade production, where relatively large allotments of clothing were made in standardized sizes.[17]

During this time, certain merchant tailors and dressmakers accumulated more capital, secured access to credit, left manual labour and hired a foreman to oversee production. They began to reorganize production within their workplace. Conditions of labour deteriorated. The emergence of sweating was part and parcel of the destruction of the traditional clothing trades. Detailed research has been conducted on Montréal, the major centre for clothing manufacture in Canada throughout most of the 19th century. There, large master tailors sought to exploit expanding markets through the extension of the division of labour. As a first step, they began to take on many more than the customary one or two apprentices. Subsequently, the traditional rounded apprenticeship was compromised as, in the interest of increasing production, boys were instructed in simply one branch of clothing manufacture. The consequences of these new divisions of labour were evident even among journeymen. Because foremen took responsibility for the most demanding task of measuring and cutting cloth, journeymen tailors increasingly were called on simply to sew. The paternal aspects of the traditional craft also declined: by 1835 journeymen no longer were benefiting from the provision of room and board in the home of their masters. At the same time, employment conditions worsened: year-long contracts were giving way to shorter terms, even to payment by piece. This enabled master tailors to lay off journeymen during slack times. Finally, larger capital requirements in clothing manufacture (tied up chiefly in cloth and readymade goods) made the path to master increasingly difficult for journeymen.[18]

From in-house division of labour it was a small step to putting out parts of the work to homes (and later, to contract shops). Because most women had experience with the needle, they were brought into the clothing trades, in competition with male garment workers, by the master tailor or contractor. They were not in a position to command the pay or labour standards of journeymen: this of course encouraged their use.[19]

By the middle of the 19th century a second group had emerged as large manufacturers of readymade garments: clothing and drygoods importers, wholesalers and retailers. While they had no experience of artisanal production of clothing, they possessed the capital to profit by expanding markets for ready-made clothing.[20] Moss Brothers exemplifies this second group of clothing manufacturers. They first entered the garment business in 1836, as importers of clothing. By 1856, they employed 800 men and women in Montréal.[21] Many other merchants followed this path. In 1888, it was observed that virtually no drygoods merchant in Montréal was without a workshop attached to his business.[22]

During the last half of the 19th century, a wide range of garment businesses developed. Economies in garment production were not achieved through the consolidation of machinery and labour; indeed, they were achieved through their dispersal. The industry was characterized by an increasingly advanced subdivision of labour which was often associated with extensive subcontracting. This practice had clear benefits for employers. Contractors could be dropped or underemployed as convenient. Competition among contractors exerted downward pressure on the prices they charged. Subcontracting enabled wholesale manufacturers to avoid the expense of recruiting and supervising workers. Both wholesale manufacturers and contractors were able to pass on to homeworkers many costs of production, including workspace, light, fuel, sewing machines, needles, and thread. Homework also permitted the circumvention of rudimentary state regulation of industrial standards.[23] Large manufacturers like Hollis Shorey claimed ignorance of the working conditions of these outworkers, even of the numbers employed.[24]

A handful of large wholesalers and manufacturers struggled successfully to control large portions of the market. In the middle, a variety of contract shops emerged. Some contractors were relatively large, employed one or two dozen people, and specialized in certain kinds of work; they were often intermediaries between wholesalers and homeworkers. Other contractors were themselves poverty-stricken, worked out of their homes, and employed in addition to family members one or two girls from the neighbourhood. At the other extreme was the woman who laboured individually, perhaps occasionally hiring a neighbourhood girl to assist her as she struggled to meet deadlines on small consignments of clothing.

By 1900, the largest clothing manufacturers employed well over one thousand workers. Of those, only a small portion were on the manufacturer's payroll. "Inside" workers, as they were called, were employed in two (often conjoint) places: in showrooms where a small number of highly skilled tailors designed clothing and cut cloth to pattern; and in warehouses, where foremen gave out cloth to outworkers, where they inspected the completed sewing, where "trimmers" finished certain lines of goods (by hemming, for instance, by correcting mistakes, or sometimes simply by cutting off loose threads), and where pressers ironed the completed garment. In these warehouses, too, large quantities of garments were stored before shipment out. Outside workers were largely on the payroll of a subcontractor (a term used interchangeably with contractor) or working on their own account.[25]

The Sweating System

The term "sweating" was introduced in Britain in the 1840s to describe the deteriorating working conditions skilled tailors had faced since the 1830s. It originally referred to the taking home of work by skilled tailors seeking to cope with falling prices, but it soon came to encompass a range of abuses including poor working conditions, irregular work and seasonal layoffs. The expression was subsequently popularized by concerned publications like the *Morning Chronicle* and *Punch*.[26]

Sweating was soon introduced to British North America where, we have seen, the labour standards of the artisanal workshop in Montréal were already under pressure. By 1852 Hamilton tailors too were cursing "the ill omened practice of sweating," which they defined as efforts by master tailors to "procure the utmost of labour from journeymen tailors for the smallest possible remuneration."[27] The growth of outwork and subcontracting in the late 1800s produced two new categories of sweated workers: those in small contractors' shops and those who laboured at home. In practice, there was little to choose between the two: the distinction between a shop and a home often was slight. These new categories of sweated workers, unlike the tailors who first faced the problem, consisted largely of women and girls.[28]

The sweating system, acknowledged the tailor and trade unionist Louis Gurofsky at the end of the 19th century, "work[ed] like machinery."[29] Clothing manufacturers decided to produce a line of clothing on their own account or obtained contracts from wholesalers, retailers, or the government. The cloth was bought wholesale. Designs were produced in the manufacturer's shop. Subcontracts were let. Often, responsibility for garment design and the letting of contracts was combined in the person of the shop foreman. The cutting of the cloth, button-sewing and buttonhole-making, the finishing of the garment (including pressing) might be let or done in-house, depending on the capacities of the manufacturer. Most sewing was done as outwork. It was let either to contractors or directly to women in their homes.[30]

Mackenzie King described in 1898 how some of the largest garment contracts of his day, government orders for military and Post Office uniforms, were filled. These garments were never manufactured "entirely upon the premises of the firms which were awarded the work." While all such firms cut the cloth, made buttonholes, and (often) put on buttons (the latter two jobs were done at trifling cost by machines tended by boys), most work was done off the premises by resort to one of three kinds of subcontract.[31]

The cut cloth might be sent to a contractor's shop, to a contractor's residence where workers were employed, or directly to an individual who laboured at home with the assistance of family members only (and sometimes one or two girls or young women from the neighbourhood). A hierarchy of skills was recognized. Needlework considered less skilled (where a minimum of fit was required) — trousers, vests, greatcoats — was consigned to homeworkers. Work which was deemed to call for greater skill — superior tunics, riding breeches — was sent to contractors' shops.[32]

Contractors proliferated. The barriers to entry were very low: the contractor simply needed access to clothing contracts on the one hand and to a pool of needleworkers on the other. One Ontario factory inspector wrote in 1897:

> The greatest tendency in the clothing trade appears to be against the establishment of large, sanitary workshops. The employers who own the present ones complain of their hands leaving them and taking rooms as workshops, and taking clothing to make at a lower price. The facilities offered for the hire of sewing machines and other necessary tools are so easy that a workman starting without any capital becomes an employer in the space of a week or two.[33]

Interaction between the custom and readymade sectors was not unknown: seasonal lulls in the custom trade often led custom shops to contract for readymade work.[34] Journeyman tailors, ordinarily employed in custom shops, did not scruple during the slack season to work for readymade manufacturers on their own account. Many skilled tailors displaced from custom work permanently joined the ranks of contractors.[35]

Immigrants were often found among clothing contractors. By the end of the 19th century they were often Jews, with some experience of the garment trades in the Old World.[36] The ranks of contractors included women, who might rise from individual homework to employ a number of other needleworkers.

Intense competition among contractors pushed prices down. "One contractor makes war upon the others, and the demand for cheapness is not satisfied," explained Ontario factory inspector Margaret Carlyle in 1897. "It has been told me by a contractor that they are compelled to accept the prices offered by the wholesalers; if they do not take it someone else would."[37] Contracting was both volatile and precarious: shops moved constantly, as the business changed owners or as contractors simply sought "to install themselves as cheaply as possible."[38] The ease of entry into subcontracting encouraged fly-by-night contractors and a range of associated abuses.[39] In many instances, Mackenzie King pointed out, contractors were nearly as miserable as those they employed.[40]

Lower prices, given the labour-intensiveness of clothing manufacture, necessarily meant downward pressure on wages and working conditions. "The contractor's principal concern is the cost of his labour, since he neither buys materials nor sells completed garments," explained F.R. Scott and H.M. Cassidy in 1935. "Consequently competition between contractors becomes almost entirely a question of competition in forcing down labour standards."[41]

The downward pressure on wages as a consequence of subcontracting was inexorable. Contractor underbid contractor, and, as Toronto's Mayor W.H. Howland explained to the Labour Commission in 1888, homeworker undercut homeworker.

> A sewing woman is taking shirts to make, for example, and getting so much for them. She goes in the establishment and says, "I want you to give me some work." She is told that they have plenty of workers and that they must keep their own people going; however after some conversation she asks what price they will give and they arrange to send her a lot at such a price a lower price than they have been paying. It is human nature and business nature for that to be done and it is undoubtedly done and the result is that when the regular worker comes in she has to take that price or she will not get the work.[42]

Falling wages, and persistently increasing working hours, produced a relentless probing of the limits of subsistence. "The political economists who base their calculations upon the living wage, that is to say, the smallest sum upon which human life can be sustained," wrote a late Victorian journalist, "would be surprised to find how small that sum may be."[43]

Accompanying the growth of the readymade clothing industry were increasing divisions of labour. These were of two kinds. The first respected traditional divisions of labour within the clothing trades, of which the most significant was the distinction between men's and women's wear. These divisions could be broken down further: customary subdivisions within the former included pantmaking, shirtmaking, collarmaking and coatmaking. Within women's wear, these included dressmaking and coatmaking. These traditional subdivisions were respected by contractors who, as A.W. Wright reported in 1896, usually "confine[d] themselves as far as practicable to the making of some particular kind of garment, coats, trousers, vests, mantles or overcoats for example."[44] Contractors might further specialize in a particular *quality* of clothing.

The extension of readymade production led to new divisions of labour, based on stages in the manufacture of a given article. These came to include the preliminary work of patternmaking, sample-making and cutting (often the prerogative of foremen and skilled men). The next stage, sewing (mostly done by female outworkers) could be highly specialized: individuals simply might sew sleeves, collars, or pockets, for instance. The sewing on of buttons and the making of buttonholes often were done by specialized workers.[45] Finishing or "trimming" was often in-house. It involved tasks such as hemming, repair work, and the trimming of loose threads. Garments would then be pressed. The final stage was the inspection of the completed goods by an official.

Divisions of labour undermined clothing workers' traditional skills, as garment manufacture was broken into various easily-mastered components. Garments were made in assortments, cut by machinery "and then each part of the work of making up and finishing [was] done by men, women and children skilled in doing that particular part."[46] Mackenzie King described in 1897 the extensive divisions of labour within larger contractors' shops.

> In a large shop there may be engaged in the manufacture of a single coat no less than 16 different individuals, each of whom works at a special line, and, after completing one stage in the process of manufacture, passes the garment on to the next, who is skilled in his line, and so on, till the article is completed.[47]

As the readymade clothing industry grew and made increasing calls for labour, the labour it demanded was ever less skilled and ever cheaper. As a consequence, more and more women and children entered the garment trades. The division of labour in the readymade sector, A.W. Wright remarked in 1896, had "practically done away with the necessity of employing completely skilled tradesmen."[48] These basic tasks could soon be well within the competence of even young and inexperienced workers.

The Technology of Garment Manufacture

Numerous key mechanical devices were introduced into the garment trades between 1850 and 1900. Significantly, however, these devices did not upset the prevailing division of labour in the clothing trades which allowed for outwork.[49]

Two aspects of garment manufacture remained in-house even with the emergence of extensive outwork in the 19th century. Cutting was the most highly skilled aspect of garment manufacture. The material had to be laid out on the cutting table with great care: an incorrect "stretch" would spoil the fit.[50] The introduction of expensive mechanical cutters encouraged the retention of cutting in-house. The "band knife" was introduced in the 1850s, making possible the cutting out of more than one garment at a time. During the 1870s "long knives," capable of cutting up to 18 thicknesses of cloth, were introduced, followed a decade later by steampowered band knives, which cut up to 24 thicknesses of cloth.[51] As well, the introduction of steam presses to replace hand irons confirmed pressing as inside work.[52]

The central innovation in the garment trades was certainly the sewing machine, whose use spread rapidly from the 1850s. It revolutionized the speed at which clothing could be manufactured. By one estimate, it took 16 hours and 35 minutes to sew a frock coat by hand. The same coat took 2 hours and 38 minutes by machine.[53] The sewing machine greatly reduced the cost of producing clothing while, in the opinion of some manufacturers, improving its quality.[54] At the same time, it was *cheap* enough for the small contract workshop or home. Various other, specialized machines were invented (such as those for pocket-stitching, making buttonholes and sewing on buttons), but a contractor could purchase one and do this work exclusively.[55]

The technical base of the industry not only allowed for extensive outwork, it encouraged it. By 1900, consequently, garment production differed from most manufacturing industries in that it was *not* becoming centralized in factories.[56] Mackenzie King estimated in 1898 that 5 per cent of men's wear (and certainly a much lower proportion of women's wear) was factory-produced.[57] Even large manufacturers like Shorey or Sanford contracted out to workers in homes or small contractors' shops, who competed fiercely among themselves for the available work. While a number of mechanical innovations had been introduced in clothing manufacture after 1850, they changed neither the industry's heavy demand for labour nor its geographical diffuseness. Into this century, Schmiechen has argued, "there was probably no industry as untouched by factory production or in which the methods of production had been standardized so little as the manufacture of clothing."[58] The industry continued to rest, as Mercedes Steedman observes, on the "systematic exploitation of a seemingly endless pool of cheap, female labour."[59]

Working Conditions of Sweated Needleworkers

Ontario factory inspector Margaret Carlyle remarked in 1899 that "most . . . garment workers in the struggle for subsistence feel obliged to accept wages that are little above subsistence."[60] In fact, wages for female needleworkers were almost uniformly below subsistence levels. One manufacturer acknowledged in 1874 that women "work very cheap."[61] For a woman without dependents, Ontario's Bureau of Industry estimated in 1889, the cost of living in Toronto was approximately $4.00

weekly.[62] Homeworkers earned nowhere near that amount. Women working in contract shops also routinely fell short of a living wage.[63]

The earliest comprehensive information on wages dates from the 1890s, when factory inspectors regularly were reporting on conditions in the needle trades, and when two federal commissions of inquiry examined sweating. Ontario factory inspector James R. Brown visited one contractor's shop which employed seven women and girls in Toronto in 1894. Some earned $1.50 weekly, some $2.00 and one, the finisher, was paid $3.00 weekly. The shop owner claimed, perhaps legitimately, that "he could not afford to pay more."[64] Louis Gurofsky testified to the Royal Commission on Sweating in 1896 that women's wages in Toronto contract shops were as low as 75 cents weekly, although $3.00 was considered a "fair" wage. The average wage failed to reach $4.00 weekly.[65] In contractors' shops in Montréal, Mackenzie King concluded in 1898, women earned between $2 and $5.30 weekly, although $3.00 was considered a good wage. Women employed in the contractor's residence earned from $1.25 to $3 weekly. As homeworkers, women could expect to earn between $1 and $2 weekly.[66]

The sweating system allowed, even encouraged, workers to exploit coworkers. Mackenzie King noted in 1898 that "[i]t was pretty generally conceded that, except by thus working overtime, or by the profits made by the aid of hired help, there was very little to be earned by a week's work."[67] He offered the examples of one woman who hired four girls to assist her at the rate of 25 cents daily (2.5 cents hourly) and another who hired five girls, some paid $2 weekly and others $1 weekly (less than 2 cents hourly).[68]

Clothing manufacturers in Montréal soon discovered that the price of subsistence was even less in outlying villages than it was in the metropolis. Québec factory inspector Joseph Lessard noted in 1897 the extension of the subcontracting network to rural areas.[69] Even Ontario contractors are reported at the turn of this century to have sent clothing to be made up in rural Québec.[70] Scott and Cassidy observed in 1935 that "a shift from town to country is a comparatively simple matter for the contractor. Cheap labour is the magnet that attracts him."[71]

Fining, the bane of homeworkers, was a further means to depress wages. A.W. Wright reported in 1896:

> When an employee in a factory or contractor's shop does imperfect work, necessitating an alteration, only the time required to make the alteration is lost. On the other hand, a person working at home must carry the goods back again, frequently losing half a day because of having to make an alteration which in actual work only requires a few minutes of time. To avoid this they are often willing to submit to a fine or reduction of wages far in excess of what the making of the alteration would be worth to them.[72]

Some warehouses made a practice of fining to reduce their wage bill. Some foremen did likewise to fatten their wallets. In either case protests from homeworkers produced a common response: "There is no more work for you."[73]

Employers' wage bills were also lowered by means of truck. Certain stores only gave women work who purchased a sewing machine from them and accepted payment in "bons" redeemable only at the stores for which the clothing was made. In Hull, for instance, about 150 or 175 seamstresses were using sewing machines in 1901 for which they had been charged $55, payable at $2.00 monthly, or in "bons" at a rate of $2.50.[74]

The hours of labour in the needle trades were irregular. Many of these trades were highly seasonal: weeks of intense labour could be followed by weeks of idleness. Seasonality was very pronounced in custom work: in millinery, perhaps the branch where it was most evident, there might be only six months' work annually.[75] The most regular employment was found in the larger workshops and factories, where the ten-hour day and sixty-hour week were standard in Toronto and Montréal in the 1890s.[76] In some cases the working days were extended during the week to allow for a half-day holiday on Saturdays.[77]

Both the larger establishments and the smaller dressmakers', milliners' and tailors' shops were subject, however, to frequent overtime in the busy season, for which there was seldom extra payment. In the custom dress shops, this pressure arose in part from customers eager to have their new garments. For "the gratification of some few hundred of inconsiderate people" complained one factory inspector, "the health of several thousand of women and girls" was jeopardized.[78] In the larger garment establishments, legal restrictions on hours of labour were circumvented by sending workers home with garments to make up.[79] Alternatively, in contract shops, "[t]he employees eat their dinner in five minutes, and put the rest of the meal hour in at work."[80]

Homeworkers, as a matter of course, were even more victimized. Mackenzie King noted that "in private houses the time is irregular and the number of hours of work usually more." He offered the example of a woman and son sewing army greatcoats at home who grossed $4 weekly on the strength of 90 hours of work *apiece*.[81] Writing in the *Globe* a few months later, King observed that 15 or 16 hour days (at as low as $3 per week) were common for home needleworkers when employed. In practice, the working day was restricted by "no limit save that of physical endurance."[82]

To the hours of sewing by the homeworker were added the hours of waiting for work. Although work was only intermittently available, homeworkers might nonetheless be required to ask at the warehouse once or twice daily, as a condition of future work.[83] One contractor (contractors were always willing to decry the iniquities of other contractors) spoke in 1896 of one shop where he had seen women kept "waiting two hours to get half a dozen pairs [of pants]."[84] Home needleworkers' time was cheap.

However poor was the pay or however long were the hours these producers worked, factory inspectors complained most persistently about needleworkers' wretched working conditions. Workshops were overcrowded; the environment was unsanitary; the air was foul. "These [small contractors'] workshops," it was reported in 1901, "are among the worst kept. Located as best they could be in old buildings or private houses, and sometimes in basements, they lack equally in light, air and cleanliness."[85] Similar accounts continued to be heard a decade later. "One feature of industrial life that is creeping into the city," wrote another factory inspector in 1911, "is underground workshops. It is almost impossible for them to be healthy. Quite a number of these places are used as tailor shops."[86] Demands by factory inspectors that contractors improve sanitary conditions often led to the abandonment of a workshop, and a clandestine move to another.[87]

Further Consequences of Sweating

The very poor conditions of labour, wretched pay, and interminable hours had further consequences for the women subject to them. They demoralized workers. They led to early exploitation of children's labour. They broke women's health. They drove some women to prostitute themselves in order to survive.

Prolonged labour under grossly depressed conditions made workers timid and fearful. A.W. Wright was told in 1896 in the course of his Royal Commission that "[i]t would be as much as any man's job was worth to be found giving information."[88] Mackenzie King was struck by the fear of dismissal of the garment workers he interviewed. "The dread of their employers, entertained by men and women alike, was in many instances distressing." King did not disclose publicly the names of his informants.[89]

The sweated clothing trades were marked not simply by the exploitation of adult labour, but also by widespread use of child labour. There was strong pressure to enlist the help of children. They spared adults work in an occupation where, literally, time was money. Even five-year-old children were capable of pulling out basting; by age ten they could perform simple sewing, such as attaching buttons. Children also were employed commonly to deliver clothing bundles.[90]

Generally, children laboured within the household. A Toronto journalist recounted in 1868 that

> frequently the industrious efforts of a whole family are employed to fill the orders of the employers. Often, in such instances, the child of eight or nine summers is made a source of material help in the construction of the coarser descriptions of men's garments that are now prepared for the ready-made clothing market. In the same way the female head of the house, a group of daughters, and perhaps

the male members of the family, if no better occupation is available, turn in
to assist the father in adding to their means of support.[91]

Into this century children were commonly employed within the family
to assist in garment manufacture. "In poor neighbourhoods," the Ontario
Committee on Child Labour reported in 1907, "piece work under sweat
shop conditions in a room of a dwelling house . . . is very common."[92]

More viciously, children were also subject to harsh exploitation by
contractors outside the family context. By the late 1800s, traditional apprenticeships had long since fallen into disuse. Children were used simply
as a cheap and docile source of labour. A.W. Wright reported in 1896:

> "Learners" are employed usually young girls and boys but the employer is under
> no obligation to teach them a trade or any part of one. Evidently such a system
> is capable of gross abuse and there are not wanting instances of such abuse
> by unscrupulous employers. I learned of one contractor, engaged in making pants
> and vests, who makes a practice of employing "learners" who engage to work
> for him without wages while they are learning the trade. These learners, usually
> girls, are kept at some trivial and easily mastered work, such as pulling out
> basting threads, sewing on buttons, or running up seams on a sewing machine,
> and then, when the term, for which they agreed to work without wages expires,
> they are discharged, without having had an opportunity to learn any trade by
> which they can earn a livelihood, their places being filled by other "learners"
> who are in turn defrauded out of several months of work and time.[93]

Contractors readily acknowledged that even in the best of circumstances,
young girls were hired simply because of the low wages they commanded.
As a rule, they were not trained in any more than one branch of clothing
manufacture. "I have twenty or twenty-five girls working for me,"
claimed one contractor in 1896, "and not one of them could make a
coat right through."[94] That year some Toronto contractors still recalled
a system of indenture, whereby girls would be apprenticed to the trade
for four years, but it was no longer practised.[95]

Needleworkers were further afflicted with a distinctive set of health
problems. Eye strain produced headaches, giddiness, fainting, hysteria,
and occasionally even total blindness. The bent posture in which they
laboured, and their lack of exercise, often led to chronic indigestion,
ulcers, dysmenorrhoea, and distortion of the spine. The foul, dusty, and
fluff-filled atmosphere of the workroom was linked with a variety of
lung complaints, including tuberculosis.[96] Sewing machines produced a
further set of problems: physical exhaustion, back and shoulder pains,
pain in the legs from use of the treadle, deteriorating vision, and "the
tremble," caused by the vibration of the machine.[97]

The seasonality of poverty has been extremely well described by Judith Fingard.[98] Winter posed particular hardships for clothing workers.

> [I]n the dead of winter, when the trade in the retail houses is slack, and the
> wholesale houses keep none but their best hands on, the prospect for those
> who are left suddenly to their own resources is, for the time, miserable indeed.
> Then, the petty savings from the busy season are anxiously hoarded, and, by
> dint of great effort are made to last till March or April, when warmer weather,

by cheapening fuel, does not so hastily deplete their scanty store, while, at the same time, the increase of work adds to the value of their labour.[99]

The seasonal patterns evident in the use of charitable agencies and public refuges almost certainly extended to prostitution.[100]

Links between needlework and prostitution were frequently drawn by contemporaries. Henry Mayhew estimated that between one-quarter and one-half of all women in readymade clothing work in London in the 1850s were forced to supplement their earnings by prostitution. In some quarters, "seamstress" almost became a euphemism for "prostitute."[101]

Far too rarely was the role played by the extremely low wages women received for needlework examined. A "full-time" prostitute offered her opinion on her "seamstress sisters" in a letter to *The Times* (of London).

> It is a cruel calumny to call them in mass prostitutes; and as for their virtue, they lose it as one loses his watch by a highway thief. Their virtue is the watch, and society is the thief.[102]

Canadians sensitive to needleworkers' plight made similar arguments. The *Labour Reformer* wrote in 1886:

> In Toronto and other Canadian cities there are many girls employed from . . . $2 per week and up . . . Does any man suppose that girls can live respectably upon such wages? Those living with their parents may do so, but it is a lamentable fact that many of these, and more who board, increase their income in ways far from honorable, and in a manner which can only result in degrading our own and future generations.[103]

During a strike against Toronto clothing contractors in 1896, one trade unionist laid out clearly what he felt to be the crux of the issue: "These men would not care if the women prostituted their bodies at night to make a living wage."[104] Mackenzie King recorded in his diary for September 18, 1897, a visit to a needlewoman earning $1.25 weekly and "supporting herself, found she was doing so by prostitution. What a story of Hell. My mind all ablaze."[105] King subsequently hinted at more direct sexual exploitation of female needleworkers: "foremen and contractors had taken a more terrible advantage of those anxious to secure work for a living . . . too terrible to admit of publication."[106]

Who Was Sweated?

Two groups of women were described by contemporaries as doing home needlework, where sweating was most evident. One group, almost certainly a minority, consisted of homeworkers whose subsistence did not depend on needlework. A Toronto journalist wrote in 1868 of women taking in sewing, "interspersing the household duties with a run at the sewing machine . . . its products . . . adding to the comforts and luxuries of their homes."[107] William Muir, a clothing contractor, echoed this view in 1874, claiming that women took in sewing "to buy finery." He continued: "These women sit down when their breakfast, dinner and supper is over, and make a garment, but are not exclusively employed at this work all day."[108] "[W]omen whose husbands are making good wages" take homework, one Toronto contractor remarked in 1896. "They want a little more money for dress and finery and compete against girls who are working for a living."[109] Home needleworkers were described in 1903 as "thrifty housewives and their just as thrifty daughters," who kept shop sewing on hand "to occupy their time in the intervals of domestic and farm work."[110]

In fact, the "typical" houseworker relied on her earnings to feed herself and her family.[111] Research focusing on the major urban centres of Montréal and Toronto has emphasized that for all but a narrow and privileged segment of the working class, the adult male's wages were inadequate to support a family — at least until well into this century. The working class family needed more than one breadwinner.[112] The "wives and daughters of mechanics" who are reported to have been engaged in homework in Montréal in 1874; or the "wives of labourers or mill hands" in Hull doing shop sewing in 1901, were almost certainly working to supplement a meagre family income.[113] Homework was one of the few means of earning an income available to women with children. Bettina Bradbury discovered that among the home needleworkers in St.-Jacques Ward in Montréal, 20 per cent had children under two; 45 per cent had children under five.[114] Families with older children would rely on them as secondary wage earners; until that point in the family life-cycle, women were necessarily employed to supplement inadequate male incomes.[115] Widows, particularly those with children, were among those most dependent on home needlework. Bettina Bradbury has calculated that 40 per cent of the widows in St.-Jacques Ward and 20 per cent of those in Ste.-Anne Ward (both in Montréal) did home sewing.[116] James Munro, Sanford's foreman, acknowledged in 1888 that among Sanford's homeworkers: "There are a great many widows and a great many who might as well be widows, as they provide for the whole house."[117]

The lack of alternative sources of income — coupled with pressing need — forced women into homework. No sooner had one contractor, William Muir, linked homework with pin-money, than he reported incongruously: "it makes my heart ache to have the women come crying for work."[118] In 1896, at a time of relentless price reductions in Toronto, one employer described women as "running — breaking their necks you might say — to get the work."[119] It is unlikely that these women were "breaking their necks" for pin-money.

Responses to Sweating

However much sweating was associated with ill-lit rooms, with needle-workers huddled together out of sight in garrets and basements, its existence was evident to anyone who cared to look. Hungry-looking people, struggling under heavy loads, were commonplace in urban centres. "Every one has seen," reported one journalist in 1895, "the large numbers of women and children winding their way up or down Bay street, carrying bundles in their arms or on perambulators."[120] Trade unionist Alfred Jury lamented in 1896 "the great number of women staggering up and down with great bundles of clothing; some of the poor creatures hardly able to walk."[121] Even without their telltale bundles, needleworkers, who spent so much of their day bent over their work, often could be identified by their stooped carriage.[122]

The first to respond to sweating were its first victims, tailors. In England, London tailors found conditions in their trade deteriorated rapidly in the wake of an unsuccessful strike against outwork in 1834. By that time, as E.P. Thompson has pointed out, they no longer enjoyed the traditional protection of the Elizabethan apprenticeship statutes, repealed in 1814. The rapid growth of the "dishonourable trades" followed: wages and working conditions in the needle trades were steadily undermined by subcontracting and outwork.[123]

In British North America, as noted above, deteriorating working conditions, including outwork, were in evidence before 1850 in Montréal. In response, tailors began to form some of the earliest unions in British North America. Locals were organized in Montréal (in 1823), Toronto (1845), and Hamilton (1854) as journeymen tailors sought to maintain working standards.[124] Conflict soon followed, generally over the allied issues of pay and contracting-out.[125]

The process of contracting-out continued into this century, as the custom sector was eroded by relatively cheap readymade production.[126] Inside needleworkers tried, generally unsuccessfully, to prevent ever more categories of clothing from being put out.[127] In the struggle against readymade interlopers, especially in tailoring, labour standards in the custom sector were constantly eroded. The suppression of outwork remained (and remains) a principal concern of garment unions.[128] Because women commonly did outwork, they were defined from an early day as undesirable and threatening by journeymen tailors.

By the end of the 19th century the Journeymen Tailors' Union (JTU) and the United Garment Workers (UGW) were the principal unions of clothing workers in North America. They had a precarious foothold in the custom sector, and among skilled workers in readymade manufacture.[129] Their commitment to organizing women was uncertain; their interest in — or even knowledge of — the sweated trades was questionable. Bernard Rose, head of the Montréal Journeymen Tailors, testified to the ignorance or indifference of the skilled custom tailors when, in 1901, he "emphatically assert[ed] that there exist[ed] no form of sweating, at least in the clothing industry of Montréal, at the present time."[130] A cutters' local of the UGW supported Montréal clothing manufacturer

Mark Workman when an outcry arose in 1899 over his contravention of anti-sweating clauses in army uniform contracts.[131]

Early efforts to organize female needleworkers, such as those made in Toronto in 1889 (by the Knights of Labor) and in 1897, 1899, and 1900 (by the Journeymen Tailors), proved abortive.[132] It was not until the great industrial unions in ladies' wear, the International Ladies Garment Workers' Union, and in men's wear, the Amalgamated Clothing Workers of America, embarked on vigorous organizational efforts after the turn of this century that garment unions enjoyed some success in (re)establishing industrial standards.[133]

Frustrations encountered by male trade unionists in organizing women made state intervention more attractive.[134] The Trades and Labour Congress (TLC) expressed its concern respecting sweatshops from its founding conference in 1883.[135] Between 1887 and 1895 a resolution in favour of the prevailing (later union) wage on all public contracts was passed annually. In 1893, a resolution calling for the abolition of the sweating system was passed. In 1895 came a successful request for a royal commission to enquire into sweating.[136]

Certainly, collective organization on the part of sweated workers was difficult. Physically isolated, homeworkers were not necessarily acquainted with each other, even those working for the same employer. Homework pitted worker against worker, as they bid against each other for work. The sweating system also held out the lure of status as an employer, which discouraged the growth of a collective sense of grievance. In contract shops, ethnic differences divided needleworkers, particularly after the turn of this century when the Jewish presence in the needle trades increased rapidly in Toronto and Montréal. The regular seasonal downturns in the clothing trades also hampered organization. Often, needleworkers were so destitute that a strike immediately meant hunger. Their low level of skill (or rather, their possession of commonly-held skills) meant that any strike would be followed by an invasion of replacements. Women faced special challenges in juggling union activity with domestic responsibilities.[137]

Although sweated workers were unlikely to end sweating unassisted, individual acts of resistance occurred. Phillips Thompson offered one example in 1900:

> a poor woman took [legal] action against her employer for her wages. She was promised twenty-five cents per dozen for making boys' pants and the money was withheld on the ground that the work was not well done.[138]

There were almost certainly others, although rare and poorly documented. The sweated seamstress, while not entirely incapable of acting to limit the extent of her exploitation, was ultimately largely dependent on the actions of others.[139]

The Middle Class and Sweating

Middle-class efforts to address the problem of sweating were often spear-headed by women's organizations. In facing the problem, Canadian women had a number of American and English models. Three general ways of dealing with sweating were advocated: the organization of sweated outworkers, agitation for protective legislation, and consumer pressure (discriminatory purchasing).[140] These suggestions were not exclusive to the middle class — trade unions at various times advocated similar tactics. Underlying most calls for reform were two convictions: first, that the worker — despite the logic of the capitalist wage market — was entitled to live by his or her work. The second reflected patriarchal unease about women, particularly those with young children, who worked for wages.[141]

Canadian middle-class concern failed to produce organizations comparable to the Women's Trade Union Leagues in the United States and the United Kingdom.[142] The National Council of Women of Canada, which dedicated itself to the advancement of Canadian women (and which, nationally and locally, often demonstrated concern for working women) said of sweating in 1901: "Canada has little or no trouble with this irregular system of manufacture."[143] Ruth Frager has remarked on the gap between early 20th-century Canadian women reformers and the concerns of working-class women, "especially where ethnic differences reinforced class differences."[144] Any local antisweating organizations formed rested heavily on the efforts of a handful of individuals and tended to be short-lived.[145] Only with the rise of the Social Gospel movement after 1900 did the Canadian middle class develop organizations committed to a comprehensive range of social reforms.[146]

Until that time, middle-class response to sweating in Canada remained individual and episodic rather than organized and sustained. Concern was often expressed in the popular press. A Toronto journalist, for instance, wrote in 1869 of a widow

> supported by her daughter, who provides food for both, by making pants at 15 cents a pair. Let the young gentlemen who adorn King street of an afternoon, and the old gentlemen who rattle their silver in their pockets, seriously reflect on that fact.[147]

By the 1890s sweating was clearly on journalists' agenda. The Montréal *Herald* was among those newspapers which followed the sweating "question" closely. It exposed in 1897 the 75- to 80-hour work weeks in "old dark tenements" needleworkers faced.

> Occupied as they are from early morning until night, they have little time, even if they had the inclination, to give a thought to the sanitary condition of their surroundings, which are often simply vile. The combination living-room and workshop offers one of the saddest spectacles which can be sought by any humanly disposed person, who seeks light on the subject of human misery.[148]

The *Herald* endorsed in 1899 a fair wage resolution by the federal government hoping that this measure would close the opportunities offered to "unscrupulous contractors of making large profits whilst paying starvation wages" and describing the consequences of sweating as "impaired health and a permanently broken system."[149] The *Herald* also reported the Montréal Federated Trades Council's call for the abolition of sweating, deploring that "little children of our city, who should be attending school, were being destroyed in the sweat shops."[150]

Fears about public (middle-class) health helped provoke wider concern about the sweated needle trades. Infected clothing was known to spread contagious disease, including scarlatina, diphtheria, and most ominously, smallpox. During the 1885 smallpox epidemic, for instance, many retailers boycotted goods produced in Montréal; Ontario provincial authorities insisted on inspecting and certifying readymade clothing from Montréal.[151] Individuals appalled by the plight of needleworkers saw this fear as a means to mobilize action against the practice of sweated clothing production. James Mitchell raised this worry in the first mention of sweating by a Québec factory inspector, in 1893.[152]

Governments and Sweating

The federal Royal Commission on Sweating was appointed in autumn 1895, largely at the prodding of the Trades and Labour Congress. It was chaired by A.W. Wright, a man of broad loyalties. An erstwhile Knights of Labor stalwart, Wright had recently edited the Canadian Manufacturers' Association's *Industrial Canada*. The Canadian decision to appoint a royal commission followed major public inquiries into sweating in the United Kingdom and in the United States during the previous decade.[153]

Wright made a number of recommendations, but the federal government failed to act on any of them. An impending election may have distracted its attention. Charles Tupper pleaded "the pressure of other business."[154] In any case, clear jurisdictional problems (most of Wright's recommendations were clearly within the purview of the provinces) invariably would have produced delays.[155]

The catalyst for federal action was William Lyon Mackenzie King. He had spent winter 1896–97 doing graduate work at the University of Chicago and living at Hull House, one of North America's earliest settlement houses. There, King was first impressed by the extent of the sweated trades. Returning to Toronto the following summer, King found work as a journalist for the *Mail and Empire*, and canvassed Toronto in search of sweated workers.[156]

King soon found them, including "a poor old crippled woman who sewed night and day."[157] He discovered that many of the homeworkers with whom he was brought into contact were making letter carriers' uniforms. Years later, he described his response:

> On questioning one of the workers as to the remuneration she was receiving for sewing machine and hand work, I found that it came to a very few cents an hour. I shall never forget the feeling of pained surprise and indignation I experienced as I learned of the extent of that woman's toil from early morning till late at night, and figured out the pittance she received.

King was further astounded to discover that this homeworker was employed by no fly-by-night subcontractor: "the contracting firm was one of high repute in the city." "As I visited other homes and shops," King continued, "I found the condition of this woman's employment to be in no sense isolated, but all too common."[158] King published his discoveries in a series of newspaper articles.[159]

Mackenzie King proceeded to parlay his family's acquaintance with Postmaster General William Mulock into an appointment as a one-man commission to enquire into the conditions under which government clothing contracts were filled.[160] In his report, first published in 1898, King argued that prices were "quite disproportionate to the amount of work done" and "insufficient to constitute a living wage" for both homeworkers and needleworkers employed in the subcontractor's residence. This intensified pressure to increase the length of the working day, which might extend to 15 hours or more. Sanitary conditions were "frequently foul and noisome."[161] In short, King was able to confirm that "the 'sweating system,' with other objectionable conditions, has accompanied for many years the manufacture of uniforms [for the post office, the militia, and the Mounted Police]."[162]

King closed the report with a warning: that sweating led women to neglect their children and "the duties of the home." He emphasized "[t]he home is still the nursery of the nation."[163] Threats to the home, it was King's conviction, constituted threats to the nation.

Even before the publication of King's report Mulock had acted. He appears to have been genuinely outraged by King's disclosures to him. "Work performed at less than living prices is almost certain to be done under conditions unfavorable to good morals, health or comfort." He required that when the Post Office let contracts, a number of conditions were to be imposed.[164] Subsequently, in March 1900, Mulock introduced "The Fair Wages Resolution" in the House of Commons. This was designed to secure to workers on government contract work a level of wage generally accepted as current in the locality where the work was carried out.[165] Daniel J. O'Donoghue capped his career as a printer, workingman's advocate, and friend to the Liberal party when he was appointed the Dominion's first Fair Wages Officer in March 1900, charged with the preparation and enforcement of fair wage schedules. In the battle against sweated labour, the federal government would act as a model employer.[166]

Both Wright and King had recognized the limits to the federal government's power of action. Wright was explicit about jurisdictional problems; King was unable to offer specific recommendations to the federal government, limiting himself instead to the claim that there existed "sufficient grounds for government interference in order that future contracts may be performed in a manner free from all such objectionable features."[167] These federal commissions made clear that in future, the key legislative action against sweating was to be taken by the provinces.

Ontario and Québec, the major sites of sweating, both had passed Factory Acts during the 1880s. Factory inspectors found the needle trades particularly vexing. The conditions they encountered were deplorable and inspectors realized that the prevalence of outwork meant that there was much they failed to see. Moreover, the Factory Acts did not apply to many of the contexts of sweated labour, something subcontractors were well aware of. Louisa King recounted her frustrations in Québec in 1898 when she requested subcontractors to provide her with the addresses of homeworkers: "ils m'ont presque toujours répondu que leur ouvrage était fait dans les ateliers de famille sur lesquels l'inspecteur n'a point de contrôle."[168]

Factory inspectors were well aware of the inadequacies of the legislation they were charged to enforce.

> While factory legislation tends to purify and improve the factories, it does so at an increased expenditure to the factory owners, while these other places [i.e., smaller shops and homes, outside the purview of the Factory Acts] are not subject to any such expense.[169]

Factory Acts, by stipulating basic labour standards, could only encourage manufacturers in their use of the small contract shops and homework which exhibited the most oppressive working conditions. Joseph Lessard told the Montréal *Herald* in 1897 that taxation and sanitary regulations were necessary "to force the workers out of tenements and into shop buildings, where they would be subject to the control and protection of Provincial legislation."[170] Margaret Carlyle echoed his proposal that same year, urging legislators to "drive [needleworkers] from the wretched places in which they now labor into well regulated factories and workshops."[171]

Following repeated requests by its factory inspectors, Ontario took a step towards tightening restrictions on sweating by amending its Shops Regulation Act in 1900. In future, every individual contracting out clothing was to keep a register of the names and addresses of individuals given work. Each article of clothing was to be labelled with the name of the individual who made it.[172] This legislation helped factory inspectors to locate homeworkers (and workers employed in small contractors' shops). It was, though, no solution to sweating. A legislative means to end sweating had to address the question of wages.

The first step in this direction took the form of resolutions on government purchasing policy. The federal government, as we have seen, was including fair wage clauses in some of its contracts from 1897 and passed its Fair Wage Resolution in 1900. Other governments followed. Ontario passed its Fair Wage Resolution in 1900 also.[173] In the United Kingdom, many municipal councils began to add fair wage clauses to their contracts in the 1890s.[174] In 1901, the Ottawa city council agreed to the request of its Allied Trades and Labour Association that it insist on the union label where possible in its purchases.[175] Workers soon discovered however that these resolutions, if inconvenient, were easily overlooked by both governments and contractors.[176]

The End of Sweating?

Recent accounts of garment workers in the United Kingdom have highlighted Parliament as the principal agent in ending sweated labour. Jenny Morris focused her study on the genesis of the Trades Boards Act of 1909.[177] James Schmiechen also closed his account of sweated labour with a discussion of this legislation, noting that in the years immediately subsequent to this act wages in the garment trades increased considerably.[178] Trades Boards, Schmiechen argued, led to "the elimination of sweated homework."[179]

Between 1917 and 1925, most Canadian provinces passed female minimum wage legislation and established minimum wage boards. Ostensibly, this action represented a key advance over the Trades Boards established in the United Kingdom, insofar as the cost of living of a single woman was to determine the minimum wage. In the United Kingdom, in contrast, the minimum wage was set on the basis of the industry's ability to pay.[180]

Yet the Canadian minimum wage acts, on account of three major limitations, were inadequate means to end sweating. First, when initially passed, they did not apply to homeworkers.[181] Second, the legislation was filled with loopholes, exempting numerous categories of female workers from its provisions.[182] Third, the onus was placed on workers to lodge complaints against employers, an action hardly likely in light of the opportunities employers had for retribution. Consequently, minimum wage legislation was both limited in scope and difficult to enforce. The Royal Commission on Price Spreads reported in 1935 that minimum wage acts were "quite inadequate" and that violations were "frequent and continuous."[183] No account of the decline of sweating in Canada, however brief, can rest very heavily on minimum wage legislation.[184]

To account for sweating's decline, a variety of causes must be identified. It is useful in facing this question to distinguish between circumstances in Ontario and in Québec, or, more specifically, between the dominant centres of clothing production, Toronto and Montréal.

In Toronto, sweating's decline after the turn of this century was closely linked with a movement on the part of clothing manufacturers toward the use of the factory for clothing production. Factories allowed for quicker production time and better coordination of the various stages of manufacture. They were also considered to produce a better quality of garment.[185]

As early as 1904, Margaret Carlyle noted "a tendency [in Toronto] to move out of the tenement houses into factories."[186] Between 1901 and 1921, the Toronto garment trades came to be dominated by a few large firms (Eaton's predominant among them), manufacturing in factories, and accounting for over two-thirds of the total value of clothing produced in the city.[187] Michael Piva has identified the 1910s as the pivotal decade. During these ten years the ratio of needleworkers employed in homes or small shops (i.e., dressmakers, tailors) to those employed in factories (as operatives) plummeted from 3.58 to 1 in 1911 to 0.53 to 1 in 1921. These figures reflect, Piva argued, "the rapid advance of the factory system and the decline of subcontracting."[188] Homework consequently diminished, although it never died out entirely.[189]

The extremely low pay, long hours, and poor working conditions associated with sweated labour were not as evident in the factory as they were in the home or small contractor's shop. A.W. Wright reported that the factory was the favoured workplace among female garment workers.[190] Work was more regular; pay was higher. On the whole, conditions of work were superior, in part because workers in factories benefited from the minimum protection offered by the Factory Acts. In addition, factory workers were more easily organized, although employers resisted collective bargaining fiercely.[191]

In Montréal, in contrast, the factory (and inside manufacture) failed to emerge at the turn of the century. Presumably its relative cost advantages were not as clear: wages in the Québec garment trades were traditionally lower than in Ontario.[192] Into the 1930s subcontracting, the contract shop and homework remained prominent features of the Montréal garment trades.[193] The Royal Commission on Price Spreads observed in 1935 that in certain sectors of the Québec clothing industry, conditions were "altogether deplorable."[194]

The onus in Québec was consequently placed far more on trade unions to bring work inside. In this task large industrial unions such as the International Ladies Garment Workers' Union and the Amalgamated Clothing Workers of America met with some success. By the end of the 1930s, Mercedes Steedman has argued, these unions "had managed to limit the use of contractors and homeworkers."[195] Union activity contributed greatly to the development of industrial standards in both Ontario and Québec. Unions were aided in this task by legislation passed by both Ontario and Québec in the course of the decade. Industrial Standards Acts allowed workers and employers representing "a preponderant group in each industry" to negotiate minimum standards of wages and hours of labour. The provincial government was empowered to impose these standards on the industry as a whole. Given the weaknesses of minimum wage legislation, Harold Logan noted, these acts were "of considerable importance."[196]

The rise of sweating, it has been argued here, was conditioned by the structured inequalities of class and gender. Sweating emerged with the growth of the readymade clothing industry over the 19th century. The capitalist imperative to reduce production costs in the context of a highly competitive clothing market, in tandem with the patriarchal marginalization of women's productive labour, produced the ruthless exploitation of countless thousands of working women described here.

Class and gender also shaped responses to sweating. The social welfare programs initiated on women's behalf — and largely without their participation — were inconsequential. The impact of protective legislation such as Factory Acts, Minimum Wage Acts and Fair Wage Acts, was slight. Only with Industrial Standards Acts did legislation begin to acquire some teeth. Sweating's decline is primarily due to factors apart from state intervention. In Ontario, capitalist calculation of profit led to the movement of the workplace from the homes and very small shops where sweating thrived to larger workplaces, including the factory, where trade unions were to enjoy some success in enforcing minimum standards of employment. In Québec, where the movement to factory production was less pronounced, the onus to fight sweating fell more heavily on unions. In both provinces trade unions enjoyed some success between the wars in eliminating the most egregious aspects of sweating.[197]

Epilogue

These curbs against sweating were only provisional. Today, the legal, regulatory and administrative regime continues to tolerate sweated homework while unions in the garment trades have weakened in their ability to enforce industrial standards. Homework has rapidly re-emerged over the last two decades, especially in Québec.[198]

NOTES

I wish to thank Del Muise, Rolina van Gaalen, Ellen Scheinberg, and Chad Gaffield for their helpful comments on earlier drafts of this paper, and invoke on their behalf the usual disclaimers. I am also grateful to *Labour/Le Travail*'s anonymous reviewers. This research was conducted under the auspices of a postdoctoral fellowship from the Social Sciences and Humanities Research Council of Canada. I wish to express my gratitude to the Council in acknowledging this support.

1. Halifax *Morning Herald*, 20 February 1889, as cited in Judith Fingard, *The Dark Side of Victorian Halifax* (Porters Lake, N.S. 1989), 159.
2. Despite their prominence, *Labour/Le Travail*, the journal likeliest to address them, contains only two items on garment workers: Irving Abella, "Portrait of a Jewish Professional Revolutionary: The Recollections of Joshua Gershman," 2 (1977), 185–213 and a research note by Jacques Rouillard, "Les travailleurs juifs de la confection à Montréal (1910–80)," 8/9 (Autumn 1981/Spring 1982), 253–9. Ruth A. Frager, *Sweatshop Strife: Class, Ethnicity and Gender in the Jewish Labour Movement of Toronto, 1900-1939* (Toronto 1992), stands as a noteworthy recent exception to a general neglect of needleworkers in Canadian working-class history.

3. Within the manufacturing sector, textile mills and shoe factories also made extensive use of women's labour. See *Census of Canada*, 1871–1881, Vol. III.
4. *Census of Canada*, 1901, Vol. III.
5. As defined in 1898 by one of its first Canadian students, William Lyon Mackenzie King, "sweating" described "a condition of labour in which a maximum amount of work in a given time is performed for a minimum wage, and in which the ordinary rules of health and comfort are disregarded. It is inseparably associated with contract work, and is intensified by sub-contracting in shops conducted in homes." See *The Daily Mail and Empire* (Toronto), 9 October 1897, 10.
6. Jacques Ferland, " 'In Search of Unbound Prometheia': A Comparative View of Women's Activism in Two Quebec Industries, 1869–1908," *Labour/Le Travail*, 24 (Fall 1989), 12.
7. Sylvia Walby, *Theorizing Patriarchy* (Oxford 1990), 20.
8. Heidi Hartmann, "Capitalism, Patriarchy and Job Segregation by Sex," in Zillah Eisenstein, ed., *Capitalist Patriarchy and the Case for Socialist Feminism* (New York 1979), 206–47; Heidi Hartmann, "The Unhappy Marriage of Marxism and Feminism: Towards a More Progressive Union," in L. Sargent, ed., *Women and Revolution* (Montréal 1981), 1–41.
9. See Sally Alexander, "Women's Work in Nineteenth Century London: A Study of the Years 1820–1850," in Juliet Mitchell and Ann Oakley, eds., *The Rights and Wrongs of Women* (Harmondsworth 1976), 77–83. On the preindustrial gender-based division of labour in Canada, see Marjorie Griffin Cohen, *Women's Work, Markets and Development in Nineteenth-Century Ontario* (Toronto 1988).
10. When the organization of women did occur at the end of the century other discriminatory practices were employed: lower pay rates for women, job segregation and ghettoization were enshrined in union contracts.
11. See Wally Seccombe, "Patriarchy Stabilized: The Construction of the Male Breadwinner Wage Norm in Nineteenth-Century Britain," *Social History*, II, No. 1 (January 1986), 53–76, esp. 66–7.
12. On these points see also Jenny Morris, *Women Workers and the Sweated Trades: The Origins of Minimum Wage Legislation* (Aldershot, Hants. 1986), 192–4.
13. See Paul Craven, *"An Impartial Umpire": Industrial Relations and the Canadian State, 1900–1911* (Toronto 1980), especially Chapter 6. For a recent study of protective legislation for women, see Mary Lynn Stewart, *Women, Work, and the French State: Labour Protection and Social Patriarchy, 1879–1919* (Kingston 1989). Stewart argues forcefully that protective legislation, passed in response to a patriarchal agenda, was inimical to women's interests, failed to improve their working conditions at home or on the job, and buttressed their secondary status in the labour market.
14. A similar convergence of forces had led to the passage of the first Factory Acts in the United Kingdom. See Michelle Barrett and Mary McIntosh, "The 'Family Wage': Some Problems for Socialists and Feminists," *Capital and Class*, No. 11 (1980), 53.
15. Jean-Pierre Hardy et David-Thiéry Ruddel, *Les apprentis artisans à Québec* (Montréal 1977), 119–20.
16. On the development of Canadian markets see H. Clare Pentland, *Labour and Capital in Canada, 1650–1860* (Toronto 1981), Chapter V.
17. Some tailors had always kept on hand small stocks of readymade goods, generally for sale to labourers. This was a sideline, however, to their principal business of custom work. Readymade clothing was often, particularly in the early decades of its manufacture, associated with a very poor quality of workmanship and material.
18. For this paragraph I am indebted to Mary Anne Poutanen, "For the Benefit of the Master: The Montreal Needle Trades during the Transition, 1820–1842," M.A. thesis, McGill University, 1985.
19. It was division of labour, not machinery, which brought women into the clothing trades in competition with men. Morris, 37. In this sense, their experience is similar to shoemaking, where women first came to be employed — as outworkers — by new divisions of labour. See Joanne Burgess, "L'industrie de la chaussure à Montréal: 1840–1870 — Le Passage de l'artisanat à la fabrique," *La revue de l'histoire de l'amérique française*, Vol. 31, No. 2 (septembre 1977), 187–210.
20. See Gregory L. Teal, "The Organization of Production and the Heterogeneity of the Working Class: Occupation, Gender and Ethnicity among Clothing Workers in Quebec," Ph.D. dissertation, McGill University, 1985, 167–9.
21. Moss Brothers also anticipated the very large Jewish presence in clothing production which emerged at the turn of this century. See Gerald Tulchinsky, " 'Said to Be a Very Honest Jew': The R.G. Dun Credit Reports and Jewish Business Activity in Mid-19th Century Montreal," *Urban History Review*, XVIII, No. 3 (February 1990), 206.
22. Royal Commission on the Relations between Labour and Capital (hereafter Labour Commission), *Quebec Evidence*, Part I (Ottawa 1889), 15.
23. In Québec, it also permitted avoidance of a business tax. See *Globe*, 19 November 1898, 1.
24. Canada, House of Commons, *Journals*, 1874, Vol. VIII, Appendix No. 3, "Report of the Select Committee on the Manufacturing Interests of the Dominion" (hereafter Select Committee Report)], 23.
25. Hollis Shorey dominated the Canadian garment industry in the late 19th century. The son of a shoemaker, Shorey was apprenticed in 1839 to a tailor in Hatley. He subsequently established his own tailoring shop in Barnston, also in the Eastern Townships of Québec. In 1861 he left for Montréal, where he was employed for a number of years as a travelling salesman. At the end of 1866 he began to manufacture on his own account. By 1870 Shorey employed 305 workers, of whom 280 were women. By 1874, Shorey's business had expanded to employ from 700 to 1000

outside workers and perhaps one-tenth that number inside. In 1888 he employed 103 inside and 1450 outside. When he died in 1893 Shorey was the largest clothing manufacturer in Canada, employing 125 workers inside and 1500 outside. Select Committee *Report*, 22–4; Labour Commission, *Quebec Evidence*, 285; Gerald Tulchinsky, "Hollis Shorey," in Frances G. Halpenny, ed., *Dictionary of Canadian Biography*, Vol. XII (1891–1900), (Toronto 1990), 968–9.

26. James A. Schmiechen, *Sweated Industries and Sweated Labor: The London Clothing Trades, 1860–1914* (Urbana 1984), 2. Similar trends were evident in contemporary Paris. See Christopher H. Johnson, "Economic Change and Artisan Discontent: The Tailors' History, 1800–1848," in Roger Price, ed., *Revolution and Reaction: 1848 and the Second French Republic* (London 1975), 87–114.

27. Hamilton *Gazette*, 28 June 1852, cited in Bryan D. Palmer, *A Culture in Conflict* (Montréal 1979), 11–12. Such abuses persisted, even in custom tailoring. See the *Labour Gazette*, February 1901, 270, on Toronto tailors and "back shops."

28. Canada, *Sessional Papers*, 1896, Vol. XXIX, No. 11 (61, 61A), *Report upon the Sweating System in Canada* (hereafter Wright Commission), 12.

29. Wright Commission, 25.

30. *The Daily Mail and Empire*, 9 October 1897, 10; *The Globe*, 19 November 1898, 1.

31. William Lyon Mackenzie King, *Report to the Honourable the Postmaster General of the Methods Adopted in Canada in the Carrying Out of Government Clothing Contracts* (Ottawa 1900) (hereafter King Commission), 6–9, 18. This report was first published in 1898, and reprinted (with minor changes in pagination) in 1899 and 1900.

32. King Commission, 6–10.

33. Ontario Factory Inspector's *Report*, 1897, 19.

34. Michelle Payette-Daoust, "The Montreal Garment Industry, 1871–1901," M.A. thesis, McGill University, 1986, 58.

35. Select Committee *Report*, 23.

36. On the attraction of immigrant Jews to garment-making, see Frager, *op. cit.* See also Robert Babcock, ed., "A Jewish Immigrant in the Maritimes: The Memoirs of Max Vanger," *Acadiensis*, Vol. XVI, No. 1 (Autumn, 1986), 136–48, and David Rome, *On Our Forefathers at Work*, New Series, No. 9 (Montréal 1978), 39–40.

37. Ontario Factory Inspector's *Report*, 1897, 23–4.

38. *Ibid.*, 1899, 23; 1913, 49.

39. Wright Commission, 21. On such swindles, see also Ontario Factory Inspector's *Report*, 1894, 14.

40. *Daily Mail and Empire*, 9 October 1897, 10.

41. F.R. Scott and H.M. Cassidy, *Labour Conditions in the Men's Clothing Industry* (Toronto 1935), 24.

42. Labour Commission, *Ontario Evidence*, 167.

43. "Knight of Labour," "Where Labor Is Not Prayer," *Walsh's Magazine* (Toronto 1895–6), 111–6, cited in Michael S. Cross, *The Workingman in the Nineteenth Century* (Toronto 1974), 153.

44. Wright Commission, 13. Montréal contractor Israel Solomon, for instance, made overcoats, employing his father and two girls. He knew nothing of the prices paid for pants or vests. Labour Commission, *Quebec Evidence*, 560.

45. This was the work undertaken by Montréal contractor Jacob Julius Rosen, who had the necessary machinery. Labour Commission, *Quebec Evidence*, 558–9.

46. Wright Commission, 13.

47. *Daily Mail and Empire*, 10 October 1897, 10.

48. Wright Commission, 11–13.

49. Even after the turn of this century, when garments for men and (a decade or two later) women became standardized, there remained a basic technical impediment to automation. Because they are made of *soft* material, garments can not be mechanically fed into a machine: human hands are needed to hold and guide the material. See Roger D. Waldinger, *Through the Eye of the Needle: Immigrants and Enterprise in New York's Garment Trades* (New York 1986), 54–5.

50. Mercedes Steedman, "Skill and Gender in the Canadian Clothing Industry, 1890–1940," in Craig Heron and Robert Storey, eds., *On the Job: Confronting the Labour Process in Canada* (Kingston and Montréal 1986), 158.

51. Gerald Tulchinsky, "Hidden among the Smokestacks: Toronto's Clothing Industry, 1871–1901," in David Keane and Colin Read, eds., *Old Ontario: Essays in Honour of J.M.S. Careless* (Toronto 1990), 272.

52. *Ibid.*, 274.

53. Martha Eckmann Brant, "A Stitch in Time: The Sewing Machine Industry of Ontario, 1860–1897," *Material History Bulletin*, Vol. 10 (Spring 1980), 3.

54. See the remarks of Hollis Shorey and William Muir in the Select Committee *Report*, 24, 39.

55. Tulchinsky, "Hidden," 274.

56. *Ibid.*, 271.

57. *Globe*, 19 November 1898.

58. Schmiechen, 26.

59. Steedman, 155–6.

60. Ontario Factory Inspector's *Report*, 1899, 26.

61. Select Committee *Report*, 36.

62. Ontario *Sessional Papers*, Vol. XXII, Part 7, 1890, *Annual Report of the Bureau of Industry*, 1889,

Part IV, "Wages and Cost of Living," 90. The estimate given was $214.28 annually. By only making provision for board, lodging and clothing, it identified the level of bare subsistence.

63. As a matter of course women were paid much less than men. "I don't treat the men bad," explained one Toronto clothing manufacturer, "but I even up by taking advantage of the women." *The Daily Mail and Empire*, 9 October 1897, 10.
64. Ontario Factory Inspector's *Report*, 1894, 14.
65. Wright Commission, 26.
66. King Commission, 12–14.
67. *Ibid.*, 19.
68. *Ibid.*, 15.
69. Quebec Factory Inspectors' *Report*, 1897, 39.
70. Ernest J. Chambers, ed., *The Book of Montreal: A Souvenir of Canada's Commercial Metropolis* (Montréal 1903), 171.
71. Scott and Cassidy, 24.
72. Wright Commission, 11.
73. Wright Commission, 26. On foremen demanding bribes, see Mackenzie King's article in *The Daily Mail and Empire* (Toronto), 9 October 1897, 10.
74. *Labour Gazette*, August 1901, 98; May 1901, 466.
75. Labour Commission, *Ontario Evidence*, 348, 358.
76. Wright Commission, 11; King Commission, 13.
77. Wright Commission, 24.
78. Ontario Factory Inspector's *Report*, 1899, 28.
79. *Ibid.*
80. Wright Commission, 24.
81. King Commission, 14–15.
82. *Globe*, 19 November 1898, 1.
83. Schmiechen, 56.
84. Wright Commission, 38.
85. Ontario Factory Inspector's *Report*, 1901, 12.
86. *Ibid.*, 1911, 19.
87. Wright Commission, 31.
88. Wright Commission, 30.
89. King Commission, 7–8.
90. Christine Stansell, *City of Women: Sex and Class in New York, 1789-1860* (Urbana 1987), 117.
91. Toronto *Globe*, 28 October 1868.
92. Ontario, *Report of the Committee on Child Labour*, 1907, 5. See also Dr. Augusta Stowe Gullen, "Child Labour," in National Council of Women of Canada, *Report of the Fourteenth Annual Meeting* (Ottawa 1907), 105.
93. Wright Commission, 10. Mackenzie King noted too the practice of discharging girls after their period of apprenticeship at little or no pay. King Commission, 10.
94. Wright Commission, 46.
95. *Ibid.*, 46.
96. Christina Walkley, *The Ghost in the Looking Glass: The Victorian Seamstress* (London 1981), 31–2.
97. Schmiechen, 50–1. Garment manufacture is still characterized by a distinctive set of health problems. See Susan Wortman, "The Unhealthy Business of Making Clothes," *Healthsharing*, Vol. 1, No. 1 (November 1979), 12–14.
98. Judith Fingard, "The Winter's Tale: The Seasonal Contours of Pre-Industrial Poverty in British North America, 1815-1860," Canadian Historical Association, *Historical Papers/Communications historiques* (1974), 65–94.
99. *Globe*, 28 October 1868.
100. See Ian Davey, "The Rhythm of Work and the Rhythm of School," in Neil McDonald and Alf Chaiton, eds., *Egerton Ryerson and His Times* (Toronto 1978), 221–53.
101. Cited in Schmiechen, 61. Seamstresses turned to part-time prostitution in contemporary Paris also, when their wages were inadequate. See Joan Wallach Scott, "Men and Women in the Parisian Garment Trades: Discussions of Family and Work in the 1830s and 1840s," in Pat Thane *et al.*, eds., *The Power of the Past: Essays for Eric Hobsbawm* (Cambridge 1984), 83–4. The "fallen" woman depicted in a series of sketches of the underside of municipal life had been a home needleworker. See *Toronto by Gaslight: The Night Hawks of a Great City* (Toronto 1884), 61.
102. 24 February 1858, cited in Walkley, 82.
103. *Labour Reformer*, 1 December 1886, cited in Lori Rotenberg, "The Wayward Worker: Toronto's Prostitutes at the Turn of the Century," in Janice Acton *et al.*, eds., *Women at Work: Ontario, 1850-1930* (Toronto 1974), 47.
104. Wright Commission, 42–3.
105. National Archives of Canada (NAC), W.L. Mackenzie King Diaries, MG 26, J 13, 18 September 1897.
106. *The Daily Mail and Empire*, 9 October 1897. On this subject, see also Frager, 126–7.

107. Toronto *Globe*, 28 October 1868.
108. Select Committee *Report*, 36.
109. Wright Commission, 51
110. Chambers, 171.
111. On this point, see also Schmiechen, 67–111; Morris, 50–79; and Lorraine Coons, *Women Home Workers in the Parisian Garment Industry, 1860-1915* (New York 1987), esp. 1-2.
112. Bettina Bradbury, "The Working-Class Family Economy, Montreal, 1861-1881," Ph.D. dissertation, Concordia University, 1984, 84–161; Terry Copp, *The Anatomy of Poverty: The Condition of the Working Class in Montreal, 1897-1929* (Toronto 1974), 30–42; Michael J. Piva, *The Condition of the Working Class in Toronto — 1900-1921* (Ottawa 1979), 27–60. By 1928, one historian has argued, "it was possible, for the first time, for the average male manufacturing worker to raise a family on his wages alone." Bryan D. Palmer, *Working-Class Experience: The Rise and Reconstitution of Canadian Labour, 1800-1980* (Toronto 1983), 192.
113. Select Committee *Report*, 36; *Labour Gazette*, August 1901, 98.
114. Bettina Bradbury, "The Family Economy and Work in an Industrializing City: Montreal in the 1870s," Canadian Historical Association *Historical Papers/Communications historiques* (Saskatoon 1979), 87.
115. On this point, see Bettina Bradbury, "Gender at Work at Home: Family Decisions, the Labour Market and Girls' Contributions to the Family Economy," in Gregory S. Kealey and Greg Patmore, eds., *Canadian and Australian Labour History* (St. John's 1990), 119–40.
116. Bettina Bradbury, "Surviving as a Widow in 19th-Century Montreal," *Urban History Review*, XVII, No. 3 (February 1989), 151. On widows and sewing, see also Lorna R. McLean, "Single Again: Widow's Work in the Urban Family Economy, Ottawa, 1871," *Ontario History*, LXXXIII, No. 2 (June 1991), 132.
117. Labour Commission, *Ontario Evidence*, 831-2.
118. Select Committee *Report*, 39.
119. Wright Commission, 37.
120. "Knight of Labour," "Where Labor Is Not Prayer," *Walsh's Magazine* (Toronto 1895-6), 111-16, cited in Cross, 157.
121. Wright Commission, 23.
122. Stansell, 113-14.
123. On the decline of the British needle trades, see Schmiechen, Chapter One; E.P. Thompson, *The Making of the English Working Class* (Harmondsworth 1968), 257.
124. Jacques Rouillard, *Histoire du syndicalisme québécois: Des origines à nos jours* (Montréal 1989), 17; Eugene Forsey, *Trade Unions in Canada, 1812-1902* (Toronto 1982), 28, 17.
125. Paul Craven, "Workers' Conspiracies in Toronto, 1854-72," *Labour/Le Travail*, 14 (Fall 1984), 54; Forsey, 28.
126. Examples of the continual growth of putting-out, and efforts by inside garment workers to prevent it, include an 1896 strike against 19 custom tailor shops in Toronto when they began to put out pants (Wright Commission, 42-3); a strike in 1912 against Toronto cloakmakers (*Labour Gazette*, February 1912, 784); and another Toronto strike against subcontracting in 1914 (*Labour Gazette*, June 1914, 1462).
127. Steedman, 165.
128. See, for instance, Rouillard, 256; Piva, 18; John Hample, "Workplace Conflict in Winnipeg's Custom Tailoring Trade, c.1887-1921," *Manitoba History*, No. 22 (Autumn 1991), esp. 6.
129. The Journeymen Tailors' Union of America, based in custom tailoring, arrived in Canada in 1889. It numbered only 300 in 1898. The United Garment Workers of America arrived in 1894 and focused its organizational efforts among cutters and trimmers. It peaked in strength between 1912 and 1915, when 3000 workers were organized in 24 locals. Forsey, 261, 266; Harold Logan, *Trade Unions in Canada* (Toronto 1948), 208.
130. *Canadian Journal of Fabrics*, XVIII, No. 4 (April 1901), 120.
131. *Montreal Herald*, 3 August 1899, 1.
132. See Gregory S. Kealey, *Toronto Workers Respond to Industrial Capitalism, 1867-1892* (Toronto 1980), 183; Wayne Roberts, *Honest Womanhood: Feminism, Femininity and Class Consciousness among Toronto Working Women 1893 to 1914* (Toronto 1976), 38. The JTU had organized at least some women in Winnipeg as early as 1892. See Hample, 5, 13.
133. Logan, 210-14.
134. This was also the experience of the "new unionists" in Great Britain, who had approached the organization of women workers with enthusiasm. Their inability to organize women led them to support the push for protective legislation. Morris, 123.
135. Labour Canada Library, Trades and Labour Congress of Canada, *Annual Proceedings*, 1883, 22.
136. Forsey, 456.
137. Many of these points are made by Arthur St. Pierre, "Sweating System et Salaire minimum," in his *Le Problème social: Quelques Éléments de Solution* (Montréal 1925), 38. See also Morris, Chapter IV; Frager, 98-107.
138. Cited in Piva, 96.

139. On the question of agency, see R.B. Goheen, "Peasant Politics? Village Community and the Crown in Fifteenth-Century England," *American Historical Review*, 96 (February 1991), 42–62, esp. 60–2.

140. "[M]ore effectual than law," said Mackenzie King of discriminatory purchasing and the union label in 1897. He later changed his mind. *Daily Mail and Empire*, 10 October 1897, 10.

141. On these points, see Morris, Chap. V, and Eileen Boris, "Regulating Industrial Homework: The Triumph of 'Sacred Motherhood,'" *The Journal of American History*, 71 (March 1985), 745–63.

142. On abortive efforts to form a Canadian WTUL in 1917–18, see Frager, 140–1.

143. National Council of Women of Canada, *Women of Canada* (Montréal 1901), 105.

144. Frager, 148. On the other hand, Nellie McClung claimed to have taken Premier Rodmond Roblin through the sweatshops of Winnipeg in 1913 as part of her campaign for the appointment of a female factory inspector in Manitoba. See Nellie L. McClung, *The Stream Runs Fast: My Own Story* (Toronto 1965), 101–6.

145. In Toronto, the Working Women's Protective Association was organized in 1893 under the dynamic leadership of Marie Joussaye. During its brief lifetime it pushed for better conditions for female workers; Roberts, 42–3. Helena Rose Gutteridge was active in Vancouver after 1911 in organizing working women and lobbying for protective legislation. Alison Prentice *et al.*, *Canadian Women: A History* (Toronto 1988), 200–1.

146. Richard Allen, *The Social Passion: Religion and Social Reform in Canada, 1914–28* (Toronto 1973).

147. *Globe*, 26 January 1869, cited in Cross, 194.

148. *Montreal Herald*, 3 February 1897, cited in Rome, 39–40.

149. *Montreal Herald*, 2 August 1899, 2, 4.

150. *Montreal Herald*, 4 August 1899, 8.

151. Michael Bliss, *Plague: A Story of Smallpox in Montreal* (Toronto 1991), 119, 142.

152. Quebec Factory Inspector's *Report*, 1893, 111; see also 1901, 166. Such concerns are echoed by A.W. Wright and Mackenzie King. See Wright Commission, 12; King Commission, 28–9; *Globe*, 19 November 1890.

153. In the United Kingdom, John Burnett conducted a major investigation into sweating in London's East End for the Board of Trade in 1887. This was followed by the striking of the "Select Committee of the House of Lords on the Sweating System," which issued five lengthy reports between 1888 and 1890. In the United States, the House of Representatives' Committee on Manufactures published its *Report on the Sweating System* in 1893.

154. House of Commons, *Debates*, 1 April 1896, 5052.

155. Most radically, Wright called for the extension of the factory acts to households "in which more than the husband and wife are employed and in which articles of any kind intended for sale are being manufactured." He further called for national standards of factory legislation. Wright also recommended that manufacturers be obliged to give factory inspectors the names and addresses of all individuals to whom work was subcontracted. Further recommendations called for protection at law for (the often unpaid) "learners," wholesalers' responsibility for the wages of (sub)contractors' employees, the labeling of "home-produced" goods (to invite consumers to pass judgement), and the licensing of dwellings (licenses were only to be granted if dwellings met certain standards of hygiene). The latter two recommendations were already law in certain American states. (Wright Commission, 17–19).

156. William Lyon Mackenzie King, *Industry and Humanity: A Study in the Principles Underlying Industrial Reconstruction* (Toronto 1973 [1918]), 54–5.

157. NAC, King Diaries, MG 26, J 13, 18 September 1897.

158. King, *Industry and Humanity*, 55–6.

159. The first of these was "Toronto and the Sweating System," published in the *Mail and Empire* on 9 October 1897.

160. King, *Industry and Humanity*, 56.

161. King Commission, 21–6.

162. *Ibid.*, 5.

163. *Ibid.*, 28.

164. Most importantly, subcontracting was banned (unless special permission was granted by the government, work was to be carried out on the contractor's own premises) and current wages were to be paid. If these conditions were not observed, contracts might be cancelled and/or the contractor fined. *Globe*, 30 September 1897.

165. House of Commons, *Debates*, 22 March 1900, 2466. Two and one-half years' delay indicates Mulock likely had difficulty convincing his cabinet colleagues of such a resolution. One member of the opposition declared that the resolution was simply a sop to the TLC by a government embarrassed by non-enforcement of the Alien Labour Act (2490–1). The Fair Wages Resolution formally passed on 17 July 1900 (10495–10502). The resolution did not have legal force until 1930, when the Fair Wages and Eight-Hour Day Act was passed. (21–22 Geo. V., Chap. 20, *Statutes of Canada*, 1930.)

166. Doris French, *Faith, Sweat, and Politics: The Early Trade Union Years in Canada* (Toronto 1962), 132. These schedules, most commonly pertaining to public works such as wharves and post offices, regularly appear in the pages of the *Labour Gazette*. See, for instance, the issue for September 1900, 15–27. For clothing contracts, see *Labour Gazette*, October 1904, 505.

167. King Commission, 31.

168. Quebec Factory Inspector's *Report*, 1898, 80. When first passed the factory acts of Québec and Ontario only applied to establishments employing more than twenty workers. Although Québec dropped this clause in 1888, it continued to exempt homework. In Ontario, although amendments in 1889 brought all establishments with at least five workers under the purview of the factory act, many contractors' shops escaped regulation because of their modest size. See *Statutes of Quebec*, 1885, Chap. 32, "An Act to Protect the Life and Health of Persons Employed in Factories"; the Act was amended in 1888 (Chap. 49). *Statutes of Ontario*, 1884, Chap. 39, "An Act for the Protection of Persons Employed in Factories"; 1889, Chap. 43, "An Act to Amend the Ontario Factories Act."

169. Ontario Factory Inspector's *Report*, 1899, 26–7.

170. *Montreal Herald*, 3 February 1897. British Fabians had long advocated the development of "large and healthy factories." See, for instance, Beatrice Potter, *How Best to Do Away with the Sweating System* (Manchester 1892), 12.

171. Ontario Factory Inspector's *Report*, 1897, 24.

172. *Statutes of Ontario*, 1900, Chap. 43, "An Act to Amend the Ontario Shops.Regulation Act." The Act also stipulated that all dwellings where clothing was manufactured were to be certified by a health inspector, who was to set limits on the number of people to be employed on the premises. This certification was revocable at any time in the event that sanitary standards were not maintained.

173. *Labour Gazette*, September 1900, 25–26. The western provinces did not pass similar resolutions until World War One. See Bob Russell, "A Fair or Minimum Wage? Women Workers, the State, and the Origins of Wage Regulation in Western Canada," *Labour/Le Travail*, 28 (Fall 1991), 72. It was only in 1936 that Ontario gave its Fair Wage Resolution teeth by requiring by law minimum labour standards on its contracts. See *Statutes of Ontario*, 1936, Chap. 26, "The Government Contracts Hours and Wages Act, 1936."

174. Morris, 130.

175. It is unclear whether the Ottawa council had the courage of its convictions. On the first contract to be tendered after the adoption of this policy, for firemen's clothing, the sole bidder offered uniforms at $21–22 with the label, and at $16.95 without. See the *Ottawa Citizen*, 1 May 1901, 2.

176. The federal government was less than diligent in enforcing the antisweating clauses in its contracts. In the affair of the large clothing contract awarded Montréal manufacturer Mark Workman in 1898–99, Laurier's government winked at Workman's failure to observe antisweating clauses. See the House of Commons *Debates* for 1 August 1899. It was to have been applied to railway contracts. (*Debates*, 22 March 1900, 2471). Railway navvies would have been surprised to have been informed of this.

177. Morris credits progressive employers like the Cadburys for the passage of key antisweating legislation in England. The Trades Boards Act, she argues, reflected "the concern of one section of the ruling class with the maintenance of the existing social order and their recognition of the harmful effect of sweated labour on social stability." Morris, 225.

178. Schmiechen, 174–9.

179. *Ibid.*, 179.

180. Margaret E. McCallum, "Keeping Women in Their Place: The Minimum Wage in Canada, 1910–25," *Labour/Le Travail*, 17 (Spring 1986), 29–56.

181. Only in 1940 did amendments to the Quebec Minimum Wage Act extend its provisions to homeworkers. *Statutes of Quebec*, 1940, Chap. 39. And only in 1968 did Ontario bring homeworkers under the purview of its minimum wage legislation in "The Employment Standards Act, 1968," *Statutes of Ontario*, 1968, Chap. 35.

182. In Ontario, for instance, a certain proportion of workers in a given' establishment were exempted as inexperienced and a certain proportion if under eighteen years of age. Only 80 per cent of pieceworkers in a shop or factory had to be paid the legal minimum wage. Special permits for exemptions were given in the case of elderly or handicapped workers. McCallum, 46.

183. Royal Commission on Price Spreads, *Report* (Ottawa 1935), 129, 111.

184. This conclusion is in line with recent interpretations of minimum wage legislation in France, which was applied specifically to homeworkers in 1915. It had little impact. See Coons, 305.

185. See Teal, 205–7.

186. Ontario Factory Inspector's *Report*, 1904, 33.

187. Daniel Joseph Hiebert, "The Geography of Jewish Immigrants and the Garment Industry in Toronto, 1901–1931: A Study of Ethnic and Class Relations," Ph.D. dissertation, University of Toronto, 1987, 203. On Toronto factories and inside work, see Scott and Cassidy, 11–12.

188. Piva, 18–20.

189. On the persistence of homework, see Veronica Strong-Boag, "Working Women in the 1920s," *Labour/Le Travailleur* (1979), 131–64.

190. Wright Commission, 8.

191. See Ruth Frager, "Sewing Solidarity: The Eaton's Strike of 1912," *Canadian Women's Studies/ Les cahiers de la femme*, 7 (Fall 1986), 96–8.

192. Mackenzie King pointed this out in 1898. (King Commission, 20.) In June 1909, the Jewish *Eagle* estimated that garment workers in Toronto earned $15–16 for a 49-hour week. In Montréal, workers

laboured 55–60 hours for $11. Cited in David Rome, ed., *On Our Forerunners — At Work. Epilogue. Notes on the Twentieth Century*, New Series, No. 10 (Montréal 1978), 130. See also Royal Commission on Price Spreads, 367, Table 33.

193. Scott and Cassidy, 30.
194. Royal Commission on Price Spreads, 112.
195. Steedman, 168. See also Logan, Chapter IX; and Frager, *passim*.
196. Logan, 220–1. See *Statutes of Quebec*, 1934, Chap. 56, "Collective Agreements Extension Act" and *Statutes of Ontario*, 1935, Chap. 28 "Industrial Standards Act." In Ontario, this legislation required homeworkers and their employers to obtain permits for their labour.
197. At the same time, it must be stressed, unions often enshrined in contract discriminatory practices with respect to women. See Steedman, 167; Frager, 125–6.
198. Michel Grant et Ruth Rose, "L'encadrement du travail à domicile dans l'industrie du vêtement au Québec," *Relations industrielles/Industrial Relations*, 40 (1985), 473–92; Carla Lipsig-Mummé, "Organizing Women in the Clothing Trades: Homework and the 1983 Garment Strike in Canada," *Studies in Political Economy*, 22 (Spring, 1987), 41–71. See also Johnson, *op. cit.* The *Globe and Mail* (2 October 1992, 1, 8) carried a report very recently of sweating's persistence, which estimated that there are now 4000 home garment workers in Ontario alone. "What's an Alfred Sung jacket that sells for $375 worth to the person who actually stitched it together? [The *Globe and Mail* informs us]: A grand total of $4."

Separate Spheres in a Separate World: African-Nova Scotian Women in Late-Nineteenth-Century Halifax County

SUZANNE MORTON

As a visible minority in a dominantly Euro-American environment, African-Nova Scotian women in the last quarter of the 19th century were conspicuous both as women and as racially different. In photographs, sketches and literary writings we can catch glimpses of black women at the Halifax city market. Court records and newspaper accounts expose "colored" women among the city's numerous prostitutes. The public nature of these particular activities distorts the diversity of the female African-Nova Scotian experience, and their high visibility to contemporaries is contrasted to their invisibility in the way that the past has been presented.[1]

The obvious public presence of African-Nova Scotian women around Halifax County and in the city streets also conflicts with predominant images of women in the 19th century. The Euro-American middle-class obsession with categorization placed women in the home and men in the workplace. This division of space, referred to as the idea of separate spheres, was supported by a host of gender-related characteristics. To some extent, this framework reflected the division of labour in society, but the ideology and values associated with it extended beyond task performance. Of course, men and women did not actually live in separate spaces, but it is impossible to deny some kind of division between public

SOURCE: Suzanne Morton, "Separate Spheres in a Separate World: African-Nova Scotian Women in Late-19th-Century Halifax County," *Acadiensis* 22, 2 (Spring 1993), 61–83.

and private existed. Men and women shared both a domestic and public life, and the idea of separate spheres was less about the physical reality than about the way that society was thought to be ordered.

African-Nova Scotian women lived in a bicultural world with two distinct historical communities shaping their identities. Evidence of the tenacity of the culture of the African diaspora was suggested by women's central participation in trade, their flamboyant taste in dress, and their skills in the art of herbal healing.[2] While folklorist Arthur Huff Fauset concluded during Nova Scotia fieldwork in the 1930s that the "pressure of western culture" had led to the loss of traditional stories, he also noted the retention of special religious customs and dialect.[3] In 19th-century Halifax County, some African-Nova Scotian women continued African traditions through activities such as making baskets, carrying them on their heads and drawing upon an extensive oral tradition of pharmacopoeia.[4] Women managed to combine the culture of the African diaspora, which included economic independence and relative sexual autonomy, with aspects of the Euro-American gender conventions such as the ideology of separate spheres.[5]

American research has suggested that while African-Americans maintained transatlantic traditions, they were strongly influenced by 19th-century Euro-American bourgeois gender conventions. Historians such as Jacqueline Jones, Evelyn Brooks Higginbotham, James Horton and Sharon Harley have argued that separate spheres ideology offered self-respect and protection to a group of women particularly vulnerable to economic exploitation and sexual harassment and assault in the public sphere. Elevating domestic culture made a great deal of sense in a hostile world. Women's low status as wage-earners encouraged them to adopt as their central identity their domestic and family roles as wives, mothers and sisters.[6] The conceptual framework of separate spheres offers insight into the experience of African-Nova Scotian women by demonstrating both the constraint and the empowerment it offered. Separate spheres ideology did not reflect the physical or material reality of their lives, nor was it the only ideology shaping their identity. Racism and sexism, however, meant that separate spheres ideology afforded women both limitations and protection. Halifax County was selected as the focus for this study because of the large concentration of African-Nova Scotians both in the city and in surrounding rural communities such as Preston, Hammonds Plains and Beech Hill, also known as Beechville.

Blacks came to Nova Scotia with European settlement as slaves, both as Loyalists and Loyalist property after 1783, as refugees during the War of 1812, and throughout the 19th century as West Indian immigrants connected by the North Atlantic economy. Many households in Halifax County originally settled on poor agricultural land around Preston and Hammonds Plains and found that subsistence farming was possible only when household production was supplemented with the day-labour wages available in the city. Rural communities continued to be important, but households and individuals attracted by wage-labour moved into the city of Halifax, concentrating themselves in the working-class Ward Five along Creighton, Maynard and Gottingen Streets or the peri-urban Ward Six community known as Africville. Urban migration rarely solved economic problems and many African-Nova Scotian men and women were among the thousands of Maritimers who left the region for better opportunities in the Boston states or Central Canada. Sources make numbers difficult to determine and the census was highly unreliable; however, in 1881 there were 1,039 Nova Scotians of African descent listed as living in the city and another 1,485 in the county and Dartmouth, for 2,524 people in the county's total population of 67,981.[7]

Research on African-Nova Scotians in the 19th century is generally hampered by the paucity of reliable sources. Descriptions by Nova Scotians of European descent are marked by racism and by a disregard that extended to government records such as the decimal census. African-Nova Scotians were seriously under-enumerated in the census and their entries marked by a high degree of inaccuracy. For example, an examination of black women buried in the Halifax Camp Hill cemetery between 1871 and 1873 and between 1879 and 1890 revealed that less than half of the 86 women interred could be matched with either the 1871 or 1881 census.[8] Sources authored by the black community are rare and generally restricted to church conventions and petitions.[9] The prominence of Peter McKerrow as historian and secretary of the African Baptist Association and family member of the household that most frequently appeared in legal sources may also distort any insights. It is impossible to separate McKerrow's personal values of respectability and appropriate behaviour from more widely-held attitudes. The absence of diaries, letters or even records of women's organizations means that we can know something about the material conditions of women's lives, but not their self-perceptions and attitudes. On the rare opportunities when we can see them, we are able only to observe their actions, never fully to understand their motivations.[10]

While Nova Scotia was a racist society in the 19th century, the circumstances were very different from those in the United States. Slavery, although important, was never widely practised. Furthermore, unlike the urban free blacks of the north, more than half the African-Nova Scotian population lived in rural areas where they were property owners, albeit of often very poor land. Wage-labour, therefore, was not as vital to community survival, as it was often mixed with subsistence agriculture or household-based manufacturing. Nor was the labour of African-Nova Scotian women in any particular demand. High levels of outmigration across Nova Scotian society suggest a surplus of local labour. In the case of African-Nova Scotian women, this meant that they competed for positions in domestic service with urban and rural women of Euro-American descent.

TABLE 1   African-Nova Scotian Population Halifax County, 1871 and 1881

	Total Population		African-Nova Scotian Population		Per cent of Total Population		African-Nova Scotian Women Over Age 12	
	1871	1881	1871	1881	1871	1881	1871	1881
Ward One	6634	7998	44	36	0.7	0.5	26	20
Ward Two	3320	3598	100	24	3.0	0.7	46	17
Ward Three	3277	2801	149	77	4.5	2.7	64	32
Ward Four	2331	1942	115	91	4.9	4.7	51	46
Ward Five	10046	13545	414	691	4.1	5.1	188	322
Ward Six	3974	6170	71	120	1.8	1.9	24	44
Total Halifax	29582	36054	893	1039			399	481
Beech Hill	407	438	66	61	16.2	13.9	23	26
Hammonds Plains	740	785	319	355	43.1	45.2	102	118
Dartmouth	4358	5673	172	252	3.9	4.4	58	81
Windsor Road	850	965	102	112	12.0	11.6	34	39
Truro Road	998	903	93	98	9.3	0.9	26	36
Preston	715	794	516	594	72.2	74.8	186	218
Other	19313	22369	27	13	0.1	>0.1	5	7
Total	56963	67981	2188	2524	3.8	3.7	833	1006

Source: Canada, *Census of 1871*, Vol. 1, Table III, "Origins of People", pp. 326-8; Canada, *Census — 1881*, Vol. 1, Table III, "Origin of the People", p. 212, and Census manuscripts [microfilm], 1871 and 1881, "Nominal Return of the Living."

With this difficulty in documentation, and the racial bias of most historians, research so far has produced relatively little insight into the 19th-century African-Nova Scotian community and, with the important exceptions of work by Judith Fingard and Sylvia Hamilton, even less specifically on women.[11] Assumptions made about the historical experiences of women have been a mix of current cultural stereotypes and imported models from American history. For example, in a published 1985 lecture James W. St. G. Walker pointed to the common stereotype that the local community had been dominated by women, who were often responsible for "family discipline, household management and even the breadwinning."[12] In an interesting construction of race and gender identity, Walker claimed that there were "more female" jobs available for black women than "black" jobs for the black man.[13] The differentiation between "black" — read male — and "female" immediately alerts us to the acceptance of a preconceived norm in which women were not supposed to be directly involved in breadwinning. This view of the past had also been reflected in the research conducted by Frances Henry in 1969 when she made the remarkable claim that dated women's paid labour outside the home as "a fairly recent phenomenon in the community."[14] Henry believed that the transformation from a subsistence to a consumer economy forced women out of the home and into the labour market to supplement the low wages available to African-Nova Scotian men. As with Walker's implicit categorization of "black" jobs and "female" jobs, Henry presumed the existence of a time when subsistence production could support a household without the need for supplemental wages or perhaps even the public economic activities of women. In this view wage-earning women outside the home were an exception to the normal gendered division of labour. Henry's identification of a well-defined sexual division of labour in which "it was generally felt the woman's place was in the home" may have been more recent than she had imagined.

The inconsistency between prevalent expectations and lived experience was further complicated by the fact that the experience of African-Nova Scotian women in late-19th-century Halifax County was by no means homogeneous. Divisions existed based on class, rural or urban residency, religion, ethnicity and more abstract criteria such as the value placed on respectability. Different waves of immigration may have carried with them distinct gender conventions. While these divisions were real, the racist nature of this society meant that these internal divisions were not perceived by the dominant Euro-American culture. The puritanical women who silently stare at us through studio photographs differed greatly from the lively market women with their multi-layered petticoats and pipes. But as late as the 1920s, a white woman in Halifax looking for help with her laundry felt free to stop any African-Nova Scotian woman on the street and request "where she could get a good girl."[15]

The example of being approached on the street not only illustrates the racist assumptions of this white woman but also her assumptions about class. Most African-Nova Scotian households in Halifax and in the county were working class and as a result many black women shared aspects of the lives of, and sometimes their actual residence with, white working-class women. But racism in fact reinforced class and, unlike their white counterparts, African-Nova Scotian women had virtually no legal wage-earning opportunities outside domestic service, taking in laundry, or sewing. Regardless of status in the community, property holdings or occupation of the husband, married women and widows charred, and young women were servants. Certainly there must have been a considerable variety of conditions under these labels. Unpredictable and irregular general day-work differed from work for regular weekly clients. Young women who lived in service in other African-Nova Scotian households may have had a dissimilar experience than their sisters and cousins who worked for white families. Indeed, one African-Nova Scotian household in Ward 5 kept a servant in 1881, even though their own daughter worked as a servant elsewhere. It is nearly impossible to understand class solely in terms of occupation as the few occupations reported offer no insight into hierarchy or power within the community. Evelyn Brooks Higginbotham has noted that racism and limited occupations among

African-Americans "skewed income and occupational levels so drastically" that social scientists have measured adherence to bourgeois conventions, including gender relations, "as additional criteria for discerning blacks who maintained or aspired to middle-class status from those who practised alternative lifestyles."[16] Racism and sexism and the resulting limited employment opportunities open to African-Nova Scotian women obscured the level of real difference within the community.

Paid work usually related to a woman's life course. Young women before marriage and widows without access to a male wage were the women most likely to work. Waged-work outside the home for married women may have been more common within the black community, but this was not necessarily reflected in the census. As the census undoubtedly missed many black women, it also missed many women's occupations, particularly when a man's occupation was provided. Relatively few married women were listed in the 1871 and 1881 censuses as engaging in paid labour; but these included schoolteacher Caroline Byers, dressmakers Mary Howell and Elizabeth Brown, and three shopkeepers — Isabel Dixon, Margaret Gleen and Catherine Gideon — whose husbands were employed in migratory occupations as seamen or ship stewards. The virtual absence of female farmers in the 1871 census conceals much agricultural work, but specifically the source of agricultural production in the many rural female-headed households. Married women who undertook occasional or casual day labour as charwomen were also severely under-represented in the 1871 census, which listed only six women. This number increased to 57 in 1881 (see Table 2). The under-representation of this form of casual employment was significant. Was casual day-labour for black women so common that no mention of it was thought necessary? Many other occupations were also missed in the census. Both Mary Ann Reid Gigi and Sarah Anderson of Hammonds Plains had no occupation listed in the census yet both worked regularly as midwives.[17] Other medical and pharmaceutical skills widely held by women also went unacknowledged. Louisa Bailey's 1891 occupation as a herbalist would have been impossible to discern without independent consultation from city directories.[18] Not surprisingly, illegal occupations such as brothel keeping, prostitution and bootlegging were absent, but these illicit occupations formed only a small part of the informal or hidden economy operating in the city and county. Residents of Halifax would have regularly seen African-Nova Scotian women at work in the informal economy, visible in public view at the Halifax market in the city's downtown. It was the perception of census enumerators that obscured the important public but informal roles women played in the economy, whether this be as vendors, boarding house operators, charwomen or midwives.

The under-representation of African-Nova Scotian women's public work was characteristic of all working-class women. While African-Nova Scotian women and working-class women of European descent shared

TABLE 2   African-Nova Scotian Female Occupations in Halifax County, 1871 and 1881

Occupations	Halifax 1871	Halifax 1881	Dartmouth and Rural 1871	Dartmouth and Rural 1881	Total 1871	Total 1881
Servant	55	80	9	45	64	125
Butler		2				2
Cook		5				5
Housekeeper		1	4	1	4	2
Pastry Cook		1				1
Charwoman	5	57	1		6	57
General Work	2				2	
Housecleaner	1				1	
Washing	27	5	4		31	5
Dressmaker	2	10	2		4	10
Basketmaker				1		1
Grocer	2				2	
Confectioner	1	1			1	1
Shopkeeper		4				4
School Teacher	1	1	2		3	1
Private Tutor	1				1	
Clerk		1		2		3
Farmer			1	12	1	12
Collector		1				1
Hairdresser		1				1
Illegible		1				1
Total	97	171	23	61	120	232

Source: Canada, Census manuscripts [microfilm], 1871 and 1881, "Nominal Return of the Living."

the lowest-paid jobs, employment for black women may have been particularly difficult to acquire and vulnerable to loss. In the limited strata of "female" jobs, African-Nova Scotians did not work in factories, and only in shops if they were family operations. The number of rural and urban Euro-American women available for domestic work meant that black women were not in specific demand as servants. Analysis of the placements of African-Nova Scotian women in Halifax households reveals that although Ward One had nearly four times the number of domestic servants as any other ward, only 11 were of African descent. Conversely, Ward Five, where households were least likely to include domestic servants and had the highest ratio of domestic servants to the general population, named 53 female black servants.[19]

African-Nova Scotians may have had difficulty acquiring positions as servants as they were disproportionately absent from the city's best residential area and over-represented in the worst area. If acquiring a position as a servant was difficult, other occupations were more blatantly blocked. Even the pretence of upward mobility was not available. Racial discrimination meant that young black women were prohibited from being trained as nurses or entering the Provincial Normal School at Truro to prepare for a teaching career.[20] Although prohibited from professional qualifications, as early as 1874 a number of local black women undertook teaching under the provision of a special permissive licence.[21]

The need for teachers in the black rural communities was constant. Few young women who had the option of residency in the city chose to return to the more difficult rural life. Good students were encouraged to get their licences, but this did not affect the supply of available black teachers nor were they necessarily successful in obtaining positions in desirable schools. In 1891 the superintendent noted the case of a young black woman at the Halifax County Academy who, upon finishing her Grade C exam, was eligible for a permissive licence, but "I could not, however, persuade her to go to the country and teach, as her prospects were much better in the city."[22] Selina Williams of Fall River was an exception. As a young black teacher with a permissive licence, she taught day school successively at North Preston and Beech Hill, in addition to her duties as a Sunday School teacher. Her unusual decision to stay in the county made her the object of Peter McKerrow's praise in his church history and in the convention minutes.[23] McKerrow concluded that "If a dozen or more of the young women in various sections of the country where these schools are organized would contemplate the good they would be doing for the race in years to come they would wake up, even now, to a sense of duty."[24] In this interesting assessment, McKerrow clearly placed the responsibility of education and "race improvement" on women, while at the same time implying the absence of this sense of duty among local young women. McKerrow's assumption that women were responsible for public education and community service drew upon the tenets of separate spheres ideology.

Education of daughters was taken seriously by many parents with at least one young woman sent to Boston when the racist policies of the Halifax school board prohibited access to education beyond grade seven.[25] But the desire for female literacy was not restricted to young girls. Forty-year-old laundress Eliza Johnston attended the Maynard Street School in the 1880s as a full-time student, achieving 100 per cent in several subjects for her efforts.[26] Rural women also cared about reading and writing. Selina Williams recalled in 1956 that when the North Preston school opened in 1897, mothers and fathers accompanied their children to class until the school inspector, concerned about overcrowding, agreed to provide lighting for an adult night school conducted three nights a week.[27]

Literacy or advanced education, however, did nothing to alter the basic fact that there were few careers open to young black women in Halifax. Many young women joined their brothers, husbands and parents or even set off by themselves to New England or Central Canada. That these women sent back to Halifax barrels of used clothes from employers suggests that even women who left the limited local opportunities still found themselves in the restricted field of domestic service.[28]

Domestic service was the most important occupation for African-Nova Scotian women as noted in the census occupational listings. It was confirmed in the racist attitudes of Anglo-Celtic middle-class women such as Mary Jane Lawson, who conceded of her black Preston neighbours that "many of the women make good domestic servants."[29] Paid domestic labour in a private household is full of contradictions. Domestic work is perhaps the ultimate form of women's work, but not when it is performed in someone else's home, and not when it is undertaken as part of a wage relationship. Women performing domestic work outside their own homes undertook work that was simultaneously public and private, productive and reproductive.[30] The widespread nature of this work was reflected in the censuses, which listed 64 African-Nova Scotian women as servants in 1871 and 125 in 1881. A similar increase was recorded in the number of women listed as charwomen, which increased from six to 57. These dramatic increases were likely the result of slightly improved record-keeping rather than any specific change in the labour market. The only occupation for African-Nova Scotian women where numbers declined from 1871 to 1881 was work as laundresses; the 31 women in this group in 1871 declined to only five women ten years later. Mary Ann Brown Thomas, widow of James Bates Thomas, may have attempted to counterattack the advent of commercial laundries that affected casual employment opportunities in this area, listing herself in the 1880–81 city directory as the proprietor of the Prince of Wales Laundry, operating from her home. Such commercial attempts were rare, and service occupations were typically private with some specialization as cooks, housekeepers and housecleaners. Specialization did not necessarily mean permanent residence with the employer. Halifax women may have preferred day labour where they did not live permanently in someone else's home and were not at the beck and call of the employer 24 hours a day. To achieve this independence and the possibility of a private life, one Hammonds Plains woman walked the eight miles into Bedford to do domestic work.[31]

Private work in someone else's home contrasted with the obviously public work black women undertook in their participation at the city market. Market activity combined domestic skills, market gardening, resourcefulness and imagination to ensure that the necessary supply of cash continued to come into the household. Surviving photographs and the classic 1872 sketch by W.O. Carlisle, "Negresses Selling Mayflowers on the Market Place," corroborate the literary evidence. Women from the county gathered wild fruits, according to one witness, from every conceivable kind of berry and flowers according to the season. In the early spring mayflowers and mosses appeared. These were followed by bouquets of ferns and little birchbark boxes. In the late fall and as Christmas approached, wreaths, evergreen swags and branches joined dyed grasses, "carefully pressed and waxed" autumn leaves, and sumach berries.[32] Throughout the year, women also sold an assortment of herbs and "roots of miraculous properties," all kinds of market vegetables and "Brooms, baskets, tubs, clothes-props, peasticks, hop and bean poles, rustic seats and flower boxes." Some vendors also sold the famous baskets,[33] and one Preston woman in the 1881 census reflected this important trade when she identified herself as a basketmaker. Preparing these goods for market meant a tremendous amount of work that combined reproductive and productive labour and the efforts of most members of the household. Various goods had to be made, grown or painstakingly gathered, and then arranged and transported into the city. In such a complex group of household activities the boundary between public productive and private reproductive work is impossible to isolate.

While separate spheres ideology limited the economic opportunities available to African-Nova Scotian women, it did not offer reciprocal financial protection. Low pay and irregular work meant that African-Nova Scotian women were dependent on access to a male wage, even if it was lower and more irregular than that available to other working-class men. Economic circumstances also meant that women were not protected from the workplace. Rural women lived and worked on their farms. The time women spent fashioning splitwood baskets or arranging bouquets to be sold at the city market was not distinct from the time spent on other household duties such as childcare or tending the garden. Likewise, urban women engaged in domestic service or employed in family business experienced no spatial differentiation between the location of work and home.

This lack of spatial differentiation was evident even among the McKerrow-Thomas family, one of the most prominent African-Nova Scotian families in the city and county. Sometime in the 1840s the Welshman James Thomas married Hannah Saunders, an African-Nova Scotian living in Preston. Thomas eventually became leader of the African Baptist Church of Nova Scotia and fathered with Hannah at least seven children. Religious leadership, business success and marriages of the children linked the Thomas family to the most respectable black families of Halifax. Among the connections of this family was the marriage of daughter Mary Eliza to Antigua-born Peter McKerrow in 1863. McKerrow was a leading member of the Morning Glory Lodge of Good Templars, the Ancient and Accepted Masons Union Lodge No. 18, trustee of Cornwallis Street African Baptist Church and secretary to the Nova Scotia African Baptist Association.[34]

In 1892 the Supreme Court of Nova Scotia heard an appeal case regarding property from the estate of Rev. James Thomas that had been lost through foreclosure and then secretly purchased by his son-in-law and estate executor Peter McKerrow. McKerrow claimed his acquisition of the property was without the knowledge of his wife or three sisters-in-law and that he was uncertain as to when they eventually discovered the transaction as he had "never discussed the matter with any of them."[35] Furthermore, McKerrow claimed his wife, Mary, had co-executed this mortgage without becoming familiar with the contents of the papers she was signing. Since one aspect of this case was the right of the female heirs to a monthly annuity from the property, it is conceivable that they feigned ignorance to strengthen their case to entitlement of monies owing. That none of these female heirs, including his wife, knew of McKerrow's financial dealings would have been quite remarkable. Three of the heirs, Rachel Thomas, Inez Thomas and Mary McKerrow, were living in the same residence as McKerrow. Working as clerks in the business at the time of the transaction, they probably possessed some knowledge of the firm's operation. On the other hand, their financial ignorance was possible and if the ideology of separate spheres, which protected women from the marketplace, was present in any African-Nova Scotian households, it was likely to be found here. The desire for respectability and possible upward mobility partially rested on appropriate gender roles, including the adoption of separate spheres ideology even when material and class circumstances did not allow for an actual separation of workplace and residence. Certainly there was not physical protection from the workplace. Three of Rev. James Thomas's daughters resided at some point at the same address as the family's hat and fur business; in addition, Thomas's son William and his second wife, Laura, not only lived beside the Sackville Street family business, but Laura had a separate listing in the city and provincial directory to advertise her business as a dressmaker and milliner.

The notion of protecting women from the economic world was also not present in the estate of John Robinson Thomas, Rev. James Thomas's oldest son and Peter McKerrow's brother-in-law. Upon John Thomas's death in 1876 he had two insurance policies of $2,000 and $1,000 that should have provided some security for his widow and three children under the age of nine. Of this amount, however, his wife, Eliza, received only $500, while $1,500 was to be invested and divided among the three children when they reached the age of majority. A further $1,000 was given to his father along with his share in the family business. Long-term support for the widow or for the children until they qualified for their inheritance did not appear to be a primary concern of John Thomas. As a result, in the 1881 census, widow Eliza Bailey Thomas was listed as a charwoman; the children were living with neighbours and their maternal step-grandmother, not the Thomas family who received the generous proportion of their father's estate.[36] The extent to which this estate was unusual, where financial protection for an aging parent took priority over providing for a young family, is unknown as so few wills were recorded. It may have been that John Thomas believed that his widow was in a better position to support herself than his aging father and mother.

The public survival skills expected of Eliza Bailey Thomas conflict with assumptions of the female character and expose the limitations of exactly which women were to be included within "women's sphere." Dionne Brand has noted that African-Americans were rarely perceived by the dominant culture as "ladies" and that the term "lady" had "predictable race and class connotations." White ladies were protected by the private sphere of motherhood and genteel domesticity, made possible by material circumstances that were beyond the resources of most black women.[37] The types of waged employment available to African-Nova Scotians were tasks that women traditionally performed, but they were with rare exception suitable work for "ladies."[38] Black women were expected to be engaged in hard physical labour such as scrubbing, thereby confirming their unladylike reputation; yet, at the same time, those who restricted their labour to the private domestic sphere and expected their husbands to act as breadwinners could be perceived as lazy.[39] In creating the image of the unladylike woman, race reinforced and worked together with class so that the bonds of womanhood were narrow.

Nova Scotian women of European descent were careful to distance and differentiate themselves from black women with racist characterizations and descriptions of their unladylike behaviour. In Margaret Marshall Saunders' depictions of black women in her journal entries and novels, she emphasized their unrestrained and therefore unladylike manners such as laughing loudly or swearing, and even alleged masculine characteristics such as smoking pipes or walking with a basket balanced on their heads.[40] Mary Jane Lawson's offensive comparison of the Preston women at market to monkeys is well-known — "chattering and like them enjoying the warmth and pleasantness of summer." Less familiar is the scorn she heaps on African-Nova Scotian women for playing at being real ladies in the festive atmosphere surrounding summer baptisms. Lawson sarcastically noted that "Before such events, there is a great demand for articles of dress: parasols, hoop-skirts, sash ribbons, veils, and fans, are all apparently necessary adjuncts of the ceremony." The fact that the symbols of femininity and middle-class womanhood were subject to mockery when associated with African-Nova Scotian women immediately attunes us to the links between racism and sex. In the late 19th century, black women in Halifax County were equally vulnerable to ridicule by their association with masculine paraphernalia such as pipes or the most feminine accessories of dress.[41]

The press also delighted in providing examples of "unladylike" behaviour among African-Nova Scotian women, such as that of the woman in 1874 found guilty of beating her husband with a potato masher.[42] The events that precipitated this reaction were irrelevant as ridicule and her unfeminine reaction became central in portraying a woman who actively defended herself. An unorganized wedding ceremony that nearly resulted in the bridesmaid and groomsman mistakenly marrying was another opportunity to exaggerate the differences between white and black women. In the confusion a white woman stepped up "who like all her sex and color, knew the ceremony well" and stopped the proceedings before the wrong couple wed. The point of this story under the sarcastic byline of "Almost Fatal Mistake" was that black women were not even familiar with the most important female ritual of the wedding.[43]

In the same way, racial stereotypes about black sexuality and the economic realities of African-Nova Scotian women could reinforce each other in the minds of the white middle class. That African-Nova Scotian women composed a disproportionate number of the city's prostitutes is hardly surprising in light of the absence of alternative occupations. While this figure may be inflated by the special attention directed at black prostitutes, the result of their visibility as a racial minority, it nonetheless underlines the lack of legal options available.[44] The association between prostitution and African-Nova Scotians may have influenced white middle-class attitudes. Judith Fingard has hypothesized that the lack of female reform agitation around this "social problem" in part may be the result of its association with the African-Nova Scotian community.[45] If this damning racism was true, it suggests the extreme extent to which white women distanced themselves from their African-Nova Scotian sisters. White women wanted to make certain that not all women were included in their sphere.

As a result of this racial malignancy and meagre economic options, it was not surprising that elements of separate spheres ideology were adopted by the black community. The ideology offered advantages beyond accommodation to the dominant culture. Sharon Harley in her work on African-American women has noted that a strictly defined sexual division of labour could be instrumental in supporting claims to middle-class status, or to what Judith Fingard might describe perhaps more appropriately as respectability. In addition to status, adherence to clearly defined gender roles could also protect single and married African-American women from racist charges of "immorality" used to undermine this femininity.[46] This interpretation appeared to be supported by the analysis of Carrie Best, born in 1903 in New Glasgow, who described her mother as "a meticulous homemaker and cook" whose duties extended beyond her home as she worked for at least one other family. But working outside the home in no way seemed to interfere with the importance she placed on her role as a wife and mother. As Best observed of her mother: "Although kind, loving and generous she was none the less a disciplinarian guarding the sanctity of the home and family safety like a lioness with her cubs. Black womanhood was held in low esteem during the early part of the twentieth century and only the home afforded the protection needed to ensure security from outside influences."[47] Best's description of her mother reveals the distinctive way that separate spheres ideology was interpreted by African-Nova Scotian women as it mixed the idea of protection offered by the private sphere with power and strength. Here was a metaphor that projected the domestic sphere not as a haven for delicate and helpless women but rather as the lair of the proud and strong lioness and her cubs.

Almost all that was happening within peoples' residences remains concealed. Although no topic in North American history has produced more debate than the discussion of the African-American family, family structure among 19th-century African-Nova Scotians is unexplored. The general debate has been largely characterized by the label of the matriarchal family, offering the false impression that women had more power than was the actual case. Matriarchy has been used as a relative term to contrast the gender relations around power in the middle-class Euro-American family. African-Nova Scotian women probably had more power within the household than their white middle-class counterparts. But as Suzanne Lebsock has cogently argued, "given this standard, women need not be the equals of men, much less men's superiors, in order to qualify as matriarchs."[48] The label of matriarchy given the black family actually offers much insight into the structure of white middle-class households. Given the American literature one would also expect to find numerous female-headed households. While there is some evidence in the frustrated notes of the census enumerator of alternative household structures, notably common-law relationships, the census data do not appear to suggest an unusually high degree of female-headed households, even in this transient port city (see Table 3).[49] In Halifax it also does not appear that women deliberately chose not to marry. Prominent widows with property who remarried included Hannah Saunders Thomas, Louisa Brown Bailey and Eliza Bailey Thomas.[50] What seems to be most distinct about the structure of African-Nova Scotian households, both urban and rural, was the number of children with different surnames than the household head, or the number of third generation children residing in the household. This fluid household structure cautions us against imposing a preconceived definition of the private family. The public/private divide may have had different boundaries as extended family and neighbours' children were frequently incorporated into what one might have considered to be the most closed and personal relationship.

Like their Euro-American counterparts, at times African-Nova Scotian women were purposely kept out of the public, particularly the political, sphere. An 1864 petition from "the coloured population of Hammonds Plains" was submitted by 40 men and on behalf of "14 Widows and some other helpless Females with Families."[51] Similarly, women did not sign the petitions criticizing racially segregated schools, although they did attend and speak at meetings on the topic.[52] To what extent this exclusion and emphasis on women reflected political power in the black community is unknown, but it seems plausible that, at least partially, women were excluded in the hope of benefiting from relief grants or better schools through conforming to the obvious patterns in the dominant culture.[53] On the other hand, while all female organizations were

TABLE 3   African-Nova Scotian Household Structure in Halifax County, 1871 and 1881

	Female-headed households with children under 12		Households with children under 12 in which a married male and female are listed		Households with children under 12 with a surname different than household head or when born after woman 50	
	1871	1881	1871	1881	1871	1881
Ward One	0	0	0	0	0	0
Ward Two	0	0	12	0	0	0
Ward Three	6	2	11	6	1	0
Ward Four	3	2	7	10	1	0
Ward Five	13	14	38	56	6	14
Ward Six	1	0	7	17	1	0
Beech Hill	2	1	8	6	3	0
Hammonds Plains	5	4	36	37	17	15
Dartmouth	2	6	22	26	5	3
Windsor Road	2	1	7	8	3	7
Truro Road	3	3	7	11	1	4
Preston	10	12	51	65	7	33
Other	1	0	2	1	0	0

Source: Canada, Census manuscripts, 1871 and 1881 [microfilm], "Nominal Return of the Living."

slow to develop within the African-Nova Scotian community, masculine institutional social life from the 1870s on was varied and included the Morning Glory Lodge of the Good Templars, the African-Nova Scotian Lodge of the Freemasons and the African Choral and Literary Association.[54] These African-Nova Scotian fraternal organizations parallelled similar associations in the Protestant and Catholic Euro-American community. In the most formal aspects of public life, there was very little space for women, regardless of race.

This contradiction between formal and informal roles was nowhere more apparent than in the African-Nova Scotian churches. Separate spheres ideology, which emphasized the special spiritual nature of women, could easily justify leadership positions within the church. Yet this leadership was primarily informal. In his history of the African Baptist Association, Peter McKerrow lists more women than men in church membership and praises their contribution as "the women . . . in most of the churches, take the lead." McKerrow, however, could not allow these words of praise to stand on their own, and women's public position in the Nova Scotia churches was justified by biblical precedent: "Good women are like the precious stones. Our saviour found no fault with the woman who went into the city and told all things that ever she did. Dorcas made clothes for the poor of her community. Priscilla, with her husband, took Apollos and instructed him more perfectly in the way of God."[55] Thus women had a historic role in the church, but the models presented were not the dynamic, independent and powerful women of the Old Testament, but the more feminine servants and teachers of the New Testament.

Like the seamstress and the teacher, the church provided women the opportunity for acceptable public roles such as Sunday School teachers, organists and singers.[56] Women, however, were perhaps less acceptable in church politics as participants in the internal split that divided the African Baptist Association throughout the 1870s. Rev. James Thomas noted women's involvement in this split in his 1871 circular letter that read: "The Church at Halifax stands true to her first organ and rules, with the exception of one male and 2 or 3 female: let us pray for them." Thomas then went on to note that "A number of the brethren and sisters in Preston sent a letter to the Association, stating that they were in a divided state."[57] Women were thus active in church politics even though they were generally excluded by formal structures of church government and religious leadership.[58]

Minutes from various meetings of the British Methodist Episcopal Church in Nova Scotia make no specific mention of women except in a motion of appreciation to the hosting clergyman "and lady" and as the subject in a charge of seduction against an Amherst clergyman.[59] Similarly, the African Baptist Association of Nova Scotia met for 37 years before its first female delegate attended the 1891 convention.[60] The following year three women were among the delegates, including Louisa Bailey and sisters Cooper and Fletcher.

The position of women within the local Baptist church had a dramatic boost in 1903 with the arrival of Rev. B.B.B. Johnson at the Cornwallis Street Church. Johnson himself was probably not unlike other American clergy who had a brief sojourn in Nova Scotia, except for one unique asset — his wife was ordained. The presence of Mrs. M.E. Johnson, temporarily at least, changed the face of public worship at the 1903 convention at East Preston. Mrs. Johnson led the convention in two prayers and joined in a temperance sermon.[61] In 1904 she perhaps unintentionally violated Nova Scotia law when she married Edward Wilson and Sophia Smith at Preston.[62] With this exception, Mrs. Rev. Johnson appears to have spent much more time with the children in Sunday School than publicly preaching the gospel.[63]

Mrs. Johnson was not the only woman to publicly speak to the African Baptist assembly. Lay leadership was frequently female and included the Nova Scotia-born Louisa Bailey. Bailey's church interests were originally directed in the area of foreign missions but later shifted to local mission fields and temperance. By the late 1880s, Louisa Bailey was twice widowed and had connections to important families in the Baptist Church.[64] She was relatively financially secure, owning property on Creighton Street and Gerrish Lane and working successively as a dressmaker, variety and second-hand shopkeeper, and finally as a herbalist from a store-front on Gottingen Street.[65] At the 1885 Baptist convention, Bailey was among the three women who addressed the meeting on temperance. According to McKerrow she "spoke admirable on the question at issue, showing the great influence that women have either for good or evil." Again, the influence of the separate spheres ideology, that women had a special role in promoting morality, was obvious in McKerrow's conclusion that "If Christian women would nobly stand up against the drink traffic wherever they go, they will be using an influence the greatness of which eternity alone will reveal, and a just recompense will be their reward."[66] In 1892 Bailey, one of the first female delegates to attend any convention, again "spoke with much force" on the important issue of temperance.[67] Her addresses to the various Baptist conventions thereafter were regular as she continued her involvement in temperance, home mission and local church operations.[68] Although there was no formal organization for home mission work, Louisa Bailey together with Charlotte Grosse of Beech Hill "gave verbal statements of work performed by them at Beech Hill and adjoining settlements." The work of Bailey and Grosse was recognized in the church's mission report and by the Africville congregation who also were touched by their hard work.[69] Whether Louisa Bailey herself upheld the ideology of separate spheres and a limited public role for women is difficult to determine. Certainly her private life was full. After her husband's death Bailey had the responsibility for her successive businesses, an aging mother and two stepgrandchildren. Similarly, her colleague in home missions, Charlotte Grosse, was able to combine active leadership outside the house with the responsibility for seven children who in the 1881 census were between the ages of less than a year and 13.[70] As for white working-class women who joined the Salvation Army, religious work provided a legitimate justification for moving beyond the domestic sphere,[71] and we must surmise that both Bailey and Grosse crossed boundaries that defined the proper place for women. At the same time, Louisa Bailey at least appears to have been cautious and aware of the potential conflict in her public leadership. At the 1907 convention, as a woman who was probably approaching her seventies, "She told how much can be done in a quiet way to advance God's Kingdom upon earth by sisters as well as brothers."[72] If Louisa Bailey actually used the phrase "quiet way" to convey the idea that the public actions of women were not completely acceptable, and this description was not the opinion of the convention secretary, the delicate balance between public and private roles for women was acknowledged.

The presence of remarkable women in "quiet" but vital leadership positions may explain why women's groups within the church were slow to develop. As early as 1883, Peter McKerrow began his campaign for the establishment of female home missionary societies in every congregation as "their labors are generally more successful than the males."[73] No action followed this call and again in 1903 an equally unsuccessful motion was presented by the "Reverend Sister Johnson." Thereafter, nothing formal was established for ten years until the creation of the Women's Missionary Society in 1913 and the Ladies' Auxiliary in 1917.[74] Quasi-women's groups had emerged in the 1890s, such as the Pastor Aid Society at the Cornwallis Street Church with Louisa Bailey as president and Mary Eliza McKerrow as vice-president. This was not a formal women's group, for although most of the executive appears to have been women, the important position of secretary was held by Peter McKerrow himself.[75] The appearance of largely women's groups with perhaps a token man was also characteristic of white women's organizations in the city.[76] Female church organization developed very late among the African-Nova Scotian women, largely because women were not fulfilling an auxiliary role but were at the centre of financial and spiritual leadership. While women such as Louisa Bailey and Charlotte Grosse stand out, less prominent women also played a crucial role. Access to paid employment meant that to a limited extent women were also able, if they so chose, to financially support their church. This financial contribution by women was impressive in the 1903 list of church members who had paid their annual tax. At the Cornwallis Street Church, 11 couples were listed, along with nine men and 16 single women. This pattern of extraordinary support from single women was repeated in the rural areas such as Beech Hill where two single men are listed beside nine women.[77]

The churches acted as both a space for women to provide financial and spiritual leadership and a buttress for those in the community who upheld a belief in separate spheres. The church also provided a haven where public behaviour was almost safe from ridicule.[78] The acceptable way for women to be strong and have an identity outside the home was spiritually. Therefore when Hammonds Plains native Caroline David died in 1903 she was described as a "kind mother, a loving wife and a true child of God."[79] Similarly, Viola Parsons remembered stories of her great-grandmother Sarah Anderson, probably born in the 1830s. Parsons was told that her great-grandfather "was an easy going man, but [great-grand] Ma was strong, courageous and a hard worker. She didn't have any fear because she was filled with the Holy Spirit."[80] This hard worker was widowed with ten children in 1871 and operated one of the most productive farms in Hammonds Plains. African-Nova Scotian women, who were often the object of ridicule, had few occasions to be presented with dignity in the white press. Yet a description of a large baptism at Africville in 1874 conceded that "the white robes of the lady converts presented quite a pleasing appearance."[81] In a specific religious moment, even the racist press could briefly see African-Nova Scotian women as ladies.

The ideological construction of separate spheres had meaning to African-Nova Scotian women, but it could not be taken at face value. The ideal of separate spheres, with its emphasis on supposedly broad-based unique characteristics, was based on the experience of middle-class Euro-American women. When these women categorized and classified black women, the veneer of sisterhood did not stand up, and separate spheres became a tool of racism to exclude women who were different. Euro-American men and women who professed a belief in separate spheres worked to ensure that gender was not to be the only primary division within society. Common links that existed between black and white working-class women and all women tied to rural subsistence production were not recognized. Separation of productive and reproductive work in most rural subsistence households was a fiction, and the segregation of work and home was equally unlikely in the city. The public lives of African-Nova Scotian women were marked by an informality and a corresponding vulnerability, which occurred in the context of a lively informal economy and lay leadership positions in the church. Gender ideology that placed women in the home offered protection and dignity within their own community, even if it could not secure recognition from the white middle class. While the ideology of separate spheres could be usefully adopted to respond to the particular needs of African-Nova Scotian women it also made them susceptible to a powerful combination of racism and sexism.

NOTES

1. I have consciously chosen to use "African-Nova Scotian" in this text to emphasize the historic presence of people who shared some form of African descent in Nova Scotia. I use "African" — in the same way that other groups of "hyphenated Canadians" are identified — with the understanding that the Nova Scotia black community did not originate in a single geographic location in Africa and that their historic identity was further shaped by the United States or the Caribbean. In the context of this study the contemporary term to describe African-Nova Scotians was "colored." This essay is not Afro-centric in its outlook as it investigates the effect of a dominant Euro-Nova Scotian cultural ideology on this community and generally overlooks what may have been more important issues for the black community such as economic survival, racism, and the impact of family separation with high levels of outmigration. As the author I should acknowledge that I am not of this community but have undertaken this research as part of my continuing interest in historical social relations in the province. I gratefully acknowledge the assistance of a SSHRC post-doctoral fellowship and the comments of Judith Fingard, the Toronto Gender History Group and my former colleagues at Queen's University.
2. Evelyn Brooks Higginbotham, "Beyond the Sound of Silence: Afro-American Women in History," *Gender and History*, 1, 1 (Spring 1989), p. 56; William D. Piersen, *Black Yankees: The Development of an Afro-American Subculture in Eighteenth-Century New England* (Amherst, MA, 1988), pp. 101-2, 84, 103.
3. Arthur Huff Fauset, *Folklore from Nova Scotia* [*Memoirs of the American Folklore Society*, Vol. XXIV (New York, 1931)], p. viii.
4. Peter H. Wood, "'It Was a Negro Taught Them': A New Look at African Labor in Early South Carolina," *Journal of Asian and African Studies*, IX, 3 & 4 (July and April 1974), pp. 160-79. Many of the black Loyalists came from South Carolina: James W. St. G. Walker, *The Black Loyalists: The Search for a Promised Land in Nova Scotia and Sierra Leone, 1783-1870* (London, 1976), p. 5.
5. Linda Kerber, "Separate Spheres, Female Worlds, Woman's Place: The Rhetoric of Women's History," *Journal of American History*, 75, 1 (June 1988), p. 26. One of the most interesting ways to examine the gender conventions of the first wave of African-Nova Scotian immigrants, the Loyalists, is to look at those who left for Sierra Leone in the 1790s. Africanists have noted that these Nova Scotian women differed greatly from Africans who lacked any experience in North America and from their fellow settlers, the Maroons. In particular, Nova Scotian women were noted for their economic autonomy and their relative sexual independence. Almost all first generation Nova Scotian women in Freetown possessed an occupation and nearly one-third of the households were headed by women. By the mid-19th century, there was at least the appearance of economic independence among Nova Scotian women in Sierra Leone that paralleled their female kin who remained in Nova Scotia. See E. Frances White, *Sierra Leone's Settler Women Traders* (Ann Arbor, 1987); Christopher Fyfe, *A History of Sierra Leone* (Oxford, 1962), pp. 143, 101, 102.

6. Higginbotham, "Beyond the Sound," pp. 56, 59; James Oliver Horton, "Freedom's Yoke: Gender Conventions among Antebellum Free Blacks," *Feminist Studies*, 12, 1 (Spring 1986), p. 58; Sharon Harley, "For the Good of Family and Race: Gender, Work and Domestic Roles in the Black Community, 1880–1930," *Signs*, 15, 2 (Winter 1990), pp. 337, 347.

7. Canada, *Census of 1871*, Vol. 1, *Census of 1881*, Vol. 1. In 1871 the population of the city was 29,582 and the county 37,008. This included 893 African-Nova Scotians in the city and 1,295 in the county and Dartmouth. By 1881 the city was more populous than the largely rural county, with the city listing 36,054 inhabitants and the county and Dartmouth only 31,863. The total population (city and county) increased by only 1,327 inhabitants, which included an increase of 336 African-Nova Scotians. Urbanization may have affected black Nova Scotians differently as the rural/urban percentage remained virtually unchanged.

8. Micro: Halifax, Cemeteries, Camp Hill (reel 10), PANS. Unfortunately, the 1891 census did not record race. The extent to which African-Nova Scotians were responsible for misinformation in the census is problematic. Enumerators were instructed that "Origin is to be scrupulously entered, as given by the person questioned": Canada, *Census of 1881 Manual*, p. 30. Judith Fingard has noted that black community leaders Peter McKerrow and his brother-in-law William B. Thomas were not recorded as African in the 1881 census. On the other hand, in this same household, other entries appeared twice. Inez and Rachel Thomas were listed both at their mother's home in Preston (120–128) and in Ward 2 (145–255) of the city, living with their brother's and sister's families. I suspect other cases of duplication among young women engaged in domestic service listed at both the family's and employer's residence. See Judith Fingard, "Race and Respectability in Victorian Halifax," *The Journal of Imperial and Commonwealth History*, 20, 2 (May 1992), p. 179.

9. Frank Stanley Boyd, ed., Peter E. McKerrow, *Brief History of the Colored Baptists of NS, 1783–1895* ([1895] Halifax, 1976). The opinions of Peter McKerrow are disproportionately prominent as he was also secretary of the African Baptist Church and the major defendant in the only civil court case I uncovered involving African-Nova Scotian women. As the son-in-law of Rev. James Thomas, Peter McKerrow was closely connected to one of the few African-Nova Scotian families who dominate recorded historical sources.

10. The paucity of sources has recently become further complicated by an appalling act of vandalism at the Public Archives of Nova Scotia. During the summer of 1990 someone stole the index cards relating to African-Nova Scotians and women. This act of vandalism placed another obstacle in the way of research on African-Nova Scotians' past. Yet so much needs to be done. This study introduces the experience of African-Nova Scotian women and reveals the need to follow up with research on residual African traditions, family structure, urban-rural movement, outmigration and female church organizations in the early 20th century. As Judith Fingard has demonstrated with court records, school records, cemetery records and detailed newspaper work promise more insight into African-Nova Scotian history. Understanding the way that race worked together with class and gender in shaping experience will not only offer knowledge of the African-Nova Scotian past, but will also lead to a better understanding of all Nova Scotian society.

11. Fannie Allison *et al.*, *Traditional Lifetime Stories: A Collection of Black Memories*, Vol. 2 (Westphal, N.S., 1990); Belle Barnes *et al.*, *Traditional Lifetime Stories: A Collection of Black Memories*, Vol. 1 (Westphal, N.S., 1987); Donald H. Clairmont and Dennis William Magill, *Africville: The Life and Death of a Canadian Black Community* (Toronto, 1974); Judith Fingard, *The Dark Side of Victorian Halifax* (Lawrencetown, 1989); Fingard, "Race and Respectability"; Sylvia Hamilton, "Our Mothers Grand and Great: Black Women of Nova Scotia," *Canadian Woman Studies/Les Cahiers de la Femme canadienne*, 4, 2 (Winter 1982), pp. 33–7; Hamilton, "A Glimpse of Edith Clayton," *Fireweed*, 18 (Winter/Spring 1984), pp. 18–20; and Marie Hamilton, "Mothers and Daughters: A Delicate Partnership," *Fireweed*, 18 (Winter/Spring 1984), pp. 64–8; Bonnie Huskins, "Race and the Victorian City: Blacks and Indians during Celebrations in Saint John and Halifax, 1838–1887," paper presented to the Canadian Historical Association, Victoria, B.C., 1990; Frances Henry, *Forgotten Canadians: The Blacks of Nova Scotia* (Don Mills, 1973); J.A. Mannette, "Stark Remnant of Blackpast: Thinking of Gender, Ethnicity and Class in 1780s Nova Scotia," *Alternative Routes*, 7 (1984); Bridglal Pachai, *Blacks of the Maritimes* (Tantallon, N.S., 1987); Pachai, *Beneath the Clouds of the Promised Land: The Survival of Nova Scotia's Blacks, Vol. 1: 1600–1800* (Halifax, 1987); Pachai, *Beneath the Clouds of the Promised Land: The Survival of Nova Scotia's Blacks, Vol. 2: 1800–1989* (Halifax, 1990); Calvin W. Ruck, *The Black Battalion, 1916–1920: Canada's Best Kept Military Secret* (Hantsport, N.S., 1987); Carolyn Thomas, "The Black Church and the Black Women," in Bridglal Pachai, ed., *Canadian Black Studies* (Halifax, 1979), pp. 234–8; James W. St. G. Walker, *The Black Identity in Nova Scotia: Community and Institutions in Historical Perspective* (Westphal, N.S., 1985), Robin Winks, *Blacks in Canada* (New Haven, Conn., 1971).

12. Walker, *Black Identity*, p. 2.

13. Walker, *Black Identity*, p. 11.

14. Henry, *Forgotten Canadians*, p. 57. She was evidently referring to married women.

15. *The Worker* (Toronto), 15 November 1924.

16. Higginbotham, "Beyond the Sound," p. 58.

17. Pachai, *Beneath the Clouds*, Vol. 2, p. 104; Viola Parsons, *My Grandmother's Days* (Hantsport, N.S., 1988), p. 18.

18. Allison *et al.*, *Traditional Lifetime Stories*, Vol. 2, p. 73; Parsons, *My Grandmother's Days*, p. 15.

19. In 1891 Ward One listed 812 domestic servants out of a total population of 8,550. Ward Five with a population of 14,347 named 188: Census manuscript, Canada, 1891. Claudette Lacelle notes that in 1871, 28 per cent of households in Ward One had servants compared to 10.1 per cent and 14.4 per cent in the two sections of Ward Five: *Urban Domestic Servants in 19th-Century Canada* (Ottawa, 1987), p. 81.

20. The first African-Nova Scotian to graduate from the Truro school was Madeline Francis Symonds in 1928. Nurse training and placement in hospitals was not available until 1946. Pachai, *Beneath the Clouds*, Vol. 2, p. 190; Donald H. Clairmont, Dennis W. Magill, *Nova Scotian Blacks: An Historical and Structural Overview* (Halifax, 1970), p. 35.

21. *Morning Chronicle*, 3 December 1874. Miss Ann Joseph taught at the Colored School in Dartmouth.

22. Nova Scotia, *Nova Scotia, House of Assembly Journal and Proceedings*, 1891, Appendix 5, Education, p. 52. Judith Fingard notes that Laura Howell taught in the Dartmouth school in 1891 and the Maynard Street School from 1896 to 1899. Martha Jones who finished her studies in 1884–5 was unable to find a position in the city. Fingard, "Race and Respectability," p. 188, fn. 81. Maria Wood of Beech Hill and Mary Bauld of Hammonds Plains are listed as school misses in 1871 and Esther Butler was listed in 1871 and 1881.

23. Nova Scotia, *Nova Scotia, House of Assembly Journal and Proceedings*, 1889, Appendix 5, Education; McKerrow, *Brief History of Colored Baptists*, p. 45; Pearleen Oliver, "From Generation to Generation; Bi-Centennial of the African Baptist Church in Nova Scotia," PANS.

24. Minutes of the 47th African Baptist Association of Nova Scotia Convention, 1900, Acadia University Archives (AUA).

25. Fingard, "Race and Respectability," p. 182.

26. Halifax School Registers, Lockman Street School, Maynard Street School, RG 14, R 1, PANS.

27. Although the county paid for lighting oil, Selina Williams taught for free: Edna Staebler, "Would You Change the Lives of These People?" *Maclean's*, 12 May 1956, p. 60.

28. Parsons, *My Grandmother's Days*, p. 27. Between 1870 and 1900 more than 90 per cent of employed African-Canadian women in Boston were classified as working in menial occupations. Elizabeth Hafkin Pleck, *Black Migration and Poverty: Boston, 1865–1900* (New York, 1979), p. 104.

29. Mrs. William Lawson, *History of the Townships of Dartmouth, Preston and Lawrencetown, Halifax County, Nova Scotia* (Halifax, 1893), p. 192.

30. Dionne Brand, "Black Women and Work: The Impact of Racially Constructed Gender Roles on the Sexual Division of Labour, Part Two," *Fireweed*, 26 (Winter-Spring 1988), p. 87.

31. Parsons, *My Grandmother's Days*, p. 21; Harley, "For the Good of Family," p. 347. Harley noted that day work permitted domestic and family life.

32. Lawson, *History of the Townships of Dartmouth, Preston and Lawrencetown*, pp. 188–9; *Novascotian* (Halifax), 17 October 1885; Margaret Marshall Saunders, *The House of Armour* (Philadelphia, 1897), pp. 287–8. Saunders noted that African-Nova Scotian women were not the only women to sell their goods at the market as she also mentions the presence of Acadian women from the Eastern Shore.

33. Joleen Gordon, *Edith Clayton's Market Basket, A Heritage of Splitwood Basketry in Nova Scotia*, photographs by Ronald Merrick and diagrams by George Halverson (Halifax, 1977).

34. Fingard, "Race and Respectability," pp. 174–6.

35. Daniel McN. Parker, Wm. J. Lewis, Wm. F. Parker Executors of last will and testament of Martin P. Black, plaintiffs and Wm. B. Thomas, Peter E. McKerrow, Thomas G.D. Scotland, Jas. T. McKerrow, Wm. B. Thomas, Peter E. McKerrow executors of last will and testament of James Thomas and Moses Vineberg, Bernard Kortosk, Jacob G. Ascher (Kortosk and Co.) and Rachel C. Sockume, Mary E. McKerrow, Inez E. Thomas, Elizabeth Ann Johnston, defendants, "A" Appeals — Supreme Court of Nova Scotia, Volume 9, 1891–92: #3360, RG 39, PANS.

36. Nova Scotia Probate Court, John Robinson Thomas, #2299, 1876. Eliza Thomas appears to have inherited property on Creighton Street from her father after his death in 1886. RG 35-102, "A", #8 1890 Street Ward Five Valuation Book, PANS.

37. Brand, "Black Women and Work: Part Two," p. 91. See Phyllis Marynick Palmer, "White Women/ Black Women: The Dualism of Female Identity and Experience in the United States," *Feminist Studies*, 9, 1 (Spring 1983), p. 153; Jacqueline Jones, *Labor of Love, Labor of Sorrow: Black Women, Work and the Family from Slavery to the Present* (New York, 1985).

38. Brand, "Black Women and Work: Part Two," p. 91.

39. bell hooks, *Ain't I a Woman: Black Women and Feminism* (Boston, 1981), p. 78.

40. Saunders, *The House of Armour*, pp. 287–8. Margaret Conrad, Toni Laidlaw, and Donna Smyth, eds., *No Place Like Home: Diaries and Letters of Nova Scotia Women* (Halifax, 1988), "Margaret Marshall Saunders."

41. Lawson, *History of the Townships*, pp. 188, 190. The important connection between finery, or dressing above one's class and the fallen woman is the subject of Mariana Valverde, "The Love of Finery: Fashion and the Fallen Woman in Nineteenth-Century Social Discourse," *Victorian Studies*, 32, 2 (Winter 1989), pp. 169–88.

42. *Morning Chronicle*, 22 September 1874.

43. *Morning Chronicle*, 22 January 1874.

44. B. Jane Price, " 'Raised in Rockhead. Died in the Poor House': Female Petty Criminals in Halifax, 1864–1890," in Philip Girard and Jim Phillips, eds., *Essays in the History of Canadian Law, Vol. III. Nova Scotia* (Toronto, 1990), pp. 200–31.

45. Fingard, *The Dark Side of Life in Victorian Halifax*, p. 97.
46. Harley, "For the Good of Family," p. 347.
47. Carrie M. Best, *That Lonesome Road* (New Glasgow, 1977), p. 43.
48. Suzanne Lebsock, *The Free Women of Petersburg: Status and Culture in a Southern Town, 1784–1860* (New York, 1985), p. 88.
49. "Their marriages are in many instances more connexion for a short season": Census manuscript, Halifax, 1871, Ward Five F-2, p. 60 (microfilm reel C10552) PANS.
50. Lebsock, *Free Women of Petersburg*, p. 52. For Hannah Thomas Colley, see May 1881, p. 85, Marriage Records, Halifax County, PANS. For Louisa Brown Bailey, see McKerrow, *Brief History*, Marriage List, 9 January 1877 and 152 Creighton St., 2 Gerrish Lane, 1890 Street Ward 5, Valuation Book, RG 35 A5, PANS. For Eliza Bailey Thomas Ewing, see Fingard, "Race and Respectability," p. 178 and 190 Creighton St., 1890 Street Ward 5, Valuation Book, RG 35, A5 PANS.
51. Terrence Punch, "Petition of the Coloured Population of Hammonds Plains," *The Nova Scotia Genealogist*, V, I (1987), p. 40. Original is in RG "p" Vol. 88, doc. 8 (microfilm), PANS.
52. Fingard, "Race and Respectability," p. 173; *Morning Chronicle*, 17 June 1892.
53. Women of European descent in the Maritimes were active petitioners: see Gail Campbell, "Disfranchised but Not Quiescent: Women Petitioners in New Brunswick in the Mid-19th Century," *Acadiensis*, XVIII, 2 (Spring 1989), pp. 22–54. Judith Fingard notes that in 1873 African-Nova Scotian mothers from Zion School petitioned the school commissioners to introduce sex-segregated classes: Fingard, "Race and Respectability," p. 181.
54. *Morning Chronicle*, 4 February 1874; Frederick Cozzens, *Acadia: Or a Month with the Blue Noses* (New York, 1877), p. 33; *Acadian Recorder*, 19 June 1879.
55. McKerrow, *Brief History of the Colored Baptists*, p. 55.
56. Minutes of the 27th African Baptist Association of Nova Scotia Convention, 1880 at Halifax, AUA.
57. Minutes of the 18th African Baptist Association of Nova Scotia Convention, 1871 at Hammonds Plains, AUA.
58. Like Euro-American women in Nova Scotia, African-Nova Scotian women in the 1790s had been important lay preachers and religious leaders: James W. St. G. Walker, *The Black Loyalists*; George Rawlyk, *Ravished by the Spirit: Religious Revivals, Baptists and Henry Alline* (Montreal-Kingston, 1984), p. 82.
59. *Minutes of the Three Annual Conferences of the British Methodist Episcopal Church, Nova Scotia — at Liverpool July 18th to 22nd, 1884* (Chatham, Ontario, 1884), p. 41, Arnett Papers, Wilberforce University, Wilberforce, Ohio, pp. 58, 101; Nova Scotia District: 31 July 1868; 2 June 1877; 18–26 May 1878; 15–19 May 1879; 7–10 May 1880; 8–11 July 1881; 18–22 July 1884.
60. Pachai, *Beneath the Clouds*, Vol. 2, p. 78; Pearleen Oliver, *Brief History of the Colored Baptists of Nova Scotia, 1782–1953* (Halifax, 1953).
61. Minutes of the 50th African Baptist Association of Nova Scotia Convention, 1903 at East Preston, AUA.
62. Register, Halifax County 1904, p. 99, No. 301, PANS. The Nova Scotia Marriage Act stated that weddings could be conducted only by men: *Revised Statutes of Nova Scotia, 1900*, Vol. 2, Ch. 111, Sn. 3, p. 220.
63. Minutes of the 50th African Baptist Association of Nova Scotia Convention, 1903 at East Preston, p. 18, AUA.
64. Louisa Brown Bailey was the widow of Rev. Alexander Bailey — a supporter of Rev. James Thomas in the religious rivalry that split the African Baptist Church and trusted friend of James Thomas as witness to his will. In addition Bailey was step-mother of John Robinson Thomas' wife, cared for two of the Thomas grandchildren and shared her house in 1871 with one of Thomas' future sons-in-law, William Johnston.
65. RG 35-102 A #5 1890 Street Ward 5 Valuation Book, PANS; *Halifax City Directory*, 1881, 1885, 1896.
66. Minutes of the 32nd African Baptist Association of Nova Scotia Convention, 1885 at Cornwallis, AUA.
67. Minutes of the 39th African Baptist Association of Nova Scotia Convention, 1892 at Dartmouth Lake Church, p. 6, AUA.
68. Minutes of the 42nd African Baptist Association of Nova Scotia Convention, 1895, AUA.
69. Minutes of the 50th African Baptist Association of Nova Scotia Convention, 1903 at East Preston, pp. 15, 20, AUA. The spellings Grosse and Grouse are both used.
70. It appears that a poem by Louisa Bailey about her mother was included in McKerrow's history of the African Baptist Church. The poem is signed only L.A. Bailey. Bailey married for a third time sometime between 1907 and her death in 1911: *Herald*, 30 December 1911, *Acadian Recorder*, 30 December 1911. In Allison *et al.*, *Traditional Lifetime Stories*, Vol. 2, Deacon Reginald Hamilton noted the importance of his grandmother Charlotte Grouse, p. 50.
71. Lynne Marks, "Working-Class Femininity and the Salvation Army: Hallelujah Lasses in English Canada, 1882–1892," in Veronica Strong-Boag and Anita Clair Fellman, eds., *Rethinking Canada: The Promise of Women's History* (Toronto, 1991), p. 198.
72. Minutes of the 54th African Baptist Association of Nova Scotia Convention, 1907, p. 4, AUA.
73. Minutes of the 30th African Baptist Association of Nova Scotia Convention, 1883 at Weymouth, AUA.
74. Oliver, *A Brief History of Colored Baptists*. In 1915 a similar organization called the Daughters of Zion was in operation at the Halifax Methodist Church: *Halifax Herald*, 1 March 1915.

75. Minutes of the 39th African Baptist Association of Nova Scotia Convention, 1892 at Halifax, p. 10, AUA.
76. E.R. Forbes, "Battles in Another War: Edith Archibald and the Halifax Feminist Movement," *Challenging the Regional Stereotype: Essays on the 20th Century Maritimes* (Fredericton, 1989), p. 81.
77. Harley, "For the Good of Family," p. 348; Minutes of the 50th African Baptist Association of Nova Scotia Convention, 1903 at East Preston, p. 12, AUA.
78. African-Nova Scotian men were also vulnerable to ridicule. Rev. James Thomas in his 1877 circular letter commented on visitors to the convention, "the strangers who had flocked from the city, and neighbouring districts; . . . some to worship others to mock and criticize": Minutes of the 24th African Baptist Association of Nova Scotia Convention, 1877 Hammonds Plains, AUA.
79. Minutes of the 50th African Baptist Association of Nova Scotia Convention, 1903 at East Preston, AUA.
80. Parsons, *My Grandmother's Days*, p. 18.
81. *Morning Chronicle*, 1 June 1874.

Providing a Woman's Conscience: The YWCA, Female Evangelicalism, and the Girl in the City, 1870-1930

DIANA PEDERSEN

As Mary Ryan, among others, has recently noted, "the provision of public space for women was a major civic project during the latter half of the nineteenth century," and women were increasingly visible and vociferous in asserting their presence in North American cities burgeoning under the impact of industrialization, rural migration, and immigration.[1] New heterosocial spaces from public parks to dance halls to department stores were designed with women's concerns in mind, but only rarely were women able to serve as architects of their own spaces and to advance their own perspective on the changing class and gender order. In late nineteenth- and early twentieth-century Canadian cities, the Young Women's Christian Association (YWCA) presented the novel spectacle of a public institution for "respectable" women, embodying a distinctly female perspective on "the problem of the city" and a commitment to what Marlene Stein Wortman has described as the domestication of the urban environment.[2] Inspired by the example of their counterparts in Britain and the United States, Canadian YWCAs constituted an organized response by committees of women from local evangelical Protestant churches and from the families of leading business and professional men to what they perceived as a growing "girl problem" in Canadian cities. Noting that "women have scarcely understood to what extent the conscience of the community has been a man's conscience," the YWCA proposed that "women must work out women's problems" and deter-

SOURCE: Adapted from Diana Pedersen, "'A Building for Her': The YWCA, Evangelical Religion, and Public Space in Canadian Cities, 1870-1930," paper given at the Berkshire Conference on the History of Women, Vassar College, Poughkeepsie, NY, 1993.

mined, thereupon, to provide young women living independently of their families with maternal supervision, a substitute for family life, and respectable homosocial recreation in a wholesome Christian setting.[3]

In contrast to the scholarship in the United States, the role of evangelicals in moral reform movements has been largely unexamined by Canadian historians, who have demonstrated until very recently a marked reluctance to recognize the centrality of evangelicalism to Canadian Protestant culture in the late nineteenth and early twentieth centuries.[4] Canadian women's historians have overwhelmingly emphasized maternal feminism — a reform ideology based on "the conviction that woman's special role as mother gives her the duty and the right to participate in the public sphere" — as the impetus underlying middle-class women's growing public presence, and have given short shrift to the evangelical component of Canadian "first-wave" feminism.[5] But like their American counterparts, many Canadian Protestant women experienced a remarkable spiritual awakening under the impact of evangelicalism and felt the urgency of the call to demonstrate their religious conviction through good works and active efforts to propagate the faith.[6] By the end of the nineteenth century, large numbers of women participated actively in the evangelical crusade to save the cities for Christ and shared the belief that the Protestant churches had an active role to play in the working out of a vision of a "manifest destiny" for Canada as that nation which would "demonstrate to the rest of the world the superiority of a nation wholly dedicated to an applied Christianity."[7] Conflating the interests of women with the interests of the Protestant churches, evangelical women championed Christianity as that religion which above all others valued women and womanly qualities, and they asserted the centrality of women to the churches' larger tasks of nation-building and saving the cities.

At the heart of the YWCA's program, and largely overlooked by historians, was a female evangelical vision of the moral regeneration of urban and national life. As Mariana Valverde has pointed out in her recent overview of moral reform in English Canada, Canadian historians have tended to characterize moral reform as "a purely negative, prohibitory project" and have failed to identify the underlying "positive" vision in which the shaping of morality was central to "a grand project that was both national and religious."[8] Such a conclusion appears warranted in the case of the YWCA whose records have been mined in recent years by both Canadian and American historians examining the development of the organized boarding house movement, "rescue work" among prostitutes, recreation reform, and other efforts to regulate prostitution and working women's sexuality.[9] By approaching the YWCA mainly from the perspective of its clientele, however, historians have failed to situate its "protective" work in the context of its evangelical vision of social transformation, leading to the observation in one recent study of working women in Chicago that organizations like the YWCA "did not hope to change the city, only to protect women from its

harsher aspects."[10] In fact, the YWCA combined protection and supervision with an attempt to constitute young women as "God's Own Cor-
nerstones," the mothers of the future generations, and the lynchpin of
the campaign for the moral and spiritual transformation of urban and
national life. The function of its "Building for Her," like the Christian
family home whose values it carried into the public sphere, was conceived
as not merely protective but also redemptive, isolating young women from
the dangers of urban public spaces, while simultaneously serving as a
base from which women, united in a common religious faith, could re-
shape the Canadian city according to the teachings of Jesus Christ and
in the interests of women, children and family life.

For many urban middle-class evangelicals in the late nineteenth century,
the traditionally rural and Protestant character of the young Canadian
nation appeared threatened by a militant Roman Catholicism, evolution-
ary theory and Biblical criticism, an increasingly self-conscious and organized working class, rural outmigration, and a massive influx of European immigrants who were neither English-speaking nor Protestant.[11]
Identifying the burgeoning cities with crime, intemperance, poverty, athe-
ism, socialism, and materialism, as well as the disappearance of the traditional rural virtues of industry, piety, thrift and self-dependence, evangelicals responded with an optimistic and aggressive fervour to the call
to save the cities for Christ. But as Carolyn Strange has recently noted,
Canadian historians have largely ignored the evangelical identification of
the city with sexual vice and the centrality of "the search for sexual order"
to urban moral reform campaigns.[12] The "narratives of sexual danger"
that enjoyed considerable currency in British and American cities were
also central to evangelical discourse on the Canadian city and resonated
with middle-class Canadians who noted with anxiety the growing numbers
of young women migrating to the cities from the rural districts and overseas in search of employment and educational opportunities.[13] For many
observers of North American cities, and particularly for evangelical
women, "the woman adrift became a symbol of the threats that industrialization and urbanization posed to womanhood and the family."[14]

In establishing the first Canadian branches of the YWCA in the early
1870s, evangelical women played a critical role in constructing the growing
visibility of young working women, increasing numbers of whom were
living independently of their families and seemingly enjoying an unprecedented period of economic and sexual autonomy, relative to their mothers
and grandmothers, as a significant "girl problem" in Canadian cities.[15]
Professing admiration for young rural women whose Protestant upbring-
ing had instilled in them a commitment to hard work and self-
improvement, the YWCA was deeply ambivalent about their arrival in
the city, recognizing the opportunities the urban environment presented
for young women, as for young men, but deeply worried about the pos-

sible dangers they faced in living apparently unsupervised and unsupported by family, community and church.[16] Sharing, and actively promoting, a widely held image of young rural women as "orphans and innocents" vulnerable to loneliness, destitution, and the machinations of white slavers, the YWCA continued a long tradition of participation in anti-prostitution campaigns by evangelical women who viewed prostitutes as the helpless victims of male lust and the double standard of sexual morality.[17] But for the YWCA, "women adrift" represented not only potential "fallen women" but also the mothers of the next generations who appeared in danger of being permanently alienated from domesticity and religion. Committed to a distinctive evangelical domesticity which attached spiritual significance to women and bourgeois family life and attributed redemptive powers to the Christian family home, the YWCA was convinced that the production of a new generation of "true Christian women" was critical to the success of the goal of national regeneration.[18] But seemingly lacking the time and the opportunity to acquire domestic skills, and prone to making unsuitable friends and drifting out of the habit of regular church attendance, young women living independently of their families appeared ill-prepared for their future responsibility as mothers, making it "necessary for those of practical bent to seek to meet the needs for preserving, in the midst of these conditions, a well-developed, all-round Christian womanhood."[19]

The YWCA's unprecedented solution to this girl problem of grave proportions was the establishment of a public institution whose mandate, according to the first annual report of the Toronto branch, was "to seek out young women taking up their residence in Toronto, and endeavour to bring them under moral and religious influences, by introducing them to the members and privileges of this Association, securing their attendance at some place of worship, and by every means in their power surrounding them with Christian associates."[20] During the nineteenth century, YWCA boarding homes featured "some of the comforts as well as such necessary restraints as are found in every well ordered family," and served a Protestant clientele, consisting largely of students, teachers, women employed in the traditional female trades such as millinery and dressmaking, and the growing numbers of women entering the new white-blouse occupations of retail sales and office work.[21] Rooms were also provided to accommodate domestic servants between situations. Of principal concern to the YWCA was the welfare of young women between the ages of seventeen and twenty-five who were newly arrived in the city, a strategy determined both by the belief that women were likely to be recruited into prostitution during their initial period of disorientation, and by the evangelical association of the experience of religious conversion with the impressionable years of youth; a woman of twenty-five was assumed to be capable of looking out for herself, and if she had not yet accepted Christ at this point in her life, she was believed to be beyond the reach of the YWCA.

In drawing attention to the girl problem as an issue of major significance to the welfare of the community and the nation that had been consistently overlooked by the churches and social reformers, and in insisting that the resolution of that problem should become the mandate of their organization, the YWCA's founders heralded a new era in the history of organized activity on the part of Canadian churchwomen. Throughout the nineteenth century, churchwomen had undertaken benevolent and charitable activities to relieve the suffering of the poor and the sick, but they had done so as individuals or in the context of denominational church societies.[22] By mid-century, their activities began to take on a more structured form and to assume greater independence from church control. Legally incorporated women's societies, capable of contracting debts and holding property, assumed responsibility for building and managing a range of charitable institutions, including orphanages, maternity hospitals and homes for the aged and the insane.[23] Such activities, however, remained purely local in scope. It was not until the 1870s that churchwomen were inspired by a new national pride following Confederation in 1867, improved transportation networks, and the example of male alliances such as the Canadian Manufacturers' Association, the Canadian Labour Union, and the Methodist Church of Canada, to organize on a national basis with a blueprint of their own for Canada's future.[24] Pioneering the methods of interdenominational cooperation, YWCAs claimed to serve as mere "handmaidens" to the churches, reaching out to young women who were beyond the churches' sphere of influence and undertaking projects that exceeded the scope and resources of any single denomination. Not incidentally, however, this strategy considerably enhanced the autonomy of churchwomen, removing them from the direct supervision of the clergy and the congregations of the denominational churches, and endowing them with unprecedented opportunities to manage and administer people, money and property.

As an institutional approach to the resolution of the girl problem, the YWCA represented a marked departure from the benevolent strategies of earlier generations of Canadian churchwomen. Under the impact of the new "scientific philanthropy," the YWCA was part of a broader movement that was transforming charity in the nineteenth century, attempting to make it less "emotional" and "impulsive," and more "businesslike," "efficient," and "scientific." Promoted by cost-conscious businessmen who took a dim view of churchwomen's traditional emphasis on relief to the sick and the destitute, scientific philanthropy emphasized the avoidance of waste and duplication of efforts, the need to distinguish between the "deserving" and the "undeserving" poor, and the importance of preventive strategies that would foster "self-dependence" and avoid further "pauperizing" the poor by disciplining them in the habits of thrift, temperance and industry.[25] During the nineteenth century, boarding homes for "self-respecting" and "self-supporting" women comprised one of a number of preventive strategies pioneered by YWCAs that were aimed at the moral transformation of working-class family life. Influenced by new theories emphasizing the inherent goodness and malleability of children that were enjoying widespread currency among evangelicals, YWCAs, like the Women's Christian Temperance Union, increasingly placed their hopes for the future in the coming generations, a strategy reflected in the founding of day nurseries and kitchen garden classes for working-class children in Montreal and Toronto.[26] They also pioneered the techniques of casework and district visitation among the poor. As several historians have noted, such activities provided nineteenth-century churchwomen with unprecedented access to the public — a license to explore urban districts that were otherwise off-limits to respectable women, legal rights through incorporation that women did not enjoy as female persons, and enhanced opportunities for fundraising and administrative work.[27]

Canadian YWCAs were organized under a variety of circumstances, at times on the initiative of a local woman who had visited an established branch in the United States, occasionally in response to an appeal from an out-of-town evangelist, and sometimes at the request of the local clergy and Young Men's Christian Association (YMCA), with which the YWCA enjoyed a close relationship.[28] That the YMCA invariably preceded the arrival of the YWCA in Canadian cities was indicative of the greater support that the churches and business sector were prepared to devote to the assistance of ambitious and upwardly-mobile young men, a problem that plagued the YWCA throughout the period under examination. Particularly during the nineteenth century, the members of local church congregations, who were regularly canvassed for funds for the boarding home, appeared both perplexed by and hostile to the notion of a public institution for respectable women. The Protestant middle class to whom the YWCA appealed had no difficulty grasping the importance of assistance to principled and ambitious young men aspiring to Christian manhood and success in business. Such men stood to become the politicians, professionals and business leaders upon whom the future of the community depended, but young women, many church members believed, would make no contribution of such obvious importance. Fortunately for the YWCA, however, its "older brother" quickly determined that its efforts to keep young men on the path of righteousness would be rapidly undermined without a pool of young women of sound Christian character to serve as their companions and prospective wives. For this reason, YMCA boards of managers, composed of prominent evangelical businessmen who were not infrequently married to members of the YWCA board, became the most enthusiastic supporters of the women's organization, offering financial advice and regular lectures on the subject of scientific philanthropy and sound business methods.

The endorsement of its male counterpart proved critical during the first two decades of the YWCA's existence in Canadian cities, when it faced an uphill battle to win the acceptance of conservative church congregations who were sometimes hostile to suggestions that young women should be supported in their attempts to make their way in the city. The YWCA was regularly accused by middle-class critics of encouraging the already alarming tendency of young women to leave their homes and live independently for purely selfish and frivolous reasons. In the face of a chronic shortage of domestic servants that plagued middle-class households throughout the turn-of-the-century decades, the YWCA was also accused of facilitating women's entry into new occupations that removed them from a more suitable home environment; the Toronto YWCA reported in 1883 that "what opposition we meet is chiefly from women, who say that we are encouraging girls to work at other things who ought to be servants."[29] The argument was regularly advanced that working women could afford to stay in hotels and consequently were in no need of any public subsidy, and that to offer them such assistance would in fact contribute to pauperization by encouraging dependence. Most problematic, however, was the prevalent association of "women" and "public" with prostitution, resulting in opposition to the provision of public funds for homes for women of dubious morals. A corollary of this belief was the conviction that a young woman "of good moral character" could navigate the city without public assistance since she was protected by the formidable armour of her virtue.

The YWCA's justification of the need for a public institution for respectable women was formulated during this initial period of skepticism on the part of its middle-class supporters. It reassured anxious observers of the continuing exodus from domestic service by assiduously promoting its pioneering classes in domestic science while publicly downplaying its corresponding experiments in the new field of commercial education. In any case, the YWCA emphasized, many of its clientele were in fact drawn from the impoverished middle classes, and were unsuited to employment as domestics by virtue of their education and delicacy. YWCAs stressed the lack of opportunities for young women in the rural districts and claimed that many new arrivals in the city were motivated by a Christian commitment to hard work and self-improvement, not the lure of city streets, and as such deserved support. YWCAs insisted repeatedly that their boarders were "self-respecting" and "self-supporting"; since all were required to pay their board, the YWCA claimed that it should not be regarded as a charity and a drain upon the public purse.

Charges that working women were in no need of publicly subsidized residences were addressed in an ongoing campaign, conducted mainly through the press, to educate the middle-class church-going public about the relationship between low wages, unsuitable living conditions, and immorality. Most emphatically, the YWCA insisted that only respectable women, as attested by a letter from a clergyman, boarded at its homes where they were further subjected to strict supervision and the requirement of regular church attendance. Virtue, in the YWCA's view, was no defence against the countless urban perils facing the inexperienced country girl who needed the protection of Christian women and suitable companionship to ward off the loneliness and desperation that the YWCA believed drove women into prostitution. Underlying all these arguments, however, was a maxim that was clearly formulated to address directly the perception that young women, particularly those who were suspect by virtue of their public visibility, had no real value to the community that justified the expenditure of public funds on their behalf. On the contrary, the YWCA, maintained, "whether we realize it or not our young women are the very foundation of society. . . . The moral, social and spiritual condition of the people will not, cannot rise above the condition of the mothers."[30]

During the initial decades of its existence in Canadian cities, the YWCA's attempts to present itself as a modern institution embodying the principles of the new scientific philanthropy co-existed uneasily with its continuing adherence to an older model of female benevolence. Many churchwomen clung to traditional female methods of fundraising until well into the twentieth century, preferring the familiar charity bazaars and pink teas to the direct and businesslike solicitation of funds advocated by the YMCA. YWCAs remained firmly committed to the nineteenth-century strategy of female institution building and to the equation of women with benevolence that was being abandoned by a new breed of female reformers beginning in the 1870s.[31] The protection of women and the adoption of sound business methods, it discovered, were not always compatible objectives given the continuing reality of women's low wages, exposing the YWCA to charges that it was unChristian if it turned destitute women away, and that it was dispensing sentimental charity if it provided them with assistance. Despite scientific philanthropy's emphasis on specialization, YWCAs in the 1870s and 1880s offered a range of programs aimed at working-class families, in addition to the boarding homes, and combined the new preventive strategies with a more traditional evangelical commitment to the rescue of prostitutes through the establishment of Magdalen homes. Although conducted on separate premises and as a completely separate department, rescue work created continuing difficulties for the YWCA by undermining its claim to support only respectable women, alienating financial supporters and driving away working women who had no wish to be associated with an institution for "fallen women."

During the 1890s, many of these difficulties were resolved as the YWCA dramatically redefined its mandate, firmly committing itself to specialization, professionalization and the necessity of preventive approaches. The Montreal Day Nursery and similar established programs legally separated from the YWCA, and the rehabilitation of prostitutes was handed over to newer organizations that specialized in such work. By the end of the nineteenth century, the YWCA had clearly defined the welfare of young women living independently as its particular mandate and set about the task of systematically establishing itself with the churches, local governments and social reformers as that organization having recognized jurisdiction in this field. At the same time, it began to target new groups of women, particularly the traveller, the recent immigrant and the "industrial girl," and expressed a new commitment to fostering the "four-fold development" of the young Canadian woman. In future, not only her spiritual needs would be addressed but all aspects of her intellectual, physical and social life would be guided by qualified Christian women. The strict rules and religious atmosphere of YWCA boarding houses had not proven particularly popular with working women during the nineteenth century and in any case permitted the organization to reach only a minute proportion of the population of working women. To the YWCA's leadership, a more effective approach seemed urgently required as increasing numbers of women were travelling from city to city, immigrants poured into the country, women formed an increasingly large proportion of the industrial labour force, and proliferating commercialized amusements appeared, from the YWCA's vantage point, to pose a threat to young women that surpassed even the danger of unsuitable living accommodations.

The YWCA's nineteenth-century facilities proved completely inadequate to the task of fulfilling this newly-defined mandate, and the commitment to four-fold development was reflected in the construction of the first buildings expressly designed for the purposes of "YWCA work" beginning in the early 1890s. In the earlier period, the organization had leased or purchased boarding houses and had rented rooms in those branches which offered classes in subjects such as domestic science, millinery, or bookkeeping for those who wished to upgrade their job qualifications. Business meetings were generally held in the building of the YMCA. The new mandate required a vastly expanded public department and, as branches multiplied in the exploding cities of Western Canada after the turn of the century, YWCAs increasingly featured reading rooms, facilities for public meetings, boarding house inspection services, employment bureaux, working women's clubs, Bible study classes, summer camps, Travellers Aid services at docks and railroad stations, expanded educational departments, classes in "physical culture," transient accommodation for women travellers, and larger boarding facilities in the face of a housing shortage that would reach crisis proportions after the First World War. While the nineteenth-century facilities had been managed by the volunteer boards, with the assistance of a paid matron and domestics who operated the boarding homes, the new programs, requiring a complex system of committees and departments, were implemented by a professional staff of college-educated YWCA secretaries who had received post-graduate training in YWCA work and "girl psychology" in the United States.

The design of the new YWCA buildings, constructed by local architects in consultation with YWCA staff and using plans obtained from the national headquarters of the American YWCA, reflected both the newly expanded mandate and the YWCA's conviction that a female public space should incorporate the best of bourgeois domesticity into a modern public facility. Descriptions of YWCA buildings emphasized that their exteriors conformed to prevailing standards of public architecture and functioned as a community monument as impressive as any public library or Board of Trade building. But, as one newspaper reporter commented on the building in Edmonton, "for all its imposing outside appearance the inside is a marvel of sheer comfort and hominess which will appeal to every living woman."[32] The hominess to which most descriptions frequently referred was created through the liberal application of such "feminine touches" as lace curtains and plants; much importance was also attached to the provision of fireplaces. Typically, the Hamilton YWCA building, on its opening in 1915, featured a marble entrance hall staircase, oiled pine floors, a rotunda and reception room with oak walls and oak and leather furnishings, a stage for theatricals, a swimming tank with shower baths, dressing-rooms and three electric hair dryers, domestic science and dressmaking rooms, a gymnasium, a laundry, a reception and reading room for residents, an oak-furnished dining room for three hundred, bedrooms to accommodate over two hundred boarders, a roof garden, house phones on each floor, cream blinds and fancy lace sash curtains, and for "the last word in bathroom-ology," two bathrooms on each floor containing provision for the use of curling tongs and an automatic electric light to heat an iron.[33]

The campaigns for the construction of YWCA buildings, which continued steadily until the end of the First World War and through a veritable YWCA building boom in the 1920s until the onset of the Great Depression, reflected a conscious decision on the part of the YWCA to reach the working woman during her leisure hours by competing directly with the new commercial amusements. To facilitate this process, most branches by the turn of the century had adopted a tiered membership system that allowed non-members, including non-Protestants, to use the YWCA's most popular facilities — particularly the cafeteria, gymnasium, and swimming pool.[34] It was hoped that in using these facilities, young women would strike up a friendly acquaintance with the members and staff and could thereby be persuaded to take out a membership and join one of the new working women's clubs where they would be brought more directly under the YWCA's influence. In this environment, the YWCA hoped that young women would be provided with wholesome recreation and suitable friends, introduced to the principles of Christian social service, recruited into a Bible study class, and ultimately persuaded to become a full member of a Protestant church of their choice. As one secretary explained, the YWCA had to work its way "into every part of the young woman's life . . . [by] showing such a complete understanding of the conditions of work and play of the young generation, that a girl will go spontaneously to the Association for sympathy in her play, advice in time of difficulty, information about her work, or for practical help if necessary in time of need."[35]

With the onset of the twentieth century and in keeping with its modern progressive facilities, the YWCA increasingly attempted to shed its maternal image and to counter public perceptions that it was a charity for working women, stressing instead a new mandate as the only organization dedicated to bringing together all women "of good character" in the community. Not "an association of one group of women working in the interests of another group," the YWCA claimed to stand as an example of "a great sisterhood, banded together in the spirit of responsibility, fellowship and service for the benefit of all."[36] Increasingly YWCAs expressed the hope that within the walls of their building all women would benefit from healthy cross-class contacts, enabling them to discover that "the things that all women have in common are many more than the things they have not in common."[37] They suggested that a shared commitment to the teachings of Jesus Christ would provide working women with the opportunity to benefit from exposure to an active model of evangelical womanhood, while encouraging middle-class women to respect the resourcefulness of the working woman facing difficult conditions and to assume the obligations of their own privileged class position by dedicating themselves to Christian social service.[38] Evangelical Christianity, teaching "love, joy and peace, patience towards others, kindness and benevolence, good faith, meekness and self-restraint" held the answer to "every girl problem" — "the problem of the hardest business woman as readily as that of the most undisciplined flapper, and that of the most restless college student no less surely than that of the most discontented society girl."[39] When the Canadian Protestant churches greeted the outbreak of the First World War as the onset of the final struggle against the forces of darkness at home and abroad, the YWCA embraced the social gospel vision of a cooperative Christian commonwealth, and its leadership envisioned a cross-class alliance of women committed to the struggle to remake Canadian society in the image of Christ's kingdom on earth.[40]

It is difficult to know to what extent Canadian working women shared the perception of the YWCA as "a great democratic sisterhood,"[41] but they were more than prepared to make use of the building on their own terms, and their preferences had an important indirect impact on the development of policies and programs. While many refused to have anything to do with what they regarded as an organization of "goody-goodies," others preferred the attractions of male company and commercial amusements, and still others remained unaware of the YWCA's existence, thousands of Canadian working women took advantage of night classes, Travellers Aid services, and summer camps. Boarding houses were filled to capacity, and homes in larger cities turned away applicants on a daily basis. In many Canadian cities, YWCAs provided the only

gymnasia and swimming pools available for the use of women, and caf-
eterias proved so popular that their revenues helped to support the less
remunerative aspects of the work. Despite the expectations of YWCA
staff, however, many women used the facilities without ever taking out
a membership, working women's clubs enrolled only a small percentage
of the clientele, and the turnout for Bible study classes was consistently
and disappointingly low. YWCAs appear to have proven most attractive
to women of Protestant background who were employed in the new white-
blouse occupations and who shared the YWCA's concern with their respectability, not infrequently a condition of their employment. For such
women, for whom the attractions of cheap amusements were not an option, the YWCA provided a welcome alternative to solitary evenings in
their rooms.

Where the YWCA had proven most successful by the early twentieth
century was in realizing its several objectives of winning public support
for the concept of an institution for respectable women, putting the girl
in the city on the agenda of the churches and moral reformers, and establishing its own jurisdiction and expertise in this field. At no time was
this success more evident than during the First World War when the
Canadian YWCA cooperated closely with the churches, governments, and
military authorities to ensure the success of what it viewed as a divine
cause and a crusade for Christianity.[42] In an alliance with the Protestant
churches, it launched the Canadian Girls in Training program, as a rival
to the unacceptably British Girl Guide movement, to mobilize adolescent
schoolgirls in service to their country and their religion.[43] Through its
Student Department, active on Canadian campuses since the 1880s, it
encouraged college women to prepare to assume the duties of the men
killed in battle and to maintain the moral and religious standards of the
nation.[44] At the request of employers in the war industries and local and
provincial governments, YWCAs across the country supervised the housing, feeding and recreation of thousands of women employed, in the face
of an acute shortage of male labour, in munitions factories and as "far-
merettes," during the harvest season. With the outbreak of war, the
YWCA saw its supreme opportunity to make women central to the larger
struggles of the churches and the nation, and to inspire women to rally
more strongly than ever before to the support of the Christian ideals
of service and self-sacrifice. Its self-appointed task of preparing "the girl
he left behind him" for national service as the wife of a returned soldier
led to cooperation with military authorities in the establishment of Hostess
Houses at military bases and to experiments with the provision of mixed
recreation in cooperation with the YMCA. At the height of wartime hysteria over venereal disease and "the girl on the street problem," the
YWCA's protective efforts extended to cooperation with police forces
in several Canadian cities in establishing female volunteer street patrols
to warn young women of the dangers of the streets, public parks and
dance halls.[45]

The YWCA's considerable success in winning recognition as an authority on the girl in the city did not come without significant compromise of its founding objectives. The expensive facilities of a modern twentieth-century YWCA required a base of financial support that extended beyond the congregations of local evangelical churches. To win the endorsement of the larger community, and particularly the business sector, the YWCA increasingly had to avoid the appearance that it was an organization for Christian women only. The homeless friendless girl in imminent moral and spiritual peril continued to figure prominently in YWCA literature but no longer sufficed as sole justification for the work since citizens who did not necessarily share the YWCA's commitment to evangelicalism had to be assured that they would benefit directly from their financial contribution. In response, and in the context of a growing concern among social welfare agencies with "the unadjusted girl," the YWCA dedicated itself to the promotion of a "normal outlook on life" among all young women of the community; it promised the citizens of Winnipeg, for example, "a Happier, Healthier Womanhood for your Daughter or Sister; a Happier, Healthier Womanhood for the Girls of Winnipeg; and therefore, because Happier, Healthier Womanhood a Better City, a Better Province and a Better Nation."[46] At the same time, with the support of the YMCA and in recognition of the fact that traditional female methods of fundraising were completely inadequate given the vastly increased scale and scope of the work, the YWCA embarked on an aggressive campaign to sell itself, and particularly its building, to the business sector and local governments as a monument to enterprising businessmen and a progressive community. Financial campaigns for "A Building for Her" emphasized not the inculcation of "true Christian womanhood," but appeals to male chivalry and promises of fit and efficient workers, the prevention of the white slave traffic, and the "Canadianization" of the thousands of incoming immigrants.[47]

While YWCAs continued to be established in cities across the country, for a total of thirty-nine branches by 1930, and successful building campaigns were conducted until the collapse of the economy with the onset of the Great Depression, the 1920s witnessed the erosion of the earlier vision of a public institution that would unite women of all classes in a common commitment to evangelical Protestantism and the moral and spiritual transformation of the community and the nation. For a brief interlude in the second decade of the twentieth century, the YWCA had come close to achieving the recognition it sought as the acknowledged authority having jurisdiction over the welfare of young women in the city, but it had done so only by making a concerted attempt to address itself to the concerns of its financial supporters and downplaying its own commitment to a female-centred vision of evangelical moral reform. By the outbreak of the First World War the YWCA had succeeded in convincing religious authorities and social reformers, as well as local governments and business leaders, that addressing the girl problem was central to the successful resolution of the problem of the city. Nonetheless, it always remained the poor younger sister of the YMCA, never able to convince the respectable Christians of Canadian cities that the protection of young women merited the same financial commitment as corresponding efforts for young men (who were viewed as needing assistance but never protection). Increasingly, too, the "modern girl" rejected the YWCA's association with "old-time religion" and preferred male companionship to its outmoded commitment to female networks and wholesome homosocial recreation. During the 1920s the very idea of public funding for an institution whose control rested in the hands of evangelical church members fell into disfavour, new secular agencies took over many of the YWCA's traditional functions and the organization was forced, by the end of the decade, into a crisis that would lead to a reassessment of the meaning of "Christian" and substantial modification of the YWCA's evangelical vision for the young women of Canada.

Deeply committed to an evangelical variant of bourgeois domesticity that attributed redemptive powers to women and family life, the YWCA sought to place the concerns of women on the agenda of Canadian moral reformers by constructing the "girl problem" as an essential component of the larger "problem of the city." Drawing upon their own experiences of middle-class family life and religious women's networks, and their critique of urban public space as male space within which women were vulnerable and victimized, they envisioned a female sanctuary in the form of a public institution embodying the values of the Christian family home. While facilitating women's attempts to negotiate the public, the YWCA simultaneously mitigated class and gender disorder by preserving women's identification with domesticity and religion, by upholding the categorization of women according to the degree of their respectability, and by promoting a community of female believers that denied class differences while being deeply rooted in class identities. In a context, however, where middle-class churchwomen lacked access to political power and economic resources in their own right, their woman-centred vision of national regeneration and domestication of the urban environment underwent considerable modification to accommodate the concerns of their male financial supporters. Nonetheless, the YWCA asserted the value of women to the community and the nation, it embodied a female perspective on the changing class and gender order and, as such, it constituted a significant effort by Canadian evangelical churchwomen to shape the public discourse on the moral regulation of urban and national life.

NOTES

1. Mary P. Ryan, *Women in Public: Between Banners and Ballots, 1825–1880* (Baltimore: Johns Hopkins University Press, 1990), 78. See also, Christine Stansell, *City of Women: Sex and Class in New York, 1789–1860* (Urbana and Chicago: University of Illinois Press, 1987); Kathy Peiss, *Cheap Amusements: Working Women and Leisure in Turn-of-the-Century New York* (Philadelphia: Temple University

Press, 1986); Joanne J. Meyerowitz, *Women Adrift: Independent Wage Earners in Chicago, 1880–1930* (Chicago and London: University of Chicago Press, 1988); Elaine S. Abelson, *When Ladies Go A-Thieving: Middle-Class Shoplifters in the Victorian Department Store* (New York: Oxford University Press, 1989).

2. Marlene Stein Wortman, "Domesticating the Nineteenth-Century American City" *Prospects* 3 (1977): 531–572. See also Linda Richter, "The Ephemeral Female: Women in Urban Histories" *International Journal of Women's Studies* 5(4) 1982: 312–328.

3. National Archives of Canada, MG 28 I240, Montreal YWCA Records, v. 39, *Annual Report*, 1915–16, 15.

4. G.A. Rawlyk, *Ravished by the Spirit: Religious Revivals, Baptists, and Henry Alline* (Kingston and Montreal: McGill-Queen's University Press, 1984), 110–111. For examples of the new scholarship on nineteenth-century evangelicalism in Canada, see William Westfall, *Two Worlds: The Protestant Culture of Nineteenth-Century Ontario* (Kingston: McGill-Queen's University Press, 1989); and Michael Gauvreau, *The Evangelical Century: College and Creed in English Canada from the Great Revival to the Great Depression* (Kingston: McGill-Queen's University Press, 1991).

5. For the definition of maternal feminism, see Linda Kealey, ed., *A Not Unreasonable Claim: Women and Reform in Canada, 1880s–1920s* (Toronto: The Women's Press, 1979), 7. For discussion of historians' reluctance to consider seriously the place of religion in the history of English-speaking Canadian women, see Diana Pedersen, "The Young Women's Christian Association in Canada, 1870–1920: 'A Movement to Meet a Spiritual, Civic and National Need' " (Ph.D. thesis, Carleton University, Ottawa, 1987), Chapter 1; and Ruth Compton Brouwer, "Transcending the 'Unacknowledged Quarantine': Putting Religion into English-Canadian Women's History" *Journal of Canadian Studies* 27(3) Fall 1992: 47–61.

6. Marguerite Van Die, " 'A Woman's Awakening': Evangelical Belief and Female Spirituality in Mid-Nineteenth-Century Canada," Unpublished paper presented to the Canadian Historical Association, Kingston, 1991. [This paper has been reprinted in this text on pages 49–68.]

7. Trevor Wigney, "Manifest Righteousness: The Presbyterian Church, Education and Nation Building in Canada, 1875–1914" in Alf Chaiton and Neil McDonald, eds., *Canadian Schools and Canadian Identity* (Toronto: Gage Educational Publishing, 1977), 89.

8. Mariana Valverde, *The Age of Light, Soap, and Water: Moral Reform in English Canada, 1885–1925* (Toronto: McClelland and Stewart Inc., 1991), 23, 27. I use the term "positive" here in Valverde's sense — "not because it was necessarily good but to distinguish it from negativity, from mere prohibition."

9. For example, Peiss, *Cheap Amusements*; Meyerowitz, *Women Adrift*; Marian J. Morton, "Seduced and Abandoned in an American City: Cleveland and Its Fallen Women, 1869–1936" *Journal of Urban History* 11(4) August 1985: 443–469; Carolyn Strange, "From Modern Babylon to a City upon a Hill: The Toronto Social Survey Commission of 1915 and the Search for Sexual Order in the City" in Roger Hall, William Westfall, and Laurel Sefton MacDowell, eds., *Patterns of the Past: Interpreting Ontario's History* (Toronto and Oxford: Dundurn Press, 1988), 255–277.

10. Meyerowitz, *Women Adrift*, 55.

11. For very different interpretations of the response to the social crisis of the late nineteenth century, see Westfall, *Two Worlds*; Valverde, *The Age of Light, Soap, and Water*; and Ramsay Cook, *The Regenerators: Social Criticism in Late Victorian English Canada* (Toronto: University of Toronto Press, 1985).

12. Strange, "Modern Babylon," 255.

13. For an analysis of several British "narratives of sexual danger," including W.T. Stead's "Maiden Tribute of Modern Babylon" and the mythic story of Jack the Ripper, see Judith R. Walkowitz, *City of Dreadful Delight: Narratives of Sexual Danger in Late-Victorian London* (Chicago: University of Chicago Press, 1992). On the entry of young Canadian women into urban wage labour, see, for example, Betsy Beattie, " 'Going Up to Lynn': Single, Maritime-Born Women in Lynn, Massachusetts, 1879–1930" *Acadiensis* 22(1) Autumn 1992: 65–86; Joy Parr, "The Skilled Emigrant and Her Kin: Gender, Culture and Labour Recruitment" *Canadian Historical Review* 68 (Dec. 1987): 529–551; Bettina Bradbury, "Women and Wage Labour in a Period of Transition: Montreal, 1861–1881" *Histoire sociale/Social History* XVII, no. 33 (May 1984): 115–131; Marilyn Barber, "The Women Ontario Welcomed: Immigrant Domestics for Ontario Homes, 1870–1930" *Ontario History* 72(3) 1980: 148–172; Alan A. Brookes and Catherine Wilson, " 'Working Away' from the Farm: The Young Women of North Huron, 1910–1930" *Ontario History* 77(4) 1985: 281–300.

14. Meyerowitz, *Women Adrift*, 42. See also Barbara Meil Hobson, *Uneasy Virtue: The Politics of Prostitution and the American Reform Tradition* (Chicago and London: University of Chicago Press, 1987).

15. Diana Pedersen, " 'Keeping Our Good Girls Good': The YWCA and the 'Girl Problem,' 1870–1930" *Canadian Woman Studies* 7(4) Winter 1986: 20–24. The YWCA was established in Britain in 1855 and within several years made its first appearance in American cities. Early Canadian YWCAs developed as part of a North American network, affiliating with one of two international committees based in New York and Chicago that were divided over the question of restricting YWCA membership to full members of evangelical churches. Making a firm commitment to evangelical control and national representation for Canada in the new World's YWCA, the Canadians withdrew to form their own national organization in 1895. On these early developments, see Pedersen, "The Young Women's Christian Association in Canada," Chapter 2; and Anna V. Rice, *A History of the World's Young Women's Christian Association* (New York: The Woman's Press, 1947).

16. For an extended discussion of the difficulties facing young women newly arrived in Chicago, see Meyerowitz, *Women Adrift*, Chapters 1 and 2.

17. For an overview of American anti-prostitution campaigns in the nineteenth century, see Hobson, *Uneasy Virtue*; and see Meyerowitz, *Women Adrift*, Chapter 3, on the images of "orphans and innocents."

18. For the concept of evangelical domesticity, see Sandra S. Sizer, *Gospel Hymns and Social Religion: The Rhetoric of Nineteenth-Century Revivalism* (Philadelphia: Temple University Press, 1978), 87. For a perceptive analysis of the image of the Christian family home, see Colleen McDannell, *The Christian Family Home in Victorian America, 1840-1900* (Bloomington: Indiana University Press, 1986).

19. Hamilton YWCA Records, Clippings, "The Young Women's Christian Association," 1902.

20. Archives of Ontario, Toronto YWCA Records, *Annual Report*, 1874.

21. Toronto YWCA Records, *Annual Report*, 1878. For an extended discussion of YWCA boarding homes, see Pedersen, "The Young Women's Christian Association," Chapter 3. On Canadian women in the new white-blouse occupations, see, among others, Alison Prentice and Majorie R. Theobald, eds., *Women Who Taught: Perspectives on the History of Women and Teaching* (Toronto: University of Toronto Press, 1991); Joan Sangster, "The 1907 Bell Telephone Strike: Organizing Women Workers" *Labour/Le Travail* III (1978): 109-130; and Graham S. Lowe, *Women in the Administrative Revolution: The Feminization of Clerical Work* (Toronto and Buffalo: University of Toronto Press, 1987).

22. Wendy Mitchinson, "Canadian Women and Church Missionary Societies in the Nineteenth Century: A Step Towards Independence" *Atlantis* 2(2) Part II (Spring 1977): 57-75; and Christopher Headon, "Women and Organized Religion in Mid and Late Nineteenth Century Canada" *Journal of the Canadian Church Historical Society* 20(1-2) 1978: 3-18.

23. For example, Patricia T. Rooke and R.L. Schnell, "The Rise and Decline of British North American Protestant Orphans' Homes as Woman's Domain, 1850-1930" *Atlantis* 7(2) Spring 1982: 21-35; and Sharon Anne Cook, "'A Quiet Place . . . to Die': Ottawa's First Protestant Old Age Homes for Women and Men" *Ontario History* 81(1) 1989: 25-40.

24. On the little-studied relationship between nationalism and feminism in English-speaking Canada, see Veronica Strong-Boag, "'Setting the Stage': National Organization and the Women's Movement in the Late 19th Century" in Susan Mann Trofimenkoff and Alison Prentice, eds., *The Neglected Majority: Essays in Canadian Women's History* (Toronto: McClelland and Stewart Limited, 1977), 87-103; and Susan Mann Trofimenkoff, "Nationalism, Feminism and Canadian Intellectual History" *Canadian Literature* 83 (Winter 1979): 7-20.

25. Robert Bremner, "Scientific Philanthropy, 1873-93" *Social Service Review* 30(2) 1956: 168-173; Joey Noble, "'Class-ifying' the Poor: Toronto Charities, 1850-1880" *Studies in Political Economy* 2 (Autumn 1979): 109-128; and especially, Lori D. Ginzberg, *Women and the Work of Benevolence: Morality, Politics, and Class in the 19th-Century United States* (New Haven: Yale University Press, 1990).

26. For a new study of the Women's Christian Temperance Union, emphasizing its educational programs for children and young people, see Sharon Anne Cook, "'Continued and Persevering Combat': The Ontario Women's Christian Temperance Union, Evangelicalism and Social Reform, 1874-1916" (Ph.D. thesis, Carleton University, Ottawa, 1990). On evangelical attitudes toward children, see Neil Semple, "'The Nurture and Admonition of the Lord': Nineteenth-Century Canadian Methodism's Response to 'Childhood'" *Histoire sociale/Social History* XIV, No. 27 (May 1981): 157-175.

27. See especially Ryan, *Women in Public*; and Ginzberg, *Women and the Work of Benevolence*.

28. The YWCA was never, as many Canadians appear to believe, a female branch of the YMCA. The two were founded as entirely separate and distinct entities with their own corresponding national and international organizations. It was not until 1927 that YWCAs and YMCAs began to share facilities in some smaller Canadian communities that could not afford two buildings. On the history of the YMCA in Canada, see Murray G. Ross, *The Y.M.C.A. in Canada: The Chronicle of a Century* (Toronto: The Ryerson Press, 1951).

29. Toronto YWCA Records, *Annual Report*, 1883, 9. On the "servant problem" in Canadian cities, see Helen Lenskyj, "A 'Servant Problem' or a 'Servant-Mistress Problem'? Domestic Service in Canada, 1890-1930" *Atlantis* 7(1) Fall 1981: 3-11; and Marilyn Barber, "The Servant Problem in Manitoba, 1896-1930" in Mary Kinnear, ed., *First Days, Fighting Days: Women in Manitoba History* (Regina: Canadian Plains Research Center, University of Regina, 1987), 100-119.

30. Ottawa YWCA Records, *Annual Report*, 1893-94.

31. Estelle Freedman, "Separatism as Strategy: Female Institution Building and American Feminism, 1870-1930" *Feminist Studies* 5(3) 1979: 512-529; Ginzberg, *Women and the Work of Benevolence*, Chapter 5.

32. Edmonton Journal, "New Y.W.C.A. Building to Be Credit to Edmonton and Province of Alberta" 5 May 1920, 6.

33. Hamilton Public Library, Spectator Scrapbooks, YWCA, "New Y.W.C.A. Building Ready for Opening," 16 January 1915.

34. Although there are few direct references in the records, it would appear that Roman Catholic and Jewish young women did use the YWCA facilities that were open to non-members. However "colored girls" were accommodated in separate programs, with Hamilton offering a class in physical culture in 1919 and Toronto opening a "colored girls' branch" in 1912, featuring a school of domestic science.

35. National Archives of Canada, MG 28 I198, YWCA of Canada Records, v. 46, *Young Women of Canada*, April 1914, 118.
36. University of British Columbia Library, Vancouver YWCA Records, *Annual Report*, 1918, 4.
37. Public Archives of Nova Scotia, Halifax YWCA Records, Clippings, "Fine Record of Local Y.W.C.A. during Year," 1917.
38. On evangelical womanhood as a lifestyle that churchwomen consciously promoted to younger women, see Anne M. Boylan, "Evangelical Womanhood in the Nineteenth Century: The Role of Women in Sunday Schools" *Feminist Studies* 4(3) 1978: 62–80.
39. YWCA of Canada Records, v. 46, *Association Outlook*, May 1918, 93.
40. On the churches' response to the war, see Michael Bliss, "The Methodist Church and World War I" *Canadian Historical Review* 49(3) 1968: 213–233.
41. Victoria, *Daily Colonist*, "Victoria Y.W.C.A. Plans and Does Much Work," 3 June 1917, 24.
42. For an extended discussion of the YWCAs of Canada and World War I, see Pedersen, "The Young Women's Christian Association," Chapter 5.
43. Margaret Prang, "'The Girl God Would Have Me Be': The Canadian Girls in Training, 1915–1939" *Canadian Historical Review* 66(2) 1985: 154–184.
44. Diana Pedersen, "'The Call to Service': The YWCA and the Canadian College Woman, 1886–1920" in Paul Axelrod and John G. Reid, eds., *Youth, University and Canadian Society: Essays in the Social History of Higher Education* (Kingston: McGill-Queen's University Press, 1989), 187–215.
45. On the wartime scares over prostitution and venereal disease, see Hobson, *Uneasy Virtue*, Chapter 7; and Jay Cassel, *The Secret Plague: Venereal Disease in Canada, 1838–1939* (Toronto: University of Toronto Press, 1987).
46. *Winnipeg Evening Tribune*, 8 April 1920, 11. On the new interest in the "unadjusted girl," see Hobson, *Uneasy Virtue*, Chapter 8.
47. Diana Pedersen, "'Building Today for the Womanhood of Tomorrow': Businessmen, Boosters, and the YWCA, 1890–1930" *Urban History Review* 15(3) February 1987: 225–242; and "The Photographic Record of the Canadian YWCA, 1890–1930: A Visual Source for Women's History" *Archivaria* 24 (Summer 1987): 10–35.

Part Three

The Promised Land? The End of the Great War to the Beginning of World War II

The Canadian interwar experience can best be described as turbulent. The transition from a wartime to a peacetime economy was a painful one, particularly for women workers; jobs generated by war production ceased, and both unemployment and inflation rose during the postwar depression. Labour militancy intensified as working men and women sought to protect or improve their standard of living. At war's end, public officials urged women to give up their employment; pressured by economic need, poor women and women from ethnic and racial minorities paid little heed.

The expanding economy of the mid- and late twenties, particularly buoyant in central and western Canada, resulted in new job opportunities and unprecedented prosperity for some segments of the Canadian population. The most significant growth occurred in the resource-related industries, but these provided few employment opportunities for women. With the return of prosperity, however, employers, especially in the growing clerical and service sectors, once again actively recruited young, single, white women.

The improved economic conditions of the mid-1920s made it possible for some male workers to support their families on their own wages — the "family wage" was becoming a reality. Yet with the onset of the Great Depression in 1929, few families could rely on one male wage earner. In many families, only wives and daughters were able to find employment; but as the Depression deepened, women found it extremely difficult to keep their paid work, and as unemployment soared, married and single women were blamed for contributing to the nation's problems by taking jobs away from men.

The wildly alternating cycles of bust–boom–bust from 1919 to 1939 created enormous demographic fluctuations. Although the population increased from nearly 9 million in 1921 to 11.5 million by 1941, the pace of growth slowed and was at its lowest during the Depression years. The number of births dropped between 1931 and 1941: there were only 2.29 million compared to 2.42 million during the previous decade. The most startling demographic change was the sharp decline in immigration after 1931, as economic conditions worsened and the Canadian govern-ment restricted immigration: a mere 149,000 immigrants arrived between 1931 and 1941, the lowest number recorded for any decade since official recording began.

Fluctuations in the nation's economy and population created an at-mosphere conducive to political change. Across the nation farmers de-serted traditional parties to support emerging political organizations. These alternative parties gave enfranchised women new avenues of po-litical involvement. At the federal level, the Co-operative Commonwealth Federation (CCF) was formed in Calgary in 1932 and, like most other leftist political organizations, officially endorsed the full participation of women. It soon became apparent, however, that women and men voters preferred the two traditional parties, particularly the Liberal party.

For the most part, women's activities and issues failed to generate the public attention they attracted during the suffrage campaign. Studies of the role and status of Canadian women during the interwar years are, however, now being undertaken by historians of women. The essays presented in this section explore, from different perspectives, women's experiences of work in the home and in the paid labour force, examine aspects of their participation in political life, and discuss the activities of some mainstream women's organizations.

Equality and Difference: Feminism and the Defence of Women Workers during the Great Depression

MARGARET HOBBS

In the summer of 1931, as Canada slipped deeper into economic de-pression, a male contributor to the *Canadian Congress Journal* commented on the angry turn of public sentiment against women and girls holding jobs. "Nowadays, any stick seems good enough to beat the business girl with," he observed with alarm. This writer, while sidestepping the con-troversial question of whether female employment was socially desirable in itself, nonetheless felt obliged, if only from a chivalrous impulse to defend the "weaker" sex against all those brandishing sticks, to point out that most young women in business had little choice but to work for pay. The depression, he argued, was paralyzing fathers' abilities to

SOURCE: Margaret Hobbs, "Equality and Difference: Feminism and the Defence of Women Workers during the Great Depression," *Labour/Le Travail* 32 (Fall 1993), 201–223. Reprinted with the permission of the editor of *Labour/Le Travail*. © Committee on Canadian Labour History.

keep their daughters at home and preventing young men from marrying them. Business "girls" would most certainly prefer to stay at home, but they could not. A young unmarried typist in an insurance office had personally assured him of this, describing wistfully the life of leisure she would choose if she were supported by some well-to-do man, either father or husband:

> If I could stay at home and have my early tea brought me by a smart parlor-maid, or butler, or whoever does these things, and get up when I liked, and spend all day playing golf or tennis, or motoring and have all the frocks I wanted, I should imagine I was in heaven.[1]

The emphasis given by both the man and the young woman to economic necessity as the magnet drawing females into employment was shared by many of those, feminist or not, who rushed to the defence of wage-earning women and girls in the 1930s. It is this line of defence which has been most noticed by feminist historians looking at the right-to-work debate, particularly in the United States, where the work of Lois Scharf on married women between the wars has been so influential.[2] Scharf found that in the 1920s a vocal group of white-collar "career and marriage" advocates resuscitated the 19th-century equalitarian tradition of feminism, a tradition which by the turn of the century had been overshadowed by the popularity of maternalist claims to women's unique nature, their "difference" from men, rather than their abstract natural rights. Equal-rights arguments, buoyed in the 1920s by new economic opportunities for women and by the entrance of more wives into employment, proved too difficult to maintain once the economy collapsed and jobs were scarce. Supporters of women workers were forced on the defensive, Scharf claims. They watered down their feminism, de-emphasizing women's "right" to choose employment and avoiding the celebration of work as personal fulfillment. Instead they highlighted the financial pressures that left most female workers with little choice but to work for pay.[3] Scharf assumes that in backing away from the language of rights and preference and embracing the language of need, 1930s feminists and others articulating this position were helping to swing the pendulum of feminist ideology from "equality" back to "difference," for the need rationale relied on a stock of traditional images of femininity. According to this interpretation, female autonomy was submerged, especially for the married woman worker, under a rhetoric that played on her familial ties and priorities, her self-sacrificing responsiveness to the economic needs of her family.

In Canada too the minority of individuals who defended women's economic roles in the 1930s more often than not framed their argument in terms of necessity, not rights or choice. Through instrumentality or personal conviction, most promoted a gender-conservative image of wage- or salary-earning wives as nurturant, self-sacrificing wives and mothers taking work outside the home only to meet the material needs of their families, and of working girls as unfortunate daughters forced to work by the absence or impoverishment of the usual male provider.

Yet it is easy to overstate ideological shifts. Although in Canada the need justification, presumed by historians to be steeped in the language of difference, gained popularity in the period, the equal-rights tradition proved more resilient than one might assume. The ascendancy of one rationale need not entail the demise of the other. Nor is there always a neat separation between those using need arguments and those articulating the legitimacy of women's choices and preferences independent of their needs. The two often overlapped.[4] Moreover, the concepts of need and choice are to a great extent relative. Clearly food and clothing constitute basic human necessities, but those who can afford to will often view holidays and entertainment as the stuff of necessity. Although one might lean to one side or the other, it was quite possible, then as now, to argue from both sides of what Ann Snitow has called the enduring feminist "divide" of equality versus difference.[5] As many scholars are currently pointing out, the splits among self-identified feminists that repeatedly occur across the divide should not obscure the fact that most people are not anchored immovably to either perspective, but are pulled in both directions. Feminists find themselves emphasizing gender differences more or less depending on the issue and the political climate, and also on which argument is most likely to win the cause. The elusiveness of philosophical consistency should be neither surprising nor lamentable. Since feminism depends on articulating the needs and interests of a gendered subject, "woman" or "women," while at the same time questioning the substance of those very categories, the tensions and inconsistencies between equality and difference are an intrinsic part of feminism as a political movement and ideological outlook.[6] I have attempted to approach the question of the defence of women workers from a perspective which recognizes these tensions, paying heed to Joan Scott's suggestion (though not taking it as far as she would) that feminist historians stop imposing the equality-versus-difference construct in ways that lock one into writing a misrepresentative history of constant oscillation from one mutually exclusive pole to the other.[7]

I

Defenders of women workers in Canada were well aware that the threats to women's economic rights were not self-contained within their own political borders. Reports of the international scope of the erosion of women's rights, especially in fascist countries where the face of anti-feminism was most severe, were carried in the national and special interest press in Canada. Feminists in particular would have been paying close attention, for since the early suffrage battle they had kept a keen eye on developments in women's status elsewhere in the western world, particularly the United States and Britain. The largest women's organizations were affiliated with internationals that, through newsletters and correspondence, encouraged information and policy sharing as well as dialogue between member countries. Many national organizations also made a conscious effort to be represented at international gatherings of women — a practice they tried to maintain despite the squeeze on their budgets in the 1930s. The swelling tide of antifeminist reaction that set in across North America and Europe on the heels of the economic crisis could not have escaped the notice of Canadians concerned with the fate of feminism closer to home. Because feminists in the depression frequently saw their concerns in an international context and were called upon by international women's organizations to join the struggle to guard women's workplace rights, it is useful to begin this examination of the defence of working women with some analysis of the response of the international feminist community.[8]

Among the middle-class women's organizations, the International Council of Women (ICW) and the International Federation of Business and Professional Women's Clubs (IFBPWC) were two of the most outspoken and consistent supporters of women workers in the western world. Established in 1888, the ICW had its roots firmly planted in the maternal feminist tradition, so much so that the organization has been dubbed by one authority "a gigantic maternal union."[9] Yet its historic investment in sexual difference did not stop it from endorsing all wives' right to paid labour in the mid-1920s.[10] The IFBPWC, unlike the ICW, was only a fledgling organization in the 1930s, although by 1937 its membership had climbed to about 100,000 commercial and professional women in 25 countries.[11] In the 1920s national and local Business and Professional Women's Clubs had been among the most active champions of the joys of work for wives. Together, the ICW and the IFBPWC stood firm during the 1930s on the principle that women, be they married or single, wealthy or poor, had as much right to jobs as men.

Although both international organizations were monitoring discriminatory actions against women early in the depression, it was 1934 before the right-to-work issue dominated the agenda at their conventions. No doubt they were spurred to stronger action then by the frightening repression of women's rights under way in several European countries, but particularly in Germany, where Hitler was throwing the full weight of the state behind a campaign to eject women from the work force and bonus their maternity function.[12] At the IFBPWC's June 1934 meeting, after listening to its Director, Canadian lawyer Dorothy Heneker, report on legislative action against women in Germany as well as in Austria, Hungary, Belgium, and Czecho-Slovakia, the Board formally registered its protest. Asserting "the right of all people to work, unhampered by restrictions of sex or social status," the conference called upon governments to cooperate and made a special plea to national affiliates to do everything in their power to fight against discrimination. One month later at the ICW's meeting in Paris, 14 international women's organizations staged a public forum on the right-to-work issue and passed three separate resolutions endorsing the principle of equality.[13] Over the next several years the IFBPWC and the ICW reiterated their positions, calling on women's organizations, particularly their own affiliates, to be vigilant watch dogs poised to spring at any state or private employers acting against women's economic interests. IFBPWC President Lena Madesin Phillips, founder of the organization and long-time activist with both the National BPWC and the National Council of Women in the U.S.,[14] spoke with particular passion on several occasions at International Federation conferences. "The right of women to work and how to preserve this right may not be the most critical problem which faces the world today," she advised her audience in 1935, "but it is one of supreme importance to business women." Echoing 19th-century American suffragists in their reliance on liberal rights rhetoric and slavery metaphors, she explained that what was at stake for women was far more than just the pay cheque:

> The fundamental question is whether women are entitled to those innate human rights for which men have fought and died or whether they, unworthy of freedom, belong in a slave class.[15]

Whatever else might divide members in the 23 countries represented in the Federation, Phillips insisted that "the underlying principle, the unifying purpose" of the Business and Professional Women's Clubs rested upon "the inherent rights and powers of every individual woman."[16]

By 1937 the language of economic need, which previously appears to have been absent from her addresses at IF conventions, had entered into Phillips' speeches. Yet, significantly, it did not overshadow her emphasis on the individualist equality principle. Even when asserting that "The business woman works because she must work," she was not restricting her understanding of "necessity" to economic matters: women, she clarified, must work "*either* for maintenance or self-expression, or both." "But whether or not economic interest is pressing," she continued, "she works because she must serve."[17] In these words one can see how Phillips drew simultaneously on equal rights and sexual difference, the latter particularly through the image of women as society's selfless handmaids.

With signs of an upturn in the world economy apparent by 1937, the IF President was anxious that women might prematurely let down their guard. Even if the return of prosperity should torpedo the more extreme of the antifeminist plans, she knew that women could easily find themselves targeted again at the first indication of another downturn. Campaigns to oust women from employment were among the "stark and primitive urges" that accompany poor economic times, Phillips reminded. A new strategy, nothing short of an international "united women's front" pledged to "eternal vigilance" was required to release women from the trap of historical repetition.[18]

II

How did Canadian women's groups respond to the directives and pleas coming from these international federations? In the United States, according to Scharf, apologists for working women may have toned down the feminism in their reasoning, but women's organizations nonetheless pulled together, in a manner unparalleled since suffrage, to hold on to past gains in female labour force participation.[19] In Canada, however, the married woman wage-earner proved no symbol of unity for women's groups in the depression. As I have shown elsewhere, many women reformers, some of whom were long-time supporters of women's rights in other matters, joined in the attacks on employed women who were either married or from well-to-do families.[20] The National Council of Women of Canada (NCWC) and its locals proved particularly timid on the question, with many women and several locals standing firmly in opposition to the employment of wives. Even in the 1920s, a decade generally more sympathetic to the presence of women in public work, the NCWC, slightly more progressive than some of its locals, would risk only cautious support for the working wife through argumentation that avoided any mention of "natural rights" or personal preference. A 1928 report prepared for the International Council on why married women worked, while acknowledging the trend for women to look increasingly to employment as an "outside interest," was nonetheless adamant that very few of even these women were working for the "purely selfish motive of a desire for personal adornment or for living in more luxurious surroundings"; rather, they were only trying to improve their standard of living or enhance their children's educational achievements. Moreover, it seemed that the bulk of the married female work force had much more modest aims: they took jobs to ensure their families had food on the table and clothes on their backs.[21]

By 1933, however, the NCWC's Trades and Professions Committee (the one most directly involved with employment and unemployment issues) underwent a change of heart. No longer was the Committee so confident about the legitimacy of working wives' motives. Undoubtedly influenced by prevailing popular opinion, nagging suspicions were voiced that married women were working for luxury and stealing jobs from the needy: men and single girls and even many older unemployed women dependent on their own resources and experiencing special hardships due to age discrimination. Under the convenership of Mary MacMahon, a confirmed adversary of working wives, the Committee all but withdrew completely its former modest support. Except when employment was a financial imperative, MacMahon insisted, a married woman's "spirit of fairness should whisper for her to remain in the home."[22] Similar sentiments surfaced the following year at the annual meeting when the ICW's trio of married women resolutions and clear call for supportive action from National Councils caused a flurry of debate.[23]

Later in the depression, a change in leadership of the Trades and Professions Committee (and possibly in its membership as well) encouraged greater tolerance. As convener, Eva McKivor used her authority in 1936 to try to sway hesitant or hostile Trades and Professions Committees within Local Councils to stand behind the wage-earning wife. "Even though we may or do believe she should not be at present in this competitive field," she reasoned in a circular to local conveners, choosing her words carefully in anticipation of resistance, "we must not criticize her right to be there."[24] If she was able to change some Council women's attitudes, the NCWC still did not accept the challenge posed by its international parent, the ICW, to form a "united women's front" in defence of women's economic rights.

A few Local Councils, however, stood apart from the National in exercising a stronger commitment to gender equality in the workplace. The Vancouver LCW, living up to its reputation as one of the boldest Councils on feminist issues, lent unqualified support to the ICW married woman resolutions, as did Councils in Victoria, Moose Jaw, Niagara Falls, and Owen Sound.[25] Yet support for the principle did not necessarily mean that the employment rights of wives was thrust to the forefront of their political agendas in their own communities. Pressured by the absence of government response to unemployed women and girls, many women's organizations felt obliged to direct their limited resources towards the provision of relief services for women. The Vancouver Council, for example, was so preoccupied with pragmatic relief-related activities, especially those concerning single jobless girls, that it seems to have had little energy left over to put much concrete action behind its various resolutions demanding all women's right to jobs.[26]

The Local Council in Montréal launched probably the most vigorous defence of women workers, despite the fact that its Trades and Professions Committee, which would normally deal with such issues, was defunct during the early years of the depression and not too active in the later years, its members apparently preferring to work closely with the local Business and Professional Women's Club.[27] Unlike many of its sister organizations in other communities, the Montréal Council did not back away from the ICW's directives on women's employment rights. In fact the Local Council sent a copy of at least one of the ICW's controversial 1934 resolutions to Montréal's mayor, Camillien Houde, after the mayor utilized the public air waves to encourage the replacement of female workers by men.[28] The Houde incident was only one of a series of antifeminist provocations prompting Montréal Council women, along with other local women's groups, to denounce publicly discriminatory attitudes and actions by 1934-5. Indeed, it was only two years before that Québec politician Mederic Martin had tried to fan the flames of antifeminism across the country by printing in *Chatelaine* an outlandish appeal to women to vacate the work force en masse in the name of patriotism.[29] Montréal Council women watched nervously but not passively over the next few years as Martin's dream of a legislative solution to the problem of women workers came perilously close to realization with the successive introduction of discriminatory bills in the Québec legislature.[30] The similarities between trends at home and events overseas in countries where drastic gender policies were gaining ground could not have escaped notice. Clearly the Montréal Council's more spirited campaign was fuelled by fears about where the erosion of women's economic autonomy was leading in other countries.

The sympathy of the Montréal Council with the ICW's equal-rights argumentation — with its emphasis on the right to work as essential to the dignity and the liberty of human beings — was consistent with its past tendency to favour equalitarian thinking over the gender-soaked maternalism of most feminists and reformers affiliated with the NCWC. On the issue of protective legislation for women workers, for example, the Montréal Council, since the late 19th century, had distanced itself from the majority stance of Canadian women reformers by rejecting the principle of special protection based on sex. Granted, some early Council members may have favoured equality of the sexes in labour matters out of conservative reluctance to interfere with employers' "rights." Others, however, like the influential Carrie Derick, were more worried that special "protection" only encouraged the replacement of female workers with men and boys not covered by the legislation. Apart from these practical concerns, Derick also embraced equality in principle.[31] Conceptualizing equality and difference as fundamentally contradictory, Derick counselled women not to expect equality in some arenas and special treatment in others. Yet despite her plea for ideological consistency, on occasion the Montréal Council could be found endorsing protective measures for women and, for whatever reason, Derick does not seem to have stood in the way.[32] Still an active member during the 1930s, Derick was the force behind a 1934 resolution denouncing the firing of women to make room for unemployed men,[33] and she undoubtedly used her influence to ensure that the Council did not lose sight of an equal-rights perspective even if it also spoke at times with an affirmation of sexual difference.

Except in a few pockets like Montréal, NCWCers were hardly the most reliable or forceful allies of women workers nervous that public resentment could cost them their jobs. More up to the task was the Canadian Federation of Business and Professional Women's Clubs (CFBPWC). The Federation was founded early in the depression when seven local BPW clubs banded together to promote the economic, educational, and social interests of its members and to encourage cooperation among this sisterhood of white-collar workers that had mushroomed during the economic developments of the previous decade.[34] Employment issues had always been of key interest to members, the majority of whom were not the privileged professionals who were often the spokespersons, but rather secretaries, stenographers, clerks, bank workers, and other low-pay, low-status white-collar workers.[35] The move to federate and the dramatic climb in the number of clubs and in their membership in the first two years — all against the background of pervasive public unease over female employment — reflects a determination to hold on to workplace opportunities they believed were rightfully theirs.[36] The relative strength of the federation, in spirit if not in dollars, may also suggest how great was the need among white-collar women for mutual emotional support against shared financial anxieties and the sting of public tirades directed at girls and women with jobs.

Unified in their commitment to single women's workplace rights, local clubs were frequently split over the place of married women in business.[37] The majority of club members were, after all, unmarried women, mostly employed but some unemployed, in an economic and ideological climate which pitted women against each other based on their marital status. Nevertheless, internal disputes about married women, particularly apparent at the local level, were not extensive enough to block the Canadian Federation from officially and strongly endorsing their presence in the workplace. By the second annual meeting, in 1931, a resolution was passed formally registering disapproval of workplace discrimination based on women's marital status.[38] The resolution stated the Federation's position simply, without couching it in the language of either need or rights.

Whatever sympathy was forthcoming from the membership for married women workers was probably due less to a political commitment to sisterhood or a feminist analysis of economic dependence than to a gut-level understanding of their own vulnerability to antifeminist attacks. The minutes of the Canadian Federation's annual meetings reveal a pragmatically motivated membership aspiring to economic security and trying to carve out for themselves — be they secretaries or medical practitioners — a legitimate claim to "professional" status. During a mid-decade thrashing out of the married woman issue at a Federation convention in Calgary, what quieted disagreements was the observation of one member that moves to cast married women aside were only "the thin edge of the wedge to get women out of positions in the professional and business world."[39] This was not depression-induced paranoia. It was fear based on an astute sense that femaleness itself was potential cause for suspicion in the work force of the depression.

Knowing full well the disastrous repercussions of gender discrimination for white-collar women already marginalized in the labour force, the Canadian Federation remained committed to winning gender battles for the women it represented. Especially wary of employer initiatives to masculinize the workforce, it urged locals to study and report on the nature and extent of discrimination in their communities. In 1933, the ugliest depression year, the President of the CFBPWC lashed out at employers and politicians using sometimes "subtle" and other times "open" propaganda to replace females with males and lower women's salaries, a practice found to be most prevalent in teaching and banking. Speaking with a passion reminiscent of the earlier generation of suffrage reformers, and nodding at their efforts on women's behalf, she impressed on her audience that female gains in the public sphere were "ours by right of a difficult conquest and painstaking labor." "O! foolish people, do they think they can stay the march of progress?" Women, she predicted, would not easily give up their hard-won trophies and crawl back to their homes in defeat, antifeminists could be certain of that. Female energy repressed in one place would erupt elsewhere with equal force. Women, for example, would counter discrimination by setting up their own all-female businesses; there were already signs of such a trend under way.[40]

The CF President was combining here an appeal to historical inevitability — an old centrepiece in feminist argumentation — with a vision of women's essential role in creating their own history. Several years later, at the 1937 meeting, discussions about women's employment seemed much more defensive. The Federation President opened the meeting insisting that "It is not so much women's right to work with which we are concerned as it is her need to work."[41] A Québec representative, still stunned from the near victory of anti-working-women forces in the provincial legislature two years earlier, thought it essential to "prove to the men" that the lingering depression was not the fault of women. Certainly appeals to the march of progress or to women's right to work for fun and self-fulfillment would not have helped exonerate women from blame. Not surprisingly, it was the economic imperative for wives to work that was referred to repeatedly by then. It constituted, for example, the backbone to a Saskatchewan report responding to the International Labor Organization's request for information about male/female wage rates and women workers' responsibility for dependents. Married women only work for necessity, the western representative told the convention, adding that there couldn't be more than fifty wives working in Regina just "because they want to."[42] If there were any married women present at the meeting with husbands securely employed or independently wealthy (and there may have been some), they did not draw attention to themselves by objecting or insisting on their right to work for fun or self-fulfillment.

Women's organizations with any inclination to defend women workers in the depression had to contend with a major obstacle: a social and cultural milieu largely sympathetic to rigorous questioning of the economic rights of women, especially married women. The increasing timidity of the Canadian Federation of Business and Professional Women's Clubs and even more so the NCWC testifies to the widely felt "gender jitters"[43] that underlay much of the campaign to oust women from jobs in the thirties. It is no coincidence that the most active organized resistance to incursions on women's earning power took place in parts of the country where antifeminism seemed to be gaining the strongest foothold, as in Québec. More support might at least have been squeezed out of some of the fence-sitters had the threat throughout Canada appeared as great as it did in the U.S., where discriminatory legislative proposals and actions were legion.[44] Without such an immediate and tangible threat, Canadian women interested in mobilizing support for the married woman worker had to contend not only with direct opposition within their membership, but also with a certain amount of apathy. While moves against women in the U.S. and much more so in parts of Europe prompted some response from women's reform organizations, many women must have felt distanced from the clouds that were gathering "over there." Certainly this was the observation of Gwethalyn Graham, who in 1936 complained to readers of the *Canadian Forum* that

> partly because of the urgency of other issues considered more vital, partly because what has been happening to the women of Germany and Italy is so much more obvious that similar conditions in our own country seem negligible by comparison, the retrogressive movement has got under way here without receiving much notice or comment.[45]

Clearly disappointed by the relatively weak-kneed response of the Canadian women's movement, Graham thought "the whole subject of Feminism" was wanting "a good airing."

III

Feminism, and in particular the question of married women's employment, had in fact received an airing in forums other than the liberal women's organizations. Debates about women's place raged in the popular press of the early 1930s, especially in the letters to the editor sections, and although the overwhelming majority of writers were camped with the forces of opposition, there were a few brave souls who dared to defend the beleaguered woman worker. A few were well-known public figures, but others were not, and some joined in the debates only under the veil of anonymity. A brief sampling of some of these voices appearing in the mainstream Toronto press as well as in national magazines like *Chatelaine*, *The Canadian Forum*, and *The Canadian Home Journal* reveals at first glance a preponderance of arguments compatible with conservative gender assumptions, reflecting the rising popularity of the politics of gender difference. But a closer look reveals an array of arguments drawing on either equality or difference, or weaving the two together. Equal-rights thinking was still alive in Canada, and not just within the Montréal Local Council of Women. Moreover, an analysis of the opinions expressed by defenders of employed women points up some limitations of sticking to a polarized frame of equality and difference to understand the contours of feminism in the period.

In the social and economic context of the depression, writers trying to defend women workers were forced into building their argument at least in part around a rebuttal of the most common charges laid against women. Accusations that women were stealing jobs from male bread-winners whose children were starving, that married women were taking jobs away from single girls who were then forced onto relief or into pros-titution, that married women were driving to work in limousines past lines of jobless outside soup kitchens, that young girls were only working for good times and fineries — these were allegations with tremendous inflammatory power that demanded response.

On a purely practical level it was important for defenders to counter the erroneous assumptions and faulty logic behind such claims. Thus the case was repeatedly made in the pages of the press, as it was often at conventions of women's organizations, that women's earnings were crucial for self or family support, especially in the working class. And, when cornered, all but the most narrow-minded antifeminists had to concede that a great many single girls were "legitimate" breadwinners and that there were also certain economic circumstances that necessitated married women's workforce involvement.[46] Besides, even if women could be persuaded to go home, what men would be willing to take their mainly low-paying, sex-typed jobs? Moreover, how many men used to manual labour or even office work were properly skilled to step right into a job that one married white-collar worker said she had spent "a lifetime learn-ing?"[47] And what would become of the new army of unemployed women? Who would support them, especially if they had no male relatives? The state?[48] Surely that was not desirable. It was also expedient for defenders of working women to argue that far from causing the unemployment crisis, employed women, of the middle class at least, were in fact con-tributing to job creation, most particularly for domestic servants, but also for men who could be hired to do odd jobs around the houses of busy double-income earners.[49] Some pushed the point to emphasize how married women's employment benefited the economy since women were the country's major consumers:

> It is generally admitted that it is women's needs and tastes and extravagances that make the wheels of industry turn. Just think of the slump in business there would be with no women on the payrolls — more men out of jobs.[50]

If it made good practical sense for working women and their sym-pathizers to refute the image of the selfish pin-money worker by drawing on these economic arguments, not all correspondents were writing in this vein merely to score political points; many were reacting on a per-sonal level to a deeply felt sense of grievance that they should be depicted as bread snatchers and home wreckers. One woman who had recently lost her job because her husband had one wanted to share with readers of the Toronto *Mail and Empire* her difficulties in keeping a family of six going when her husband made only $26 a week and had no steady work all winter. In producing her monthly budget for critics to scrutinize she appealed for understanding of her family's need of additional income.[51] Another woman, married and employed, whose husband's 72-hour work week driving a cab pulled in only ten dollars if he was lucky, wrote in to the Toronto *Telegram* to let single girls know she was not working for fun or extras. "It's no picnic," she cried, especially when going out to work meant leaving her small baby for others to enjoy. What choice did she have, she asked, if she wanted her child to be fed and clothed?[52] One can read between the lines her fear of being judged not only an illegitimate worker but also a bad mother.

Defenders of working women possessed a good understanding that the attacks on women workers were not just motivated by rational assessments of who were and were not the rightful breadwinners. The "real" issue, the *Canadian Forum* editorialized, was the old belief "that woman's place is in the home."[53] Efforts by defenders to cast the working woman, especially the working wife, as selflessly bound to home and family, pursuing paid labour only out of economic necessity, reflect a desire to soothe public fears — and perhaps for some their own fears as well — that the traditional gender order and the family itself were not breaking down under the weight of the unemployment crisis. Some other common arguments tending to shore up conservative gender ideology were that employment keeps girls good and out of "trouble," that employment made wives better companions for their husbands, that discrimination against married women was contributing to the decreasing marriage rates confirmed by studies of youths (since not many youths could get by on just one income) and also to the increase of extra-marital sex.[54]

Despite the prevalence of what might be interpreted as a defensive and conservative retreat, an open embrace of gender difference, working women and their supporters can also be found appealing to the principle of equality and critiquing restrictive notions of masculinity and femininity, including the gender division of labour in the depression family. Perhaps unemployed men, not working women, should be the ones to go home, one woman boldly suggested in *Chatelaine*:

> Their mothers or sisters or wives who have jobs and are away from home all day would be only too glad if they would stay home and clean up the house, wash the dishes or look after the baby.[55]

Other women declared that it was simply "unfair" to treat women differently from men, that this was a relic from an outmoded time when women truly were the economic dependents of fathers or husbands, and that discriminatory policies would represent an erasure of years of struggle by feminists and a denial of women's fundamental rights as independent beings.[56] Gwethalyn Graham, referred to earlier lamenting the slipping away of feminism, argued for a rejection of the narrow biologism poking its head through popular psychology, and urged readers to confront squarely the question of "whether or not women shall be entitled, as individuals, to work for the sake of the work itself."[57]

While Graham came down hard and clear on the side of the equalitarian tradition, many other writers drew simultaneously on equal rights and maternal thinking. Preferring to grab at whatever arguments seemed to do the trick, they showed none of the unease with the ideological contradictions that had prompted Montréal's Carrie Derick to advise women they could not have it both ways, expecting equality on the one hand and special privileges on the other. For example, one of the letter-writers who wrote to the Toronto *Star* in defence of women's hard-earned "rights" also thought it might be true that women's first duty was to home and family.[58] And it was commonplace to combine arguments based on "fairness," equality, and individual choice with those based on the imperative of financial need. Harriet Parsons, a Toronto journalist for the *Canadian Home Journal*, utilized the language of rights, embraced the importance of women working for pleasure and fulfillment (observing "Not being needed is worse than not being fed"), argued that men and women shared identical interests in the economic crisis and that businesses should revoke any married woman bans. Yet despite her commitment to equality principles Parsons, like so many others, could also be found reasserting gender difference, suggesting for example that young men's salaries be raised as a strategy to encourage more youth to marry.[59]

IV

The blurring of boundaries between those arguing from an equal-rights perspective and those relying on conceptions of gender difference can also be seen by looking at the thinking of two influential and highly visible spokespersons for women's interests in the interwar period, one from the west and one from the east: Helen Gregory MacGill and Agnes Macphail. MacGill, an outspoken Juvenile Court Judge in Vancouver for over 20 years (from 1919 to 1929 and again from 1934 to 1945), had also chaired the Mother's Pension Board in the 1920s, served on the B.C. Minimum Wage Board for 17 years, briefly sat on its replacement, the Board of Industrial Relations in 1934, and served on the Mayor's Unemployment Committee from 1930 to 1931. One of Canada's best known early feminist reformers, she has generally been portrayed as a maternal or "social" feminist, more concerned with welfare and other reform measures affecting women and children than with principles of women's rights, more interested in the vote as a tool for social reform than a symbol of women's equality.[60] Although she may have leaned more to this side, her public statements on female employment during the depression suggest that she cannot be parked too rigidly on the side of difference alone.

Undeniably, she downplayed the joys of jobs for women and avoided arguing in the abstract about rights. Instead, led by a legal mind sticky about logic, MacGill first exposed the fallacious thinking of those who saw in women both cause and cure for economic depression, beginning with the fact that no exodus of female workers could make a dent in male unemployment since most men would not do "women's work," such as domestic service and stenography. Compelled to respond to prevailing cynicism about why women took work outside the home, MacGill chose to emphasize economic factors more than social and personal ones, portraying women and girls as crucial economic contributors to their families and as indispensable workers to industry. Drawing on her years of experience in the Juvenile Court and on the Minimum Wage Board she observed how much more familial in orientation were young working girls than boys; they poured their wages and their energies back into families which depended on the economic, social, and emotional roles they took on. In her descriptions of employed wives she underlined a similarly selfless female preoccupation with family welfare, pointing to women who used their pay to put food on the table, to help with the bills, to give their children more opportunities for education and a higher standard of living, or to save for old age.[61]

But there is also an emphasis in her writing on women's "sameness" to men. Like men, she insisted, women have always worked — they have just not always been paid for it — and when they are remunerated they have a right to equal pay for equal work. Like men, women experience need: "Being jobless is not a matter of sex, and suffering caused by hunger or cold is not limited to either men or women."[62] Like men, women often had dependents to support. It angered her that married women were singled out as undeserving workers presumed to be living with male providers, and she reminded readers of the woman with an unemployed or underemployed husband, and of the woman with a sick, disabled, incompetent, irresponsible, or lazy husband who, along with the children and often an older parent or relative, was dependent on her. Untroubled by the presence of a much smaller number of non-needy women in employment, MacGill pointed to the double standard that questioned the employment rights of women but not those of men, some of whom were independently wealthy or supported by others, and some of whom were without dependents:

In the case of the man seeking a professional position, the firm does not ask if he needs the work or if he has an income of his own or if his wife inherited money. . . . According to the theory applied to the married woman . . . unless he is penniless, should he be allowed to work, on the theory that if he was not working some other poorer man or some unmarried woman who needed it more might have his position.

If he is wealthy it is still not held that he should not hold a position or job. He is not urged to stay at home and be the perfect husband helping with the dishes, firing the furnace and playing golf in the afternoon.[63]

Not only should we conclude that MacGill drew arguments from the feminist traditions of equality as well as difference, we should also notice how the economic-need argument itself does not belong solely in the interpretive category of difference, where it has generally been placed by feminist historians. If MacGill used the need rationale to breathe life back into the image of women as nurturing mothers and dutiful daughters, different from men in their selfless commitment to family life, clearly she also used it to establish women's sameness to men and so to reinforce women's claim to equal consideration and treatment. Given the strength of popular fantasies depicting men's wages feeding hungry bellies and women's wages buying frivolous extras from silk stockings to fancy cars, it was important to remind people of the basic economic realities that led the majority of women *and* men to view paid work as primarily, though not necessarily exclusively, a means to live. MacGill knew well from her own life, which was marked by financial insecurity,[64] that however enjoyable and stimulating work might be, it was the pay cheque, not the personal fulfillment, that enabled survival. In stressing the economic significance of work MacGill was also echoing the priorities of many working-class women, whose paid work in no way matched the glamorous image held dear by "career feminists." In fact MacGill was joined in her emphasis on economic factors by some Communist Party supporters who defended married woman workers of the working class not from respect of their "choices," but from the understanding that their husbands' low wages left them no other alternative but to try to find work themselves.[65]

If MacGill is generally seen too one-dimensionally as a social or maternal feminist, Agnes Macphail, Canada's first woman MP, pacifist, feminist, and advocate for farmers and labourers, has sometimes been classified too narrowly as an equal-rights feminist. In his recent biography, Terry Crowley suggests the classic liberal texts of Mary Wollstonecraft and John Stuart Mill molded Macphail's understanding of feminism and she became by the late 1920s Canada's "foremost advocate of women's equality based on fundamental human rights." Her commitment to "absolute equality," he argues, remained unshaken during the depression; it was only later in her life, after World War II, that she modified her ideas slightly to embrace a politics of "equality through difference."[66]

Although her own decision not to marry reflected uncertainty about the possibilities for female independence within marriage, and more specifically a concern that the duties of wife and mother generally encroached on women's career plans, Macphail was uncompromising in her insistence on women's rights to both family and employment, regardless of the state of the national economy or their personal financial need. She assumed that increasingly most women wanted both marriage and paid work,[67] and that despite antifeminist attempts to restrict women to the former, there was not enough work left in the modern home to warrant women's full-time presence.[68] In contrast to MacGill's concern that Canadians recognize women as economically needy and so worthy breadwinners, Macphail worried that such an argument could backfire, lending weight to the conservative notion that economic pressures were the *only* legitimate ground for female employment. This fear could lead Macphail on occasion almost to dismiss the economic significance of women's wages, even though her close work with farmers and labourers, and her well-developed class politics, meant that in reality she was totally cognizant of the importance of women's contributions to family survival. "Nor is work a matter of bread and butter," she said to a gathering of women in Montréal in 1936, her real point being somewhat more subtle: that work means more than just wages to women. "Every person, man and woman, boy and girl, desires to find satisfaction and happiness through useful and purposeful work."[69] Every chance she got, she hammered home this message. While not disagreeing with the content of the MacGill argument, Macphail shifted the focus to legitimize women's spiritual and personal interest in work and so to support explicitly the principle of equality itself:

> It is not because women are generous with their money to parents, children, nieces and nephews, brothers and sisters, an aged aunt or uncle — although these things are true — that I defend her right to work for pay.
> It is not that women are good spenders and spending keeps money in circulation that I defend women's right to work.
> It is that women, to be spiritually happy, must work — she must make her contribution to the highest good in any way that seems to her best.[70]

This was a courageous position to take amidst the social and economic conditions of the depression and she never backed away from it.

Despite her clear debt to equal-rights thinkers, Macphail also espoused elements of maternalism that should not be overlooked. She was not averse to drawing on the familiar housekeeping metaphors when pushing for women in politics, and especially when addressing the issue of women and peace, one can see her making assumptions about women's unique capacity for nurturance and pacifism that borrowed not just on an analysis of social conditioning but also on women's different "nature." "Woman," she insisted, "is by nature, constructive — to produce and to preserve life is her great function — all destruction is an offence to her womanhood."[71]

Macphail's dues to both equality and difference are best combined in her reliance on familiar arguments about the historical inevitability of women's involvement in paid work outside the home.[72] As Nancy Cott has observed, this was an argument that bridged the equality and difference divide for it "gave weight to economic need, and demand factors in the economy, as much as 'rights,' bringing women into the labour market."[73] Indeed, Macphail, and for that matter MacGill, can be read as constituting what Mary Poovey has called "border cases," women who in thought and in life straddled the divide and so expose for us the artificiality of its binary construction.[74] Not only did some women draw on the broad traditions of both equality and difference, the cases of MacGill and Macphail suggest that we miss some of the complexities if we rigidly strap the need argument to difference and the fulfillment argument to equality. Both working for need and working for fulfillment could be read as assimilation to the male model and hence as expressions of women's sameness and equality to men, since ultimately a man's right to work was presumed to lie both in his need to support dependents and, although less acknowledged in the depression, in his obligation and desire to perform a useful job in society.

V

In Canada during the 1930s there was not as much of a unified defence of the woman worker as there was in the United States, but nor does there appear to have been such a unified campaign against women. Among defenders of working women a shift in emphasis is discernible during the depression from the language of rights and personal preference, which received some attention in the twenties, to the language of economic need, but this shift is not as pronounced as historians have discovered in the U.S. Since equal-rights feminism has never been as strong in Canada as it has in the U.S. or Britain, it is perhaps not so surprising to see less of a rigid break with the past in this period. But this paper reminds us that equal-rights thinking is not entirely absent from the Canadian right-to-work debate.

Despite our tendency to impose the equality-versus-difference construct on both our writing of feminist history and our feminist activism, most organizations and individuals have not in fact argued consistently from one perspective or the other. Instead, as Scott observes, feminists (and, we might add, their supporters who may not always identify themselves as feminists) have tried "to reconcile theories of equality with cultural concepts of sexual difference." Certainly such reconciliation was evident in the defence of women workers in Canada of the thirties.[75] One might hypothesize that a rigid dichotomy between equal rights and difference has been forced on the past by contemporary feminist historians, for as suggested above although historians have commonly read the argument from need as an assertion of women's family ties, and hence a reinforcement of separate-spheres ideology, it can also be interpreted as an attempt to assimilate the woman worker into the male-worker model, since what was being demanded was women's right to work on the same economic grounds that men's right to work was presumed to rest, namely on the basis of his need to support himself and his dependents. So assimilated, it was hoped that women could establish their claim not just to jobs but also to relief. Since the very category "worker" was presumed to be male in the depression, with single women only included because their need for self-support likened their situation to that of men, sharp reminders of women's breadwinner roles were necessary statements about the sameness of women to men. Thus, although the need argument came in the thirties to dominate the feminist defence of women's employment rights, this did not in itself signal a conservative retreat from feminist principles of equality advocated more boldly in the previous decade. Women's investment in employment in the depression needed to be articulated from an economic and a social perspective. Unfortunately, there were too few in Canada like Macphail who insisted on the legitimacy of both.

NOTES

I would like to thank Ruth Roach Pierson and Joan Sangster for their assistance with this article.

1. "Why Girls Work," *Canadian Congress Journal* X, 8 (August 1931), 88.
2. See Lois Scharf, *To Work and to Wed: Female Employment, Feminism, and the Great Depression* (Westport 1980), especially chs. 1–3. This interpretation is also apparent in Scharf and Joan M. Jenson, "Introduction" to Scharf and Jenson, eds., *Decades of Discontent: The Women's Movement, 1920–1940* (Boston 1987); Susan Ware, *Holding Their Own: American Women in the 1930s* (Boston 1982), ch. 4; Winnifred Wandersee, *Women's Work and Family Values, 1920–1940* (Cambridge 1981), 120.
3. Although the choice-and-fulfillment argument seems more feminist to Scharf, one has to wonder, given the crucial importance of wages to working-class families and the poor conditions under which most women laboured, how relevant it was to all but an elite group of women in certain business occupations and the professions. However, for the purposes of this paper I am more concerned with the implications of her thesis for feminist debates over equality and difference.
4. See Veronica Strong-Boag, *The New Day Recalled: Lives of Girls and Women in English Canada, 1919–1939* (Toronto 1988), 45–6. On Canadian suffragists' use of both maternalist and equalitarian arguments a few decades earlier see Strong-Boag, "'Ever a Crusader': Nellie McClung, First-Wave Feminist," in Strong-Boag and Anita Clair Fellman, eds., *Rethinking Canada: The Promise of Women's History* (Toronto 1986).
5. Ann Snitow, "A Gender Diary," in Marianne Hirsch and Evelyn Fox Keller, eds., *Conflicts in Feminism* (New York 1990). Snitow reminds us that the equality/difference divide has been variously named and re-named by feminist theorists in the past as the debate between "minimizers" and "maximizers" of gender, between radical and cultural feminists, between essentialists and social constructionists, between cultural feminists and poststructuralists, and between "motherists" and feminists. Karen Offen's identification of "relational" and "individualist" traditions also invokes this dualist paradigm. See Karen Offen, "Defining Feminism: A Comparative Historical Approach," *Signs* 14, 1 (1988), 119–57.
6. See Snitow, "A Gender Diary" and many of the other articles in Hirsch and Fox Keller, eds., *Conflicts in Feminism*. See also Denise Riley, *"Am I That Name?" Feminism and the Category of "Women" in History* (Minneapolis 1988).
7. Joan Scott, *Gender and the Politics of History* (New York 1988), 176.
8. In this section of the paper I deal only with two influential middle-class international reform organizations and their national affiliates in Canada. Other organizations, however, in particular those associated with the radical Left, were also active on behalf of working-class women workers. Single women and girls tended to receive the most attention, but many Communist women and the Communist Party of Canada newspaper, *The Worker*, can be found defending the working-class wife in industrial employment. The Left's response is only mentioned briefly later in this paper but receives fuller coverage in my dissertation.
9. Veronica Strong-Boag, *The Parliament of Women: The National Council of Women of Canada, 1893–1929* (Ottawa 1976), 74.
10. Provincial Archives of Ontario (PAO), Toronto Local Council of Women Papers, MU6373, series F, box 12, *Bulletin,* (ICW), July 1934, 8.
11. National Archives of Canada (NAC), MG 30 C128, Dorothy A. Cummins (Heneker) papers (hereafter Heneker papers), vol. 1, file: Correspondence, 1932–1951, Heneker to Secretary General of League of Nations in Geneva, 16 September 1937.
12. See Tim Mason, "Women in Germany, 1925–1940: Family, Welfare and Work," parts I and II, *History Workshop* (Spring and Summer 1976), 74–111, 5–32; Claudia Koonz, *Mothers in the Fatherland: Women, the Family, and Nazi Politics* (New York 1987); Leila J. Rupp, "Mother of the Volk: The Image of Women in Nazi Ideology," *Signs: Journal of Women in Culture and Society*

3, 2 (Winter 1977), 362–79; Gisela Bock, "Racism and Sexism in Nazi Germany: Motherhood, Compulsory Sterilization, and the State," *Signs* 8, 3 (Spring 1983), 400–21.

13. PAO, Toronto Local Council of Women Papers, MU6373, series F, box 12, *Bulletin* (ICW), July 1934, 3 and 8.

14. Susan D. Becker, *The Origins of the Equal Rights Amendment: American Feminism between the Wars* (Westport 1981), 198.

15. NAC, CFBPWC Papers, vol. 82, file: IFBPWC — Proceedings . . ., Proceedings of Board of Directors (IF), Brussels, 23–26 September 1935, 9. See also vol. 4, Acc. #81/401, file: *The Business and Professional Woman*, 1935, 1937–41, "14 Countries Attend International Meet," *The Business and Professional Woman*, December 1935, 6.

16. *Ibid.*, 10.

17. NAC, CFBPWC Papers, vol. 82, file: IFBPWC — Proceedings . . ., Proceedings of the 7th Annual Meeting of the Board of Directors, Stockholm, 15–18 July 1937, 28. (emphasis mine)

18. NAC, MG 28 155, vol. 82, file: IFBPWC — Proceedings of Meetings 1930–53, Proceedings of 7th Annual Meeting of the Board of Directors, Stockholm, 15–18 July 1937, 7–8.

19. Scharf, *To Work and to Wed*, 59. See also Scharf, "'The Forgotten Woman': Working Women, the New Deal, and Women's Organizations," in Scharf and Jenson, eds., *Decades of Discontent*. Scharf, in her insistence on the unity of feminism, seriously underplays the significance of the splits that divided interwar feminists on the question of the employment of wives.

20. Margaret Hobbs, "Rethinking Antifeminism in the 1930s: Gender Crisis or Workplace Justice? A Response to Alice Kessler-Harris," *Gender & History* 5, 1 (Spring 1993), 4–15.

21. NCWC *Yearbook*, 1928, 95–6. This study of why married women worked was continued the next year and included a survey of 300 married women stenographers. See *Yearbook*, 1929, 109–10.

22. NCWC *Yearbook*, 1933, 105.

23. NCWC *Yearbook*, 1934, 121, 137.

24. NAC, RG27, vol. 3350, file 10, McKivor to Local Conveners, 16 October 1936.

25. NCWC *Yearbook*, 1934, 121.

26. See Mary Patricia Powell, "A Response to the Depression: The Local Council of Women of Vancouver," Michiel Horn, ed., *The Depression in Canada: Responses to Economic Crisis* (Toronto 1988).

27. NAC, MG 28 1164, Montreal Council of Women Papers, vol. 5, file: Annual Reports . . ., *Fortieth Anniversary Issue and Annual Report, 1933–34*, November 1934, 57; NCWC *Yearbook*, 1936–1937, 55.

28. NAC, Montreal Council of Women Papers, vol. 5, file: Annual Reports . . ., *Forty-First Year Book and Annual Report, 1934–35*, November 1935, 23.

29. Mederic Martin, "Go Home, Young Woman!" *Chatelaine* (September 1933), 10 and 37.

30. NAC, Montreal Council of Women Papers, vol. 5, file: Annual Reports . . ., *Forty-First Year Book and Annual Report, 1934–35*, November 1935, 45, and vol. 6, file: MCW History, "Areas of Interest of Montreal Council of Women," compiled by A. Hooper.

31. On Derick's struggle for equal treatment in her own scientific career in academe see Margaret Gillett, "Carrie Derick (1862–1941) and the Chair of Botany at McGill," in Marianne Gosztonyi Ainley, ed., *Despite the Odds: Essays on Canadian Women and Science* (Montréal 1990), 74–87.

32. On the Montréal Council's involvement in the ongoing debate over protective legislation see Margaret Hobbs, "'Dead Horses and Muffled Voices': Protective Legislation, Education and the Minimum Wage for Women in Ontario," M.A. thesis, University of Toronto, 1985, 27–30.

33. NAC, Montréal Council of Women Papers, vol. 6, file: MCW Resolutions 1916–60.

34. NAC, CFBPWC Papers, vol. 1, Acc. #81/401, file: Annual Convention — Programmes — 1930–33, 1939, Program of First National Convention, Winnipeg, 2–5 July 1930.

35. Although I was unable to locate data indicating the precise occupational distribution of members, the predominance of office workers is apparent from the minutes of Canadian Federation meetings. In the U.S. too this class of worker predominated: Nancy Cott claims that almost half of the total membership of the American Federation were in clerical employment. Nancy Cott, *The Grounding of Modern Feminism* (New Haven 1987), 91. Apart from the clerks, stenographers and secretaries, there were also waitresses and other working or lower-middle-class women in similar low-pay, low-status fields. Susan Becker, *The Origins of the Equal Rights Amendment: American Feminism between the Wars* (Westport 1981), 225.

36. The number of clubs in the Federation doubled by the second year from 7 in 1930 to 13 in 1931. (The number for 1931 is listed variously in the records as 13 or 20, but the former figure is more likely to have been correct.) Affiliated clubs increased to 19 in 1932 and 20 in 1933. The combined membership rose from 732 in 1930 to 1132 in 1931, 1595 in 1932, and then dropped to 1451 in the bleak economic year of 1933. NAC, CFBPWC Papers, vol. 43, Minute Book, Annual Conventions, "Minutes. First Session of the Fourth Annual Convention," Hamilton, 10 July 1933, 5.

37. The BPW Clubs in Kamloops and Brantford, for example, proved especially unwilling to lend support to married women, NAC, MG28 155, CFBPWC Papers, vol. 10, Acc. #81/401, file: Newsletter of CFBPWC 1932, "Actions and Re-Actions," *Newsletter*, 2, 1 (June 1932), 15; NCWC *Year Book* (1936), 122.

38. NAC, CFBPWC Papers, vol. 1, Acc. #81/401, file: Annual Convention — Minutes 1931, Minutes of the Second Session of the Second Annual Convention of Business and Professional Women's Clubs, Montreal, 4 July 1931, 2.

39. NAC, CFBPWC Papers, vol. 43, Minute Book 1, Minutes of 5th Convention, CFBPWC, Calgary, 3–6 July 1935.
40. NAC, CFBPWC Papers, vol. 43, Minute Book, Annual Conventions, Minutes, Fourth Annual Convention of the CFBPWC, Hamilton, July 1933, President's Report, 2.
41. NAC, CFBPWC Papers, vol. 43, Minute Book 2, Minutes of 6th Convention, CFBPWC, Niagara Falls, 12–16 July 1937, 5.
42. NAC, CFBPWC Papers, vol. 43, Minute Book 2, Minutes of 6th Convention, CFBPWC, Niagara Falls, 12–16 July 1937, 80.
43. The phrase is a variation on Ruth Pierson's "wartime jitters over femininity." See Ruth Roach Pierson, *"They're Still Women After All": The Second World War and Canadian Womanhood* (Toronto 1986). For an analysis of the gender crisis affecting both masculinity and femininity see Hobbs, "Rethinking Antifeminism."
44. The discriminatory Section 213 of the National Economy Act together with the rash of proposed married persons' clauses that swept through state legislatures served as a focal point for concrete feminist action. Women's organizations were successful in repealing the offending Section 213 and only one state managed to pass a married persons bill. See Scharf, *To Work and to Wed*, 46–59.
45. Gwethalyn Graham, "Women, Are They Human?" *Canadian Forum* XVI, 191 (December 1936), 21.
46. See for just a few examples Letter to the Editor from Trade Union, Toronto *Telegram*, 19 January 1931; Letter to the Editor from "Auntie," Toronto *Mail and Empire*, 4 October 1930, 8; Letter to the Editor from "Live and Let Live," Toronto *Mail and Empire*, 23 October 1930, 6.
47. "Can You Shackle Woman Again?" Response by W.A. Parker, *Chatelaine* (November 1933), 44; Letter to the Editor from "A Married Business Woman," Toronto *Mail and Empire*, 25 September 1930, 8.
48. Letter to the Editor from "A Married Business Woman," Toronto *Mail and Empire*, 25 September 1930, 8.
49. "Persecution of Married Women," Editorial, *Canadian Forum*, XII, 137 (February 1932), 164; Letter to the Editor from "A Married Business Woman," Toronto *Mail and Empire*, 25 September 1930, 8; Harriet Parsons, "Canada Needs Her Woman Power," *Canadian Home Journal* (July 1933), Harriet Parsons Papers, Metropolitan Toronto Public Library, Baldwin Room.
50. Letter from Alice Brown in "Can You Shackle Woman Again?" Readers' Responses to Mederic Martin, *Chatelaine*, November 1933, 26.
51. Letter to the Editor from "London, Ontario," Toronto *Mail and Empire*, 30 September 1930, 8.
52. Letter to the Editor by Married Woman Worker, Toronto *Telegram*, 7 November 1930, 6.
53. "Persecution of Married Women," 164.
54. "Can You Shackle Woman Again?" Response from Patience Strong, *Chatelaine* (November 1933), 44; Letter to the Editor from "Experienced," Toronto *Mail and Empire*, 6 October 1930, 10; "Persecution of Married Women," 164; Parsons, "Can Youth Afford to Marry?" 14–15, 45–7 and "Canada Needs Her Woman Power," Harriet Parsons Papers, Metropolitan Toronto Public Library, Baldwin Room. Parsons referred in her article, "Can Youth Afford to Marry?" to a survey conducted by the YMCA of 184 young men in ten Ontario cities which fuelled fears that the majority of youths could not afford to marry.
55. "Can You Shackle Woman Again?" Response from "An interested reader," *Chatelaine* (November 1933), 26.
56. Letter to the Editor from "Experienced," Toronto *Mail and Empire*, 6 October 1930, 10; Letter to the Editor from "A Woman," Toronto *Star*, 22 July 1931, 6.
57. Gwethalyn Graham, "Women, Are They Human?" *Canadian Forum* XVI, 191 (December 1936), 22.
58. Letter to the Editor from "A Woman," Toronto *Star*, 22 July 1931, 6.
59. Parsons, "Can Youth Afford to Marry?" 14–15, 45–7.
60. Naomi Black, "Introduction" to Elsie Gregory MacGill, *My Mother the Judge* (Toronto 1981), xix.
61. See Helen Gregory MacGill, "The Jobless Woman," *Chatelaine* (September 1930), 5, 47–8, and "What of the Wage-Earning Wife?" *Chatelaine* (March 1930), 8–9, 64–6.
62. MacGill, "The Jobless Woman," 48.
63. MacGill, "What of the Wage-Earning Wife?" 9.
64. MacGill supported her first husband through medical school in the United States. He died young, leaving her the sole support of her two small sons and her mother. These two years before she remarried must have been difficult, but interested readers will not find many details of this period in the biography by her daughter, Elsie Gregory MacGill. Her second husband, initially a "good provider," later dove into financial difficulties that left him broke by the mid-1910s, and although he was able to pull himself up again he spent years paying off debts. When he died in 1939 he left no estate. Throughout their marriage and beyond, MacGill's public roles, though prestigious, offered limited financial security. In fact her 17-year stint on the B.C. Minimum Wage Board brought no remuneration, nor did her chairship of the Mother's Pension Board or many other of her public duties. See Elsie Gregory MacGill, *My Mother the Judge: A Biography of Helen Gregory MacGill* (Toronto 1981 [1955]).
65. For sympathetic portrayals of the plight of married women workers see the following articles in *The Worker*: "Working Women Support Communist Candidate," 26 July 1930; untitled piece, 4 January 1930; "Working Women Demonstrate!" prepared by the Women's Department, WUL,

4 April 1931; "International Women's Day," by Fred Raymond, 27 February 1932; "Organizational Problems: a Better Attitude towards Women Is Needed," by C.S., Port Arthur, 7 October 1933. Despite this evidence of support for married women, the Communist Party restricted its empathy for married women workers to those of the working class and never joined forces with middle-class women trying to mount a wider campaign on behalf of married women. On the whole women and men in the radical Left in the thirties paid more attention to the needs of single women workers than married women workers. Because married women were not a real priority for Communists, I have not attempted a detailed consideration of their occasional efforts to defend the employment rights of wives.

66. Terry Crowley, *Agnes Macphail and the Politics of Equality* (Toronto 1990), 90, 208. See Ch. 10 for his discussion of this shift, which he traces especially through her initial rejection of gender-specific protective legislation and affirmative action as "special privilege," to her full support for pay equity.

67. "Almost every woman," she wrote, "wants a mate, children and the opportunity of doing work which she enjoys and that is increasingly work outside the home." NAC, MG27 III C4, Macphail Papers, vol. 10, file #23, "What Is Woman's Objective?" n.d.

68. In a manner that must have been irritating to many full-time housewives exhausted with the demands of children and husbands, Macphail referred often to the modern home as the "workless home." See for example NAC, MG27 III C4, Macphail Papers, vol. 10, file #23: "Whither Woman?" Address to the Canadian Alliance for Women's Vote in Québec, Montréal, March 1936.

69. NAC, MG 27 III C4, Macphail Papers, vol. 10, file #23: "Whither Woman?" Address to the Canadian Alliance for Women's Vote in Québec, Montréal, March 1936.

70. NAC, MG 27 III C4, Macphail Papers, vol. 10, file #23: "Women — What Now?" Address to Hamilton Civic Women's Club, 2 October 1939. See also in the same file "How Far Can Women Help Solve National Problems?" CBC, 21 May 1939; "What Should Women Do Now?" Address to Ottawa Local Council of Women, 20 March 1939.

71. NAC, MG27 C4, Macphail Papers, vol. 10, file #23: "Women — What Now?" Address to Hamilton Civic Women's Club, 2 October 1939. See also in the same file "Women in the Present World," 1936; "Women in Government," n.d. [1939?], where she stated amidst a lengthy list of women's qualities, good and bad, that "Women are not good fighters" . . . "Not too good at sustained mental effort."

72. See, for example, NAC, MG27 C4, Macphail Papers, Vol. 10, file #23: "Women — What Now?" Address to Hamilton Civic Women's Club, 2 October 1939; "Women in Government," n.d. [1939?]; "Whither Woman?" Address to the Canadian Alliance for Women's Vote in Québec, Montréal, March 1936.

73. Nancy Cott, *The Grounding of Modern Feminism* (New Haven 1987), 119.

74. Mary Poovey, *Uneven Developments: The Ideological Work of Gender in Mid-Victorian England* (Chicago 1988), 12.

75. For another study challenging polarized conceptions of feminist politics of equality and difference in the interwar years in Canada, see the recently published biography of the well-known Winnipeg public figure Margaret McWilliams: Mary Kinnear, *Margaret McWilliams: An Interwar Feminist* (Montréal 1991).

"A Thing of the Past": Teaching in One-Room Schools in Rural Nova Scotia, 1936–1941

DIANNE M. HALLMAN

My mother writes:

> I taught six years, most of them in the thirties. . . . In most cases the country one-room school was approximately 20 feet by 30 feet. The entrance was divided into two porches, one for the girls, and one for the boys. In the centre of the room there was a rectangular box-type cast iron stove (wood-burning). Attached

SOURCE: Dianne M. Hallman, "'A Thing of the Past': Teaching in One-Room Schools in Rural Nova Scotia, 1936-1941," *Historical Studies in Education* 4, 1 (1992), 113-132.

to the back of the school room there was a shed with a slanted roof. This is
where the wood was stored for the winter months . . . out back there were two
small buildings commonly called "outhouses" — one for the girls and one for
the boys . . . Most schools had two rows of seats on either side of the stove.
Each seat or desk accommodated two pupils. These desks were on metal frames
which were fastened to the floor with screws. Under the top of the desk was
a divided compartment where the pupils kept their scribblers, books, pencil
boxes, etc. There were no ballpoint pens. The higher grades sometimes used
fountain pens which had to be filled from a bottle of ink. As there was no
electricity, the school room had three large windows on two opposite sides. The
blackboards were between the windows and were just ordinary boards painted
black. The cross-lighting caused a glare which made it difficult for the pupils
to copy assignments for the next day, for the younger ones to see their math
questions, or any other work that was taught from the board.[1]

With consolidation, the "not-so-good old school days," as my mother
refers to them, became a "thing of the past."[2] And the one-room schoolhouses in Nova Scotia where those days unwound, morning and afternoon, day after day, two hundred days of the year, are mostly gone too . . .
some, victims of simple disuse and deterioration, others of a good soak
in kerosene and a well-aimed match. The place where my three brothers
and one sister began their schooling has long since been obliterated, probably by the latter means. The present hardy growth of alders where the
schoolhouse formerly stood successfully conceals any feature of the landscape which might stir a memory of other presences — effaces any hint
of the easy-going, intimate familiarity that generations of children had
with the trees, rocks, and coarse grasses there — children whose learning
included where to look for the first spring mayflowers, and the biggest
wild strawberries. These schools, the material surroundings of my mother's work as a teacher, have become, to borrow my mother's words again,
a "thing of the past." I call attention to the singular form because I
think it is particularly revealing that the enormous subtleties of experience within teaching, its material conditions, and the myriad unseen
political and administrative structures which organized that experience
are compacted and reduced by historical convention to a "thing." It is
this "thing of the past" — which is not one thing but many — that I
begin the work of uncovering in this essay.

This paper is based on a personal history of teaching as recorded
by Margaret Elizabeth Johnston (my mother). Margaret Johnston graduated from the Provincial Normal College, Truro, Nova Scotia, with a
"B" licence in 1935, and taught in one-room rural schools in three different counties in Nova Scotia until her marriage in 1941. I have used
the recorded recollections of my mother to inform my questions about
how the public education system in Nova Scotia was constituted at that
time, and to act as a sounding board for ideas gleaned from present-
day accounts of the history of female teachers.[3]

Historiographers of education in Nova Scotia by and large have studied the structures and personalities of officialdom, but have ignored the
individual teacher, except perhaps to confirm *her* general shortcomings.[4]

The day-to-day work of teachers and their personal evaluations of that work — what was rewarding, frustrating, commonplace, or tedious — have received short shrift in the historical record of education in Nova Scotia. Oddly enough, however, glimpses into the personal lives of teachers sometimes emerge from the pages of the Annual Reports of the Superintendent of Education. The many photographs of country schools, and brief descriptions of events such as Saturday morning weaving classes for teachers, evoke an almost tangible, if fleeting, sense of the nature of some of teachers' daily activities.[5] However, the thoughts and feelings of the women who got up each morning, who bathed in water drawn from a well and heated on a wood stove, and who then walked a half mile or more to teach school all day, have not been the priority of the province's educational historians. This study focuses on the work experience of one such woman, while also explicating some of the economic and administrative variables that ordered that experience.

In other parts of Canada, the United States, and Australia, interest in the history of teachers, specifically the experience of female teachers, has generated a vibrant literature which highlights the close mesh between the personal and political aspects of teachers' lives. This literature has led me to consider my mother's teaching career from a variety of angles and with respect to a number of issues: the image of the female rural schoolteacher as a pawn and a pauper; gender inequity in pay scales; the question of a bar against married female teachers; the numerical dominance of women in the teaching profession; the numerical dominance of men in the administration of teaching; and the ways in which broadly based administrative concerns affected the individual teacher. The questions that I put to my mother in order to draw out pertinent information along these lines did not always elicit what I expected. Part of the work of this essay, then, is to consider the ways that my mother saw her work as typical (or not) of her time and place, and to assess how her impressions are confirmed, elaborated, or called into question by the literature; alternatively, how the literature is confirmed, elaborated, or called into question by her recollections.

The dialectic between experience and interpretation of that experience occurs on at least two levels throughout the paper: first, my mother has mulled over her memories of teaching, and has selected, shaped, pruned, and written what she considered significant for a daughter's research project. Both her memories and her interpretation of those memories have no doubt been affected by the events of the intervening fifty years, in ways that would be virtually impossible to discern. Other influences on her decisions about what to record are likewise inaccessible. Second, from my mother's written recollections, I have pulled out the elements that I consider important for a research project — selected, shaped, pruned, and written a story that is ultimately neither mine nor my mother's. One source of my interpretation is an intertextual frame of reference formed from the annual reports, historical articles, and theses on the development of public education in Nova Scotia, and revisionist history which brings a feminist analysis to bear on the work of women teachers. Another is the ongoing dialogue I have with my mother as I test the impressions received from texts against her recollections of her experience.

As I set about the work of saying something about what it was like to teach in rural one-room schools in Nova Scotia during the 1930s, I realize that there are any number of ways I could render my mother's experience; there are any number of ways that my authorial voice can "talk over" my mother's — suppressing, ignoring, or misconstruing what she has to say. The complexity of attempting a fair representation of someone else's "lived actuality" is a lesson in epistemological and methodological humility.[6] I am deeply aware that there are divides I cannot cross, and depths I cannot plumb. Moreover, I feel like something between a pirate and a pope: pilfering from my mother's memory bank a "usable" past; making official pronouncements about what is historically relevant. Yet I know that when I "contextualize" her experience, I am being incredibly presumptuous. Beware!

The female rural schoolteacher, Margaret Nelson suggests, is "one of our favourite victims."[7] Low pay, adverse working conditions, isolation, loneliness, and restrictive rules governing behaviour are themes that pervade the literature on rural schoolteachers, factors which combine to create an image of a hapless schoolmarm. J. Donald Wilson begins one of his articles on rural women teachers in British Columbia with an account of the death of Mabel Jones, a young schoolteacher in the Cowichan Lake District, who in 1928 was driven to take her own life. It was widely believed that the insurmountable difficulties of her teaching situation in isolated, hostile surroundings provoked her final, desperate act. Although Jones' response to her working conditions was extreme, Wilson's use of this example in his introduction sets the tone for what is to follow in the remainder of the article — a focus on rural female schoolteachers in dire straits during the period from 1929-34.[8] Similarly, Robert Patterson's essay on the experiences of novice rural schoolteachers on the Canadian Prairies between the two World Wars concentrates on the trials and tribulations of these young, and for the most part, female teachers.[9]

In addition to the above studies, the general tenor of quantitative work done in the United States and Canada on the debilitating effects on teachers of the economic hard times of the 1930s provides a broad outline of despair in terms of abundance of candidates for positions; low salaries — sometimes even no salaries at all; worsening working conditions; and no job security. Furthermore, female teachers are considered to have been hurt by the Depression even more than men. They were more vulnerable partly because of their higher numbers in the profession, and partly because of specific policies directed toward squeezing them out. In Lois Scharf's study of the effects of the Depression on American working women, for example, the chapter on teachers is entitled "Even Spinsters Need Not Apply . . ."; a caption which epitomizes the negative effects of retrenchment policies on female teachers who, in 1930, had constituted four-fifths of the teaching force in the United States.[10] Scharf points out how "economic competition, structural changes, and public sentiment all worked to the advantage of men at the expense of female teachers generally."[11] This was a legacy that was to last well beyond the Depression years.

Taken together, these studies give support to the tendency to approach the experiences of all female rural schoolteachers with the expectation of hearing some variation of a familiar narrative of epic struggle against adversity. While I in no way want to diminish the very real difficulties women teaching in rural areas generally faced, or to discount regional variations in the types of problems with which they had to contend, I believe that a willingness to privilege the dramatic over the mundane misses much of the story. Margaret Nelson found, for instance, that what was disclosed in her oral interviews of women who taught in rural Vermont prior to 1950 challenged the impression obtained from the written records of the teacher as a proper object of pity or scorn. The women's reflections on their teaching experience brought to light a sense of their own agency in creating the circumstances of their employment: pride in their work, striving to improve conditions, and manipulation of constraints to their own advantage. They felt respected by the community and worked hard to keep that respect.[12]

My mother's account of her teaching experience also counters the received notion of the country schoolteacher as the pawn of trustees, the subject of gossip, and the community drudge. The theme that runs throughout her account is one of mutual respect: respect for her work on the part of the community; and respect on her part for the children and communities she served. To explain why she wanted to be a teacher my mother says: "In those days, much more than now, the teacher was a role model much respected and looked up to."[13] She appears never to have been disillusioned on this score. Tangible signs of this respect are discernible throughout her career.

As a teacher, completing the work for up to twelve grades made for "difficult days"; yet my mother frequently remarks that "it was amazing how cooperative those students were." She habitually went to her boarding home for the midday meal, leaving the children unsupervised. On this point, she says:

> During my six years of teaching, I never had any noon-time problems. The children mostly were well disciplined in their homes, so therefore they were well behaved in school and had respect for their teacher as well as their elders.[14]

Boarding places were generally arranged for her before she arrived. Although they lacked running water and indoor bathrooms (conveniences she had had in her own rural home), she says that she adjusted quickly. Otherwise she comments:

> The food was excellent even in those hard times. In one home deer meat and cranberries were quite prevalent, but I really liked both very much. . . . The teacher wasn't expected to lift a hand to do anything, but I usually enjoyed drying dishes and exchanging the news of the day.[15]

Her description of her work reveals a close and lively connection to the community:

> The fun time of the year was the preparation for a Christmas concert. All the pupils took part, even the youngest. They loved it and we all worked hard to make it the best concert around. In May we had Arbor Day. This was clean up day. Everyone worked at it, washed the windows, washed the woodwork, washed the desks, and scrubbed the floor. The boys cleaned and raked the yard. They also carried the water from the nearest home which was heated on the school stove for the cleaning. There was no water or electricity in the school. . . . When everything at the school was spic-and-span, the rest of the day was spent having a picnic. There were games, races, and lots of good food. Not much money was available to spend on the school room. Teachers often organized and had pie sales to raise money for this purpose. I was able one year to completely paint the interior, have a cement step made, and a school sign painted which I did myself.[16]

Although my mother agrees that the prevailing expectation was that the teacher had to "maintain a good reputation," this did not seem to be particularly problematic for her, or cause her undue worry. She portrays relations with the schools' communities as clear sailing:

> It was easy for a teacher to make friends in the community where she taught . . . especially families who had children in school were very pleased to have the teacher visit the home, often inviting her for the evening meal. Sometimes there would be card parties and other social get togethers. The more the teacher participated the better she became acquainted and the more popular she became.[17]

Many of the relationships my mother formed while teaching were to continue many years beyond her teaching career. One that she made in her first year of teaching was especially enduring — he was later to become her husband, and they have been together for more than fifty years.

The diminutiveness of teachers' salaries in the United States and Canada was legendary in these times. In 1930, according to Lois Scharf's U.S. study, the median salary for a teacher in a one-room rural school was $788; by 1935, the salaries of rural teachers were cut by an average of 33%.[18] Many schools were unable to meet even this reduced payroll. In Canada, one of the provinces hit hardest by the Depression was Saskatchewan, where farmers not only had to contend with the general economic exigencies but with one crop failure after another. John E. Lyons compares the school taxes collected in 1929 ($11 million) to those collected in 1937 (less than $4.5 million) to show emphatically the impact of the Depression on public schools in Saskatchewan.[19] Here teachers' salaries dropped 50% or more in six years. In 1930, a female rural schoolteacher holding a first-class certificate would have earned on average $1,142; by 1936, this had fallen to $407.[20] Wage cuts during the Depression were perhaps not quite so dramatic in Ontario, but nonetheless significant, with the brunt of the wage loss borne by female teachers. Judith Arbus highlights how the Depression exacerbated gender inequities and discrimination against women in hiring and promotion, and notes that the teaching salaries were reduced by 55% for women during the period from 1930 to 1936, whereas men's salaries were reduced by only 38%.[21]

Salaries for teachers in Nova Scotia before the 1930s were among the lowest in Canada. The Depression brought even harder times, but it is a time-honoured phrase in Nova Scotia that it suffers less from recessions in the economy than other places, because "rock bottom" is never far away. The decrease in teachers' salaries was not as precipitous or as severely detrimental to women as what appears to have been the case for Ontario and Saskatchewan. The overall average salary for teachers decreased 4.4%, from $754 in 1931 to $721 in 1934, its lowest point. The average salary of female teachers as a whole decreased 4.6% from its 1931 level of $709. The average salary for male teachers declined about 15% in this period from a high of $1,194, and continued to decline for a year or two after women's salaries stabilized. In the ten years surveyed, from 1931 to 1941, the lowest average salary for women teaching in rural schools was $518 in 1934, a 5.4% decrease from the 1931 level; for men in rural schools it was $606 in 1935, a 4.5% decrease. It would appear that men teaching in urban areas bore the brunt of wage cuts. Their average salaries dropped 16%, from a high of $1,912 in 1932 to a low of $1,598 in 1935. However, in comparison to the wages of most teachers, their predicament was far from pitiable.[22]

According to the Annual Report of 1935, the year my mother entered teaching, the average salary for female teachers in rural schools was $519, inclusive of provincial aid.[23] What appears statistically as an average salary may be a far cry, however, from what the "average" teacher gets to put in her pocketbook. In my mother's recollection, the salaries ranged from $300 to about $500 or $600 a year, plus a provincial grant paid directly to the teacher and based on the level of certification (about $160 for a "B" licence such as my mother had). A teaching job in a "poor section" would certainly not net the elusive average wage.[24] During these years, she notes, "teachers were very plentiful," and teachers changed schools often in order to "try and better their situation," a practice that drew criticism from school inspectors, but went on nevertheless.[25] My mother taught in five different schools during her six years of teaching, expressing the view that this was a matter of course.

The ultimate test of earning a livelihood is not how much you make, but how much you can buy with what you make. Discussion of Depression retrenchment policies generally neglect to compare teachers' relative standard of living before and after the wage cuts. The loss in real spending power represented by wage reductions cannot be adequately addressed here, but a brief profile of my mother's standard of living can. My mother paid three to five dollars a week for board ($120 to $200 a year for a 40-week school year). She generally spent summers at the home of her parents. Being a single woman with no dependants, she was able to save enough in three years to buy a car, and from then on, often travelled to her parents' home for weekends. She found the pay low, but reasoned that "men in the thirties (labourers) with families worked at any kind of work they could get for *$1.00 a day* often walking several miles to and from jobs."[26] Like the women Judith Arbus interviewed, she was "grateful to be working."[27]

When asked to comment specifically on gender differentials in the rates of pay, my mother replied:

> Men received the same wages as women with the same qualifications. If they held the position of Principal, they received more. A female Principal would receive the same as a male if they had the same qualifications. Usually men were chosen to be Principal with the general belief that they could assert more control [than women].[28]

Nova Scotia's adherence to the widespread belief that maleness was a prerequisite for effective principalship came as no surprise to me, but how did my mother receive the impression that equity in pay between men and women existed when the documentary evidence appears to give such overwhelming support to the contrary? However, a close look at the official statistics reveals that salary differentiation on the basis of gender was a subtle, ambiguous issue. It must be considered in conjunction with teacher qualifications, length of teaching experience, and placement in rural or urban schools, factors which are difficult to unravel and isolate with respect to sex from the departmental data.

When my mother started teaching in 1935, the average salary for women teachers was 69% of that of men. Yet women with a "B" licence made 89% of what men with the same licence made. At that time teaching licences were ranked in accordance with years of study and/or Normal College training beyond provincial examinations. An "Ac" licence was at the top and required a university degree plus professional training or teaching experience; an "A" licence required two years of training beyond Grade XII; a "B" licence one year plus a summer school course beyond Grade XI; and the "C" and "D" licences were of a temporary or permissive status and signified even shorter periods of training. Teachers with "B" licences were the largest group in the teaching force (36%).

Female teachers in rural and village schools made 85% of what men similarly placed did. It was in the urban schools that the disparity between men and women widened considerably, with female teachers making only 59.5% of what male teachers made. At this time, men comprised only about 14% of the total number of teachers, so they must have held a high proportion of the top-grade "Ac" and "A" licences, and have been concentrated in the better-paying urban schools in order to have tipped the average salary differential so dramatically in their favour.[29] This would appear to have been the case for the school year 1937-38. The data compiled by the Dominion Bureau of Statistics shows that 66.9% of the men teaching had Class 1 or higher certificates ("A" or "Ac" licences) compared to 36% of the women.[30] It can also be seen that the largest group of teachers (786 out of a total of 3,393) were paid in the range of $400-$499. Of these teachers, 715 were women. However, of the 73 teachers that were in the top range of salaries (over $2,000), 66 or 90% were men. No woman earned over $2,500 whereas 21 men did. Men made up 27% of those commanding mid-range salaries ($1,000-$2,000), and only 13% of those making below $1,000.[31]

An historical snapshot such as that provided by the *Biennial Survey of Education* cannot be relied upon to show trends, but the statistics given for the length of tenure in schools create the impression that women in general stayed in the profession longer than men. It has been generally assumed, however, that women's stay in the teaching profession was shorter than men's due to their customary retirement upon marriage. In rural schools women with fifteen years of experience or more accounted for 3.9% of all teachers, whereas men in the same tenure category comprised only 0.9% of all teachers. These teachers would have been in schools of more than one room, for there were almost no teachers with over seven years' experience in one-room rural schools. In urban schools women with fifteen or more years of experience accounted for 23% of all teachers compared to men at 2.8%. Even when the greater number of female teachers in the profession as a whole is taken into consideration, it still holds true that higher numbers of women stayed in the profession longer than men: 27.8% of all female teachers in urban schools had fifteen years of experience or more, compared to 18.4% of all male teachers. In rural schools, it would appear that men may have taught longer: 6.9% of male teachers had over fifteen years of experience compared to 4.5% of female teachers. However, in the case of rural schools, the actual number of teachers with a long tenure was very small for both sexes.[32]

When my mother left teaching in 1941, women were faring even more poorly in comparison to men than they had in 1935; their average salary in Nova Scotia as a whole was only 65% of what men earned (although this was a slight improvement over 1931 when it was only about 60% of the male average). The average salary for all teachers had increased 10% between 1935 and 1941 but men's had increased by 12% whereas women's had risen by only 8%. Women with a "B" licence were making 5% less than they had in 1935, but a startling 13% more than their male counterparts. However, this differential likely reflected a movement of more experienced teachers upward, and their replacement by less experienced teachers at a lower salary, with the then-current group of male "B" teachers being newer to the job. By this time, those with "A" licences comprised the largest group of teachers (43%); while those with "B" licences remained relatively constant at 35%. Men still made up about 14% of the teaching force, and the greatest discrepancy in salaries remained in the urban schools, with women losing ground slightly, making 59% of what men earned.[33]

Unfortunately, grades of licences, years of experience, and numbers of teachers in urban and rural schools were not analyzed by sex in the annual reports or the *Biennial Survey* in such a way that one can determine the relative salary of men and women with the same teaching licence, same years of experience, and teaching in the same type of school. Although a precise picture is impossible to draw from the statistics available, it would seem that the lower salaries accorded to women were not merely a function of their overrepresentation in rural schools, lower qualifications, or fewer years of experience. This would agree with Arbus' Ontario finding that the most prestigious and best-paid jobs were the preference and the prerogative of men.[34] Yet from the perspective of my mother — a teacher with a "B" licence in a rural school — men's and women's salaries would have appeared to be tolerably matched.[35]

The retirement of female teachers upon marriage was a complex phenomenon determined not only by administrative policies, employment opportunities, and social conventions and constraints, but also by each individual woman's peculiar accommodation to her perceived possibilities and constraints. My mother remarks that some of her female classmates continued to teach after marriage. Many, like herself, did not. She does not remember any sort of a bar against married women teaching, or an active discouragement of mixing marriage with teaching on the part of the administrators. In her case, her marriage was followed by the birth of four children in relatively quick succession (including a set of twins); and as well she ran a post office, cared for two aging parents in her home, helped to run a farm, and did all the cooking, cleaning, canning, and gardening, for several years without the benefits of running water or electricity. Teaching, itself at least a ten-hour-a-day job, was not a practical option. By the time the family responsibilities lightened, the higher qualifications then required of teachers would have been an obstacle to her return. By 1956 an "A" licence had become the minimum required standard.[36] However, to assume that my mother's retirement from teaching signalled her retirement from the public sphere would be seriously misleading. She continued, and continues to this day, to lead a very active life in the community and the church; and for many years, her juggling of conflicting demands always included some form of paid part-time work — from running a post office to doing surveys for the Dominion Bureau of Statistics.

My aunt, on the other hand, who also graduated from Provincial Normal College with a "B" licence about the same time as my mother, went back to teaching shortly after her third child was born, after a ten-year absence. Having fewer children farther apart, and a husband whose regular waged employment allowed the family freedom from a dependence upon farming for its livelihood, she was able to overcome the domestic impediments to her return to teaching. The different adaptations of these two women to their particular circumstances are a caution against generalizing a "typical" response by female teachers to marriage. The shortage of teachers after the start of World War II might also have allowed some women more room than they had before to negotiate working conditions, including work after marriage, during pregnancies, and after childbirth.[37]

While several facets of the so-called feminization of teaching have been considered in the scholarly literature, a question which has received little attention is how women managed to maintain their numerical dominance in the teaching profession during the Depression. In Nova Scotia more male teachers were highly desired, according to the rhetoric of both the Superintendent's office and the Nova Scotia Teachers' Union;[38] they enjoyed higher salaries on average than female teachers; and even the poorest school offered as much as the labourer's going rate of pay of "a dollar a day." Yet throughout my mother's teaching career, male teachers made up only between 14% to 16% of the teaching force. Why were men not breaking down the doors to get into teaching? My mother's only brother, Gerald, who taught for one year, provides some interesting clues. He finished Grade XI in the spring of 1930, went to the Provincial Normal College summer school in Truro, and received a Temporary licence. He writes:

> I thought it [teaching] would give me a bit better income as any jobs I took around Clarence [his home] paid fifteen cents per hour, ten hours a day — nine dollars per week. . . . I had a single-room school with 45 pupils from primary to Grade 11. . . . My pay from the school was $300 and a Provincial Grant of $150, and from that I had to pay board for a short week. I felt I could do better, so the next year I went to the Nova Scotia Agricultural College and took a degree course in two years. The Agricultural College year was short, so I had time to work on the farm in the summer, and I also went to Army Camp for 10 days each summer and worked my way up to C.S.M., then I took my Commission and qualified as a Lieutenant. When war was looking close, we were called in — actually the 28th August 1939. When I was called in I was working full time in a warehouse at fifteen cents per hour, ten hours a day, and six days a week. On the 28th August I got five dollars per day, seven days a week, so that was more what I wanted.[39]

The army offered this young man economic opportunities unavailable elsewhere in his locale, a chance to get ahead, a relatively secure future. For many men who took up this opportunity, it turned out to be either a very short future, ending abruptly on the battlefield; or, as in Gerald's case, a long lifetime of suffering the effects of a permanent war injury and chronic ill health. Yet at 26 years of age, the chance to make $35 per week, compared to $9 per week, was clearly irresistible. The army, then, may have drawn some men away from teaching. Yet Gerald had already been drawn away before he joined the army, first by the Agricultural College, and then by the type of job he was hoping to avoid by going into teaching in the first place. Therefore the economic attractions of the army as an alternative occupation do not satisfactorily explain men's staying away from the classroom in droves. The nature of the relationship between teaching and farming, and between the Provincial Normal College and the Agricultural College in terms of female/male entry into different occupations, would be extraordinarily difficult to unravel, but a very promising area of inquiry in terms of solving the puzzle as to why men in Nova Scotia typically did not teach.

Another insight into the apparent male reluctance to enter teaching was offered by my mother. Most men, she said, were expected to work in order to support themselves and help out their families before they acquired enough schooling to get a teaching licence. Finishing Grade XI and a year at Normal College (the minimum requirement starting from 1933) was an impossible luxury for young men whose obligations to provide, in the straitened economic circumstances of the 1930s, often coincided with puberty. On the other hand, perhaps the Depression merely exacerbated a pattern of male early-leaving already established, a practice that was also evident in nineteenth-century rural Quebec.[40] In any case, this explanation does not account for those men (like Gerald) who did have the academic qualifications to teach, but who chose other occupations over teaching, even though they were not necessarily more lucrative.

One area where men were definitely numerically dominant was in the administration of teaching. The implications for female teachers of a practically all-male inspectorate have yet to be fully explored. Robert S. Patterson's article leaves the impression that teachers on the Canadian prairies customarily discovered the Inspector to be distant and of little practical assistance.[41] Wayne E. Fuller's study of rural schools in the American context also confirms the infrequency of visits by the county superintendents, the American equivalent to inspectors, and further suggests that their calls precipitated great anxiety in inexperienced teachers.[42] Moreover, through her case studies of women teaching in Vermont, Margaret Nelson has begun to document the vulnerability of female rural schoolteachers to sexual harassment by their supervisors.[43]

About the inspectors for whom my mother worked, she says equivocally: "Some you were glad to see come; others not so glad." One was a particular favourite and he literally became a household word for many years as she named her horse after him. She describes him as having been there to help, not to criticize . . . a description that hopefully fitted the inspector better than it did the horse. She enjoyed the few occasions that he would take over the class, finding it interesting to watch "how he dealt with some of the crazy answers the kids gave you." Still, one could rarely expect a visit more than the twice-yearly norm, although the submissions to the annual reports of this particular inspector detail as many as four visits a year to some schools. About one in the "not-so-glad-to-see" category, she recalls asking for help with an algebra problem of a type that she had never encountered before:

> He took off his bowler hat and sat at the desk for about fifteen minutes with the book. Then he put on his hat, handed me the book on the way out the door, saying, "here, take this home with you tonight — you'll figure it out."[44]

My mother's conclusion was that he did not know how to do the problem either. Ignorance on the part of inspectors of the curriculum teachers were required to teach was a frequent complaint of the teachers Patterson interviewed.

During the 1930s and 1940s, two major themes were reiterated throughout the annual reports to the legislature by the Department of Education. One was the applauding of higher standards of certification for teachers; the other, the promotion of the larger municipal unit. Both were couched in the rhetoric of progressive education then in vogue throughout North America. Improved teacher training seems to have been seen as somewhat of a panacea for all the ills of the education system.

The Minimum Professional Qualification, which had allowed prospective teachers with as little as Grade X education to teach without further professional training, was abolished in 1926. That same year three universities instituted a one-year programme of professional teacher training beyond the Arts and Science degree programmes which led to an Academic or "Ac" licence. It continued to be possible to obtain a "Temporary" licence after successful completion of Grade X examinations and a Normal summer school, or a "C" licence after a half-year course at the Provincial Normal College until 1933. In 1933, a "B" licence became the minimum standard. This required a full one-year Normal School training plus a summer school session beyond successful completion of Grade XI examinations. Normal-trained teachers accounted for 86% of the teaching force in 1935, when my mother began teaching, and 92% of the teaching force in 1941, when she retired. The following table shows the distribution of teachers according to grade of licence for the years 1935–41, and documents a steady increase in the proportion of teachers with Academic and "A" licences, a relatively stable proportion with "B" licences, and a significant decrease in the percentage of teachers with "C" and "D" licences. Licence requirements were downgraded for a period during World War II when candidates for teaching were in

Distribution of Teachers according to Grade of Licence								
Year end	# of teachers	Normal trained	University Graduates	Ac.	A	B	C	D*
1935	3649	3166	577	105	1077	1328	944	145
1936	3659	3284	571	101	1190	1371	865	132
1937	3714	3395	600	110	1293	1421	769	121
1938	3794	3507	628	121	1422	1436	669	146
1939	3829	3495	645	140	1510	1441	601	137
1940	3868	3651	644	148	1634	1432	525	129
1941	4016	3732	669	165	1740	1406	488	217

*Temporary or Permissive.
Source: *Annual Report for 1941*, xxvii.

short supply. Although there was a temporary increase in the number of teachers with the lowest category of licence, those with an "A" licence — which required two full years of Normal College training beyond Grade XII — were in the majority by 1941 (43%). Enrolment in the Normal College during the war dropped by as much as 41% from pre-war levels, precipitating a shortage of teachers and slowing down (but not reversing) the upward trend in teacher qualifications. In 1956, an "A" licence became the mandatory minimum.

Commenting on the upward movement of academic standards and professional standards, Henry Munro, the Superintendent of Education from 1926 to 1948, stated:

> As the trained teacher is the pivotal factor in the field of education, it is encouraging to note how our teachers are equipping themselves for their important task. . . . It may be added that the men now engaged in teaching are in growing numbers taking it up as a permanent profession and qualifying themselves on both the academic and professional sides.[45]

As has been previously noted, most teachers "equipped themselves for the task" through training at the Provincial Normal College in Truro, Nova Scotia. My mother attended PNC for one year following completion of her Grade XI Provincial examinations. This is how she described her year:

> I took two classes in Maths, two in English, Health, Music, Art, and Industrial Arts. All these classes were methods of teaching the different subjects to all grade levels. Each class lasted about forty minutes with ten minutes to change to the next class. At quarter to 12:00 noon, all classes met in the large assembly room with Dr. Davis, the Principal, for comments, instructions, and announcements. Afternoon classes lasted from 1:30 to 3:30 p.m. Each night we had to prepare lesson plans. Next day, someone in the class would be called upon to teach the lesson. This continued until Christmas, giving each student an opportunity to teach every subject at least once.
>
> Most every Friday night a social evening was held. If a dance was planned they often invited the Agricultural students who were mostly boys. [The Ag-

ricultural College was in the same town.] PNC had nearly four times as many girls as boys.

Christmas was really the first break when everyone got the chance to go home. After Christmas teaching practice began in earnest. Each class was divided into groups of five or six. Friday mornings, the group along with their Instructor went out to a local school, and one in the group taught the assigned lesson. On our return, the Instructor praised or criticized the teaching and pointed out the mistakes. This teaching practice continued until all in the group had taught a lesson in each subject in different local schools.

By the end of May, the graduation list was posted. Then we were given the names of schools requiring teachers. Each student sent out several applications, and many received positive replies before leaving for home. Much preparation went into the graduation exercises which were held in the theatre by the middle of June. It was a proud and memorable day for all the graduates.[46]

My mother's favourite class was Industrial Arts. The purpose of this course was to enable teachers to instruct boys in the elements of woodworking and similar manual work. The contradiction in training women to teach a course meant only for boys went without remark. At any rate, my mother was never able to teach her favourite subject due to the lack of appropriate facilities and equipment. The travelling "shopmobiles" designed to enable instruction in mechanical science to rural boys came too late for her to utilize.[47]

In his submission to the Annual Report for 1935, Principal Davis of the Provincial Normal College stressed that the training in all departments was directed towards the needs of rural schools (even though 37.7% of all teachers at that time taught in urban schools). He wrote, "while it is not incumbent on teachers in the rural schools to be farmers, all should be able to discuss freely and feel emotionally the right relation of man and land in Nova Scotia."[48] How the needs of rural schools were perceived and how the notion of "right relation" was conceptualized embodied many unspoken assumptions and contradictory ideas. Where, for instance, did women fit into this concept of right relation and with what implications for their education? Moreover, the promotion of an educational ideology and practice aimed to keep Nova Scotians on the land, coexisting with one aimed to make rural students competitive workers in an industrial economy, seems, at first glance, to have been contradictory. Furthermore, by 1938 the number of urban students almost matched that of rural students.[49] Were the urban students also educated to stay on their non-existent farms? Explication of the nature and scope of these contradictions will have to await further study.

The promotion of the larger municipal unit was articulated in terms of extending equality of opportunity to all children. Read in the light shed by later revisionist history which views schools as the means through which the state moulds its future workers, and through which class and gender-based inequities are reproduced, there is a tendency to be suspicious of rhetoric portending the democratization of education. On the other hand, the inequities produced by the local administration of schools were very real and increasing yearly, as urban schools grew richer and rural schools poorer.

Each rural community had its own "school board," made up of three trustees and a Secretary-Treasurer, which budgeted the teacher's salary, school repairs, and wood for the fire in the expenditures drawn from the school portion of the local property taxes. This system of administration had existed virtually unchanged for over fifty years and, in the official circles of the Department of Education, it was blamed for most of the inequalities in education in the province. The fiscal policies of trustees were typically viewed as miserly, a reputation that was probably well deserved. Loran DeWolfe's 1915 assessment of trustees was one that he maintained throughout his long career in the Rural Science Department and Rural Education Division of the Department of Education (1913–43):

> If always the most intelligent and progressive men (or women) in the section were elected trustees the system would be fairly good. But it frequently happens that those elected are ignorant of school law, of educational progress, of twentieth century ideals — in fact, of everything except that they should hire the cheapest teacher who applies.[50]

My mother's assessment of trustees was less severe, pointing out that their efforts were circumscribed by limited funds. They had little incentive to spend a lot of money on a teacher, and a lot of incentive to spend little money.

An enormous amount of energy was expended by the Department of Education over the years in attempts to redress this situation of regional inequity. The move towards the larger unit was a pet project of the Superintendent of Education, Henry Munro. Every one of his submissions to the annual reports during these years alludes to the disparity and wasteful duplication of services involved in maintaining one-room schoolhouses, and speaks to the educational advantages and economic viability of consolidation.[51] A full history of the consolidation of schools in Nova Scotia has yet to be written, but it is known that it was a very long and slow process. Munro did not live to see the full fruition of his efforts. Mine was the first class in my home area to complete all its elementary schooling in a consolidated school, beginning in 1960–61. In remote sections this would have occurred even later.

And yet it was with this steady, irrevocable change towards consolidation that, as my mother puts it, "the not-so-good old school days" became "a thing of the past."[52] There are ways in which my mother's teaching experience belongs to an era so distant and different from that which occurs in today's schools that it can only be dimly imagined. Yet it had its own subtle gradations of satisfaction and of frustration, a range of practical tasks to be negotiated daily, and was connected in obvious and less obvious ways to a changing administrative bureaucracy. The mutability of these aspects of teaching is missed in the tendency to treat rural school teaching as a solitary historical phenomenon — a thing of the past. Reflective readings of my mother's experience can provide a fresh perspective on public education in Nova Scotia, and confirmation of, as well as challenge to, some of the present-day literature on female rural schoolteachers.

NOTES

This paper is dedicated to the memory of Gerald F. Johnston. His contribution to this paper was greatly appreciated. I would like to thank my mother, Margaret Johnston Miller, for her generous sharing of her time and her memories. I would also like to thank Dr. Alison Prentice for her comments on an earlier version of this paper. I gratefully acknowledge the financial support of the Social Sciences and Humanities Research Council and the Ontario Institute for Studies in Education.

1. Margaret Elizabeth Johnston, Lansdowne, Nova Scotia, to Dianne M. Hallman, Oakville, Ontario, 28 Feb. 1991. Personal letter retained by Dianne M. Hallman. It is interesting to note that "movable chair desks" were a highly esteemed innovation for a rural school. In 1929, Hillsborough School won the School Improvement Contest for providing movable desks. It was apparently the first rural school in Nova Scotia to have them; see Jane M. Norman, *Loran Arthur DeWolfe and The Reform of Education in Nova Scotia, 1891–1959* (Truro, Nova Scotia: Atlantic Early Learning Productions, 1989), 147.

2. Johnston to Hallman, 1991.

3. I asked my mother to write about her recollections of teaching. Her response became the basis for further questions and discussion through letters and telephone conversations. Direct quotations are taken from her letters, which were combined, transcribed, and dated 28 Feb. 1991.

4. Historical works consulted were Norman, *DeWolfe*; Arthur Thomas Conrad, "Educational Development in Nova Scotia under Henry Fraser Munro" (M.A. thesis, St. Mary's University, 1960); John Earle, "The Development of the Teaching Profession in Nova Scotia" (M.A. thesis, St. Mary's University, 1960); A. George MacIntosh, "The Development of Teacher Education in Nova Scotia" (M.A. thesis, St. Mary's University, 1964); Robert Alexander MacKay, "The Development of Rural Education in Nova Scotia, 1900 to the Present" (M.Ed. thesis, St. Francis Xavier University, 1966); Grace Helen Whitman, "The Development of the Public Schools of Nova Scotia, 1920–1940" (M.Ed. thesis, Acadia University, 1965). None of these works challenge the view that defects in the educational system were at least in part traceable to defects in the teacher, almost invariably referred to as "she" when the author was being critical.

5. Copies of the *Annual Report of the Superintendent of Education for Nova Scotia* were surveyed for the years 1935–41.

6. The concept of epistemological and methodological humility is outlined in Uma Narayan, "Working Together across Difference: Some Considerations on Emotions and Political Practice," *Hypatia* 3, 2 (Summer 1988): 37.

7. Margaret Nelson, "Using Oral Histories to Reconstruct the Experiences of Women Teachers in Vermont, 1900–1950," in *Studying Teachers' Lives*, ed. Ivor Goodson (New York: Routledge, Teachers' College Press, 1992).

8. J. Donald Wilson, "'I Am Ready to Be of Assistance When I Can': Lottie Bowron and Rural Women Teachers in British Columbia," in *Women Who Taught: Perspectives on the History of Women and Teaching*, ed. Alison Prentice and Marjorie R. Theobald (Toronto: University of Toronto Press, 1991), esp. 203–4. For a more comprehensive account by the same author see "The Visions of Ordinary Participants: Teachers' Views of Rural Schooling in British Columbia in the 1920s," in *A History of British Columbia: Selected Readings*, ed. Patricia E. Roy (Toronto: Copp Clark Pitman, 1989), 239–55.

9. Robert S. Patterson, "Voices from the Past: The Personal and Professional Struggle of Rural School Teachers," in *Schools in the West: Essays in Canadian Educational History*, ed. Nancy M. Sheehan, J. Donald Wilson, and David C. Jones (Calgary, Alberta: Detselig, 1986), 99–111.

10. Lois Scharf, *To Work and to Wed: Female Employment, Feminism, and the Great Depression* (Westport, Connecticut: Greenwood Press, 1980), 66.

11. Ibid., 85.

12. Nelson, "Using Oral Histories," 21–22.

13. Johnston to Hallman, 1991.
14. Ibid.
15. Ibid.
16. Ibid. The Rural Education Division of the Department made a big effort to reward communities for improvements made to their schools through prizes and letters of recognition. It is interesting that my mother does not recall anything of the work of this division, headed by Loran DeWolfe. See Norman, *DeWolfe*, chap. 7, esp. 146–54.
17. Johnston to Hallman, 1991.
18. Scharf, *To Work and to Wed*, 69.
19. John E. Lyons, "Ten Forgotten Years: The Saskatchewan Teachers' Federation and the Legacy of the Depression," in *Schools in the West: Essays in Canadian Educational History*, 114.
20. Ibid.
21. Judith Arbus, "Grateful to Be Working: Women Teachers during the Great Depression," in *Feminism and Education: A Canadian Perspective*, ed. Frieda Forman, Mary O'Brien, Jane Haddad, Dianne Hallman, and Philinda Masters (Toronto: Centre for Women's Studies in Education, OISE, 1990), 182.
22. *Annual Report of the Superintendent of Education for the Year Ending July 31, 1935* (Halifax: King's Printer, 1936), xxii; and *Annual Report of the Superintendent of Education for the Year Ending July 31, 1941* (Halifax: King's Printer, 1942), xxvii.
23. *Annual Report for 1935*, xxii.
24. Poor sections were areas where there were few taxpayers to support a school, and which relied on government assistance. Teachers were paid the bare minimum. In 1935 grants to assisted schools totalled $15,560 over and above regular grants, just over 1% of all expenditures. Out of 1,764 sections, 353 received assistance.
25. Johnston to Hallman, 1991. Throughout the Annual Reports for the period, Inspector T.A.M. Kirk reiterates this concern: "The frequent changing of teachers is not desirable and I have been impressing on trustees and teachers alike that it is unwise and inefficient to change when conditions are mutually satisfactory." *Annual Report for 1939*, 39.
26. Johnston to Hallman, 1991.
27. Arbus, "Grateful to Be Working," 178, 180.
28. Johnston to Hallman, 1991.
29. *Annual Report for 1935*, xxii.
30. *Biennial Survey of Education, Elementary and Secondary, 1936–38*, compiled by the Dominion Bureau of Statistics (Ottawa: King's Printer, 1940), 58.
31. Ibid., 52.
32. Ibid., 58.
33. *Annual Report for 1941*, xxvii.
34. Arbus, "Grateful to Be Working," 187.
35. Considerable work has been done comparing urban and rural teachers which addresses the gender politics of teacher placement and salary differentials. For a Canadian example, see Marta Danylewycz, Beth Light, and Alison Prentice, "The Evolution of the Sexual Division of Labour in Teaching: A Nineteenth-Century Ontario and Quebec Case Study," *Histoire sociale/Social History* XVI, 31 (May 1983): 81–109; for an American one, see David F. Labaree, "Career Ladders and the Early Public-High School Teacher: A Study of Inequality and Opportunity," in *American Teachers: Histories of a Profession at Work*, ed. Donald Warren (New York: Macmillan Publishing Company, 1989), 157–89.
36. Conrad, "Educational Development in Nova Scotia," 93.
37. Margaret Nelson makes the point that women in Vermont had considerable latitude in negotiating their work after marriage and childbirth, even in the thirties. See "Using Oral Histories," 9–13.
38. MacIntosh, "The Development of Teacher Education," passim.
39. Gerald F. Johnston, Yarmouth, Nova Scotia to Dianne M. Hallman, Oakville, Ontario, 26 Mar., 1991. Personal letter retained by Dianne M. Hallman.
40. Danylewycz, Light, and Prentice, "The Evolution of the Sexual Division of Labour," 91.
41. Patterson, "Voices from the Past," 109.
42. Wayne E. Fuller, "The Teacher in the Country School," in *American Teachers: Histories of a Profession at Work*, 105, 113.
43. Margaret K. Nelson, "The Threat of Sexual Harassment: Rural Vermont School Teachers, 1915–1950," *Educational Foundations* 2, 2 (Summer 1985).
44. Johnston to Hallman, 1991.
45. *Annual Report for 1935*, xxi.
46. Johnston to Hallman, 1991.
47. *Annual Report for 1941*, xi.
48. *Annual Report for 1935*, 87.
49. There were 55,486 urban students, compared to 60,952 rural. See the *Biennial Survey of Education, 1936–38*, 31.
50. "Report of the Director of Rural Science, 1913–14," *Journal of the House of Assembly* (1915): 101, quoted in Jane M. Norman, *DeWolfe*, 44.
51. See Conrad, "Educational Development in Nova Scotia," passim.
52. Johnston to Hallman, 1991.

"If You Had No Money, You Had No Trouble, Did You?": Montréal Working-Class Housewives during the Great Depression

DENYSE BAILLARGEON

The profound effects of the Great Depression on Québec society are well known.[1] However, most of the research that has been done on the Depression has analysed activities and organisations in the public sphere.[2] In contrast, little is known about the effects of these difficult years on the private sphere, and specifically on the family lives of workers.[3] This article reports the results of an oral history study which was designed to remedy this gap in our knowledge through an exploration of the experience of a group of working-class Montréal housewives. Because women during this period bore the primary responsibility for feeding, clothing and generally looking after the welfare of the family, a study of the domestic activities of working-class housewives during the 1930s provides an opportunity to introduce a new dimension. This study was designed to elicit information about the ways in which women engaged in a range of strategies in order to make up for the decline in their husbands' earning power and also to examine the way in which the Depression influenced motherhood, the working conditions of housewives and the division of labour within the family.

The study is based on an analysis of interviews with 30 women, all of whom lived in Montréal. Montréal was selected as the locus of the study because it was the industrial centre of the Province and also because 60% of unemployed Québécois lived there.[4] Because the Depression had its greatest impact on workers and especially on unskilled workers, I drew my sample from those women who had lived through the decade of 1929–39 in a working-class district of Montréal. All my respondents were of French Canadian origin, and were Roman Catholic. Since the study was designed to examine family life, all the women were married, and all had been married before 1934.[5] The employment patterns of their husbands were variable: some of the husbands were employed during these years while others were unemployed.

The first section of the interview questionnaire was designed to obtain information about the women's lives, from their birth to the Second World War. Thus, data on family of origin, school attendance, participation in paid labour and apprenticeship to domestic work before marriage

SOURCE: Denyse Baillargeon, "'If You Had No Money, You Had No Trouble, Did You?': Montréal Working-Class Housewives during the Great Depression," *Women's History Review* 1, 2 (1992), 217–237.

were gathered. In the second part of the questionnaire, I looked for information pertaining to the couple's courtship, the preparations for the
wedding, and the marriage itself, up until the family felt the effects of
the Great Depression. The final section concerned the family economy
during the 1930s, and raised questions about the contribution of paid
and domestic labour, the state, the family, and all the other survival strategies to which the interviewees resorted during that decade.[6]

An Introduction to the Respondents in the Sample

All the women interviewed were born between 1897 and 1916, 14 of
them in rural areas. However, all lived in Montréal and Verdun (a
working-class suburb of Montréal) at the beginning of the Depression.
Most were daughters of workers or farmers, and most grew up in poor
families with a relatively large number of children, where the low income
and irregular employment patterns of the father rendered the work of
the children critical to the family's survival:[7]

> We were not rich, not even well-off. We barely made ends meet. [. . .] In
> those days, wages were low. We managed, but I can't say that we were com-
> fortable. In those days, people had no money. You started to work young. I
> think that my oldest sister began when she was twelve.[8]

For the majority of these women, school was thus but a brief interlude
preceding their integration into the workforce. In fact, 21 of the women
interviewed had left school on or before their 14th birthday.[9] With the
exception of three respondents who lived on the farm until their wedding
and a fourth, raised by her well-to-do grandparents, all these women
worked for a wage before they got married. A few were teachers or clerks
in stores or offices, but most were employed as servants or workers.[10]
All these women were educated to become wives and mothers, but the
interviews revealed that their early integration into the labour force did
nothing to develop their skills as housewives. Indeed, being employed
outside the home cut short the time during which they could have become
familiar with the most complicated housework tasks, like cooking and
sewing. Many respondents, but especially those who left school for the
factory or the office, acknowledged that their skills in these areas were
quite limited and that they felt ill-prepared to keep house once married.[11]
Actually, 16 of them did not know how to sew at that time, even though
all their mothers were skilled enough to make most of the garments for
their families. Seven would never acquire this skill, while the others would
be forced to set about it after marriage, when a tight budget would give
them no choice. Some of them, who had to learn by themselves, found
it particularly difficult to become proficient seamstresses:

> I was not a very good seamstress. I sewed for my children only, that is the
> youngest ones [. . .]. Since I had two boys in a row, I started sewing for them.

I managed to learn, but how many times did I lean over my machine in tears? I was discouraged you know? I had no idea how to go about it, and I was not one to ask for help. (R23)

Eighteen of the respondents were married before 1929, ten between 1930 and 1932, and the other two in 1933 and 1934, respectively. Two early weddings, celebrated after 1929, came as a result of unexpected pregnancies, and the bride of 1933 had to postpone her wedding day for three years because her fiancé was unemployed. Since the social network of Québec youth during the early decades of the century was centred around the district or the village, a strong social and geographical endogamy governed the respondents' choice of marriage partners.[12] For instance, in 22 cases, the couples originated from the same or a neighbouring district or locality. Moreover, differences in income and living standard between the family of origin of the couples were slight: in 16 cases, the father and father-in-law of the respondents had a similar job or trade, while 17 of the couples were formed of wage-earners of the same category. Most of the couples married with slender means and settled with a minimum of belongings: the bride's trousseau, the wedding gifts and furniture for two or three rooms, generally second-hand or bought on credit. Lack of savings and low income made it necessary for 18 of them to cohabit with in-laws for some time, in most cases with the husband's side of the family.

A survey of the employment status of the husbands reveals that most were workers or low-echelon salaried employees[13] while three had a small business (one owned a barber shop, one a *restaurant-dépanneur*, and a third was the owner of two taxis). These last three men did not, however, enjoy a higher standard of living. Among the sample as a whole, only five of the men earned as much as $25 a week; some earned as little as $10 and more than half of them earned less than $20. Data from the Federal Department of Labour shows that in December 1929, a family of five in Québec needed a minimum income of $20.18 a week to cover food, heating, lighting and lodging.[14] This illustrates that even before the Depression set in most of these couples were living below the poverty level and suggests that even if the main provider of the family was employed, the family could not survive without intensified domestic production and a very tight rein on the budget. Even then, help was needed from in-laws and family; often, husband and wife had to take in additional work or resort to alternate strategies to bring in more cash. Women's paid work and strategies will be examined in the next section, but those of the men also deserve a few words since this was not a marginal phenomenon.

Thirteen of the husbands had a "side-line" during the thirties. A mechanic repaired cars at home, after his regular work hours; an office clerk worked during the week-end on the maintenance of the sports club where he worked during the week. A third man organised small lotteries where the prize, advertised at his grocer's, was a chequer-board he had made, while another one sold hockey game score cards to his workmates, both in violation of the law prohibiting lotteries. A fifth man worked as a book-keeper for a grocer in addition to his regular work as a municipal civil servant. The restaurant owner worked during the day as a salesman in a shoe store while his wife worked in the restaurant. A man employed in a department store opened a little snack bar for his workmates, with the permission of the store owners. During the Second World War, he also made figurines for Christmas displays since the store could not order them from Italy. In addition to these regular side-lines, the husbands who became unemployed during the thirties engaged in other wage-earning activities such as excavation work or washing walls and ceilings for neighbours, removing snow in the well-to-do districts of the town, and selling home-made alcohol.

Most of the husbands of the respondents were unemployed or under-employed during the 1930s. Of the three business owners, only one — the barber shop owner — kept his business: the other two had to sell out before going bankrupt. Cash flow difficulties brought them brutally back into the ranks of the unemployed, confirming that their ownership status did not set them apart from the other working people on whom they depended for their living. Among the salaried men, only four avoided unemployment, reduced time employment or salary cuts. Four had to accept a shorter work week and three others suffered wage cuts of as much as 20%. Seven were without steady jobs for more than three years, six for periods of one to two years, and the last, the luckiest one, was without work for a few months only. In all, 15 of these young couples lived on welfare for more or less prolonged periods.

There is, therefore, no doubt that most of the sample families saw their financial situation deteriorate during the 1930s. Further proof of this is that the welfare benefits represented only 50% of what was nec-essary in 1933 to cover the basic needs of a family of five.[15] Obviously, the families of the unemployed could not subsist on welfare benefits and, to fill the gap, turned back to strategies they already knew or had to learn. My research reveals the extent to which these family strategies relied on the skills and resources of the wife.

Domestic Work and the Family Economy during the 1930s

For my respondents, maternity was in theory the prime object of marriage and sexuality, which is not surprising if one remembers the religious and medical dogmas of the time. As one of them said: "It was a woman's life to bear children" (R24). However, in actuality, bearing and raising children often became a very heavy burden, particularly when financial resources were severely limited. After two or three children, most women admitted they were hoping to postpone further additions to their families and despite the precepts of the Church, some of them did have recourse to methods of birth control: "After my third [child], I said: we should take a little break or we will never make it! We didn't have that much money in those days and with three children, there was a lot more to do" (R23).

On the whole, the 28 women in the sample who were able to bear children averaged five children each, which is two less than their mothers who averaged 7.2 babies. This average conceals, however, great differences between the women, five of whom had more than eight children, three had more than ten, and six had less than three. Most often, however, that is in 11 out of 28 cases, they had three to five children. The 15 women who controlled their fertility had an average of four children, while the others had six. The number of pregnancies is a little higher: 6.3 for all fertile women in the sample. Those who did not take contraceptive measures had 7.5 pregnancies, while for those who practised some form of family planning the figure was 5.4.

We can surmise that during these years, the respondents' decision to use contraception had some connection with the economic difficulties of the 1930s. In fact, the majority of couples who tried to control their fertility experienced cuts in wages or had to live on welfare for more or less prolonged periods. However, a complexity of motivations was involved. For instance, few women spoke only of economic reasons to justify their decision to limit the size of their family, but also referred to the amount of work a larger family would entail and to their wish to give proper care and education to each child. A typical response was as follows:

> I said to myself, God gave me children but I don't want to see them suffer later on. Larger families always meant hard times [. . .] So I said, we could avoid that. My husband and I both decided that. Because my husband earned so much and I wanted to give them a good education. [. . .] I said, I prefer to have a small family and be able to give them what they need. I was thinking of their education. (R16)

On the other hand, several couples in the sample who also faced serious financial difficulties did not see fit to limit the number of their children, which indicates that a lower income is not always the main motivation for birth control. The families who practised contraception made a deliberate decision to do so, a decision that involved the co-operation of the husband: the contraceptive methods used — condoms in three cases, or coitus interruptus in 8 cases out of 15 — left the women no choice but to depend on their husbands.[16] In the case of the Ogino-Knauss method, the goodwill of the husband was equally essential.[17] For families who did not practise contraception, religious background combined with an ignorance of birth control methods, a rural background and a large number of children in both of the families of origin appear to have produced a fatalistic acceptance of large numbers of children, in spite of the economic difficulties engendered by the Depression: "There was nothing and you heard of nothing to prevent pregnancies. Physically, it is tough being pregnant but you could not do otherwise. Sometimes you would think about it: if only there was something. Some had methods, or so they said, but I found out too late" (R3); "To prevent pregnancies was out of the question. It was the law of the Church. You had to have children" (R29).

For the women in the sample who did practise contraception, the Great Depression was in part responsible for a lessening of their work load as mothers. But it must be remembered that in the religious climate of the times, recourse to a contraceptive method created a profound moral crisis: most women had a deep sense of guilt in transgressing the Church's teaching and continued to confess their perceived "sin" to their priest, at the risk of not being shriven: "Going to confession was cruel. It was no picnic having to confess using birth control . . . I had no choice . . . The priests would lecture us" (R5). Some of them developed different strategies to be absolved without trouble, like whispering or going to confession at the end of the day, when the priests were tired and probably bored stiff. One of the women related:

> Once, during Holy Week, I went to confession with my husband. He said: I'll go before you, and when he came out, he nodded "no": he hadn't received absolution. Oh yes! They refused to give us absolution! Once, we even saw three priests! Finally we found one . . . I don't know if he was tired, it was late, he was probably hungry and eager to get out of the confessional . . . Anyway, he was in such a rush that I don't even know if he heard our confession. Besides, we would whisper as low as possible . . . anyway. (R10)

On the other hand, those who did not use birth control often endured anxiety and discouragement throughout their pregnancies, feeling they could not fulfil their children's needs: "He worked until 1933 . . . After that there was no more construction, and there was a new born baby every year. That's tough. They had to be fed you know? When your man is out of work" (R12). Whatever the choice, it is obvious that for these women, maternity brought more anxieties than joys during the years of the Depression.

While several couples were willing to transgress the Church's rules in order to practise birth control, they generally refused to consider any new sharing of roles, even though their economic circumstances were considerably worsened. Having said this, it is necessary to point out that even before the Depression set in, family division of labour based on sex did not always scrupulously follow the pattern of a strict separation of the roles of male provider and female housewife. Indeed, when they got married, it was generally agreed that the wife should leave her job to take care of the house and of the expected children, while the husband should become the sole breadwinner. In practice, however, 18 women in the sample worked for pay during the 1930s. Five were employed outside the home, while the others carried on some type of paid activity in the home: for example sewing, laundering, taking in boarders, doing house cleaning, selling home-made pastries or managing a small business.

Therefore, most of those who contributed to the family income during the decade of the Depression had begun to work even before their husband lost his job or suffered a cut in pay:[18] only three respondents took paid employment because their husband was out of work.

On the other hand, nine husbands lost their jobs for periods of several months or several years and the question of their wives supplementing the family income never arose.[19] The respondents offered many reasons for this, such as the number of dependent children in the family and the unlikelihood that the women would find work. However, opposition by the husband to the wife's employment appears constantly and often simultaneously in the testimonies, which reveal a great ambivalence on the part of the women interviewed. Women as well as men were reluctant to engage in a role reversal at variance with the socially accepted division of labour. One of them stated: "I wanted to go to work; he didn't want me to. Besides, the children were too young, and I could not leave them on their own. In those days, you didn't leave your babies" (R20). Thus, the presence of small children seemed to be a main deterrent, even if the unemployed father could have been available to look after them. Most of these women also said there was no work to be found, though they admitted not having tried to find any:

> Back then, there was no more work for women than there was for men. Besides, I would have been at a complete loss going about looking for a job. My mother-in-law had never worked out of the home. As for myself, I guess I felt obliged to do the same thing. (R19)

In fact, in the nine couples where the wife had never contributed to the family income before the husband lost his job, the division of labour based on sex was such an inborn and rigid concept that it precluded any new outlook on seeking new sources of income.

A closer look at the five women who worked outside the home shows that only two of them became the main breadwinner. Moreover, they had a maximum of two children and someone other than the father took care of them, even though he was out of work. For their part, those women who took in paid work in the home before their husbands became unemployed continued and even intensified their work load whenever possible.[20] But none of them even considered the possibility of exchanging paid work within the home for outside employment. According to their own statements, their husbands would not have allowed it. An informant declared: "During the crisis I sewed for others in order to make money for the household. I helped my husband a lot; he did the best he could and so did I." However, when asked if she considered working for wages she replied: "My husband would have never allowed me to. He would have said that a woman should not work outside . . . You could only be hired to work as a housekeeper" (R5).

Male inactivity due to unemployment did not bring about any increase in the men's sharing of housework.[21] In the same way that women did not seek to replace their husbands as the main provider, the men did not take a greater part in the housework, except to do tasks that had already been incorporated into the family pattern (like shopping, looking after the children or washing the floors). At any rate, according to their wives, they spent most of their time outside the home, looking for work. Moreover, it is clear that the women considered that the house was their domain and even if their husbands were unemployed, they did not ask for more help:

> Oh no! Like I said, in those days men would never, ever have done housework. I would never have wanted him to either. I enjoyed doing my own thing. Women were all the same back then. I was an early bird and I always managed to get my work done in time, so there was no need for help. (R29)

Thus, if it can be said that the Depression did not modify the division of labour within the family along sex lines — that is no changes were made at all as to the roles and responsibilities that already prevailed in the family — this does not mean that they were strictly based on the breadwinner/housewife pattern.[22] As we have seen, paid work among married women was not a marginal phenomenon, even if a majority of the wage-earner wives worked within the home. On that matter, the testimonies confirmed what many researchers have already intimated: that many women contributed financially to the family income while still assuming all the responsibilities related to motherhood and housekeeping.

However, it is difficult to determine exactly what part of the total family income was provided by women. In most cases, the respondents could not remember very clearly what they earned because their work varied constantly as did the time devoted to it within any one week: "It was an extra; it didn't give me a steady income" (R22). Yet even these partial recollections allow us to estimate these contributions as between $3 to $10 a week — which in some cases was as much as 50% of the breadwinner's wages. This money was all the more important because it could make the difference between living under or just a little above the poverty level. "It didn't pay much but it gave me a little income at the end of the week. When my husband didn't have enough, I would either help pay for the rent or buy clothes for the children" (R17).

According to a time-honoured working-class tradition, in Québec as elsewhere, women were generally the ones who managed the budget.[23] Despite what they were able to earn, the sums they were managing were generally very small because these supplements were in most cases added to very low incomes. Making ends meet was a real balancing act for the majority of the respondents. To achieve this goal, they established priorities which they respected most rigorously. Heading the list were those expenses which could not be tampered with, like rent and electricity, which they considered as debts that must be met. Next came food, fuel and then whatever could be spent on clothing, transportation, insurance or leisure, if they had any money left. Very few could even consider savings.

Checking and double-checking the prices, buying only the bare minimum, avoiding any waste and debts were the *mots d'ordre* brought up constantly in the testimonies: "I never wasted anything" (R1); "Every cent was accounted for" (R2); "You know, we never bought anything we didn't need. We never wasted anything" (R26). This means that they were always doing very intensive housework, usually in the most inadequate conditions with inefficient appliances. The wood or coal stove was used for both cooking and heating. All meals were home-made, from soups to pastries, and many made preserves, pickles and jams. Women who had learned to sew made most of their own clothes and those of their children, often remaking hand-me-downs. They also sewed all the household linen: sheets, tablecloths, tea towels, bed linens, bed covers, drapes, curtains, etc. Most of them owned a footpedal sewing-machine, even if they only used it for repairing clothes, but most waited till after the second or third child before acquiring a washing machine. Even those lacking this appliance never used commercial laundry services in any regular way. This means that, for varying lengths of time, most of the women did all their washing by hand with washboards, in tubs or bathtubs if they were lucky enough to have one in their lodgings.

What they could afford for rent might vary from $12 to $18 a month,[24] which meant low-quality lodgings: poor lighting, poor insulation, softwood floors that were hard to keep clean, etc. Lodgings were often infested with rats or cockroaches. While all these lodgings had municipal water and electric facilities, they were rarely connected to natural gas. Less than half of the respondents lived in lodgings with a bath and the vast majority could not afford to rent or buy a water heater.[25] Inadequate income also meant that the lodgings were always too small and the parlour often had to serve as a bedroom. Some children even slept in the kitchen, or in the hallway on cots which were folded and made up daily.

This brief account shows that for these women, budgeting was practically an obsession, while housework represented harsh, physically demanding labour, which had to be done in unpleasant conditions, often without adequate facilities. In fact, their domestic work consisted of such a varied number of tasks and services that when the Depression came, it was hard to find anything they could add to what they were already doing. Unlike women in the middle income groups, who, for instance, could substitute their own labour for ready-made consumer products — like clothes or food — the majority of women in this sample had not yet become mass consumers. They could not return to methods of saving from which they had never departed.[26] On the contrary, lack of income and inadequate welfare payments caused them to give up some of the work they used to do, such as making preserves, jams or pickles, for in order to make these, they would have had to buy products in bulk which they could not afford: "We didn't have money to buy anything. How could we buy all it took to make ketchup and things like that? We were allowed only one sugar ration. In order to make jam you needed a lot more; so we didn't make any" (R19). However, there is no doubt that for these women, lower incomes and, above all, inadequate welfare benefits led to serious difficulties in providing food and clothing, and to a deterioration or at the least a lack of improvement in their working conditions.

Because they already bought only the bare necessities, the Depression days forced them to cut expenses in crucial areas, where alternatives had to be found. This is particularly true where food was concerned, since then the lack of money often meant looking for new sources of savings, which generally resulted in a lowering of both the quantity and quality of foodstuff. In order to get cheap meat, some did their shopping at the slaughterhouse rather than at the local butcher. A few dollars would get them several pounds of meat, but the nutritional value was not necessarily the best: "In those days, you could buy your meat [at the slaughterhouse]; soup bones were available and other such things as sausages, blood-pudding, nothing expensive as you can imagine, however 99 bought a whole lot" (R19). Others shopped at their regular butcher but late on Saturday evening.[27] Few butchers had refrigeration in those days and often they preferred to cut prices rather than keep meats until Monday, which might have meant a total loss. Another way of cutting costs in food was to buy damaged or no longer fresh fruits and vegetables, even if it took greater care and time to prepare them: "As you can imagine, it was a lot more work. Sometimes it was slightly spoiled. But as long as it was edible" (R5). Surprisingly, the respondents did not turn to baking their own bread. One said she tried three or four times, but it was a long and complicated task and lack of experience increased the risk of poor results and loss of costly ingredients. It was more economical to buy from the commercial bakers at the end of the day, when the delivery trucks would bring back unsold loaves which the companies were willing to sell at bargain prices:

> We would go to the bakers once the trucks came back from their run at 4 o'clock in the afternoon. For 25¢, we had a pillow-case full of bread. People would pass by the street corner carrying a folded pillow-case under their arm. Others had bags; they were all going to M . . . (R20)

It is evident that it took considerable skill and imagination to prepare tasty and nutritious meals under those circumstances. Despite their care and inventiveness, many interviewees were often forced to eat only slices of bread — sometimes spread with mustard or sugar — or do without food at all for entire days in order to feed their children: "We can't say that we ate well [. . .] We barely had enough to eat, and most of the time, we left what we had for the children" (R27). So it can be stated that where food is concerned, the Great Depression certainly complicated the tasks of the housewife in both the buying and the preparation of food. An even more serious consequence was the fact that the diet of the wife, and often that of the children and the husband, was frequently totally inadequate.[28]

For the unemployed, buying clothes and sewing material were the first budget cuts they made. This meant that women and their husbands alike had to wear out their clothing completely in order to find money with which to dress their growing children. Two of the respondents, who had never sewed before, learned to do so because of the Depression:

> That's when I learned to sew. At first, I bought clothes for my children but after, [when my husband lost his job] I couldn't afford to. I learned to sew by taking apart old clothes and remaking them. I didn't have a sewing-machine, so in the evenings I would go to my mother's to sew while my husband looked after the children. (R12)

In most cases, however, women who did not know how to sew relied on parents or charity organisations such as the Salvation Army or Saint-Vincent-de-Paul.

Lower incomes forced half of the respondents to move, often more than once, to ever less expensive and less comfortable homes.[29] Thus the Depression generally lowered the standard of living of the whole family, but even more so that of the women for whom home was at once both work and living space. For these women, moving also meant additional heavy work. The new home had to be found, possessions had to be packed and unpacked and the new place had to be thoroughly cleaned. If money was available, moving also entailed painting or wallpapering, sewing new curtains, and so on. Tight economic conditions did not encourage small landlords to maintain their rented premises properly or to undertake major renovations. In fact, the number of building or renovation permits sharply decreased during the Depression. Therefore, not only did the Depression increase the number of moves a family made, it also postponed any improvement in the workplace for these working-class housewives.[30]

The Great Depression also deprived some of the interviewees of a number of home appliances. For instance, many could not get repairs done. Others saved on electric bills by reducing their use of electric appliances. Two of the respondents had their power cut off; this made their work all the more difficult, because they had to postpone tasks to the evening, as they could then illegally hook up the wires with less fear that the company inspector might drop in.[31] Finally, two went back to live on the farm because their husbands could not find any work. Without electricity or running water, they had to put their electric irons, toasters and washing machines in storage and go back to making by hand a number of products that they were used to buying ready-made. Both these women had previous experience of farm life so it was easier for them than it might otherwise have been. However, they certainly experienced a serious set-back in the quality of their working conditions.[32]

Finally, the Great Depression also postponed any buying of furniture or appliances. In the 1940s, as soon as their income improved, one of the first acquisitions for most of the respondents was a new, more efficient gas cooker which replaced the old wood stove.[33] It should be noted that such purchases also meant that they were living in better equipped, more expensive accommodation. Those who had not yet acquired a washing machine would buy one during the war or immediately after. Others exchanged older models for newer electric ones. Also, in the 1940s, many of the households became subscribers to the telephone system.[34] Because refrigerators were very expensive, these were amongst the last appliances to enter their homes. In most cases, they were not acquired until the 1950s.[35]

Despite having to move more often, do laundry more frequently because they had fewer clothes, facing greater difficulties in feeding their families, and generally searching constantly for ways and means with satisfy the needs of all their family members, these women were not unanimous in their assessment as to how the Depression had affected their lives. Many felt that lack of money had not really entailed that much more work. Others conceded that they had to work more but hastened to add that they could cope with it very well: "Housework never bothered me" (R6); "Yes, [it meant more work], but like I said, it was part of a routine. It didn't bother me. I managed to cook with what I had . . ." (R29). In fact, their testimonies attest once more to the courage and self-sacrifice of which women are capable as they raise their families and also their pride in overcoming whatever hardship they have to face. The evidence reveals that women have a very elastic conception of their working time and capacity, which renders the task of evaluating the impact of the Depression on their housework all the more difficult. More than a living memory of responsibilities, their statements reflect pride in having ensured their family's well-being in spite of adverse economic conditions.

It is obvious, however, that for most of these families, and especially for those who lived on welfare for many years, it would have been impossible to cope were it not for their parents' support. Of course family solidarity did not begin with the Great Depression; it was always present, particularly among low income families.[36] Yet, the interviews indicate that there was a difference in kind during economic hard times. In normal times, for instance, shared child care and the exchange of clothing was natural enough, as well as the sharing of certain work tools, such as washing or sewing machines and the use of the telephone. The Great Depression increased the sharing of goods and services amongst family members, particularly gifts of food and fuel, as well as loans or gifts in money and the sharing of living space. Such help obviously went further than the traditional exchanges. Many of the respondents felt as humiliated by their need to seek such help as by having to ask for government welfare assistance, which was a last resort for most of them: "It was my mother who supported me. She would send us food and things, because we had nothing to eat and he didn't work" (R27); "That, I didn't like. It would have been okay if there had been only me but there was my husband and my son to consider" (R9).

The evidence from the respondents underlines the fact that the immediate family played an essential role in supporting those most stricken by the Great Depression. The rule was that government welfare only went to those who were absolutely destitute and who could not be helped by their families. In practice, however, families helped in many ways to fill the gap between the actual needs and what the welfare provided. Having exhausted their own resources and cut their expenses to the bone, couples then turned for help to their close families. The use of the traditional family network, which relied on the domestic work of the women of the previous generation, was therefore intensified during the Great Depression, and it is clear that the contribution of these women to the well-being of families on the dole was as essential as that of the state. Thus all women within the extended family and not only the housewives whose husbands were unemployed bore the brunt of the Depression.

Solidarity between neighbours was different. In fact, women were suspicious about their neighbours and kept their distance. They did not have the time to chat with neighbours and beside, they feared gossips: "I didn't bother with neighbours [. . .] I would stay home, and quietly do my chores. Besides, I figured that our distress was our own business, and nobody else's" (R22). This attitude reflects their desire to protect their private life and to conceal their poverty, which was perceived as shameful. Yet, help was not totally absent but as an interviewee put it, neighbours tried not to interfere with each other's lives: "When in need, they would help us, but each minded their own business" (R16). It consisted for the most part of exchanges of services to help reduce the burden of household chores, rather than of outright material aid. There were of course exceptions. One respondent who was particularly poor could depend on her landlord to provide her with coal. Another, who suffered a fire, found temporary refuge with a neighbour. However, most often, when one needed money, food, clothing, a roof over one's head or fuel, the immediate family was the safest bet.

The Depression did not bring about major changes in this respect, any more than it noticeably increased the level of indebtedness. Most working-class families frowned on the use of credit, especially for consumer goods.[37] In fact, the lack of social security measures to compensate for loss of income was such that these women and their partners were acutely aware of their financial limitations:

> We never had debts. I never bought anything on credit because I figured that
> if there was no money today, there wouldn't be any more tomorrow. If we had
> accumulated debts, I don't know how we could have paid for them. In our

days we always wondered whether or not the salary would still be there tomorrow. There was nothing you know; you couldn't rely on anyone but yourself. That's why most of the time, we deprived ourselves of many things we wished for. (R17)

The poor labour market, particularly during the thirties, increased the fear of not being able to pay off their creditors. Avoiding credit was also considered as proof that the wife was a good manager and that a family could meet its essential needs.

During the Depression, a few of the respondents had bought clothing from travelling salesmen who offered credit, with interest payments; another few incurred debts at the grocer, to their landlord or with the doctor; but most preferred to turn to the Salvation Army or the Saint-Vincent-de-Paul for food, furniture or clothing when the immediate family could not help. The amounts of the debts incurred were small indeed compared with today's standards; they rarely represented more than the wages of a week or two. In fact, it can be said that most of these households preferred to restrict their desires according to their means.[38] For these women, the essential was to feed, clothe and house the family.

Few of the interviewees complained about their precarious finances or the fact that the Depression further reduced their purchasing power. This can be attributed to a certain form of fatalism, but for the most part the women simply accepted that they were "living like everyone else." This is why, despite their many hardships, most of these women do not recall the 1930s as a particularly tragic period of their lives. The relative poverty of most of these households in the pre-Depression years meant that while family survival during the Depression itself involved cutting essential elements from the family budget, poverty had prepared them for deprivation: their previous experience had taught them to live frugally and to depend on the paid work, the domestic labour and the managing strategies of the wife in order to survive. Their pre-existing poverty meant that the conditions they endured during the Depression were not so drastically different from their previous standard of living. Moreover, most of the women had grown up in relatively poor households. Inured to poverty since childhood, they had learned to deal with it and knew ways and means of overcoming it.

It should also be borne in mind that the Depression struck early in the life-cycle of most of the families in the sample. At this stage in the life-cycle, it was still possible for some couples to postpone having children and thus to limit their expenses. Few among them had been able to acquire much that could be lost because of the Depression. Because it came early in their adult lives, they could hope for better days ahead and this certainly helped them to face hardships, and therefore, the difficulties of the decade 1929–39 left a temporary impression rather than a lasting impact. All the respondents did indeed remember the hardship of the time and the widespread unemployment, but the more closely they were questioned, the more measured their comments were as to the effects of the Depression on their experience. As one respondent said when asked if the Depression had left any particular impact on her life:

> No, as I said before, I don't know if it is because we were young but I can't say it marked us. We always hoped that things would change. I think if it had happened in times like now, we would have panicked more because we've been spoiled. That is the difference. In those days, we were content with very little, just the essentials so to speak. The ones who had lost most were the ones who had money. Some of them committed suicide; that was very bad. But, if you had no money, you had no trouble, did you? (R29)

NOTES

This article was drawn from my Doctoral thesis "Travail domestique et crise économique. Les ménagères montréalaises et la crise des années trente" (University of Montréal, 1990), which was subsidised by the Fonds FCAR (Québec). Many thanks to Danièle Dionne who translated a shorter version of the paper and to Hélène Houle who faced the delicate task of translating the excerpts of interviews. Finally, I am especially grateful to Professor Deborah Gorham of Carleton University for her useful comments and careful revision of this paper.

1. For instance, researchers have shown that between 1929 and 1933, Canadian manufacturing production decreased by a third, the index of consumer goods dropped by 25%, wages for non-exporting production dropped 37%, while the unemployment rate reached between 27 and 33%. During the winter of 1933, 1.5 million Canadians, that is 15% of the total population, were living on the dole, while in Montréal, this figure rose to 28% for the whole population of the city, but up to 38% for the francophone community. In Montréal the marriage and birth rates decreased, respectively, from 9.8 to 6.9 per thousand and from 28.4 to 22.1 per thousand between 1929 and 1933. See Allen Seager & John H. Thompson (1985) *Canada, 1922-1939, Decades of Discord*, p. 196 (Toronto: McClelland & Stewart); A.E. Safarian (1970) *The Canadian Economy in the Great Depression*, p. 103 (Toronto: McClelland & Stewart); James Struthers (1983) *No Fault of Their Own. Unemployment and the Canadian Welfare State (1914-1941)*, p. 215 (Toronto: University of Toronto Press); Michiel Horn (1972) *The Dirty Thirties. Canadians in the Great Depression*, p. 10 (Toronto: Copp Clark); *Rapport de la Commission d'enquête du chômage*, pp. 33-37 (Montréal, 1937); *Annuaire Statistique (ASQ) 1930 and 1934*, pp. 75, 80 (Québec, 1930, 1934).
2. The stagnation of the agricultural sector in the Western Provinces, industrial unemployment, labour unrest, the On-to-Ottawa trek of the single men working in the relief camps, the measures taken by the different levels of government to deal with unemployment, and the creation of the Canadian welfare state have especially interested historians. In addition to the titles already cited, see, for example, Michiel Horn (Ed.) (1988) *The Depression in Canada. Responses to Economic Crisis* (Toronto: Copp Clark Pitman); L.C. Marsh (1940) *Canadians in and out of Work: A Survey of Economic Classes and Their Relation to the Labor Market* (Toronto: Oxford University Press). In connection with the ideological and political situation in Québec, see Bernard Vigod (1979) "The Québec Government and Social Legislation during the 1930s: A Study in Political Self-destruction," *Journal of Canadian Studies/Revue d'études canadiennes*, 14, pp. 59-69; Andrée Lévesque (1984) *Virage à gauche interdit. Les communistes, les socialistes et leurs ennemis au Québec, 1929-1939* (Montréal: Boréal Express). On the administration of direct relief in Montréal, see June MacPherson (1976) " 'Brother can you spare a dime?' The Administration of Unemployment Relief in the City of Montréal, 1931-1941," M.A. thesis, Concordia University. On social policies, see Claude Larivière (1977) *Crise économique et contrôle social: le cas de Montréal, 1929-1937* (Montréal: Editions coopératives Albert Saint-Martin); Michel Pelletier & Yves Vaillancourt (1975) *Les politiques sociales et les travailleurs, Cahier II: les années 30* (Montréal).
3. During the winter of 1932-33, 54.9% of the unemployed in Montréal were manual and unskilled workers; 16.9% were semi-skilled and 15.5% were skilled workers (Marsh, *Canadians in and out of Work*, pp. 345-346).
4. In 1931, 42.7% of Québec labour power was living in Montréal (Lévesque, *Virage à gauche interdit*, p. 15).
5. For a more precise description of the methodology employed, see Denyse Baillargeon (1990) "Travail domestique et crise économique. Les ménagères montréalaises durant la crise des années trente," Ph.D. thesis, University of Montréal, pp. 77-102.
6. For a detailed review of the interview guidelines and a succinct biography of each of the respondents see Baillargeon, "Travail domestique et crise économique," Appendices A and B, pp. 419-433.
7. Note that the majority of women in the sample, that is 16 out of 30, had grown up in families of six to nine children; seven were from families comprising five children or less and seven were

from families of more than ten children. The very large family with more than ten children, which was often portrayed as the normal French Canadian family for that period, made up only a small proportion of the sample. On that matter see Marie Lavigne (1983) "Réflexions féministes autour de la fertilité des Québécoises," in Nadia Fahmy-Eid & Micheline Dumont (Eds.) *Maîtresses de maison, maîtresses d'école. Femmes, famille et éducation dans l'histoire du Québec*, pp. 319-338 (Montréal: Boréal Express).

8. Excerpt from the interview with respondent number 29. Thereafter, each excerpt drawn from the interviews will be followed by an R and the number associated with the respondent (in this case: R29).

9. Many authors have stressed the low school attendance of French Canadians and the lack of legislation enforcing compulsory school attendance before the forties. See Louis Philippe Audet (1971) *Histoire de l'enseignement au Québec*, 2 vols. (Montréal: Holt, Rinehart & Winston); Thérèse Hamel (1984) "Obligation scolaire et travail des enfants au Québec, 1900-1950," *Revue d'histoire de l'Amérique française*, 38, pp. 39-58; Dominique Jean (1989) "Familles québécoises et politiques sociales touchant les enfants de 1940 à 1960: obligation scolaire, allocations familiales et travail juvénile," Ph.D. thesis, University of Montréal. On girls' education see Micheline Dumont & Nadia Fahmy-Eid (1986) *Les Couventines. L'éducation des filles au Québec dans les congrégations religieuses enseignantes, 1840-1960* (Montréal: Boréal Express).

10. It is interesting to note that with the exception of two women who were teachers and a third who was a nursing assistant, most of them changed jobs many times. In all, 11 were employed as clerks in offices and stores; 14 worked as unskilled workers and 7 as servants. Working as a servant was especially disliked by the women, who preferred to work in a factory. Their appraisal of domestic service was similar to those of the women quoted in David M. Katzman (1981) *Seven Days a Week: Women and Domestic Service in Industrializing America* (Chicago: University of Illinois Press).

11. Such findings led the bourgeois ladies of the Fédération nationale Saint-Jean-Baptiste to set up some cooking and sewing classes for the female industrial workers in Montréal. See Nicole Thivierge (1982) *Ecoles ménagères et instituts familiaux: un modèle féminin traditionnel*, p. 122 (Québec: Institut québécois de recherche sur la culture [IQRC]). On the apprenticeship of domestic work see also Denise Lemieux & Lucie Mercier (1989) *Les femmes au tournant du siècle 1880-1940. Ages de la vie, maternité et quotidien*, pp. 67-107 (Québec: IQRC). On the role of mothers in the apprenticeship of domestic work, see also Lynn Jamieson (1986) "Limited Resources and Limiting Conventions: Working-Class Mothers and Daughters in Urban Scotland," in Jane Lewis (Ed.) *Labour and Love. Women's Experience of Home and Family, 1840-1940*, pp. 49-69 (Oxford: Basil Blackwell).

12. Horace Miner (1985) *St-Denis: un village québécois* (Montréal: Hurtubise HMH); Lucia Ferretti (1985) "Mariage et cadre de vie familiale dans une paroisse ouvrière montréalaise: Sainte-Brigide, 1900-14," *Revue d'histoire de l'Amérique française*, 39, pp. 233-251.

13. One was without a job when he married in 1927; eleven were industrial workers; three worked in the construction trade (one bricklayer and two labourers); six were employed in the commercial and services sectors as manual workers and six as non-manual workers.

14. *ASQ, 1930 and 1934*, pp. 400, 426; Canada, ministère du Travail, *La Gazette du Travail*, February 1933, p. 249. Twenty dollars a week, which covers only the bare necessities, was thus a strict minimum for a family of five. It took $1500 a year, that is more than $28 a week, to attain a level of decency (Lévesque, *Virage à gauche*, p. 22).

15. For a family of five, the Montréal Unemployment Commission paid $8.50 for the rent to the landlord and gave $7.15 a week in winter and $6.55 in summer to cover all other expenses. In 1933, according to the *Labour Gazette*, it took a minimum of $14.29 a week for a family of two adults and three children to survive (Montréal, *Commission du chômage. Renseignement à l'usage des chômeurs nécessiteux et des propriétaires*, pp. 10-11; Canada, ministère du Travail, *La Gazette du Travail*, February 1933, p. 249).

16. Those methods were the most widely used everywhere in Canada. According to Angus McLaren & Arlene Tigar McLaren, during the twenties and the thirties: "The birth rate was brought down, not because of any technological break through, but because more couples intent on limiting their fertility conscientiously employed traditional methods." Angus McLaren & Arlene Tigar McLaren (1986) *The Bedroom and the State: The Changing Practices and Politics of Contraception and Abortion in Canada, 1880-1980*, p. 22 (Toronto: McClelland & Stewart).

17. The understanding of the ovulation cycle by those two doctors in the late 1920s enabled couples to determine in which period of the month they should avoid intercourse. It should be recalled that during the thirties the Catholic Church finally accepted this method because it was associated with abstinence. However, the couples who wanted to use it had to obtain the permission of the Church. (McLaren & Tigar McLaren, *The Bedroom and the State*, pp. 130-131; Andrée Lévesque [1989] *La norme et les déviantes. Des femmes au Québec pendant l'entre-deux-guerres*, p. 31 [Montréal: Editions du Remue-ménage].) It should also be noted that the testimonies reveal that the physicians were not so eager to explain its workings, even to the couples to whom they recommended no other pregnancies (Baillargeon, "Travail domestique et crise économique," pp. 214-215).

18. Veronica Strong-Boag had noted the same phenomenon for English Canadian women between the wars: "The incorporation of paid work into domestic routines appeared relatively commonplace in both the 1920s and 1930s, a good index of how tough times were not restricted to the Great Depression" (Veronica Strong-Boag [1988] *The New Day Recalled: Lives of Girls and Women in*

English Canada, 1919-1939, p. 125 [Toronto: Copp Clark Pitman]). Elizabeth Roberts also reports a large variety of strategies used by English working-class women between 1900 and 1940 to supplement the family income (Elizabeth Roberts, "Women's Strategies, 1890-1940," in Lewis, *Labour and Love*, pp. 223-247.)

19. On the question of role reversal during the Great Depression, see Mirra Komarovsky (1971) *The Unemployed Man and His Family* (New York: Arno Press); Ruth Milkmann (1976) "Women's Work and Economic Crisis: Some Lessons of the Great Depression," *Review of Radical Political Economics*, 8, p. 85.

20. That was not always possible; for instance many seamstresses lost a part of their clientele because of the economic crisis.

21. Many authors have observed that phenomenon for English Canada and the United States. See Strong-Boag, *The New Day Recalled*, p. 50; Komarovsky, *The Unemployed Man*, pp. 28-30.

22. See especially Komarovsky, *The Unemployed Man*.

23. Meg Luxton (1980) *More Than a Labor of Love: Three Generations of Women's Work in the Home*, pp. 161-199 (Toronto: Women's Press); Strong-Boag, *The New Day Recalled*, pp. 133-144; Elizabeth Roberts (1984) *A Woman's Place: An Oral History of Working-Class Women, 1850-1940*, pp. 125-168 (Oxford: Basil Blackwell); Pat Ayers & Jan Lambertz, "Marriage Relations, Money, and Domestic Violence in Working-Class Liverpool, 1919-39," in Lewis, *Labour and Love*, pp. 195-219.

24. In fact, more than half of the respondents paid less than $15 a month for a four-room apartment at the beginning of the thirties. According to the *Labour Gazette*, the lease for a six-room apartment without modern conveniences in Montréal amounted to between $16 and $25 a month in 1929 and between $15 and $18 a month in 1933, while the same apartment with all the conveniences was rented for between $25 and $40 a month in January 1929 and between $18 and $33 in January 1933 (Canada, ministère du Travail, *La Gazette du Travail*, February 1929, p. 256, and February 1933, p. 257).

25. A municipal inquiry in 1936/37 led to the conclusion that of the 4216 leases visited, 91.5% had softwood floors, 15% were infested with rats, 17% with bugs, and 23% with cockroaches. Many were located in basements, attics, backyards, or old stables. Only 1716 had a completely isolated toilet while in 1431 cases, it was added after the construction in a corner of the kitchen, in 112 cases it was to be found in the parlour, in 536 cases in a bedroom and in 239 cases in the hallway. On the other hand, only 32% were equipped with a bath and 11% had running hot water. Real Belanger, George S. Mooney & Pierre Boucher (1938) *Les vieux logements de Montréal*, pp. 10-12 (Commission Métropolitaine de Montréal, Département d'urbanisme et de recherche).

26. See Milkmann, "Women's Work and Economic Crisis"; Susan Ware (1982) *Holding Their Own. American Women in the Twentieth Century* (Boston: Twayne).

27. It should be recalled that during this period, stores were closing at 11 p.m. on Saturday nights.

28. According to Marjorie Spring Rice, the working-class women in England during the thirties also deprived themselves the most in order to feed and clothe their husbands and children: "Naturally they suffer [. . .] from the lack of sufficient food and clothes [. . .] but it is undoubtedly true that even in these respects the mother will be the first to go without." Marjorie Spring Rice (1980) "Working-Class Wives," in Ellen Malos (Ed.) *The Politics of Housework*, p. 96 (New York: Allison & Busby).

29. The number of moves in Montréal was steadily rising during the first years of the crisis: 54,000 in 1930, 55,000 in 1931, 65,000 in 1932 and nearly 82,000 in 1933 according to the data provided by the Montréal Light Heat and Power Company (*La Patrie*, 17 April 1931 and 17 April 1933, p. 3). Moreover, most of the families were looking for cheap rent because of the economic crisis. During this period, the best living places remained vacant while a surplus of population was observed in old quarters. For more information see Marc Choko (1980) *Les crises du logement à Montréal*, p. 109 (Montréal: Editions coopératives Albert Saint-Martin).

30. The number of construction and renovation permits issued in Montréal decreased from 5755 in 1929 to 2196 in 1933. This number increased to 2981 in 1939. The most affected sector was new home construction where the number of permits fell from 4116 to 875 between 1929 and 1933. Moreover, a large number of houses located in working-class areas were demolished to be replaced by public service buildings or utilities: Atwater market, Jacques-Cartier bridge, etc. (construction statistics from Montréal in Choko, *Les crises du logement*, pp. 107, 146).

31. Note that Montréal Light Heat and Power was the sole company distributing electricity in the region, maintaining high prices. It could therefore cut the power, without recourse, to the clients that did not pay their bills. According to Robert Rumilly, more than 20,000 families saw their electricity cut at the worst of the crisis. Robert Rumilly (1974) *Histoire de Montréal* (Montréal: Fides), quoted in Larivière, *Crise économique*, p. 175).

32. Between 42,000 and 54,000 persons went back to the farm during the thirties. This means that the fate of my two respondents was shared by a lot of women some of whom were not as well prepared to face these changes (Paul-André Linteau et al. [1989] *Histoire du Québec contemporain*, Vol. 2; *Le Québec depuis 1930*, p. 41 [Montréal: Boréal Compact].)

33. In 1941, 17.7% of the Montréal households used wood or coal as fuel for cooking and only 8.2% in 1951 (Canada, *Recensement du Canada 1941*, Vol. V, pp. 51-62 and *Recensement du Canada 1951*, Vol. III, pp. 22-3). There are no data on this topic in the 1931 Census. On the other hand, the municipal inquiry already mentioned concludes that nearly all the households visited were heated

only by a stove. For 68.6% of the cases, wood and coal were used as the fuel (Belanger et al., *Les vieux logements*, p. 11).

34. In 1931, 10.5% of the Québec households had a telephone; in 1941, 44.9% of the Montréal households had one, while in 1951, this percentage rose to 77.1% (Canada, *Recensement du Canada 1931*, Vol. I, p. 1417; *Recensement du Canada 1941*, Vol. V, p. 84; and *Recensement du Canada 1951*, Vol. III, p. 42).

35. In 1941, 25.1% of Montréal households had a refrigerator; 61.1% in 1951 and 89.7% in 1958 (Canada, *Recensement du Canada 1941*, Vol. V, p. 79; *Recensement du Canada 1951*, Vol. III, p. 38; and Canada, Dominion Bureau of Statistics, *Household Facilities and Equipment*, 1958, p. 16).

36. See Andrée Fortin (1987) *Histoires de familles et de réseaux. La sociabilité au Québec d'hier à demain* (Montréal: Editions Saint-Martin); Marc-Adélard Tremblay (1977) "La crise économique des années trente et la qualité de vie chez les montréalais d'ascendance française," in Académie des Sciences Morales et Politiques, *Travaux et Communications*, Vol. 3: *progrès techniques et qualité de vie*, pp. 149-165 (Montréal: Bellarmin).

37. Note that buying furniture on an Instalment Plan was not considered as using credit because there was no interest charged; however, the purchase price was generally higher (Baillargeon, "Travail domestique et crise économique," p. 405; Strong-Boag, *The New Day Recalled*, p. 115). According to the 1941 Census, 65.9% of the appliances, furniture and radios were bought on hire-purchase that year (Canada, *Recensement du Canada 1941*, Vol. X, pp. 374-377).

38. Marc-Adélard Tremblay goes as far as to state that: "Au moment de la crise économique, les normes de consommation portent principalement sur les besoins primaires et ont une très grande stabilité. La publicité commerciale existe à peine et les nouveaux modèles de consommation des sociétés urbaines et industrialisées pénètrent à peine dans les milieux plus à l'aise et chez les familles urbaines de longue date" (Tremblay, "La crise économique des années trente," p. 156). This takes for granted that the working-class families were living in isolation without radios or newspapers or catalogues to remind them of the large variety of products available on the market. This seems highly improbable.

Mothering in a Newfoundland Community: 1900-1940

CECILIA BENOIT

Introduction

In much of the prolific literature on women published in the past two decades, there has been a tendency to focus on the home as a sphere of production instead of merely an enclave of retreat from the "world of 'work.'"[1] In addition, feminist historians have begun to re-examine historical records in an attempt to discover women's hitherto hidden history.[2] Attention has also been drawn to the position of women in societies undergoing modernization and to the individual and collective political behaviour of women — within and outside the household.[3] Much of the literature on women, however, has remained abstract and theoretical. We still lack substantive evidence, for example, for a theory of gender hierarchies, in part perhaps because we have only begun to become familiar with the socio-economic and cultural circumstances of the lives of rural women. Only such substantive evidence can lead to a fuller understanding of the paradoxical position of women throughout history.[4]

SOURCE: Cecilia Benoit, "Mothering in a Newfoundland Community: 1900-1940," in Katherine Arnup, Andrée Lévesque, and Ruth Roach Pierson, eds., *Delivering Motherhood: Maternal Ideologies and Practices in the 19th and 20th Centuries* (London and New York: Routledge, 1990), 173-189.

I will describe below one historical case of women's subordination in a Newfoundland community immediately prior to modernization at the onset of World War II. In particular, I will examine the political economy of mothering and attempt to demonstrate that women's unequal status in family and community was associated with social and economic processes which excluded women from most forms of wage labour. While males found employment in the market economy, their female kin remained within the bounds of the community as "procreators" and "homemakers," statuses closely regulated by economic structures and religious institutions. Nevertheless, these women managed to survive and find satisfaction in informal networks of production and friendship.

My focus in this paper is the problem of mothering (as an institution and as a personal encounter)[5] in one historical instance, as experienced by the women themselves. The time span is the period from 1900 to 1940, still within the lived experience of older people in the community, and just prior to the opening of an American air force base at the beginning of World War II, an event which changed the community virtually overnight into a modern town. By use of the snowball technique, informal tape-recorded interviews were conducted with approximately twenty women and ten men (age 65-95). Typical of the general population as a whole, many of my female interviewees were widows, living either alone or with one of their adult children. Whenever husbands and wives were interviewed, separate time was allotted for each, since the women and men were generally reluctant to discuss "private matters" (e.g., sexuality, birth control, pregnancy) in the company of the other sex. The interviews ranged from one to two hours, and a few were repeated. Census data and other archival materials, in addition to local and cross-cultural studies on the topic, were consulted in order to substantiate the interview data.

The Setting

> I was born ten years before the new century came in — not yesterday, hey? We had a lovely house back off the pond, around two miles from the church and the merchant's store. In 1900 there wasn't much very big around here. No way for a woman to earn a cent really. No doctor, just the midwife to take care of the folks. The road was really not much more than a cow path and unless you were a man or grown boy, you didn't get to see what the other side of the Bay was like.
> (Housewife, born 1890)

The situation of women in Stephenville, Newfoundland, between 1900 and 1940 illustrates some of the dilemmas of motherhood. Although in some ways this small community was unlike other outport communities in Newfoundland during this period,[6] most of its structural features can be found in cultural settings elsewhere.[7] In this Catholic community of Scots, Acadians and Micmac Indians, mothers and daughters rarely left their community while husbands and sons were absent for long periods each year. This situation resulted in an extremely sharp division of labour between women and men and, in consequence of the prolonged periods of separation, in a ruptured bond between many husbands and wives. The sexes were indeed "worlds apart":[8]

> Women from Stephenville were born to work and stay put and so we lived with it. Work was your story and so you bit your lip and got on with it. We women had what it took to make a good frame. And then we helped each other. Sometimes I wonder, though, as I sit here getting old, how we conquered it all.
> (Housewife, born 1898)

Stephenville men were commonly known as "Jacks-of-all-trades." They tried their hands at farming, fishing, lumbering and hunting, often at a combination of several of these. Nevertheless, they were always "in the red" with the local shop owners, and hence in constant search of paid work. After 1925,[9] men were increasingly able to sell their labour on the open market in return for a low wage, a bunk bed in a lumber camp, and perhaps three meals a day. After the fall harvest they usually left their community and did not return before Christmas. Soon thereafter they would be gone again until spring planting time. Despite their hard work, the men earned a few dollars at most for a twelve-hour day. Bad weather or a poor tree crop sometimes meant that they returned home with nothing more than "the shirts on their backs." They would help the women with the garden, cut firewood, perhaps hunt or fish, and soon start the cycle once again. The women watched their male kin come and go with the seasons, never quite sure where they were, always fearful that they would return without enough money to settle accounts with the merchant.

Which forces, we may ask, kept the women bound to their community? And what economic contribution did they make to the survival of their families? As I will argue below, their non-wage labour often meant the difference between minimal comfort and destitution. Women frequently bartered their crafts for food at the merchant store. They also performed the tasks necessary for the upkeep of the Church and the priest. Their many other productive activities, too, were essential for the well-being of their families:

> One thing was sure, the people here were not ill-fed or ill-clothed. All the women worked together like a team. At least we could plant our basic food and gather enough berries for winter preserves. Then we had hens and lots of fresh milk. No, we didn't get through the rough times on salt fish alone.
> (Housewife, born 1898)

Community Women

Stephenville women conceived life as a cyclical process and such notions as individual freedom (or "women's rights") were foreign to them. They were daughters and usually mothers, always tied to some household, whether married, spinstered or widowed. Their lives were tightly inter-woven with significant others. They lived on the edge of the modern world familiar only to their male kin. All this is not to say that these women did not experience change. In fact, their lives were continuously in flux. There was the precariousness of the community economy, and there were the rhythms of the seasons, of birth, puberty, marriage, mén-opause and old age. They lived each day at a time, investing their hopes for change in their children and getting by on the friendship and support they freely gave each other:

> You were a respected woman if you worked hard and tended to the family and had a brood of youngsters. It was your assigned lot in life as a woman. Work and having babies after marriage was all we had, except [for] each other.
> (Housewife, born 1898)

While the Newfoundland census for the period under examination records a variety of males "gainfully occupied" (farmers, fishermen, me-chanics, loggers, sawmill operators, miners, factory workers and fish cur-ers, as well as "professionals" such as civil servants and teachers),[10] the only recorded "gainfully occupied" females are a small number of fish curers (forty-eight in 1911, eighteen in 1921). The sole profession men-tioned is teaching, "gainfully occupying" one to three females. No women are recorded as otherwise employed, although my interviewees frequently mentioned the midwife, who sometimes received money for her services. They also spoke of a woman apprenticed by the government to the local priest, eventually performing the duties of post office mistress (while dou-bling as the priest's domestic help). All other women, according to the census, were "homemakers," without salary or wage. This societal def-inition of women as "homemakers" included all single women keeping house for their male kin, single mothers living within their fathers' house-holds, re-adopted widowed daughters and so forth — in addition, of course, to the married women. It is important to note that throughout this period the yield of agricultural and animal products was consistently high. In attempting to understand women's subordination to men two interconnected spheres must be examined in which women lacked ef-fective control: sexuality and procreation, as well as the institution of marriage.

Sexuality and Marriage

The Stephenville Catholic hierarchy strongly believed that a woman should be "protected" by a man — either by a father, a husband, a male relative, or at least by the local priest. Marriage was the highest goal for woman, other than entering the convent. Since prior to World War II, few labouring families had sufficient financial resources to send a daughter to a convent (or a male to a seminary), the option of "spiritual marriage" to the Church was closed to Stephenville women.

My female interviewees point out that, according to the religious orthodoxy of the time, "good women" were supposed to be asexual and virtuous and to suffer through the sex act without moving as much as a muscle. While enjoying sex was seen as a vice in the case of women, it was regarded as a "natural" male urge assigned to men by nature. Not surprisingly, sex was frequently regarded as yet another form of labour expected of married females, along with domestic work, church work, garden work, and so forth. When a woman married and set up house with a man, she often did so not out of love but in order to achieve the status of a legitimate mother:

> Women were told that "once you find some man to take you to be his wife, you made your bed and now you lay in it." Well, let me tell you this much, the women from around here didn't have any soft beds to choose from. As a single girl, sex and your period were dirty and evil, not proper discussion for "virgin" ears. I was fourteen when I started comin' around, you know, when a girl starts changing. I recall my mother saying that the best years of any woman's life were before the change.
> (Housewife, born 1900)

Stephenville women, during this period, had virtually no way of disassociating pregnancy from sexuality. Unexpected pregnancy was a constant worry for both married and non-married women. If a single woman's lover were a Catholic boy willing to marry her, then her status remained intact. But if he were not Catholic, perhaps someone she had met through her lumberjack brothers at the fall harvest or a traveller en route elsewhere, marriage was virtually impossible, even if he was willing:

> I had my only child when I was seventeen. I wasn't married, you know. My little child, she only lived a month and two days. It was probably the best for the both of us. Now I really wanted to marry that fellow. But I was scared to death 'cause he was a "black" Protestant. Father and the priest went wild. I got the strap for my sin and then had to do nine months of penance at Sunday mass. It was a mortal sin, my dear, the blackest sin of all. For the rest of my life I had to live with it. After that, I just kept away from men.
> (Single mother, born 1916)

In brief, whichever direction these women turned, their hands were tied. Since mixed marriages were unheard of then, such a pregnant woman was marked for life.[11] However, because marriage was economically crucial for achieving the social status "woman," and also because it was difficult to meet a non-kin male since a woman was usually tied to the community, she was forced to take her chances — at a time when there was no effective birth control. Nor was medically safe abortion available. This situation placed single women in a very vulnerable position:

> Sometimes my brothers would come back home with a bunch of lumberjacks they met in the woods and have a lot to drink and brag about. When a fellow

comes out of the lumberwoods after living in bunk houses with perhaps five hundred to a thousand men and blackarding[12] and gambling their spare time away, you can well imagine the state their minds and body was in when we laid eyes on them. All they wanted to do is drink and party and have someone to run after them. And, imagine, they were about the only fellows you had to choose from for a husband. A girl had to be real careful, 'cause once she got in trouble, her life was done for.
(Spinster, born 1910)

A young girl finding herself pregnant, with an extremely strict father to deal with and the priest to face (if her lover were a Catholic and not a close relative), experienced a genuine trauma. Nevertheless, there was community pressure on the man to marry her. If he chose to support the child financially, however, no further social pressure was applied:

Fellows used to say, "If you don't give in to me, I'll leave you 'cause there's lots more of your kind dying to grab hold to a husband around here." These fellows were just out for themselves and a bit of fun. Well, it wasn't much to laugh about being left in trouble with a bad name and a bastard child on the way. Sometimes the fellow would sincerely promise to marry you if you let him get close and then, after he had his bit, he'd clear out to the woods or God knows where. They were always trying to corner you.
(Housewife, born 1903)

Some women caught in such circumstances without a "legitimate" male partner tried drastic and occasionally fatal measures:

I sometimes heard tell of some girls taking stomach salts or jumping from the loft and things like that. Poor things, they didn't have it very easy. I heard talk of one who took the scissors to herself. It's no wonder, 'cause back in those times you got punished some bad for your misdeed. You had to go up to the front of the altar at Sunday mass and do penance before the entire congregation. You were an utter disgrace and your poor child, after all that, had to suffer. For without a real father, it had to go without being baptized, and the government would make note in the books that it was not normal, and for the rest of its days it was labelled. For sure, this wasn't right. I think that the Church and most of the old men were too strict with the womenfolk.
(Midwife, born 1889)

Stephenville women who "chose" to avoid men entirely were at least able to avoid the trauma associated with unwed motherhood. "Spinsterhood," however, as one woman put it, "was no bed of roses either." A society which measured women's status according to the frequency of her pregnancies within marriage gave little praise to a woman who did not make her biology her destiny. Such a woman was labelled an "old maid" and remained a servant and perpetual minor in her parents' house, despite her age, life experience and productive labour. Even the married women tended to view her as somehow "abnormal" since she did not mother children.

As mentioned above, the unavailability of eligible partners was a problem for both sexes. The lack of opportunity for women to leave their community, however, made their situation even more desperate than it was for their male counterparts. By the late 1930s, according to one respondent,

> There was no one in Stephenville for a girl to marry. Before the war came, things were so bad that a girl couldn't get married unless she ended up marrying her first or second cousin. We were all really blood relatives. But what were we all to do? Everyone was a streak of relations.
> (Widow, born 1909)

Marriage, then, while wanted by most women, also meant sacrifice. As an institution, it was full of contradictions. But the women who "escaped" marriage had trials of their own to endure. And neither could avoid productive labour without monetary reward.

Women's Productive Labour

Work — both inside the household and on the family farm — was the common experience of all women. Childhood freedom frequently ended as early as age eight or nine. Young girls, like their male siblings, might leave school after the second or third grade.[13] Prior to World War II, few finished high school. As one female interviewee put it, "by the time you were up to your mother's apron pocket, you were ready for hard work." While boys were off with their male kin, every morning at dawn mothers and daughters were already working, no matter what season:

> A young girl was like an apprentice or helper to her mother or big sister. I suppose it was a good practice for when we got married and had babies of our own. I had to stand on a chair to do the first batch of dishes I washed. We made butter with a hand churn, baked lovely biscuits and molasses buns for the crowd and washed with a scrubbing board. All this before you were perhaps nine years of age.
> (Spinster, born 1910)

Without male support, the women took over the "hard" work, in addition to the other activities of their sex. They planted seeds, weeded, doctored animals, put the cattle out to pasture, gathered driftwood at the shore, thus keeping the entire family and farm operating until the men returned:

> We knew all about the winds and the sea. We could tell the time by the sun and the weather by the moon. We knew just where to find the best berries and wild plants. Two women could break forty gallons of tame strawberries in a hard day's work. We were not easy. There was no slacking about.
> (Housewife, born 1900)

Inside the household there was constant activity: a diaper to change, a cup of tea for grandpa, a bandage for an injured soul, and so on. It was only after the children and old folks had gone to bed and the dishes were washed that these women took out their looms and spinning wheels to begin their other activities, such as making clothes and quilts:

My dear, we made it all. We'd soften up brinebags and make them into diapers.
I was at the loom by the age of twelve. My mother was some marvelous spinner.
We also used a sewing machine, the kind with the pedal. We would rip out
a worn pair of trousers for a pattern. It was all rough, but real warm. We used
to make lovely crochet and needlework and knit sweaters with our own homespun
wool. Some of it we donated to the Church. The merchant would trade for
staples only when we were in dire straits.
(Midwife, born 1889)

The women called these occasions of communal craft production
"frolics" or "bees" (the male equivalents were the communal construction
of a barn or house). Their productive labour during these spare moments
in their daily cycle, as well as the food they collected and harvested,
provided many of the basic necessities of survival. The use value of the
things they produced or collected cannot be overemphasized, even if the
merchant assigned little exchange value to them. As one woman put it,
"we had no commodities back then. What we made by hand wasn't worth
a dime outside the family. Still, without all of it, we wouldn't be here
today." In brief, these women's reproductive and productive lives consisted of an endless series of tasks during each day and year of their
lifetime. From childhood onwards they were tied to the soil, the household, the laws of the community, and ultimately to the biological rhythms
of their bodies.

Yet this is not to say that their male kin did not face hardships as
well. Wage labour forced the men to live for long periods outside their
community. This sharp sexual division of labour often had devastating
effects on family life.[14] Under the impact of the dual stresses of separation
and poverty, marriage and families were seldom sustained by bonds of
intimacy or love. When the men returned to their families, they usually
desired a rest from the hardships of communal living. And their still
relatively traditional society, based as it was on the laws of the Church,
which justified women's subordination, was a welcome break from the
alien world where they were periodically forced to sell their labour. The
community and the extended family provided these men with emotional
security and a means of livelihood during periods of unemployment. At
home they had some real power: power over women. Within the family
they could set down rules and demand to be served. And the community
elders, especially the priest and the aging family patriarchs, sanctioned
such dominance of men over women.

My female informants were rather sober in their assessment of their
relationships with men. They have few romantic reminiscences, and are
usually quick to state that they would never wish their kind of marriage
or their own father-daughter relationship on anyone else. Many felt
"runned to death" as the servants of men rather than seeing themselves
as their equals.

There were, nevertheless, ways for women to find at least some limited degree of satisfaction or even happiness. Since their primary role
was to reproduce and to maintain the kin group, and since their husbands,

brothers and fathers were mostly working-class men spending much of their time away from home, these Stephenville women sought out the company of other women. It is, therefore, important to examine this hidden side of their lives, left out of the records of the past, for it was precisely in their own restricted sphere that these women made sense of the forces they could not change. In their "separate" world of frolics, spinning bees, childbirth, doctoring and death, they were a "power to be reckoned with."

The Safety Net of Women's Experience

In Stephenville prior to 1940, it was virtually impossible to obtain medical attention. One doctor periodically visited rural people and examined them for signs of an epidemic, or he came upon the request of a merchant family who could afford to pay for his services. The closest hospital (after 1933) was more than twenty miles away and connected by an often impassable gravel road. Consequently, few women left home during childbirth. The members of the community made do with herbal medicines and the aid of the local midwife, who was important to every person's health and who was well respected, sometimes even loved:

> We usen't to bother with the company doctor. I had the midwife, Auntie Elizabeth, for all my babies. There was no limit to the things she used to handle — curing measles and yellow jaundice with a brew made from sheep dung; sour-duck seeds for anybody with hay fever; and yellow root for the cramps. She was so kind and sweet to us all.
> (Housewife, born 1910)

These women had never heard of invalidism. Nor had they heard of gynaecology and obstetrics. Urban women, especially of the upper classes, might have been told by (male) medical professionals that "the uterus was the real heart of woman, from which all her other parts sprung," that "women by *nature* were essentially frail, weak and nervous creatures whose main purpose in life was to have sons as heirs," or that they would continuously experience "bouts of illness caused by their wombs."[15] Stephenville women, in contrast, were "layin-in" nearly every year for eleven days or so under the watchful eye of the midwife, returning to their work as soon as humanly possible:

> Don't worry, we were some tough. We would be down at the beach or in the garden until we went into labour. Having babies was only one part of it. It never kept me bedridden for long.
> (Widow, born 1901)

These women did not long remain confined within the narrow walls of their homes. They saw family as interrelated spheres of production, reproduction, and consumption, as a part of the non-market economy in which they exchanged the goods they had made and the medical skills they had learned from each other. They cared for each other's children during sickness and childbirth, and they provided friendship during difficult times:

> I first learned to doctor the women and others in the village from my dear mother. I learned to give a newborn a steeped brew from weeds — caraway seeds perhaps. I was always present during birth, consoling and guiding my expectant mother. All the women used to help out: some cooked; others kept house; others washed and fed the kids. Together we were a strong team.
> (Midwife, born 1889)

The midwife or "granny," as she was called, like all the other women, had little contact with medical professionals. She possessed her own common sense knowledge about the human body. She saw childbirth as one among many changes in a woman's life, as part of a continuous life process of reproductive moments. Pregnancy and menopause were not diseases but natural and inevitable events in the lives of women. Knowledge about the granny's own body rhythms complemented the advice she had received from the midwife whom she had succeeded. She had no ambition to become a professional health care worker but merely aspired to guide the community members along a path of well-being:

> I always made my expectant mothers stay confined for ten days. That was my only rule. After childbirth, I often gave them boiled juniper or senna tea. A warm drink did wonders. I did lose some babies, but not very many, and few mothers. The women used to trust me. Of course, I didn't have any fancy doctor instruments for plucking out babies. But my homemade remedies served the purpose most of the time.
> (Midwife, born 1889)

Although ignorant of modern obstetrics and without access to medical back-up services, the grannies nevertheless succeeded in gaining the respect of most community members, not least because they were in many ways companions who shared their knowledge rather than professionals in positions of power vis-à-vis their clients. During the evenings, sitting in the kitchen of an expectant mother while spinning, weaving, or knitting with a group of neighbouring women, the granny tended the woman in labour without dominating her or speeding up the birth process. She was not, like professionals,[16] "a cut above the average folk"; she received no government payment, and often even her nominal five to ten dollar fee was replaced by a piece of woven cloth or some vegetables, or payment was postponed to some later date. She performed other health care activities in a similar manner: pulling teeth, mending broken bones, nursing colds, and even doctoring the villagers' animals. During this period, Stephenville would have indeed hardly managed without her non-wage labour.

Many other productive activities — such as weaving, spinning, carding or gathering — were performed by these women in a similarly informal manner, frequently out of sheer economic necessity. During their frolics at home, along the seashore or in the garden, they could talk about their problems, share intimacies and laugh a little, while teaching their daughters future skills:

> At our matting and spinning bees we used to talk about it all. We would complain about the merchant and often about the priest as well. We also had our little laughs. One woman swore that every time her husband hung his pants on the bed post, she ended up pregnant again. It eased the hardships, having each other. (Housewife, born 1902)

In both the productive and reproductive areas of women's lives, the joys were frequently closely tied to the pains. Poverty and family life were burdens which nevertheless did not prevent frequent moments of enjoyment. Little pleasures, such as seeing the first plants break the soil in the early summer, giving their kinfolk a handmade quilt and, of course, giving birth, *were* concrete satisfactions, even if these women were forced to contend with a subordinate position in the presence of their male relatives and of the religious authorities. However, even where women achieved independence in some spheres of work (for example, as midwife, gardener or weaver), this neither led to equality within the family during the off-seasons when the sexes mixed nor to their right to reformulate the rules of the Church or of the traditional law which formally subordinated them to men.

Conclusion

I have tried to show that the lives of rural women are worth examining. Studies of the relationship between the sexes in Western pre-modern societies may well contribute to the badly needed substantiation of present generalizations concerning gender hierarchies.

The concept of "motherhood" has had a long, though hidden, career. Women, as procreators, have often been rendered subordinate, both by their biology and by patriarchal social systems. This is well demonstrated by the community in which I conducted my interviews. There, as elsewhere, mothering has involved ambiguous and even contradictory features: on the one hand, we confront a relatively isolated community with a limited degree of economic development, in which most people led an existence of toil, in which women had to survive for long periods without the presence and support of their male kin, and certainly without the amenities now taken for granted in welfare states. On the other hand, poverty and a sharp sexual division of labour paradoxically also permitted a kind of independence which women now frequently lack in modern suburban communities. Furthermore, the knowledge shared by the midwife and the other women was of crucial importance for their physical and emotional well-being (and indeed for the health of all community members), constituting a means of coping with daily life and contributing to a network of skills and intimacies from which men were excluded.

In brief, pre-modern motherhood, while clearly involving economic exploitation and patriarchal domination, was rarely just misery; for rural mothers their sorrows were balanced by genuine joys, both of which joined them together in sisterhood.

NOTES

1. For an examination of the "domestic labour debate," see Jean Gardiner, "Women's Domestic Labour," *New Left Review* 89 (January/February 1975), 47-58; Margaret Coulson, Bianka Magas and Hilary Wainwright, "The Housewife and Her Labour under Capitalism — A Critique," *New Left Review* 89 (January/February 1975), 59-71. Also see Margrit Eichler, "Women's Unpaid Labour," *Atlantis* 3, 29, pt. II (Spring 1978), 52-61, and Bonnie Fox, ed., *Hidden in the Household: Women's Domestic Labour under Capitalism* (Toronto: The Women's Press, 1980).
2. For an account of women's history "in the cracks," as Elise Boulding puts it, see her *The Underside of History* (Boulder, Colorado: Westview Press, 1976); see also Gerda Lerner, "Placing Women in History: A 1975 Perspective," in Berenice Carroll, ed., *Liberating Women's History: Theoretical and Critical Essays* (Urbana: University of Illinois Press, 1975), pp. 357-67.
3. Concerning economic and industrial change and its impact on working women, see, in particular, Louise A. Tilly and Joan W. Scott, *Women, Work and Family* (New York: Holt, Rinehart and Winston, 1978). Concerning women's power positions, see Mary Beard, *Woman as Force in History* (New York: The Macmillan Company, 1946) and Michèle Barrett, *Women's Oppression Today* (London: Verso, 1980).
4. Ruth Pierson and Alison Prentice argue that:
   > The critical task of feminism . . . is to examine the structures of women's inequality. When and where has systematic subordination of women existed? What have been the social, economic and political mechanisms of women's oppression? [However], because an exclusive preoccupation with these mechanisms could lead to a distorting and purely negative picture of women as victims, it is equally a task of feminism to reclaim, elucidate and re-evaluate the positive aspects of women's experience in the present and the past.

   See Ruth Pierson and Alison Prentice, "Feminism and the Writing and Teaching of History," *Atlantis* 7, 2 (Spring 1982), 38.
5. For an analysis of giving birth and rearing children, see Adrienne Rich, *Of Woman Born* (New York: W.W. Norton & Company, 1976) and Jessie Bernard, *Women, Wives and Mothers: Values and Options* (Chicago: Aldine Publishing Co., 1975).
6. For a general history of social and economic conditions in other areas of Newfoundland, see James Faris, *Cat Harbour: A Newfoundland Fishing Settlement* (St. John's: Institute of Social and Economic Research, Memorial University, 1966); David Alexander, "Development and Dependence in Newfoundland, 1880-1970," *Acadiensis* 4, 1 (1974). There have been several recent attempts to correct and broaden our understanding of women's lives in Newfoundland, especially Ellen Antler, "Women's Work in Newfoundland Fishing Families," *Atlantis* 2, 2, pt. II (Spring 1977), 106-13. See also Hilda Chalk Murray, *More Than 50%: Woman's Life in a Newfoundland Outport, 1990-1950* (St. John's: Breakwater Books, 1979).
7. See John Berger and Jean Mohr, *Seventh Man* (London: Writers and Readers, 1972); Marilyn Porter, "Worlds Apart: The Class Consciousness of Working Class Women," *Women's Studies International Quarterly* 1, 1 (1978); Carol Stack, *All Our Kin* (New York: Harper and Row, 1974).
8. As Carroll Smith-Rosenberg notes, however, such a division of women and men is hardly atypical:
   > In hundreds of cultures around the world and across time, women have lived in highly sex-segregated communities; spending their time with other women; developing female rituals and networks. . . . This is true among Tiwi aborigines, Victorian ladies, Nazi women, and working-class women in London in the 1960s.

   Carroll Smith-Rosenberg, "Politics and Culture in Women's History," *Feminist Studies* 6, 1 (Spring 1980), 61.
9. At this time, a pulp and paper mill opened in the nearby town of Corner Brook, employing males from the surrounding areas to cut logs to supply the mill. This work was seasonal in nature, generally occurring in the late fall and winter months. The men had to supply their own transportation and tools, and their room, board and doctor bills were subtracted from their earnings. Payment was made by the cord of wood cut (between 1 and 2 dollars per cord was the norm). According to my interviewees, the average worker was lucky to make a dollar a day and often less when cutting in areas of slow tree growth or when the demand for logs was low.
10. *Census of Newfoundland*, 1901, 1911, 1921, 1935. The population of Stephenville showed a gradual increase during this period, from 643 to 926 persons. It was roughly equally divided by sex. Most families owned their own dwellings, which housed on the average six persons. Twice as many females were widowed as males, although the percentage was low for both sexes. While in 1901 approximately one-fifth of the adult population over 20 years remained single, in 1911 and 1921 the figure was

approximately one-third and by 1935 it had risen to nearly fifty per cent. Given that the community during this period was virtually totally Catholic, it is not surprising that divorce and separation appear in the census only once — in 1921 when two such persons were recorded.

11. Stephenville males did not have to confront such a problem, even when they fathered a child with a non-Catholic woman, since they did not reside in the same community as the mother-to-be. In fact, the religious elite and family patriarchs of their own community were often totally unaware of such "illegitimate offspring."

12. In the Newfoundland dialect of the French Shore (west coast of the island), "blackarding" means cursing or using "dirty" words.

13. Between 1900 and 1920, almost two-thirds of the population between the ages of five and fifteen were *not* in school, while after this time up to 1940 the reverse was the norm. See *Census of Newfoundland*, 1901–11, 1921, 1935.

14. Ethnographics of blue-collar marriages highlight similar relationships between spouses as a result of a sharp sexual division of labour. See M. Komarovsky, *Blue Collar Marriage* (New York: Vintage Books, 1962); Lillian Breslow Rubin, *Worlds of Pain: Life in the Working-Class Family* (New York: Basic Books, 1976). For a fictionalized account of the strong negative emotions within a Newfoundland family, see P. Janes, *House of Hate* (Toronto: McClelland and Stewart, 1970).

15. See Barbara Ehrenreich and Deirdre English, *For Her Own Good: 150 Years of the Experts' Advice to Women* (Garden City, New York: Anchor Press/Doubleday, 1978); C. Smith-Rosenberg, "Puberty to Menopause: The Cycle of Femininity in Nineteenth-Century America," *Feminist Studies* 1, 3–4 (Winter/Spring 1973), 58–72.

16. The same kind of non-professional approach was also taken by the midwife and by the village women in regard to other reproductive moments in their lives, such as menstruation and menopause. For a cogent description of the non-medical understanding of menopause in another Newfoundland community, see Dona Lee Davis, *Blood and Nerves: An Ethnographic Focus on Menopause* (St. John's: Memorial University of Newfoundland, Institute of Social and Economic Research, 1983). For a discussion of communal and professional types of control, see T. Johnson, *Professions and Power* (London: Macmillan Press, 1972).

White Female Help and Chinese-Canadian Employers: Race, Class, Gender, and Law in the Case of Yee Clun, 1924

CONSTANCE BACKHOUSE

In early October, 1924, the Regina City Council voted to deny Yee Clun a licence that would have allowed him to hire white female waitresses to work in his restaurant. It was obvious to all observers that the vote was motivated solely on the basis of Yee Clun's Chinese-Canadian racial identity. The Council ruling followed the enactment in 1912 of a Saskatchewan statute, colloquially known as the "white women's labour law," which prohibited the employment of white women by Asian-Canadian males (see Appendix A). Controversy had attended the passage of the statute almost from the outset, and the litigation which ensued from Yee Clun's application continued the tradition in which members of the Asian community challenged the discriminatory measure, attempting to force the Canadian legal system to live up to its rhetorical claims of fairness and equality. The "white women's labour law" and the consequent

SOURCE: Constance Backhouse, "White Female Help and Chinese-Canadian Employers: Race, Class, Gender and Law in the Case of Yee Clun, 1924," *Canadian Ethnic Studies* xxvi, 3 (1994), 34–52.

dispute surrounding Yee Clun's application constitute a critical moment in the history of Canadian race relations, in which law functioned as a crucible for melting and reforging prevailing perspectives on race, gender and class. This provides a marvellous backdrop against which to examine the role of law and legal institutions in the creation of racial stereotypes in Canada.

1. Initial Enactment of the Legislation

In order to appreciate the significance of the Yee Clun case, it is necessary to provide rather extensive detail about the legal context in which the case was heard. First I will discuss the initial enactment of the "white women's labour law"; second, the earliest, precedent-setting prosecutions under the act; and third, the legislative amendments passed to alter the statute in certain important respects. The Saskatchewan Liberal government enacted the anti-Asian statute in March of 1912, in response to an intense lobby campaign from a diverse group of constituents (Backhouse, 1993). Small businessmen and male trade-unionists had banded together to protest what they believed to be unfair competition from immigrant Chinese workers whose long hours and hard work had begun to make inroads into the business profits and wages of white men. Although the legislation did not directly bar Asian entrepreneurs from operating restaurants, laundries or other businesses, it prohibited them from hiring white women, something which was intended to have significant economic consequences. Due to the gendered nature of discriminatory pay scales, female employees earned less than males in the labour force. One group of less expensive female workers — white women — would now be off-limits to Asian employers. It would have been difficult for Asian employers to hire women of colour, for they were few in number in the Canadian west at this time. Restrictive immigration laws and the hostile treatment accorded racially diverse newcomers had combined to retard the arrival of Asian and Black women to the area. In addition, systemic barriers constricted the job market for First Nations' and Métis women who continued to live in the west. The ban on hiring white women meant that Asian employers were limited to hiring more expensive male workers, at considerable jeopardy to their competitive position (Backhouse, 1993: 7-10).

Protestant moral reformers and middle-class white women's groups had joined the small businessmen and trade unionists who campaigned for the legislation. Clergy and lay members of various "social and moral reform" councils aligned themselves with the National Council of Women, the Regina Council of Women, the Woman's Christian Temperance Union and the Y.W.C.A. to support the measure. Concerned about reports (often exaggerated) of Chinese plural marriage and concubinage, they embellished racist stereotypes which depicted Chinese men as addicts of opium and inveterate gamblers. Fearful of the implications of the pronounced sexual imbalance within the Asian-Canadian community, they decried racial intermarriage and fretted over the potential for coercive sexuality that suffused the employment relationship. White women were called into service as the "guardians of the race," a symbol of the most valuable property known to white society, to be protected at all costs from the encroachment of other races (Backhouse, 1993: 10–19). The combined lobby forces of organized labour, business, religion, moral reform, and feminism — all white — crossed class and gender boundaries in their efforts to impede Asian-Canadian men who might have wished to hire white female employees.

Similar coalitions in other provinces resulted in the passage of identical or similar statutes in Manitoba, Ontario and British Columbia over the next seven years (see Appendix B).

2. Early Prosecutions

The first prosecutions under the Saskatchewan act occurred in May, 1912. Quong Wing and Quong Sing, Chinese-Canadian men who operated two restaurants and a rooming house in Moose Jaw, were charged with employing three white women: Nellie Lane and Mabel Hopham as waitresses, and Annie Hartman as a chambermaid. The cases were hotly contested at trial, with defense counsel arguing that it was impossible to know with any certainty what the legislature meant by the term "Chinese." Various witnesses offered suggestions that the designation might relate to birth in China, birth of one's parents in China, physical presence ("standing on Chinese soil"), citizenship, reputation within the community, proficiency in the Chinese language, and visual appearance. The defence lawyer insisted that the absence of any racial definition within the statute rendered it too vague to enforce. He was backed up by the testimony of Nellie Lane, one of the white waitresses, who stubbornly refused to make any racial designation at all of her employer, Quong Wing, insisting instead that "I treat him as myself."

The notion of "race" is not a natural, biological or trans-historical feature, but a sociological classification situated in a particular time and context (Fryer, 1988; Montagu, 1942; Bolaria and Li, 1988; Davis, 1991; Anderson, 1991; Harris, 1993; Pascoe, 1991). As Anderson (1991: 3–12) notes, "racial" differences cannot be conceptualized as absolute because genetic variation is continuous. Racial categories form a continuum of gradual change, not a set of sharply demarcated types; there are no natural or intrinsic isolating mechanisms between people, and given the geographic dispersion of populations over time, the concept of "pure" human "races" is nonsensical. It is almost impossible to define "Chineseness" as a fixed concept, transported without variation across generations and location, to identify equally a Chinese person in Hong Kong, a Chinese person in mainland China, an immigrant of Chinese origin living in Saskatchewan, a second-generation person of Chinese origin living in South Africa, and a third-generation Canadian of Chinese origin living in Vancouver (Anderson, 1991: 16). Anderson (1991: 18) has used the term "racialization," a concept of greater utility, to refer to "the process by which attributes such as skin colour, language, birthplace, and cultural practices are given social significance as markers of distinction."

The prosecutions in Moose Jaw represented a successful effort on the part of the state to "racialize" Quong Wing and Quong Sing, who were pronounced "Chinese" by the presiding police magistrate without serious consideration of any of the defence arguments. Although the witnesses might have had difficulty articulating what they meant by "Chinese," most were adamant in their observations that the two defendants were such. Rooted in this particular historical context, racial distinctions took on a certain "common sense" quality, an unconscious, often visceral reflection of community assumptions. The magistrate felt so certain of his ground that he felt no need to offer any rationale or analysis of the matter whatsoever in his judgment.

Members of the Asian community were outraged over the new enactment and the verdicts. Many of them had put down permanent roots in Saskatchewan, taking out naturalization papers, converting to Christianity and investing considerable labour in developing successful business ventures in the province. They were both insulted and economically disadvantaged by the new law which restricted their opportunity to hire female employees. A number of Chinese merchants organized to raise money to finance appeals. Despite their best efforts, the legislation and the verdicts were upheld by the Supreme Court of Saskatchewan in 1913 and the Supreme Court of Canada in 1914 (Backhouse, 1993).

An equally significant test case was tried in Saskatoon in August, 1912. Charges had been laid against the Asian proprietor of a local restaurant who employed three white waitresses. There was some debate at trial over the racial identity of the defendant, Mr. Yoshi, who had immigrated to Saskatoon from Tokyo with his wife seven months earlier. The Saskatoon *Daily Star* recounted the amusement of observers, who found the entire line of questioning absurd:

> The mirthful side of the case was revealed when Kabayshi, a cook for Yoshi, was in the witness stand. [. . .] Cross-examined by counsel for the defence, Kabayshi found himself in a Chinese puzzle when asked how he knew that the defendant was a Jap. "He is a Jap because I know he is a Jap," said witness. He then said that Yoshi's wife told him he was a Jap. Finally, amidst much laughter, witness said that another reason why he knew the defendant was a Jap was because he had heard him tell the girls in the kitchen at the restaurant that he was. (*Daily Star*, 1912a).

The matter of the "whiteness" of the female employees was settled with less despatch. The question was complicated by the ethnic origins of the women concerned, who were described as "Russian" and "German." Since the statute contained no definition of "white woman," Crown Attorney MacKenzie endeavoured to supply one, arguing that the court should "give these words the meaning which is commonly applied to them; that is to say the females of any of the civilized European nations." Professing great confusion, Saskatoon police magistrate Brown reserved on the issue and adjourned the trial (*Daily Star*, 1912b).

Racial visibility, which is politically and socially constructed, can change dramatically over time. People may be seen as objects of racial difference in one place and time, but find themselves shuffled and re-categorized, or rendered invisible in others. The divisions in Canada between the English and French, the Jews and Gentiles, now viewed as linguistic, religious, or culturally based, have historically been depicted in "racial" terms. The boundaries of racial designation that seem obvious in one setting, become more elusive in another. One witness testifying before the 1902 Canadian Royal Commission on Chinese and Japanese Immigration announced: "I never call Italians white labour." A Saskatchewan historian, writing in 1924, claimed that Slovaks (or Polaks), Germans, Hungarians, Scandinavians, Finns, and Serbians were each discrete groups in a "racial sense" (Backhouse, 1993). In early 20th-century Saskatchewan, residents of English or Scottish origin would have been hard-pressed to identify racially with Russian or German immigrants in matters of employment or social interaction. What was at stake in this trial was whether the latter should be "racialized" as "white" in contra-distinction to Asian immigrants, in the context of the "white women's labour law."

Endeavouring to provide some assistance to the court, one Saskatoon resident wrote the following letter to the editor of the Saskatoon *Daily Star*:

> Sir — Having in mind the adjournment of the [Yoshi] case . . . I take the liberty of offering enlightenment as to the definition of the term "white". . . . Fingier, the famous ethnologist, says that the white races or Caucasians include Europeans, Armenians and Russians, other than Tartars who are included in the Yellow or Mongolian class. The white races as defined above, are opposed to the black or Negroids, the brown Malays, the red or American aborigines, and the yellow or Mongolians, including the Chinese and Japanese.
>
> This information can be readily obtained from any good encyclopaedia, and the writer humbly suggests that some reference be supplied the magistrates in this city, as it is deplorable that such culpable ignorance should delay or prevent the dispensation of justice. [. . .]

> One Who Has Lived in China (*Daily Star*, 1912c).

Whether he was prompted to reach a decision by the letter or not, the police magistrate issued his ruling the next day. He had decided to settle the question "by taking his own opinion," he announced, and the names of the waitresses turned out to be key. The names revealed Russian and German nationality, claimed the magistrate, and although "he did not think it necessary to go into the classification of the white race," he was of the view, by way of "illustration," that "Germans and Russians were members of Caucasian race" (*Daily Star*, 1912d). Although the defendant spoke of an intention to appeal his conviction, no further legal records survive. The ruling would stand as a hallmark of the utility of law in consolidating various strains of national groups into a central "white" Canadian identity, constructed in stark opposition to the "Chinese" other.

3. Legislation Amendments

Within months of the Yoshi trial, pressure from the Japanese government resulted in amendments to the act. An imperial power of relatively greater military and commercial significance than China, Japan was able to convince the legislature to delete all references to "Japanese" or "other Oriental persons" from the text as of 11 January 1913 (see Appendix A; Backhouse, 1993: 20). The Chinese government continued to voice its concern over being singled out in the statute, and as its international stature improved after World War I, the protestations ultimately became more forceful. In 1919, Saskatchewan restructured its "white women's labour law" to disguise the anti-Chinese focus. The new law deleted all explicit reference to Chinese or other Asian employers, leaving it up to individual municipalities to determine whether to license restaurants or laundries in which white women were employed (see Appendix A).

Attorney General Turgeon explained that the bill was necessary because of pressures brought to bear for "the removal of this discrimination on the ground of the racial susceptibility of the Chinese." The change was one of "form" only, he assured his fellow legislators, since the government intended no substantive alteration in policy, but wished to achieve its ends without "singling out" the Chinese (*Morning Leader*, 1919a). George Langley, the member for Redberry and Minister of Municipal Affairs, advised that "it was the hope of those responsible for the bill" that no municipality would "grant the privilege" contained in the new act (*Morning Leader*, 1919b).

4. The Yee Clun Application

It was late in the summer of 1924, when Regina City Council found itself first confronted with an application for a licence from Yee Clun, the proprietor of the Exchange Grill on Rose Street. Yee Clun had been one of the first Chinese residents in the area, settling in Regina around 1901, purchasing property, and opening a restaurant which would achieve a reputation as "one of the best" in the city. One of few Chinese men to live with his wife in Canada, Yee Clun was also widely acknowledged as "the leader of the Chinese community in Regina" (*Morning Leader*,

1924a, 1924b). In 1922, he had been elected president of the Regina branch of the Chinese National Party, a non-sectarian fraternal organization with a membership of one hundred and fifty Chinese residents from the city (*Morning Leader*, 1924c, 1924d).

On 6 August 1924, Yee Clun appeared before City Council, to request a licence allowing him to employ white women in his restaurant and rooming house. According to the newspaper reporters who covered the case with considerable interest, Yee Clun explained that many Chinese restaurateurs required the services of white female employees because "they can't procure boys of their own nationality on account of the tightening up of immigration laws" (*Morning Leader*, 1924a). Asian employers were indeed facing marked labour shortages. Access to Asian women had always been limited, due to the sharp gender disparities in the composition of the immigrant population. With the passage of the federal Chinese Exclusion Act in 1923, a virtual stranglehold had been placed upon all Chinese immigration — male and female — which would last for more than twenty years, dislocating families and further drying up the labour pool for Asian employers (Chinese Immigration Act, 1923; Andracki, 1978; Angus, 1937; Li, 1980; McEvoy, 1982). White men, who were not included in the protective legislation, would have made prohibitively expensive employees within labour-intensive enterprises run on marginal profit (Backhouse, 1993). White women had become by necessity the residual group of potential employees.

Yee Clun obviously realized that his application would be received in the nature of a test case, and he had taken care to obtain prior approval from the city licence inspector and the chief constable of Regina. He also received support from Alderman Cooksley, who pointed out Yee Clun's twenty-three-year residency in the city, and stressed that he "had always borne an exemplary character." Cooksley noted that Chinese cooks and waiters were already employed in most restaurants in Regina, where they worked side by side with white women (*Morning Leader*, 1924a).

Alderman Dawson was less impressed. He declared that "there was all the difference in the world between hiring help and being hired help," and charged that it would be "a dangerous precedent" for council to "permit any Chinese to employ white women." Dawson moved that the matter be tabled until the next meeting to give any organization that might be opposed to the proposal "an opportunity to express their views." In an attempt at compromise, the council voted to give preliminary approval to the application, subject to ratification at the next council meeting (*Morning Leader*, 1924a).

Alderman Dawson's delaying tactics were apparently designed to provide local community groups an opportunity to intervene. Many Saskatchewan whites seem to have been harbouring deep suspicions about the Chinese, a perspective undoubtedly bolstered by persistent press reports of their narcotics and gambling activities. Chinatowns were alleged to harbour murderers, gamblers, and those who would traffic in liquor and the "abomination" of narcotics (*Morning Leader*, 1924e). When Chinese residents were prosecuted for drug offences they found their convictions given great prominence in the newspapers, without any apparent recognition of the racially-selective enforcement which often led to their detection and capture (Anderson, 1991: 101; see, for example, *Morning Leader*, 1924f). The Regina *Morning Leader* was given to recounting "sordid and revolting" stories about young white women who were introduced to Chinese men in Sunday school classes, only to come "under the influence of the stronger personalities" of the would-be converts and find themselves tragically transformed into "drug fiends" (*Morning Leader*, 1922a).

The gender implications of such racist propaganda, with its focus on the dangers inherent in encounters between Asian men and white women, were not lost on the women's organizations of the time. Some of the most prominent of Regina's organized feminists harboured particularly virulent anti-Chinese sentiments. Among the first to debate the matter of Yee Clun's application were the executive members of the Woman's Christian Temperance Union (W.C.T.U.), whose concerns revolved around racial intermarriage. The executive of the three Regina W.C.T.U. branches called a special meeting on 12 August 1924, to discuss the issue. Their various members decried "instances of girls marrying their Chinese employers," insisting that "intermarriage of the races should not be encouraged." There were some voices of dissent, with a few arguing that it was unjust to oppose racial intermarriage when immigration regulations made it virtually impossible for Chinese men to bring Chinese wives and families to Canada. At least one woman spoke out to assert that she would "rather marry some Chinaman than some white men," but the general sentiment of the meeting was that "there was no desire to see the practice common." Barring white women from Chinese employment would deter "close contact" between the races, it was thought. Those who expressed concerns about limiting job opportunities for women were met with brash assurances: "There was other work to be had which was honest and less fraught with danger." At the end of the day, a resolution was passed that "it was not in the best interests of the young womanhood of the city to grant the request of the restaurateur," and a Mrs. Rankin was designated to head the delegation to carry the message to city council (*Morning Leader*, 1924g, 1924h).

The Regina Local Council of Women (L.C.W.) was somewhat slower off the mark, with the press reporting that "efforts to call a meeting" on the matter had "proved abortive owing to the absence of the officers from the city on vacation." The L.C.W. more than made up for its tardiness when the meeting was finally held, with members voting unanimously and without discussion to lobby city council to ensure that no licences be issued to Chinese men (*Morning Leader*, 1924g, 1924i). The

L.C.W. would schedule a special lecture on racial intermarriage for later in October, when Reverend Hugh Dobson would inform them that such liaisons were "growing in number in Canada." Although Reverend Dobson would caution that such trends were "nothing to worry overmuch about," the women of the L.C.W. were clearly of a different view (*Morning Leader*, 1924j).

The Regina L.C.W. comprised a coalition of middle- and upper-middle-class women, first founded in 1895. The group made it its mission to confer frequently with government officials on matters of education, social welfare, and labour law. Well known as the founders of the first hospital in Regina, and the organizers of the Children's Aid Society, reception facilities for immigrant women and a milk fund for needy children, the L.C.W. women also lobbied for industrial homes and separate courts for women, as well as the appointment of women to the hospital and library boards (Griffiths, 1993: 48, 70, 96, 184; Saskatchewan Labour Women's Division, n.d.).

The resolution to oppose Yee Clun's licence seems to have been championed by the L.C.W. president, Mrs. Maude Bunting Stapleford. A native of St. Catharines, Ontario, Mrs. Stapleford had graduated from Victoria College, University of Toronto, with an honours in modern languages in 1907. That same year, she married Dr. E.W. Stapleford, moving with him to Regina when he was appointed president of Regina College. The mother of four children, Mrs. Stapleford was one of the pre-eminent club women in the province. She had served successively as president of the Women's University Club, president of the Women's Educational Club, president of the Regina Local Council of Women, president and convenor of laws and legislation of the Saskatchewan Provincial Court of Women, and was active as well with the W.C.T.U. and the Methodist church (*Pioneers*, 1924: 80; Provincial Council of Women, 1955). When she urged that a "strong contingent" of L.C.W. members attend the city council meeting in support of the anti-Chinese lobby, Maude Bunting Stapleford spoke with the authoritative voice of one of the most active leaders of the Saskatchewan women's community.

In taking this position, Mrs. Stapleford was behaving well within the bounds of accepted convention within the organized women's movement. Prohibitions on the hiring of white women by Asian-Canadian men had been debated and endorsed by branches of the Y.W.C.A., by the Local Council of Women in Saskatoon, and by the federal umbrella group, the National Council of Women. The latter organization would do a full-scale investigation of the problem in the mid-1920s, noting that employment bureaux discouraged white women from taking such positions, advising that social service workers were "emphatic in desiring the bar raised against such employment," and concluding that the legislation was essential for the "protection of white girls" (Saskatchewan Local Council of Women, 1921, 1926–31; National Council of Women of Canada, 1927: 88; 1928: 97; Backhouse, 1993: 11–18).

When City Council reconvened on 19 August 1924, more than twenty representatives of women's organizations were present to speak to Yee Clun's application. Those opposed to granting the licence included several new groups such as the Gleaners Ladies Orange Benevolent Association of Saskatchewan, the Sons of England Benevolent Society, and the Salvation Army Women's Hostel (*Morning Leader*, 1924k). Most vociferous of all were the spokeswomen from the Regina Women's Labour League.

The Regina Women's Labour League (W.L.L.) was one of a number of left-wing organizations established during the second decade of the 20th century to give women more voice within the labour movement. Loosely affiliated with the Communist Party of Canada, the leagues were primarily made up of middle-aged wives of trade-union men and single career women such as teachers and journalists (Roome, 1989; Lindstrom-Best, 1989: 207; Prentice, 1988: 219, 278; Collette, 1990; *Searchlight*, 1920a). Although the W.L.L.'s main focus was the economic exploitation of women, the analysis the organization adopted was suffused with the maternal feminism which marked the beliefs and practices of more middle-class women's organizations. The primary aim of most Women's Labour Leagues was to support the families of striking workers, and their approval of the concept of a "family wage" led them to lobby for prohibitions on the employment of married women and night work for all female employees (Roome, 1989: 98; *Searchlight*, 1920b). Some even advocated compulsory medical examination for "mental defectives" before marriage (*Morning Leader*, 1924i). The Women's Labour Leagues existed on the fringe of the male trade-union world, as the decision of the Trades and Labour Congress of Canada to deny their federation membership in September 1924 so eloquently illustrated (*Labour Gazette*, 1924: 852). But the anti-Asian sentiments that laced the activities of the male labour movement, which had lobbied so successfully for the enactment of the "white women's labour law" in the first place, seem to have infected the perspectives of the left leaning women from the W.L.L. as well.

On behalf of the Regina Women's Labour League, Mrs. W.M. Eddy gave the opening address to City Council on the evening of 19 August 1924, flanked by sister members Mrs. K. Cluff and Mrs. W.J. Vennele. Regina women were proud of the title "Queen City of the West," she announced, and had no wish to see their city be dubbed the "queer city of the west." Employment of white women by Chinese men was "not in the best interests of white women or the community in general," claimed Mrs. Eddy, and if the Chinese required service, "they could get it from men." Regina Mayor Burton began to play devil's advocate at this point, and the following exchange ensued on the floor of the council chamber:

> Mayor Burton: Have you any evidence that conditions are not right in other places where white help is employed by Chinese?
>
> Mrs. Eddy: We are not here as a court of morals, but to voice our protest from the economic standpoint. Judging by the Chinese laundries, conditions are not as good as they might be, and if it is allowed, we feel there will be an influx of an undesirable class of women into the city.
>
> Mayor Burton: Your objection is mainly sentimental?
>
> Mrs. Eddy: Not by any means, Mr. Mayor. We feel this is only the thin edge of the wedge and that if this application is granted, there will be an influx into the city of an undesirable class of girl. Male help might just as well be employed. Employment of white women by Chinese might lead to mesalliances. In a rooming house there are many opportunities of temptation, more perhaps than in a restaurant. (*Morning Leader*, 1924h, 1924k).

There were a few lone voices in support of Yee Clun. Mrs. Reninger and Mrs. Armour, teachers from the Chinese Mission in Regina, declared that they had known Yee Clun as "a very faithful" and "conscientious man," and claimed that "any girl would be safeguarded in his company." Indeed, "more was expected" from the Chinese than "any other nationality," they asserted. The city licence inspector attested that "the women of the city had nothing to fear" from Yee Clun, and promised that he would cancel the licence forthwith if "there was the slightest appearance of wrong" in the future (*Morning Leader*, 1924k).

The most forceful advocate for Yee Clun was the Regina City Solicitor, G.F. Blair. His support came as something of a surprise to the Regina *Morning Leader*, which described Blair's position as a "bombshell." It was Blair's opinion that council was wrong to assume that it could arbitrarily grant or refuse a permit "except on the ground that the applicant is an undesirable character." "Whether the applicant was Chinese, Japanese, Irish or Greek," insisted Blair, "did not enter into the question." Mayor Burton seemed somewhat nonplussed by this legal advice, and asked point blank: "If this man is a respectable citizen with a good character recommended by public officials, then we have no right to refuse his application?" Blair retorted: "You have no right in the world to discriminate." If the council ruled otherwise, cautioned Blair, it "would be inviting litigation." With that last announcement, council adjourned the matter until October (*Morning Leader*, 1924k).

When the debate resumed on 7 October 1924, the Local Council of Women took the rather extraordinary step of bringing along legal counsel to put forth their case. D.J. Thom, who acted as the L.C.W. solicitor, opened by noting that they were not asking the council "to originate any discrimination against the Chinese." The federal government had taken the lead in this, with its long-standing network of legislation which discriminated against the Chinese with respect to immigration, taxation and suffrage (for details, see Backhouse, 1992). Thom's argument was overtly and unabashedly racist. "Chinatowns," he asserted, "have an unsavory moral reputation," and "white girls lose caste when they are employed by Chinese." The authority he cited for this proposition was none other than Mrs. Emily Murphy, Canada's first female magistrate and an internationally renowned feminist. Murphy had published an influential anti-narcotics book in 1922, in which she profiled Chinese involvement in drug trafficking, and warned that entrapment was likely to occur in Chinese "chop-suey houses" and "noodle parlors" (Murphy, 1922). In December, 1922, Emily Murphy had written a letter to the Regina *Morning Leader* about the rapid spread of the narcotics traffic into Saskatchewan, and mentioning the interracial nature of opium and cocaine use amongst both Chinese men and white women (*Morning Leader*, 1922b). Given information such as this, claimed Thom, regardless of Yee Clun's upstanding character references, "the reputation of the city was at stake" (*Morning Leader*, 1924b).

In an attempt to counter the L.C.W., the Chinese residents of Regina had banded together to retain the services of solicitor A.G. MacKinnon. He appeared on their behalf before the council, but he directed his arguments solely to his client's honourable reputation. Yee Clun was "the leader of the Chinese in Regina, a man of the highest type, and a law-abiding citizen," claimed MacKinnon. In this, Yee Clun reflected his people, whom MacKinnon asserted tended to be convicted in the courts at a substantially lower rate than people of other nationalities. MacKinnon took a more cautious approach than City Solicitor Blair. He did not argue that it would be unlawful for city council to base their decision on race, merely advising that "the city was not bound by any law to discriminate" against Yee Clun, and urging them not to do so (*Morning Leader*, 1924b).

The city council was finally called upon to issue its decision in this remarkable case, which had attracted an unprecedented amount of public intervention and media attention. With all but four aldermen opposing the application, council voted to refuse Yee Clun the licence (*Morning Leader*, 1924b). Possibly realizing that he should have taken a more forceful legal position in front of the council, A.G. MacKinnon immediately announced his intention to appeal the ruling to the courts (*Morning Leader*, 1924l).

MacKinnon's resulting action to void the ruling of city council was not heard by the Saskatchewan Court of King's Bench until 14 November 1925. At the trial, the mayor and various aldermen from Regina's council took the stand to give evidence why they had refused Yee Clun a licence. All admitted that the decision was based upon racial grounds. "It was because he employed a number of Chinamen on his premises," they testified, "who, owing to the restrictions placed upon them by our federal laws, have not been permitted to bring their wives into this country." The danger, claimed the witnesses, was that "such employees would constitute a menace to the virtue of the white women if the latter were allowed to work on the same premises with them." Yee Clun himself, they conceded, posed no particular threat, given the presence of his wife in Regina and his "excellent" character. But his Chinese employees were another matter entirely (*Yee Clun*, 1925: 234).

This logic seemed to elude Saskatchewan judge Philip Edward Mackenzie, who appears to have been more inclined to take the position advanced much earlier by Alderman Cooksley. Describing the council's argument as "fallacious," Judge Mackenzie wrote:

> [I]t suggests that if the plaintiff, instead of employing Chinamen, had employed an equal number of white men, matrimonially unattached, no member of the council would have considered it, though the menace to the virtue of the white women might well be greater in the latter event, since there would exist no racial antipathy to be overcome between them and the white men. . . . [I]t is common knowledge that white restaurant keepers do frequently employ Chinamen on their premises, which suggests the seemingly absurd conclusion that when a Chinaman is employed by a Chinaman, however respectable the latter may be, the former is a menace to the white women's virtue, while, when the white man employs him, he is not. (*Yee Clun*, 1925: 235).

Recounting the legislative history of the Saskatchewan statute, Mackenzie noted that the 1919 amendment had removed the racial discrimination contained in the original law. Whether he was unaware of the politicians' real motives, or whether he knew but chose to repudiate them, Mackenzie asserted that the legislative intent was to "abolish the discriminatory principle," and added that "it would be strange if the municipalities . . . could now go on and maintain the discriminatory principle which the Legislature had been at such pains to abolish." Judge Mackenzie ordered the city council to grant Yee Clun his licence forthwith (*Yee Clun*, 1925: 236–7).

With this decision to impose race-neutral enforcement of the statute, Judge Mackenzie's ruling cut against the prevailing political grain in the province. It departed as well from the earlier court conclusions that the "white women's labour law" was constitutional in spite of its discriminatory impact. But Mackenzie's judgment was strangely consistent with a string of earlier decisions from British Columbia judges who had struck down anti-Chinese provincial statutes and municipal by-laws in the late 19th century. John McLaren (1991) has argued that the first British Columbia judges were motivated by a concern to "check the excesses of 'responsible' government," foster the economic contribution of the Chinese, and protect the formalistic "rule of law." Others have argued that where judges ruled against racist legislation, they typically did so not to advance equality, but to protect the interests of white capital. Ryder (1991a; 1991b) and Grove and Lambertson (1994) claim that laws which restricted white employers from access to Asian labourers were frequently offensive to judges, while laws which restricted Asians in their rights to vote or carry on business as entrepreneurs were not. Given the impact of the decision in the Yee Clun matter, which prohibited a municipality from impeding the business interests of a Chinese employer, it would appear that McLaren's rationale may be more applicable in this case.

Whatever Judge Mackenzie's motivations may have been, the Saskatchewan legislators were clearly of the view that municipalities ought not to be stopped from applying the racially neutral language of the 1919 statute in a racially biased manner. Before more than two months had passed, the legislature voted in favour of a further enactment to shield Saskatchewan municipalities from any judicial review of their licensing decisions. The 1926 statute expanded the scope of the law to encompass lodging houses, boarding houses, public hotels and cafes, along with the traditional restaurants and laundries. Curiously, this time the off-limit workers were no longer identified by race; the hiring of any "woman or girl" could subject an employer to municipal scrutiny (see Appendix A). Presumably this, too, was a change in form and not in substance, since access to potential employees who were women of colour remained strictly limited.

Although Yee Clun was not mentioned by name, the new enactment explicitly empowered the city council to revoke the court-ordered licence he had been issued. The statute authorized any municipal council to "revoke a license already granted," and admonished that any such revocation "shall be in its absolute discretion; it shall not be bound to give any reason for such refusal or revocation, and its action shall not be open to question or review by any court" (Appendix A).

It is not clear what action, if any, the Regina City Council actually took to revoke Yee Clun's licence. But records indicate that government officials continued to harass Yee Clun for some time after the litigation was over. Prosecuted and convicted for failing to make proper tax returns for his business, Yee Clun would be forced back to court in 1928, seeking judicial review of this ruling as well. Once again, the Saskatchewan King's Bench overturned the initial decision, finding that the authorities who secured the original conviction had failed to follow proper procedures (*Yee Clun*, 1929).

The "white women's labour law" stayed on the books for years. Manitoba was the first to repeal its act in 1940, with Ontario following in 1947, but British Columbia let the statute stand until 1968. The Saskatchewan statute, veiled in racially neutral language, was not repealed until 1969 (Appendices A and B). Working-class white womanhood had proven to be a stalwart symbol in the forging of political, social and economic hierarchies. The enforcement of the "white women's labour law," in the context of racist attacks on the economic opportunities and social freedoms of Chinese men, illustrates the powerful influence of Canadian law in the shaping of historical and contemporary understandings of race, class and gender.

Appendix A

SASKATCHEWAN "WHITE WOMEN'S LABOUR LAW," 1912

"An Act to Prevent the Employment of Female Labour in Certain Capacities," Statutes of Saskatchewan 1912, chapter 17.

First reading was held 26 February 1912, second reading on 1 March 1912, and debate and third reading on 4 March 1912: *Journals of the Legislative Assembly*, 1912, at 68.

Section 1 provided: No person shall employ in any capacity any white woman or girl or permit any white woman or girl to reside or lodge in or to work in or, save as a *bona fide* customer in a public apartment thereof only, to frequent any restaurant, laundry or other place of business or amusement owned, kept or managed by any Japanese, Chinaman or other Oriental person.

SASKATCHEWAN "WHITE WOMEN'S LABOUR LAW," 1913

"An Act to Amend an Act to Prevent the Employment of Female Labour in Certain Capacities," Statutes of Saskatchewan 1912–13, chapter 13.

Royal assent, 11 January 1913.

This amendment deleted all references to "Japanese" or "other Oriental persons."

SASKATCHEWAN "WHITE WOMEN'S LABOUR LAW," 1919

"An Act to Prevent the Employment of Female Labour in Certain Capacities," Statutes of Saskatchewan 1918–19, chapter 85.

First reading was given on 15 January 1919, second reading on 17 January 1919, and it went through Committee of the Whole and received third reading on 21 January 1919. The bill was granted royal assent on 27 January 1919, to come into effect 1 May 1919.

Section 1 read: No person shall employ any white woman or girl in any capacity requiring her to reside or lodge in or to work in any restaurant or laundry without a special license from the municipality in which such restaurant or laundry is situated, which license the council of every municipality is hereby authorized to grant.

SASKATCHEWAN "WOMEN'S LABOUR LAW," 1926

"An Act Respecting the Employment of Female Labour," Statutes of Saskatchewan 1925–26, chapter 53, sections 3, 4.

First reading was held 11 January 1926, second reading 20 January 1926, third reading 28 January 1926, and royal assent granted 28 January 1926. Annual licences were required, and section 4 stated:

The council may grant or refuse a license under section 3, or revoke a license already granted either under *The Female Employment Act*, chapter 185 of *The Revised Statutes of Saskatchewan, 1920* or under this Act. The grant, refusal or revocation shall be in its absolute discretion; it shall not be bound to give any reason for such refusal or revocation, and its action shall not be open to question or review by any court.

See also Revised Statutes of Saskatchewan 1920, chapter 185; Statutes of Saskatchewan 1925–26, chapter 53, sections 3, 4; Revised Statutes of Saskatchewan 1930, chapter 257; Revised Statutes of Saskatchewan 1940, chapter 309; Revised Statutes of Saskatchewan 1953, chapter 269.

The act was not repealed until passage of the "Labour Standards Act, 1969," Statutes of Saskatchewan 1969, chapter 24, section 73. See also "An Act to Protect Certain Civil Rights," Statutes of Saskatchewan 1947, chapter 35, as amended by "An Act to Amend the Saskatchewan Bill of Rights Act, 1947," Statutes of Saskatchewan 1949, chapter 29, which may have offered an impediment to the continuation of a racially-based application of the labour statute.

Appendix B

MANITOBA

"An Act to Prevent the Employment of Female Labour in Certain Capacities," Statutes of Manitoba 1913, chapter 19.

The Manitoba statute, passed on 15 February 1913, stipulated that it was only to come into force "upon proclamation of the Lieutenant-Governor-in-Council," and all indications are that it was never actually proclaimed. Revised Statutes of Manitoba 1913, Schedules B and C, list the statute as unproclaimed, and there is no reference to it in the listing of proclaimed statutes in the yearly volumes of legislation between 1913 and 1940. With respect to the failure to proclaim, see Walker (1989: 7 and 16). See also Lai (1988: 94) claiming that the failure to proclaim resulted from the opposition mounted by the Chinese communities, who united to fight these statutes throughout the late 1910s.

The 1913 statute was not contained in the Revised Statutes of Manitoba 1913, the Consolidated Statutes of Manitoba 1924, or the Revised Statutes of Manitoba 1940. It was expressly repealed in "An Act to Repeal Certain Enactments Which Have Become Obsolete," Statutes of Manitoba 1940, chapter 35.

ONTARIO

"An Act to Amend the Factory, Shop and Office Building Act," Statutes of Ontario 1914, chapter 40.

Section 2(1), stated: "No Chinese person shall employ in any capacity or have under his direction or control any female white person in any factory, restaurant or laundry." Section 2(2) provided that "subsection 1 shall not come into force until a day to be named by proclamation of the Lieutenant-Governor in Council."

The Toronto *Globe* (1914: 1) noted: "Hon. James Duff's bill to amend factory, shop and office building act passed through Committee and it was agreed to proclaim the clause regarding employment of women by orientals should Privy Council decision in Saskatchewan case [Quong Wing] be favourable." Despite the fact that the courts upheld the Saskatchewan act as constitutional, actual proclamation in Ontario did not occur until 2 November 1920, with the provision to come into effect 1 December 1920. A copy of the unpublished order-in-council is held by the Ontario Cabinet Office; see also *Executive Council Ontario* (1928: 193) which lists the section as proclaimed: "Proclamations: Bringing into force section 31. Factory & Shops Act (re employment of white women by Chinese)." The Ontario Cabinet Order-in-Council proclaiming the section noted that this was "upon the recommendation of the Honourable the Minister of Labour." A lobby from organized labour seems to have been important: see *Labour* (1928) which notes: "Labour has long sought this regulation and it expects the Ontario government to enforce the law."

When the act was reprinted in the Revised Statutes of Ontario 1927, as "The Factory, Shop and Office Building Act," Revised Statutes of Ontario 1927, chapter 275, section 30, the proclamation subsection was no longer included. This seemed to cause some surprise, since few authorities appear to have been aware of the proclamation: see Department of Labour (1928) where various provincial and federal officials, newspapers, and agents of the Chinese consulate state that no proclamation was ever given. Due to strenuous representations from the Chinese Consulate General in Ottawa, the Ontario legislature passed an amendment in 1929, Statutes of Ontario 1929, chapter 72, section 5, reinserting the proclamation requirement, and making it retroactive to 31 December 1927, the day on which the Revised Statutes of 1927 came into force. The provisions were continued in this form by Statutes of Ontario 1932, chapter 35, section 29 and Revised Statutes of Ontario 1937, chapter 194, section 28, unproclaimed; "Table of Public Statutes: Table B, Acts or Parts Thereof Unproclaimed," Statutes of Ontario 1946, at 928. They were repealed in Statutes of Ontario 1947, chapter 102, section 1.

BRITISH COLUMBIA

"An Act to Amend the 'Municipal Act,'" Statutes of British Columbia 1919, chapter 63, section 13.

Patterned after the Saskatchewan act subsequent to its deletion of the clause relating to "Japanese or other Oriental persons," the statute prohibited the employment of "any white woman or girl" in restaurants, laundries, places of business or amusement owned, kept, or managed by "any Chinese person."

In 1923, British Columbia replaced the racially specific terminology with more neutral language, deleting all reference to Chinese employers and leaving it to the discretion of police officials whether white women were to be allowed to work in restaurants and laundries: "An Act for the Protection of Women and Girls in Certain Cases," Statutes of British Columbia 1923, chapter 76. The 1923 act, for the first time, also included "Indian" women and girls as "protected" categories of employees: section 3.

See also Revised Statutes of British Columbia 1924, chapter 275; Revised Statutes of British Columbia 1936, chapter 309; Revised Statutes of British Columbia 1948, chapter 366; Revised Statutes of British Columbia 1960, chapter 410; repealed by "An Act to Amend and Repeal Certain Provisions of the Statute Law," Statutes of British Columbia 1968, chapter 53, section 29.

I have as yet been unable to locate any similar American statutes although Mears (1927: 306-7) notes that the Oregon legislature considered prohibiting the employment of white females in restaurants or grills "owned or operated by Orientals." A bill to this effect, introduced in 1919 by W.G. Lynn, was defeated in the legislature due to the combined forces of Chinese hotel and restaurant proprietors and the press. Concerns about constitutionality were apparently a factor.

REFERENCES

I am greatly indebted to the following for their advice and assistance: Ken Leyton-Brown, Bruce Ryder, John R. Wunder, Elizabeth Higginbotham, Marianne Welch, Georgina Taylor, and Peter S. Li. Kristen Clark, Anna Feltracco, Alexandra Hartmann, Kevin Misak, Bev Jacobs, John Hill, Linda Charlton and Signa Daum Shanks provided remarkably helpful research assistance on various aspects of this study. Funding from the Law Foundation of Ontario and the Social Sciences and Humanities Research Council of Canada is gratefully acknowledged.

Anderson, Kay J. 1991. *Vancouver's Chinatown: Racial Discourse in Canada, 1875–1980*. Kingston and Montreal: McGill-Queen's University Press.

Andracki, Stanislaw. 1978. *Immigration of Orientals into Canada, with Special Reference to Chinese*. New York: Arno Press.

Angus, Henry F. 1937. "Canadian Immigration: The Law and Its Administration," in Norman Mac-Kenzie, ed., *The Legal Status of Aliens in Pacific Countries*. London: Oxford University Press, 58–75.

Backhouse, Constance. 1992. "Gretta Wong Grant: Canada's First Chinese-Canadian Female Lawyer." Unpublished manuscript.

———. 1993. "The White Women's Labour Laws: Anti-Chinese Racism in Early 20th-Century Canada." Unpublished manuscript.

Bolaria, B. Singh, and Peter S. Li. 1988. *Racial Oppression in Canada*, 2nd edition. Toronto: Garamond Press.

Chinese Immigration Act. 1923. Statutes of Canada, chapter 38.

Collette, Christine. 1990. "For Labour and for Women: The Women's Labour League, 1906–18." *Labour/Le Travail* 26: 230.

Daily Star. 1912a. "What Is White Woman? Definition Puzzled Magistrate and Lawyers in Case of Orientals in Court," Saskatoon, p. 3, August 14, 1912.

———. 1912b. "Counsel for Defence in Orientals Case Questions Authority of Provincial Legislature to Pass Act," Saskatoon, p. 3, August 15, 1912.

———. 1912c. "Letters to the Editor: The White Help Question," Saskatoon, p. 3, August 19, 1912.

————. 1912d. "Judge Finds Law Valid in Oriental Help Case and Gives Decision against Chinamen and Jap Which Counsel Announces He Will Appeal," Saskatoon, p. 3, August 21, 1912.

Davis, F. James. 1991. *Who Is Black? One Nation's Definition*. University Park, Pennsylvania: Pennsylvania State University Press.

Department of Labour. 1928. "Canadian Laws Governing the Employment of Women," an undated memorandum appended to correspondence dated 28 September 1928, Public Archives of Canada, RG 25, Vol. 1524, file 867, "Employment of Women by Chinese in Canada," correspondence and memoranda.

Executive Council Ontario. 1923. *Consolidated Indexes to Orders in Council Formerly Titled the Journals of Executive Council Ontario*, Consolidated Index No. 6, p. 193, 1 Nov. 1919 to 15 July 1923.

Fryer, Peter. 1988. *Black People in the British Empire: An Introduction*. London: Pluto Press.

Globe. 1914. p. 1, April 8, 1914.

Griffiths, N.E.S. 1993. *The Splendid Vision: Centennial History of the National Council of Women of Canada, 1893–1993*. Ottawa: Carleton University Press.

Grove, Alan, and Ross Lambertson. 1994. "Pawns of the Powerful: The Politics of Litigation in the Union Colliery Case [*Union Colliery v Bryden* case]." *B.C. Studies*, 103: 3–31.

Harris, Cheryl I. 1993. "Whiteness as Property." *Harvard Law Review* 106: 1707.

Labour. 1928. "Law Prohibits Working of White Girls with Chinese," September 8, 1928.

Labour Gazette. 1924. "Resolution Refused to Women's Labour Leagues," p. 852, October, 1924.

Lai, Chuenyan David. 1988. *Chinatowns: Towns within Cities in Canada*. Vancouver: UBC Press.

Li, Peter S. 1980. "Immigration Laws and Family Patterns: Some Demographic Changes among Chinese Families in Canada, 1885–1971." *Canadian Ethnic Studies* 12: 58–73.

Lindstrom-Best, Varpu. 1989. "Finnish Socialist Women in Canada, 1890–1930," in Linda Kealey and Joan Sangster, eds., *Beyond the Vote: Canadian Women and Politics*. Toronto: University of Toronto Press: 196–216.

McEvoy, F.J. 1982. "A Symbol of Racial Discrimination: The Chinese Immigration Act and Canada's Relations with China, 1942–1947." *Canadian Ethnic Studies* 14: 24–42.

McLaren, John. 1991. "The Early British Columbia Supreme Court and the 'Chinese Question': Echoes of the Rule of Law," in Dale Gibson and W. Wesley Pue, eds., *Glimpses of Canadian Legal History*. Winnipeg: Legal Research Institute, University of Manitoba: 111–53.

Mears, Eliot Grinnell. 1927. *Resident Orientals on the American Pacific Coast: Their Legal and Economic Status*. New York: Institute of Pacific Relations.

Montagu, M.F. Ashley. 1942. *Man's Most Dangerous Myth: The Fallacy of Race*. New York: Columbia University Press.

Morning Leader. 1919a. "Municipalities Will Decide on Employment," Regina, January 18, 1919.

————. 1919b. "Employment Agencies to Vanish Now," Regina, January 22, 1919.

————. 1922a. "Spreading the Drug Habit," Regina, p. 4, April 7, 1922.

————. 1922b. "The Narcotics Traffic," Regina, p. 16, December 30, 1922.

————. 1924a. "Allow White Female Help in Chinese Restaurants," Regina, p. 1, August 8, 1924.

————. 1924b. "Council Turns Down Request of Yee Klung," Regina, p. 3, October 8, 1924.

————. 1924c. "Chinese National Party Reorganizes," Regina, p. 9, December 29, 1924.

————. 1924d. "Chinese Society to Move Quarters," Regina, p. 17, December 16, 1924.

————. 1924e. "Chinatown at Vancouver to Get Cleanup," Regina, p. 1, October 3, 1924.

————. 1924f. "Seek to Have Drug Peddler Deported Soon," Regina, p. 9, November 6, 1924.

————. 1924g. "Protest White Girl Help in Chinese Restaurants," Regina, p. 1, August 12, 1924.

————. 1924h. "Women Object to Yee Clun's Application," Regina, p. 1, August 13, 1924.

————. 1924i. "City Women Oppose White Female Help for Chinese," Regina, p. 9, September 24, 1924.

————. 1924j. "Is Not Alarmed at Inter-Marriages," Regina, p. 2, October 29, 1924.

————. 1924k. "May Not Treat Chinese Apart from Others," Regina, p. 1, August 20, 1924.

————. 1924l. "Court to Decide Chinese Rights," Regina, p. 9, October 22, 1924.

Murphy, Emily. 1922. *The Black Candle*. Toronto: Thomas Allen.

National Council of Women of Canada. 1927. "Report of the Committee on Trades and Professions for Women," *The Yearbook of the National Council of Women of Canada*. Ottawa: NCWC.

————. 1928. "Report on Trades and Professions," *The Yearbook of the National Council of Women of Canada*. Ottawa: NCWC.

Pascoe, Peggy. 1991. "Race, Gender, and Intercultural Relations: The Case of Interracial Marriage." *Frontiers* (Summer) 12: 5–18.

Pioneers and Prominent People of Saskatchewan. 1924. Toronto: Ryerson Press.

Prentice, Alison, et al. 1988. *Canadian Women: A History*. Toronto: Harcourt Brace Jovanovich.

Provincial Council of Women of Saskatchewan. 1955. *History of the Provincial Council of Women of Saskatchewan, 1919–1954*. Regina: Commercial Printers Ltd.

Roome, Patricia. 1989. "Amelia Turner and Calgary Labour Women, 1919–1935," in Linda Kealey and Joan Sangster, eds., *Beyond the Vote: Canadian Women and Politics*. Toronto: University of Toronto Press: 89–117.

Ryder, Bruce. 1991a. "Racism and the Constitution: The Constitutional Fate of British Columbia Anti-Asian Immigration Legislation, 1884–1909." *Osgoode Hall Law Journal* 29: 619.

————. 1991b. "Racism and the Constitution: The Constitutional Fate of British Columbia Anti-

Asian Legislation, 1872-1922." Unpublished manuscript. Copy on file at Osgoode Hall Law School Law Library.

Saskatchewan Labour Women's Division. n.d. *Saskatchewan Women, 1905-1980*. n.p.

Saskatchewan Local Council of Women. 1921. *Minute Books* Saskatchewan Archives Board (S.A.B.), S-B82 I.3. March 21, 1921, p. 3-4; April 14, 1921, p. 1; April 28, 1921, p. 1-2.

———. 1926-31. *Minute Books* S.A.B., B-82 I.4. April 3, 1926, p. 24; December 18, 1927, p. 81; April 25, 1930, p. 191; May 27, 1930, p. 193.

Searchlight. 1920a. "Women's Labor League Active," Calgary, p. 4, January 23, 1920.

———. 1920b. "Work of the Women's Labor League in Calgary," Calgary, p. 3, September 4, 1920.

Walker, James W. St. G. 1989. "'Race' Policy in Canada: A Retrospective," in O.P. Dwivedi et al., *Canada 2000: Race Relations and Public Policy*. Guelph: University of Guelph: 1.

Yee Clun, 1925. *Yee Clun v. City of Regina*, Saskatchewan Law Reports, vol. 20, p. 232.

———. 1928. *Rex ex rel Eley* v. *Yee Clun and Yee Low*, Saskatchewan Law Reports, vol. 23, p. 170.

Populism and Gender: The UFA and Social Credit Experiences

ALVIN FINKEL

"The state," writes sociologist R.W. Connell, "is not inherently patriarchal, but is historically constructed as patriarchal in a political process whose outcome is open." He adds:

> The process of bureaucratization is central here, as concentrated bureaucracy is a tight fusion of the structure of power and the division of labour. Together with selective recruitment and promotion, these structures form an integrated mechanism of gender relations that results in the exclusion of women from positions of authority and the subordination of the areas of work in which most women are concentrated.[1]

But, one can ask, what happens in a situation where most women are concentrated in the same areas of work as men — for example, on the farm — and what happens when the process of bureaucratization is challenged by a mass political movement which accedes to state power? Do gender roles within populist movements and gender attitudes on the part of populist governments reflect greater equality than do conventional, bureaucratized political movements and governments? In seeking answers to these questions, this paper examines the experience of the United Farmers of Alberta (UFA) and Social Credit in Alberta, assessing the extent to which patriarchal norms were affected by mass-based movements in western Canada in the first half of the twentieth century.

Populism, broadly defined, refers to grass-roots political movements that call for popular control over "a network of concentrated political and/or economic institutions allegedly wielding unwarranted power."[2] Usually the expression of political protest by farmers and lower-middle-class elements, such movements depend for their success on the mass participation of ordinary citizens rather than the finances and organ-

SOURCE: Alvin Finkel, "Populism and Gender: The UFA and Social Credit Experiences," *Journal of Canadian Studies* 27, 4 (Winter 1992-93), 76-97. Reprinted with permission.

izational power of small elites. The ideology of populists is fairly un-
sophisticated and fluid relative to that of Marxist socialists or of
conservatives.

Indeed, some political scientists distinguish between right-wing populists whose critiques of existing economic relations are narrow (focusing
on supposed bankers' conspiracies or on Jews), and left-wing populists
whose critiques are closer to those of socialists (focusing on monopoly
capitalists as the people's oppressors). In practice, populist movements
can be seen as existing on a continuum between right and left; the place
of individual movements on this continuum shifts over time. On the political spectrum, the United Farmers of Alberta leaned to the left and
Social Credit leaned to the right, though the UFA always represented
a variety of farmers' perspectives, and Social Credit, until the early 1940s,
reflected the views of an assortment of individuals united only by their
common belief that monetary reform had to be a crucial part of any
attempt to reform the economic system.[3] The focus in this essay is upon
women's self-activity within these organizations and the extent to which
women attempted to use these movements to promote gender-based goals.
The paper examines the limitations placed on any project that opposed
patriarchy by both the overarching ideological perspectives and the structures of such male-dominated populist movements.

The UFA was formed in 1909 by a merger of two existing farm
organizations for the purpose of promoting cooperation among farmers
so "that the moral, intellectual and financial status of the farmer may
be improved thereby." Its goals included lobbying governments to win
legislation favourable to farmers and promoting cooperative efforts to reduce production costs and increase prices for farm products.[4]

When it was formed the UFA was open only to men, but in 1912
the annual convention moved unanimously that:

> Whereas the women in the rural homes of Alberta are sharing equally with the
> men the burden of the struggle for better conditions and equal rights, and
> Whereas we believe that under the law our women should enjoy equal privileges
> with the men
> Therefore be it resolved that we believe that the wives and daughters of our
> farmers should organize locally and provincially along the lines of the UFA for
> the improvement of rural conditions, morally, intellectually and socially and we
> would urge all our members to assist in every way the development of such
> an organization.[5]

The sentiments of this resolution support once-popular and now generally
disproved notions that the Prairie farm frontier experience greatly weakened patriarchy.[6] It was argued that men working side-by-side with
women to build farms and rural communities did not assert their traditional gender privileges. In practice, while women did much of the
same work as men, they also did the usual housework tasks alone and
held the same inferior legal status as elsewhere in the country. The resolution demonstrates only that, rhetorically, farm men were willing to

admit women's crucial role in the Prairie rural economy. In fact, the record of the UFA as a movement and as a government in recognizing women's equality with men was less than impressive.

While the UFA amended its constitution in 1913 to allow women to join, it waited three years after passing the resolution before it attempted to organize a Women's Auxiliary. In 1915, a year after the Saskatchewan Grain Growers Association created a Women's Auxiliary, a meeting called by the UFA was held in McDougall Church in Edmonton. Addressed by Nellie McClung, among others, the majority of the 58 delegates from existing rural women's clubs decided to affiliate with the UFA.[7] But the leaders of the new Auxiliary were not content with the status the UFA men had conferred upon them and they lobbied for the creation of an autonomous women's branch. "A great deal of insistence and patience on the part of our Auxiliary officials and members" led to the creation of the United Farm Women of Alberta (UFWA) in 1916.[8] This campaign for autonomy was greatly aided by the democratic goals characterizing the UFA political organization. Since the UFA's major objective was to increase farmer involvement in politics rather than to achieve a set political program, it had a stake in encouraging democratic practices that would bring more farm people into the movement. While some male members regarded a separate women's organization as a threat to the unity of the male-dominated farm movement, the consensus was that openness of the movement to differing perspectives was a strength rather than a weakness.

Key figures in the push for autonomy for the women's section were the organizers of a Country Women's Club in Alix, Alberta, in 1914. Leona Barritt, the president of that club, and Irene Parlby, its secretary, were elected delegates to the McDougall Church meeting (though illness prevented Parlby from attending) and they became activists in the new auxiliary group. Well-educated, articulate farm women, both were proponents of equal legal rights for women and men.[9] Parlby became the first president of the UFWA and Barritt its first secretary. At that time, the UFWA counted only 745 of the 15,217 members of the UFA, though some women in areas where a UFWA club had not formed had become members of men's locals.[10]

The constitution of the UFA, as amended in 1917, indicated that while the UFWA was to be autonomous from the UFA — it would organize its own locals and hold its own convention — such autonomy was limited. While its convention could occur either simultaneously with the men's convention or at another time (in practice, they were always held simultaneously), and could "discuss any matter not inconsistent with the objects of the Association as set forth in Section 3 hereof . . . it shall not be competent for them [the UFWA] to petition Parliament or the Legislature on any matter independently of the Central."[11] The UFWA was also given responsibility for the youth section of the UFA. Just as women took responsibility for children at home, the UFA expected them to look after children in the organization. A similar practice of placing the youth group under women's supervision was followed in other provinces' farm organizations.[12]

By failing to provide a salary for the president of the UFWA, the UFA demonstrated its belief that the women's organization was not equal to the men's. While the UFA president received a salary of $4,000 per year in 1925, a princely salary by the standards of the time, the UFWA president received only reimbursement for her expenses up to $500 per annum ($250 less than the UFA president's expense account). The UFWA was, however, assigned a secretary. She was paid less than the UFA secretary and was expected to help the latter with her work. An attempt in 1923 by the UFWA executive to boost their secretary's salary was rejected by the UFA executive as outside the powers of the UFWA.[13]

The UFWA leaders joined with other women's movements in the province in the campaign for female suffrage. They also became the leaders of the movement for dower rights. Elizabeth B. Mitchell made the following observation in 1915:

> The special trouble which has turned the prairie women's mind to politics is connected with the land. The woman so obviously shares with her husband in making the "improved farm" out of the 160 acres of original prairie that it is felt to be an injustice that this product of their joint labour becomes the sole property of the man and that he can, if he chooses, sell it and break up the home without his wife's consent. Cases where this has been done have raised a great deal of feeling, among men as well as women, and a Bill was actually introduced lately into the Saskatchewan Legislature making the wife's signature as well as the husband's necessary for the validity of any deed, whether of mortgage or sale, affecting the farm.[14]

Convinced of the need for improved legislation regarding women's property rights and of women's mission to improve the sparse social and educational infrastructure of the western provinces, the UFWA pioneers worked tirelessly to encourage women to form UFWA locals — five women in a district was the minimum number required — and to join in campaigns for women's rights and improved community services. Parlby, president from 1916 to 1920, and her successor, Marion Sears, criss-crossed the province, shrugging off complaints from male chauvinists who argued that they must be neglecting their family duties. Using the kind of language with which social feminists often justified women's entry into the public sphere, Sears told the men at the UFA convention in 1924: "Word was sent to me last summer that instead of organizing locals, I should be home darning socks. Had we concerned ourselves with the forces that determine the price of socks, we might not have found as much public mending to be done."[15]

The double burden of home and farm work allowed fewer women than men to participate in such organizations. Among farm women who did have some time to participate, more preferred to be involved in the rural Women's Institutes which emphasized the "social importance of women's work in the home" than in the UFWA, which was committed, however modestly, to "reforming the economic and legal framework of society."[16] Nonetheless, by 1921, the UFWA counted 4,536 members in 309 locals. While only a small proportion of the 37,721 members in the total UFA organization, it may have included more committed members than the male section of the organization. As UFA membership declined during the 1920s, women's membership as a percentage of the total increased. In 1925, for example, the UFWA accounted for 2,172 of 11,079 memberships, or over 20 percent of the total, whereas four years earlier the women's section enrolled only 12 percent of the total.[17] The UFWA leaders were consciously feminist but no overarching ideology held their movement together. Naomi Black indicates that feminists may be divided into two groups, equity feminists and social feminists, the former stressing equal rights for the sexes, the latter "the movement of women into the public sphere in the extension of their domestic role."[18] While earlier writers tended to treat the equity feminists as the more radical of the two groups,[19] because the social feminists emphasized women's mothering role, more recent analysts, including Black, have reversed this judgment. Social feminists, who stress women's differences from men, are, they note, in a better position than equity feminists to press the goal common to all feminists of "freedom from gender-based control."[20] Their calls for women's control over an expanded domestic sphere have often posed greater challenges to patriarchy than equal rights demands that the social realm created by patriarchy allow women to staff positions and enjoy privileges once reserved for men.

Like other women's movements closely allied with a male-dominated movement, the UFWA often subordinated its feminism to the interests of that movement.[21] But the feminist goals which had led to the creation of a separate wing for women in the farmers' political movement were never completely lost. These "first wave feminists," while at times interested in winning equal rights for women with men, were also interested in social feminist causes such as reproductive rights and the women's peace movement. Even the movement for expanded dower rights, though sometimes phrased in equity feminist language, was often presented in social feminist terms: the farm home, the locus of the farm woman's responsibility and authority, should not be put in jeopardy via male control over property.

UFWA feminism was conditioned by a strong class consciousness that led its leaders to be suspicious of middle-class organizations like the National Council of Women of Canada.[22] Leona Barritt, the cofounder and first provincial secretary of the UFWA, was not atypical in drawing a line between class-based organizations of women and other women's organizations. Addressing the Social Services Council in Edmonton in 1920, she observed:

> Along with Labor the farmer has been the underdog. He has been the victim of exploitation by elevator companies, packers, machine companies, wholesalers

and retailers, and he has been discriminated against by legislation directed by
the big interests. I would rather belong to the United Farm Women of Alberta
or its sister organizations in other provinces, or to a labor union than to any
other women's organization in Canada.[23]

The "equal rights" campaign of the UFWA had several thrusts. At
the federal level, these included calls that "the inequalities in our laws
as between men and women in the matters of divorce, domicile, homestead
and personal naturalization be equalized."[24] Provincially, the push was
for joint custody of children after a divorce and for a tough dower law
that would require a spouse's signature before any financial transaction
involving farmland or a home could be concluded.

The federal campaign bore little immediate fruit. But the UFWA
was able to convince the UFA men to support women's rights to take
up a homestead, a right denied under the Dominion Lands Act of 1872.
When control over public lands passed from the federal to the provincial
government in 1930, the provincial government passed legislation to give
both sexes equal rights to apply for a homestead.[25]

The UFA government, however, proved unwilling to respond to the
other equal rights demands of the UFWA women, despite the constant
prodding of Irene Parlby, elected to the Legislature in 1921 and a cabinet
minister — always without portfolio — throughout the 14 years of UFA
administration. The campaign for improved dower rights proved largely
futile. A Dower Act, passed in 1917 by the provincial Liberal government
in response to a concerted campaign by a variety of women's organizations, provided limited protection for farm wives. Husbands could no
longer sell the family home without their wives' consent; however, consent
was not required for the husband to sell or dispose of furniture, farm
equipment, livestock, seed or indeed any item other than the family home.
The law also provided no recognition of the contribution to the family
farm of wives who separated from or divorced their husbands and were
forced to leave the farm. Court decisions weakened still further the limited
property rights that the Act provided for women.[26]

Support within the UFWA to change this state of affairs was strong
but by no means unanimous. A strongly-worded resolution in 1920 by
the Calgary local of the organization to make wives co-equals with their
husbands in the disposition of all farm assets occasioned a long debate
after which approval in principle was passed; later, however, it was rescinded in favour of tabling the motion. It took two more years for the
UFWA convention to adopt a position in favour of "the principle of
community [of] interest of husband and wife with regard to property
acquired as a result of their common labour and effort . . . [to apply]
in coverture, in separation and at the death of either [spouse]." Nevertheless, to mollify men who might regard such a principle as a challenge
to their rule in the household, the UFWA advocated, in contravention
of this principle, that "the husband shall have the management of the
community property but shall be restricted as to selling or mortgaging

real estate, or leasing it for more than one year, without the concurrence of his wife."[27]

Discussions between the UFWA and Irene Parlby led to the drafting of a Bill based on the above two conflicting principles. Parlby brought it forward as a private member's Bill in 1925, but it received only one reading and was not debated in the Legislature.[28] She simply lacked the support to proceed and agreed to let the Bill be studied by a committee. That committee had a feminist majority and the UFWA leaders were confident that it would recommend some version of Parlby's original Bill.[29] But, in 1928, when the committee reported, it was clear that a committee majority had retreated from support of the "community of property" idea. While the hostility of the male legislators to the concept was no doubt the real cause of this retreat, the committee also mentioned that many women's groups and individuals had protested against clauses in the Parlby Bill that made men the heads of the community of property and that removed women's control over income earned from property acquired before the marriage.[30] Indeed, they claimed that the Bill in its original form was unacceptable to most Alberta women for these reasons.

The committee's recommendations included a call "that the principle of matrimonial equality should be embodied in any legislation passed for the recognition of the economic value of a wife's contribution."[31] A spouse would be expected to provide the marriage partner with the "necessaries" of food, clothing, shelter and medical care. The wife's consent would be required for a chattel mortgage, and in the case of a forced sale of a homestead under mortgage, the wife would receive half of any surplus remaining. Finally, the province was asked to appoint qualified mediators who could attempt to head off divorces and legal separations.

As Catherine Cavanaugh observes: "In the end, feminists' arguments based on home protection superseded the married woman's rights as a result of her individual contribution to the family's assets arising from her work in the home and in the fields." As a result, "while many women could support the concept of partnership in principle, most stopped short of an equal division of the 'husband's' property. What they sought was equal status, not economic equality."[32] The degree of women's opposition expressed before Parlby's committee to men being placed in charge of a community of property suggests that many women didn't stop short of this concept. Clearly, however, Parlby realized that the time was not right for a bold assertion of farm women's economic equality. The leaders of the UFWA reluctantly accepted this verdict and the modest resolutions of the Parlby committee.[33] During its remaining seven years in office, however, the UFA government took no notice of these recommendations. The battle for women's equal claim on the farms and farm homes had been lost and the UFWA simply dropped the issue. This was ironic in view of its centrality in spurring the formation of the UFWA, but in keeping with the general desire of the farm feminists to maintain class and organizational unity even at the expense of the fight for gender parity. Indeed, Elizabeth Wyman, the long-time and generally tough-minded convener of the UFWA's legal committee, asked vapidly at the end of a summary of the Parlby committee's report,

> But are we not, to some degree at least, asking our Government to do something for us that we do not always do for ourselves, that is recognize within ourselves the full value and importance of the work we are doing as homemakers. . . . When we as homemakers realize that the bringing of little children into this world and rearing them, and making the folks around us happy and comfortable is just as divine; and assume the dignity of our high calling, then would not this attitude of mind bring about an outer manifestation that would be recognized in all places?[34]

The glorification of motherhood in her statement was not atypical of UFWA discourse, but the implied rejection of legislation as a necessary protector for women certainly was. Wyman was merely announcing that the UFWA would not prove sore losers in an area where they had confidently expected to make gains. By the end of the 1920s, however, few would be able to express with confidence the traditional claim that Prairie farm men were more egalitarian than men generally. Marion Sears expressed this traditional view in her presidential address in 1923:

> Since women have been admitted to the practice of law, property rights for women and children have been investigated. There is very much [a] need for more just laws in regard to these rights. In older settled regions the fight is long and bitter. We do not look for a similar experience with farmer governments. Pioneering together on the prairie gives men and women a mutual regard for the rights and privileges of one another.[35]

The campaign for women's property rights was not the only feminist campaign undertaken by the UFWA. From an early date, farm women became active in the campaign for legalizing contraceptive devices and spending government money to disseminate information about contraception. As with property rights, the issue touched a raw nerve with conservative women within the UFWA. Their 1923 convention received three resolutions in favour and two against the idea of legalizing birth control information and devices.[36] Susan Gunn, the organization's president from 1925 to 1929, recalled the debate of a pro-contraception motion many years later:

> Those opposed, and there were many, were vociferous in their demands that it be voted down. With flushed cheeks and heated voices they proclaimed that such a suggestion was irreligious, immoral, decadent and shameful. . . . Those for the motion with great restraint opposed these arguments as being an untold blessing to mothers who would thereby space the birth of their children. Every child would be a loved and wanted baby. The health of the mother would be safeguarded and instead of a new baby every year regardless of every consideration of the mother's health and vitality, or the number of little children requiring her care. . . . The discussion raged for 2½ hours. At the end the resolution was passed by a substantial majority.[37]

But that majority was unable to persuade the UFA government to act. "This subject was so far ahead of its time it didn't have a hope," wrote Gunn. Nonetheless, the birth control advocates persevered and began to demand that governments not only legalize birth control information but disseminate it as well. In 1933, the UFWA convention agreed to petition the Department of Health to establish birth control classes "for those married women who desire information on family limitation and for those whose health and welfare it is deemed advisable."[38] Government representatives encouraged the women to believe they were working with other provinces to enact legislation in this area but in fact no legislation was forthcoming. The UFWA also lobbied for sex education as part of the hygiene course in the schools.[39]

Interestingly, the UFWA was more progressive than the women's section of the Dominion Labour Party on the birth control issue and perhaps more surprisingly on the issue of employment for married women. A resolution passed by a UFWA local against the employment of married women was set aside by the provincial board because "Mrs. Ross [vice-president and later president of the UFWA] thought as we had been fighting for equal rights for women, that it would be going against this principle to pass this resolution."[40] The socialist Women's Labour League in the cities felt no such inclination to recognize married women's labour rights. Meanwhile, within the Dominion Labour Party, Amelia Turner, a Labour school trustee who was also a bridge to the UFA through her work as assistant editor of *The UFA*, the organization's official organ, fought unsuccessfully to win support for married women's rights to seek employment and to limit births. Whereas most of the younger generation tacitly shared Turner's view that married women's rights included the opportunity to employment, equal pay, and access to birth control, older leaders like Marion Carson strongly opposed the idea of married women working and refused to place birth control on the agenda of the DLP Women's Section meetings.[41]

Although the UFWA activists were to be disappointed in the UFA's reluctance to improve the legal status of women or to legalize and disseminate birth control information, they had important victories in their campaigns for improved community services. Both before and during the UFA's tenure in office, UFWA campaigns had been a key factor in the establishment of municipal hospitals, travelling health clinics, and a system of public health nurses. Such campaigns had also been conducted by rural women in the other Prairie provinces and in the western United States, incited in part by the high rates of maternal and infant mortality in the countryside relative to the cities. Many of the UFWA's ideas for a more practical, less drill-oriented school curriculum, were adopted by the Department of Education.[42] Writing of the western states Joan Jenson notes, "organizing around education . . . could also give women an expanded role as local community leaders."[43] So, the politically active farm women, who emphasized the rudimentary character of health, educational and recreational services in their communities, took pride in the legislative achievements won by their lobbying. It was hoped that, by improving rural services, bright young people would be encouraged to remain on the farms.[44] Indeed, the fear that the farming areas might become the homes of only the stupid and lazy fit in with the UFWA's fairly unpleasant fixation (a concern evident in its first two presidents) upon the need for sterilization of the "mentally unfit." While the UFWA activists were not the only farm leaders who advocated "culling the stocks" — Irene Parlby's phrase for practices of institutionalizing and sterilizing "mental defectives" — they counted the Sterilization Act passed by the UFA among their achievements.[45]

Apart from its social service achievements, the UFWA took pride in its creation of an egg and poultry pool, on the model of the wheat pool established by the UFA.[46] It was the cooperative ethic that underlay both UFA and UFWA activities. For the UFWA militants, the cooperatives they established and the improvements their efforts brought to community facilities compensated for their inability to force male legislators to grant greater legal and sexual freedom to women. Jill Vickers observes: "First-wave feminism worked with a theory of politics that placed a high value on citizenship but in which claims to it rested as often on perceived obligations as on abstract theories of rights. In their actions, many of these feminists clearly believed in a norm of service that involved the Christian duty to help others and in the concepts of self-help and community building."[47]

In the Depression years, however, when the communities they had helped to build were threatened by economic collapse, the UFWA activists embraced a socialist philosophy as an extension of the cooperative philosophy of their organization. This paralleled a similar development in the UFA organization, one which created a distance between the organization and the government bearing the same name.[48] The embrace of socialism did not lead UFWA women to extend their implied critique of patriarchy in the earlier years; indeed it seemed to mute that critique. The UFA and UFWA conventions in 1933 supported the new Cooperative Commonwealth Federation (CCF) and adopted a long, radical "declaration of ultimate objectives" that made no mention whatsoever of gender roles or women's rights.[49] An attempt by a UFWA local in 1934 to have the organization press for equal land property rights between spouses was stopped cold by the UFWA board.[50] Nonetheless, the UFWA women, like CCF women generally, "quite honestly saw their politics as militant and unique."[51] Eleanore Price, the UFWA president, forcefully summed up the women's case for socialism in her 1934 address to the UFA convention:

> What would a Co-Operative Commonwealth bring to the farm women of the prairies? The possession of a home and if public utilities were operated for public benefit instead of private profit, the electric power would be there to make the

tasks of the farm easier and give to us a little of that long sought leisure. There would be a planned economy which would take our surplus products for fair compensation and we could purchase warm clothing, house furnishings and other things so necessary for comfort. We would have socialized health services. Women wouldn't be using their husbands' glasses because they could not afford a pair of their own and needed medical services would no longer be neglected for with socialization of finance there would be the necessary purchasing power. In a planned social order there would be a place for the youth of today. There would be freedom, social justice and a foreign policy designed to obtain international economic co-operation and to promote disarmament and peace.[52]

Indeed, the promotion of peace became a particular focus of the UFWA, as it often has been for women's organizations. Taken up by the UFWA in the 1920s, the peace issue became even more dominant in board and convention discussions in the 1930s. There were calls for "a new idea of patriotism" in which "national greatness" would be seen "not in terms of territory and wealth but rather in terms of fair dealing and international good will." The Department of Education was called upon to promote peace studies in the curriculum.[53] Women's roles as peacemakers in the home and community were alluded to as fitting them particularly for a campaign to stop men from using warfare to settle arguments. Eleanore Price's 1934 address indicates the militant tone of the farm women's anti-war campaign:

Are we women going to let nationalism, greed, suspicion, fear, warmindedness, the lust for territory or markets, stampede us into another war? We stand appalled at the mad race in armaments. The world spends annually four and a half billion dollars in military establishments. This misappropriation of wealth upon implements of human destruction at a time when poverty, hunger and destitution are rampant throughout the whole world, shows the degree of insanity reached by present-day civilization. We women have learned the fallacy of war to end war; of war to make the world safe for democracy.[54]

The focus on the socialization of wealth as the key to women's emancipation and the promotion of peace caused the UFWA to place more attention on federal politics. The increasing conservatism of the UFA government made the provincial picture, in any case, look bleak. It also opened the door to a new populist organization, Social Credit, which rallied behind its banner individuals of a variety of reformist beliefs who accepted William Aberhart's call for monetary reform at the provincial level. While supporting monetary reform, UFWA activists rejected the notion that it was a panacea; they were politically sophisticated enough to reject the majority view among Albertan voters that the province could constitutionally legislate in the areas of banking and currency.[55]

The Social Credit movement in Alberta had its origins in the monetary reform propaganda that leading UFA figures undertook in the 1920s. Influenced by Major C.H. Douglas, the British engineer who propounded social credit ideas, as well as by American monetary reformers, leading UFA figures such as MPs William Irvine and Henry Spencer spread the notion that farmers, workers, and small businessmen were the victims of an unjust financial system. The banks, it was argued, restricted credit to maintain their own power and left ordinary citizens unable to qualify for needed loans except at exorbitant interest rates. By the early 1930s, Irvine and Spencer, never one-issue reformers, had subsumed their critique of financial institutions within a broader socialist framework attacking concentrated private wealth.[56] But William Aberhart, a Calgary high-school principal and popular evangelical radio preacher, became a convert to social credit ideas in 1932, and the combination of his charisma and the existing popularity of monetary reform ideas produced a new mass movement in Alberta. Initially a series of study clubs, Social Credit moved into the political arena in 1935 and swept out of office a UFA administration discredited by scandals and by its timidity in dealing with Depression hardships.[57]

Before 1937, women had no separate Social Credit organization though there was an assortment of women's clubs. Any 10 people in a constituency could form a club and some women had chosen to avoid mixed-sex groups. Women, however, played a major role in popularizing Social Credit and silencing its critics. Several of the party's main organizers in the early years were women like Edith Gostick, Edith Rogers and Mrs. D.L. McCulloch.[58] In the rural areas, according to one Social Credit cabinet minister, women used threats of consumer boycotts to intimidate businessmen who were hostile to Social Credit from voicing their criticisms publicly.[59] If Aberhart had been able to deliver on his pie-in-the-sky promise of a social dividend for all adult Albertans of $25 per month, women would have been among the major gainers. Few married women, in particular, enjoyed incomes separate from their husbands' control. Aberhart promised them an independent income. His *Social Credit Manual* justified his plan to grant income to individuals rather than families. Posing the rhetorical question: "Would basic dividends make the women too independent?" Aberhart replied: "Economic security is the right of every citizen, male or female. Women were never intended to be slaves, but helpmates. There would, no doubt, be more wholesome marriages consummated. They would not need to marry for a meal ticket."[60]

Apart from promising all women separate incomes, Social Credit made some attempts to appeal directly to working women. The *Social Credit Chronicle*, the organ of the movement in its early days, included testimony from "working girls" about the need for social credit for women. One department store worker, who earned "six bucks a week" wrote that she was "the main support of two young brothers, one baby sister, a somewhat sickly mother and a real strong healthy father who has been on relief for the past three years." Having described a workplace of heartless, lecherous managers, she concluded:

> . . . the ordinary average "Woiking Goil" don't know much about Social Credit, they are so darned tired when they get home at night after a long day in the store they have not got enough ambition to read about Social Credit or even

hear about it. But they do say this if it's going to better conditions and remove the everlasting fear of being "fired" and then following the firing, a future of "God knows what," they are one hundred per cent behind it.[61]

Inside Social Credit some women played leading roles, but most were relegated to bake sales, teas and making tissue flowers for floats in parades. While this paralleled women's fate in the traditional political parties, it was a departure from the roles women had assumed in the UFWA. The UFA was an organization more committed to farmers' participation in politics than it was to a specific set of policies; this gave women in the organization considerable room to manoeuvre. Social Credit, by contrast, was committed to a specific economic program, convinced that a huge conspiracy existed to prevent the implementation of that program. As a result the party was less willing to accept dissent and gave party women less room to manoeuvre than their UFWA counterparts enjoyed. Not surprisingly, then, when the Social Credit Women's Auxiliaries (SCWA) were formed in 1937, the question of their autonomy from the "male-stream" Social Credit organizations along the lines of the UFWA-UFA relationship never arose. Edith Rogers, by then an MLA, was the major force behind the Auxiliaries and her concern was neither with women's issues nor with organizing bake sales. Instead, she was devoted to the notion of political education of women and believed that more would feel comfortable learning Social Credit principles inside an exclusively women's group than in mixed-sex party clubs. The Auxiliaries' attitude to male leadership at the outset is reflected in its official history: "Mr. Aberhart's encouragement and help were important in getting the groups off to a good start. The women never forgot his patience in teaching them the principles of Social Credit. Some said he spoiled them! But Mr. Aberhart said 'I am always glad to help anyone who wants to learn.' "[62]

This was, no doubt, disingenuous. Women such as Edith Gostick and Edith Rogers were far more familiar with Social Credit ideology than the charismatic Premier, whose ignorance of its fine points was often commented upon by Major Douglas. Yet the women's leaders chose to act as if they learned all they knew from the "great man." There were nonetheless glimmers of feminist thinking in the movement. Cornelia Wood, a long-time Social Credit MLA and Mayor of Stony Plain, was a social feminist. Equity feminism was demonstrated at early Auxiliaries conventions that called for minimum wages for domestic servants and for female police magistrates.[63] But, as Veronica Strong-Boag observes, "Social Credit's ambivalence about women's place in the modern world can be seen by contrasting a 1938 resolution, arguing that married working women with employable husbands be taxed at a rate of fifty percent to support unemployed single women, with the tabling in 1939 of a reso-lution that asked that women be placed on an equal basis before the law."[64]

The early Auxiliaries joined the UFWA in making the promotion of peace a special concern. The two populist women's organizations shared with Aberhart the view that wars resulted from the machinations of financiers and industrialists. At the December 1939 Women's Auxiliaries convention, the Social Credit women passed the following resolution, which subsequently was accepted by the party convention in January 1940:

> [The SCWA] are opposed to profiteering out of the sale of armaments and also opposed to profiteering out of the sale of foodstuffs, clothing and the necessities of life. . . . Be it therefore resolved that conscription of capital and finance must precede any other form of conscription that the exigencies of war may make.[65]

This would prove the last radical resolution from a provincial SCWA convention. In its early days, the Social Credit movement had attracted a wide variety of social reformers. But the conservatism of the Aberhart government on issues such as Workmen's Compensation and the treatment of individuals and families on relief disillusioned many women and men who had been attracted to its egalitarian rhetoric before the election of 1935.[66] Party membership declined from a peak of 41,000 in 1937 to fewer than 4,000 in 1943. While it rebounded to almost 8,000 for the election of 1944, Social Credit was never again a grass-roots party.[67] The populist anti-bankers rhetoric soon became of secondary importance as the party leaders assumed the mantle of militant cold warriors.[68] Many reform-minded women felt compelled to leave the party.

Among those attracted to Social Credit's early radicalism and disillusioned by its post-1940 conservatism was Leona Barritt, whose role in shaping the early UFWA was second only to that of Irene Parlby. Barritt was a socialist when she wrote her history of the UFWA in 1934 and had not, apparently, changed her views when she was invited by Aberhart to serve as the only female member of his five-person panel which acted as the final decision-maker in the selection of constituency candidates in 1935.[69] Alienated by the right-wing turn of Social Credit ideology in the early 1940s, however, Barritt drifted away from the party and back to the UFWA. Ethel Baker, secretary-treasurer of the Social Credit League's Calgary constituency association in the late 1930s, was a like-minded drop-out. A department store clerk of many years, she was in charge of Social Credit's municipal campaign in 1938. As a result of Aberhart's denouncing of the Calgarians' platform of public spending on housing, slum clearance, and support for trade unionism, Baker left Social Credit; she became, instead, an activist in a left-wing municipal coalition in Calgary and a campaigner for a national public pension scheme that eliminated the means test.

The most public defection of a prominent woman activist was that of Edith Rogers, who had campaigned across the province for the League in the years leading up to the 1935 election. Rewarded with a legislative nomination, she was one of two women elected as a Social Crediter in 1935. A former school teacher and bank clerk who had developed a mistrust of financial institutions, Rogers was committed to a program of state-financed medical care and to providing citizens with the financial means necessary to abolish poverty. After her defeat in 1940, she became disillusioned with the party's rightward drift and had joined the CCF before the 1944 election. Serving in executive positions for the CCF and unsuccessfully seeking election to the Legislature under its banner, she later enjoyed a long and distinguished career as an Edmonton school trustee. While none of these three defectors from Social Credit emphasized gender issues within the party, all three, by focusing on social welfare issues such as housing, were particularly attentive to women's concerns. Those women who remained in Social Credit were increasingly, like the men in the organization, lower middle-class, religious, small-town dwellers whose politics were conservative on issues other than monetary reform.[70]

The Women's Auxiliaries fell in line with the new party conservatism after 1940. They became a model organization of right-wing women who unquestioningly accepted stereotyped views of women's roles and indeed defended them with vigour. During this period, the UFWA continued, though with thinned ranks, to pursue an agenda that combined concerns for the welfare of all agriculturists as a class, with the particular concerns of farm women. In the latter case, a campaign for legalized midwifery was significant.[71] The Auxiliaries maintained their interest in world peace although they accepted implicitly Canada's role as a combatant in World War II. The focus during and after the war was on the creation of a durable peace, not through force of arms, but through international cooperation and understanding.[72]

By contrast, the SCWA pursued an agenda dependent on government priorities. The pledge which members were required to make, beginning in 1941, left little room for organizing around gender-specific issues or indeed any issue outside the government's agenda. The pledge read: "I believe that Social Credit is the only solution for our present economic problems, and I am determined to stand shoulder to shoulder with our Government in this great fight for Financial Freedom. I will also endeavour to cooperate in every way possible with the members of this Auxiliary, in any work they shall deem necessary to promote this cause." Mrs. Muriel Jury, SCWA president in 1943, told the organization's sixth annual convention that the Auxiliaries' chief responsibilities were "to assist the [Social Credit] league, to assist the Government in carrying out their mandate which was given them in 1935, and renewed in 1940."[73] A major preoccupation for the SCWA women during the war was sending parcels of knitted articles, canned goods and confections to the men and women in the Canadian armed forces overseas. The war over, the Auxiliaries set up a Goodwill Depot, the rationale for which was described as follows:

> The Social Credit Woman's Auxiliary, recognizing the need for a centre in which the hundreds of young Edmonton women, particularly young war brides who are now starting out to establish homes, can meet, talk over their problems with

some older and more experienced women and receive practical assistance in the
business of homemaking and family care, have undertaken to establish here, in
downtown Edmonton, just such a centre, and the name by which it will be known
is "The Goodwill Depot."[74]

In general, the Auxiliaries in the 1940s and 1950s concentrated on promoting the Social Credit provincial regime and extolling the role of mothers. The leadership undertaken by wives of cabinet ministers and MLAs
in the SCWA made unlikely any criticism of government policies affecting
women. At the same time, the Social Credit government followed a variety
of policies that created hardships for single mothers, mothers in common-
law relationships, widows, and women with husbands requiring hospital
care or who required hospitalization themselves. These women received
little attention from the Auxiliaries, though in the 1960s Social Credit
women did develop a more positive attitude to women in the labour force.
They did not, however, campaign for legislative changes to accommodate
women workers.[75]

Despite Aberhart's embrace of the notion of an independent income
for women, neither his government nor those led by his Social Credit
successors, Ernest Manning and Harry Strom, proved willing to enhance
the legal or economic position of women. Indeed, the government maintained a policy of rejecting married female applicants for positions, in
total disregard of a 1930 UFA law called the Sex Disqualification Removal
Act.[76] The women's extension program, begun by the government in 1938,
concentrated on women as consumers and mothers and made no attempt
to augment rural women's opportunities for off-farm work. Neither wom-
en's legal rights nor daycare ever became priority items for Social Credit
governments.[77] Accordingly, the Social Credit governments failed to aid
women who wished to earn independent incomes in the paid workforce.
Nor did they provide them with a direct source of independent income.
Not until 1957 and 1958 did the government issue social dividends and
these were for only $20.00 a *year*, a far cry from the $25.00 per *month*
promised in 1935.[78] Generally, Social Credit extolled individualism and
opposed welfarist policies. Its "co-insurance" hospitals policy required
hospitalized people to pay a daily fee, a fee which broke many families
and left many widows with debts for their husbands' health care long
after their deaths. While seven women were elected under the Social
Credit banner between 1936 and 1971, no more than three served at
any one time and only one, Ethel Wilson, achieved cabinet rank. That
did not occur until the 1960s, and like Irene Parlby before her, Wilson
was made minister without portfolio. While several of the female members
of the Social Credit caucus fought for greater consideration for widows
and wives of injured workers, only Wilson, a former union official, appears
to have been a defender of women in the labour force. Her efforts
were responsible for the establishment of the Women's Bureau in 1966
though it proved to be a toothless body, only able to do research on
women's legal and economic position.[79] In fairness, women's gains

in other provinces during the period of Social Credit tenure were also slight. In this regard, Social Credit's conservative attitude to gender-related issues reflected the prevalent patriarchal views of the period.

Overall, then, the achievements of Alberta's two populist governments in expanding the legal and economic opportunities and protections for women were slight. Still, the experience of the women's organizations, or at least the UFWA, need not be seen in a negative light. The UFWA's feminism, while it did not represent a consistent body of theory, embraced both social feminist and equity feminist perspectives. While the UFWA was ultimately disappointed in its campaigns for women's rights, it could point to many improvements in health and social services as its contribution to the betterment of the lives of women and men in Alberta communities. The legacy of its campaigns for women's property rights, legalization of birth control, legalized midwifery, sex education in the schools, etc., was not forgotten; all these campaigns were taken up by feminists a generation later.

The radical differences between the UFWA and the SCWA ought not to be understated. Reflecting the cooperative, left-leaning philosophy of the UFA, the farm women exhibited a collective consciousness on the levels of both gender and class. They sought improvements in women's legal position (via changes to patriarchal laws) and in women's economic position, by means of legal and economic changes. Their socialism and peace activism in the 1930s, while it at times jeopardized their gender consciousness, did reflect their consistent stand in favour of collectivism as opposed to individualism. While the early Social Credit movement was initially too hazy in its ideological leanings to represent a dramatic contrast to the UFA and the UFWA, it had, by 1940, developed an increasingly individualist philosophy hostile to collectivist notions. It was within this framework that the SCWA developed, eventually proving itself unable to confront the problems faced by women either as women or as members of certain social classes.

In conclusion, then, left-wing and right-wing populist organizations in Alberta spawned completely different women's organizations in ideological terms. While the former made at least a gentle attempt to weaken patriarchy, the latter pointedly defended it. It might be argued as well that the UFWA could have fought better for its aims had it not been forced to mute its activities so as not to offend the patriarchal UFA. But it is unlikely, given the level of farm women's consciousness at the time, that a feminist organization of farm women outside of the framework of the male-controlled parties could have achieved the acceptance of an important body of women. As it was, the farm women's movement was able to take advantage of the general interest in political life created by the populist UFA to organize women into a class-and-gender-conscious organization which politicized a large section of a generation of Alberta women. The movement was not, however, able significantly to weaken patriarchy, which has simply been assumed by male populist movements to be eternal and not open to question.

NOTES

The author wishes to thank participants at the Gender, Family and the West conference in Banff, February 1990, for useful suggestions in revising this paper, particularly Georgina Taylor, Randi Warne and Patricia Roome.

1. R.W. Connell, *Gender and Power: Society, the Person and Sexual Politics* (Stanford: Stanford University Press, 1987), 129.
2. John Richards, "Populism: A Qualified Defence," *Studies in Political Economy* 5 (Spring 1981), 6. The best overall survey of the thinking of populists on the Canadian Prairies is David Laycock, *Populism and Democratic Thought in the Canadian Prairies* (Toronto: University of Toronto Press, 1990).
3. On the politics of the United Farmers of Alberta, see C.B. Macpherson, *Democracy in Alberta: Social Credit and the Party System* (Toronto: University of Toronto Press, 1962); W.K. Rolph, *Henry Wise Wood of Alberta* (Toronto: University of Toronto Press, 1950); Carl F. Betke, "Farm Politics in an Urban Age: The Decline of the United Farmers of Alberta after 1921," in *Essays in Western History*, ed. Lewis H. Thomas (Edmonton: University of Alberta, 1976), 175–89; and David Laycock, *Populism and Democratic Thought*. On the politics of Social Credit see Alvin Finkel, *The Social Credit Phenomenon in Alberta* (Toronto: University of Toronto Press, 1989); Macpherson, *Democracy in Alberta*; David R. Elliott and Iris Miller, *Bible Bill: A Biography of William Aberhart* (Edmonton: Reidmore, 1987).
4. Provincial Archives of Alberta (PAA), *Winifred Ross Papers*, Box 1, File 9, "Constitution and By-Laws" of United Farmers of Alberta, 1917.
5. PAA, *Susan Gunn File*, Gunn to Leslie Robinson, n.d. Gunn's letter indicates that she quotes this resolution from the 1912 UFA convention report.
6. On equality between men and women, see Elizabeth B. Mitchell, *In Western Canada before the War: Impressions of Early Twentieth Century Prairie Communities* (1915; Saskatoon: Western Producer Prairie Books, 1981), 46, 48. Catherine Cleverdon's classic work on the winning of the suffrage, *The Women Suffrage Movement in Canada* (Toronto: University of Toronto Press, 1950), 46, also asserted that the frontier levelled gender differences. The limits to equality for farm women are discussed in, among others, Veronica Strong-Boag, "Pulling in Double Harness or Hauling a Double Load: Women, Work and Feminism on the Canadian Prairie," *Journal of Canadian Studies* 21, 3 (Fall 1986), 32–52; Linda Rasmussen et al., *A Harvest Yet to Reap: A History of Prairie Women* (Toronto: Women's Press, 1976); Catherine Anne Cavanaugh, "The Women's Movement in Alberta as Seen through the Campaign for Dower Rights, 1909–1928," M.A. thesis, University of Alberta, 1986.
7. Origins of the UFWA are discussed in Susan Jackel, "Introduction" to Elizabeth B. Mitchell, *In Western Canada before the War*, xxiii. There are several histories of the UFWA, two in pamphlet form produced by the UFWA itself. These are Mrs. R.W. Barritt, *History of United Farm Women* (1934); and Eva Carter, *Thirty Years of Progress: History of United Farm Women of Alberta* (1944). The Barritt history can be found in PAA, *T.R. McCloy Papers*, Item 2; copies of Carter are included in PAA, *Winifred Ross Papers*, Box 2, File 31. See also Leslie Robinson, "Agrarian Reformers: Women and the Farm Movement in Alberta, 1909–1925," M.A. thesis, University of Calgary, 1979.
8. Eva Carter, *Thirty Years*, 22–23.
9. PAA, *Winifred Ross Papers*, Box 1, File 10, "United Farmers of Alberta Annual Report," 1917, presents biographies of the leading UFWA figures, including Parlby and Barritt.
10. PAA, *Winifred Ross Papers*, Box 3, File 53, "Minutes of the 15th Annual Convention of the United Farmers of Alberta," 1923. Also PAA, *Winifred Ross Papers*, Box 1, File 10, "United Farmers of Alberta, Annual Report and Year Book," 1920, Report of Anna Archibald, secretary of UFWA.
11. "Constitution and By-laws of UFA."
12. Women's supervision of the youth group in the United Farm Women of Ontario is discussed critically in Pauline Rankin, "The Politicization of Ontario Farm Women," in *Beyond the Vote: Canadian Women and Politics*, ed. Linda Kealey and Joan Sangster (Toronto: University of Toronto Press, 1989), 317.
13. UFA salaries are indicated in PAA, *Winifred Ross Papers*, Box 1, File 1, "Minutes of UFA Board Meeting," 24 January 1925. The thwarted UFWA attempt to increase its secretary's salary is reported in *Ross Papers*, Box 1, File 1, "Minutes of UFWA Executive Meeting," 13–16 February 1923.
14. Elizabeth B. Mitchell, *In Western Canada before the War*, 56.
15. "Minutes of the 15th Annual Convention of the United Farmers of Alberta," 1923.
16. See Strong-Boag, "Pulling in Double Harness"; Marilyn Barber, "The Servant Problem in Manitoba, 1896–1930," in *First Days, Fighting Days: Women in Manitoba*, ed. Mary Kinnear (Regina: Canadian Plains Research Center, 1987), 100–19; and Rasmussen et al., *A Harvest Yet to Reap*, 122.
17. "Minutes of the 15th Annual Convention of the United Farmers of Alberta," 1923; PAA, *Ross*

Papers, Box 2, File 15, "Minutes of the 18th Annual Convention of the United Farmers of Alberta," 1926.

18. Naomi Black, *Social Feminism* (Ithaca, New York: Cornell University Press, 1989), 26.

19. Typified by Aileen Kraditor, *The Ideas of the Woman Suffrage Movement, 1890–1920* (New York: W.W. Norton, 1970).

20. Black, *Social Feminism*, 23. It should be noted that social feminists often used maternalist rhetoric to achieve an equal rights agenda. Ernest Forbes makes this point strongly in his review essay "The Ideas of Carol Bacchi and the Suffragists of Halifax: A Review Essay on *Liberation Deferred? The Ideas of the English Canadian Suffragists, 1877–1918*," *Atlantis* 10, 2 (Spring 1985), 119–26. See also Dolores Hayden, *The Grand Domestic Revolution: A History of Feminist Designs for American Homes, Neighbourhoods and Cities* (Cambridge, Mass.: MIT Press, 1981).

21. Naomi Black, writing about the Women's Co-operative Guild of England, for example, observes: "The facilitating effect of cooperative beliefs and structures is in conflict, as I show, with the WCG's feminism and its desire for independent action. Loyalty to party and movement finally destroyed feminism in the organization." Black, *Social Feminism*, 5.

22. The UFWA was only one of several western and rural women's groups that withdrew from the NCWC in the early 1920s. "By World War I western farm women also were increasingly unhappy with the Council's urban, pro-business and central Canadian sympathies." Veronica Strong-Boag, *The New Day Recalled: The Lives of Girls and Women in English Canada, 1919–1939* (Toronto: Copp Clark Pitman, 1988), 192.

23. *Edmonton Free Press*, 10 January 1920, 8. The problems faced by women in attempting to effect feminist changes from within mixed-sex political organizations are discussed in Sylvia Bashevkin, "Independence vs. Partnership: Dilemmas in the Political History of Women in English Canada," in *Rethinking Canada: The Promise of Women's History*, ed. Veronica Strong-Boag and Anita Clair Fellman (Toronto: Copp Clark Pitman, 1986), 246–75. The co-existence of equal rights and maternal-feminist perspectives among "first wave" feminists generally is explored in Deborah Gorham, "The Canadian Suffragists," in *Women in the Canadian Mosaic*, ed. Gwen Matheson (Toronto: Peter Martin Associates, 1976), 24–26; and Forbes, "The Ideas of Carol Bacchi."

24. PAA, *Ross Papers*, Box 2, File 19, "Minutes of the 11th Annual Convention of the United Farm Women of Alberta," 1925.

25. Susan Jackel, "Introduction" to Georgina Binnie-Clark, *Wheat and Woman* (Toronto: University of Toronto Press, 1979), xxi–vi.

26. Cavanaugh, "The Women's Movement," 58, 60–64.

27. *Ibid.*, 71; PAA, *Ross Papers*, Box 2, File 19, "Minutes of the 8th Annual Convention of the United Farm Women of Alberta," 1922.

28. *Journals of the Legislative Assembly of the Province of Alberta*, 1925, 90; Index, 7.

29. The seven members of the committee included three of the women who had brought the famous Persons case to the Judicial Committee of the Privy Council of the United Kingdom, Parlby, Emily Murphy and Henrietta Muir Edwards, the legislative convener of the UFWA, a feminist female lawyer, a male lawyer who had drawn up the Parlby bill, and the French consul in Calgary. PAA, *Ross Papers*, Box 2, File 19, "Reports and Addresses Delivered to the 15th Annual Convention, United Farm Women of Alberta," 1929; Legislative Report, Mrs. Wyman. See also PAA, *Ross Papers*, Box 2, File 19, "Reports and Addresses Delivered to the 12th Annual Convention, United Farm Women of Alberta," 1926. The UFWA secretary's report, indicating the introduction of the Community of Property Bill in the Legislature, commented: "Unquestionably as a result of this general thought, a law will be evolved protecting the wife's interest in the home she has helped to found."

30. "Reports and Addresses Delivered to the 15th Annual Convention, UFWA," 1929: Legislative Report, Mrs. Wyman.

31. *Ibid.*

32. Cavanaugh, "The Women's Movement," 92.

33. "Reports and Addresses Delivered to the 15th Annual Convention, UFWA," 1929: Legislative Report, Mrs. Wyman.

34. *Ibid.*

35. PAA, *Ross Papers*, Box 2, File 15, "Reports and Addresses Delivered to the 9th Annual Convention, UFWA," 1923.

36. PAA, *Ross Papers*, Box 2, File 15, "Minutes of the UFWA Convention," 1923.

37. PAA, *Susan Gunn File*, Gunn to Robinson, 31 October 1977.

38. PAA, *Ross Papers*, Box 2, File 19, "Minutes of the 19th Annual Convention of the UFWA," 1933.

39. PAA, *Ross Papers*, Box 2, File 19, "Minutes of the 20th Annual Convention of the UFWA," 1934; and PAA, *Ross Papers*, Box 1, File 5, "Minutes of the Board Meeting of the UFWA," 25 January 1932.

40. PAA, *Ross Papers*, Box 1, File 5, "Minutes of the Board Meeting of the UFWA," 24 January 1931.

41. Patricia Roome, "Amelia Turner and Calgary Labour Women 1919–1935," in *Beyond the Vote*, 99.

42. Barritt, *History of United Farm Women*, 6. Barritt notes Irene Parlby's central role in the campaigns for reforms in the area of health. On the western states, see Joan M. Jenson, *With These Hands: Women Working on the Land* (Old Westbury, New York: Feminist Press, 1981), 144–56.

43. Jenson, *With These Hands*, 149.

44. Leona Barritt noted that when she was secretary of UFWA, the organization had circularized its locals regarding recreation facilities and the quality of community life in rural Alberta. The only recreation available generally was dancing and pool-playing. Gymnastics, organized sports, and Boy Scouts were generally absent. Church services were often limited. Barritt believed that a wider range of activities and services were needed "to create a wholesome rural life." *Edmonton Free Press*, 10 January 1920, 8. Irene Parlby, extolling the cooperative movement as the means of improving rural life before the 1927 UFWA convention, regretted that the cleverest boys and girls were leaving the farm for good. "Reports and Addresses Delivered to the 13th Annual UFWA Convention," 1927.

45. Barritt, *History of United Farm Women*, 7; PAA, *Department of Public Health Records*, "Mental Deficiency: An Address Delivered by the Honourable Mrs. Parlby before the UFWA," January 1924.

46. PAA, *Ross Papers*, Box 2, File 19, "Reports and Addresses Delivered to the 12th Annual UFWA Convention," 1926, President's Report: Mrs. R.B. Gunn.

47. Jill Vickers, "Feminist Approaches to Women in Politics," in *Beyond the Vote*, 20.

48. Finkel, *Social Credit Phenomenon*, 21–22.

49. PAA, *Ross Papers*, Box 2, File 15, "Minutes of the 25th Annual Convention of the United Farmers of Alberta," 1933.

50. PAA, *Ross Papers*, Box 1, File 5, "Minutes of the UFWA Board Meeting," 24 January 1934.

51. Joan Sangster, "The Role of Women in the Early CCF," in *Beyond the Vote*, 135. On women in the CCF, see also Joan Sangster, *Dreams of Equality: Women on the Canadian Left 1920–1950* (Toronto: McClelland and Stewart, 1989); and Georgina M. Taylor, "The Women . . . Shall Help to Lead the Way: Saskatchewan CCF-NDP Women Candidates in Provincial and Federal Elections, 1934–1965," in *"Building the Cooperative Common-wealth": Essays on the Democratic Socialist Tradition in Canada*, ed. J. William Brennan (Regina: Canadian Plains Research Center, 1985), 141–60.

52. PAA, *Ross Papers*, Box 2, File 15, "Minutes of 26th Annual UFA Convention, 1934": Address of UFWA President (Eleanore Price) to UFA Convention.

53. PAA, *Ross Papers*, Box 2, File 20, "Minutes of 21st Annual UFWA Convention," 1935. On women's role in Canadian peace movements generally, see Barbara Roberts, "Women's Peace Activism in Canada," in *Beyond the Vote*, 276–308.

54. "Minutes of 26th Annual UFA Convention, 1934": Address of UFWA President (Eleanore Price) to UFA Convention.

55. The 1935 UFWA Convention rejected Aberhart's version of social credit by 90 to 3, an even greater margin than the rejection provided by the UFA Convention. "Minutes of the 27th Annual UFA Convention, 1935," and "Minutes of the 21st Annual UFWA Convention, 1935."

56. Finkel, *Social Credit Phenomenon*, 22–23. On Irvine see Anthony Mardiros, *William Irvine: The Life of a Prairie Radical* (Toronto: Lorimer, 1979).

57. Social Credit won 56 of 63 seats in the 1935 provincial election while the UFA failed to elect a single member.

58. Larry Hannant, "The Calgary Working Class and the Social Credit Movement in Alberta, 1932–35," *Labour/Le Travail* 16 (1985), 105.

59. Glenbow-Alberta Institute Archives, *John Hugill Papers*, Box 2, File 43, Hugill to D. Morkeberg, Markerville, Alberta, for the information of the Danish ambassador to Canada, 22 September 1942.

60. William Aberhart, *Social Credit Manual as Applied to the Province of Alberta* (n.p. 1935), 51.

61. *Social Credit Chronicle*, 12 January 1935, 4.

62. PAA, *Social Credit Women's Auxiliaries Papers*, File 21, *Stars in Time: A History of Alberta Social Credit and Women's Auxiliaries*, 1974, 9.

63. PAA, *Social Credit Women's Auxiliaries Papers*, Report of the First to Third Annual Provincial Conventions of the SCWA to the Alberta Social Credit League, 1938–40.

64. Strong-Boag, *The New Day Recalled*, 201.

65. PAA, *Premiers' (Aberhart) Papers*, File 1117 B, "Report of Social Credit Convention," January 1940.

66. Finkel, *Social Credit Phenomenon*, 52–59.

67. PAA, *Premiers' (Aberhart) Papers*, Files 1117 B, 1118, 1124.

68. Finkel, *Social Credit Phenomenon*, 104–13.

69. Judging by her letters in the late 1930s to *People's Weekly*, the CCF-supporting newspaper, edited by Elmer Roper and William Irvine.

70. PAA, *Premiers' (Aberhart) Papers*, File 1079, R.D. Ansley to Aberhart, 28 May 1942. Wrote Ansley:
    I had planned on seeing Mrs. Barritt also on the Mirror trip as she is vice-president of the Lacombe Constituency. But from others at both Mirror and Lacombe I was informed that she had been greatly influenced with the accompanied propaganda which came with Russia's entrance in the war. Of course she is still actively associated with the league. But as she and I have had very hot personal arguments over socialistic philosophy in past years I thought it unwise for me to go out of my way to discuss matters with her at this time.
    Two years later, the "Minutes of the 30th Annual UFWA Convention," 1944, indicate that Barritt had become again a director of the UFWA. Ethel Baker's dispute with Aberhart is outlined in PAA, *Premiers' (Aberhart) Papers*, Vol. 1115, Ethel Baker to Aberhart, 4 October 1938; Aberhart to Ethel Baker, 7 October 1938. Rogers' defection to the CCF is chronicled in various issues of *People's Weekly* in 1944 and 1945.

71. *Ross Papers*, Box 2, File 20, "Minutes of the 27th Annual UFWA Convention," 1941.

72. *Ross Papers*, Box 2, File 20, Minutes of the UFWA Conventions 1939–48.

73. PAA, *Social Credit Women's Auxiliaries Papers*, "Program of Topics for 1941"; and "Minutes of 6th Annual Convention," December 1943.
74. *Stars in Time*, 19.
75. Finkel, *Social Credit Phenomenon*, 145–46; *Stars in Time*, 25.
76. PAA, *Premiers' (Aberhart) Papers*, File 782, M.W. Robertson, Civil Service Commissioner, to Bill McLean, Edson, 22 March 1941. Wrote Robertson:

> The only married women that (sic) are permitted to work are those whose husbands are cripples and are unable to do any kind of employment, or if the husband is not crippled but is sick or temporarily unable to gain employment. Then a woman is given only temporary employment until such time as the husband becomes employed.

77. PAA, *Premiers' (Aberhart) Papers*, File 650, Government of the Province of Alberta, Department of Agriculture, "Some Reasons for the Establishment of Women's Extension Programme," 10 November 1938. The Women's Cultural and Information Bureau Act in 1966 was the government's only response to increased public demands for protection of women's rights. But the Bureau limited itself to information gathering and disseminating and had no powers either to deal directly with discrimination or take cases of discrimination before the courts. PAA, Alberta Department of Labour, Research Division, "A History of Labour and Social Welfare Legislation in Alberta," 1972.
78. *Statutes of the Province of Alberta*, 1957, Chap. 64, An Act to Enable Citizens of Alberta to Participate Directly in the Benefits Arising from the Development of the Oil and Gas Resources of the Province; Statutes of the Province of Alberta, 1959, Chap. 60, An Act to Amend the Oil and Gas Royalties Dividend Act.
79. *Stars in Time*, 52–54.

Part Four

The Unfinished Revolution:
World War II to the Present

Between 1939 and 1995, Canada was transformed from a small, staid, white Anglo-Saxon and conservative country of just over 11 million inhabitants into a dynamic, officially bilingual, and multicultural society of more than 28 million inhabitants. In the wave of immigration that began immediately after World War II, North American and European immigrants were joined by large contingents from the West Indies, Asia, and Latin America; by 1990 more than 70 percent of immigrants were from non-traditional locations. The majority were women, for after 1958 female immigrants outnumbered male immigrants in most years.

World War II brought the Great Depression to a close. Then, after the continuous, unprecedented prosperity of most of the 1950s and 1960s, the economy experienced a series of slowdowns. Inflation, rising unemployment, and sky-rocketing interest rates were among the problems faced by Canadians. In the early 1980s, and again in the early 1990s, most regions of the country had to fight a full-fledged recession and the effects of worldwide economic restructuring.

By the end of the 1980s the transformation of Canada from a rural and agricultural nation to an overwhelmingly urban society was completed. The movement from an industrial to a post-industrial society was signalled as early as the 1950s by the declining importance to the national economy of primary, resource-based industries, and of secondary industry such as manufacturing, accompanied by the continuous growth of the service and clerical sectors. After the war, women's participation in the paid labour force had decreased, though less so than in the United States. The expansion of the tertiary sector, however, created massive employment opportunities for women, so that in spite of widespread opposition to their working for wages, increasing numbers of married women entered the labour force. By the 1960s it had become widely accepted that childless married women, or those whose children were in school, could be in the labour force. By the mid-1980s, the majority of women with preschool children were working outside the home, although facilities for child care lagged far behind demand.

The 1960s began a period of social change and social upheaval unprecedented in the country's history. American investment in Canada grew rapidly, provoking increased concerns about the nation's sovereignty, so that "American imperialism" became a key political issue. In growing numbers, Canadian women participated in the protest against the war in Vietnam and against the nuclear armaments associated with the Cold War. Francophones, Native peoples, students, and women struggled, sometimes together but most often on parallel or even conflicting courses, to achieve a larger share in economic and social resources and, above all, a larger voice in the allocation of those resources. A resurgent women's movement, bringing together old established groups and a host of new ones, launched public actions on behalf of women themselves.

In the last section of this reader we have attempted to represent the diversity of women's self-identifications in the most recent period of Canadian history — a focus in which we reflect the current direction of feminist historical research. In addition, as always, the essays include attention to women's experience in the paid labour force and in the family.

Women and Income Security in the Postwar Period: The Case of Unemployment Insurance, 1945–1962

ANN PORTER

Federal labour market policies after World War II crucially shaped both the nature of women's labour force participation and their access to the postwar welfare state's social security provisions. This article explores how Canadian federal policy helped shape women's economic status during that period by examining how they fared in the unemployment insurance (UI) scheme from the end of the war until the early 1960s. It is argued that the federal state, in part through the implementing of the UI plan, played a critical role in reinforcing women's marginal economic position. In the case of UI, this occurred by channelling women into low-wage sectors and by limiting women's access to income security benefits. The latter resulted, in particular, from a special UI regulation for married women which was in effect from 1950 to 1957. The rationale for this regulation, its implications for women, and the factors leading to its eventual revocation are a major focus of the article.

A second focus concerns the question of the formation of and impetus for change in state policies, particularly with regard to women. The lit-

SOURCE: Ann Porter, "Women and Income Security in the Post-War Period: The Case of Unemployment Insurance, 1945–1962," *Labour/Le Travail* 31 (Spring 1993), 111–144. Reprinted with the permission of the editor of *Labour/Le Travail*. © Committee on Canadian Labour History.

erature examining UI's implementation has tended to present state policies as the result variously of direct pressure from the business class,[1] state mediation between different classes with the goal of ensuring the long-run stability of the system,[2] or the autonomous decisions made by bureaucrats and other state officials.[3] Such analyses, however, cannot explain adequately either changes in state policies or what the implications of those changes may have been for women. Such an explanation requires greater understanding of the role of gender relations, including not only an examination of changes in the prevailing ideology, but also an assessment of the political organization of women and their relation to other social forces. The 1950s is commonly viewed as a period of retrenchment when the ideology of domesticity prevailed and women were relegated to the home. In fact, however, the position of women changed considerably during this period. Women, especially married women, entered the labour force in growing numbers, while women's organizations and trade unions became increasingly concerned with equality rights for female workers, and attitudes concerning the proper role of women began to evolve. It is these changes which must be examined in order to understand the change in UI policy with regard to married women workers.

The 1940 UI Act was one of the key pieces of legislation to shape Canada's postwar welfare state. It was seen as a way to maintain demand, to bring about greater industrial stability, and to provide workers with some form of income security in times of unemployment. Under the scheme, benefits were calculated as a proportion of earnings and were to be paid to unemployed workers who had contributed for at least 180 days during the two years immediately preceding the claim and who showed that they were capable of and available for work but unable to find suitable employment.[4] The plan was to be based on insurance principles and thus to have a sound actuarial basis.

Overarching responsibility for administering the UI program was vested in the Unemployment Insurance Commission, made up of a chief commissioner, a commissioner representing employees, and one representing employers. An Unemployment Insurance Advisory Committee (UIAC) was established to advise the Commission and to make recommendations regarding the Insurance Fund and the coverage of those not insured under the Act. It was made up of a chairperson and from four to six other members with an equal number of representatives of employers and employees, appointed by the Governor-in-Council in consultation with their respective organizations. As well, structures were devised to allow for the appeal of decisions made by UI officers. Those whose claim was disallowed had the right to appeal to a tripartite Court of Referees, again made up of representatives of employers, employees, and the government. Under certain conditions the decision of these Courts could, in turn, be appealed to an Umpire chosen from the judges of the Exchequer Court and the Superior Courts of the provinces.[5]

Although the origin of the UI system has been the subject of some debate,[6] until recently little attention has been paid to its implications for gender relations. This question has been addressed by Ruth Roach Pierson, who writes that "gender pervaded the 1934–40 debate on UI, and was inscribed in every clause of the resulting legislation."[7] Specifically, she found that the UI contribution and benefit structure of the 1940 Act reproduced sexually unequal wage hierarchies; women's employment patterns and childcare responsibilities meant they were disadvantaged both in their ability to qualify and in the length of time they were able to draw benefits; women were virtually excluded from the higher levels of the administrative structure; and the prevailing ideology of the "family wage," which assumed that the male was the head of the household and that married women would be supported by their husbands, led to the inclusion of dependants' allowances in the UI benefit structure. Pierson suggests that, in the framing of the legislation, women's principal access to benefits was to be indirectly through dependants' allowances.[8]

During World War II, women entered the labour force to an unprecedented degree. Their employment shifted from low-wage jobs in domestic service and unskilled occupations to higher-paid, skilled positions in manufacturing, and their average weekly earnings increased dramatically.[9] For example, women's overall labour force participation increased from 24.4 per cent in 1939 to a high of 33.5 per cent in 1944,[10] while their average weekly earnings rose from $12.78 to $20.89 in the same period.[11] Given these developments, to what extent did conceptions change concerning women's access to income security benefits?

Despite the upheavals brought about by the war, the federal government documents which helped to shape the postwar period continued to view women's role in much the same way as had been the case prior to 1939: women's place was seen as being primarily in the domestic sphere and the husband was viewed as the chief wage earner.[12] Both Leonard Marsh's *Report on Social Security for Canada* (1943) and the *White Paper on Employment and Income* (1945) expected that a large number of wartime women workers would retire voluntarily from the labour market either to resume or to take up their domestic role.[13] To Marsh, the social security system applied to a woman primarily "in her capacity as housewife."[14] And the 1943 Subcommittee on the Post-war Problems of Women (a subcommittee of the federally appointed Advisory Committee on Reconstruction), even while calling for "equality of remuneration, working conditions and opportunity for advancement" for women, believed nonetheless that either marriage or settlement on farms would be the best solution to the problem of large numbers of unemployed single women after the war.[15]

Federal government policy during the postwar reconstruction period reflected these views. Various measures were aimed at reducing women's, especially married women's, attachment to the labour force. These included the closing of daycares,[16] the renewal of civil service regulations barring married women from federal government work,[17] and income tax changes which provided a disincentive to married women to work for pay.[18] Other measures tended to steer women from the relatively well-paid jobs they had occupied during the war to the low-wage service sector — for instance, laid-off women were encouraged to undertake postwar training in such areas as domestic service, household management, waitressing, and hairdressing.[19]

These measures were designed largely to ensure jobs for men at the end of the war. They were introduced amid fears that the high levels of unemployment that had characterized the Depression would recur, as might the unrest that had followed World War I.[20] The result was that women's labour force participation dropped from the 1944 high of 33.5 per cent to 25.3 per cent in 1946, and remained between 23 per cent to 24 per cent for the next nine years before increasing once again.[21] What is clear from these measures is that the postwar goal of maintaining a "high and stable level of employment and income"[22] really applied only to men. The notion of full employment was not only limited by the modest goal of a "high and stable" level, but was further restrained through its being applied only to a particular sector of the labour force. As one government document of the period noted, "women are encouraged only to enter the labour market when economic activity is at such a level that their employment will not prevent men from obtaining positions."[23] This meant that for women there was no attempt to ensure either employment or income, and indeed, that such security could be achieved for men only if large numbers of women were encouraged or coerced into leaving the labour force.

Thus, the state was involved in rebuilding a particular type of labour market structure which involved women moving from relatively highly paid and highly skilled wartime manufacturing jobs into part-time and insecure jobs in the low-paid manufacturing and the growing service sectors. This had the effect of maintaining women in a marginal position within the economy and in a status of economic dependence in the family. This, in turn, ensured the existence of a sizeable labour reserve. That women fulfilled this function was explicitly recognized by, for example, a Department of Labour document from the period which referred to women as the "number one worker reserve" to be "drawn into employment under emergency conditions."[24]

Two particular aspects of the postwar UI scheme contributed fundamentally to women's increased dependence on the male head of the household and their concentration in low-wage job ghettoes. This occurred first through the channelling of women into low-wage sectors and secondly through the introduction in 1950 of a regulation imposing additional requirements on married women.

The UI scheme helped channel women into low-wage sectors partly through the way in which it was administered. Records of decisions made by the UI Umpire register numerous cases for the immediate postwar period in which women were disqualified from UI benefits for a specified interval because they had refused to accept work at a fraction of the pay they had been receiving during the war. Often they were expected to accept work in either the service sector or low-wage, female-dominated manufacturing sectors, although they previously had been employed either in the more highly paid manufacturing sectors or by the government. For instance, in 1946 a woman who had been employed as a radio examiner doing war work at 74.58 cents an hour was disqualified for four weeks after refusing general factory work at 45 cents an hour.[25] Another woman, employed as a brewery packer during the war at $33.15 a week, was disqualified for six weeks when she declined a job as a confectionery packer at the industry's prevailing weekly wage of $15.40.[26] Similarly, a woman employed by the Dominion government from 1940 to 1947 at $152 a month was notified after almost six months of unemployment of a job as a ward aide at a local hospital for $75 a month plus one meal a day for a 48-hour week. When she refused to apply on the basis that she knew nothing of the work and that she had spent time and a considerable amount of money obtaining mechanical drafting training, she was disqualified for six weeks because she had refused to apply for work at a suitable employment.[27] The four- or six-week disqualification in these cases was significant not only for the immediate loss of benefits, but because it indicated the expectations concerning the appropriate work for women even as it held out the threat of further disqualification should similar work be refused in the future.

Some indication of the extent to which women in particular were expected to accept work at reduced wages and in occupations other than those for which they had immediate experience is disclosed by surveying the UI Umpire's decisions for 1945–46. Of the 138 appeals heard by the Umpire in this period, 22 were from women who had been disqualified (generally for six weeks) for refusing to accept work at drastically reduced wages and often in a completely different line of work.[28] The Umpire lifted the disqualification in only five of these cases, generally either because the woman had been unemployed for less than a month, or because the wages were considerably less than the prevailing wage in the industry.[29] During the same period, only two men appealed for somewhat similar reasons. In one case, the Umpire ruled that the man was justified in refusing the lower-paid and less-skilled job and the disqualification was lifted.[30] In the other, while the man initially refused the work offered because the wages were too low and the hours of work long, his appeal reveals little about the question of accepting work at lower wages. He appealed on the grounds that the doctor told him not to do strenuous work. In his case, the appeal was rejected because of an inadequate medical certificate.[31]

The issue of women being expected to accept work at low rates of pay was raised in the House of Commons by CCF members Stanley

Knowles (Winnipeg North Centre) and Angus MacInnis (Vancouver East). Knowles noted that Ottawa married women who took temporary jobs during the war were required to pay UI, even though some asked to be exempted on the grounds that their jobs were only temporary. While women who were laid off from wartime jobs initially were granted UI when they met the usual conditions — that is, they were available for other work similar in character, and work was unavailable for them — women who subsequently applied for UI were offered wholly dissimilar jobs at much lower rates of pay. When they proved unwilling to take such jobs, they were told that they were thereby disqualified from benefits. Knowles referred to stories of

> married women who had become grade 2 or grade 3 stenographers and who were offered such positions as charwomen, assistants in laundries, ironers, work at slicing bread, icing cakes, baby sitting, housekeeping and so on. When they report that they are unwilling to take positions of this kind and feel that they should not be asked to take them within the meaning of the words "suitable employment," they are simply told by the people in the offices to whom they appeal that nothing can be done about the matter.[32]

MacInnis noted that one directive sent to him from the UI office in 1946 stated that an offer at a wage rate of 5 cents an hour lower than the former rate might be considered suitable after three weeks of unemployment, and that 10 cents an hour lower might be suitable after four weeks (the equivalent of about $16 a month).[33] It appeared, however, that this directive did not apply to women. MacInnis cited the example of a woman who had been earning $160 a month who was disqualified because she refused to accept a job at $100 — a drop of $60 a month. She appealed to the Court of Referees. They sustained her disqualification because she had placed a restriction of $125 a month on her services. The employment officer who gave evidence swore that no positions for "girls" that had been listed at the office carried a salary of $125 a month.[34] To some extent private industry clearly played an important role in steering women into low-wage sectors through their reluctance to retain or advertise higher-paid positions for women once the war was over.[35] But, state policy, including the UI system, also had a role to play in this regard.

The policy which most blatantly discriminated against women, however, was the 1950 regulation imposing additional requirements on married women who claimed UI benefits. During the first two and a half months that it was in operation, 10,808 women were disqualified.[36] The regulation remained in effect for seven years, during which time between 12,000 and 14,000 women annually were disqualified at a saving to the UI Fund estimated by the UI Commission at $2,500,000 per year.[37]

Regulation 5A was brought into force by order-in-council P.C. 5090 effective November 15, 1950, following an amendment by the House of Commons to the UI Act (Section 38(1)(d)), empowering the Commission to make regulations with regard to married women. The regulation itself provided that a married woman would be disqualified from UI benefits for a period of two years following her marriage unless she fulfilled certain conditions that would prove her attachment to the labour force. Specifically, beyond the general requirements of being unemployed, capable of and available for work, and unable to find employment, a married woman had to work for at least 90 days (a) after her marriage if she was not employed at the date of her marriage, or (b) after her first separation from work after her marriage if she was working at the time of her marriage. She was exempt from the regulation, however, if her separation from work was due to a shortage of work or an employer's rule against retaining married women, if her husband had died, become incapacitated, had deserted her, or if she had become permanently separated from him. The regulations subsequently were amended somewhat. For instance, the 90-day requirement was reduced to 60, first for those required to work after the first separation after marriage (1951), and later in all cases (1952). The exemptions were also expanded, for instance, to include women who had left employment voluntarily with just cause for reasons solely and directly connected with their employment (1951).

Where did the impetus to enact such a regulation come from? Discussion of special UI provisions for married women had occurred as early as the 1930s. Pierson noted that it was assumed at the time that married women would be provided for by their husbands. Therefore, for married women to claim UI was "a contradiction in terms or, what was greatly feared, a way to defraud the system."[38] R.B. Bennett's 1935 UI Act (declared *ultra vires* of the federal government and never implemented) empowered the UI Commission to impose additional conditions on "special cases," which included married women. The 1940 Act, however, contained no such provision.[39] The framers of the 1950 married women's regulation cited similar strictures embodied in the British UI Act of 1935 and in a number of U.S. states.[40]

Renewed pressure to enact such a regulation in Canada began as early as 1946 when large numbers of women, especially married women, were being laid off from former war industries or forced to leave full-time work due, for instance, to lack of childcare provisions or the reinstatement of bans on employing married women. Adding insult to injury, it was then suggested that married women were responsible for draining the UI Fund.[41] Pressure to enact such a regulation continued, however, well past the time when women war workers would have been collecting UI, and certainly, by the time it was enacted in 1950, few would have been in this category. Young married women in general, however, became targeted as abusers of the UI Fund.[42]

To some extent, the renewed interest in a regulation for married women can be seen as a continuation of the ideology, never really abandoned, of the family with a male breadwinner and a dependent wife. Pressure to enact such a regulation arose from a context of heightened emphasis on women's domestic role and on the idea that now that the war was over, women should choose once again between employment and marriage, and that it was improper for those who chose the latter to collect UI benefits. This certainly was the view publicized in an Edmonton newspaper in 1946:

> . . . it was never intended, surely, that a young woman quitting work in order to get married should thereupon become eligible to draw unemployment benefits. In such a case, the employe [sic] makes her choice between employment and marriage. If she choses [sic] the latter, she can hardly be said to be unemployed, in fact or theory . . .[43]

In addition, two groups actively called for such a regulation. The first consisted of business associations such as the Canadian Manufacturers' Association (CMA) and the Canadian Construction Association (CCA). These two groups submitted briefs in 1949 to the UI Advisory Committee (UIAC) which expressed concern about the large amount of unemployment benefits paid out during 1948–49 and which attributed this partly to the abuse of the UI Fund by married women and pensioners who, they argued, did not really wish to find work.[44] The CCA went so far as to argue that "the virility of the nation will suffer if people can receive support in this manner."[45]

The second source of pressure came from the UI Commission and the UIAC. Both bodies took up the view that married women were draining the Fund. In its report to the Governor-in-Council for the fiscal years 1946–47 through 1948–49, the UIAC drew attention to the amount of benefits disbursed to recently married women who they suggested were representing themselves as unemployed when in fact they had actually withdrawn from the labour market, had no serious intention of working, and were not obliged by economic circumstances to obtain employment.[46] In July 1949, the Commission proposed a regulation stipulating that married women would be entitled to a benefit only if they contributed to the Fund for an additional period of time following marriage to prove their commitment to the labour force.[47] That same month, the UIAC endorsed this proposal in principle and recommended UI Act amendments empowering the Commission to make such a regulation.[48]

A.D. Watson, the actuarial adviser (responsible for assessing the financial basis of the Fund), also played a role in pointing to married women as the source of a drain on the Fund. The concerns expressed in his December 1949 report virtually mirror those of the two business associations, pointing to the amount paid out in claims in 1947 and 1948, two years with extremely low levels of unemployment, and suggesting that married women and pensioners may have been guilty of drawing on the Fund when they had really left the field of employment.[49] He stated that

> . . . persons who are not available for insurable employment on account of some necessary work about the home . . . or on account of illness, personal or in the family, or on account of a birth, marriage or death in the family . . . have no right to benefit.[50]

This clearly targeted many women, not just because of their general, everyday domestic responsibilities, but because women have tended to assume a greater share of responsibility in times of illness or death of family members. Watson was concerned, too, about possible abuse because of extending benefits to seasonal workers. Here again, women were singled out: "[t]his is an area where married women may prove to be very effective claimants unless controlled by sound regulations."[51] Clearly the "actuarial ideology"[52] included a particular view of women — a view which coincided with that of the business organizations.

The attitude of state officials beyond the Commission and the UIAC was somewhat mixed, but generally supportive of the regulation. While one state official called it an "unjustifiable discrimination,"[53] the Deputy Minister of Labour, A. MacNamara, did not take this view. While stating on one occasion that "personally I am not of the opinion that the skulduggery reported to be going on in regard to married women is as extensive as we have been led to believe,"[54] nevertheless on other occasions he stated that the regulations were not unfair and that he recommended them.[55] At yet another time, he adopted a fairly patronizing attitude, and clearly did not view as a cause for concern any harm that the regulation was likely to do to women. In a reply to Fraudena Eaton[56] (one of the few people who might have been considered by the government to be a spokesperson on women's employment issues), who had expressed concern about the regulation, he stated:

> I suppose that there are quite a number of girls who have no intention of working after they get married who will be glad to have Unemployment Insurance Benefits to pay the instalment on the Washing Machine — or is it a new Television set?[57]

The UIAC labour representatives played a somewhat ambiguous role in the implementation of the regulation for married women. The minutes of the July 1949 meeting at which the regulation was approved in principle record no objection from any of the three labour representatives: George Burt (Canadian Congress of Labour), Percy Bengough (President of the Trades and Labour Congress), and Romeo Vallee (Canadian and Catholic Confederation of Labour).[58] At a subsequent meeting in July 1950 when a draft of the regulation was discussed and approved, both Burt and Bengough were absent[59] and thus neither the CCL nor the TLC had any representation.

It is significant that while the committee endorsed a proposal to require additional conditions for married women, it failed to agree on a similar proposal with respect to pensioners and older workers.[60] Clearly, organized labour's strong representation on the latter issue was a critical factor. The UIAC labour members unequivocally opposed this proposal.[61] Also, the Dominion Joint Legislative Committee of the railway transportation brotherhoods presented a brief voicing strong opposition, arguing that it would be unfair to pensioned railroaders to adopt the proposed requirement that they be eligible for benefit following compulsory retirement from the railway only after working an additional 15 weeks to prove their attachment to the labour force. The brief suggested that many would be denied benefits because they would be unable to find work and thus the principle on which benefits are normally paid would be reversed. The brotherhoods stated that "this obvious violation of the principles of the Act and the destruction of the equity and right of the potential claimant, when in need, must be recognized."[62] Their statement, however, refers only to pensioners and there does not seem to be a similar concern on the part either of the railway brotherhoods, or UIAC labour members, about the violation of principles as far as married women were concerned. It is also significant that following the proposal to impose additional conditions on pensioners, the labour bodies were able to secure an amendment to the UI Act to increase the size of the UIAC, so that by July 1950 the railway brotherhoods (along with the railway companies) had direct representation.[63]

Also, there clearly was discussion of the possibility of a trade-off whereby, in exchange for regulations regarding married women or pensioners, other workers would be treated more liberally. The UIAC secretary noted that

> . . . the thought has been that if the Fund could be protected against the drain arising from fraudulent claims and claims from groups whose attachment to the labour market is not continuous or genuine, it would probably be possible to meet the demands of organized labour for a reduction of the waiting period and a change in the provisions governing non-compensable days.[64]

It is not clear, however, to what extent the labour unions participated in this discussion.

In the period immediately following the announcement of a possible regulation, the TLC and the CCL took somewhat different positions. Despite the silence or absence of the CCL representative on the UIAC, there were other indications that at least some of the CCL members were opposed to such a regulation, and the CCL as a whole quickly took a position of strong opposition. At its October 1949 convention (following the acceptance in principle of the regulation), the CCL adopted a recommendation (ironically, from the Committee on UI, chaired by Burt) that the "Congress oppose any attempt to impose special qualifications [for UI] on pensioners and married women."[65] Individual staff members indicated their opposition to a married women's regulation,[66] while the March 1950 CCL brief to the federal government called the amendment which placed married women in a special category "a retrograde step."[67] At the September 1950 convention, the CCL Committee on UI stated that it viewed the new section of the Act allowing for the married women's regulation as "discrimination and restrictive, calculated to work an injustice on married women who out of economic necessity must remain in the labour market."[68] The Committee "strongly urged that the elimination of this section be sought and that the Congress strongly oppose all further attempts to enact such provisions into the Act."[69]

Two points clearly emerge from the CCL discussion of the issue. First, while there was concern about discrimination against married women, a more fundamental issue — expressed in the statements at the conventions, in the brief to the federal government, and by individual members — was that such a regulation was simply the thin edge of the wedge that would open up the possibility of similar actions being taken against other groups, particularly pensioners, and that the Act as a whole might be undermined.[70] Secondly, it is clear that when the regulation was first proposed in UIAC deliberations, there was neither the interest nor the ability to oppose a regulation for married women in the same way that there was for pensioners.

The TLC took a position that was somewhat more ambiguous. Its September 1950 convention resolved to express concern about the possible restriction of benefits for pensioners and married women and to urge "the Advisory Committee of the UI Commission to allow the payments of benefits to remain as they are at present" (i.e., prior to the enactment of the regulation). [71] Nevertheless, Percy Bengough, a month later, in a memo to Deputy Minister of Labour MacNamara, stated that the married women's regulation was "both necessary and well thought out."[72] It seems that considerable weight was given to this latter position, for MacNamara stated that "in view of his attitude I think there should be no hesitation about putting through the regulations."[73]

In summary, the introduction of the married women's regulation must be seen in the context of a renewed emphasis on the prewar ideology that married women belong in the domestic sphere. A policy restricting married women's right to UI was in keeping with the notion that they did not belong in the labour force, and that their status as dependants meant that they had more limited need for income security. The enactment of the regulation also reflected in part the overriding concern of both the business associations and the actuarial adviser (and through this person the UI Commission along with several UIAC members) with the scheme's actuarial soundness and the health of the UI Fund, their very limited conception of income security, and their belief that, given any chance, workers will be quick to defraud the system. This led to a somewhat contradictory view of women. On the one hand, the ideology of domesticity presented the image of the housewife content to take care of her family, worrying about their nutritional needs and providing the foundation for "true democracy."[74] On the other hand, the image presented by the promoters of the married women's regulation was that of the conniving married woman, calculating how to abuse the UI Fund to the maximum and who had to be "controlled by sound regulations."

The enactment of the regulation also has to be seen in the context of the constraints of the postwar economy, where limited employment opportunity was available, and where the enactment of "high employment" policies required the withdrawal of large numbers of women from the labour force. In the late 1940s for many women it was an economic necessity to work, but unlike during wartime, women, especially married women, had difficulty finding employment. To some extent, in a classic case of blaming the victim, married women were then singled out as extensive users of the system.

Finally, it is important to assess the nature of the organization and relative strength of the various social forces both inside and outside the state. The fact that the government's final position coincided with that of the business associations and the sections of the state whose views closely mirrored those of business (for example, the actuarial adviser) suggests the strength of the business position. At the same time, an assessment of the relative strength of different sections of the working class is critical in explaining why regulations were enacted against married women, but not other groups of workers. Reflecting no doubt both the attitude and membership of trade unions at the time, the interests of married women workers were not well represented by labour, and opposition equivalent to that concerning pensioners was not mounted. Nor were married working women well represented by women's organizations. Two that were particularly active at the time were the National Council of Women and the Canadian Federation of Business and Professional Women, both of them overwhelmingly middle class in membership. As will be seen below, these groups initially did not speak out in opposition to the regulation. This meant that the interests of women workers were represented neither by the groups pressuring the state to enact particular policies, nor within the institutions of the state itself which were responsible for implementing UI.

It is significant that when the UIAC was established in 1940 there was a "woman's representative."[75] In 1947, however, the position for a woman on the UIAC was dropped.[76] The inability of women to retain representation on this latter body speaks to the relatively weak position of women in this period. As the Conservative MP Ellen Fairclough (Hamilton West) was later to point out, a large percentage of women in the labour force were not organized. Women were working as clerks in stores and in small places which were not unionized. Most had no voice in the administration of the Act, whether through labour unions, management, or as individuals. Thus it was "comparatively easy for the administration to legislate against them for the purpose of disqualification, whether justified or not."[77]

What did this regulation mean for the women concerned? Two sources provide some indication of how it affected individual women. A number of cases were raised in the House of Commons. In addition, further evidence is provided in the decisions of the UI Umpire. A provision to which many objected was the requirement to work 90 days (later 60 days) *after the first job separation* subsequent to marriage. This meant that women who were recently married and who left or were laid off from their jobs and did not meet the exemption requirements had to find *another* employment for 90 days before being able to collect their benefits, even if they had been working and paying contributions for many years. CCF member Clarence Gillis (Cape Breton South) provided an example of what this entailed in his region:

> For example, the Maritime Telephone and Telegraph Company put in a dial system. When that happened a lot of women were let out. Many of them were married, and had gone back to work. Some of them had been working for as long as four or five years. But when they registered for unemployment insurance they were told that since this was their first separation after being married, they must go back and take employment for 60 days in order to qualify. That is the way it was administered. For many, many months we wrestled with that particular problem and it was never cleared up.[78]

CCF member Stanley Knowles pointed out that women not only had to be unemployed, but also had to find work in order to be eligible for benefits:

> . . . you require of married women . . . not only that they be available and not only that they report once a week; you require that they actually be at work. If a married woman needs work, wants it, and tries her best to get it but cannot get it then you deny her unemployment insurance benefits to which she is otherwise entitled because she has not proven her attachment to the labour market by actually being at work.[79]

Although women who became unemployed because of a shortage of work were exempt from the regulation, there were many other situations in which women who were laid off were disqualified for the two-year period following their marriage. For example, one case involved a woman who worked as a folder in a shirt and overall manufacturing company who said she had been laid off for not working overtime although she had not been told to do so, while the employer claimed that she was dismissed because her work was not satisfactory. She was disqualified for a period of two years from the date of her marriage.[80] Another situation brought forward by two locals of the United Electrical, Radio and Machine Workers of America (UE) involved 80 women who refused to be strikebreakers by returning to work under the employer's terms. The two women who were recently married were disqualified for the two years following marriage, while the other 78 were able to claim benefits while seeking employment elsewhere.[81] In another case, a woman writing to Stanley Knowles explained that she lost her job at the T. Eaton Co. when she got married because the policy of the department she was working in was not to employ married women. However, she did not qualify for an exemption to the married women's regulation since Eaton's stated that they had no *over-all* store policy with regard to married women. She was therefore disqualified from receiving UI for two years from the date of her marriage.[82] In her letter to Knowles she noted that the cost of living is so high that my husband and I find it very difficult to get along with only one of us working. For the past three months I have tried to get a job but have been unable to do so. An Insurance Officer told me in an interview that it was almost impossible to place me now that I was married and this same person also told me that I would have to work 90 days before I could claim benefits. When I appealed my case I asked the court how they expected me to work for 90 days if I was unable to find a job and they said "That is the $64.00 question. We can't answer that."[83]

Many cases involved women who had left their employment or been laid off because of pregnancy. The Act had no specific provisions concerning pregnancy (whether in the case of recently married women, or others). By administrative ruling, however, insurance officers generally disqualified women for a six-week period before the expected date of confinement and for six weeks after it, on the grounds that they were not available for work.[84] Under the married women's regulation, however, married women who left or were laid off (as many were)[85] because of pregnancy were disqualified for a period of two years following marriage.

Clarence Gillis spoke of a case of "rank miscarriage of justice" where a "little girl" in Sydney had paid into the UI fund for five years, had worked for more than 90 days after marriage, but was laid off because she was pregnant and had "slowed up a bit in her work." She was barred from UI benefits for two years.[86] (She would have had to find work for 90 days *after the first separation* subsequent to marriage in order to qualify.) While the regulation was amended in 1955 to allow an exemption if the separation from employment was due to "illness, injury or quarantine," this did not include pregnancy. In the words of the UI Umpire who ruled on the issue, "there can be no question of incapacity for work due to illness in the case of a mere pregnancy."[87] It seems that pregnancy was still considered a voluntary state, and that women who chose to enter that condition were not deserving of an independent source of income security.

One of the exemptions to the regulation was for those who voluntarily left their job for reasons solely and directly connected with their employment, such as a dangerous work situation (1951 revision). A number of cases cited involved women who left their jobs in order to follow their husbands to another city. They were disqualified for a period of two years following marriage, however, because they voluntarily left their jobs for personal rather than employment-related reasons.[88] (Other people who voluntarily left their employment without just cause generally were disqualified for a period of up to six weeks.)[89] This section of the regulation was later amended (1955) so that a woman moving to another city would qualify, but only if there were "reasonable opportunities for her to obtain suitable employment" in that area. The latter phrase meant that many women were still disqualified.[90]

Thus, in all these cases, it can be seen that the consequence of the regulation was to deny an independent source of income security to married women who otherwise were entitled to benefits. Married women were presumed guilty of abuse until they were able to prove otherwise, by finding employment subsequent to marriage.[91] The regulation, which implied that married women did not really need the money and therefore should not be entitled to UI, was contrary to the basis of the scheme, according to which benefits are a right, not something for which a means test should be applied.[92] The over-all consequence for women of the measure was to increase their income instability, to increase their dependence on the male head of the household, and to reinforce the view that women's place was primarily in the household, where they were responsible for meeting the domestic requirements of the family.

What was the reaction of various groups and political actors after the regulation was enacted? Business organizations several times expressed their approval of the regulation.[93] Both the Commission and the actuarial adviser also went to considerable lengths to justify the regulation. For example, Watson, in his report of July 1954, calculated that while the number of married women in insurable employment was about half the number of single women, the number of benefit days paid to them was more than three times as great.[94] While seeming oblivious to the possibility that this might reflect the difficulty married women faced in finding permanent jobs, he argued that the claims of married women on benefit were excessive both as to number and duration.[95] The UI Commission took up this theme and stated that the proportion would be even higher if the regulation were not in force to control unjustified claims.[96] It also suggested that married women were using various tactics when they were sent to jobs to cause employers to reject them, so they could remain on UI. For instance, "trained stenographers who have been taking shorthand for years have suddenly found they have lost their knowledge."[97]

On the other hand, there were numerous protests against the regulation by labour organizations and women's groups, as well as by various members of the House of Commons. Ellen Fairclough, who appears at the time to have been the parliamentary spokesperson for women's organizations, was probably the most persistent of the MPs at calling for its elimination. She also urged on numerous occasions that there be provision for the representation of women on both the UI Commission and the UIAC, and on more than one occasion proposed amendments to that effect.[98] Stanley Knowles and Clarence Gillis of the CCF also, as noted above, played an important role in urging that "this discrimination against married women . . . be eliminated."[99]

Of the central labour bodies, the CCL continued to play the most active role in protesting against the married women's regulation and in urging its repeal. Although the regulation did not top its list of concerns about UI in the 1950s (generally being listed after such issues as the extension of coverage to other occupations, the increase in benefit rates, and so on), the CCL nevertheless had the most visible role (along with

MPs) in calling for its repeal. CCL annual conventions consistently passed resolutions reiterating its opposition to the regulation.[100] In its annual brief to the federal government, its submissions to the UIAC and to the UI Commission, the CCL repeatedly expressed its opposition to the discriminatory treatment of married women claimants and called for the elimination, or at least drastic revision, of the married women's regulation and Section 38(1)(d) of the Act allowing the Commission to make regulations regarding married women.[101] Protests against the married women's regulation were also registered at meetings of the labour representatives on the Courts of Referees (attended by the CCL, TLC, and CCCL). This was particularly the case for meetings in Quebec, where for example, "the members . . . insisted that the regulation be repealed."[102]

One of the major labour initiatives on the issue was a 1951 joint submission to the UI Umpire by the three labour bodies (CCL, TLC, and CCCL), undertaken at the behest of the CCL.[103] The labour representatives argued that Section 38(1)(d) and Benefit Regulation 5A had resulted in "unjustifiably discriminatory action against certain married women"; had introduced an inconsistency in the Act by creating a "class of persons" distinguishable not by the nature of their employment or by their wage arrangement, but merely by marital status; that the blanket disqualification of married women meant that the innocent were being made to suffer; that "this is flagrantly contradictory to our whole concept of justice and to the practice of law in this country" and "is a gross abuse of authority by the Commission and a strengthening of the dead hand of the bureaucracy."[104] The labour submission further objected to the fact that the regulation was applied retroactively and that it was so restrictive that neither the Courts of Referees nor the Umpire had much leeway to modify the insurance officer's decisions. Thus, argued the labour delegation, it curtailed and inhibited the right of appeal provided for in the Act.[105]

The Canadian and Catholic Confederation of Labour also clearly voiced its opposition to the married women's regulation. In addition to participating with the other labour bodies in presentations to the UI Umpire and the UI Commission in which it urged the elimination of the regulation,[106] the CCCL, in its annual brief to Cabinet, regularly requested the abolition of the sections of the UI Act and the Regulations which placed married women in a special category.[107] Indeed, in 1951 the CCCL devoted a whole section of its brief (considerably more than the other labour bodies) to the married women's regulation, declaring that it could not agree to "the disqualification in advance of a whole category of insured persons simply because it is more difficult to verify their good faith."[108]

The TLC, on the other hand, was somewhat less active in opposing the regulation. Resolutions continued to be brought forward and passed at TLC conventions expressing opposition to and urging the repeal of the married women's regulation and accompanying statutes.[109] The TLC executive, however, appeared at best lukewarm in its opposition to the regulation. Unlike the CCL, it did not raise the issue in submissions to the UIAC.[110] In a 1951 joint meeting of labour representatives with the UI Commission, the TLC — unlike the other two labour bodies — did not argue that the married women's regulation should be revoked. It simply urged that the words "after her first separation" be dropped so that the additional 90 days that a married woman would have to work would simply be after her marriage.[111] The TLC executive council annual convention reports regularly recommended changes to the UI Act, but it was only in 1955 that one urged the removal of the married women's regulation.[112] Similarly, each year in its brief to the federal government, the TLC recommended changes to the UI provisions. But it was not until 1952 that this included changes to the married women's regulation, and then it simply was stated that the regulation "should be given more sympathetic consideration" and that the 90 days required to establish benefit rights should be reduced to 60.[113] It was only in 1954 and 1955 that their brief called for abolishing the married women's regulation altogether.[114]

The Canadian Labour Congress, formed with the CCL-TLC merger of 1956, seems to have taken up the former CCL's strong opposition to the married women's regulation. For example, a 1957 brief strongly urged the removal of such regulations, stating that they "perpetuate inequities and discrimination, result in anomalies and undermine confidence in the Act."[115] Individual union locals also played a role in representing their members before the Courts of Referees and the Umpire and urging that the regulation be rescinded.[116]

Women's organizations had a much less institutionalized forum for expressing their views on unemployment insurance than did the labour organizations. Again, this reflected their relative strength and organization at the time. Not only did organized labour have representation on the UIAC and the UIC, but it often made submissions to the UIAC. Women's organizations, on the other hand, had a much less visible presence. It seems they usually were not notified of hearings on the subject of UI or invited to attend.[117] Nevertheless, both individual women and women's organizations as a whole eventually came to play an important role in urging the repeal of the regulation. Two groups which took a stand on the issue were the National Council of Women of Canada (NCW) and the Canadian Federation of Business and Professional Women's Clubs (BPW).

The National Council of Women was an umbrella group to which a range of organizations — church-based, professional, and other — were affiliated.[118] While their meetings to some extent were concerned with arranging social functions, they also discussed and passed resolutions on many important matters of the day, ranging from the guaranteed annual wage to international peace. They supported equal rights and greater opportunities for women in many fields, including the appointment of women to the civil service commission, the Senate and the UI Court of Referees;[119] the right of women to serve on juries; and equal pay legislation.[120] On labour issues, however, their positions often reflected the middle-class bias of their membership. For example, the Economics and Taxation Committee of the NCW suggested that "women of Canada might use their influence to discourage wage demands."[121] On the issue of unemployment, their concern largely took the form of an effort to have their homes redecorated or renovated during the winter months. This was at least in part at the urging of the federal government which had undertaken a campaign to stimulate winter employment.[122]

On the question of the married women's regulation, there was little recorded discussion until the mid-1950s. When a resolution was passed on the issue by the Council of Women of West Algoma in 1951, it was not brought forward to the annual NCW meeting because members of the executive who were in contact with the UI Commission expressed the view that the Commission was dealing with the issue and thus "they did not think anything would be gained by Council action at the present time."[123] In 1953 the issue was discussed in a number of local councils.[124] There is little indication of the content of these discussions, although the Winnipeg Trades and Professions Committee did note that "since recent amendments to this Regulation there appears to be a minimum of hardship imposed on married women. . . . The benefit fund . . . is definitely *not* a subsidy. . . . "[125]

At the 1954 annual NCW meeting, a resolution was nevertheless brought forward by the Trades and Professions Committee of the Toronto Council of Women that Regulation 5A be rescinded and that the "UI Commission take the same action to protect the Unemployment Insurance Fund against unjust claims from married women as is taken with other categories of claimants."[126] The government's case that married women were claiming a disproportionate amount of benefit was presented by Ruth Hamilton, UIC adviser on women's employment,[127] and after some discussion, the resolution was defeated by 139 to 41 votes.[128] This position was reversed, however, when the same resolution passed at the NCW's 1956 convention.[129] Subsequently, the NCW made representations requesting that the married women's regulation be rescinded both to the labour minister[130] and to Prime Minister Louis St. Laurent.[131]

The BPW brought together women in business and the professions and thus tended to be more focused on the issue of women's employment opportunities. They also passed resolutions on a variety of issues that would improve the position of women. They urged the introduction of equal pay legislation, the removal of discrimination against married women in the federal civil service, the appointment of women to the Senate, the establishment of a women's bureau by the federal government, and so on.[132] On numerous occasions, the BPW passed resolutions urging the federal government to appoint a woman to the UI Commission[133] and that the UI Act be amended to include "sex" as a basis for non-discrimination in referring applicants to employers (this already was the case with respect to race, creed, colour, ancestry, and origin).[134] Resolutions at both the 1954 and 1956 biennial conventions were passed urging the revocation of the married women's regulation.[135] Representations urging the repeal of the regulation were subsequently made to the federal Minister of Labour, to the Industrial Relations Committee examining the 1955 revisions to the UI Act, and to both Prime Ministers St. Laurent and John Diefenbaker.[136]

The married women's regulation was revoked on 15 November 1957 by PC 1957-1477, shortly after Diefenbaker's Conservative government came to power. Labour Minister Michael Starr, announcing the order-in-council, cited two reasons for it: a dislike of discrimination, and the continually increasing importance and permanence of married women as working women.[137] In addition, as noted above, both labour and women's groups played a critical role in pushing for the revocation of the regulation. While labour had been more consistently and for a longer period of time urging the abolition of the married women's regulation, the addition in the mid-1950s of the voice of women's organizations was nevertheless crucial.[138] The position of women's groups was given added weight by the fact that Ellen Fairclough, a member of the BPW who for many years had spoken out against the discrimination against women in this regulation, had become a cabinet minister (although not directly responsible for UI) in the new Diefenbaker government.[139]

The question of a special regulation for married women remained a contentious issue into the early 1960s. The issue came up again in the UIAC where, at the request in 1959 of one of the employer representatives, the Commission prepared a memorandum outlining the history of the married women's regulation, providing figures that showed that the proportion of married women claiming benefit had increased since the regulation had been revoked[140] (which is hardly surprising, given the number that had been excluded), and reasserting that "many married women are claiming benefit when they are not really unemployed and available for employment and unable to find work."[141] The Commission also suggested a number of possible solutions, including a return to the old regulation; that a married woman could be excluded from receiving benefit if her husband was employed; that a married woman could be disqualified as not available for employment if she had children under school age, and so on.[142] Unlike a decade earlier, however, UIAC members were unable to agree on a recommendation to reinstate some form of regulation for married women. While the employer-members were in favour of such a regulation, the labour representatives were opposed to it. Thus, in the end, no recommendation was forthcoming.[143]

There were also attempts on the part of the Canadian Manufacturers' Association to bring back the regulation. For example, in the CMA's 1959 brief, it was stated strongly that "abuses must be eliminated . . .

or the Fund will be drained by special minority groups at the expense of the majority of contributors," and that "[a]lthough the Married Women's Regulations were reasonable and designed solely to limit a manifest abuse, they were attacked by women's organizations and labour unions which claimed that married women were being discriminated against."[144] This was followed in 1960 by a virulent letter to the labour minister which argued that UI Act changes had "resulted in dangerous dissipation of the Unemployment Insurance Fund," and identified seasonal workers and "certain types of workers who have left the labour force such as housewives and retired persons" as the source of the drain.[145]

The question of the status of unemployed married women and their use of the UI system also surfaced at the 1960 hearings of a Senate special committee on manpower and employment. Dr. Warren James[146] cited figures to show that a disproportionate number of those registering at UI offices for jobs were married women, particularly under the age of 45, young people, and men over 65.[147] For example, he found that the proportion of women registered for jobs at UI offices who were married (67 per cent) was much greater than the proportion of married women in the labour force as a whole (46 per cent).[148] He also calculated that two-thirds of married women had a "somewhat tenuous attachment to the labour market,"[149] and concluded that "there are some systematic influences at work which lead many of these people to register for jobs although their membership in the labour force is clearly often marginal."[150]

The economist Sylvia Ostry, appearing before the Committee as an academic expert, similarly drew attention to the phenomenon she referred to as "schizoid respondents" — married women, elderly men, and seasonal workers who classified themselves as "unemployed and seeking work" for the purpose of collecting UI, but not when asked the question by the monthly labour force survey administered by the Dominion Bureau of Statistics.[151] Both of these studies were taken up in the Senate committee's report, which suggested that the high proportion of married women registering for jobs at UI offices "reflects some features of the unemployment insurance system which merit attention."[152]

The actual use that these experts made of the statistics is, it should be noted, highly questionable. It repeatedly was pointed out that the concept of unemployment used in the Dominion Bureau of Statistics labour force survey could not be compared to that used for UI purposes.[153] For example, in the labour force survey, if a person had been laid off because of bad weather, or with instructions to return to work within 30 days, he or she was not considered unemployed, yet was entitled to draw UI benefits. Similarly, a person working at all during the survey week, even for part of a day, was not considered as unemployed, but could be drawing UI.

What is lacking in these studies from the period is any analysis of the particular employment situation of married women, or any suggestion that perhaps both the high rate of claims and the high proportion reg-istering for work at UI offices might reflect the difficulty such women had in obtaining jobs, and their concentration in vulnerable employment areas, where they were more likely to be laid off. That such might have been the case was suggested, for instance, in various statements during the early 1950s by the Women's Division of the National Employment Service (the section of the UI Commission that referred people to jobs). For example, the division reported that in 1950 there was a steady in-crease in the number of female applicants registered at local offices of the Commission for whom it was not possible to find suitable employ-ment. This situation was attributed at least in part to the rising cost of living in Canada and the necessity for married women to find work in order to augment family incomes.[154] In both 1951 and 1952, the division had difficulty filling orders for secretaries, stenographers, and typists although competent women with good qualifications were available:

> . . . it was generally the experience of placement officers that most of these applicants were married or in the older age brackets, and thus could not meet requirements of employers' orders in many instances. Despite efforts of em-ployment officers to persuade employers to consider such applicants, the general trend was for single women well under thirty years of age.[155]

The Women's Division reported in 1954 that the number of unplaced female job applicants had steadily increased, while the number of job vacancies had decreased.[156] Women also appear to have been over-represented among those placed in casual jobs by the UI employment service, and therefore would be more likely to have renewed claims for benefits. In 1952, women accounted for 36.3 per cent of regular place-ments, but 63 per cent of casual placements.[157]

In fact, it appears that women as a whole were not drawing a dis-proportionate number of claims. Svanhuit Josie, a labour economist ap-pearing at a later round of hearings, pointed out that when account was taken of both single and married women (and many married women had previously contributed as single women), it was evident that a much smaller proportion of women were drawing benefits than were in the insured population and that the proportion of UI money they received was even less. Specifically, she calculated that between 1942 and 1959 women made up from 25 per cent to 34 per cent of the insured labour force, but accounted for a minimum of 13 per cent and a maximum of 26 per cent of those drawing benefits, and that the proportion of money paid out that went to women varied from 11 per cent to 26 per cent.[158] What her figures show is that, far from being a drain on the UI Fund, women as a whole in fact were *subsidizing* it! Nor is there any indication that the UI Fund was actually being drained. The balance in the Fund rose steadily from the time it was started to a peak of $927 million in December 1956.[159] It reached such a high point that the CCL suggested it was over-funded and that the benefit rate consequently should be increased.[160]

The subject of married women's regulations came up a final time during the 1961 hearings of the Committee of Inquiry into UI (the Gill Commission). The committee was set up in part because by the end of the 1950s, unemployment had risen to 7 per cent and for the first time there was a depletion of the UI Fund. Its terms of reference included determining "the means of correcting any abuses or deficiencies that might be found to exist." A long list of business organizations accused married women (again, along with older workers and seasonal workers) of draining the Fund and urged the reinstatement of married women's regulations.[161] This included the Canadian Manufacturers' Association and the Canadian Construction Association (both of which seemed to have changed their position little in the intervening 10 years) as well as the Canadian Retail Federation, the Canadian Chamber of Commerce, the Canadian Life Insurance Officers' Association, the Canadian Metal Mining Association, the Canadian Lumberman's Association (which claimed that "the greatest abuse is from married women"), and the Canadian Pulp and Paper Association (which argued that "secondary" wage earners should be subjected to more stringent requirements than heads of families). Office Overload, describing itself as giving employment to more than 15,000 mostly married women every year and one of the largest employers of female office workers in Canada, while not calling specifically for regulations for married women, did state that "coming into daily contact as we do with so many temporary workers — as most of these married women are in the labour force for a relatively short period of time . . . we are exposed to perhaps more than our share of abuses of the U.I. Fund."[162]

Yet, a number of organizations rejected the reinstatement of regulations for married women. In some respects the tenor of the hearings with respect to women had changed considerably since the time the regulation first was enacted. First, women, both as individuals and as members of organizations, had a more visible presence. Of the two major women's organizations, the NCW in this instance provided the stronger statement with regard to the possibility of a new regulation for married women, declaring that they were "unalterably opposed to any change in regulations which would be prejudicial to the rights and interests of women, whether married or single."[163] The BPW brief contained no specific reference to the question of regulations for married women, but did recommend the inclusion of "sex" in clauses preventing discrimination in employment.[164] A second change was greater support from labour unions on the issue. The National Legislative Committee of the International Railway Brotherhood, which 10 years previously had represented only the interests of pensioners, now stated "its opposition to discrimination against any particular group."[165] A number of other groups and individuals appearing before the committee expressed similarly strong and unequivocal opposition to the reinstatement of regulations restricting benefits to married women. This included the CLC, the Government of Saskatchewan, and Svanhuit Josie, who appeared as an individual before the committee and expressed concern about "the attacks on working women — most of them unfounded."[166]

Thus, despite the studies of the experts and the requests from business groups, the married women's regulation was not reinstated.[167] This change in state policy reflected a shift in two respects in the position of working women — especially married working women. First, changes were beginning to occur in the prevailing ideology concerning the proper role for women. Between 1951 and 1961, women's overall labour force participation role increased from 24 per cent to 29 per cent while that of married women doubled from 11 per cent to 22 per cent and it had increased more than five times (from approximately 4 per cent) since 1941.[168] Married women were becoming an increasingly important source of labour both for the growing service sector and the state. This development meant that the idea that women only worked for a short time before marriage and then belonged in the home no longer corresponded to the reality of women's lives. It seemed increasingly anomalous for state policy to be based on such a notion. That changes were beginning to occur in the prevailing ideology is evidenced, for example, in the statement by the Labour Minister, Starr, in announcing the revocation of the regulation, the increased acceptance of the notion that women should be paid equally for work that they perform and so on.[169]

Secondly, there was beginning to be a change in the representation of women's interests in the political arena, later to become more clearly articulated in the "second wave of feminism" of the 1960s. As women came to play an increasingly important role in the paid labour force, their interests came to be better represented both by labour and by women's organizations. While figures on the number of women in unions are not available for this period,[170] increased concern about women workers on the part of labour by the late 1950s can be seen in the growing number of discussions on the role of women in trade unions, the formation of white-collar organizing committees, and the establishment of women's committees in some of the central labour bodies.[171] Women's organizations also had a renewed interest in equality rights for women workers, as evidenced not only by their actions with respect to UI, but also through their efforts to have equal pay legislation introduced, to have a woman's bureau established in the federal Department of Labour, and so on. Particularly important, on certain issues, labour and women's organizations now had a commonality of viewpoint. The result was that whereas in 1950 it was possible to enact a regulation that disqualified a large number of married women from receiving UI benefits, by 1960 this was no longer possible.

Conclusion

It has been seen that the postwar UI scheme contributed in two ways to the tendency to restrict both employment possibilities and income security for women. The first was that in the years immediately following the war, women — unlike men — were disqualified for a period of time from receiving UI unless they accepted work in low-wage sectors, often at a fraction of the pay they had received during the war. The second was the introduction in 1950 of a regulation imposing additional conditions on married women. These policies combined had the effect of disqualifying a large number of women from receiving benefits to which they were otherwise entitled, denying many married women an independent source of income security, and contributing to the concentration of women in low-wage job ghettoes. The consequence was to increase women's dependence on the male head of the household and to reinforce the view that women's place was primarily in the domestic sphere.

A second concern of the article has been the question of the formation of state policies and the dynamic of their change, particularly with regard to women. In this respect, a greater understanding of the role of gender relations, including changes in the prevailing ideology as well as in the relative strength and political representation of women, is important. The married women's regulation was introduced in the context of the economic constraints of the postwar period, where there was a renewed emphasis on the idea that married women belonged in the domestic sphere, but not in the labour force. As the 1950s progressed, however, there was a considerable erosion in this ideology of domesticity. As married women entered the labour force in increasing numbers, the idea that they belonged exclusively in the home no longer corresponded to the reality of their lives. It became more difficult to justify a policy that was based on such an assumption. In addition, in the late 1940s, working women, who constituted a relatively small part of the labour force, were not well represented either by labour or by women's organizations. By the late 1950s, however, both groups began to pursue more actively the issue of equal rights for women workers. The combined opposition of both these groups to a policy that discriminated against certain women was key both in the revocation of the married women's regulation and in ensuring that a similar one was not later reinstated.

NOTES

1. Alvin Finkel, *Business and Social Reform in the Thirties* (Toronto 1979), ch VI.
2. Carl Cuneo, "State Mediation of Class Contradictions in Canadian Unemployment Insurance, 1930–1935," *Studies in Political Economy*, 3 (1980); Carl Cuneo, "State, Class and Reserve Labour: The Case of the 1941 Canadian Unemployment Insurance Act," *Canadian Review of Sociology and Anthropology*, 16(2) (1979).
3. Leslie A. Pal, "Relative Autonomy Revisited: The Origins of Canadian Unemployment Insurance," *Canadian Journal of Political Science*, XIX:1 (March 1986); Leslie A. Pal, *State, Class and Bureaucracy: Canadian Unemployment Insurance and Public Policy* (Montreal 1988).

4. For an overview of the provisions of the 1940 UI Act see Gary Dingledine, *A Chronology of Response: The Evolution of Unemployment Insurance from 1940 to 1980*, prepared for Employment and Immigration Canada (Ottawa 1981); Leslie Pal, *State, Class and Bureaucracy*; Ray Brown, "Unemployment Insurance and the National Employment Service," *Labour Gazette* (September 1950).

5. Dingledine, *Chronology*, 13.

6. See, for example, Finkel, *Business and Social Reform*, ch VI; Cuneo, "State Mediation"; Cuneo, "State, Class and Reserve Labour"; Leslie A. Pal, "Relative Autonomy Revisited"; Carl Cuneo, "Restoring Class to State Unemployment Insurance," *Canadian Journal of Political Science*, XIX:1 (March 1986); Pal, *State, Class and Bureaucracy*; James Struthers, *"No Fault of Their Own": Unemployment and the Canadian Welfare State, 1914–1941* (Toronto 1983).

7. Ruth Roach Pierson, "Gender and the Unemployment Insurance Debates in Canada, 1934–1940," *Labour/Le Travail*, 25 (1990), 102.

8. *Ibid.*, 93–5.

9. For a discussion of the recruitment of women into the labour force during the war, see Ruth Roach Pierson, *"They're Still Women after All": The Second World War and Canadian Womanhood* (Toronto 1986), ch 1.

10. Labour Canada, Women's Bureau, *Women in the Labour Force: Facts and Figures (1973 Edition)* (Ottawa 1974), 227. The proportion of the female labour force in manufacturing increased from 27 per cent in 1939 to 37 per cent in 1943, while that in domestic service dropped from 18.6 per cent to 9.3 per cent. Canada, Department of Labour, *Canadian Labour Market* (June 1946), 20.

11. Canada, Department of Labour, *Canadian Labour Market* (December 1946), 16. Before the war, the highest weekly wage paid to women was an average of $15.83 in the fur goods industry. In contrast, during the war, in aircraft manufacturing, shipbuilding and ship repairs, women received an unprecedented average of $31.81 per week. *Ibid.* (June 1946), 20–1.

12. See, for example, Leonard Marsh, *Report on Social Security for Canada, 1943* (Reprinted Toronto 1975), especially the chapter devoted to "women's needs," 209–14.

13. *Ibid.*, 212; Canada, Department of Reconstruction, *Employment and Income with Special Reference to the Initial Period of Reconstruction* (Ottawa 1945), 3.

14. Marsh, *Report on Social Security*, 210. The Marsh Report also discusses the suggestion (present in the Beveridge Report) that women's retirement from the labour force might be encouraged by a general marriage grant or bonus, or allowing previously employed women, on marriage, a commutation of all unemployment insurance contributions paid into the fund. He makes no recommendation on the subject however. *Ibid.*, 212–13.

15. Gail Cuthbert Brandt, "'Pigeon-Holed and Forgotten': The Work of the Subcommittee on the Post-war Problems of Women, 1943," *Histoire sociale/Social History*, XV, 29 (May 1982), 253, 250.

16. Pierson, *"They're Still Women,"* 55–60.

17. *Ibid.*, 82.

18. *Ibid.*, 49.

19. *Ibid.*, 83–88.

20. Brandt, "'Pigeon-Holed,'" 239–40.

21. Labour Canada, Women's Bureau, *Women in the Labour Force* (1973 edition), 227.

22. Canada, Department of Reconstruction, *Employment and Income*, 1.

23. Canada, Department of Labour, *Canadian Labour Market* (June 1946), 23.

24. *Ibid.* (August 1951), 1.

25. Canada, Unemployment Insurance Commission, *Decisions of the Umpire, 1943–1948*, CUB-168, 29 November 1946, 196.

26. *Ibid.*, CUB-122, 6 September 1946, 158.

27. *Ibid.*, CUB-317, 5 February 1948, 327.

28. *Ibid.* It should be noted that the Umpire's decisions record only those cases which went through to a second level of appeal, and not all instances of a particular type of disqualification.

29. Significantly, in the 1945–46 period approximately 43 per cent of cases coming before the Umpire were brought by women, even though they made up only 34 per cent of the insured population. (Canada, Dominion Bureau of Statistics, *Annual Report on Current Benefit Years under the Unemployment Insurance Act*, 1945, table A, 6.) In addition to refusing to accept work at reduced rates of pay, a number of women were disqualified for a certain period of time for such things as wanting to restrict hours of work because of domestic responsibilities, or leaving their job to follow their husbands to another city. In general, it seems that the UI scheme was designed with the male worker as a model, and that in a number of instances the position of women created certain anomalies and meant that they did not fit comfortably within the guidelines laid out by the Act.

30. Canada, Unemployment Insurance Commission, *Decisions of the Umpire, 1943–1948* (Ottawa nd), CUB-165, 22 November 1946, 194.

31. *Ibid.*, CUB-113, 25 July 1946, 149.

32. Canada, House of Commons, *Debates*, 14 July 1947, 5637.

33. *Ibid.*, 5638.

34. *Ibid.*

35. A government document noted that in 1946 the greatest demand for women was concentrated in the lower-paying occupations such as service work, textile work, and unskilled positions. Canada, Department of Labour, *Canadian Labour Market* (June 1946), 21–2.

36. Canada, House of Commons, *Debates*, 19 February 1951, 453.
37. Canada, Committee of Inquiry into the Unemployment Insurance Act (Gill Commission), *Report* (Ottawa 1962), 31.
38. Pierson, "Gender," 95.
39. *Ibid.*
40. See, for example, National Archives of Canada (NAC) Unemployment Insurance Commission (UIC) Records, RG50, vol. 53, 18th meeting UIAC, July 1950, UI Commission to UIAC, 27 June 1950.
41. See, for example, NAC, UIC Records, RG50, vol. 59, file 1, UIAC Correspondence 1946–1947, J.G. Bisson, Chief Commissioner to Hon. Humphrey Mitchell, Minister of Labour, 30 August 1947. Bisson noted that several people at the July 1947 meeting of the UIAC argued that the increase in total benefit paid out during the previous year largely reflected the laying off of married women and older persons employed during the war who would not ordinarily have been working or have built up benefit rights.
42. See NAC, UIC Records, RG50, vol. 53, 16th meeting UIAC, July 1949, C.A.L. Murchison, Commissioner UIC to UIAC, 11 July 1949. Murchison suggested that there were two reasons for the drain on the Fund by married women. The first was married women who were laid off after the war, but by 1949 this group had practically ceased to be a problem. The second was the many young women who, on marriage, had no intention of continuing to work, but because job opportunities were not readily available, were able to draw benefits.
43. NAC, UIC Records, RG50, vol. 60, UIAC Reports 1941–1947, "Raiding Jobless Insurance Fund," *Edmonton Journal and Edmonton Bulletin*, 20 December 1946.
44. NAC, UIC Records, RG50, vol. 53, 16th meeting UIAC, July 1949, submission from Canadian Manufacturers' Association to UIAC 13 July 1949; submission from Canadian Construction Association to UIAC 16 July 1949.
45. NAC, UIC Records, RG50, vol. 53, 16th meeting UIAC, July 1949, submission from Canadian Construction Association to UIAC 16 July 1949, 2.
46. Canada, Unemployment Insurance Commission, *Annual Report* (1951), 37.
47. NAC, UIC Records, RG50, vol. 53, 16th meeting UIAC, July 1949, C.A.L. Murchison, Commissioner, UIC to UIAC, 11 July 1949.
48. NAC, UIC Records, RG50, vol. 53, 16th meeting UIAC, July 1949, "Minutes of the Meeting," 9.
49. NAC, UIC Records, RG50, vol. 53, 17th meeting UIAC, January 1950, "Actuarial Report for the UIAC," 23 December 1949, 24, 28.
50. *Ibid.*, 28.
51. *Ibid.*
52. Leslie Pal argues that the administrative expertise involved in an insurance scheme took the form of an "actuarial ideology" which was largely removed from class forces. See Pal, "Relative Autonomy Revisited"; Pal, *State, Class and Bureaucracy*.
53. NAC, Department of Labour Records, RG27, vol. 3458, file 4-11, pt. 5, M.M. Maclean, Director, Industrial Relations Branch to A. MacNamara, 3 October 1950.
54. *Ibid.*, MacNamara to W.A. Mackintosh, Chairman, UIAC, 4 October 1950.
55. *Ibid.*, MacNamara to N. Robertson, Clerk of the Privy Council, 12 October 1950.
56. During the war Fraudena Eaton was the head of the Women's Division of the National Selective Service agency created to oversee the recruitment and allocation of labour. See Alison Prentice *et al.*, *Canadian Women: A History* (Toronto 1988), 297. In 1956 she became president of the National Council of Women. Rosa L. Shaw, *Proud Heritage: A History of the National Council of Women of Canada* (Toronto 1957).
57. NAC, Department of Labour Records, RG27, vol. 3458, file 4-11, pt. 5, MacNamara to Mrs. Eaton, 1 April 1950. Another exchange of letters is carried on in a similar vein. In response to a question about the case of "a girl" who marries her employer, the UIC legal adviser notes that "of course . . . she may obtain relief if her husband becomes incapacitated, dies or is permanently separated from her and I do hope that this provision will not encourage self-imposed widowhood and reveal whatever criminal tendencies a woman may possess." MacNamara takes this up and notes that "possibly the best thing for the girl to do would be to send off the attractive male." *Ibid.*, Claude Dubuc to MacNamara, 28 October 1950; MacNamara to Bengough, 30 October 1950.
58. NAC, UIC Records, RG50, vol. 53, 16th meeting UIAC, July 1949, "Minutes of the Meeting." At least one state official expressed surprise at labour's position, noting that it seemed odd that the labour members of the UIAC had approved such a regulation, even in principle. NAC, Department of Labour Records, RG27, vol. 3458, file 4-11, pt. 5, M.M. Maclean, Director, Industrial Relations Branch to MacNamara, 3 October 1950.
59. NAC, UIC Records, RG50, vol. 53, 18th meeting UIAC, July 1950, "Minutes of the Meeting."
60. NAC, Department of Labour Records, RG27, vol. 3458, file 4-11, pt. 5. G.M. Ingersoll to A. MacNamara, 23 November 1949. The issue was also raised at the meeting of the UIAC, January 1950, and the Committee agreed not to recommend amendment of the Act in this regard. NAC, UIC Records, RG50, vol. 53, 17th meeting UIAC, January 1950, "Minutes of the Meeting," 8.
61. NAC, Canadian Labour Congress (CLC) Files, MG28 I103, vol. 25, file 2 United Automobile, Aircraft and Agricultural Implement Workers of America, George Burt, 1947-50. Burt to A.R. Mosher, President, CCL, 9 August 1949.

62. NAC, UIC Records, RG50, vol. 53, 17th meeting UIAC, January 1950, "Minutes of the Meeting"; submission, Dominion Joint Legislative Committee, Railway Transportation Brotherhoods.

63. *Labour Gazette* (April 1950), 534; (June 1950), 792.

64. NAC, Department of Labour Records, RG27, vol. 3458, file 4-11, pt. 5. Ingersoll to MacNamara, 7 October 1950. See also *Ibid.*, Ingersoll to MacNamara, 23 November 1949. A similar point was made at a meeting of the UIAC by the chairperson of the Committee. NAC, UIC Records, RG50, vol. 53, 17th meeting UIAC January 1950, "Minutes of the Meeting."

65. Canadian Congress of Labour, *Proceedings of the Ninth Annual Convention* (October 1949), 96, 98.

66. See, for example, NAC, CLC Files, MG28 I103, vol. 25, file 2, Andy Andras to Pat Conroy, Secretary Treasurer CCL, 7 March 1950; *Ibid.*, vol. 238, file 238-16, Sam Wolstein to Pat Conroy, 4 March 1950.

67. *Canadian Unionist* (April 1950), 80.

68. CCL, *Proceedings of the 10th Annual Convention* (1950), 76.

69. *Ibid.*, 76-77.

70. For example, the CCL brief to the federal government expressed the concern that such a regulation "is likely to lead to the undermining of the Act by the imposition of restrictions against other classes of workers." *Canadian Unionist* (April 1950), 80. See also NAC, CLC files, MG28 I103, vol. 25, file 2, Andras to Conroy, 7 March 1950; CCL, *Proceedings of the 10th Annual Convention* (1950), 76.

71. Trades and Labor Congress of Canada, *Report of the Proceedings of the Annual Convention* (September 1950), 444. The resolution was brought forward by the New Brunswick Federation of Labour.

72. NAC, Department of Labour Records, RG27, vol. 3458, file 4-11, pt. 5, Bengough to MacNamara, 24 October 1950.

73. *Ibid.* MacNamara to Norman Robertson, Clerk of the Privy Council and Secretary to the Cabinet, 26 October 1950. He is referring both to the married women's and to another regulation.

74. The term is from the Subcommittee on the Post-war Problems of Women, Brandt, "'Pigeon-Holed,'" 249.

75. NAC, UIC Records, RG50, vol. 59, Ingersoll to A.H. Brown, 30 April 1947. This was Miss Estelle Hewson, from the Border Branch of the Canadian Red Cross Society, Windsor.

76. It is not clearly specified why this change took place. At this time the number of employer and employee representatives was increased from two to three and it was argued that this did not leave room for a women's representative, since the maximum number on the Committee was six plus the chairperson. It appears that the change may have been to ensure regional representation and to allow the addition of a representative from the Quebec labour movement. See *Ibid.*, MacNamara to V.R. Smith, 23 June 1947; Mackintosh to Stangroom, 20 August 1946; Ingersoll to Brown, 30 April 1947.

77. Canada, House of Commons, *Debates*, 10 June 1955, 4625. See also Canada, House of Commons, Standing Committee on Industrial Relations, *Minutes of Proceedings and Evidence*, 26 May 1955, 187-8.

78. Canada, House of Commons, Standing Committee on Industrial Relations, *Minutes of Proceedings and Evidence*, 6 June 1955, 475.

79. Canada, House of Commons, *Debates*, 18 May 1951, 3203.

80. Canada, Unemployment Insurance Commission, *Digest of the Decisions of the Umpire* (Ottawa 1960), CUB-848, 21 August 1952.

81. Canada, House of Commons, Standing Committee on Industrial Relations, *Minutes of Proceedings and Evidence*, 26 May 1955, 262.

82. NAC, Stanley Knowles Papers, MG32 C59, file 19-A, UIC cases, correspondence 1942-1952, Mrs. Dora Doersam to Stanley Knowles, 10 May 1951; Milton F. Gregg, Minister of Labour to Stanley Knowles, 11 June 1951. In a subsequent similar case where a woman lost her job at the T. Eaton Co. because of department policy not to keep on married women, the decision to disqualify her was successfully appealed and the woman was therefore able to collect benefits. See Decision of the Umpire CUB-859, 5 September 1952. Quoted in *Labour Gazette* (January 1953), 118-19.

83. NAC, Stanley Knowles Papers, MG32 C59, file 19-A, UIC cases, correspondence, 1942-1952, Mrs. Dora Doersam to Stanley Knowles, 10 May 1951.

84. See NAC, UIC Records, RG50, vol. 53, 16th meeting UIAC, July 1949, C.A.L. Murchison, Commissioner, UIC to UIAC 11 July 1949. See also NAC, Department of Labour Records, RG27, vol. 3458, file 4-11, pt. 7, J.G. Bisson, Chief Commissioner, UIC, to Minister of Labour, 3 September 1954.

85. See for example, Canada, Unemployment Insurance Commission, *Digest*, CUB-1101, 8 December 1954. In this case an employer laid off a pregnant woman six months before her due date and she was disqualified for two years from receiving UI.

86. Canada, House of Commons, *Debates*, 13 June 1952, 3197-8.

87. CUB-1215, 9 February 1956, reported in *Labour Gazette* (April 1956), 428.

88. Canada, Unemployment Insurance Commission, *Digest*, CUB-772 and 773, 6 December 1951.

89. Dingledine, *Chronology*, 13. Regulation 5A also went much further than the general provision of the Act in recognizing as just cause for leaving employment only those reasons solely and directly connected with employment.

90. See, for instance, Canada, Unemployment Insurance Commission, *Digest*, CUB-1457, 7 February 1958. This issue was also brought up a number of times in the House of Commons. See, for example, Mr. Bryce in Canada, House of Commons, *Debates*, 11 August 1956, 7452.

91. This was later pointed out by the CLC at the 1961 hearings of the Committee of Inquiry into the UI Act. See NAC, Gill Commission Records, RG33/48 vol. 10, Submission to the Committee of Inquiry into the Unemployment Insurance Act by the Canadian Labour Congress, 58.

92. This was pointed out by Svanhuit Josie. NAC, Gill Commission Records, RG33/48, vol. 10, Submission to the Committee of Inquiry into Unemployment Insurance, 31.

93. See, for example, NAC, UIC Records, RG50, vol. 54, 24th meeting UIAC, July 1954, "Minutes of the Meeting." The Canadian Manufacturers' Association stated that "it would be unsound to consider . . . any changes in the Act or Regulations which would have the effect of increasing the drain on the Fund."

94. NAC, RG50, vol. 54, 24th meeting UIAC, July 1954, "Actuarial Report," 8–10.

95. *Ibid.* He also made the suggestion that married women were contributing to the recorded rate of unemployment since they were only registering as unemployed for the purpose of collecting benefits and did not genuinely want employment.

96. Canada, House of Commons, Standing Committee on Industrial Relations, *Minutes of Proceedings and Evidence*, 6 June 1955, 463–8. Brief from Mr. Barclay, UI Commission. He noted that while married women made up 33.9 per cent of the insured labour force in 1954, they accounted for 51.4 per cent of all female claimants. *Ibid.*, 468.

97. *Ibid.*, 464. This caused Ellen Fairclough to call Barclay's brief a "slander against women in employment." *Ibid.*, 469. The UI Commission also argued that since in the first month after they came into effect 18 per cent of women kept alive their application for employment, 5 per cent reported finding work and 77 per cent allowed their application to lapse, this proved that they were not really interested in finding employment. Canada, Unemployment Insurance Commission, *Annual Report* (1951), 38.

98. See, for example, Canada, House of Commons, *Debates*, 18 June 1952, 3397. Canada, House of Commons, Standing Committee on Industrial Relations, *Minutes of Proceedings and Evidence*, 26 May 1955, 183–7.

99. Knowles, Canada, House of Commons, *Debates*, 4 June 1952, 2913.

100. In addition to the resolutions passed at the 1949 and 1950 conventions (see notes 65, 68), resolutions on the subject were passed in 1951–1954. See CCL, *Proceedings of the Annual Convention* (1951), 98; (1952), 71; (1953), 87; (1954), 94. In all cases the recommendation to abolish or significantly modify the married women's regulation is part of the Report of the Committee on Unemployment Insurance, which had consolidated the resolutions on the subject. In 1955 the Committee simply expressed surprise that amendments to the regulation recommended by the UIAC and the UI Commission were turned down by Cabinet. *Ibid.* (1955), 97–8.

101. For the annual briefs, see *Canadian Unionist* (April 1950); (April 1951); (April 1952); (March 1953); (November 1954); (December 1955). On the CCL submissions to the UIAC see NAC, UIC Records, RG50, vol. 53, 19th meeting UIAC, July 1951; 21st meeting UIAC, July 1952; 23rd meeting UIAC, July 1953; RG50, vol. 54, 24th meeting UIAC, July 1954. On the submission to the UI Commission see NAC, CLC Files, MG28 I103, vol. 238, file 238-19; UIC "Minutes of the Meeting with Representatives of Labour Organizations, May 10, 1951."

102. NAC, CLC Files, MG28 I103, vol. 239, file 239-11, "Minutes of a Meeting of the Employees' Representatives on the Courts of Referees in the Province of Quebec," 29 March 1952. See also *Ibid.*, file 239-9, "Report on the Conference of Employee Members of the Courts of Referees in the Province of Quebec," 18 February 1951; file 239-12, "Conference of Employee Nominees of the Courts of Referees in Ontario," 19 April 1952. In the latter case only modifications in the regulation were recommended.

103. NAC, CLC Files, MG28 I103, vol. 284, file UI part 5, 1951–1952, J. Marchand, CCCL to A. Andras, CCL, 7 March 1951; A. Andras to P. Conroy, 16 March 1951.

104. NAC, CLC Files, MG28 I103, vol. 238, file 238-20. A. Andras to P. Conroy, 16 March 1951; "Joint Submission to the Umpire Re Appeals against Disqualification under Benefit Regulation 5A," 1–6.

105. *Ibid.*

106. NAC, CLC files, MG28 I103, vol. 284, file UI part 5, 1951–1952, J. Marchand to A. Andras; *Ibid.*, vol. 238, file 238-20, "Joint Submission to the Umpire"; *Ibid.*, vol. 238, file 238-19, UIC, "Minutes of the Meeting with Representatives of Labour Organizations," 10 May 1951.

107. *Labour Gazette* (May 1951), 647; (April 1952), 411; (April 1953), 542; (December 1954), 1705; (January 1956), 50; (January 1957), 154.

108. CCCL brief to the federal government. Quoted in *Labour Gazette* (May 1951), 647.

109. Trades and Labor Congress of Canada, *Report of the Proceedings of the Annual Convention* (1951), 196, 276–7; (1952), 173–4; (1954), 475; (1955), 377.

110. See, for example, NAC, UIC Records, RG50, vol. 53, 19th meeting UIAC, July 1951, TLC submission to the UIAC. The CCL presented submissions to the UIAC far more frequently than did the TLC.

111. NAC, CLC Files, MG28 I103, vol. 238, file 238-19, UIC, "Minutes of Meeting with Labour Organizations," 10 May 1951.

112. Trades and Labor Congress of Canada, *Report of the Proceedings of the Annual Convention*, 1949–1955.

113. *Trades and Labor Congress Journal* (April 1952), 14.

114. *Ibid.* (November 1954), 8; (January 1956), 9–10.

115. NAC, UIC Records, RG50, vol. 54, 32nd meeting UIAC, July 1957, CLC submission to the UIAC, 3.
116. The United Electrical, Radio and Machine Workers of America (UE) appears to have been particularly active in this regard. For example, it appeared along with the CCL before the Umpire and requested that the Umpire recommend that Regulation 5A and the authorizing statute be rescinded. See CUB-655, March 22, 1951, reprinted in full in *Labour Gazette* (May 1951), 711–13. Two locals of UE, as noted earlier, also appeared before the 1955 hearings on the amendments to the UI Act to protest about the case of two married women denied benefits and to urge the elimination of the regulations. Canada, House of Commons, Standing Committee on Industrial Relations, *Minutes of Proceedings and Evidence*, 26 May 1955, 262.
117. It appears, for example, that they were not initially notified of the 1955 hearings on amendments to the UI Act. The issue was raised by Ellen Fairclough, Canada, House of Commons, Standing Committee on Industrial Relations, *Minutes of Proceedings and Evidence*, 17 May 1955, 61.
118. For an analysis of the National Council of Women in an earlier period see Veronica Strong-Boag, *The Parliament of Women: The National Council of Women of Canada, 1893–1929* (Ottawa 1976). See also Rosa L. Shaw, *Proud Heritage*.
119. See, for example, NAC, National Council of Women (NCW) Papers, MG28 I25, vol. 97, file 7, Brief to Prime Minister St. Laurent December 1953; vol. 93, file 9, Milton F. Gregg to Mrs. R.J. Marshall, 5 September 1951.
120. See, for example, NAC, NCW Papers, MG28 I25, vol. 97, file 11, Resolutions, 1953–54.
121. NAC, NCW Papers, MG28 I25, vol. 97, file 12, Annual Report, Economics and Taxation Committee, 1953–54.
122. NAC, NCW Papers, MG28 I25, vol. 99, file 4, Newsletters 1954–55, January-February 1955, 7; vol. 100, file 16, Newsletters 1955–56, February 1956; vol. 125, file 2, Correspondence 1957–58, Michael Starr to Mrs. Eaton, 9 October 1957; vol. 125, file 3, Correspondence 1958–59, Mrs. Rex Eaton to "Dear President."
123. NAC, NCW Papers, MG28 I25, vol. 92, file 4, Agnes Reau, Chairman, Committee on Resolutions to Mrs. D.F. Duncan, Corresponding Secretary, Fort Williams, 30 April 1951. The view that the UI Commission was dealing with the matter was expressed by Mrs. Finlayson, NCW representative to the National Employment Committee of the UI Commission, and Mrs. Turner Bone, representative "to the Montreal branch."
124. This was at the request of Isabel Finlayson, who suggested that the Local Laws and Trades and Professions Committees find out about the application of Regulation 5A in their locality. NAC, NCW Papers, MG28 I25, vol. 96, file 7, I. Finlayson to "Madame Chairman," 6 November 1953.
125. NAC, NCW Papers, MG28 I25, vol. 96, file 10, Local Councils of Women, 1953–1965, "Report of Trades and Professions Committee Presented to Winnipeg Council, 23 April 1954." See also *Ibid.*, vol. 97, file 12, Standing Committees, 1953–1954, "Report of the Committee on Laws"; "Report of the Trades and Professions Committee, June 1954."
126. NAC, NCW Papers, MG28 I25, vol. 96, file 1: Annual Meeting, 1954, "Minutes, 61st Annual Meeting June 25–July 1, 1954," 4.
127. Women had somewhat more representation in the employment section of the UI Commission than they did with respect to the administration and coverage of the insurance itself. For example, not only was there an adviser on women's employment within the UI commission administrative structure, but women also had representation on the National Employment Committee which oversaw the operations of the employment offices under the jurisdiction of the UI Commission. For example, the NCW had a representative on this committee in the 1950s. Rosa L. Shaw, *Proud Heritage*, 199.
128. NAC, NCW Papers, MG28 I25, vol. 96, file 1: Annual Meeting 1954, "Minutes, 61st Annual Meeting June 25–July 1, 1954," 4.
129. The convention proceedings do not reveal the reasons for this abrupt change. See NAC, NCW Papers, MG28 I25, vol. 100, file 1: Annual Meeting, "NCW, Resolutions for Annual Meeting, 1956"; vol. 103, file 7, PM and Cabinet: Correspondence, 1956–57, Milton F. Gregg to Mrs. F.F. Worthington, 30 October 1956, acknowledging receipt of recommendation that the married women's regulation be rescinded.
130. NAC, NCW Papers, MG28 I25, vol. 103, file 7, PM and Cabinet: Correspondence, 1956–57, Milton F. Gregg to Mrs. F.F. Worthington, 30 October 1956.
131. *Labour Gazette* (March 1957), 267.
132. See, for example, NAC, Papers of the Canadian Federation of Business and Professional Women's Clubs (BPW Papers) MG28 I55, vol. 44, "Minutes of the 13th Biennial Convention, July, 1952."
133. See, for example, NAC, BPW Papers, MG28 I55, vol. 44, "Minutes of the 10th Convention, July, 1946," 3; vol. 65, Resolutions: 15 June 1948; vol. 45, "Minutes of the Meeting of the Board of Directors 4 June 1955," 6.
134. NAC, BPW Papers, MG28 I55, vol. 12, "Report of Chairman of Standing Committee on Legislation, 1950–52."
135. NAC, BPW Papers, MG28 I55, vol. 44, Minutes of the Biennial Convention, July 1954, 38; Minutes of the Biennial Convention July 1956, 19; vol. 45, Reports 1954–56.
136. At Fairclough's request, the Ontario BPW sent a telegram urging the deletion of discriminatory clauses against married women to the labour minister as the 1955 amendments to the UI Act

came before the House. See NAC, BPW Papers, MG28 I55, vol. 34, 1955 Correspondence, BPW of Ontario, Ontario Provincial Conference, 30 September–2 October 1955, Report of the Provincial President. The representation to the Industrial Relations Committee took the form of a telegram from the BPW sent to both the labour minister and Fairclough. Canada, Standing Committee on Industrial Relations, *Minutes of Proceedings and Evidence*, 6 June 1955, 472–3. On the meetings with Prime Ministers St. Laurent and Diefenbaker, see NAC, BPW Papers, MG28 I55, vol. 81, *The Business and Professional Woman*, XXV (May–June 1957), 6; XXV (January–February 1958), 16.

137. Canada, House of Commons, *Debates*, 15 November 1957, 1171–2.

138. The role of these groups is frequently cited in assessments of why the regulation was eventually revoked. See, for example, Canada, Committee of Inquiry into Unemployment Insurance (Gill Committee), *Report*, 38. NAC, Gill Commission Records, RG33/48, vol. 10, Svanhuit Josie, Submission to the Committee of Inquiry into Unemployment Insurance, 1961, 32; NAC, CLC files, MG28 I103, vol. 285, UI Misc. Inquiries 1959–1960, part 2, Andras to O'Sullivan, 9 February 1960.

139. Fairclough's role was recognized by Fraudena Eaton, President of the NCW when, in a letter to Fairclough she noted "I recognized that your firm hand on this matter strengthened the hand of the Minister of Labour." NAC, NCW Papers, MG28 I25, vol. 125, file 2: Correspondence 1957–58, Mrs. Rex Eaton to the Honourable Ellen Fairclough, 19 December 1957.

140. NAC, UIC Records, RG50, vol. 56, 38th meeting UIAC, April 1960; UI Commission to UIAC, 12 July 1960, "Impact of Benefit Regulations to Married Women," 3. The memorandum noted that benefit payments to single women increased by 60 per cent between 1957 and 1958, while payments to married women rose by 80 per cent.

141. *Ibid.*, 6.

142. *Ibid.*, 6–7.

143. NAC, UIC Records, RG50, vol. 56, 40th meeting UIAC, October 1960, "Special Report of the UIAC Resulting from Meeting October 27, 1960."

144. NAC, Department of Labour Records, RG27, vol. 3458, file 4-11, pt. 8, Submission to the Standing Committee on Industrial Relations of the House of Commons on Bill C-43, An Act to Amend the Unemployment Insurance Act by the Canadian Manufacturers' Association, 21 May 1959, 13, 16.

145. NAC, Department of Labour Records, RG27, vol. 3458, file 4-11, pt. 8, J.C. Whitelaw, General Manager, Canadian Manufacturers' Association to Michael Starr, Minister of Labour, 20 December 1960.

146. Dr. James was formerly of the Dominion Bureau of Statistics, then working for the Department of National Defence.

147. Canada, Senate, *Proceedings of the Special Committee of the Senate on Manpower and Employment*, 1960, 217–18.

148. *Ibid.*, 218. The figures on married women registered for jobs is from a survey conducted at the UI offices; those on the proportion in the labour force are from the monthly labour force survey administered by the Dominion Bureau of Statistics.

149. *Ibid.*, 238. This was based on the number indicating that it was not financially necessary to work (and included those indicating that "the extra money is desirable and useful" or that they "like to have something useful to do"), who preferred part time or temporary work, and the proportion whose husbands were working full time. *Ibid.*, 209, 236–8.

150. *Ibid.*, 252.

151. *Ibid.*, 364–6. Such a comparison had also appeared in early reports of the Commission. For example, Barclay, one of the UI Commissioners, noted that in 1946–49 more women were claiming UI benefits than were reported by the labour force survey as without jobs and seeking work. Canada, House of Commons, Standing Committee on Industrial Relations, *Minutes of Proceedings and Evidence*, 6 June 1955, 464.

152. Canada, Senate, *Report of the Special Committee of the Senate on Manpower and Employment* (Ottawa 1961), 65.

153. This was pointed out, for example, by a staff person at the UI Commission. See NAC, UIC Records, RG50, vol. 53, 18th meeting UIAC, July 1950, W. Thomson, Supervisor of Analysis and Development Division UI Commission to Chief Commissioner, 20 July 1950. Ostry also notes some of the differences between the two measures, but nevertheless compares the two. Canada, Senate, *Proceedings*, 356–63. The differences are also indicated in Canada, Senate, *Report of the Special Committee of the Senate on Manpower and Employment*, 14.

154. Canada, Unemployment Insurance Commission, *Annual Report* (1951), 25.

155. *Ibid.* (1952), 14. See also *Ibid.* (1951), 25.

156. *Ibid.* (1954), 14. The division does not distinguish between married and single female applicants.

157. Quoted by Ellen Fairclough. Canada, House of Commons, *Debates*, 18 June 1952, 3396–7.

158. NAC, Gill Commission Records, RG33/48, vol. 10. Submission to the Committee of Inquiry into the Unemployment Insurance Act by Svanhuit Josie 1961, 34.

159. Canada, Committee of Inquiry into the Unemployment Insurance Act, *Report* (Ottawa 1962), 1.

160. The point was made by Stanley Knowles, quoting a CCL document. Canada, House of Commons, *Debates*, 4 June 1952, 2913.

161. NAC, Gill Commission Records, RG33/48, vol. 10 for all briefs.
162. NAC, Gill Commission Records, RG33/48, vol. 10, Submission to the Committee of Inquiry into the Unemployment Insurance Act from Office Overload Co. Ltd., October 1961.
163. NAC, Gill Commission Records, RG33/48, vol. 10, Submission from the National Council of Women.
164. NAC, Gill Commission Records, RG33/48, vol. 10, Submission from the Canadian Federation of Business and Professional Women's Clubs.
165. NAC, Gill Commission Records, RG33/48, vol. 10, Submission from the National Legislative Committee, International Railway Brotherhood.
166. NAC, Gill Commission Records, RG33/48, vol. 10, Submission from Svanhuit Josie, 11.
167. The Gill Committee recommended that no special regulations be enacted relating to married women, although they did suggest more active claims supervision. Canada, Committee of Inquiry into Unemployment Insurance, *Report*, 12.
168. Sylvia Ostry, *The Female Worker in Canada* (Ottawa 1968), 3–4.
169. By 1961 equal pay laws had been enacted by eight provinces and by the federal government. *Labour Gazette* (June 1965), 518.
170. The Department of Labour in their publication *Labour Organization in Canada* did report on the percentage of trade union membership made up of women until the early 1950s. They noted, however, that the figures were unreliable since many of the local labour unions did not differentiate on the basis of sex in their membership records. See, for example, *Labour Organization in Canada* (1948), 19; (1949), 21. In 1953 they discontinued the reports. When the *Labour Gazette* produced a special issue on women in the labour force in 1954, they requested, but were unable to obtain, this information from the central labour bodies. For examples of both the TLC and CCL inability to provide such figures, see NAC, CLC files, MG28 I103, vol. 269, Dept. of Labour, Misc. Part 2, 1952–56, Bengough to H.J. Walker, 19 February 1954; vol. 190, file 6: Federal Dept. of Labour correspondence, Part 1, 1950–54, Burt to Dowd, 3 February 1954. In 1954 the CCCL estimated that more than a third of its members were women. *Labour Gazette* (March 1954), 389. In 1963 women accounted for 16.3 per cent of trade union membership. Canada, Ministry of Trade and Commerce and Dominion Bureau of Statistics, *Annual Report under the Corporations and Labour Unions Return Act, Part II: Labour Unions, 1963* (Ottawa 1966) 37, table 15A.
171. For example, in 1959 a special course on the role of women in trade unions was held for the first time at the CLC Ontario summer school, and it was also noted that each year the number of women enrolled in various courses had increased. *Labour Gazette* (September 1950), 910. In 1952 the CCCL decided to reserve one of its vice-presidencies for a woman, and it also established a women's committee that was active from 1952 to 1956 and from 1960 to 1966. See Lucie Piché, "Entre l'accès à l'égalité et la preservation des modèles: Ambivalence du discours et des revendications du Comité Féminin de la CTCC-CSN, 1952–1966," *Labour/Le Travail*, 29 (Spring 1992); *Labour Gazette* (March 1954), 389. In 1960 a women's committee was also established in the Ontario Federation of Labour. *Labour Gazette* (December 1960), 1290. In 1959 the CLC established a committee to coordinate white collar organizing. *Labour Gazette* (August 1959), 797. Individual unions had already established office worker departments. For example, Eileen Tallman was the head of the Office Workers Department of the United Steelworkers of America from 1952 to 1956. It should be noted that while women clearly formed a high proportion of white collar workers, organizing in this area was not necessarily presented as a "women's issue."

Remembering Lesbian Bars: Montreal, 1955–1975

LINE CHAMBERLAND

Retracing lesbian meeting places, mainly bars and other drinking establishments, takes on more than historical importance. It facilitates studying the sociological significance of the emergence of lesbian subcultures by examining the actual conditions under which they flourished and then locating them within existing sex and class relationships. My

SOURCE: Line Chamberland, "Remembering Lesbian Bars: Montreal, 1955–1975," in Rommel Mendès-Leite and Pierre-Olivier de Busscher, eds., *Gay Studies from the French Cultures: Voices from France, Belgium, Brazil, Canada, and The Netherlands* (New York: The Harrington Park Press, 1993), 231–269.

research on the social aspects of lesbian life in Montreal between 1955 and 1975 analyses these social spaces as indicators of the existence of lesbian networks and of subgroups within the lesbian world.[1] I also examine the strategies and the interplay of allegiances which permitted certain sites to be appropriated by lesbians, as well as the ways lesbians dealt with the specific repressive measures they encountered from the moment their social existence was, in this particular way, made public. Finally, since the use of physical space is largely a function of social class which determines access to space as well as the kind of activities that can be practised in public or private spaces, this variable was constantly taken into consideration.[2]

In this essay, I will first address the nature of the differences between lesbians and gay men in their relationship to public space in the urban environment. Next I will focus on the bars and other public meeting places for francophone Montreal lesbians. Taking into account class differences, I will describe the development of these establishments as a form of the appropriation of urban public space. I will distinguish two periods (the emergence of the earlier lesbian meeting places in the 50s and early 60s and their transformation in the late 60s and 70s) and describe briefly two bars typical of each period, the *Ponts de Paris* and *Baby Face Disco*. Then by comparing these two bars, I will look at the strategies which made this appropriation possible and the specific role played by working-class lesbians in this process. Following this, I will discuss the role of bars in the development of a lesbian culture and class-related differences in the way these places are inscribed in lesbian memories. Finally, I will suggest explanations for class-related differences in bar-going habits and ways of expressing lesbian identity.

Lesbian Invisibility in the Urban Environment

The emergence of homosexual communities in larger North American cities transformed the relationship of gay men to the urban environment. To be sure, certain public places had long been used as venues for anonymous sexual encounters. In the 20th century, however, numerous businesses and institutions appeared, which eventually formed the basis of an economic, social, and sexual exchange matrix. In some cities, this led to a parallel concentration of local residents who openly identified themselves as gay. Gay territoriality then contributed to the gay world's greater visibility and accessibility. In some cases, gay ghettoization of space has caused tension among the general population and competition for a piece of urban turf. It also facilitated the rise of a corresponding political power (Altman, 1982; D'Emilio, 1983; Kinsman, 1987; Murray, 1979).[3]

Studies of lesbian culture have not revealed such marked territoriality. Gay men had access to public places that have traditionally been out of reach for women, where for the entire class of women admission was either prohibited (in the case of certain drinking establishments), restricted by threat of harassment to certain hours or types of use (the inability to walk down the street or stroll through a park at night without a male escort), or tabooed (women frequenting certain entertainment venues, such as theatres, clubs, and billiard rooms, unless accompanied by men).[4] Some studies asserted that lesbians didn't frequent bars intensely or regularly (Bell and Weinberg, 1978; Hanley et al., 1978; Hedblom, 1973; Hooker, cited by Lisagor, 1980; Moses, 1978).[5] Others noted that contrary to that of gay men, lesbian involvement in bar life began only after the emergence of an individual's lesbian identity and was variable through time (Eisner, 1982; Schäfers, 1976). Spatial concentration has taken place only for certain women's communities: white, feminist, and middle-class, and even then, to a considerably less significant extent than for gay men (Ettore, 1980; Wolf, 1980). Lesbian commercial outlets and institutions remain few in number and not very visible. They are frequently advertised as gay or feminist, not explicitly lesbian. On the whole, whether autonomous or not, they tend to mask the nature of their enterprises and rarely publicize their existence as clearly or as widely as comparable gay male businesses and institutions. As in society generally, lesbian culture is only faintly visible in the urban environment, which at times makes locating it difficult (Hanley et al., 1978).

THE EMERGENCE OF PUBLIC MEETING PLACES FOR LESBIANS IN MONTREAL

In Quebec, public places frequented by lesbians prior to the 50s have left little trace. However, vocabulary in use during the 50s in written documents and personal stories indicates that some lesbians adopted Butch/Femme roles and were socially visible as such earlier than that. Allusions to Butch/Femme roles were present in the childhood memories of some of my respondents, as well as in sensationalist publications of the time (Higgins & Chamberland, 1992). In current Quebec French, the term *butch* refers to lesbians who opted for masculine dress and manners, going so far as to pass for men. In the language of lesbians who adopted these roles, nouns and pronouns for butches were masculinized: thus, one said *un butch*, not *une butch* and *il* (he), not *elle* (she). Many butches had masculine nicknames and some insisted on being addressed as *Monsieur* (Mister). Another word was *femme-homme* (mannish woman) to refer specifically to those who frequently passed as men. The terms designating the feminine partner are less specific: primarily the word *femme* was used, sometimes accompanied by a possessive pronoun, as in *ma femme* (my wife). Note that in French, *femme* has the double meaning of woman and wife. Sometimes *femelle* (female) was used, as well as certain expressions, such as *être (ou vivre) en ménage avec . . .* (set up house with . . .). The most common term for lesbians in this era, however, was *femmes-aux-femmes*, which might be translated as "women who like women." This term was commonly used as a label and left no doubt as to the exact nature of the relationship between the two women, including the sexual component. This vocabulary is different from that used in France, where lesbians were frequently called *gouines* and butches were called *Jules*, terms that were never heard in Quebec.

From the 50s on, cabarets, bars, and other drinking establishments, including clandestine venues and billiard rooms, were used by francophone lesbians in Montreal for the purposes of meeting and socializing. These establishments figured among the most disreputable of their type, but the services offered, operating costs, material organization, and other commercial characteristics were not significantly different from other businesses of a similar nature. They were situated in the eastern part of the city, in or near a well-circumscribed area known as the Red Light District or the Main.[6] The sphere of influence enjoyed by a given establishment and its customers fluctuated a lot, and the absence of written sources makes it extremely difficult to recreate a definitive portrait.[7] Nevertheless, it is possible to identify the most popular long-term venues of the 50s and early 60s: the *Ponts de Paris* (first known as *Aux deux canards*), the *Zanzibar*, the *Blue Sky* (which became the *Café Only*), and the *New Orleans*. Located directly on Main were the *Café St-John*, renamed the *Saguenay*, the *Canasta*, and the *Rodéo* (later the *Lodéo*). Lesbians also frequented *Le Bérêt bleu* and the *Hi Lo*, as well as the *Casa Loma*, one of the city's leading night clubs, where occasional drag shows attracted a large mixed clientele. Given the social characteristics of the respondents, bars which were frequented mainly by anglophones have not been studied. The best known was the *Tropical*, mainly a gay men's bar located in the anglophone western part of downtown. For a more complete portrait, francophone and anglophone lesbian meeting places would have to be compared, and the interaction between the two groups examined.

The area in which these earlier lesbian meeting places were located had a long-established reputation for illicit or semi-licit sexual activities (striptease, prostitution, etc.) as well as vice and crime. The Red Light District's cheap hotels rented inexpensive rooms for all kinds of sexual encounters, paid or unpaid. For decades, the legal and illegal activities of this sector were carried out under the eyes of the neighbouring, mainly working-class population, and under the control of local organized crime elements, which until the 70s benefited from the collusion of the police and the implicit tolerance of municipal authorities.[8] With its numerous night clubs, bars, and cafés, Montreal was known as a wide-open city for many decades and throughout eastern North America.[9] In the hierarchy of entertainment venues, the cabarets located in the French-speaking eastern part of the city were seen as more outrageous and less respectable than the ones in the English West.

In most of the bars they patronized, lesbians represented but a small proportion of the clientèle, which was made up, in varying degrees, of heterosexual couples, single men, prostitutes, inveterate alcoholics, small-time criminals, homosexual men, transvestites, and transsexuals. Most of the lesbians who went regularly to the bars and clubs of the district came from, and still belonged to, the working class. They worked in nearby factories, hotels, and restaurants, or held low-level positions in the white-collar sector or in a number of artistic fields. Butches tended to hold non-traditional jobs in warehouses, taxi-driving, transportation, building maintenance, etc. Some got by on government welfare or unemployment payments and others lived off petty criminal activities. Lesbians from other classes also came once in a while. Many never came back after a first visit. There were also "housewife lesbians" who visited the bars on occasion. These were women who had opted for marriage as a social inevitability and a means of surviving economically, while they continued to have secret homosexual affairs, whether intermittent or long-term, taking advantage of the room to manoeuvre that their institutionalized heterosexual status provided.

During this period, relationships between lesbians and sex-industry workers developed on a number of levels. Members of both groups came from a working-class or agricultural milieu. Jobs performed by strippers and prostitutes prior to entering the sex-industry were similar to those of working-class lesbians: unskilled labourer, clerk, waitress, cleaning woman, etc. (Limoges, 1967). It is nearly impossible to judge how many sex-industry workers engaged in regular homosexual activity, but research interviews attest to their large number. As well, the conditions for the practice of prostitution in this sector (soliciting in clubs that paid off local gangsters and decentralized control resulting from nonprofessional pimps for whom prostitution was merely a quick source of hard cash) left the prostitutes a certain degree of autonomy in their work and the actual possibility of giving their pimp the slip. It was not unheard of for him to be replaced by a "butch protector."[10] Lesbians and sex-industry workers found themselves shoulder to shoulder in many different establishments: on one hand, butches went to heterosexual clubs to visit or court those who were working, or to keep their eye on those they were "protecting"; and on the other, dancers and prostitutes went into lesbian bars or hung around with lesbians to avoid male solicitation or to temporarily get away from their pimp. All these women were subject to the same double repression, by the police on one hand, because of the women's criminalized sexual activities, and by men in general because they were the only women who walked the streets after dark in this part of town without an escort and were thus liable to be targets of aggression.

These earlier meeting places had a bad reputation as being rough and dangerous. Although the risk of brawls with other lesbians and police raids seems to me exaggerated, they did in fact occur and could have very disastrous consequences. It is very hard to estimate the actual incidence of fighting in lesbian hangouts. In general, my sources consist more of hearsay or "I was afraid that . . ." than actual memories of raids or brawls. This was especially the case for women who went to these bars only a few times, and who were quite apprehensive about the likelihood of such incidents, primarily because they would not have known what to do, or been able to fight back. According to the narrators' memories, some of the fights between lesbians involved newcomers who didn't yet know the rules and were perceived as competitors. They got a rude initiation. Newcomers often failed to return after their first encounter with the brutality of the milieu or because of the trouble they got into through ignorance of its rules. Other altercations happened late at night, fuelled by excessive drinking and sexual rivalry. I have also heard about fights that started because heterosexual women and even some lesbians made fun of butches and femmes. There were also attacks by men and fights related to the criminal activities.

Although lesbians were rarely convicted of gross indecency under Canadian law, those who went to bars and were visible on the streets were arrested under various pretexts such as underage drinking, vagrancy, or disorderly conduct. Police often checked ID and collected names for their files. When they left bars, lesbians were sometimes interrogated by policemen without any charge being issued. They were also sexually insulted by them on the streets, while being arrested or during court appearances. In one case, eighteen lesbians were arrested at *La Cave* on a Sunday afternoon under false charges of gross indecency (like putting their hands in each other's pants). Such charges might be dropped or changed after some time in prison. While in jail, lesbians underwent the same medical exam as prostitutes.

Opened in 1956, the *Ponts de Paris* was among the oldest and certainly the best known of these earlier meeting places. Its interior and exterior appearance was typical of the cabaret clubs of the 50s which offered live entertainment and remained unchanged throughout the 60s and the 70s. A brightly lit sign next to the street entrance announced the star and other performers. The shows were hosted by a locally known M.C. and included many types of acts: singers, dancers, acrobats, drag, musical soloists, etc., from Montreal and other cities. Some performers were known to be gay men or lesbians. There was no explicit homosexual content in the shows but there were drag shows and veiled allusions. The bar boasted two orchestras, one for the show and one for dancing. Special events included New Year's parties and Mardi Gras costume balls and the bar was sometimes rented to celebrate lesbian weddings. In short, the *Ponts de Paris* was a lively cabaret with a lot of activities going on.

The layout of the establishment was crucial to its internal dynamics. The large raised stage was the centre of attraction and served as a dance floor between shows. It was surrounded on three sides by large tables which could accommodate groups. The *Ponts de Paris* attracted a diversified clientèle composed of lesbians, gay men, heterosexual couples, and single men. A different section was assigned to each. Lesbians were seated on the left side and, if that was full, in the front of the centre, near the stage. This section was for women only.[11] Some narrators recall that meeting new lesbians was not as difficult because they were seated together at large tables. The heterosexual and gay male clientèle shared the tables in the rear centre and the right-hand section.[12] The bar ran along the rear wall. Its stools as well as a few tables near it were used by customers, male and female, looking for various kinds of paid sexual encounters. These included older lesbians who gave money to or provided drinks, meals, etc., for younger ones. Prostitutes might agree to sexual exchanges with men or women, but conventional prostitution wasn't nearly as common as in other establishments like the *Blue Sky*. Customers arriving at the *"Ponts"* were instantly sized up by the doorman. They were shown to seats in the appropriate section according to his perception of their sexual identity. The quality of the seats given to them varied according to the size of the tip, whether they were regulars who had a good personal relationship with the door man, etc. For heterosexual couples, the best seats not only gave a good view of the show but also of lesbian couples on the dance floor. The detailed rules of interaction between these two groups will be discussed below. Here it is sufficient to add that customers were not allowed to stand up or move around in the bar, except in the aisle between the bar and the tables.

Retracing these earlier lesbian meeting places clearly demonstrates that links between lesbians and the sexual and criminal underworld existed not only in the discourse of moralists. They were a concrete reality for working-class lesbians who worked in or frequented these bars. A large number of butches lived in the Red Light District. Despite the heterogeneity of the cliques which mingled there, from thugs to effeminate homosexuals and transvestites, sharing the same territory and the same social ostracism created a sense of belonging which is manifested by the appearance of a definite "us-versus-them" relationship to the outside world.[13] For the general public, including lesbians who didn't frequent these places, the association of lesbianism with vice and criminality was reinforced by the yellow press, which presented this world as common to all lesbians and gay men. These papers were the only ones to provide significant coverage of gay people during the 50s and 60s in Montreal. Analysis of a sample of yellow papers shows that they were not fabricating their views of homosexuality out of nothing. While attacking homosexuality and building a negative and stereotyped image of lesbians and gay men, they provided factual information about the homosexual meeting places and based their stories on the observable behaviour of the most visible members of the homosexual minority (Higgins & Chamberland, 1992).

THE EVOLUTION OF THE PUBLIC MEETING PLACES DURING THE SIXTIES AND EARLY SEVENTIES

Towards the end of the 60s, the picture changed considerably. The Red Light District gradually lost its population of working-class families, and more and more marginal individuals, including sexual outcasts, began to move in, taking over its cheap rooms and frequenting its cafés, brasseries, and billiard rooms.[14] Organized crime began to lose interest in the area, since it was reorganizing its activities elsewhere and extending them over a larger territory.[15] But the association of this part of the city with all forms of sexual immorality became even more pronounced. Lesbian meeting places changed in response to the same combination of economic, legal, and cultural factors as other establishments. The most notable changes were the disappearance of clubs that offered live entertainment — this having become uneconomical — and the appearance of discotheques. The *Ponts de Paris* remained open but, as in other cabarets, the shows were on a much smaller scale. One singer, accompanied by one or two musicians, repeated her performance twice a night. Juke boxes replaced the orchestras. Another change was the opening up of the taverns (renamed *brasseries*) to a female clientèle in the early 70s.

Gay men's establishments began to proliferate; some opened their doors to a female clientèle but the number of lesbians was usually insignificant. However, the creation of some mixed gay bars with a primarily female clientèle was a new phenomenon. In these places, the sharing of space inside between men and women was not rigidly controlled. Lesbians and gay men usually occupied different areas but they might occasionally mix together. Though interaction was minimal, they got along amicably. Proximity to the Red Light District and contact with prostitution networks continued unabated.[16]

From 1968 on, clubs and discotheques for women only began to appear; men were not allowed in if the place was managed by lesbians, but might be permitted in occasionally if the managers were men.[17] These new spaces were located away from the Red Light District, in the west end of the city, which was English-speaking and considered well-to-do. They had more indirect and fluctuating contacts with organized crime. There was a more modern look to the exterior of the buildings. Dress codes (e.g., no jeans) as well as rules of conduct once inside were enforced in order to give the appearance of a clean, respectable, middle-class establishment. Because of the non-mixed clientèle, there was a greater protection against male voyeurism, attacks by men, and social stigmatization. All these factors helped to attract a new clientèle composed of secretaries, technicians, teachers, nurses, and other professionals, as well as artists, students, and activists.

Baby Face Disco was typical of the lesbian bars of this period. It was Montreal's first lesbian-only drinking establishment, created and managed by a butch known as Baby Face, who had extensive experience in other bars.[18] As in other discotheques, the space was equipped with a juke box, a small dance floor, and strobe lights, which required only a minimal investment. There were few tables, so customers stood or walked around. This movement made it easy to meet new people. Baby Face herself acted as bouncer, choosing whom to let in and keeping a watchful eye on her customers. The clientèle was made up of many different groups: lesbians from different classes and ethnic backgrounds, older butches and femmes and younger lesbian-feminists, anglophones and francophones. Each social group behaved according to its own rules and rituals. Dress, etiquette, and patterns of interaction were quite different between those who were into roles and those who were not. The former usually sat in the same area, mostly in couples and groups. They still cruised by having the waitress take someone a drink or — with permission of the butch if needed — by asking a woman to dance. These older ways of sexually approaching other women coexisted with new models. For younger lesbians, standing near someone, inviting her outside to smoke pot together, or dancing alone in a sensuous manner were preferred. These cultural differences were puzzling for both sides.

In the 70s, lesbian bars opened in various parts of the city. The early years of the decade were a transitional period. One popular bar at the time, *Chez Madame Arthur*, benefited from a convergence of favourable conditions: police surveillance was at a minimum, the feminist and gay movements were in full swing, and a number of regular customers were developing a collective sense of lesbian identity. In terms of age, ethnic origin, and social status, the club attracted a more varied clientèle than its predecessors.[19] As the lesbian clientèle expanded, the establishments became somewhat specialized. After a few years, a hierarchy of bars emerged. At one end of the scale, there were private clubs, not necessarily stylish but requiring paid membership, and therefore reserved for a select clientèle composed primarily of professionals. At the other end, there were the brasseries of the Main "where you could still see butches playing pool and drinking beer all day long," in the words of one of the interviewees. Others characterized the regulars at bars they did not frequent, as, on one hand, "the intellectual elite" or "the stylish ones, who think they are better than everybody else," and on the other, as "the cheap, unattractive, vulgar ones who have no taste." Meanwhile, new kinds of lesbian spaces were created by politicized feminist lesbians who were dissatisfied with existing bars and rejected Butch/Femme roles. Huge spaces were rented as meeting places where different kinds of activities took place: dances, games, parties, etc. Here again, class splits and political disagreements about lesbian visibility continued, but that's another story.

STRATEGIES FOR APPROPRIATING URBAN SPACE

Not only did the working-class lesbians form the core of patrons at the earliest lesbian-identified bars and clubs, but they also played a crucial part in securing these public spaces for lesbians, and thus in the eventual development of bars for lesbians only. We now turn to the processes by which these public spaces were appropriated for lesbian use. In making themselves visible as Butch/Femme couples, by meeting in public places, working-class lesbians faced a double repression, that of heterosexual men and that of the judicial system. The former considered it legitimate to harass and ill-treat women who transgressed the socially imposed limits even though they didn't know them and had no personal ties with them. Sexual insults were particularly frequent, sometimes followed by threats or actual violence. Various strategies were developed in order to establish lesbian visibility as well as deal with its consequences. First we will examine Butch/Femme roles which were a key factor in putting these strategies into effect.[20] Next, we will compare the *Ponts de Paris* and *Baby Face Disco* and see how these two bars managed to recruit a lesbian clientèle and to protect it from stigmatization and harassment by men. Finally, we will look at the alliances made with organized crime in order to counteract police repression.

Butch/Femme roles can be seen as a way of living one's lesbian identity during an extremely repressive era by juggling gender categories and thus selectively making visible or concealing lesbian existence, depending on the circumstances. Ideologically and symbolically, these roles represented a double transgression. There was first the denial of the exclusivity of gender categories. Butches adopted identifiably masculine attributes in their appearance (suits, rings, tattoos of the beloved's name, etc.). By pitching their voices low, walking with a swagger, and being ready to fight at the least provocation, they obliterated the supposedly natural distinctions between men and women. In a context of rigidly genderized behaviour models, these characteristics signified to others their determination to get into men's world, whether by working in traditional male jobs or walking the streets at night. They also clearly indicated that they were able to compete on equal terms with men in order to gain access to male prerogatives. Secondly, entering into a Butch/Femme relationship implied that the two individuals, in conducting and presenting themselves as a "couple," asserted their right to all the elements of such a relationship, including the sexual component. Unlike the exchange of affection under the guise of female friendship, these roles were a revealing and unambiguous mark of lesbian identity. Role behaviour worked perfectly to counteract lesbian invisibility, the primary form of oppression. The message was clear and there was no mistaking it. As one lesbian put it, "Otherwise, people would have found any number of reasons to avoid saying that these were lesbians."

Though butches usually got (and still get) more attention, it should be remembered that femmes contributed to the visibility of the lesbian relationship as well. In their dress and behaviour, femmes were far from conforming to the dominant moral code.[21] Flashily dressed and sexy in appearance, femmes' public image expressed sexuality in too flagrant a way for them to be taken for pure young girls or respectable wives. Like prostitutes, many femmes used too much make-up or wore revealing strapless dresses or had tattoos on hidden parts of their bodies. In their interaction with butches, femmes acted like other women in public (cigarettes were lit for them, drinks paid for, etc.). These small gestures symbolically gave the butch the status of a protective partner, one who would take care of the femme and protect her against other men's sexual advances and aggression. Women who adopted the femme role publicly agreed to being seduced, loved, and fought over by other women. In general, their femaleness was never in doubt, so it was possible for femmes to pass for ordinary women in many situations. But when they went to the clubs or walked the streets with their butch partner, femmes manifested their rejection of the dominant norms that denied women any sexuality.

For butches or Butch/Femme couples, the roles left little room to conceal, manage, or negotiate personal identity in order to avoid stigmatization in many social contexts. Their advantage lay in the fact that they reproduced conventional gender categories so completely that butches managed to pass for men. Especially in public and impersonal situations (for example, while strolling along the street), the couple was treated as such, or there was enough surprise and consternation to create a sense of a misunderstanding and neutralize the risk of ostracism. One interviewee reported:

> Two feminine women, they can't hold hands on the street and what have you, but me, when I had on my suit and tie, like when I was with my girlfriend, well, I could hold her hand and I didn't feel like people were staring at us. . . . If we went to a restaurant, most of them . . . they didn't even notice; they said "Madam" to her and "Sir" to me, and we sat down. . . . They didn't notice because in those days it was too taboo.

On the other hand, in prolonged social interaction or face-to-face encounters, roles constituted a risk, since the meaning behind them, once discovered, was so obvious that the only possible outcome was direct confrontation.[22] One narrator, who frequently passed as a man and was fearful of fights, recounted how she constantly had to be tactful and on her guard when she went into heterosexual clubs, to the point of mixing with men in order not to be discovered.

In broader social terms, the message of roles was unequivocal. Establishments where large numbers of butches and femmes congregated gained a reputation as lesbian spots. As a result, such places provided social space for lesbians who did not engage in roles, as well as other women who came for a variety of reasons (curiosity, bisexuality, sexual adventure, uncertainty about identity after having been labelled a lesbian, etc.).

Butch/Femme roles were strategic not only in making lesbian existence socially visible, but also in securing and defending the lesbian space that had been won. The use of public places required the reconciliation of opposing demands. On one hand, exposure was needed in order to ensure that lesbian bars became known and accessible. Knowing that such places existed and discovering where they were was a problem. On the other hand, concealment was necessary in order to escape repression. In the two clubs considered, *Les Ponts de Paris* in the 50s and *Baby Face Disco* in the late 60s and 70s, the problem was solved in different ways. In both, the fight against repression relied on Butch/Femme roles.

Les Ponts de Paris cabaret had a wide range of customers including tourists from all over North America. Its openness to a wide public had contradictory implications. For one thing, it became widely known (and denounced) as a lesbian hang-out. There were many ways to learn of its existence. Like other cabarets, its shows were advertised in the newspaper. The presence of lesbians, made evident by visibly Butch/Femme couples, was an added attraction. People would learn about this by hearsay. For tourists, the word was spread by taxi drivers, hotel employees, etc. References in guide books and in the sensationalist press also alluded to the *Ponts'* unusual clientèle. All in all, it became so well known, and to such a large segment of the population, that several lesbians found themselves being told about it by their friends or families, who often had no inkling of their sexual orientation. Once you knew the name or had a vague indication about its location, finding the place was easy.

However, this increased public awareness maximized the exposure for lesbians who went there. They were exposed to the voyeuristic eyes of heterosexual customers. One narrator didn't want to go back after a first visit because she hated being an exhibit. Others did return, but many disliked being shown like zoo animals or rare specimens. Lesbians also feared being recognized by people they knew, as happened to one woman who lost her job when her boss saw her in this club. A third problem was harassment by men, both for butches and for femmes. As one interviewee put it: "The butches got harassed and insulted. The femmes got bothered because they were gay and all the guys wanted to get them into bed." Finally, the police regularly inspected the club and its vicinity. Lesbian customers risked being spotted or arrested by them. The openness which made it possible for lesbians to learn about the existence of the *Ponts* also had the consequence that those who came to visit it ran the risk of being labelled, ridiculed, humiliated, harassed, and arrested.

As a result, protective measures were put into effect. Both the heterosexual owners/managers and the butches who frequented the bar or worked there as waitresses, bouncers, or in other capacities cooperated in enforcing these measures. Butches and femmes needed a place to meet other lesbians, as well as a place to go for entertainment. Owners/managers had a vested interest in protecting lesbians because they were regular customers: they accounted for a substantial proportion of the business and they attracted other customers. Central to this protection was the creation of a separate section for lesbians, as mentioned above. It is not unusual for a bar to have different sections, each being occupied by distinct groups of customers. But in the *Ponts*, this separateness became an enforced rule. I haven't been able to retrace when this rule was put in place, but it was crucial in terms of establishing a specialized, secure, and easy-to-find (newcomers identified as lesbians were automatically seated there) space for lesbians. In order to counter the risk of verbal and physical attack by men, male customers were never allowed in this area, under any conditions. Stocky doormen watched over the flow of people inside the establishment and made sure that this rule was enforced. Moreover, butches guarded the security of the section. If necessary, they responded to verbal aggressions from men and provided physical protection for other lesbians. They also kept an eye on the dance floor, the entrance to the club, and the nearby streets. Men insulting lesbians or trying to interfere with women dancing together were quickly put in their place. Occasionally, butches protected prostitutes from their pimps.

In addition to physical segregation, everyone had to abide by another special rule of conduct. In all social interaction, remarks were to be addressed first to the Butch, whether they concerned the couple (e.g., an invitation to join a table) or just the partner identified as the Femme (e.g., inviting her to dance). When a heterosexual couple wanted to find lesbian partners for sex, only the woman could go into the reserved section, and she made the invitation to the butch. This was a form of protection against solicitations, which were often too numerous, demanding, or simply dishonest.[23] Butches were part of all the interactions with outsiders; the contact with them acted as a warning to would-be troublemakers. Their appearance, their toughness, and their aggressiveness were enough to prevent many intrusions and attacks by men. Generally, these measures were sufficient to defend lesbians' space and safety but were of little use against labelling and social stigmatization.

In *Baby Face Disco*, these problems were dealt with differently. When Baby Face opened her lesbian-only bar at the end of the 60s, she counted on the diversification and expansion of the lesbian clientèle to "make the place pay." Her bar used absolutely no advertising. It was located in an area far from the Red Light District. There was no sign on the outside; you had to know where it was. The discretion of the bar as well as the exclusion of heterosexuals, men and women, greatly reduced the risk of assault and of exposing lesbians' identity. Finding enough lesbian customers to insure the survival of the bar was possible because the social and legal context had become less repressive.[24] The existence of specialized gay men's and lesbian bars began to be taken for granted. Established networks now existed among lesbians, facilitating the circulation of information about places to meet in a variety of different ways: word-of-mouth, printed publicity, through feminist or lesbian organizations, etc.

At the beginning of *Baby Face Disco*, Butch/Femme roles were still crucial in marking the space as a lesbian one and in defending it. But within a few years, they became less essential to the internal dynamic of the establishment. As we have seen, roles worked as open displays of lesbian identity. They served to identify a bar as a lesbian meeting place and encouraged attendance by other lesbians. They also made it easy for Baby Face, acting as doorman, to distinguish lesbians from other women, sexual tourists in these times of "sexual revolution," or casual visitors who might be unaware of the real nature of the place. Because of this, the manager was to greet with suspicion the arrival of the new androgynous lesbian feminists at the beginning of the 70s; she suspected they were not really lesbians. As other ways of expressing lesbian identity developed, butches and femmes weren't the only visible lesbians any more. When it came to defending the premises against male aggression, the butches who worked at *Baby Face Disco* carried on their role insuring the protection of the place.[25] But inside the establishment, the defensive role of butch customers was rendered superfluous. The toughest and most violent ones were no longer required, either inside the club or in its immediate vicinity. Moreover, Baby Face, hoping to improve the image of lesbian clubs, imposed codes of dress and conduct. Customers wearing jeans were not permitted to enter. Putting one's feet on a chair was not allowed, nor was having too much to drink. These rules were necessary to build up the clientèle. At *Baby Face Disco*, butches didn't have to look tough and aggressive any more, nor were they welcome if they acted that way. Butch/Femme roles became less pronounced. Other sets of behaviour models and interaction patterns began to emerge.

In the face of legal repression, defensive strategies in both bars relied on an arrangement with organized crime in order to avoid police interference. Butches served as intermediaries with the underworld, either as managers and employees of the clubs, as active participants in vice activities, or as accomplices in them. In the earlier club, *Les Ponts de Paris*, these links were overt. The owners/managers were directly involved in organized crime. They were expert in counteracting police efforts against illegal activities in drinking establishments (e.g., underage drinking, prostitution, gambling). Essentially, various attempts were made to reduce the frequency and impact of police raids. Officers were bribed to give advance notice of their visits or to neglect to pay a visit at all. Male and female detectives infiltrating the club were sniffed out (waitresses became expert at this task, and the regular customers were rapidly initiated). Washrooms, the dance floor, and other sites where acts of public indecency might occur were systematically watched (and such activities tolerated or not, depending on the imminence of a police raid).[26] Finally, fights between lesbians were immediately broken up in a manner that was both firm and paternalistic. The goal was to avoid giving the authorities an excuse to take action without alienating the regular customers or impeding petty criminal activities. Disruptive, unmanageable men could be safely expelled from the club since the male clientèle was easily replaced. But lesbian trouble-makers were thrown out only as a last resort.

At *Baby Face Disco*, the connection with organized crime was more indirect. The manager was able to run an establishment protected from police raids in return for a minor involvement in criminal activities. In order to maintain an untainted reputation for her bar and keep the police at bay, the manager, Baby Face, insisted on keeping the place clean and under control. All illegal activity was prohibited, at least when customers were present. Drugs, fights, prostitution, consumption of alcohol by minors, indecency, and corruption of minors were forbidden.[27] To avert disorder, the manager, Baby Face, imposed her authority from the very first contact at the entrance of the club. She was also very strict about the rules defining how customers were supposed to behave. Disruptive women, or those given to fighting, were simply banned from the club for indeterminate periods. Baby Face attempted to identify and disperse troublesome cliques that might form. In short, she did everything possible to guarantee the respectability and the safety of the establishment. Police surveillance appears to have been minimal, at least until the approach of the 1976 Olympics, when a new city clean-up operation was unleashed.

In summary, Butch/Femme roles served to make lesbian existence visible, to control interaction with the surrounding environment, and to defend the safety and security of lesbians and their property against police repression and male aggression. In a more liberal context, where repression was less direct and less fierce, and where other avenues existed for socializing and making lesbian existence visible, Butch/Femme roles were more and more called into question.

Taking Our Place in Time: The Debate over Lesbian Memory

For a number of decades, bars and similar establishments have been part of the public milieu where lesbians socialized, but the question of their role and importance is open to interpretation. After a brief look at academic research, I will examine how this question became controversial among feminist lesbians interested in the reconstruction of our lesbian past. Then I will turn to my own research, which has revealed similar splits in how lesbian bars, especially the earlier ones, are inscribed in lesbian memory.

Researchers who focus on culture or collective identity point to bars as places to meet and find support. They see the bar as an institution which fosters a subculture that in turn provides a structure for, and validates, lesbian life experience (Jay, 1983; Kallen, 1986; Lisagor, 1980; Pratt, 1966). Bar life is analysed as a collective universe with its own rules, rituals, and language. Different functions of bars mentioned are: initiation into lesbian behaviour and life-style, sociability, formation of support groups, social construction of sexuality, reinforcement of personal lesbian identity, neutralization of negative societal judgements, and legitimization of sexual choices.

Among feminists, the discussion of the pre-feminist bar milieu and of Butch/Femme roles is the subject of acute controversy.[28] For some, this world was one in which sexual stereotypes imposed from outside (exemplified by Butch/Femme roles) were acted out, tarnishing the image of the majority of lesbians who, in fact, did not frequent the bars. I myself was part of the early 70s politicized lesbian feminist generation that rejected these earlier types of lesbian spaces. We had many reasons for doing so at that particular moment of our history. On one hand, we didn't want to stay closeted or confine ourselves to small private circles as had many lesbians, including nearly all professionals. We wanted to live our lesbian lives openly, to belong to a community, and to make a political revolution that would change all sexual and gender identities as well as the nature of personal relationships. On the other hand, we didn't want to pay the traditional price for leading an openly lesbian life: downward mobility or at least no chance of upward mobility. We had been to school, had aspired to better jobs, and had distanced ourselves from our original milieu. As for all women, the feminist movement gave us the confidence to want everything. Our political goal was to extend our possible choices as women and as lesbians. We struggled side by side with heterosexual women over common goals. But we were also pursuing our own immediate personal interest as lesbians, creating new places to meet other lesbians, forging networks, spotting educated lesbians with whom we had political affinities, etc. The renewal of feminism also provided us with an ideological framework within which we could legitimize our sexual choices as well as build new identities for ourselves and a new public image for our community. So we defined ourselves as a new generation of women-loving-women and of radical-feminist-lesbians fighting against patriarchal oppression. In the process, we distanced ourselves from the older lesbian generation and harshly criticized Butch/Femme roles.

Controversy erupted a few years later when we began to reconstruct our lesbian history. Some historical research on the reproduction of Butch/Femme roles among working-class lesbians viewed bars as the central focus of an authentic lesbian culture, as well as a site for confrontation with the outside world and resistance to oppression prior to the advent of the lesbian feminist movement (Davis and Kennedy, 1986 and 1989; Nestle, 1987). Sexual desire for other women, open display of lesbian sexuality, creation of autonomous social spaces, rejection of traditional feminine roles and of submissiveness were praised as characteristics of lesbian identity. Butch/Femme roles were reinterpreted as a fundamental organizing principle of lesbian culture, providing a guide for self-presentation and personal interaction both within the community and with outsiders.

Other researchers have defined lesbianism as an identification with a female world and downplayed its sexual component. In an effort to valorize lesbian experience, they documented many historical examples of friendship, solidarity, and romantic love between women. They argued that emphasis on bar life would reinforce popular stereotypes and negative images of lesbians, linking them with other illicit and pathological forms of sexuality. Butch/Femme roles were seen as an imitation of stereotypical models imposed by male writers or as symptoms of alienation. They maintained that an authentic historical lesbian culture should incorporate feminine and feminist values as they understood them.

My own research examines these issues in the specific case of Montreal lesbian history. It reveals distinct divisions related to social class and, more specifically, to the kinds of occupations practised, in relation to the frequenting of certain public places and making lesbian existence visible in the urban environment. The difference between the classes cannot be reduced to the fact of knowing or not about the existence of bars. Most of the women I have interviewed knew about them to some degree. There isn't any real difference as to the minimal knowledge and therefore access to such places.[29] But there are sharp differences in the extent to which these places were frequented, in the attitudes toward Butch/Femme roles, and in the manner in which these places are subsequently inscribed in lesbian memory. An analysis of the interviews shows that there was no such thing as a homogeneous lesbian culture, even if we consider varying degrees of participation and integration as dependent on different factors, among them class of origin and current class position. Instead, the subcultural arrangements I was able to discern were differentiated along class lines.[30] By this, I mean working-class lesbians and those who were professionals had different ways of recognizing each other, of manifesting their lesbian identity, and of constituting social networks. These arrangements also included differing models and rules for behaviour, specific vocabularies, knowledge of books, movies, etc., as well as frameworks for interpreting sexual and love relationships. Integration into an openly lesbian network and bargoing habits were among the most glaring differences regarding the ways in which lesbians from different classes experienced these manifestations of their subcultures. These differences are clearly expressed in the ways in which lesbian bars are remembered today.

I was astonished by the divergent and even contradictory testimonies about bar life. The only common point is that the clubs and cafés of the 50s and 60s were recalled as being part of a violent milieu, where the toughest imposed their own laws, where making a place for oneself required both strength and diplomacy. During the 70s, frequenting lesbian bars became a much less dangerous activity. Police harassment diminished, and inside the bars and discos the atmosphere became more relaxed. Recollections of this period focused primarily on interpersonal relationships and pleasant occasions.

The most striking differences in recalling the earlier bars takes us back to the issue of class. For teachers, nurses, journalists, librarians, and other professionals, the clubs of the 50s and 60s were "dives," sordid, vulgar, unwholesome places, frequented by women with whom they wished to have no contact of any kind. The first visit to such a club disgusted and frightened them. They listed many reasons that kept them away from these lesbian hangouts: the bad reputation of all the clubs and cabarets in that period; the association with the Red Light District; the fact that most had never been initiated into night-life, either by their families or by their co-workers; the rudeness of the patrons, including the lesbians; the humiliation of being on display for heterosexual men and couples; the danger of being recognized by heterosexuals; and their own rejection of Butch/Femme roles. These lesbians began to go to lesbian bars at the end of the 60s with the opening of lesbian-only places. They identified with the more respectable middle-class image that these bars presented. Some narrators recalled the presence of other lesbian professionals, some of whom were well-known journalists, writers, etc., while others stressed how different the clientèle was between the older places and the new ones. Furthermore, the new bars were considered safe places, protected from intrusion by outsiders. These lesbians were extremely resistant to having the earlier bars included in lesbian history. For them, those places did not count then and should not count now.

As for Butch/Femme roles, most professionals who are lesbians said they had always rejected them, that they found them incompatible with their idea of love between women. They often used derogatory terms to speak of the lesbians who were into roles, referring to them as "caricatures," women wearing absurd costumes whose behaviour was ridiculous and exaggerated.[31] They described the butches in particular as alcoholics, rough and aggressive, always ready to fight or to size up other women as sexual. Because butches thought of themselves as men, they weren't real lesbians, some of them said. But these lesbians also distanced themselves from the ultra-feminine Femme. Femininity (wearing makeup, jewels, sexy dresses, etc.) was seen by them as a means of attracting men and expressing sexual availability. While conforming to social expectations and not revealing themselves as lesbians, for these women, carefully de-emphasizing feminine appearance was their way of showing a total absence of interest in men and a veiled expression of their lesbian identity.[32]

In contrast, working-class lesbians who frequented the bars remembered them positively and generally demonstrated a more accepting attitude. They didn't deny the toughness or the links with organized crime, but they knew the rules and felt at ease there. The positive elements were related particularly to the possibilities for socializing offered by clubs and bars, entry into social circles which provided friendship and support, sexual encounters, a sense of solidarity when confronted with social ostracism, confirmation and valorization of one's sexual identity. The chance, as one woman put it, "to be with my own kind." These narrators recounted with pride their confrontations with men or with the police, at least the ones where they were victorious. Those who were patrons of the *Ponts de Paris*, for example, remembered it as a warm place, where they had fun, celebrated lesbian weddings, and met friends. They compared it to a large family. One narrator recalled feeling sympathy for a male doorman who was murdered in a clash between gangs: she said he was very protective of her and her friends. Others remembered feeling protected against verbal and physical harassment by men. Even those who were not strong were unafraid during fights because of the bouncers' ability to put an end to them quickly without having to call the police. Not all working-class lesbians went to these bars and clubs, or at least not regularly, but even when they were not patrons, they were not as baffled by their atmosphere as were lesbians from other classes, nor intimidated by the toughness of the milieu.

All the working-class narrators now distanced themselves from Butch/Femme roles; but rather than totally rejecting them, they assessed roles in all their aspects (sexuality, division of labour in the couple, dress code, visibility, violence, etc.).[33] They reminisced about the advantages of roles but they also remembered the price one had to pay and the restrictions resulting from roles. Developing a tough exterior and being aggressive were highly useful qualities when deflecting male insults and blows but proved to be less desirable when it came to settling differences with one's partner or expressing other emotions.[34] Not surprisingly, working-class lesbians made few comments about lesbians from other classes, since they had no contact with them. Lesbian professionals did not exist socially because they were not visible, either to society at large or to other groups of lesbians, so working-class lesbians didn't take their existence into account. However, lesbian professionals had to deal with the public image given by visible working-class lesbians and consistently dissociated themselves from the masculine butches.

In summary, class differences are reflected in differences in remembering. Any attempt to reconstruct a homogeneous lesbian culture, a common past or collective identity representative of a community, is precluded by the diversity of individual memories, multifaceted and contradictory. Some wish to bury once and for all the very sites that others, without wishing to idealize them, recognize as landmarks in their history. These divergences are parallel to the opposite positions in the intense debate that took place during the 80s about the definition of lesbianism and the markers of lesbian identity and of lesbian culture. For some lesbians, the old bar culture was part of their own personal lives; reclaiming their past is a matter of integrity and respect. Others consider the search for respectability and association with socially recognized values and behaviour as the most efficient strategy for bettering the social situation of lesbians; they don't want to include the pre-feminist bar culture (which was denigrated by mainstream society) in our collective past and still express disdain for Butch/Femme experiences. For other reasons but with similar results, some militant lesbians believe that the authentic history of lesbian communities is equated with the story of their own radicalism and therefore limited to the post-feminist era.

CLASS AND JOB-RELATED CONSTRAINTS ON LESBIAN EXPERIENCE

The controversy over the importance of bars during the 50s and 60s indicates that it lies at the juncture of several emotional debates: the various approaches based on class and race in studies of lesbian community which often bear an unacknowledged bias, the definition of lesbianism and the signs or indicators of lesbian existence, sexual practices, the quest for social respectability as a strategy in the struggle against homophobia. Depending on the point of view, Butch/Femme roles are either to be disparaged or defended; those who were at one time either Butch or Femme find themselves subjected to value judgements which do not always take into consideration the constraints of the times in which they lived or the complexity of their experiences. Obviously, a historical approach cannot ignore these ethical and ideological debates because they shed light on and enrich one's findings. As a sociologist, what interests me are the underlying explanations for the differences in how lesbians recall class-related lesbian life experiences. Here, I would like to suggest two explanations, one related to the effects of class-based cultural background, the other to the practical implications of different occupations.

Growing up working class in the central part of the city could mean exposure to lesbians at an early age. Working-class girls might be warned against butches' sexual advances by a parent, a brother, or a work-mate when they began to work in nearby factories. Butches were part of the urban environment. Young women might see them on the streets, inside the billiard halls, or even in the homes of family members. Such was the case for one narrator who, at fourteen, became friendly with a butch who lived at her uncle's and worked in the same factory as she did. For those whose parents belonged to the lowest strata of the working class, going to clubs and cafés was often part of the regular activities of their immediate family, extended family, or neighbours, and it was not uncommon for them to join in before they reached the legal drinking age. This kind of initiation was inconceivable for young women of traditional petty bourgeois Catholic families, for whom such forms of recreation were strictly forbidden.

Another cultural factor relates to the type of sports practised by lesbians from different classes. Playing and watching team sports (broomball, softball, etc.) was common among working-class lesbians and often included going to hotels and bars after games. Large loose groups, open to newcomers, developed around sporting activities; some were overtly lesbian while others included many lesbians. Lesbians from petty bourgeois backgrounds tended to prefer individual sports such as skiing, horse-back riding, and sailing. Most of their recreational time was spent with their partners and a few selected friends. No doubt one could find other differences in the cultural habits and sociability patterns linked to the different kinds of recreational activities enjoyed by the different social classes.

The second explanation relates to current class position and the expectations associated with particular types of work. According to the narratives collected, integration into the work force was a critical element in the life paths of women who acted on their sexual desire for other women. It gave them a minimum of economic independence and permitted them to either bypass marriage completely or leave their husbands (Roy, 1985). It also helped them to become physically and geographically mobile and thus evade the controls imposed by primary groups like the family.

Integration into the work force demanded more than specialized knowledge and skills; it called for other qualities, depending on the occupation. The case of teachers illustrates this very well. Because part of a teacher's job is to inculcate the young with society's values, she must exemplify these values in her personal life or at least appear to do so in the eyes of the school authorities. It was also a matter of professional credibility, since teaching youngsters required feminine capacities (or qualities) that only a "true woman" possessed. In Quebec, until the middle of the 60s, the majority of the educational institutions were run by religious orders; the moral requirements were particularly strict and impinged heavily on teachers' private lives.[35] Until the 50s, women had to present a certificate of good conduct signed by their priest to be admitted to teacher's college. For all teachers, any involvement in night life, like going regularly to the clubs, whether lesbian or otherwise, meant running the risk of moral condemnation and the loss of employment with no possibility of getting another job in any Catholic school. All the testimonies by lesbian teachers stress the strict separation between private life, about which all the lay teachers were silent when they were at school, and the facade of respectable morality that they maintained at school. In their local environment, teachers were widely known. Lesbian teachers were afraid of being recognized by present or former students if they went to bars with a large mixed clientèle or even to a lesbian-only bar. One narrator's experience illustrates the operation of social control by the nuns. When a jealous ex-lover sent passionate letters to the nuns she had worked for in the West Indies, she felt it necessary to defend her job in Quebec by convincing them that this was part of a draft novel since the order could and would communicate with her current employers.

In the world of journalism, job-related constraints were completely different. In the period studied, journalists were critical of Quebec's traditional elite groups and their moral codes; they adopted a more liberal way of thinking and projected an image of themselves as modern and tolerant. Moreover the structure of this economic sector facilitated professional mobility. There were lots of temporary and contractual jobs in media firms undergoing rapid competitive development. Losing one's job was not that terrible because you could always find another one, possibly a better one, in a more open-minded firm where they didn't care about your personal life. However, journalists who were publicly known as columnists or television reporters had to watch their public image. They felt free to disclose their lesbian identity to most of their colleagues, but going to the bars meant risking being publicly identified as a lesbian. That could slow down a career, to say the least, since they couldn't count on their open-minded colleagues or bosses to defend them in such circumstances.

Other sectors such as hotels and restaurants also had particular requirements. Women who worked with the public as hostesses or waitresses had to present a heterosexual front, sometimes even to the point of looking sexy and appearing sexually available. However, since this was considered part of the services for which (male) customers paid, you didn't have to conform to this code outside business hours, and employers didn't enquire much about your private life as long as you performed well. Furthermore, as in the media industry, jobs were unstable and losing one because of the disclosure of one's sexual identity implied only temporary unemployment. The chances of finding another job in the same sector weren't compromised.

As for butches, many worked in jobs traditionally held by men, for example as unskilled labourers in the transportation industry. These jobs required characteristics that were opposite to traditional femininity. Butches had to be strong and aggressive. Bosses kept them because they were good workers. They also had to defend their personal space and integrity against male co-workers. Butches also worked in factory jobs, where the only important requirement was manual dexterity and the general productivity of the work force. The moral requisites for all these jobs were minimal.

Other empirical studies have established links between employment and integration into homosexual subcultural networks. In her study of the female homosexual subculture in Toronto in the early 60s, Pratt

(1966) noted the specialization of the lesbian-identified drinking establishments along class lines and the predominance of Butch/Femme roles among lower-working-class lesbians. She found that the degree to which women adopted a butch image depended on whether they had a job or not and what kind of job. In his study of 50s gay male society in Montreal, Leznoff (1954) identified visibility versus secrecy as the main factor in the structuring of homosexual networks. Class and occupation, or more precisely occupational vulnerability, were the most significant factors for differentiating between overt and covert homosexuals who formed different subgroups within gay men's subculture. However, lesbian networks seem to have been more strictly divided along class lines while gay male networks crossed them because there were sexual exchanges between members of the different networks.

My research shows that bar-going habits, attitudes towards Butch/Femme roles, participation in openly lesbian networks and thus lesbian visibility in general are all clearly linked to occupation. Getting and keeping a job was a matter of economic survival. Job-related constraints were concrete and inescapable. Lesbians may have had some choice at one point in their lives, but once in a given situation, the compatibility between integration into particular lesbian subgroups and the requirements of a particular job were not under their personal control.[36]

Jobs also provided positive opportunities in relation to expression of lesbian identity. For example, a librarian could secretly develop an interest in lesbian literature as long as this activity was hidden (or shared only with lesbian friends who also kept it secret). Professional status gave women the resources that were needed to pursue such interests: education, money, access to libraries and bookstores, information to retrace lesbian books, trips to France where censorship was not nearly as strong as in Quebec, etc. These opportunities also varied according to occupation. Journalists had access to all kinds of information about books, known individuals' private lives, the artistic world, etc. On the other hand, in traditional men's jobs, butches learned physical and manual skills that gave them strength and confidence when confronting men on the streets. They knew their tricks and shortcomings. Waitresses often met gay men as co-workers since the latter were numerous in this employment sector; they might exchange information about meeting places and help each other. And we could go on. Class and occupational status both put objective limitations on and offered potential resources for the development of lesbian identity and participation in different subcultural arrangements.

Conclusion

An aspect of the history of a social group is anchored in the history of the premises it has occupied or, in various ways, made use of. The processes by which lesbians appropriated public places not only indicate the group's position in society but help to identify the repressive elements confronting lesbians in their pursuit of the right to exist socially. Whatever their class, all lesbians were oppressed by the social condemnation of their sexual choices and hampered in their capacities to live the kind of life they wanted because of the limitations imposed on them as women and as lesbians. They all had to evade these social controls and fight for personal and private spaces where they could live their lesbian lives. One way of doing so was to keep their sexual preference secret. But to exist socially, to create its own culture, an oppressed group must occupy social space within which a collective life can grow. Doing so potentially changes the oppressive nature of its situation into one of direct repression. Oppression manifests itself by an internalized struggle to conceive, express, and act upon lesbian desires that are constantly denied or condemned. To make a public demonstration of the existence of lesbianism as a sexual choice and show that there exists a possibility of leading a lesbian life will provoke a confrontation with groups and institutions whose interest is to reproduce heterosexual patterns and the sexual subordination of women. It is also through this confrontation that lesbians have built a collective identity. Working-class lesbians thus played a key role in developing a lesbian culture in Montreal because they were the first to appropriate public spaces for lesbian use and to be socially visible as a collectivity. These were two crucial advances for lesbians.

The reconstruction of our past must not exclude any class or ethnic background. Obviously it is easier to find written traces of the lives of well-educated lesbians, or of those who came from rich and well-known families. Much attention has justly been given to the collective contribution of lesbian writers and artists to the development of lesbian identity and culture. Some of these women constituted small lesbian collectivities and were visible in the artistic world. They created salons, supported each other's creative work, published or translated lesbian literature, etc. Their personal interests as well as the means they have used to open up new social spaces for lesbian use — in this case cultural spaces — were different from those of working-class lesbians. My basic point is that our collective past is composed of diverse experiences. Focusing on only some of them will lead to distortion. It will also exclude lesbians coming from groups which have occupied a subordinate position in society and whose contribution to history has always been neglected. My research demonstrates the importance of working-class lesbian contributions in establishing our existence as a social group.

NOTES

The author wishes to thank her thesis director, Nicole Laurin; Nicole Lacelle and Louise Toupin for their comments; Joyce Rock; Monik Audet for her love and support; and all the lesbians who trusted her in telling her their life stories. She is very grateful to Ross Higgins, from the Gay Archives of Québec, who was doing research on gay men's history in Montreal during the same period of time. We exchanged much information and he gave constant support and useful criticism.

The Social Sciences and Humanities Research Council of Canada has provided financial assistance for this study.

This text was translated from the French by Marlene Wildeman and Ross Higgins.

1. This research is based primarily on 25 interviews with 39- to 65-year-old lesbians who had lived in Montreal for at least a few years between 1955 and 1975. Most of them are of French Canadian ethnic origin and were raised in the Catholic religion; one is of Hispanic origin and another comes from the local black community. Those who were of other ethnic origins were nevertheless integrated into francophone social networks. Their geographic and class origins varied considerably, as did their occupations: teachers, nurses, and other professionals, factory workers and technicians. Others held jobs as blue-collar workers, office clerks, or salesclerks, while still others lived off minor criminal activities. Two of them had been married for a certain length of time, one with, one without children. Two others were single mothers and one was a nun for nine years. They all nevertheless participated in homosexual activities. Among the available written sources about the bars were certain sensationalist newspapers (Higgins & Chamberland, 1992), tourist guides, and the literature on prostitution and organized crime in Montreal.

2. Rich people have greater physical mobility and access to various forms of protected spaces through ownership of one or more residences with large fenced-off yards, membership in private clubs, etc. The richer you are, the less other people can intrude on these spaces or even get close enough to see into them. Conversely, poor people have smaller homes and carry on more activities, such as socializing, in public settings. They are also more vulnerable to the gaze of the onlooker, be it that of the passerby, the police officer, or the academic observer. I have heard that some very rich lesbians living in Montreal during the 50s and 60s used to fly to far-away places, like Paris and Capri, where they could freely and openly live their lesbian lives. I had no way of making contact with them either as a lesbian and feminist militant or as a professional researcher.

3. Specifically, electoral power, because in Canada and the United States, voting takes place in a territorial framework. For example, in Montreal, at all levels of government, the representatives of the electoral district that includes the "gay village" are officially gay or pro-gay. All candidates have to at least pretend that they favour gay rights in order to have a chance of being elected. This was demonstrated again in the summer of 1990, when all the candidates for a federal election there participated in a march against police brutality which happened to take place during the campaign. The term "gay" ambiguously refers to men and women but there has never been any openly lesbian or specifically pro-lesbian candidate in Montreal.

4. In Quebec, for example, women were prohibited by law from entering taverns until 1971. Access to taverns was one of the women's rights issues fought for by the Quebec feminist movement in 1970. Conversely, because of their exclusively male clientèle, taverns were among the first meeting places for gay men.

5. Both Hanley et al. and Hedblom refer to Gagnon and Simon's work, which was biased by the characteristics of their informants, mainly Daughters of Bilitis members who rejected bars and were engaged in creating an alternative to bar life.

6. The term Red Light District, in Quebec French le Red Light, dates back to the turn of the century when red lights allowed customers to easily locate the brothels (Lévesque 1989). The Main, or La Main, designates a particular street within this zone, St. Lawrence Boulevard, the dividing line that separates Montreal into East and West.

7. During my interviews, I have found that memories about bar life are numerous and vivid when it concerns the depiction of the place, of its atmosphere, of the clientèle, as well as personal impressions and incidents that occurred. A first visit to a bar always left an impression, whether one decided to return or to reject the place completely. Only the narrators who were regular patrons of specific bars could describe accurately and credibly rituals, rules, and patterns of interaction among the lesbian customers and with outsiders. Memories proved vague and ineffective when it came to administrative and commercial details, such as type of permit, the year a bar opened and when it closed, opening and closing times, ownership, sales, profits, etc., as well as relationships between owners/managers, police authorities, and organized crime.

8. Organized crime's control of drinking establishments was carried out either directly, through ownership and overt control over all activities, legal or illegal, which took place on the premises, or indirectly, through protection rackets imposed on the establishment or its workers (waiters, waitresses, prostitutes, etc.). Before 1970, none of these establishments could escape the monopoly held by organized crime. City clean-up campaigns served only to bolster the moral reputation of future municipal councillors, long enough for them to get elected, or put on a show for the duration of international events like Expo '67 (Brodeur, 1978; Champlain, 1986; Turmel, 1974).

9. Maclean's magazine speaks of "two dozen first-class night clubs" and counts no less than "70 second-floor bistros" ("Montreal Night Out," vol. 64. Nov. 15th 1951: 16–17, 61–63). Two articles from the Canadian Time magazine, in 1946 and 1949, describe Montreal as an open city. The latter compares it to "a little Paris" and mentions its "organised vice" (cited by Plante). Caprio (1963) includes Montreal among the cities where you could easily find lesbian pornographic performances (Caprio: 96–97). During the 50s, the Catholic Church constantly denounced the pro-

liferation of cabarets and erotic shows which gave Montreal — the "city of one hundred steeples" — its reputation as a very well organized erotic centre in some American cities.

10. Among the eleven interviewees who had frequented bars regularly, three had had a relationship with a prostitute and one of these had assumed the role of "protector." According to one testimony, it seems that some butches occasionally participated in paid sexual activities themselves. In a study by Thérèse Limoges (1967), a criminologist who conducted prison interviews with twenty prostitutes who had worked in this area, fifteen had participated in homosexual activities and four had worked under a female "protector." This study confirms my own findings. Texier and Vézina (1978) noted the same phenomenon for the 1970s. In Toronto, Pratt (1966) also noted links between prostitution and the working-class lesbian subculture in the early 60s. She says that for butches who didn't want to work, criminal activities, including prostitution and pimping, were an alternative way of making a living.

11. The women's washroom was also located on the left side, which reinforced the separateness of this part of the bar. It was watched over by a woman employee who also sold toilet paper as well as products ranging from combs to marinated pork tongues and pickled eggs.

12. The importance of the gay clientèle seems to have fluctuated throughout the years and is estimated diversely by the narrators.

13. "Us guys, the downtown dykes" — "In this part of town, we understand each other; we're all one people." — "We were a real mixed bag; there were straights, gays, prostitutes, you name it . . . everybody who hung out on The Main." (Excerpts from interviews.)

14. Sensationalist newspapers described this transformation of the Red Light District by pointing out that it was no longer "the headquarters of the underworld" but "the preferred hang-out of lesbians and homosexuals [who] are congregating in the rooming houses of St. Lawrence Boulevard" (*Nouvelles et polices judiciaires*, 1969, 15[7]: 6).

15. There were several reasons why organized crime decided to carry on their illegal activities elsewhere: running drinking and gambling establishments gave way to less visible activities such as the sale of drugs; growing police repression, particularly evident during the world's fair, Expo '67; reorganization of the police force in an attempt to reduce corruption and murderous rivalries between gangs. All these factors combined to reduce the hold organized crime had on the drinking establishments, making it possible, from that time on, for new bars to open outside of its control (Champlain, 1986; Turmel, 1974). Finally, the "call-girl" system gradually came to replace prostitution in the clubs during the course of the 1970s (Texier and Vézina, 1978).

16. For example, one such mixed bar, the *Bâton rouge*, was located right next to a hotel used by prostitutes, and the prostitutes spent their time alternately working at the hotel and relaxing in the bar.

17. This policy of occasionally letting men in depended entirely on the manager or doorman, who from time to time let his friends in. It provoked the anger of the lesbian clientèle on numerous occasions, to the point where they picketed one bar, *Madame Arthur*, in 1974.

18. Baby Face, whose real name is Denise Cassidy, arrived in Montreal in the middle 50s, coming from a small French-speaking town. She worked in factories and as a professional wrestler. One of her friends at that time told me that she had always dreamed of opening a lesbian-only bar. She began her lesbian-bar career as a bus-girl at the *Ponts de Paris*, became a waitress at *La Cave*, a mixed gay bar, and then manager of two predominantly lesbian bars and discos, *La Source* and *La Guillotine*. She became well enough known to give her own name to the places she managed during the 70s and the 80s: the clientèle followed her when the bar moved, which happened a couple of times. She has now retired from the bar business.

19. At *Madame Arthur*, the level of education was significantly higher than in previous bars; white-collar workers were numerous but blue-collar workers were not. Marie-Claire Blais' novel *Nights in the Underground* provides an evocative description of *Madame Arthur*. Blais also refers to *Baby Face Disco* and the *Ponts de Paris* (called *Moon's Face* and *Chez Madame Jules* in the novel).

20. Obviously, these strategies were not conscious or intentional. Roles are examined here as an organizing principle with respect to relationships between lesbians and their environment, and not from the perspective of a subjective identification with the roles or the degree of conformity to them. According to the participants' statements, these two aspects varied considerably depending on the individual. Comparing the 40s with the more repressive decade which followed, Davis and Kennedy (1986) noted a growing inflexibility in Butch/Femme roles, which seemed to go along with the increasingly repressive social climate, and, as well, greater pressure from the lesbian community on butches to look and act even tougher.

21. At that time in Quebec, it was still frowned on for a woman to use much make-up or to make any display of her sexuality even with her husband. Prior to World War II, even lipstick was condemned. In the 50s, discreet lipstick and face-powder were allowed but smoking, wearing slacks, showing off bare skin, or wearing too much jewellery were censured. The Catholic Church vigorously opposed the inroads of the cosmetics industry, which it saw as a manifestation of invading American materialism.

22. On the negotiation of stigmatized identity in different structures of face-to-face interaction, see Goffman (1963).

23. The narratives do not give the point of view of the female heterosexual. However, some narrators claim that it sometimes happened that bisexual women or married lesbians took advantage of the

situation to initiate liaisons which excluded their husbands. On the other hand, heterosexual women who made advances anticipating a mixed orgy without explicitly saying so were identified and black-listed. To my knowledge, few lesbians agreed to participate in these events, unless they themselves had set them up for money.

24. In 1969, the Omnibus Bill changed Canadian laws on sodomy and gross indecency: acts committed in private between two consenting adults, i.e., over 21 years of age, were decriminalized. The actual legal consequences were minor for lesbians, but many interviewees perceived the Bill as a step towards the social legitimation of homosexuality. This legal change also coincided with a lessening of police harassment.

25. In the first years, *Baby Face Disco* was located on the second floor, over another bar frequented by male customers who sometimes got drunk and tried to enter upstairs.

26. Like other establishments, lesbian bars used special lights to signal the arrival of the police. New customers were immediately told what the devices were for. For instance, at *La Cave*, a mixed gay club which existed around 1967, at the flashing of certain lights, gays and lesbians ceased any compromising activities, and rearranged themselves at other tables to form mixed groups and couples, in order to put on a heterosexual face.

27. Even though the legal age for drinking alcohol was 18 from 1971 on, the age required by the manager for admission to the club was 21 because of laws concerning the corruption of minors.

28. This question was the subject of lively debate at workshops on this theme at the International Scientific Conference on Gay and Lesbian Studies: *Homosexuality, Which Homosexuality?* Amsterdam, December 1987.

29. Of the twenty-five lesbians interviewed, only three didn't know that such places existed. Before the 70s, five interviewees — including these three — had never set foot in the clubs or bars, nine went rarely, and eleven frequented one or more bars regularly, including one who worked in a bar for a short period. All of them visited lesbian bars during the 70s.

30. Because of the respondents' ethnic homogeneity and class diversity, my research was particularly suited to reveal the differences in lesbian experience related to class.

31. This illustrates exactly the point made by Deb Edel and Joan Nestle (in Loulan, 1990: 24). The way these women used the word "role" was denigrating and condescending because of its connotations of superficiality and masquerading. Lesbians who were into roles didn't feel that they were artificial. On the contrary, they felt that they were just being themselves, that they were expressing who they really were, including their desire for other women. While I agree with Edel's and Nestle's comment, I have retained "role" as a sociological term and I am not discussing the subjective identification with Butch/Femme roles, as I mentioned earlier.

32. It also enhanced their professional credibility because it conveyed the message that they were more interested in their jobs than in getting married. Conversely, it was their way of spotting other lesbians at work or elsewhere, trying to find how non-heterosexual they were in different aspects of their lives: no husband or fiancé, no interest in getting one, no submissiveness to men, etc. Only after that first inquiry did they begin to approach a woman and ask more direct questions about her private and sexual life.

33. This distancing could have been, in some cases, a product of the interview situation. Narrators' accounts may have been shaped by the fact that they identified me with the feminist movement of the 1970s. Some spoke of Butch/Femme roles as something related to people other than themselves, a technique that allowed them to dissociate themselves from stigmatized behaviour. When this problem arose, I played along with it, even as I made an effort to demonstrate my neutrality towards and my interest in roles, and in certain aspects of behaviour associated with roles.

34. The contrast between the Butch's tough exterior and vulnerable inner feelings was one of the themes of popular American lesbian literature of the time ("lesbian pulp romances"), exemplified by Beebo Brinker, the tender-hearted Butch in Ann Bannon's novels.

35. Didi Khayatt (1992) offers an excellent analysis of what is at stake for lesbian teachers in primary and secondary schools in Ontario: their legitimacy and their credibility as teachers, and the terrible consequences of a disclosure of their lesbian identity.

36. It is impossible to say which comes first, integration into a particular lesbian subculture and finding a compatible job, or the reverse. It depended on particular circumstances of an individual life and was a matter of choice in a socially determined context. In other words, some butches have stuck to factory work in order to be able to dress as they wished, but others didn't have much choice to begin with. In contrast, lesbians who identified with the many so-called masculine attributes but had better job opportunities had more to gain in adapting themselves to a straight working environment.

REFERENCES

Altman, D. (1982). *The Homosexualization of America. The Americanization of the Homosexual.* New York: St. Martin's Press.

Bell, A., & Weinberg, M. (1978). *Hommosexualities: A Study of Diversity among Men and Women*. New York: Simon & Schuster Inc.

Blais, M.-C. (1979). *Nights in the Underground*. Don Mills, Ontario: Musson Book Co.

Brodeur, J.-P. (1978). *Les commissions d'enquêtes publiques sur la police au Québec*. Unpublished doctoral dissertation, University of Montreal, Montreal.

Caprio, F.S. (1963). *Female Homosexuality — A Modern Study of Lesbianism*. New York: Grove Press Inc.

Champlain, P. de (1986). *Le crime organisé à Montréal (1940–1980)*. Montreal: Editions Asticou.

Commission d'enquête sur le crime organisé (1976). *Rapport officiel — La lutte au crime organisé*. Montreal: Edition Stanké & Quebec Official Editor.

Davis, M., & Kennedy, E.L. (1986). "Oral History and the Study of Sexuality in the Lesbian Community: Buffalo, New York, 1940–1960." *Feminist Studies*, 12(1), 7–26.

Davis, M., & Kennedy, E.L. (1989). "The Reproduction of Butch/Femme Roles: A Social Constructionist Approach." In Kathy Peiss & Christina Simmons with Robert A. Padgug (Eds.) *Passion and Power: Sexuality in History* (pp. 241–256). Philadelphia: Temple University Press.

D'Emilio, J. (1983). *Sexual Politics, Sexual Communities: The Making of a Homosexual Minority in the United States, 1940–1970*. Chicago: University of Chicago Press.

Eisner, M. (1982). *An Investigation of the Coming-out Process, Lifestyle, and Sex-Role Orientations of Lesbians*. Unpublished dissertation, York University, Toronto. Ettore, E.M. (1980). *Lesbians, Women and Society*. London: Routledge and Kegan Paul Ltd.

Gilmore, J. (1988). *Swinging in Paradise — The Story of Jazz in Montreal*. Montreal: Véhicule Press.

Goffman, E. (1963). *Stigma: Notes on the Management of Spoiled Identity*. Englewood Cliffs, New Jersey: Spectrum Books.

Hanley, S., Schlesinger, B., & Steinberg, P. (1978). "Lesbianism: Knowns and Unknowns." In Benjamin Schlesinger (Ed.) *Sexual Behavior in Canada* (pp. 126–147). Toronto: University of Toronto Press.

Hedblom, J.H. (1973). "Dimensions of Lesbian Sexual Experience." *Archives of Sexual Behaviour*, 2(4): 329–341.

Higgins, R., & Chamberland, L. (1992). "Mixed Messages: Gays and Lesbians in Montreal Yellow Papers in the 1950s." In Ian McKay (Ed.) *The Challenge of Modernity: A Reader on Post-Confederation Canada* (pp. 422–431). Toronto: McGraw-Hill Ryerson Limited.

Jay, K. (1983). "Life in the Underworld: The Lesbian Bar as Metaphor." *Resources for Feminist Research/ Documentation sur la recherche féministe — The Lesbian Issue*, 12(1): 18–20.

Kallen, E. (1986). "In and Out of the Homosexual Closet: Gay/Lesbian Liberation in Canada." *Culture*, 6(2): 49–63.

Khayatt, M.D. (1992). *Lesbian Teachers: An Invisible Presence*. Albany, NY: SUNY Press.

Kinsman, G. (1987). *The Regulation of Desire — Sexuality in Canada*. Montreal: Black Rose Books.

Lesselier, C. (1987). *Aspects de l'expérience lesbienne en France, 1930–1968*. Unpublished dissertation, University of Paris VIII, Paris.

Lévesque, A. (1989). *La norme et les déviantes — Des femmes au Québec pendant l'entre-deux-guerres*. Montreal: Editions du Remue-ménage.

Leznoff, M. (1954). *The Homosexual in Urban Society*. Unpublished dissertation, McGill University, Montreal.

Limoges, T. (1967). *La prostitution à Montréal*. Montreal: Editions de l'homme.

Lisagor, N. (1980). *Lesbian Identity in the Subculture of Women's Bars*. Unpublished doctoral dissertation, University of Pennsylvania.

Loulan, J. (1990). *The Lesbian Erotic Dance*. San Francisco: Spinster Book Company.

Morgan, J.-L., & Stanké, A. (1972). *Pax-Lutte à finir avec la pègre*. Montreal: Editions La Presse.

Moses, A. (1978). *Identity Management in Lesbian Women*. New York: Praeger Press.

Murray, S. (1979). "The Institutional Elaboration of a Quasi-Ethnic Community in Canada." *International Review of Modern Sociology*, 9(2): 165–177.

Nestle, J. (1987). *A Restricted Country*. Ithaca, New York: Firebrand Books.

Newton, E. (1985). "The Mythic Mannish Lesbian: Radclyffe Hall and the New Woman." In Estelle Freedman and others (Eds.) *The Lesbian Issue — Essays from Signs* (pp. 7–25). Chicago: University of Chicago Press.

Plante, P. (1950). *Montréal sous le règne de la pègre*. Montreal: Edition de l'Action nationale.

Pratt, J.-A. (1966). *A Study of a Female Homosexual Subculture*. Unpublished dissertation, University of Toronto, Toronto.

Roy, C. (1985). *Les lesbiennes et le féminisme*. Montreal: Edition Albert St-Martin.

Schäfers, S. (1976). "Sexual and Social Problems of Lesbians." *Journal of Sex Research*, 12(1): 50–69.

Texier, C., & Vézina, M.O. (1978). *Profession: prostituée — Rapport sur la prostitution au Québec*. Montreal: Editions Libre expression.

Turmel, Jean (1974). *Police de Montréal — Historique du Service*. Montreal: Montreal Urban Community Police Services.

Wolf, D. (1980). *The Lesbian Community*. Berkeley, California: University of California Press.

Canada's Immigration Policy and Domestics from the Caribbean: The Second Domestic Scheme

AGNES CALLISTE

Introduction

Employment in domestic service was one of the few ways by which black women from the Caribbean could immigrate to Canada before 1962. The role of domestic service in the immigration of Caribbean blacks has been historically significant. In the period 1922 to 1931, 74 percent of the 768 Caribbean blacks who immigrated to Canada came as domestics. Between 1955 and 1961 domestics comprised 44 percent of the 4,219 independent Caribbean immigrants; many of these immigrants also sponsored the entry of their family members to Canada.[1] The proportion of Caribbean domestics is even higher than these statistics indicate, since many of the sponsored wives of immigrants who are listed as "dependents" entered the labour market; they had to work because of economic necessity given their husbands' low wages.[2] Despite the significance of domestic service for the immigration of Caribbean blacks, little has been written on Caribbean domestics in Canada.[3]

This study examines the Caribbean Domestic Scheme in Canada from 1955 to 1966 and argues that the growing demand for cheap domestic labour in Canada was the crucial stimulus for the Scheme; at the same time, other economic and political factors played a role in the initiation and continuation of this immigration scheme. Caribbean people, both in Canada and in the Caribbean, had pressured the Canadian government to liberalize its discriminatory immigration policy and regulations against people from the area. The Department of Immigration agreed to the Domestic Scheme in order to maintain Canada's preferential trade and investment in the British Caribbean; this agreement also reflected imperial ties between Canada and the Caribbean.[4]

The Domestic Scheme did not indicate liberalization of Canada's immigration policy; on the contrary, it indicated the racial, patriarchal and class biases underlying Canadian policy. Prior to 1962, the entry of black immigrants had been severely restricted except when they were needed as a cheap pool of labour. They provided a reserve army of labour for predominantly unskilled work which white workers were not willing

SOURCE: Agnes Calliste, "Canada's Immigration Policy and Domestics from the Caribbean: The Second Domestic Scheme," in Jessie Vorst et al., eds., *Race, Class and Gender: Bonds and Barriers* (Toronto: Between the Lines, 1989), 133–165.

to do (these jobs included working in the coke ovens in the Sydney steel plant, and working as domestics).[5] As the Superintendent of Immigration, W.D. Scott, stated to the Minister of Immigration:

> Coloured labour is not generally speaking in demand in Canada and it is not only regarded as the lowest grade, but it is the last to be taken on and the first to be discharged in most enterprises.[6]

Scott's description of the 1918 situation was still relevant in 1955. Despite the critical shortage of labour during the post-war industrial boom,[7] Canada turned to the West Indies as a source of cheap domestics only when it became evident that Europe could not satisfy the urgent demand for domestics; adding to the problem, many Europeans who emigrated as domestics left domestic work soon after their arrival in Canada.[8]

Utilization of the Domestic Scheme reflected some of the strategies adopted by Caribbean women (as well as other immigrant women) to enter Canada in order to improve their economic and social position.[9] These developments also provide some insights into race, class and gender relations in Canada. We will begin by outlining the conceptual framework for this study of the Domestic Scheme. Then we will discuss Canada's immigration regulations and policy in relation to Caribbean blacks, focusing on those factors which influenced the Domestic Scheme. Finally, we will examine the operation of the Scheme and look at its impact on the lives of Caribbean women.

Conceptual Framework

Canada's immigration policies have been shaped by the demand for cheap labour, as well as racial, ethnic, gender and class biases which have discriminated against women of colour, particularly black Caribbean women. Recent studies[10] suggest that international labour migration is a result of uneven capitalist development: massive accumulation of capital and concentration of productive resources in some countries and underdevelopment and dependence on those countries by others (i.e., the "centre-periphery" relationship). This dependence is partly the product of direct exploitation by the "centre" of the "periphery's" resources through colonialism and imperialism.

Sixteenth-century European settlers in the Caribbean first tried to enslave indigenous people to cultivate tobacco. When this population proved unsuited, the settlers brought over indentured workers from Europe. With the change of the primary crop from tobacco to sugar cane in the mid-17th century, settlers began to import African slaves as a cheap, abundant and easily controllable labour force to work on the sugar plantations. After emancipation and the introduction of an apprenticeship system in 1838 indentured workers were imported predominantly from China and India.[11] Colonialism and slavery moulded plantation societies in the Caribbean in the interest of the metropolitan countries. Their economic legacy in the Caribbean has been underdevelopment, with high levels of unemployment (over 25 percent in some countries),[12] limited opportunities, low wage levels and poverty for the majority of the population.[13] Governments in the Caribbean encouraged emigration as a means of reducing overpopulation and unemployment as well as improving the economic condition of emigrants and their families.[14] Thus, Caribbean people have had a migratory tradition since the time of emancipation, as they responded to employment opportunities within the Caribbean (e.g., migration from the smaller Windward and Leeward islands to Trinidad, Guyana and Panama) and opportunities abroad to support themselves and their families.[15]

The legacy of slavery produced a low status for blacks. While Africans were enslaved for economic reasons,[16] the ideology of racism — that blacks were inferior — was used to justify slavery. Colour was also used as an effective means of social control;[17] the colour stratification in the Caribbean, which associated blackness with class disprivilege and powerlessness, was maintained after emancipation. In the Caribbean, as well as in Canada, blacks remain one of the most disadvantaged groups due to institutional racism and systemic discrimination. Colonialism and slavery have affected labour migration, race relations and gender relations. People from colonial and less developed societies, particularly blacks, were more vulnerable to exploitation; they were more likely to be perceived as inferior and therefore as undesirable immigrants. Thus, blacks were more likely to retain their subordinate position in the country of immigration and to be subjected to economic, political and social control. Working-class women of colour from colonial societies were the most vulnerable.

Despite Canada's demand for cheap labour, its immigration policies were selective in terms of race, ethnicity and gender — according to the needs of the labour market. Race and gender ideologies were used to justify the domination, exclusion and restriction of blacks and other people of colour, particularly women. For example, prior to 1955, stereotypes about black women being promiscuous and single parents were used to restrict the immigration of Caribbean domestics.[18] The ideology of racism was constructed to justify slavery, colonialism and imperialism. As this ideology was reproduced, it perpetuated the belief that different racial and ethnic groups had inherent attributes which suited them to particular jobs.

Racism interacted with sexism and class exploitation in the labour market. Prior to the mid-1950s in Canada, black men were pictured mainly as porters and black women as domestics. The latter reflected the stereotype of the "black mammy" or the traditional Aunt Jemima.[19] In 1911, for example, some employers in Québec recommended the immigration of domestics from Guadeloupe, not only because they were cheap but also because they were "fond of children," "knew their place," and "providing they remain in the country as servants."[20] The Québec mistresses' evaluation of their domestics also reflected class relations and the fragmentation of gender along class lines.

The ideologies of racism and sexism were so pervasive that even some British Caribbean people seemed to have shared the stereotypical conceptions about black women. For example, a Caribbean trade official in Canada criticized Canada's discriminatory immigration policy against British Caribbean people because of its refusal to admit domestics into "a field of employment" he believed to be "admirably suited to West Indians."[21] Similarly, another Caribbean minister made a proposal to the Department of Immigration to recruit Caribbean women as "children's nurses" because they were "temperamentally well suited" for these positions.[22]

In advanced capitalist and patriarchal societies racism and sexism are used to maximize profits in several ways: through segregated labour markets in which racial minorities and women, particularly women of colour and immigrant women, are concentrated in low status and low paying jobs; and through the split labour market where women of colour are paid less than white workers and men for doing the same work.[23] Specifically, Caribbean domestics have been paid less than their Canadian and European counterparts. In 1910–11, for example, Caribbean domestics received a monthly wage of $5.00 compared to $12.00–$15.00 paid to other domestics. Even when we add the $80.00 cost of transportation from Guadeloupe to Québec, Caribbean domestics were still cheaper to hire since they had two-year contracts.[24]

The classic cycle of structural discrimination reproduces itself. Discrimination in employment affects the wider society; discrimination in the areas of education, housing and immigration serves to perpetuate inequality. Blacks were stigmatized as unassimilable and undesirable for permanent settling because of racist ideology. The Department of Immigration used the depressed conditions of blacks in Canada, particularly in Halifax, to justify its restrictive immigration policy against Caribbean people.[25] In reality, the low socio-economic position of blacks in Nova Scotia and more generally in Canada reflects a history of oppression: slavery, discrimination in employment and housing, as well as segregated schools. Black poverty, a result of structural conditions, was attributed by many whites to cultural and personal characteristics, such as laziness and inability of blacks to maintain themselves.[26]

Organized labour — feeling threatened by a cheap labour pool of non-unionized workers that might depress wages[27] — has historically discriminated against blacks (including those from the Caribbean) and other people of colour by formally excluding them from unions or by relegating them to auxiliary and segregated locals.[28] Labour opposed liberal immigration policies. Thus, the working class was fragmented along racial lines.

Working-class immigrant women of colour face a fourfold oppression. Their immigrant status interacts with race, class and gender. Many immigrant women have been relegated to the worst jobs, such as domestic service.[29] With its low wages, social isolation and undesirable working conditions,[30] domestic service is increasingly being performed by women from the Third World (particularly the Philippines and the Caribbean) on work permits. Live-in domestics are super-exploited. As Arnopoulos points out,

> [they] usually earn less than half the minimum wage, work long hours with little time off, and are clearly the most disadvantaged group among immigrant women in the Canadian labour market.[31]

As in other aspects of the gender division of labour, the racial and class position and the immigrant status of women affect their reproductive role. Women provide "the future human and labour power and the citizens of the state" as well as of the racial and ethnic collectivities.[32] The stereotype about working-class Caribbean women as single parents has been used to justify the restriction and exclusion — even deportation — of Caribbean domestics since 1911. In that year, for example, seven domestics from Guadeloupe were barred from entry because they were single parents. The immigration officer surmised that they were likely to become pregnant again and would probably become a public burden.[33] The stipulation that Caribbean domestics who came on the Scheme were to be young (ages 21 to 35), single and without children[34] had economic advantages for both employers and the state. The women were likely to be strong and healthy. Without their families in Canada, they would be more dependent on employers. This also represented a substantial saving in social capital such as housing, schools, hospitals, transportation and other infrastructural facilities.[35]

This policy reflected the double standard in society, as well as an ethnocentric and patriarchal bias in immigration policy. Leah and Morgan point out that male immigrants and migrants were not required to be single and without children.[36] Immigration regulations and policy which prohibited the entry of Chinese women (except for the wives of those classes of Chinese that were exempt from the Act, i.e., members of the diplomatic corps, merchants and students)[37] and the entry of American black migrant porters' wives and families prior to 1943,[38] suggest racial, class and patriarchal biases in immigration policy which have inhibited the reunification of families of people of colour. These biases in Canadian immigration policy have also shaped the migration of black women from the Caribbean as domestics.

Canadian Immigration Policy and the Domestic Scheme

Caribbean blacks began migrating to Canada in very small numbers at the turn of the century. In Nova Scotia they came to work predominantly in the Cape Breton steel mills and in the coal mines. The Caribbean women were in great demand as domestics: with industrialization and urbanization, Canadian women were leaving domestic service to work in the emerging manufacturing and service sectors (e.g., in factories and shops) which provided higher status and greater freedom because their work time was clearly established.[39] The first Caribbean Domestic Scheme consisted of the recruitment of approximately 100 women from Guadeloupe in 1910–11 to help fill the demand for cheap labour in Québec.[40] Despite favourable reports from employers, who recommended that the Scheme be continued as a solution to the chronic shortage of domestics, it was stopped ostensibly because of rumours that some of the women were single parents.[41] Another reason for discontinuing the Scheme was the view that domestic service was not vital to the economy.

In his recommendation to the Minister that the Scheme be discontinued, W.D. Scott, superintendent of immigration, also emphasized the need for the exclusion of black immigrants, especially from among the Americans going to Saskatchewan and Alberta as homesteaders.[42] An Order-in-Council, P.C. 1324 of 1911, was passed to prohibit black immigration for one year. However, the order was cancelled because "it was inadvertently passed in the absence of the Minister."[43] Such an order would have raised undesirable diplomatic problems with both the United States and the Caribbean. It would have antagonized black voters in Ontario and Nova Scotia who had traditionally supported Liberal candidates. Moreover, the informal restrictions instituted by the Department were probably considered sufficient to exclude blacks.[44]

Some of the domestics from Guadeloupe and the British Caribbean were subsequently deported when it seemed likely they would become public charges. This occurred particularly during the recession in 1913–15 when it was reported that there were scores of unemployed Canadian women in the cities and towns who were willing to do domestic work. Moreover, immigration officers were instructed to exclude all Caribbean blacks (e.g., as likely to become a public charge) even when they complied with the Immigration Act.[45] The deportation of domestics, particularly from Guadeloupe, was used for decades to justify the restricted entry of Caribbean women.[46]

Even when there was a demand for Caribbean domestics, for example during the wars, their immigration was strongly discouraged because they were not regarded as a "permanent asset."[47] Blacks were stereotyped as lazy, backward, more criminally inclined and less productive than whites.[48] During economic slack, they were likely to be fired to make room for unemployed whites. As Scott argued during World War I, when there were many requests to nominate Caribbean domestics:

. . . . It seems to me that Canada would be adopting a very short-sighted policy to encourage the immigration of coloured people of any class or occupation. At its best it would only be a policy of expediency and it is altogether unnecessary, in view of the present upheaval in Europe, which will unfortunately throw upon the labour market a large number of women of a most desirable class, who can be utilized for the permanent advantage of Canada . . . there is no use booking these coloured domestics because they are bound to meet with difficulties.[49]

One of the most effective regulations used to restrict the immigration of Caribbean blacks was Order-in-Council P.C. 1922-717 which prohibited the landing of immigrants except farmers, farm labourers and domestics, the wife and minor children of residents in Canada, and British subjects from white English-speaking countries (Britain, Newfoundland, New Zealand, Australia and South Africa) and American citizens.[50] This regulation practically excluded Caribbean blacks except dependents and domestics going to assured employment.[51] Thus, in the period before World War II the entry of Caribbean blacks was small and sporadic. Altogether, between 1904 and 1931 only 2,363 were admitted — largely as labourers and domestics.[52] Immigration almost ceased during the Depression.

In the immediate post-war period, the immigration of Caribbean blacks was restricted to sponsorship by close relatives.[53] Section 61 of the 1952 Immigration Act gave the Governor-General-in-Council authority to exclude people on the basis of nationality, citizenship, ethnic origin, occupation, geographical area of origin and probable inability to become readily assimilated.[54] This section of the act was rigidly applied to restrict black immigration. For example, Order-in-Council P.C. 1950-2856 defined British subjects eligible for admission as those born or naturalized in Britain, Australia, New Zealand and South Africa. British subjects from the Caribbean, and other non-white countries, could enter only under special arrangement or quota or if they satisfied the Minister that they were suitable immigrants (for example, that they could be integrated into the Canadian community within a reasonable time after their entry).[55] The Order reduced immigration of Caribbean blacks from 105 in the fiscal year 1949–50 to 69 in 1950–51, although the number of applications had doubled. Ethnic origin, not geographical area, mattered. Therefore, whites from the Caribbean were admitted: in 1951–52, 414 whites compared to 65 blacks.[56] Since miscegenation (racially mixed marriage) was unacceptable in Canada, immigration policy required married white applicants to supply family photographs in order to avoid non-white wives and children coming through chain migration.[57]

Pressures for Increasing Immigration from the Caribbean

The restriction of blacks and other people of colour from the British Caribbean antagonized Caribbean people, particularly after World War II. They put pressure on the Canadian trade commissioners in Jamaica and Trinidad, who were responsible for implementing immigration regulations and policy, to liberalize Canadian immigration regulations and policy. This intensified pressure resulted from the movement toward self-government, an increasing level of education and high unemployment,[58] especially after the McCarran-Walter Act of 1952 further restricted Caribbean immigration to the United States. The trade commissioners recommended to the Department of Immigration that it should develop a tolerant immigration policy which would permit the entry of a restricted number of people from the British Caribbean, irrespective of their ethnic origins; the commissioners also called for greater diplomacy in responding to applicants, particularly the influential professional and business people, in order to develop closer commercial relations. As the Canadian Trade Commissioner in Trinidad, T.G. Major, stated to the Acting Director of Immigration in 1950:

> ... We must be very careful not to offend local susceptibilities. ... It must always be kept in mind that the peoples of the British Caribbean when not hampered by exchange difficulties buy up to $40 per head per annum of Canadian goods, even now the figure is close to $25 per capita or about $43 million per annum. As the colonies are moving steadily in the direction of self government and federation Canadian public relations must be handled with care. ... There have been occasions when I have not been too happy about the phraseology used in "refusal" letters sent directly from Ottawa and have had to soothe ruffled feelings. ... Canada is looked upon as the "big brother" of the British Colonies in these parts ... the accumulated good will is such a valuable asset to Canada that it must be carefully tended. Sooner or later immigration from the British Caribbean will have to be dealt with in accordance with a yet to be determined policy rather than on an ad hoc basis.[59]

In the period following World War II, Canada had, indeed, more trading and investment interests in the Caribbean than in any other Third World country. Over 1,500 Canadian firms and companies had commercial connections in the Caribbean with a volume of exports which, despite exchange difficulties during the war and immediate post-war period, ranged between $30 and $80 million.[60] Canada–Caribbean trade was very important to the Atlantic provinces. The Caribbean was the most important market for salt fish; Nova Scotia's exports in 1963 to the English-speaking Caribbean were valued at $14,246,000 or 10.8 percent of the province's total exports for that year. Moreover, Canada imported raw materials (e.g., petroleum, bauxite and sugar) from the Caribbean. But more important to the Canadian economy was Canadian investment, particularly in the field of banking and insurance. Canadian banks began to move into the British Caribbean by 1889 to serve the bilateral trade and spread quickly throughout the area. For many years, three Canadian banks (Royal Bank, Bank of Nova Scotia and Canadian Imperial Bank of Commerce), together with Barclays Bank of England, had a monopoly of the banking business of the Caribbean. While intended to serve the interests of Canadian traders, these Canadian banks soon became an indispensable internal banking service for the Caribbean — only on the deposit side, since loans were generally restricted to traders.[61] Consequently, "the West Indies suffered a net drain in funds that helped [to] perpetuate their underdevelopment,"[62] at the same time that the Canadian economy was being developed. Moreover, the banks' entry into consumer loans in the 1950s and 1960s reinforced the region's heavy dependence on imports.

Canadian insurance companies began to move into the Caribbean in 1880, and controlled approximately 70 percent of the insurance business in the region by the 1950s. Since 1955 Canadian investment has also played an important role in mining and manufacturing, particularly the Aluminum Company of Canada (ALCAN). In its Jamaican operations alone, ALCAN has invested more than $130 million.[63]

Given Canada's economic interests in the Caribbean, it was important to appease Caribbean people, whether in the Caribbean or in Canada (such as the Negro Citizenship Association in Toronto), who were very critical of Ottawa's discriminatory immigration policy. Thus in 1951 the Departmental Advisory Committee on Immigration recommended to the Minister that Canada establish an annual quota of 150 Caribbean blacks who were professionals, skilled workers or close relatives sponsored by residents and who would contribute to the economic and cultural development of this country. The committee expected such immigrants to become exceptional citizens and help make blacks more acceptable in Canada.[64] Although Cabinet did not agree to a formal quota, it decided to admit a small number of immigrants from the Caribbean "of exceptional merit" (i.e., professional and skilled immigrants) on humanitarian grounds and by executive direction.[65] Out of 122 applicants from the Caribbean admitted in 1952–53, for example, 56 were skilled and professional immigrants.[66] This class bias in immigration policy was designed to serve the needs of the Canadian economy.

Canada's refusal to agree to a Caribbean quota (similar to those for India, Pakistan and Ceylon)[67] reflected racism against blacks. It probably also reflected the Caribbean's colonial status which increased the probability that Caribbean people would be perceived as inferior (i.e., that they could not govern themselves). Moreover, as colonies they did not have representatives at the United Nations who could help to put international pressure on Canada. Besides admitting immigrants on the basis of "exceptional merit," the Department of Immigration decided to be more diplomatic and, if possible, more specific when explaining the rejection of Caribbean applicants on occupational grounds (i.e., where it appeared that applicants had no employment offer or that they did not have a skill which would make them readily employable in Canada).[68]

Given the insatiable demand for domestics, it became increasingly difficult to reject Caribbean domestics on occupational grounds. As labour force opportunities grew for women — with the shift from primary to secondary industries and expansion of the tertiary or service-producing industries — women tended to leave domestic work because of undesirable working conditions, low wages and the low value placed upon domestic work.[69] The increased participation of women in the paid labour force,[70] the affluence which accompanied the post-war industrial boom, and the baby boom also strengthened the demand for domestics. Canadians, particularly those who had visited the Caribbean, put pressure on the federal government for the admission of Caribbean domestics as a cheap and reliable labour supply.[71] The publicity given to the exclusion of Caribbean domestics[72] probably also served to pressure the Canadian government to modify its immigration policy with respect to Caribbean domestics.

The pressure to change immigration regulations and policy came increasingly from within the Canadian black community. In the immediate post-war period this group had assisted Caribbean immigrants in trouble, particularly those threatened with deportation, and facilitated the immigration of relatives of residents in Canada. By 1954 the community had developed a program to challenge immigration policy. The Negro Citizenship Association coordinated the efforts of existing black organizations with the support of mainstream organizations, such as church groups, the Brotherhood of Sleeping Car Porters and the Ontario Labour Committee for Human Rights.[73] The association focused attention on immigration policy, arguing that it demonstrated second-class status and was a structural barrier to integration. The black community held public meetings and invited Caribbean politicians visiting Canada to give public lectures. They demonstrated and sent petitions to Ottawa. A delegation presented a brief to Prime Minister Louis St. Laurent in 1954 with explicit proposals for policy reform: equal treatment of applicants from the British Caribbean with other British subjects, definition of "exceptional merit," and the need for an immigration office in the Caribbean.[74]

Racial provisions in the immigration regulations were challenged before the Supreme Court of Canada in 1955 when Harry Narine-Singh's family was ordered deported to Trinidad because Caribbean people of South Asian origin could not be admitted to Canada unless they were sponsored by close relatives.[75] Although the appeal was dismissed with costs on the basis that the immigration regulations which permitted exclusion or restricted entry because of ethnicity were legal, "the regulations were amended and 'Asian' was deleted." Thus, women of South Asian origin were eligible to apply to Canada on the Domestic Scheme. As the Director of Immigration informed the Labour Commissioner in Guyana, "there would be no objection to including a few" of them in the Domestic Scheme.[76] The discriminatory immigration policy against British Caribbean people was also periodically attacked by the official opposition.[77] However, the Immigration Department did not liberalize the regulations and policy. It simply sought "to eliminate certain irritants."[78] Thus, the Domestic Scheme was designed and shaped by both economic and political interests. In addition to serving the needs of the Canadian labour market, the Scheme was intended to further Canada's economic interests through trade and investments in the British Caribbean. It was also influenced by local and international politics, and by the need to appease the official opposition and people from the British Caribbean, both in Canada and in the Caribbean.

The Second Caribbean Domestic Scheme

The second Caribbean Domestic Scheme was based on the Canadian government's racist and sexist assumptions about black Caribbean women. Given that black women were perceived as promiscuous or as single parents likely to become a public burden, the Domestic Scheme began as an experiment with black immigration acceptable only under certain conditions: a limited number of migrant workers would be allowed as a short-term solution to the chronic shortage of domestics. The Department of Immigration's original intent was to admit Caribbean domestics as migrant workers for one year, with a possible one year extension on the understanding that they would remain in domestic service. The Ministers of Trade and Industry of Jamaica and Barbados, who negotiated the Domestic Scheme with the Department of Immigration through the Colonial Office, had guaranteed the return of the domestics at the end of their contract.[79] An economic advantage to such a rotating migrant system is that employers and the state would have the greatest possible degree of control over that labour power so that it could be utilized only for domestic service and no longer than justified by economic demand. The use of migrant domestics would thus ensure that Canada did not have to meet the cost of their original production (nurturing and educating them), nor the expense of maintaining them in times of recession.[80] Furthermore, the Department of Immigration did not want the Domestic Scheme to open the door to Caribbean immigration. As late as January 1955, the Director of Immigration blatantly argued against an immigration agreement with the British Caribbean. In his words:

> . . . It is from experience, generally speaking, that coloured people in the present state of the white man's thinking are not a tangible asset, and as a result are more or less ostracised. They do not assimilate readily and pretty much vegetate to a low standard of living . . . many cannot adapt themselves to our climatic conditions. To enter into an agreement which would have the effect of increasing coloured immigration to this country would be an act of misguided generosity since it would not have the effect of bringing about a worthwhile solution to the problem of coloured people and would quite likely intensify our own social and economic problems.[81]

However, the Immigration Department decided to admit Caribbean domestics as landed immigrants. This change was made for two reasons: first, in response to criticisms that admitting domestics as migrant labour was a discriminatory policy similar to indentured labour; and second, because officials thought that, unlike Europeans, Caribbean domestics were not likely to leave domestic service at the end of their one year contract. Moreover, the Department felt that administrative controls would provide sufficient sanctions to prevent abuse of the Scheme. For example, any domestic found "undesirable" (e.g., who might become pregnant during her first year) or who broke her contract was to be deported at the expense of the Caribbean government.[82]

The perception of Caribbean women as career domestics was based on discrimination in the labour market and the stereotypical perception of black women as domestics. In 1963, for example, when the Ministry of Development, Trade, Industry and Labour in Barbados offered to recruit 300 nurses to supply the growing demand in Toronto, the Central District superintendent assumed that Barbados could not afford to send so many trained nurses. Based on a racist stereotype, the superintendent suspected that these women were either domestics or at best nurses' aides.[83]

The emigration of skilled labour actually indicated the limited job opportunities available in Barbados; such emigration caused a brain drain from Barbados to Canada — an economic loss incurred by Barbados from educating and training professional and skilled people who subsequently migrated without contributing directly to the country's economic activity. Canada, on the other hand, economized on the reproduction of high-cost labour by importing ready-made workers, since it is cheaper and quicker to import foreign nurses than to produce them domestically.

Caribbean governments facilitated the brain drain. They instituted a rigorous selection process to ensure that candidates for the Domestic Scheme would establish a good name for Caribbean people in Canada; in this way, the Domestic Scheme would continue. It was also felt that the selection process would reduce or eliminate the probability of Caribbean governments having to pay the return fare of any domestic who might be deported during the first year after her arrival in Canada.[84] Unlike preferred immigrants from northern and western Europe, Caribbean domestics were not eligible to apply for interest-free travel loans from the Canadian government under the Assisted Passage Loan Scheme[85] of 1950. Since the Domestic Scheme provided almost the only opportunity for many black women from the Caribbean to enter Canada, and given the lack of educational and employment opportunities in the Caribbean, some skilled and semi-skilled workers (e.g., civil servants, nurses and teachers) used the Scheme to immigrate to Canada in order to further their education and to seek other fields of employment.[86] Frances Henry found in her study of 61 domestics in Montréal who came on the Scheme that only 12 percent of those previously employed had worked as domestics.[87] According to *The Trinidad Chronicle*, the selection process placed greater emphasis on the women's educational background and ambition than on their domestic skills.[88] This policy of brain drain from the periphery to the centre to do unskilled work was depicted in a cartoon about Caribbean girls' aspirations: "I'll be a Civil Servant when I grow up and get a chance to go to Canada as a Domestic Servant!"[89]

In 1956 the Department of Labour described the Scheme as an excellent experiment that had provided the best group of domestics to enter Canada from any country since World War II. According to the government, all of the 100 women were still in domestic service and 84 percent were still in their first job approximately nine months after their arrival. Those who had transferred did so for higher wages and better working conditions or to be located close to friends. Employers were enthusiastic about the Scheme. They found their employees to be more educated, "fond of children," obliging and less demanding than other domestics.[90] Thus, the Scheme was extended from 100 in 1955 to 200 in 1956 and to 280 by 1959 to include Guyana and the islands of the Caribbean Federation. Between 1955 and 1966, 2,940 domestics came to Canada on the Scheme.[91]

Unlike their employers, many Caribbean domestics were very disappointed. They found the work harder, the working hours longer and the pay much less than they had expected. They were surprised that Canadians hired only one domestic — a general domestic — instead of several who would share the work load and perform specialized duties. The first group found it more difficult than subsequent groups to leave domestic work at the end of their contract. This might be attributed to several factors, including greater inequality in employment, the lack of recognition of education, skills and work experience from non-European countries, the stigma attached to people engaged in domestic work, and the lack of networks among Caribbean women. Thus, three years after their arrival, many of the women were still working as domestics — they were trapped in dead-end jobs.[92]

However, by the late 1950s different areas of employment were becoming accessible to blacks, due in part to post-war social changes and legislation. Some blacks were able to leave domestic service.[93] Caribbean domestics developed their own networks in order to be supportive of one another and to prepare new arrivals for life in Canada. They met these women at the airport or train station, quickly exchanged addresses and telephone numbers and tutored them on working conditions and wages, in order to put them on their guard. One domestic told a new arrival:

> If you don't like your bosses, you are allowed to switch right away . . . Thursday is the regular day off; they will try to change it when it's convenient for them, don't let them do it. For big jobs such as washing windows, walls and scrubbing floors, let them bring in a char.[94]

Members of succeeding groups were more likely to assert their rights, to ask for higher wages, to transfer from one domestic job to another — because of unsatisfactory working conditions or isolation in the suburbs or because it was too far to travel to night classes — and to leave their position at the end of their contract.[95]

Those who were skilled or semi-skilled in other occupations (approximately 25 percent) tended to leave domestic service at the end of one year; others did so at a slower rate — as they upgraded their education through night classes or correspondence courses or tried to save money to sponsor some members of their family. Sixty percent of the 1958 group, for example, left domestic service in less than two years. Less than 25 percent of each group remained in domestic service after three years.[96] Caribbean women found employment in the following areas: the service sector; secretarial services; the textile industry; laundry; hairdressing and restaurants; as nurses and nurses' aides in hospitals; and, to a lesser extent, in sales, accounting and teaching. In some cases the new job was more physically exhausting and the net pay was lower than in domestic service, but the women's work time was clearly established and they had greater freedom.[97]

The educational qualifications required of Caribbean domestics was changed from Grade 8 to some high school in 1961, to prevent the immigration of low-skilled people from the Caribbean through sponsorship and to facilitate the retraining of domestics, if necessary.[98] This change reflected the general educational upgrading of the labour force; it also recognized the likelihood that Caribbean women might leave domestic work.

Although Caribbean women remained in domestic service longer than Europeans who came on similar schemes, some officials of the Departments of Immigration and Labour were disappointed by the former group's high mobility rate out of domestic service, particularly during the downturn in the economy and the high unemployment rates in semi-skilled and unskilled jobs in 1958–59. Even more disturbing to the officials was the sponsoring by some women of their family members.[99] Although the number of Caribbean applications was negligible compared to the influx of unskilled immigrants from Southern Europe,[100] immigration officials complained that Caribbean immigrants were swelling the semi-skilled and unskilled labour force through chain migration. In 1961 there were 107 applications from the 1959 and 1960 groups of Caribbean domestics to sponsor their fiances and close relatives, including five "illegitimate" and three "legitimate" children.[101] Since only single women without children were allowed on the Scheme, mothers who had failed to list their children on their application forms needed legal counsel if they wanted to sponsor them.[102] The eventual case of the "Seven Jamaican Women" (who were ordered deported in 1977 when they applied to sponsor their children) occurred during a period of economic decline and after the establishment of a new policy of recruiting domestics on work permits. At this time, Caribbean women were considered to be expendable.[103]

Immigration officials' negative attitudes toward Caribbean women's sponsorship of their families reflected race, class and gender biases: the nuclear, patriarchal family was regarded as the norm in Canada and men were expected to be the main wage-earners. Order-in-Council P.C. 1950-2856 provided for a resident to sponsor the entry of his fiancee "provided the prospective husband is able to support his intended wife."[104] This assumed that immigrant women were likely to be dependent. However, the evidence suggests that because of immigration policy regarding Caribbean blacks, namely a predominance of single women as domestics (and nurses), women were more likely to sponsor their prospective spouses and other relatives.[105] Some of the Caribbean men who came to Canada, sponsored by women already immigrated on the Domestic Scheme, had difficulty finding work.[106] In these cases, the women were the main wage-earners. Black women have always worked (in paid occupations) proportionately more than white women. Similarly, black women have had responsibility for financially supporting their children and grandchildren more often than have their white counterparts.[107]

The need for professional and skilled immigrants, as well as ethnic selectivity in immigration policy, militated against the immigration of low-skilled Caribbean men. The Negro Citizenship Association made representations to the Department of Immigration to admit a comparable number of Caribbean males to balance the sexes. The Department responded that it would prefer to admit professional and skilled Caribbean men to better meet the needs of the labour market; given the class differences between the sexes, such immigration would not satisfy the women's needs for companionship and marriage.[108]

There was, indeed, a gross disproportion of the sexes. The problem was even more acute since young Caribbean men present in Canada were predominantly university students who wanted to keep their social distance, at least publicly, from domestics. Because of class bias some students did not welcome domestics at their parties and one student organization almost banned them from attending. Some members of another Caribbean student organization preferred to disband their choir because of inadequate numbers, rather than admit domestics to it. Some female students also kept their social distance from domestics because they did not want to be mistaken for having that profession, given the stereotype about Caribbean women as domestics.[109] Thus, race and gender were fragmented along class lines. This phenomenon was less common among students from the smaller islands where there was less anonymity and where they probably had met the women and/or their relatives before migrating to Canada. One woman recalled that a student, whom she had known in the Caribbean, allowed her and her friends to use his room on Thursdays until they rented their own room in the same building.[110]

The loneliness and isolation of Caribbean domestics were partially counteracted by community and women's organizations, and by the women's own initiative. Some domestics in Toronto, Montréal and Ottawa organized their own clubs, which met at the Young Women's Christian Association (YWCA). Some domestics in Montréal started two netball teams. Another group, the Pioneer Club, met at the Negro Community Centre (NCC) where community workers organized activities such as sewing and craft classes, and arranged for visiting speakers. The Pioneer women organized some social functions at the NCC such as talent shows. The group which met at the YWCA in Ottawa occasionally attended the Pioneer Club's functions, thus widening the network.[111] The initial contact between the Centre and domestics was made by some employers in Québec living outside of Montréal (e.g., in Chateauguay) who were concerned about their employees' loneliness on Thursday afternoons. The Department of Labour's evaluation of the Domestic Scheme in 1956 indicates that some employers had expressed concern about the limited social contacts that domestics had outside of employment.

The immigration policy of recruiting single women, causing the black community to experience an imbalanced sex ratio in certain age categories, has implications for aging: in the next decade some of the women who came on the Domestic Scheme will have become senior citizens — without having any immediate family in Canada.[112] There is need for further research in this area.

Caribbean domestics traditionally preferred to work in Montréal and Toronto. These cities had higher wages, a greater demand for domestics, and better educational and employment opportunities; the women were also more likely to have friends and/or relatives in these cities. Between 1955 and 1961, 580 out of the 1600 women chose Montréal.[113] After 1958 deliberate efforts were made to place domestics across the country, albeit in small numbers. Based on a racist supposition, this was done to prevent racial concentration: domestics tended to band together. Immigration officers sometimes spirited women away from their friends (meeting them at the airport in Montréal) who might have influenced them to remain in the city.[114] This manipulation of Caribbean domestics was probably intended to make them more controllable; it also served to fill requests for domestics in small towns and in western Canada. Historically, it was difficult to get domestics to work in small towns and rural areas.[115] Despite the wider placement, some domestics migrated to Montréal and Toronto. In the 1959 group, for example, 34 moved to Toronto during their first year.[116]

Criticisms of the Domestic Scheme

By 1961 the Department of Immigration was becoming ambivalent about the benefits of continuing the Domestic Scheme. Some officials suggested that the Scheme should be discontinued because "the rapid movement" out of domestic service did not serve the long-term economic need for domestics. Moreover, the Scheme, like other special group programs, was perceived to have become unnecessary because of the proposed changes to immigration regulations in 1962. The latter emphasized education, skills, the ability of immigrants to establish themselves successfully in Canada (e.g., with pre-arranged employment), and the elimination of explicit racial qualifications for admission.[117] This view was also supported by the Caribbean Association in Ottawa, which argued that "to enter into a formal agreement with a government of a predominantly white country in which non-whites enter this country in a socially inferior role" encourages racism. The association suggested that since there was no apparent need for the continuation of the Domestic Scheme, which labelled and condemned Caribbean women to second-class status in Canada, Caribbean governments should cancel it and domestics should be treated as a skilled group under Canada's preferred immigration policy.[118] In the Canadian government's assessment, though, eliminating or reducing the quota of Caribbean domestics would likely cause greater tension in Canada–Caribbean relations, since the new regulations had not led to a substantial increase in Caribbean immigration to Canada[119] — due partly to the administration of the regulations. The evidence suggests that, apart from the Domestic Scheme, Canada did not actively recruit or officially encourage immigrants from the Caribbean until 1967, when immigration offices were opened in Jamaica and Trinidad.[120]

The Scheme had other political benefits for Caribbean government officials who did the initial selection of domestics.[121] Although the Department of Labour wanted the Scheme to continue because of the need for domestics, some immigration officials thought that professional and skilled immigrants would be more beneficial to the Canadian economy.[122] The Canadian government's dilemma was well expressed by G.F. Davidson, Deputy Minister of Immigration:

> Our chief dilemma seems to be that we are ambivalent as to what it is we are trying to do. Are we trying to pick domestics whose attitude to household service is good and who will be content to remain in household service and be good domestics on a career basis? Or are we using the domestic movement as a means of selecting a higher class of girl who will not stay in domestic service any longer than necessary but will move out after a year into the occupation for which she is best suited, and be in the long run a greater credit to herself, her race, and to Canada?[123]

Support for the continuation of the Domestic Scheme as a means of maintaining Canada–Caribbean relations also came from the Canadian government's representatives in the Caribbean. For example, the Assistant Under-Secretary of State for External Affairs in British Guyana, Arnold Smith, was very patronizing in his support for the Scheme. In his words:

> . . . nothing that Canada has ever done for B.G. is so well and favourably known, or has given Canada as much kudos as this Domestic Workers Plan, which has had the very modest achievement of sending for the past 10 years a total of 30 B.G. (per year) girls to work in Canadian homes as servants. I have noted Department of Immigration rumblings somewhere to the effect that they are considering discontinuing the plan. Notation is made here that if this becomes a real intention it must be combatted in the strongest possible fashion. Why should such a mild scheme — which is working in doing something towards filling a labour shortage in Canadian homes, is doing much to prove no discrimination because of colour, and which is pleasing to the B.G. people — be eliminated?[124]

Smith did not recognize the race, class and gender biases of the Domestic Scheme. However, these were clear to blacks, particularly during the

Civil Rights Movement and the movement for political independence in the Caribbean.

The immigration issue was a constant source of embarrassment and friction in Canada–Caribbean relations, particularly on the politically independent islands. Eric Williams, Prime Minister of Trinidad and Tobago, criticized Canada and other predominantly white Commonwealth countries for discriminating against people of colour as if they were "poison or disease":

> Today the world has worked out the curious hybrid of juridical equality of states and racial inequality of peoples. . . . Canada eases its conscience by accepting a handful of domestic servants; in Britain the contemporary slogan is "keep Britain white," the very Britain which was built up by African and Asian labour in Africa, Asia and the West Indies. Whatever the Commonwealth may be in theory, it is in practice being increasingly tainted with a racial limitation.[125]

Williams' criticisms prompted a Canadian Member of Parliament, David Orlikow, to propose the issuing of a white paper to amend the Immigration Act and regulations, eliminating racial discrimination and convincing people of colour that the Canadian government believed in racial equality.[126]

Some blacks criticized the Scheme as a form of indentured labour in which Caribbean domestics were expected to work harder at much less pay than their Canadian and European counterparts. One critic estimated the wage difference at $150 per month.[127] Blacks argued that the benefits of the Scheme were questionable for several reasons. First, the small number of women who emigrated under the Scheme could not significantly reduce unemployment and population pressure in the Caribbean. Second, the Scheme did not provide great opportunities for black women, since they often did not have the time to upgrade their education. The evidence suggests that after initial surprise at domestics' attending night classes, many employers agreed to give their employees time off for this purpose, even though they thought that the women's educational and occupational expectations were too high. Some employers, though, refused to do so; in a few cases the relationship became very strained once employers had found out that domestics were attending classes. Obviously, some employers held very negative stereotypes about Caribbean women which influenced their perceptions about what jobs were appropriate for them.[128] These negative stereotypes and employers' attempts to limit their employees' educational and occupational expectations reflected race, gender and class biases, as well as the desire for cheap and controllable labour. Such a mistress-servant relationship is a challenge to the women's movement.[129]

A third criticism of the Scheme was that Caribbean domestics were being treated as third-rate citizens in Canada who were not allowed to integrate. Caribbean governments were criticized for their sexism and for supporting the centre-periphery relationship by sending young women — including skilled and semi-skilled workers — to Canada as domestics. The editor of *The Barbados Advocate*, for example, argued that pay inequity in the Caribbean was pushing skilled and semi-skilled women to emigrate on the Domestic Scheme. He called for pay equity for women and an end to the brain drain.[130] Thus, both Canadian and Caribbean governments were being asked to re-examine the effects of the Domestic Scheme.

Despite these criticisms the Domestic Scheme seemed to be popular in the Caribbean;[131] it gave some women the chance to emigrate to a legendary land of opportunity and it enabled them to send much needed remittances home.[132] Emigration was also perceived as a relief from unemployment and overpopulation.

In a remarkable development Guyana relinquished its annual quota of 30 domestics in 1965 as part of its repatriation program. The Guyanese government asked Ottawa to implement a program which would educate Guyanese women and men, and which would be mutually beneficial to the Canadian and Guyanese people (e.g., by training 25 women as stenographers and 25 men as agriculturalists to help meet the country's development needs).[133] This request reflected a policy shift in Canada–Caribbean relations — from trade preference to an aid program.[134] The Caribbean Domestic Scheme was approved annually by Order-in-Council until the introduction of the points system in 1967.[135]

Since 1973 the Canadian Employment and Immigration Commission (CEIC) has been admitting domestics (and seasonal agricultural workers) predominantly on temporary work permits. This policy shift reflects two factors: the number of women leaving domestic work at the end of their contracts and the lack of industrial expansion. The goals of this new system are twofold. First, it ensures that the women's labour power is utilized only for domestic work. Second, because domestics from the Third World are regarded as expendable, they can be sent back to their home countries when the demand for domestics falls. Thus, women on permits are even more marginalized than those women who came on the Scheme.

Caribbean women seem to be even more vulnerable than some other Third World women. Recruitment of domestics from the Philippines has increased significantly in recent years, while there has been a decrease from the Caribbean. For example, 30 percent of the 5,021 new entrants in 1985 were from the Philippines compared to 13 percent from Jamaica and Guyana, the two Caribbean countries included in the ten leading source countries. Filipinos comprised 42 percent of the 8,175 new entrants in 1987, with Jamaicans comprising only 2 percent. In 1986 and 1987 Jamaica was the only Caribbean territory in the ten principal countries of origin for domestics.[136] Plausible explanations for the employers' preference for Filipinos compared to Caribbean domestics are: the former tend to be younger, they are probably cheaper, and they are more likely to show, if not feel, deference to their employers. Research has shown that employers expect submissiveness from domestic workers.[137]

Under the 1981 regulations live-in domestics who have been here for two years and who have achieved a potential for self-sufficiency are allowed to apply for landed immigrant status; however, older Caribbean women with children are less likely than others to be granted landed immigrant status.[138] These disadvantages experienced by Caribbean women have several causes. Racism may be a factor, given that blacks are lower on the stratification ladder and have more negative stereotypes (e.g., they are likely to be single parents) than Asians. Moreover, CEIC officials may evaluate older Caribbean women with dependent children as less likely to become self-sufficient. Further research is needed on the current immigration policy, its implementation, employers' preference for domestics and the question of whether types of domestic service vary by ethnicity.

Conclusion and Evaluation

Although the Domestic Scheme provided opportunities for some Caribbean women and their families to emigrate to Canada, it reinforced the racial, class and gender stereotypes about black women being inherently suited to domestic work. This did not stop Caribbean women in their struggle for upward mobility. They upgraded their education and moved into jobs with higher status and pay. Currently, some of the women are in nursing, teaching, accounting, small business and secretarial services; at least one studied medicine after teaching for a number of years and two are educational administrators. Some of the women migrated to the United States.

On the whole, though, the Domestic Scheme reinforced the oppression of black working-class women. It also contributed to the Caribbean's dependency on Canada. While some Caribbean governments recognized that the Scheme was demeaning to black women, they regarded it as a partial solution to such domestic problems as unemployment and over-population. Despite some advantages of emigration, it could not significantly reduce unemployment or provide a solution to the Caribbean's under-development. Indeed, by sending some skilled and semi-skilled women on the Scheme, Caribbean governments were perpetuating their under-development and dependency through the brain drain. Caribbean women were thus being oppressed by colonialism and neo-colonialism in the Caribbean, and by racism, sexism and class bias in Canada.

Although we do not know the long-term psychological effects of the Domestic Scheme on the women and their families, there is a suggestion that some domestics found such work very demeaning, particularly those from a higher social class background in the Caribbean and those whose families had employed domestics themselves. Some Caribbean domestics described their jobs as being in a prison — they felt as if they were trapped. Moreover, the stigma attached to doing domestic work, and the racism, sexism and class bias that the women had to endure, may well have contributed to psychological problems. Some women who have achieved upward mobility will not admit that they came on the Scheme; they would prefer to forget about it.[139]

Keith Henry's study of black politics in Toronto indicated that the overwhelming majority of females — particularly domestics — were politically disadvantaged because of racism and sexism; women's participation occurred predominantly in the church and in social clubs.[140] While this may have been the case in the 1950s and early 1960s, since the late 1960s — with the increased influx of people from the Caribbean to Canada and policies promoting multiculturalism — some Caribbean domestics, whether current or former, have been very active on the boards and executives of community and women's organizations. A few former domestics have even been elected national presidents of organizations, and some have served on provincial and federal advisory councils.

This paper on Canada's immigration policy and the second Caribbean Domestic Scheme is part of a larger study of the social history of Caribbean domestics in the period 1900 to the present. The paper also provides some of the historical background for understanding the experiences of some black Caribbean women in Canada. There is a need for further research on the social consequences of the Domestic Scheme for Caribbean women and their families, the effects of immigration policy on ethnic stratification, and the policy implications for the aging of Caribbean women. Given that domestic service was the only job open to many black women before the late 1950s, it would be interesting and useful to conduct a comparative analysis of Caribbean domestics and indigenous black Canadian domestics. Such a study might focus on the experiences of black Nova Scotians who work in white communities adjacent to their black communities. Special attention should then be directed to the implications of domestic service for the family and the community.

NOTES

The author would like to thank the women and men whom she interviewed; and the nine reviewers, particularly Ronnie Leah, for their useful comments.

1. Canada, Department of Immigration and Colonization, *Annual Report*, 1922–1931; Canada, Department of Citizenship and Immigration, *Annual Report*, 1955–1961; Public Archives of Canada (hereafter PAC), Immigration Branch Records, RG 76, Vol. 475, File 731832; Vols. 566–67, File 810666; Vol. 830, File 552-1-644; Vol. 838, File 553-36-563.

2. S. Arnopolous, *Problems of Immigrant Women in the Canadian Labour Force* (Ottawa: Canadian Advisory Council on the Status of Women, 1979); R. Leah, "Immigrant Women: Double Victims — A Study of Working Class Immigrant Women in the Canadian Labour Force." A paper presented at the Annual Meeting of the Canadian Sociology and Anthropology Association, Montréal, 1980; Confidential interviews, May–August, 1982, 1983; July 12, 1988.

3. For preliminary work or case studies on Caribbean domestics, see Y. Bled, "La Condition des Domestiques Antillaises à Montréal" (M.A. thesis, University of Montréal, 1965); F. Henry, "The West Indian Domestic Scheme in Canada," *Social and Economic Studies* 17:1 (1968), pp. 83–91; M. Silvera, *Silenced* (Toronto: Williams-Wallace, 1983); J. Turritin, "Networks and Mobility: The

Case of West Indian Domestics from Montserrat," *Canadian Review of Sociology and Anthropology* 13:3 (1976), pp. 305–20.

4. PAC, RG 76, Vol. 830, File 552-1-644; Vol. 838, File 553-36-556; File 553-36-644.

5. Canada, Department of the Interior, *Annual Report*, 1906–1917; Department of Immigration and Colonization, *Annual Report*, 1918–1931; Department of Citizenship and Immigration, *Annual Report*, 1955–1961; PAC, RG 76, Vol. 556, File 810666, W.D. Scott to L.M. Fortier, August 10, 1916; Vol. 830, File 552-1-644; Vol. 838, File 553-36-556; File 553-36-644; RG 76, Acc. 83-84/349, Box 107, File 5750-5, Part 1, the Director of Immigration to Crerar, Minister of Immigration, April 17, 1942.

6. PAC, RG 76, Vol. 566, File 810666, W.D. Scott to W.W. Cory, April 25, 1918.

7. A. Green, *Immigration and the Postwar Canadian Economy* (Toronto: Macmillan, 1976).

8. PAC, RG 76, Vol. 838, File 553-36-644; F. Iacovetta, "'Primitive Villagers and Uneducated Girls': Canada Recruits Domestics from Italy, 1951–52," *Canadian Woman Studies* 7:4 (1986), pp. 14–18.

9. Canada, House of Commons, *Debates*, 1948, Vol. 6, pp. 5811–12; F. Iacovetta, "Canada Recruits Domestics from Italy"; PAC, RG 76, Vol. 838, File 553-36-644.

10. M. Burawoy, "The Functions and the Reproduction of Migrant Labor: Comparative Material from Southern Africa and the United States," *American Journal of Sociology* 81:5 (1976), pp. 1050–87; M. Castells, "Immigrant Workers and Class Struggles in Advanced Capitalism: The Western European Experience," *Politics and Society* 5:1 (1975), pp. 33–66; R. Miles, *Racism and Migrant Labour* (London: Routledge and Kegan Paul, 1982); A. Portes, "Migration and Underdevelopment," *Politics and Society* 8:1 (1978), pp. 1–48.

11. F. Augier, S. Gordon, D. Hall and M. Reckford, *The Making of the West Indies* (Trinidad: Longman, 1960); E. Williams, *Capitalism and Slavery* (New York: Capricorn Books, 1966).

12. The official unemployment rate of 25 percent disguises seasonal patterns and underemployment.

13. G. Beckford, *Persistent Poverty: Underdevelopment in Plantation Economies of the Third World* (New York: Oxford University Press, 1972).

14. PAC, RG 76, Vols. 566–67, File 810666; F. Bodsworth, "What's Behind the Immigration Wrangle?" *Maclean's*, May 14, 1955, p. 127.

15. G. Beckford, *Persistent Poverty*; G. Lewis, *The Growth of the Modern West Indies* (New York: Modern Reader Paperbacks, 1968).

16. E. Williams, *Capitalism and Slavery*.

17. G. Beckford, *Persistent Poverty*.

18. PAC, RG 76, Vol. 475, File 731832; Vols. 566–67, File 810666; RG 76, Acc. 83-84/349, Box 107, File 5750-5, Pt. 1, the Director of Immigration to Crerar, April 17, 1942.

19. A. Davis, *Woman, Race and Class* (New York: Vintage Books, 1983); B. Hooks, *Ain't I a Woman* (Boston: South End Press, 1981); *The Winnipeg Tribune*, August 4, 1904; August 20, 1905; January 30, 1906.

20. PAC, RG 76, Vol. 475, File 731832, G.A. Marsolais to W.D. Scott, May 20, 1911; E. Dufresne to W.D. Scott, May 20, 1911; F.X. Dupuis to W.D. Scott, May 22, 1911; R. Morin to W.D. Scott, May 22, 1911; A. Rivet to W.D. Scott, May 22, 1911; C. Laurendeau to W.D. Scott, May 23, 1911; G. Boudrias to W.D. Scott, May 23, 1911.

21. F. Bodsworth, "The Immigration Wrangle."

22. PAC, RG 76, Vol. 847, File 553-110, the Office of the Commissioner for Canada to the Under-Secretary of State for External Affairs, December 29, 1961.

23. E. Bonacich, "A Theory of Ethnic Antagonism: The Split Labor Market," *American Sociological Review* 37 (1972), pp. 547–59; "Abolition, the Extension of Slavery, and the Position of Free Blacks: A Study of Split Labor Markets in the United States, 1830–1863," *American Journal of Sociology* 81:3 (1975), pp. 601–28; "Advanced Capitalism and Black/White Relations in the United States: A Split Labor Market Interpretation," *American Sociological Review* 41 (1976), pp. 34–51; A. Phizacklea, ed., *One Way Ticket: Migration and Female Labour* (London: Routledge and Kegan Paul, 1983).

24. *The Montreal Herald*, April 8, 1911. See also PAC, RG 76, Vol. 475, File 731832; Vol. 566, File 810666; A. Clarke, *The Meeting Point* (Toronto: Macmillan, 1967); *The New Nation*, May 31, 1964.

25. PAC, RG 76, Vol. 830, File 552-1-644, the Director of Immigration to the Minister, September 12, 1951.

26. *The Black Worker* (March 1952); D. Clairmont and D. Magill, *Nova Scotian Blacks: An Historical and Structural Overview* (Halifax: Institute of Public Affairs, Dalhousie University, 1970); D.C. Corbett, *Canada Immigration Policy: A Critique* (Toronto: University of Toronto Press, 1957), pp. 36, 195; H. Tulloch, *Black Canadians: A Long Line of Fighters* (Toronto: N.C. Press, 1975); R. Winks, *The Blacks in Canada: A History* (Montréal: McGill-Queen's University Press, 1971).

27. PAC, RG 76, Vol. 830, File 552-1-644, the Director of Immigration to the Minister, September 12, 1951.

28. A. Calliste, "Sleeping Car Porters in Canada: An Ethnically Submerged Split Labour Market," *Canadian Ethnic Studies* 19:1 (1987), pp. 1–20; "Blacks on Canadian Railways," *Canadian Ethnic Studies* 20:2 (1988), pp. 36–52; R. Marshall, *The Negro and Organized Labor* (New York: John Wiley, 1965); H. Northrup, *Organized Labor and the Negro* (New York: Harper and Brothers, 1944).

29. R. Leah, "Immigrant Women"; A. Phizacklea, ed., *One Way Ticket*; P. Rothenberg, ed., *Racism and Sexism: An Integrated Study* (New York: St. Martin's Press, 1988).

30. S. Arnopoulos, *Problems of Immigrant Women*; G. Leslie, "Domestic Service in Canada, 1880–1920,"

in *Women at Work: Ontario, 1850–1930*, J. Acton, P. Goldsmith and B. Shepard, eds. (Toronto: Canadian Women's Educational Press, 1974), pp. 71–126.

31. S. Arnopoulos, *Problems of Immigrant Women*, p. 23.
32. F. Anthias and N. Yuval-Davis, "Contextualizing Feminism — Gender, Ethnic and Class Divisions," *Feminist Review* 15 (1983), pp. 62–75.
33. PAC, RG 76, Vol. 475, File 731832, W. Klein to W.D. Scott, July 21, 1911.
34. PAC, RG 76, Vol. 838, File 553-36-644, L. Fortier to the Permanent Secretary, Ministry of Labour, Jamaica, August 1955; C. Smith to R. Mapp, Minister of Trade, Industry and Labour, Barbados, July 25, 1956.
35. M. Burawoy, "Reproduction of Migrant Labor"; R. Miles, *Racism and Migrant Labour*.
36. R. Leah and G. Morgan, "Immigrant Women Fight Back: The Case of the Seven Jamaican Women," *Resources for Feminist Research* 8:3 Pt. 2 (November 1979), pp. 23–4.
37. "An Act Respecting Chinese Immigration," *Statutes of Canada* (Ottawa, 1923), Chapter 38, pp. 3–4.
38. A. Calliste, "Sleeping Car Porters in Canada."
39. PAC, RG 76, Vol. 475, File 731832, M.D. to L.M. Fortier, c. May 22, 1911; Vol. 566, File 810666, F.B. Williams to W.D. Scott, June 29, 1909; J. Gilchrist to W.D. Scott, April 1, 1915; M. Barber, "The Women Ontario Welcomed: Immigrant Domestics for Ontario Homes, 1870–1930," *Ontario History* 72 (September 1980), pp. 148–72; G. Leslie, "Domestic Service in Canada."
40. PAC, RG 76, Vol. 475, File 731832, E.B. Robertson to G.W. Elliott, August 15, 1910; G.W. Elliott to W.D. Scott, September 10, 1910; Regimbal to W.D. Scott, April 10, 1911; R. Morin to W.D. Scott, May 22, 1911; *La patrie (Montréal)*, April 7, 1911; *The Montreal Herald*, April 7, 1911.
41. PAC, RG 76, Vol. 475, File 731832, W.D. Scott to F. Oliver, June 2, 1911.
42. Ibid.
43. PAC, RG 2/1, Vol. 769, P.C. 1324, "Prohibiting Negro Immigrants from Landing in Canada," August 12, 1911; Vol. 772, P.C. 2378, October 5, 1911.
44. Canada, House of Commons, *Debates*, 1911, Vol. 1, col. 608; R. Brown and R. Cook, *Canada, 1896–1921* (Toronto: McClelland and Stewart, 1974), p. 62.
45. West Indians had the highest deportation rate, particularly in 1913–15 when 91 were deported. Between 1909 and 1916, one in every 30 West Indians was deported. PAC, RG 76, Vol. 566, File 810666, L. Fortier to W.D. Scott, June 30, July 27, 1914; W. Egan to J. Cormack, April 24, 1925; *The Canada Year Book, 1915* (Ottawa, 1916), p. 114.
46. PAC, RG 76, Vol. 566, File 810666, W.D. Scott to E. Mousir, secretary, the Canadian-West Indian League, September 8, 1914; Scott to W. Givens, November 11, 1914; Scott to Melville-Davis Steamship and Touring Company, September 24, 1915; Scott to F. Knight, April 25, 1916; Scott to J. Webster, May 16, 1916; Scott to F.B. Harrison, June 1, 1917; RG 76, Acc. 83-84/349, Box 107, File 5750-5, Pt. 1, the Director of Immigration to Crerar, April 17, 1942.
47. PAC, RG 76, Vol. 566, File 810666, W.D. Scott to Pickford and Black, June 17, 1915.
48. R. Winks, *Blacks in Canada*, pp. 292–98.
49. PAC, RG 76, Vol. 475, File 731832, W.D. Scott to Hone and Rivet, May 11, 1915.
50. P.C. 1922-717 was amended several times, e.g., P.C. 1923-183, P.C. 1931-695, P.C. 1950-2856. PAC, RG 76, Acc. 83-84/349, Box 107, File 5750-5, Pt. 1, April 17, 1942; J. Cameron, "The Law Relating to Immigration" (L.L.M. thesis, University of Toronto, 1943); Canada, House of Commons, *Debates*, 1922, Vol. 3, pp. 2514–17; cited in *Debates*, 1931, Vol. 4, pp. 3124–25.
51. Canada, Department of Immigration and Colonization, *Annual Report, 1922–31*; PAC, RG 76, Vol. 566, File 810666, F.C. Blair to the Royal Mail Steam Packet Company, September 20, 1922.
52. Canada, Department of Citizenship and Immigration, *Annual Report, 1954*; Department of the Interior, Annual Report, 1906–17; Department of Immigration and Colonization, *Annual Report, 1918–31*.
53. An average of 82 West Indian blacks were allowed in annually in the fiscal years 1945–52. Canada, Department of Mines and Resources, *Annual Report, 1945–49*; Department of Citizenship and Immigration, *Annual Report, 1950–52*; PAC, RG 76, Vol. 830, File 552-1-644.
54. "An Act Respecting Immigration," *Prefix to Statutes, 1952* (Ottawa: Queen's Printer), p. 262.
55. Canada, House of Commons, *Debates*, 1950, Vol. IV, pp. 4449–50; *Debates*, 1922, Vol. 3, pp. 2514–17; *Debates*, 1931, Vol. 4, pp. 3124–5; J. Cameron, "The Law Relating to Immigration"; D. Moore, *Don Moore: An Autobiography* (Toronto: Williams-Wallace, 1985); PAC, RG 76, Acc. 83-84/349, Box 107, File 5750-5, the Director of Immigration to Crerar, April 17, 1942.
56. PAC, RG 76, Vol. 830, File 552-1-644, "Immigration from the British West Indies since World War II Showing Partial Breakdown of Ethnic Origin," January 1, 1958.
57. PAC, RG 76, Vol. 567, File 810666, C. Smith to A. Joliffe, May 28, 1948.
58. PAC, RG 76, Vol. 567, File 810666, T. Major to H. Choney, January 26, 1948.
59. PAC, RG 76, Vol. 830, File 552-1-644, T.G. Major to the Acting Director of Immigration, May 17, 1950. See also, T.G. Major, "Immigration from the British Caribbean," August 31, 1951; E.M. Gosse to the Director of Immigration, October 9, 1951.
60. PAC, RG 76, Vol. 830, File 552-1-644, T.G. Major, "Immigration from the British Caribbean," August 31, 1951; E.M. Gosse to the Director of Immigration, October 9, 1951.
61. C.B. Fergusson, "The West Indies and the Atlantic Provinces: Background of the Present Relationship," in *The West Indies and the Atlantic Provinces of Canada* (Halifax: Institute of Public Affairs, Dalhousie University, 1966), p. 32; E. Nash, "Trading Problems of the British West Indies,"

in *The Economy of the West Indies*, G. Cumper, ed. (Kingston: United Printers, 1960), pp. 223–42.

62. T. Naylor quoted in R. Chodos, *The Caribbean Connection* (Toronto: James Lorimer, 1977), p. 110.

63. C. Callender, "The Development of Capital Market Institutions in Jamaica," *Social and Economic Studies* 14:3 (1965), Supplement; R. Chodos, *Caribbean Connection*; D. Fraser, "The West Indies and Canada: The Present Relationship," in *The West Indies and the Atlantic Provinces of Canada*, pp. 33–41.

64. PAC, RG 76, Vol. 123, File 3-33-21, L. Fortier to Cabinet, October 13, 1951.

65. PAC, RG 76, Vol. 123, File 3-33-21, P. Baldwin to the Deputy Minister, December 22, 1951; C. Smith to the Deputy Minister, March 28, 1952; W. Harris, Memorandum to Cabinet, June 10, C. Smith to the Deputy Minister, May 26, 1954; 1952; D. Moore, *Don Moore*.

66. Canada, Department of Citizenship and Immigration, *Annual Report*, 1953, pp. 34–35.

67. After India, Pakistan and Ceylon became independent, Canada agreed to accept 150, 100 and 50 immigrants from these countries, respectively. This decision was a result of international pressure. PAC, RG 76, Vol. 123, File 3-33-21, L. Fortier to Cabinet, October 13, 1951.

68. PAC, RG 76, Vol. 830, File 552-1-644, the Director of Immigration to the Minister, September 12, 1951.

69. S. Arnopoulos, *Problems of Immigrant Women*; M.P. Connelly, "Canadian Women as a Reserve Army of Labour" (Ph.D. dissertation, University of Toronto, 1976).

70. M.P. Connelly, "Women as a Reserve Army."

71. PAC, RG 76, Vol. 567, File 810666; Vol. 838, File 553-36-644.

72. F. Bodsworth, "The Immigration Wrangle"; "Here's Ottawa's Side of Negro Ban Story," *The Financial Post*, July 12, 1952, p. 12.

73. For information on the Ontario Labour Committee on Human Rights, see A. Bruner, "The Genesis of Ontario's Human Rights Legislation: A Study in Law Reform," *University of Toronto Faculty of Law Review* 37:2 (1979), pp. 234–55; A. Calliste, "Sleeping Car Porters in Canada."

74. PAC, RG 76, Vol. 123, File 3-33-21, the Director of Immigration to the Deputy Minister, May 26, 1954; Vol. 830, File 552-1-644 Brief presented to the Prime Minister by the Negro Citizenship Association, April 27, 1954; *The Black Worker* (March 1952); D. Moore, *Don Moore*, pp. 87–120.

75. Harry Narine-Singh was a draughtsman who applied for landed immigrant status when he was on a visit to Canada. "Immigration and 'Race,'" *Canadian Labour Reports* (July-August 1955), p. 4.

76. PAC, RG 76, Vol. 830, File 552-1-644, the Director of Immigration to the Deputy Minister, September 12, 1958.

77. Canada, House of Commons, *Debates*, 1952, Vol. 3, pp. 2803–4; *Debates*, 1952–53, Vol. 4, pp. 4348–53; *Debates*, 1957–58, Vol. 4, pp. 3382, 3670–71; F. Hawkins, *Canada and Immigration: Public Policy and Public Concern* (Montréal: McGill-Queen's University Press, 1972).

78. PAC, RG 76, Vol. 830, File 552-1-644, the Director of Immigration to the Deputy Minister, September 12, 1958.

79. PAC, RG 76, Vol. 830, File 552-1-644, W. Dawson to A. Brown, May 10, 1955.

80. M. Burawoy, "Reproduction of Migrant Labor"; R. Miles, *Racism and Migrant Labour*.

81. PAC, RG 76, Vol. 830, File 552-1-644, the Director of Immigration to the Deputy Minister, January 14, 1955.

82. PAC, RG 76, Vol. 838, File 553-36-644, Department of Citizenship and Immigration to Cabinet May 1955; interview, January 26, 1989.

83. PAC, RG 76, Vol. 847, File 553-110, Pt. 2, Central District Superintendent to the Acting Chief, Settlement Division, April 3, 1963; Note, April 17, 1963.

84. PAC, RG 76, Vol. 838, File 552-1-644, the Department of Citizenship and Immigration to Cabinet, May 1955.

85. The Assisted Passage Loan Scheme provided interest-free loans — initially to single workers and heads of families migrating from Europe, and since 1955 also to their wives and dependent children — to cover the cost of passage to their Canadian destination of those immigrants who qualified because they were in occupations which were considered to be in short supply in Canada.

86. PAC, RG 76, Vol. 838, File 553-36-644, Pt. 2, G. Haythorne to L. Fortier, March 13, 1956.

87. F. Henry, "The West Indian Domestic Scheme."

88. *The Trinidad Chronicle*, October 28 and November 2, 1956.

89. *The Evening News*, May 30, 1960.

90. One woman who had changed jobs three times was making the highest salary in the group: $125.00 per month compared to the average wage of $75.00. PAC, RG 76, Vol. 838, File 553-36-644, G. Haythorne to L. Fortier, March 13, 1956.

91. Computed from PAC, RG 76, Vol. 838, File 553-36-563.

92. Confidential interviews, July 9–16, 1988.

93. Canada, *Prefix to Statutes, 1952–53* (Ottawa: Queen's Printer, 1953), pp. 27–29; H. Potter, "The Occupational Adjustment of Montréal Negroes, 1941–48" (M.A. thesis, McGill University, 1949); confidential interviews, May-August, 1982, 1983; July 15, 1988.

94. Confidential interview, July 13, 1988.

95. PAC, RG 76, Vol. 838, File 553-36-563, The West Indian Domestic Scheme, November 20, 1963; interviews, July 9–17; V. King, "Calypso in Canada," *Canadian Welfare* (November 1958), pp. 178–83; Y. Bled, "Domestiques Antillaises."

96. PAC, RG 76, Vol. 838, File 553-36-556, W. Baskerville to R. Smith, January 5, 1960; File 553-36-560, C. Isbister to the Minister of Immigration, November 20, 1963; File 553-36-563, A. Ewen, "Household Service Workers from the West Indies and British Guiana," October 6, 1961.
97. Confidential interviews, July 9–17, 1988.
98. PAC, RG 76, Vol. 838, File 553-36-560, W. Baskerville to R. Smith, December 12, 1961.
99. PAC, RG 76, Vol. 838, File 553-36-563, A. Ewen, "Household Service Workers from the West Indies and British Guiana," October 6, 1961.
100. K. Levitt and A. McIntyre, *Canada–West Indies Economic Relations.* (Montréal: The Centre for Developing-Area Studies, McGill University, 1967), pp. 90–101.
101. PAC, RG 76, Vol. 838, File 553-36-563, A. Ewen, "Household Service Workers from the West Indies and British Guiana," October 6, 1961.
102. Confidential interviews, July 16, 1988.
103. R. Leah, "Immigrant Women."
104. Canada, House of Commons, *Debates,* 1950, Vol. 4, p. 4450.
105. Interviews, July 12–16, 1988.
106. A. Clarke, *The Meeting Point;* Y. Bled, "Domestiques Antillaises."
107. D. Brand, "A Working Paper on Black Women in Toronto: Gender, Race and Class," *Fireweed* 19 (Summer/Fall 1984), pp. 26–43; A. Davis, *Woman, Race and Class.*
108. PAC, RG 76, Vol. 838, File 553-36-563, The West Indian Domestic Scheme, November 20, 1963.
109. PAC, RG 76, Vol. 838, File 553-36-563, The West Indian Domestic Scheme, November 20, 1963; Y. Bled, "Domestiques Antillaises"; L. Diebel, "Black Women in White Canada: The Lonely Life," *Chatelaine* (March 1973), pp. 38–39, 84, 86–88; D. Handelman, "West Indian Associations in Montréal" (M.A. thesis, McGill University, 1964), pp. 40–45; G. Lamming, "The West Indians: Our Loneliest Immigrants," *Maclean's,* Nov. 4, 1961, pp. 27, 52, 54–56; interviews, July 9–17, 1988.
110. Interviews, July 12–14, 1988.
111. PAC, RG 76, Vol. 838, File 553-36-644, Pt. 2, G. Haythorne to L. Fortier, March 13, 1956; Y. Bled, "Domestiques Antillaises"; T. Das Gupta, *Learning from Our History* (Toronto: Cross-Cultural Communication Centre, 1986), p. 57; V. King, "Calypso in Canada"; interviews, July 9–17, 1988.
112. Interviews, December 1988.
113. Y. Bled, "Domestiques Antillaises."
114. PAC, RG 76, Vol. 838, File 553-36-563, Location of West Indian Domestics, 1961; interviews, July 24, 1983; July 16, 1988.
115. PAC, RG 76, Vol. 566, File 810666, J. Gilchrist to W.D. Scott, April 1, 1915; M. Barber, "Immigration Domestics."
116. PAC, RG 76, Vol. 838, File 553-36-563, Location of West Indian Domestics, 1961; interviews, July 28, 1983; July 16, 1988.
117. Order-in-Council, P.C. 1962-86; House of Commons, *Debates,* 1962, Vol. 1, pp. 9–12.
118. PAC, RG 76, Vol. 839, File 553-36-644, B. Myers to the Chief Minister, St. Lucia, December 2, 1964.
119. PAC, RG 76, Vol. 838, File 553-36-560, C. Isbister to the Minister of Immigration, November 20, 1963.
120. In 1961, 1,126 West Indians were admitted. In 1962, the number increased to only 1,480 and in 1963 to 2,227. In 1964 Canada permitted 112,606 immigrants to come to Canada. Of these only 1,493 were from the Caribbean. Canada, House of Commons, *Debates,* 1966, Vol. 6, p. 5963; *The Globe and Mail,* November 5, 1963; F. Hawkins, *Immigration,* p. 382; K. Levitt and A. McIntyre, *Canada–West Indies Relations,* p. 93.
121. PAC, RG 76, Vol. 838, File 553-36-560, C. Isbister to the Minister of Immigration, November 20, 1963; File 553-36-563, the Deputy Minister of Immigration to W.R. Baskerville, June 16, 1961; W.R. Baskerville to the Deputy Minister, June 27, September 26, 1961.
122. PAC, RG 76, Vol. 838, File 553-36-563, W. Baskerville to the Deputy Minister, June 27, 1961; September 26, 1961.
123. PAC, RG 76, Vol. 838, File 553-36-563, G.F. Davidson to the Acting Director of Immigration, August 29, 1961.
124. PAC, RG 76, Vol. 838, File 553-36-560, A. Smith to C. Isbister, July 3, 1964.
125. Canada, House of Commons, *Debates,* 1966, Vol. 3, p. 2319; Vol. 6, p. 5963; *The Globe and Mail,* May 21, 1965.
126. Canada, House of Commons, *Debates,* 1966, Vol. 3, p. 2319.
127. *The New Nation,* May 31, 1964.
128. Y. Bled, "Domestiques Antillaises"; interviews, July 24, 1983; July 12–16, 1988.
129. S. Arat-Koc, "In the Privacy of Our Own Home: Foreign Domestic Workers as Solution to the Crisis in the Domestic Sphere in Canada," *Studies in Political Economy* 29 (Spring 1989), pp. 33–58.
130. *The Barbados Advocate,* April 6, 1964; *The New Nation,* May 31, 1964.
131. PAC, RG 76, Vol. 838, File 553-36-560, S. Hubble to the Under-Secretary of State for External Affairs, May 7, 1965.
132. For a discussion of the importance of remittances for the Gross Domestic Product in the Caribbean, see G. Lewis, *The Modern West Indies.*

133. PAC, RG 76, Vol. 838, File 553-36-560, C. Merriman to M. Gregg, May 1965; R. Curry to H. Moran, July 13, 1965; Note for file, July 13, 1965.
134. Canada's aid program in the British Caribbean began with the West Indian Federation in 1958. R. Chodos, *Caribbean Connection*; D. Fraser, "The West Indies and Canada."
135. Data on the year in which the Scheme ended are contradictory. According to K. Levitt and A. McIntyre, *Canada–West Indies Relations*, p. 92, in July 1966, Canada announced a 100 percent increase in the number of entries permitted under the Domestic Scheme. However, others indicate that the Scheme was terminated in 1966. J. Turritin, "West Indian Domestics," p. 308; interview, July 16, 1988.
136. Canada, Employment and Immigration, "Foreign Domestic Movement: 1985 Statistics Highlights"; "Foreign Domestic Movement Statistical Review, 1986" (July 1987); "Foreign Domestic Movement Statistical Highlight Report, 1987" (December 1988); Interview, June 26, 1989. In both years England and Germany ranked second and third respectively of the top leading source countries. In 1987 seven European countries and Australia accounted for 32 percent of the new entrants.
137. L. Martin and K. Segrave, *The Servant Problem: Domestic Workers in North America* (Jefferson, N.C.: McFarland Publishers, 1985); J. Rollins, *Between Women: Domestics and Their Employers* (Philadelphia: Temple University Press, 1985).
138. J. Ramirez, "Good Enough to Stay," *Currents* 1 (1983-84), pp. 17-19; M. Silvera, *Silenced*, p. 29; *Winnipeg Free Press*, November 25, 1983; interview, June 26, 1989.
139. PAC, RG 76, Vol. 839, File 553-36-644, L. Fortier to A. Brown, June 8, 1960; Y. Bled, "Domestiques Antillaises"; interviews, July 12-16, 1988.
140. K. Henry, *Black Politics in Toronto since World War I* (Toronto: The Multicultural History Society of Ontario, 1981), p. 35.

Race, Class, Gender, and Work Experience of South Asian Immigrant Women in Atlantic Canada

HELEN RALSTON

This paper investigates the lived experience of South Asian immigrant women in Atlantic Canada. It focusses specifically on the relationship of gender, race and class to their lived experience in the paid labour force.

The 1986 Census gave a population of roughly 3,800 South Asians scattered throughout the four Atlantic provinces, which then had a total population of approximately two and a quarter million. About half the South Asian population resided in Nova Scotia, with nearly forty per cent in Metro Halifax. The second most heavy concentration of South Asians was in Metro St. John's, Newfoundland. The sample for my study comprises 126 first-generation South Asian immigrant women over the age of 15 years, one-tenth of the estimated total population of South Asian women of that age in the Atlantic region. It is drawn proportionately to their distribution in the four provinces. Names have been selected at random from a directory. My approach in the research is to emphasize qualitative in-depth biographical case studies rather than quantitative statistical or comparative analyses. The preliminary findings presented here relate to 101 cases of the total sample.

SOURCE: Helen Ralston, "Race, Class, Gender and Work Experience of South Asian Immigrant Women in Atlantic Canada," *Canadian Ethnic Studies* 33, 2 (1991), 129-139.

The Conceptual Framework

Following the theorizing of Dorothy Smith (1987) and Roxana Ng (1984, 1986, 1989), the concept "lived experience" refers to the practical activities of the women's daily lives (such as doing housework, cooking meals, ferrying children to and from schools and activities, working in various full-time or part-time, paid or unpaid job-related activities, doing volunteer work, participating in various cultural and social organizations), rather than to the more conventional connotations of people's perceptions of and attitudes toward situations in which they find themselves.

An important theoretical point is that the experience of being a South Asian immigrant women in these activities is a social construction, not an individual attribute. Being South Asian refers not so much to the personal qualities of individuals (who come from India, Pakistan, Sri Lanka, Bangladesh or whatever foreign country), but rather to social characteristics which are constructed and reconstructed in the historical and ongoing social processes of relationships in specific social, economic and political contexts. Things like national origin, skin colour, language, religion, culture, food customs, dress and work activities become organized as "differences" which have important consequences for individuals and groups. In fact, the term "South Asian" itself is a social construction to encompass distinctly different ethno-cultural groups who trace their origins to the Indian sub-continent.

In much the same way, the term "immigrant woman" refers not so much to legal status as to the processes of social construction in everyday life which describe some women who are visibly "different" in those same characteristics (skin colour, language, religion, dress, customs, work activities and the like). On the one hand, in legal terms, the women may be Canadian citizens who have been permanent Canadian residents for more than twenty years. On the other hand, the term "immigrant woman" is seldom applied to white anglophone Western women who have entered Canada from Australia, New Zealand, Northern Europe, or the United States.

In this theoretical approach, again following Roxana Ng's (1989) conceptualization, gender, ethnicity, race and class are also understood as social attributes which are defined, constructed and reconstructed in social relationships. Although analytically distinct concepts, they are dynamically inter-related. They arise over time and are continually being reconstructed in the processes of production and reproduction in the development of the Canadian state.

In analyzing the experiences of South Asian women in Atlantic Canada I have also drawn on the growing body of Canadian literature on immigrant women (Arnopolous, 1979; Jacobson, 1979; Cassin and Newton, 1979; Ghosh, 1979, 1981a, 1981b, 1983; Naidoo, 1980a, 1980b, 1985a,

1985b, 1987; Naidoo and Davis, 1986, 1988; Indra, 1981; Roxana Ng, 1981, 1982, 1984, 1986, 1989; Ng and Das Gupta, 1981; Ng and Ramirez, 1981; Silvera, 1981; Ramkhalawansingh, 1981; Johnson and Johnson, 1982; Winnie Ng, 1982; Khosla, 1983; Boyd, 1984, 1986; Agnew, 1986; Burnet, 1986; Das Gupta, 1986; Estable, 1986, 1987; Stasiulis, 1986, 1987, 1990; Ng and Estable, 1987; *Resources for Feminist Research*, 1987). This research has highlighted that immigrant women are not a homogeneous group. Immigrant women have different biographies and histories. The lived experience of women who come from India, Pakistan, Vietnam, the Philippines, Trinidad or El Salvador is different from those who come from the United States, Britain, New Zealand, Australia, Scandinavia, or the Netherlands. Those who enter Canada as physicians and scientists have a different experience from those who come as farm workers or domestics. Those who speak English and were educated in a British system are in a different situation from others of another language and educational system. Race, class and language interact as significant variables to determine the actualities of everyday life. Above all, they contribute to the differential work experience among white and non-white immigrant women.

While the majority of immigrant women — especially if they are non-white — tend to be in the lower-paid, less skilled and less secure traditionally female occupations (Boyd, 1975, 1984, 1986; Ng and Ramirez, 1981), previous research has indicated that white immigrant women in Canada are bimodally distributed in the occupational structure (Arnopoulos, 1979; Boyd, 1975, 1986; Stasiulis, 1986), a high percentage of them being concentrated in the more skilled and professional occupations. For some non-white immigrant women — including South Asians — the bimodal occupation distribution is replicated (Stasiulis, 1986, 1987). In other words, a high percentage of South Asian women are employed in more skilled and professional occupations.

A further point I make is that in analyzing the lived experience of immigrant women it is important to consider *where the women have settled* as well as their origins. Rarely has this been done in previous research. The assumption is often made that what is true for women in Ontario or British Columbia is true for the rest of Canada. My argument is that one has to take into account the uneven capitalist economic development of Canada. This uneven development has had a significant impact on the destination of South Asian immigrants, the kind of work they do, and their experience in the work world. Indeed, it has had an impact on immigration policies and practices themselves. According to 1976 revisions of the Immigration Act, the setting of annual immigration levels by the Minister of Employment and Immigration is made in consultation with the provinces and in terms of regional demographic and labour market needs.

Profile of the Immigrant Women

The one hundred and one women who participated in the interviews have been in Canada an average of seventeen years, the longest resident having immigrated in 1956, the most recent having arrived in 1988. They were born in India (62), present-day Pakistan (17), Sri Lanka (3), Burma (2), West Indies (2), Uganda/Kenya (7), Singapore (1), Indonesia (1). Their religious affiliation was as follows: Hindu (56), Sikh (13), Muslim (14), Christian (16), Zoroastrian (1) and Jewish (1).

The youngest person interviewed was 23 years; the oldest, 74 years, with the mode being in the early forties. All but one woman had married; three were widowed. Only eleven women were not married at the time of their arrival in Canada. Over three-quarters of the married women had arranged (or what some chose to call "semi-arranged") marriages. By "semi-arranged" they meant that their parents had consulted relatives and members of their own caste and religious community or had placed advertisements in newspapers to find potential candidates for marriage with their daughter. The woman might or might not have been previously acquainted with any one of the candidates. She was free to agree or disagree with the proposed marriage and she could express preference among the candidates. The man had similar freedom to accept or reject the proposed marriage. Most of the women entered Canada as dependent immigrants, both legally and actually. Many were sponsored for entrance to the country as dependents, after their husbands were already settled and working in Canada. In many cases, the immigrant husband returned to the Indian sub-continent to find a partner in an arranged marriage. He then made application to the Canadian Immigration Commission for his wife's admission as a permanent resident whom he was able to maintain financially. The wife was given permanent resident status in Canada under what is now called the "family class" category of immigrant.

In terms of educational level, the majority of the women were highly educated at the time of their entrance to Canada. In this they reflected the 1986 Census data which gave 81 per cent of South Asian women as university-educated. Twenty-nine (29) of the women I have interviewed had post-graduate doctoral, master's or equivalent professional degrees; forty (40) had college degrees or teaching, nursing or other professional diplomas; fifteen (15) came with some college education or as university students; thirteen (13) had high school education; two (2) had only elementary school education; two (2) had no formal school education at all. Eighty-one (81) had considerable knowledge of and fluency in English on arrival in Canada; twenty (20) had little or no knowledge of English on arrival and still had some difficulty in speaking it. Some who had considered themselves completely fluent in English before migrating to Canada had difficulty with variations in Canadian accent, pronunciation and vocabulary.

Despite the relatively high level of education of the women on entrance to Canada, at the time of the interviews, only fifty-two (52) women were working in the paid labour force; two (2) women had retired; forty-seven (47) others were not working in the paid labour force. I deliberately sought to interview women in working-class jobs but I had great difficulty in locating any such women. I found only two in Metro Halifax, one in Moncton, New Brunswick, and none in St. John's or elsewhere in Newfoundland. Ten (10) women (1 in Metro Halifax; 4 elsewhere in Nova Scotia; 1 in Metro St. John's; 1 elsewhere in Newfoundland; 3 in New Brunswick) were paid employees in their husband's professional practice or business.

Of the fifty-two (52) women who were working in the labour force at the time of the interview, twenty-six (26) worked as medical or health care professionals, as social workers or counselors, and as teachers and librarians; seven (7) were other salaried professionals; two (2) were self-employed business people; one (1) was a skilled tradesperson; eight (8) were secretaries or book-keepers; six (6) were clerks, salespersons or cashiers; one (1) was a factory worker; one (1) was a trained and certified homemaker.

The Immigrant Experience

Immigrants who settle in the Atlantic region have a different experience from those who settle in highly industrialized regions of Canada. Since the early 1960s, immigration policies and practices have favoured the entrance to Canada of South Asians, particularly South Asian men, who have professional and technical skills and who have been highly educated in English-language institutions. The 1986 census data reveal that India was second only to the United States of America as a leading source country of immigration to Canada (Kalbach, 1990: 26). Some of these immigrant men were desirable for well-paid professional jobs in the less industrialized peripheral regions of the country where native-born Canadians did not wish to go. In other words, it would seem that immigration policies favoured men who could successfully integrate economically into western industrial society. As Kalbach (1990: 40) has pointed out, however, the facilitation of economic integration does not necessarily ensure successful social integration nor moderate ethnic and racial prejudice of other Canadian residents.

Such immigration policies have had important consequences for immigrant women. Immigrant women have a different experience from immigrant men. Not only are immigrant women usually legal and actual dependents of their husbands, but they tend to be more isolated than immigrant men from participation in the mainstreams of society. They carry disproportionate responsibility for household activities and child care; they have fewer opportunities for learning or improving the English language; they have more limited employment and job-training opportunities (Law Union of Ontario, 1981: 234). Moreover, immigrant women who settle in the Atlantic provinces will not have the same level of informal networks and organized support services as those who settle in Metro Toronto or in Metro Vancouver, two metropolitan centres where over three per cent of the population is South Asian.

Although most of the women I have interviewed were highly qualified, the majority of them did not enter Canada in the category of independent migrants. Legally, they came as dependents of their husbands. As I have noted already, for most of them, migration to Canada followed upon an arranged marriage. Moreover, marriage generally implied a religious-legal union in which the wife agreed to the husband's control over gender relations in the family. India, for example, does not have a uniform civil code, despite ongoing efforts of the middle-class women's movement to obtain such a code. Marriage and family affairs of each religious community in India are governed by what is called "personal law"; that is, the law is based on the religion of the community. Hindus are governed by Hindu Law; Muslims by Muslim Law; Christians by Christian Law; and so forth. "Personal" marriage and family laws most characterize the gender subordination of Indian women, particularly in the domestic sphere.

When the immigrant women settled in Canada, culturally-defined gender relations learned in their country of origin dictated that they were totally responsible for transmission of the culture to the children and for work inside the home, whether or not they worked outside the home as well. Their dependent gender status was socially maintained and reproduced in the day-to-day activities of the household and the work world. Moreover, as Djao and Ng (1987) have noted, their legal status as "family class" immigrants sometimes made them ineligible for English language classes and for job-training programmes.

Among the immigrant women I have interviewed, paid (or unpaid) work outside the home was vital to offset the isolation or boredom of domesticity and the traumatic break from customary familial relations which resulted from migration. The gender and class ideology in the home country permitted women to enter the medical, health and teaching professions. Their superior class position probably favoured their arranged (or "semi-arranged") marriages with professional men of a similar caste/religious community background. Their marriage and subsequent migration maintained their subordinate gender position. When they formed Western-style nuclear families in Canada, without the servants middle-class families customarily employed in Third World countries, the entire burden of the household fell on the woman. In Canada, as Ng (1989: 14–15) has reported from her investigation of immigrant women, the content of domestic work and the social relations within which the work was performed were different. The woman's household activities were governed by the husband's work schedule, children's school and extracurricular activities, transportation systems, the number of household cars, access to shopping facilities, the degree of household mechanization, and so forth. The sexual division of labour changed for the women in that many of them contributed to family finances by working outside the home (or for their husband's business or profession inside the home). It did not change for most men, who made no contribution to household work.

Lived Experience in the Paid Labour Force

It was when the women entered (or tried to enter) the paid work world that their experience of being "different" was most marked. Forty-two (42) women said that they had experienced difficulties in trying to get a job. Many of them found that they were socially defined as "different" because of educational qualifications, language, Third World origin, skin colour, work experience (or lack thereof), and the like. And "different" was all too often construed as inferior.

The experience of frustration in getting paid work outside the home in Atlantic Canada was greater for women with graduate degrees who had worked in their home country than for those women who were less highly qualified. One woman said quite bluntly, "I didn't want to come to Canada; I had a good job in India." Yet she had agreed to an arranged marriage with full knowledge that it would entail migration to Atlantic Canada, where her husband was already working. At the moment of choice, she evidently preferred marriage, with uncertain job opportunities, to remaining single in a highly skilled, well-paid job. Three women spoke of the complete lack of job opportunities in their geographical area for women with their advanced science qualifications. Not only could they find no research jobs, but they were also designated as "too qualified" for some teaching jobs or else told that there was a surplus of teachers. Similarly, some women who had practiced as medical doctors in the home country found it impossible to work as such in Atlantic Canada: either they could not get an internship or they were unable to take the necessary time for studying and sitting for certification exams. In several cases, the wife was unable to take accreditation exams because it was assumed that the husband had priority for similar studies and exams. Gender subordination and the sexual division of labour operated materially by giving the woman responsibility for housework and child care and by placing the man in the paid work force. Ideological female subordination was ensured through socio-cultural myths and traditions of female subservience.

Many women were underemployed and had a sense of being undervalued. The superior class position they had held in their home country because of their educational qualifications was discounted in Canada. They found that they had to have a superior performance in exams or work just to be treated equally with other Canadians. As one woman put it, "You have to be first among the first to succeed as well as a [native-born] Canadian." Another stated, "It's hard to be a foreigner; I have to get 100 per cent to get a job." And again, "For women of colour it's difficult to find jobs, particularly in a place where few jobs are available." Several women who had worked in factories and fish plants and as cashiers in supermarkets in the past came to Canada as fully-qualified teachers or school administrators. For many women, factory work was not an option for the simple reason that there is little or no factory work available in poorly-industrialized Atlantic Canada. Paid domestic work is usually performed by other (usually visible) minorities in the region. Some women, comparing the situation of relatives and friends in Toronto, made the point that "in Toronto jobs were practically looking for them"; but they then added the rider, "ordinary jobs to keep occupied." For these women, at least, the purpose of work outside the home was clearly to offset isolation and boredom. Where paid work outside the home was unavailable (or unobtainable), many women took on various kinds of voluntary work activities. Staying in the home was the one thing to be avoided, even if one was aware of the exploitation of women volunteers as unpaid labour. The wry comment of one person was: "That's one place where they don't ask you 'What is your qualification?' or 'How old are you?' They'll have you whatever way they can have you."

There were some paid-work success stories among the women I interviewed. One who held a high-status, well-paid job as a financial comptroller found that gender rather than race was the salient characteristic which demanded over-achievement to hold a superior position in the work world. "You have to be three times as good [as a man] to get the same kind of job and the same kind of money. . . . You have to prove yourself," she said. This same woman related that her daily activities included total responsibility for domestic work, and, in addition, management of the family finances.

Another woman was unusual, not only in being highly paid as a production shift-worker in a large industrial plant, but also in living in an extended family with women to care for her children and a husband who supported her particular job outside the home. This woman took great pride and gained considerable satisfaction in her work activities. In this family, gender roles for the respondent at least, if not for the older generation of women, had been redefined.

Other women whom I interviewed were indignant when Canada Manpower officers had suggested that they "get a file-clerk's job and work your way up." Unless there was dire financial need in the family, they refused to take this route of accepting a low-status job for which they were over-qualified and they persistently sought work (occasionally successfully) on their own account. Another source of frustration in looking for work was the complete negation of experience in the home country and the demand for "Canadian experience" in their work record. One woman expressed succinctly the salience of socially constructed "difference" for structural discrimination in the work force: "It is not essentially [being] South Asian, but being *not* Canadian." Women found that they were treated differently in terms of their ethnic or racial background, people from non-English-speaking countries experiencing more discrimination than others. Liddle and Joshi (1986: 188–90) have argued that the notion of Indian women's inferiority to Western women is to be understood in the context of cultural imperialism and the power relations between the West and the Third World.

Conversely, some women who *did* get jobs met explicit racial antagonism and resentment, expressed in remarks such as the following: "How do *you* get a job when so many people here are unemployed?" Another respondent stated, "Women of colour always have difficulty [getting a job]." On the other hand, "Indian women [who have jobs] are often resented because they work so hard. Canadians don't work as hard. They wonder how we can get what we have," said another. In fact, several women I interviewed claimed that many South Asian women will not seek work in the normal job market or they will work for their husbands precisely because they have experienced devaluation or discrimination in jobs or else they have heard of and expect racial discrimination and undervaluation of their credentials.

For many women, gender relations in the domestic sphere compounded the experience of frustration with respect to the work world. "Men don't even like to think the problem exists; they wouldn't even stop to consider it," said one woman. Women's work outside the home was dominated by the cultural patterns of gender relations in marriage. For the most part, women had to be submissive and deferential to men's needs. They found that the disadvantages of the subordinate gender position were more salient than the relatively high position in the class hierarchy which their educational and work qualifications gave them.

Conclusion

Although the one hundred and one women I have interviewed had unique stories to tell about being an immigrant to Canada, the preliminary findings have indicated some similar patterns in their everyday life experience as well as some different work experience in terms of where they have settled. Their work experience has suggested that the women faced situations that were sometimes unique to them as immigrant women belonging to a visible minority group; for example, the need for top performance in competition with native-born Canadians to obtain scarce jobs. At other times, their experience was shared with other native-born Canadian women; for example, the need for top performance to get a typically "man's" job, such as financial comptroller.

Being a South Asian immigrant woman was experienced above all as being "different" from other Canadians — not only in visible and audible characteristics like skin colour and accent, respectively, but also in such social characteristics as educational and work experience prior to migration. Distinct cultural groups have been identified in terms of their ancestral origins in the Indian sub-continent as being generally "different" from Anglo-Canadians.

The dynamic interconnectedness of gender, race, ethnicity and class in the lived experience of these immigrant women in the paid work force requires further analysis. Stasiulis (1990) has explored the possibilities and problems inherent in analyses that seek to conceptualize the links among relations organized by these variables. The present research has indicated support for Stasiulis's contention that women cannot be treated as a homogeneous racial category. Race interacts with gender in the work experience of these middle-class immigrant "women of colour." Furthermore, the work experience of middle-class South Asian immigrant women in Atlantic Canada differed from that of working-class South Asian immigrant women in Toronto. Comparison with the work experience of white Canadian-born women, further analysis in terms of period of arrival in Canada and corresponding changes in Canadian immigration policies, regulations and practices, together with a closer look at variations in work experience in larger and smaller (or more- and less-industrialized) settlements should cast light on the links between ethnicity/race, gender, class and lived experience and the development processes over time in Atlantic Canada. The very different circumstances of working-class South Asian immigrant women who do shift work in Toronto factories, where, according to Das Gupta (1986), they are exploited and divided on the basis of race and ethnicity, compared to the circumstances of middle-class educated South Asian immigrant women in the metropolitan centres of Atlantic Canada, illustrate the complexities of the interconnections between gender, race and class in the Canadian context. Moreover, one has to take into account not only the dynamic interrelationships of race, class and gender, but also their interconnectedness in specific Canadian contexts; namely, the location of the immigrant women (and men, for that matter) at the centre or the periphery of the Canadian political economy. The uneven economic development of Canada has had a significant impact on the destination of migrants (especially Asian migrants), the kind of work they do, and their work experience.

REFERENCES

I acknowledge the helpful comments of two anonymous reviewers and funding for research by the Social Sciences and Humanities Research Council of Canada.

Agnew, Vijay. 1986. "Educated Indian Women in Ontario." *Polyphony. Women and Ethnicity* 8, 1-2: 70-2.

Arnopoulos, Sheila McLeod. 1979. *Problems of Immigrant Women in the Canadian Labour Force.* Ottawa: Canadian Advisory Council on the Status of Women.

Boyd, Monica. 1975. "The Status of Immigrant Women in Canada." *Canadian Review of Sociology and Anthropology* 12: 406–16.

———. 1984. "At a Disadvantage: The Occupational Attainments of Foreign-Born Women in Canada." *International Migration Review* 18-4: 1091–1119.

———. 1986. "Immigrant Women in Canada." Pp. 45–61 in Rita J. Simon and Caroline B. Brettel (eds.), *International Migration: The Female Experience.* Totowa, NJ: Rowman & Allanheld.

Burnet, Jean (ed.). 1986. *Looking into My Sister's Eyes: An Exploration in Women's History.* Toronto: Multicultural History Society of Ontario.

Canada. Statistics Canada. 1987. *The Daily Addendum.* Dec. 3. Ottawa.

Cassin, Marguerite, and Jennifer Newton (eds.). 1979. "Immigrant Women." *Special Issue of Multiculturalism* 2, 4.

Das Gupta, Tania. 1986. "Looking under the Mosaic: South Asian Immigrant Women." *Polyphony. Women and Ethnicity* 8, 1–2: 67–9.

Djao, Angela W., and Roxana Ng. 1987. "Structured Isolation: Immigrant Women in Saskatchewan." Pp. 141–58 in Kathleen Storrie (ed.), *Women — Isolation and Bonding.* Toronto: Methuen.

Estable, Alma. 1986. *Immigrant Women.* A Background Paper Prepared for the Canadian Advisory Council on the Status of Women.

———. 1987. "Immigration Policy and Regulations." *Resources for Feminist Research* 16, 1: 28.

Ghosh, Ratna. 1979. "Women and the Politics of Culture: South Asian Women in Montreal." *Resources for Feminist Research* 8, 3: 21–2.

———. 1981a. "Social and Economic Integration of South Asian Women in Montreal, Canada." Pp. 59–71 in G. Kurian and R. Ghosh (eds.), *Women in the Family and the Economy.* Westport, Conn.: Greenwood Press.

———. 1981b. "Minority within a Minority: Being South Asian and Female in Canada." Pp. 413–26 in G. Kurian and R. Ghosh (eds.), *Women in the Family and the Economy.* Westport, Conn.: Greenwood Press.

———1983. "Sarees and the Maple Leaf: Indian Women in Canada." Pp. 90–99 in George Kurian and Ram P. Srivastava (eds.), *Overseas Indians: A Study in Adaptation.* Delhi: Vikas Publishing House.

Indra, Doreen M. 1981. "The Invisible Mosaic: Women, Ethnicity and the Vancouver Press." *Canadian Ethnic Studies* 13: 63–74.

Jacobsen, Helga E. 1979. "Immigrant Women and the Community: A Perspective for Research." *Resources for Feminist Research* 8, 3: 17–21.

Johnson, Laura C., and Robert E. Johnson. 1982. *The Seam Allowance: Industrial Home Sewing in Canada.* Toronto: Women's Educational Press.

Kalbach, Warren E. 1990. "A Demographic Overview of Racial and Ethnic Groups in Canada." Pp. 18–47 in Peter S. Li (ed.), *Race and Ethnic Relations in Canada.* Toronto: Oxford University Press.

Khosla, Prabha. 1983. "Profiles of Working Class East Indian Women." *Fireweed* 16: 43–8.

Law Union of Ontario. 1981. *The Immigrant's Handbook: A Critical Guide.* Montréal: Black Rose Books.

Liddle, Joanna, and Rama Joshi. 1986. *Daughters of Independence: Gender, Caste and Class in India.* London, UK: Zed Books.

Naidoo, J.C. 1980a. "Women of South Asian and Anglo-Saxon Origins in the Canadian Context: Self-Perceptions, Socialization, Achievement, Aspirations." Pp. 50–69 in Cannie Stark-Adamec (ed.), *Sex Roles: Origins, Influences and Implications for Women.* Montreal: Eden Press.

———. 1980b. "East Indian Women in the Canadian Context: A Study in Social Psychology." Pp. 193–218 in K. Victor Ujimoto and Gordon Hirabayashi (eds.), *Visible Minorities and Multiculturalism: Asians in Canada.* Toronto: Butterworths.

———. 1985a. "Contemporary South Asian Women in the Canadian Mosaic." *International Journal of Women's Studies* 8, 4: 338–50.

———. 1985b. "Cultural Perspectives on the Adjustment of South Asian Women in Canada." Pp. 76–92 in I.R. Lacqunes and Y.H. Poortinga (eds.), *From a Different Perspective: Studies of Behavior across Cultures.* Lisse, The Netherlands: Swets and Zeitlinger.

———. 1987. "Women of South Asian Origins: Status of Research, Problems, Future Issues." Pp. 37–58 in Milton Israel (ed.), *The South Asian Diaspora in Canada: Six Essays.* Toronto: The Multicultural History Society of Ontario.

Naidoo, Josephine, and J. Campbell Davis. 1986. "South Asian and Anglo Saxon Women in Canada: Attitudes toward Multiculturalism." Pp. 73–103 in Victor Ujimoto and Josephine Naidoo (eds.), *Asian Canadians: Contemporary Issues. Selections from the Proceedings, Asian Canadian Symposium VII, University of Manitoba, June 4–7, 1986.* Guelph, Ont.: University of Guelph.

———. 1988. "Canadian South Asian Women in Transition: A Dualistic View of Life." *Journal of Comparative Family Studies* 19: 311–27.

Ng, Roxana. 1981. "Constituting Ethnic Phenomenon: An Account from the Perspective of Immigrant Women." *Canadian Ethnic Studies* 13, 1: 97–108.

———. 1982. "Immigrant Housewives in Canada." *Atlantis* 8, 1: 111–17.

———. 1984. "Sex, Ethnicity or Class? Some Methodological Considerations." *Studies in Sexual Politics* 1: 14–45.

———. 1986. "The Social Construction of 'Immigrant Women' in Canada." Pp. 269–86 in Roberta Hamilton and Michelle Barrett (eds.), *The Politics of Diversity: Feminism, Marxism and Nationalism.* Montreal: The Book Centre Inc.

————. 1989. "Sexism, Racism and Canadian Nationalism." Pp. 10–25 in Jesse Vorst et al. (eds.), *Race, Class, Gender: Bonds and Barriers. Socialist Studies/Etudes Socialistes. A Canadian Annual 5.* Toronto: Between the Lines.

Ng, Roxana, and Tania Das Gupta. 1981. "Nation Builders? The Captive Labour Force of Non-English-Speaking Immigrant Women." *Canadian Women's Studies/Les cahiers de la femme* 3, 1: 83–5.

Ng, Roxana, and Alma Estable. 1987. "Immigrant Women in the Labour Force: An Overview of Present Knowledge and Research Gaps." *Resources for Feminist Research* 16, 1: 29–33.

Ng, Roxana, and J. Ramirez. 1981. *Immigrant Housewives in Canada.* Toronto: The Women's Centre.

Ng, Winnie. 1982. "Immigrant Women: The Silent Partners of the Women's Movement." Pp. 249–56 in Maureen Fitzgerald, Connie Guberman and Margie Wolfe (eds.), *Still Ain't Satisfied: Canadian Feminism Today.* Toronto: The Women's Press.

Ramkhalawansingh, Ceta. 1981. "Language and Employment Training for Immigrant Women." *Canadian Ethnic Studies* 13, 1: 91–6.

Resources for Feminist Research. 1987. "Immigrant Women in Canada." 16, 1 (March): *passim.*

Silvera, Makeda. 1981. "Immigrant Domestic Workers. Whose Dirty Laundry?" *Fireweed* 9 (Winter): 53–9.

Smith, Dorothy E. 1987. *The Everyday World as Problematic: A Feminist Sociology.* Toronto: The University of Toronto Press.

Stasiulis, Daiva. 1986. "Anti-Racism and Black Feminism in the Canadian Context." Paper presented at the 10th annual meeting of the Canadian Research Institute for the Advancement of Women, Moncton, New Brunswick, Nov. 7–9.

————. 1987. "Rainbow Feminism: Perspectives on Minority Women in Canada." *Resources for Feminist Research* 16, 1(March): 5–9.

————. 1990. "Theorizing Connections: Gender, Race, Ethnicity and Class." Pp. 269–305 in Peter S. Li (ed.), *Race and Ethnic Relations in Canada.* Toronto: Oxford University Press.

The Politics of Obstetric Care: The Inuit Experience

JOHN O'NEIL AND PATRICIA A. KAUFERT

Inuit in remote communities of the Canadian North have experienced, within the space of three decades, a transition from birth in the context of home and family, to birth under the care of a nurse-midwife in a community clinic, to birth under the control of physicians in hospitals in southern Canadian cities. This article is concerned with the political apects of this history. It discusses obstetric policy as one aspect of the penetration of southern institutions and controls into the lives of people living in the Canadian North.

The politics of one woman's birth experience and the politics of Inuit relationships with Western medical institutions and the larger Canadian society are inextricably linked. Personal feelings of alienation during confinement in southern hospitals reflect macro-political negotiations for greater community control over birthing options: namely, the struggle against the system of internal colonialism that has characterized northern Canada (O'Neil, 1988).

The data for the article derive from a research project initiated in response to questions about the evacuation of women for childbirth put

SOURCE: John O'Neil and Patricia A. Kaufert, "The Politics of Obstetric Care: The Inuit Experience," in W. Penn Handwerker, ed., *Births and Power: Social Change and the Politics of Reproduction* (Boulder, CO: Westview Press, 1990), 53–68.

by Inuit from the Keewatin communities to senior health officials. Their concerns included the loneliness of women confined in southern hospitals for several weeks, the impact of this separation on family well-being and the implications that an out-of-territory birth certificate might have for cultural survival (O'Neil et al., 1987). A team of health researchers, administrators, clinicians and Inuit leaders came together and held a series of meetings in each community to discuss these problems. The outcome of the meetings was the development of the research project which is now in progress; it includes a detailed medical record audit and a prospective survey of Inuit women's experience of pregnancy and birth.

This article explores the historical and political background to the changes in obstetric policies which have taken place in the Keewatin over the past fifteen years. It uses archival data, government reports and statistics on the place of birth, plus transcripts of the community meetings and material from a series of interviews with physicians, nurses, administrators and Inuit women.

Evacuation for Childbirth

The Keewatin region lies along the western shore of Hudson Bay and is part of the Northwest Territories. A population of approximately 5,000 Inuit live in an area of 225,000 square miles. There are seven communities lying between 200 and 800 miles north of Churchill and ranging in size from 200 to 1,100 people. Churchill itself is 600 miles north of Winnipeg, the site of the nearest tertiary care hospitals. A 30-bed secondary level hospital is located in Churchill and each community has a "nursing station." Nursing stations are best described as outpatient primary health care clinics staffed by one to five nurses, some of whom have training as nurse practitioners or, more rarely today, as nurse-midwives.

The annual number of births for all the communities in the Keewatin between 1970 and 1985 ranged from 105 to 161. Routine prenatal care is provided at the nursing stations with most women being seen by a visiting physician at least once or twice during pregnancy. There has been a gradual but steady decline in the number of births in nursing stations between 1971 and 1985 (Kaufert et al., 1987). While a few births still occur in the communities rather than the hospital, these are usually the result of a woman going into labor before the date set for her evacuation south. Official policy no longer supports childbirth in the nursing station as an elective option. Women are sent to either Churchill or Winnipeg two or three weeks before their expected date of confinement with a few leaving much earlier. High-risk women are sent to Winnipeg and low-risk women to Churchill (only 40% of all births to Keewatin residents in 1986–87 were in Churchill [Gershman, 1987]).

Physicians and health administrators explain the drift towards hospital birth by the efforts of the medical community and government to lower infant mortality and morbidity rates, coupled with the adoption by obstetricians of more and more rigorous definitions of what constitutes risk in childbirth. This explanation strips away and ignores the social, political and historical contexts which are the setting for changes in obstetric policy in the Keewatin. The core argument of this article is that the displacement of the traditional Inuit way of birth and the assumption of medical control over childbirth are not isolated phenomena, but part and parcel of the wider history of northern health care and northern politics. The nurse-midwife is a pivotal figure in this account, yet her position in the North is also a chapter in another political history, that of midwifery in Canada and the occasional challenge to the medical monopoly over childbirth.

Health, Health Care and Colonialism

The medicalization of childbirth in the Keewatin is one dimension of the extension of southern power into northern Canada and of the relationship between illness and colonialism. Any understanding of present policies of obstetric care or of the perception of these policies within the communities must begin with the history of medical care in the Keewatin and the emergence of a Western hegemonic institutional presence in the health arena.

Traditional Inuit ideas about sickness and health have been described as continuous in contrast to the disassociative model of Western biomedicine (Wenzel, 1981). Inuit sought explanations for illness and misfortune in terms of the individual's relationship with his physical, social and spiritual environment. These explanations were both sociological and historical in the sense that misfortune brought about a critical examination of the social order. The healer's role was to facilitate this examination and assist in the construction of new social understandings. The ideology that validated the healer's role and activities emerged through community consensus rather than being imposed to support the interests of a dominant elite.

With the arrival of missionaries and fur traders in most parts of the Canadian Arctic in the 1940s and 50s, illness and health emerged as commodities which could be traded for the spiritual and economic loyalties of the Inuit population. Early missionaries and traders made their meagre medical resources available in exchange for either conversion to Christianity, or monopolistic control over the fur trade. Scheffel's (1983) work in Labrador on the Moravian mission demonstrates clearly that the Moravians selectively withheld medical assistance when members of the surrounding Inuit communities were slow to convert. Gradually, the treatment of illness became a factor in the negotiations surrounding the spiritual and economic orientations of Inuit. This process had a secularizing impact on Inuit understandings about illness and well-being and resulted in less attention being paid to the maintenance of interpersonal codes for social behaviour.

Formal western medicine was first introduced in the Canadian North in the 1950s when physicians began to accompany the various ships supplying the missions and trading posts scattered across the Arctic coast (Brett, 1969). The standard response to infectious disease epidemics such as tuberculosis was to remove infected individuals from their communities and relocate them to southern hospitals and sanatoria for extended periods of time. Other options such as encouraging the population to redistribute itself into smaller traditional groups were sometimes proposed by field staff, but were rejected by southern authorities (Lee, 1975; Graham-Cumming, 1969). By separating survivors from their families and dependents, the health care system exacerbated the social damage already incurred as a result of these epidemics and the accompanying high levels of mortality (Hodgson, 1982).

Implicit in this treatment approach was the message that responsibility for decisions regarding the type and location of treatment for diseases was now entirely in the hands of the colonial power. In the name of medical care, government claimed the authority to disrupt family life and traditional patterns of social organization. This demonstration of power had far-reaching ramifications in shaping Inuit expectations. Instead of viewing sickness as an event which, with the help of a healer, resulted in increased social harmony and integration, illness was feared not only as a threat to life, but also as a threat to social continuity and autonomy. Sickness facilitated the intrusion of the colonial power into the intimacies of family life, and its paternalism was reproduced continuously in the highly emotional context of the medical encounter, the evacuation of the patient and the breaking apart of families.

The Traditional Way of Birth

In traditional terms, beliefs surrounding childbirth were constructed parallel to general understandings of illness and misfortune. Specific ritual avoidances of particular foods and social contacts were prescribed, and problems in childbirth were regarded as the outcome of a failure to observe these rules. Although shamans were rarely midwives, difficult births sometimes required shamanistic intervention. In the wider context, problems of fertility, the production of males and infant mortality were all linked to the general sociological framework of standards for interpersonal behaviour.

The risks of traditional childbirth are central to the current debate over childbirth in the North. For governmental and medical authorities, a reduction in infant mortality from the "traditional" (i.e., pre-settlement) period is the justification for all the changes which have been made in obstetric care in the Keewatin. For the Inuit, the belief that "traditional" (i.e., pre-contact) birth was safe is basic to their demand for control over childbirth. The distinction between pre-contact and pre-settlement is an imposed one, for the current discourse blends both periods and reconstructs historical memory to fit ideological needs. The preservation of traditional beliefs in relation to pregnancy and childbirth is part of the re-affirmation of Inuit culture, but it is also a political act. As such, memories of the past are being collected, redefined and shaped to meet the political and symbolic needs of the present community.

The following assertion of the competence of traditional ways is taken from a statement made at one of the meetings held in the Keewatin.

> Inuit people do not believe that having a child, being pregnant, birthing is a disease. It's not an illness. It's a way of life, a normal function of a human being. And in the sense that it's not a disease, then they don't think that you absolutely have to be in the hospital. . . . They [the Inuit] have delivered babies before for centuries and centuries.

After talking to older women about their own experience, we found no one model of traditional birthing, in the sense of a set of prescribed procedures which define where birth should be, who should be present or how it should be managed. Certainly, there were traditional midwives, some of whom are still alive. But women also describe births managed by the woman alone; in other cases, they talk about being helped by their husbands or by other women.

> Once one woman found out that someone was in labor, she told other women and they just came to assist because they wanted to. They knew that the woman in labor was scared so they would come to assist.

Systematic differences in birthing traditions between groups among the Inuit have been described in the ethnographic literature (Freeman, 1984: 680; Dufour, 1987), but variations in the accounts we have collected so far seem often to be a function of the characteristics of a particular birth or of who was available at a particular time. In this nomadic hunting society, the latter usually depended on the season.

Yet, although there is no single model, certain themes are common to many of these accounts and recurred whenever Inuit women talked to us about childbirth and the past. One is a sense of competence. The emphasis was on personal strength and responsibility. Women birthed babies in a hastily constructed snow house, or "beside the sled." Often they continued travelling or returned to regular activities shortly after the birth. Their memories reflected a feeling that life was hard, but childbirth was relatively easy and straightforward; a normal event in an otherwise difficult existence.

Managing birth by oneself, or helping other women birth, emerged as a source of pride for women, a public sign of virtue. Competence was linked with the possession of knowledge.

> Back then, the women had the knowledge to take care of a woman in labor . . . we were informed by our elders on what to do and what not to do (Meeting at Rankin Inlet).

Often a comparison was drawn between the present situation in which health professionals claim a monopoly over obstetric knowledge and this traditional time when information about childbirth was disseminated throughout the community, passing from one generation to the next. Another theme is control; the contrast was made between hospital birth, hooked up to machines, and the traditional right of a woman to choose the position in which she would labor.

In these reconstructions of the past, traditional birth is a communal event, rather than an individual and anomic experience in a southern hospital. Whereas hospital birth is disassociated from the community, traditional birth was integrative. Saladin d'Anglure (1984: 494) describes the importance of such relationships in northern Quebec.

> The midwife (*sanaji* "she who makes") occupied an essential place in the kinship system, as the cultural mother responsible for the role and for settling the sex of the infant (it was believed that male babies could transform themselves into girls at birth, and sometimes the reverse) and for presiding over all the important rites of passage accompanying the first performances of the child, receiving important presents on such occasions. Terms derived from or resembling kinship terms accompanied the relations between the midwife and the children she delivered, and between children delivered by the same midwife; thus *uitsiaq* "husband-in-law" and *nuliatsiaq* "wife-in-law" were used reciprocally by a boy and girl with the same midwife.

Participation in birth was the nexus, therefore, of a series of relationships, linking the midwife to the woman she had delivered and to the child. (As a boy grew into a hunter, he would bring part of his "first catch" to his midwife; a girl would give something she had sewn.) The removal of birth out of the community and into the hospital spells the loss of these relationships.

The Nursing Station and the Nurse-Midwife

Infant mortality rates for the Keewatin in the fifties and early sixties are not known, but they were high according to government reports. These were the years when people were moving from nomadic camps into permanent settlements. Housing conditions were poor, nutrition was deteriorating and levels of infectious disease, particularly tuberculosis, were high. Many of the women giving birth had lived through the periodic famines of the 1950s. The circumstances were unique and the "pre-contact" traditional mortality rate may have been much lower (Fortuine, 1976).

Prior to 1960, Inuit women in the Keewatin could go to the military hospital in Churchill or to a Catholic mission hospital in Chesterfield; most did neither. The annual *Report on Health Conditions in the Northwest Territories* (1966) estimated that 66% of Inuit births occurred outside hospitals or nursing stations in 1964. (This percentage was calculated on the number of live births known to the authorities; the real figures were probably higher.) "Capturing" childbirth became a critical dimension in the relationships of colonialism and the domination by one society over another.

The first step in the medicalization of childbirth lay in the transfer of births out of the local setting and into the nursing station. Construction of the nursing stations began in 1960 and was completed in 1970. They were staffed by foreign trained nurse-midwives (predominantly British), a group known as the "come-from-aways" in Labrador (Benoit, 1988). They were hired to provide emergency and primary medical care as well as midwifery (O'Neil, 1986; Scott, 1978).

Through their training, professional ties and ideology, the nurse-midwives brought governmental and medical institutions into the communities. The nursing station was government territory and the nurse a government employee. As such, she held a position in a hierarchy which included physicians and administrators working in northern health care and which stretched from the nursing stations to Ottawa. Nurses had to accept and implement directives from higher up the system rather than respond to the demands of the community in which they were working.

Nurses were nonetheless expected to adopt a public health perspective which relied on personal knowledge of individuals and families. This knowledge was often, however, constructed ahistorically and without consideration for broader structural conditions. Labels of "good" and "bad" were based on assessments of personal hygiene, morality and industriousness. These attributes were generally evaluated in terms of an assimilationist model (i.e., in comparison to those Inuit who lived a "White" lifestyle) or a romantic vision of traditionalism with little regard for the conditions of colonialism. Many nurses had little understanding of the tremendous uprooting and readaptation required in the process of resettlement. Nor did they fully appreciate the extremely poor environmental conditions with which women had to cope.

Not understanding Inuit culture, nurses tended to devalue women's roles and functions. This ignorance was sometimes corrected by time and the gradual accumulation of knowledge about the communities in which a nurse worked as a midwife, but only a few nurses stayed longer than a year or two. Turnover was generally high and communities had to continually renegotiate relationships with new nurses. On the one hand, nurses were often blamed by Inuit for policy issues beyond their influence and control. On the other hand, nurses tended to support medically dominated health policy that contributed to medicalization and southern control of northern health. The occasionally idealized view of the nurse-midwife in the North has to accommodate this notion of the nurse as enforcer of government policy in a community of which she had only limited understanding.

Childbirth and the Nursing Stations

Reminiscences of the very early years suggest that nurses attended births only by invitation, going to wherever the birth was taking place, be it snow house or summer tent. Lee describes her experiences as a nurse in Baffin Island in 1957:

> [I] had been alerted to the fact that Oola and Pitsuala were the settlement's two official midwives, but so far had not been asked for obstetrical help. [I] was relieved. [I] worried about faulty hygiene, of course, but felt it wise to leave the Inuit to deal with childbirth as they had always done. The most sensible way of handling the ignorance you've brought to the Arctic, Dorothy, [I told myself] firmly, is to impose it on others as little as possible (Lee, 1975: 101).

This attitude of respect for traditional ways was soon replaced by the self-assurance of a government convinced it "knew" what was needed. Mason (1987) quotes from an interview with Otto Schaefer, a physician who worked for the Federal Government in the Canadian Arctic. He described the situation in the late 1960s in the following terms:

> There was a push from above for more hospital deliveries, and deliveries in nursing stations instead of in tents and igloos. I do not say that I was one hundred per cent convinced that there was a great need for it, but eventually it was inevitable (Mason, 1987: 224).

The pressure was effective; according to the annual *Report on Health in the Northwest Territories* for 1968, 97% of births in the Keewatin occurred in a hospital or a nursing station.

The criterion for deciding eligibility for birth in a nursing station in the 1970s was a relatively informal assessment of the likelihood that birth complications might develop. With slight variations, the following statement was included in each of the annual reports from 1969 until 1977 (emphasis added):

> We have continued the policy that see all primagravida and grand multiparae (fifth or subsequent infants) evacuated to a hospital for delivery as are all complicated pregnancies or anticipated complications. Provided no complications ensued at the birth of the first infant or *if all else is well*, second, third or fourth babies are delivered in nursing stations.

Although the criteria for evacuation were not officially changed throughout the 1970s, a gradual and steady decline in the number of nursing station births occurred throughout this period. By the early 1980s, official policy was against any births taking place in the nursing stations.

The community view of the history of these changes is neatly summarized in a comment made at one of the meetings:

> When all the nursing stations moved into our communities, they told us the first child had to be born in the hospital in Churchill or Winnipeg . . . the next five could be born in the settlement . . . every child born after that had to be away to the hospital. Okay, we accepted that. And then what really started this wanting to have children in the settlement was that everybody for any number of children had to go out. There were no more deliveries in town.

Implicit in this statement is a question — why did the shift to hospital birth take place? One set of answers lies in the improvements in transportation which made it easier to plan an evacuation. Better communication systems brought the nurse into closer contact with physicians and administrators to the south and allowed them closer oversight of her work. Changes in obstetric technology increased the apparent gap between nursing station and obstetric ward (Kaufert et al., 1987). But another explanation is that midwifery had few, if any, supporters, except among women and within the communities.

To explain why midwifery in the North went relatively undefended requires a brief digression into the history of midwifery in Canada.

Canada and Midwifery

The nurse-midwives of the Keewatin were working within one of the few countries in the world where midwifery is not legal. Each of the provinces of Canada has a medical act, dating back to some time in the late 19th century, which gives monopoly rights over childbirth to physicians. Medical Services in the Keewatin was a federal government agency and outside provincial jurisdiction, but even so the use of midwives went unchallenged by the medical profession only because of the special conditions of the North. There was no change in the official attitudes of the profession towards midwifery.

As Biggs (1983) has shown for Ontario, the medical profession worked hard throughout the latter half of the nineteenth century all across Canada to gain control of childbirth and to have midwifery declared illegal. While similar battles were fought in other industrialized countries, the profession achieved monopolistic control over childbirth only in Canada. Mason (1987) suggests that the reason lies in the rural nature of most of Canada which inhibited the development of an organized midwifery resistance movement, such as those which served to protect and sustain midwifery in the more urbanized countries of Europe.

Certainly, Canada was not without midwives or without a demand for their services. Biggs' (1983) work in Ontario and Benoit's (1988) in Newfoundland and Labrador have shown that the "lay" or "granny" midwife was active in the remote rural areas and among the urban poor. Such women had their staunch defenders in the press and in the provincial legislatures, but were powerless against a politically strong and well-organized medical profession (Biggs, 1983; Mason, 1987).

While the physicians claimed that the issue was safety, the underlying motivation for the legislation against midwives was economic survival for an over-supply of country doctors (Biggs, 1983; Mason, 1987). At a time when most people relied almost entirely upon their own resources in dealing with illness, birth offered a way for the doctor to gain access to the family. Mason quotes a letter to the *Canada Lancet* in 1874 in which a physician argues strenuously against an amendment to the Medical Act which would allow provinces to license midwives:

> Where I am located I have to contend with two of these old bodies and a quack, who I must say have been pretty successful in their attendance, as they get about 60 cases a year, which would amount in my hands to a very decent living for my small family (Mason, 1987: 204).

As Benoit has shown, the "granny" midwives continued to operate among the poor and in the remote rural areas; but the Provincial Medical Acts effectively prevented the development of formal training programmes or a system of licensing for midwives on the European model. The medical monopoly was occasionally challenged by individual women (such as Lady Aberdeen) and by formally organized groups (such as the Victorian Order of Nurses). For example, in 1910–1911, the V.O.N. promoted a plan modelled on the midwifery training programme in New York, only to have it defeated by an opposition which combined the medical profession and the nursing associations. According to Biggs (1984: 117):

> Efforts to introduce a system of midwifery in Canada were circumscribed by the professional interests of nurses who wished to retain their recently earned professional status and by physicians who wished to protect their financial interests as well as maintain their monopoly over childbirth.

One could say that the irony of the history of midwifery in the North is that the new demands for midwifery services in the South emerged as this enclave of practising midwives started to disappear from the North.

Nurse-Midwifery in the North

The decision to staff the new nursing stations with nurse-midwives has to be seen against this historical background. It explains, for example, why the federal government had to hire abroad. Canadian training programmes did not exist. This history also meant that Canadian physicians, unlike their European counterparts, were not trained alongside midwives. Relationships between the midwives and physicians working in the Keewatin were somewhat eased whenever the latter were British and familiar with midwifery. But the official position of the medical profession was always that the nursing station was a poor alternative to physician-attended, hospital birth. In the medical view, a midwife-managed birth did not count as medically attended.

The Canadian system with its historical rejection of midwifery undoubtedly worked against the survival of the midwife in the North. As described earlier, her ability to function was increasingly circumscribed, as stricter guidelines for justifying a birth in the community were adopted. By the early eighties, none were eligible, regardless of how low a woman's risk status.

For a number of reasons there was no organized opposition to the change in policy among northern nurses. First, the nurse-midwives who worked in the North were isolated not only in the physical sense, but due to their foreign training, they lacked informal ties which would link them into Canadian nursing networks. Given the Canadian system, they were also without professional colleagues among southern nurses and the status of their midwifery qualification within professional nursing associations was ambiguous.

As policy changed, any nurse-midwife who might have regretted the ending of midwifery in the North would have had few natural allies among her nursing colleagues. The midwives working in the North were few in number and had always been a transitory, relatively unorganized group with a very high turnover. Starting in the mid 1970s, the representation of midwives among northern nurses was diluted as nursing stations were staffed increasingly by Canadian nurses. Then, in the early 1980s a change in immigration policy set restrictions on the hiring of nurses abroad, including the nurse-midwives for the North.

The Canadian nurses working in the Keewatin in the early 1980s were trained in a medical tradition which said all births should be in hospital. Indeed, the role of the nurse in the community was seen very differently by these new nurses. They were trained in the emerging theoretical paradigms of a school of nursing which emphasized the collaborative role of the health care practitioner in encouraging people to engage in self-help activities (Cardenas and Lucarz, 1985). This training, combined with a more professional attitude (i.e., as contrasted with the missionary motivation of earlier nurses), contributed to conflict between the two nursing traditions in the North. Hence, there was not only a lack of concerted support for midwifery among nurses, but any nurse who still wanted to provide a midwifery service was as likely to be criticized by her colleagues as by the administration.

The demise of midwifery carried costs for the relationships between the nursing station and the community. Seen from the community perspective, the loss of nurse-midwives (and the loss of local birth options) has significantly undermined nurses' roles in northern communities. Nurses' credibility from the community perspective has also suffered. Some loss of confidence in nursing staff is attributable to a community-based perception that nurses who can't deliver babies are not qualified to provide primary health care.

Politics and Childbirth

Obstetric policies in the Keewatin delineate struggle in two arenas; first, the politics of North-South colonial relationships; second, the politics surrounding demands by women for midwifery care in childbirth. For the Inuit, the trend towards southern control over childbirth is considered not only as a hardship for women and their families, but as a threat to long-term cultural identity and survival. These concerns include a persistent worry over children with birth certificates showing they were born outside the Northwest Territories.

> Most of the people are worried that too many of the Inuit children are being born in the district of Manitoba. During the deliberations for Nunavut, they would like to try to settle this so that it could be included in the settlement before anything is done.
> I am worried that if I was born in a place like Coral Harbour and if my baby is born in Churchill, does that mean even though we're same blood, are we considered non-relatives? I am asking this because of the Alaska settlement where anyone born after 1971 was not included in the agreement.

Although assured by various territorial, provincial and federal officials that a Manitoba birth certificate will not affect entitlement to NWT economic benefits, the history of Native-Government relations in North America leaves many Inuit unconvinced. Special status entitlements (as determined by disk numbers, treaty status, band and, in the case of Alaska, corporate enrollments) have played an important historical role in determining eligibility for economic benefits. For many Inuit, the birth certificate issue symbolizes the extent to which these special entitlements have been determined and manipulated by forces external to their communities.

Inuit see the medicalization of birth as a threat to cultural and political autonomy on another level. Concerns range from loss of traditional skills and knowledge, to identity issues, to political entitlement. These concerns are illustrated in the following comment taken from community meetings held in 1986 in various Keewatin communities.

> Nowadays we are told, forget about our Inuit traditional ways. My concern is that when there's a healthy pregnancy, couldn't the mother have her child in her home town with the older Inuit women who have been midwives and with a younger person who has never had experience in delivering babies to help her along, to watch and to observe. Because that would teach the younger generation what our ancestors used to do.

Loss of knowledge is equated with a loss of competence and, therefore, vulnerability; independence lies in regaining control over decision making.

> If the government should suddenly stop giving assistance to the Inuit, where is that going to leave us? We should start doing something about midwives. Should all the assistance be cut back, then at least we would have another alternative to turn to.

Loss of knowledge and the ability to be responsible for oneself is expressed as a sense of profound deprivation in this statement taken from an interview with one of the traditional midwives:

> It's demeaning to a woman to take her rights away, in a sense killing one of the reasons for living, for her purpose was to help with birthing, and birthing was a part of woman's responsibility, and when you take responsibility away from a person, she becomes a worthless person.

This sentiment might also be expressed by those nurse-midwives who would still like to practise in the North, if it were feasible for them to do so.

Clearly, the efforts of nurses (particularly nurse-midwives) to establish themselves as independent practitioners in the Canadian context are threatened by the growing medical control over northern primary health care. It is easy to see the changes in obstetric policy in the North as part of a struggle between nursing and medicine for professional dominance in the primary health care arena. Seen in its historical context, the demise of the northern midwife is part of a much older competition for control over childbirth between the medical profession, on the one hand, and women and midwives, on the other hand.

The struggle by Inuit for control over childbirth and the struggle for midwifery in Canada have much in common. We suggest that until northern nurses and Inuit see themselves as victims of the same institutional and historical processes, the trends towards medicalization of childbirth, and health in general, will continue to occur.

REFERENCES

This research was supported by grants from the National Health Research and Development Program (6607-1412-49) and a Health Scholar award to O'Neil (6607-1379-48). The authors are grateful for the assistance of their co-investigators on the project, Drs. B. Postl, M. Moffatt, P. Brown and B. Binns, Ms. Rosemary Brown and particularly our Inuit collaborators, Eva Voisey and Peter Ernerk. However, the conclusions expressed here are those of the authors, and not necessarily shared by our co-investigators. We also thank the people of the Keewatin region for taking the time to discuss the issues described here with us. We are grateful to our Winnipeg and northern research staff, in particular Dr. Penny Gilbert, Ms. Jackie Linklater, Charlotte St. John and Nellie Kusugak, for their assistance.

Benoit, Cecilia. 1988. "Midwives in Passage: A Case Study of Occupational Change." Ph.D. dissertation (Toronto: University of Toronto). Biggs, C. Lesley. 1983. "The Case of the Missing Midwives: A History of Midwifery in Ontario from 1795-1900." In *Ontario Historical Society — Ontario History*, Vol. LXXV, No. 1.

———. 1984. "The Response to Maternal Mortality in Ontario, 1920-1940." Thesis submitted in conformity with the requirements for the degree of Master of Science in the Division of Community Health at the University of Toronto.

Brett, H. 1969. "A Synopsis of Northern Medical History." *Canadian Medical Association Journal* 100: 521–525.

Cardenas, B., and J. Lucarz. 1985. "Canadian Indian Health Care: A Model for Service." In *Community Health Nursing in Canada*. Stewart et al. (eds.). Toronto: Gage.

Dufour, Rose. 1987. "Accoucher dans un Iglou." In *Accoucher Autrement*. F. Saillant et M. O'Neil, eds. Montreal: Editions Saint Martin.

Fortuine, Robert A. 1976. "The Health of Eskimos as Portrayed in the Earliest Written Accounts." *Bulletin of the History of Medicine* 45: 97–114.

Freeman, Milton M.R. 1984. "The Grise Fjord Project." In *Arctic, Handbook of North American Indians*. David Damas (ed.). Washington: Smithsonian Institution.

Gershman, Stuart. 1987. "Obstetrical Admissions to the Churchill Health Centre of Inuit Women from the Keewatin District, N.W.T.: A Descriptive Analysis." Unpublished manuscript, Department of Community Health Sciences, Faculty of Medicine, University of Manitoba.

Graham-Cumming. 1969. "Northern Health Services." *Canadian Medical Association Journal* 100: 526–531.

Hodgson, Corinne. 1982. "The Social and Political Implications of Tuberculosis among Native Canadians." *Canadian Review of Sociology and Anthropology* 19(4): 502–512.

Kaufert, Patricia A., P. Gilbert, J.D. O'Neil, P. Brown, R. Brown, B. Postl, M.M. Moffatt, B. Binns, and L. Harris. 1987. "Obstetric Care in the Keewatin: Changes in the Place of Birth, 1971–1985." Paper prepared for presentation at 7th International Congress on Circumpolar Health, June 8–12, Umea, Sweden.

Lee, Dorothy. 1975. *Lutiapik*. Toronto: McClelland and Stewart.

Mason. 1987. "A History of Midwifery in Canada." In *Report of the Task Force on the Implementation of Midwifery in Ontario*. Appendix I, Ontario Ministry of Health.

O'Neil, John D. 1986. "Health Care in the Central Canadian Arctic: Continuities and Change." In *Health and Canadian Society: A Sociological Perspective* (2nd ed.). D. Coburn et al. (eds.). Toronto: Fitzhenry and Whiteside.

————. 1988. "Self-Determination, Medical Ideology and Health Services in Inuit Communities." In *Northern Communities: The Prospects for Empowerment*. Gurston Dacks and Ken Coates (eds.). Edmonton: Boreal Institute for Northern Studies.

O'Neil, John D., P.A. Kaufert, P. Brown, E. Voisey, M.M. Moffatt, B. Postl, R. Brown, and B. Binns. 1987. "Inuit Concerns about Obstetric Policy in the Keewatin Region, N.W.T." Paper prepared for presentation at 7th International Congress on Circumpolar Health, June 8–12, 1987, Umea, Sweden.

Report on Health Conditions in the Northwest Territories, 1966, 1968–1977. Medical Services, National Health and Welfare Canada, Yellowknife, Northwest Territories.

Saladin D'Anglure, Bernard. 1984. "Inuit of Quebec." In *Arctic, Handbook of North American Indians*. David Damas (ed.). Washington: Smithsonian Institution.

Scheffel, David. 1983. "Modernization, Mortality, and Christianity in Northern Labrador." *Current Anthropology* 24(4): 523–524.

Scott, Cora, L. 1978. "Canada's 'Barefoot' Midwives." *The Canadian Nurse* 74(9): 41–42.

Wenzel, G. 1981. "Inuit Health and the Health Care System: Change and Status Quo." *Perspectives on Health* I 5(1): 7–15.

Contributors

Constance Backhouse is a professor in the Faculty of Law at the University of Western Ontario.

Denyse Baillargeon is an assistant professor in the Department of History at l'Université de Montréal.

Cecilia Benoit is an associate professor in the Department of Sociology at the University of Victoria.

Agnes Calliste is an associate professor in the Department of Sociology and Anthropology at St. Francis Xavier University.

Line Chamberland teaches at Collège Maisonneuve in Montreal.

Carol Cooper teaches Native history at the University of Waterloo.

Nadia Fahmy-Eid is a professor in the Department of History at l'Université du Québec à Montréal.

Alvin Finkel is a professor of history at Athabaska University.

Dianne M. Hallman is an assistant professor in the Department of Educational Foundations at the University of Saskatchewan.

Margaret Hobbs is an assistant professor in the Women's Studies Program at Trent University.

Patricia A. Kaufert is an associate professor in the Department of Community Health Sciences at the University of Manitoba.

Loraine Littlefield is a Ph.D. candidate in the Department of Anthropology at the University of British Columbia.

Royden K. Loewen teaches in the Department of History at the University of Manitoba.

431

Robert McIntosh works in the Government Archives Division of the National Archives of Canada.

Suzanne Morton is an assistant professor in the Department of History at McGill University.

Jan Noel is an assistant professor in the Department of History at the University of Toronto, Erindale College.

John O'Neil is an associate professor in the Department of Community Health Sciences at the University of Manitoba.

Diana Pedersen is an assistant professor in the Department of History at Concordia University.

Ann Porter is a Ph.D. candidate in the Graduate Program in the Department of Political Science at York University.

Helen Ralston is a professor emerita in the Department of Sociology at St. Mary's University.

Elisabeth Tooker is a professor emerita in the Department of Anthropology at Temple University.

Marguerite Van Die is an associate professor at Queen's Theological College, Queen's University.

Reader Reply Card

We are interested in your reaction to *Canadian Women: A Reader*, by
Wendy Mitchinson, Paula Bourne, Alison Prentice, Gail Cuthbert
Brandt, Beth Light, and Naomi Black. You can help us to improve this
book in future editions by completing this questionnaire.

1. What was your reason for using this book?

   ☐ university course   ☐ continuing education course   ☐ personal interest
   ☐ college course   ☐ professional development   ☐ other _____

2. If you are a student, please identify your school and the course in
   which you used this book.

3. Which chapters or parts of this book did you use? Which did you
   omit?

4. What did you like best about this book?

5. What did you like least about this book?

6. Please identify any topics you think should be added to future
   editions.

7. Please add any comments or suggestions.

8. May we contact you for further information?

   Name: _____
   Address: _____
             _____
   Phone: _____

(fold here and tape shut)

MAIL ⮞ POSTE

Canada Post Corporation / Société canadienne des postes

Postage paid
If mailed in Canada

Port payé
si posté au Canada

Business Reply

Réponse d'affaires

0116870399   01

0116870399-M8Z4X6-BR01

Heather McWhinney
Publisher, College Division
HARCOURT BRACE & COMPANY, CANADA
55 HORNER AVENUE
TORONTO, ONTARIO
M8Z 9Z9